1985

CONTEMPORARY ISSUES IN BUSINESS ETHICS

CONTEMPORARY ISSUES IN BUSINESS ETHICS

JOSEPH R. DES JARDINS

Villanova University

JOHN J. McCALL

St. Joseph's University

Wadsworth Publishing Company
Belmont, California
A Division of Wadsworth, Inc.

Philosophy Editor
Kenneth King

Production Editor
Harold Humphrey

Managing Designer
Paula Shuhert

Designer
Lois Stanfield

Signing Representative
Winston Beauchamp

Printed in the United States of America

1 2 3 4 5 6 7 8 9 10——89 88 87 86 85

ISBN 0-534-03693-7

Library of Congress Cataloging in Publication Data

Des Jardins, Joseph R.
  Contemporary issues in business ethics.

  1. Business ethics—Addresses, essays, lectures.
I. McCall, John J., 1951–   II. Title.
HF5387.D39   1985   174'.4   84-10446
ISBN 0-534-03693-7

*P*reface

It is always a bit presumptuous to add a book to a field already well populated by a variety of texts, anthologies, and casebooks. One must try to do either something a little bit different or a little bit better. Then one must hope that others in the field share your prejudices and overlook your immodesties. Here is what we think that we do differently.

A Greater Emphasis on Social and Political Philosophy

We have tried to replace the more standard ethical theory that usually begins business ethics anthologies with a focus on those normative issues commonly covered in social and political philosophy. Of course, we still treat important questions of ethics (e.g., the origin and extent of rights). Those questions appear, however, not as isolated discussions but within the context of an argument about the place of business within our social environment.

We think that there are two benefits to this emphasis on social and political topics. First, by doing this we introduce philosophy at a lower level of abstraction. In our experiences, this not only helps students to grasp philosophical concepts more easily, but it also makes philosophy more obviously relevant to students (perhaps, especially, to business students).

We also believe that an emphasis on ethical theory encourages an overly narrow view of the range of moral issues in business. Students often see ethical issues only as a question of standards for individual personal behavior. In our approach, students are asked to confront not only the questions "What should I do?" and "What values should I accept?" but also "What sort of society is best to live in?" and "What sorts of institutions ought society to value?" We emphasize that individuals in business make not only personal decisions, but also decisions that have wide-ranging effects throughout society. We believe that our emphasis upon social and political concepts will help students recognize that most business decisions have a moral component.

Our anthology's emphasis on social and political issues appears in a number of ways. Most generally, we have woven throughout the book a continuing discussion of how rights arising from business ownership and management need to be integrated with other rights that are recognized within a democratic society. This emphasis on business as a social institution within a broader social environment is reflected in the first two chapters, where we try to defend a general theory of the responsibilities associated with the control of corporate property. Subsequent chapters amplify this theme by (1) introducing important public policy concepts (e.g., due process and strict liability), (2) pursuing arguments about the appropriate forms of government regulation, and (3) describing current legal debates over issues central to business operations.

New Topics and Approaches

We believe that employee rights are among the most important topics in business ethics. It was that belief that initially caused us to propose this anthology, since most other texts ignore this area or treat it in a single chapter where different proposed employee rights are given only cursory consideration. We have included a major section on employee rights, in which separate chapters, including a chapter on the topic of employee rights to participate in corporate decision making, allow us to give careful and extended attention to five important prospective employee rights.

Our first two chapters also provide a novel approach by integrating both text and articles. We hope that the textual analysis of two classic articles will introduce the student to philosophical analysis in a way that is both less abstract than text alone and more systematic than articles alone. We also attempt to use these first two chapters to provide a model for student analysis of the anthologized articles of the following chapters.

We believe that our treatments of law and business-government interaction also have new twists. We do not discuss government regulation in the abstract. Instead we consider regulation only within the various chapters where the arguments are tied to the particular problems of specific government regulations. Our treatment of the legal material also is new. We do not reprint excerpts from judicial decisions as do most other anthologies. Rather, we have chosen to include law journal articles which survey changes in the law. We think that these articles will provide the student a better sense of business-related law as the evolving product of social and political debates within our society.

Greater Empirical Content

Philosophers working in the general area of applied ethics always run the risk of engaging in mere armchair analysis. No matter how elaborate, interesting, or logical their reasoning, many philosophical contributions in these fields strike the general reader as bizarre, unrealistic, or irrelevant. We hope to overcome these problems by including empirical research by sociologists, economists, psychologists, and political scientists, as well as the more standard fare of philosophical and business representatives. We think that the hard data provided by these interdisciplinary readings will force class discussions down from an unfortunately-all-too-common level of pure speculation to a level of real and documented consequences.

Another standard method for addressing this problem of armchair analysis is to include case studies. We include a carefully chosen case for most chapters because we believe that cases are

helpful teaching tools for stimulating student interest. However, we believe that brief cases alone are not enough. Some who agree lengthen cases into elaborate and detailed studies. In contrast, we think that short cases along with careful empirical research provide the best antidote to armchair analysis.

Philosophical Substance

As the field of business ethics has developed in recent years, the quality of writing in this field has improved considerably. We have tried to include the best philosophical articles we could find. Sometimes this meant reprinting recent contributions in business ethics, sometimes we have chosen articles written for more general philosophical audiences, and sometimes we have commissioned articles specifically for this anthology. In all cases, we try to include the article in its entirety and strive to avoid editing the philosophical precision and substance out of the piece.

Teaching Aids

We also have tried to make this book a helpful teaching tool. Some of the teaching aids are:

1. Substantive chapter introductions to supply unity and structure both within and between chapters

2. Case studies, usually from actual cases, to begin most chapters by raising the important questions found in the anthologized articles

3. Study questions that do not simply ask for repetition of facts but that also aim at stimulating further analysis of the topics covered

4. Two introductory textual chapters that both provide demonstration of how one critically analyzes articles and argue for a view of business as a social institution with a particular set of responsibilities

5. Articles that have been used successfully in our own classes

Acknowledgements

Support and encouragement come from a variety of sources and in many different guises. We continue to benefit in many ways from our association with that community of scholars that we call "Notre Dame philosophy." We also have received great support from our present colleagues. At Villanova University, special thanks for financial support must be offered to Rev. Lawrence Gallen, O.S.A., Vice President for Academic Affairs; Rev. John O'Malley, O.S.A., Dean of Arts and Sciences; and Tom Busch, Chairman of Philosophy. At St. Joseph's University, thanks are due to Dr. Richard Passon, Vice President for Academic Affairs, for support for typing and photocopying expenses. We should also thank Norman Bowie; Fran Gillispie, S.J.; Kenneth Goodpaster; Chris Gowans; Tom Grassey; Joe Hill; Tom Joad; John Serembus; Dana Ward; and Clarence Walton for their suggestions, assistance, and/ or inspiration in the creation of this anthology.

To the following people who reviewed the manuscript at various stages, thank you for your effort, time, and suggestions: Vere Chappell, University of Massachusetts; John Atwell, Temple University; Paul Roth, University of Missouri; Clifford Williams, Trinity College; George Brenkert, University of Tennessee; Mark Pastin, Arizona State University; and Thomas Carson, Virginia Polytechnic Institute.

The Eichs of Big Fish Lake, Minnesota graciously provided the ideal vacation spot for finishing the manuscript, while the Davis clan in Ames, Iowa provided a place to release those pressures that built up as the manuscript deadline approached.

Some years ago we noticed that the prefaces of many Wadsworth philosophy texts contained a special thanks to Ken King. They usually said something about Ken being especially encouraging and talented and quite perceptive about knowing when to apply pressure and when to back off. Well, that, and a whole lot more, is all true. Thanks Ken. Hal Humphrey deserves special thanks as our production editor. He also made a wise decision when choosing a copy editor.

Finally, Linda Eich Des Jardins deserves greater thanks and acknowledgement than can be expressed in a preface. But we'll try anyway. Thanks, Linda, for the technical, substantive, and emotional support.

Contents

PART ONE
BUSINESS
AND MORALITY

CHAPTER ONE

IS MORALITY RELEVANT TO BUSINESS?

Introduction

*"**B**USINESS ETHICS IS* a contradiction in terms." "What does business have to do with ethics?" Although such statements are overused clichés, they accurately describe the views of many people in today's society. For various reasons, many people believe that ethics is irrelevant to business. The first challenge that a book or course in business ethics must overcome, therefore, is to show that business and ethics can be combined and that there is a legitimate area of study called *business ethics.*

As a first step in meeting this challenge, we must point out an ambiguity in the claim that ethics is irrelevant to business. On the one hand, some will claim that business practices are, for the most part, *unethical.* In this view, business is corrupt and the study of business ethics is, at most, a study of that corruption. No doubt this is the understanding implicit in the first cliché mentioned above: that "business ethics," like "terrorist ethics" or "criminal ethics," involves two concepts opposed to each other. On the other hand, others will claim that business practices are, for the most part, *non-ethical.* In this view, business practices are ethically neutral and the attempt to apply ethical standards to business is as inappropriate as applying ethical standards to brushing one's teeth or tying one's shoes. Typically, this would be the view implicit in the second cliché mentioned above.

From this we can derive two different understandings of the claim that ethics is irrelevant to business: (a) ethics is irrelevant to business because business is *unethical* (or, ethically corrupt); and (b) ethics is irrelevant to business because business is *non-ethical* (or, ethically neutral).

Statement (a) will be ignored in this book. At best it represents an open question, to be decided by careful argument and debate. (The sort of argument and debate that characterize the selections in the chapters that follow.) It would be cynical and intellectually irresponsible simply to assume that such a position is true. For that reason, we will disregard this view.

Statement (b) is more instructive for our present purposes. It is possible to defend this claim in two distinct ways. First, someone might argue that there is something special about business that exempts it from ordinary ethical evaluation. As do etiquette or games, business might have its own rules independent of ethical norms. Accordingly, just as it would be a mistake to say that there is an ethical significance to deciding on which side of the plate a fork is placed, so it would also be a mistake to think that there is an ethical significance to business decisions. We shall refer to this defense as the *ethically neutral* approach to business.

A second strategy would be to argue that ordinary ethical standards are nothing more than personal feelings or emotions and that, accordingly, it would be inappropriate to allow such subjective factors to interfere with the functioning of business. This second strategy we shall call the *ethical relativist* approach.

Not surprisingly, there are many people who think that both of these strategies can successfully demonstrate the irrelevance of ethics to business. To defend the legitimacy of business ethics, therefore, it is necessary to respond to both approaches. The following well-known article raises these and other objections to the relevancy of ethics to business. Let us turn to that article and return later to an examination of these two views of business and ethics.

ALBERT CARR

Is Business Bluffing Ethical?

A respected businessman with whom I discussed the theme of this article remarked with some heat, "You mean to say you're going to encourage men to bluff? Why, bluffing is nothing more than a form of lying! You're advising them to lie!"

I agreed that the basis of private morality is a respect for truth and that the closer a businessman comes to truth, the more he deserves respect. At the same time, I suggested that most bluffing in business might be regarded simply as game strategy—much like bluffing in poker which does not reflect on the morality of the bluffer.

I quoted Henry Taylor, the British statesman who pointed out that "falsehood ceases to be falsehood when it is understood on all sides that the truth is not expected to be spoken"—an exact description of bluffing in poker, diplomacy, and business. I cited the analogy of the criminal court, where the criminal is not expected to tell the truth when he pleads "not guilty." Everyone from the judge down takes it for granted that the job of the defendant's attorney is to get his client off, not to reveal the truth; and this is considered ethical practice. I mentioned Representative Omar Burleson, the Democrat from Texas, who was quoted as saying, in regard to the ethics of Congress, "Ethics is a barrel of worms"—a pungent summing-up of the problem of deciding who is ethical in politics. I reminded my friend that millions of businessmen feel constrained every day to say *yes* to their bosses when they secretly believe *no* and that this is generally accepted as permissible strategy when the alternative might be the loss of a job. The essential point, I said, is that the ethics of business are game ethics, different from the ethics of religion.

He remained unconvinced. Referring to the company of which he is president, he declared: "Maybe that's good enough for some businessmen, but I can tell you that we pride ourselves on our ethics. In 30 years not one customer has ever questioned my word or asked to check our figures. We're loyal to our customers and fair to our suppliers. I regard my handshake on a deal as a contract. I've never entered into price-fixing schemes with my competitors. I've never allowed my salesmen to spread injurious rumors about other companies. Our union contract is the best in our industry. And, if I do say so myself, our ethical standards are of the highest!"

He really was saying, without saying it, that he was living up to the ethical standards of the business game—which are a far cry from those of private life. Like a gentlemanly poker player, he did not play in cahoots with others at the table, try to smear their reputations, or hold back chips he owed them.

But this same fine man, at the very time, was allowing one of his products to be advertised in a way that made it sound a great deal better than it actually was. Another item in his product line was notorious among dealers for its "built-in obsolescence." He was holding back from the market a much-improved product because he did not want it to interfere with sales of the inferior item it would have replaced. He had joined with certain of his competitors in hiring a lobbyist to push a state legislature, by methods that he preferred not to know too much about, into amending a bill then being enacted.

In his view these things had nothing to do with ethics; they were merely normal business practice. He himself undoubtedly avoided outright falsehood—never lied in so many words. But the entire organization that he ruled was deeply involved in numerous strategies of deception.

PRESSURE TO DECEIVE

Most executives from time to time are almost compelled, in the interests of their companies or themselves, to practice some form of deception when negotiating with customers, dealers, labor unions, government officials, or even other departments of their companies. By conscious misstatements, concealment of pertinent facts, or exaggeration—in short, by bluffing—they seek to persuade others to agree with them. I think it is fair to say that if the individual executive refuses to bluff from time to time—if he feels obligated to tell the truth, the whole truth, and nothing but the truth—he is ignoring opportunities permitted under the rules and is at a heavy disadvantage in his business dealings.

But here and there a businessman is unable to reconcile himself to the bluff in which he plays a part. His conscience, perhaps spurred by religious idealism, troubles him. He feels guilty; he may

develop an ulcer or a nervous tic. Before any executive can make profitable use of the strategy of the bluff, he needs to make sure that in bluffing he will not lose self-respect or become emotionally disturbed. If he is to reconcile personal integrity and high standards of honesty with the practical requirements of business, he must feel that his bluffs are ethically justified. The justification rests on the fact that business, as practiced by individuals as well as by corporations, has the impersonal character of a game—a game that demands both special strategy and an understanding of its special ethics.

The game is played at all levels of corporate life, from the highest to the lowest. At the very instant that a man decides to enter business, he may be forced into a game situation, as is shown by the recent experience of a Cornell honor graduate who applied for a job with a large company:

This applicant was given a psychological test which included the statement, "Of the following magazines, check any that you have read either regularly or from time to time, and double-check those which interest you most. *Reader's Digest, Time, Fortune, Saturday Evening Post, The New Republic, Life, Look, Ramparts, Newsweek, Business Week, U. S. News & World Report, The Nation, Playboy, Esquire, Harper's, Sports Illustrated.*"

His tastes in reading were broad, and at one time or another he had read almost all of these magazines. He was a subscriber to *The New Republic*, an enthusiast for *Ramparts*, and an avid student of the pictures in *Playboy*. He was not sure whether his interest in *Playboy* would be held against him, but he had a shrewd suspicion that if he confessed to an interest in *Ramparts* and *The New Republic*, he would be thought a liberal, a radical, or at least an intellectual, and his chances of getting the job, which he needed, would greatly diminish. He therefore checked five of the more conservative magazines. Apparently it was a sound decision, for he got the job.

He had made a game player's decision, consistent with business ethics.

A similar case is that of a magazine space salesman who, owing to a merger, suddenly found himself out of a job:

This man was 58, and, in spite of a good record, his chance of getting a job elsewhere in a business where youth is favored in hiring practice was not good. He was a vigorous, healthy man, and only a considerable amount of gray in his hair suggested his age. Before beginning his job search he touched up his hair with a black dye to confine the gray to his temples. He knew that the truth about his age might well come out in time, but he calculated that he could deal with that situation when it arose. He and his wife decided that he could easily pass for 45, and he so stated his age on his resume.

This was a lie; yet within the accepted rules of the business game, no moral culpability attaches to it.

THE POKER ANALOGY

We can learn a good deal about the nature of business by comparing it with poker. While both have a large element of chance, in the long run the winner is the man who plays with steady skill. In both games ultimate victory requires intimate knowledge of the rules, insights into the psychology of the other players, a bold front, a considerable amount of self-discipline, and the ability to respond swiftly and effectively to opportunities provided by chance.

No one expects poker to be played on the ethical principles preached in churches. In poker it is right and proper to bluff a friend out of the rewards of being dealt a good hand. A player feels no more than a slight twinge of sympathy, if that, when—with nothing better than a single ace in his hand—he strips a heavy loser, who holds a pair, of the rest of his chips. It was up to the other fellow to protect himself. In the words of an excellent poker player, former President Harry Truman, "If you can't stand the heat, get out of the kitchen." If one shows mercy to a loser in poker, it is a personal gesture, divorced from the rules of the game.

Poker has its special ethics, and here I am not referring to rules against cheating. The man who keeps an ace up his sleeve or who marks the cards is more than unethical; he is a crook, and can be punished as such—kicked out of the game or, in the Old West, shot.

In contrast to the cheat, the unethical poker player is one who, while abiding by the letter of the rules, finds ways to put the other players at an unfair disadvantage. Perhaps he unnerves them with loud talk. Or he tries to get them drunk. Or he

plays in cahoots with someone else at the table. Ethical poker players frown on such tactics.

Poker's own brand of ethics is different from the ethical ideals of civilized human relationships. The game calls for distrust of the other fellow. It ignores the claim of friendship. Cunning deception and concealment of one's strength and intentions, not kindness and openheartedness, are vital in poker. No one thinks any worse of poker on that account. And no one should think any worse of the game of business because its standards of right and wrong differ from the prevailing traditions of morality in our society.

DISCARD THE GOLDEN RULE

This view of business is especially worrisome to people without much business experience. A minister of my acquaintance once protested that business cannot possibly function in our society unless it is based on the Judeo-Christian system of ethics. He told me:

> I know some businessmen have supplied call girls to customers, but there are always a few rotten apples in every barrel. That doesn't mean the rest of the fruit isn't sound. Surely the vast majority of businessmen are ethical. I myself am acquainted with many who adhere to strict codes of ethics based fundamentally on religious teachings. They contribute to good causes. They participate in community activities. They cooperate with other companies to improve working conditions in their industries. Certainly they are not indifferent to ethics.

That most businessmen are not indifferent to ethics in their private lives, everyone will agree. My point is that in their office lives they cease to be private citizens; they become game players who must be guided by a somewhat different set of ethical standards.

The point was forcefully made to me by a Midwestern executive who has given a good deal of thought to the question:

> So long as a businessman complies with the laws of the land and avoids telling malicious lies, he's ethical. If the law as written gives a man a wide-open chance to make a killing, he'd be a fool not to take advantage of it. If he doesn't, somebody else will. There's no obligation on

him to stop and consider who is going to get hurt. If the law says he can do it, that's all the justification he needs. There's nothing unethical about that. It's just plain business sense.

This executive (call him Robbins) took the stand that even industrial espionage, which is frowned on by some businessmen, ought not to be considered unethical. He recalled a recent meeting of the National Industrial Conference Board where an authority on marketing made a speech in which he deplored the employment of spies by business organizations. More and more companies, he pointed out, find it cheaper to penetrate the secrets of competitors with concealed cameras and microphones or by bribing employees than to set up costly research and design departments of their own. A whole branch of the electronics industry has grown up with this trend, he continued, providing equipment to make industrial espionage easier.

Disturbing? The marketing expert found it so. But when it came to a remedy, he could only appeal to "respect for the golden rule." Robbins thought this a confession of defeat, believing that the golden rule, for all its value as an ideal for society, is simply not feasible as a guide for business. A good part of the time the businessman is trying to do unto others as he hopes others will *not* do unto him. Robbins continued:

Espionage of one kind or another has become so common in business that it's like taking a drink during Prohibition—it's not considered sinful. And we don't even have Prohibition where espionage is concerned; the law is very tolerant in this area. There's no more shame for a business that uses secret agents than there is for a nation. Bear in mind that there already is at least one large corporation—you can buy its stock over the counter—that makes millions by providing counterespionage service to industrial firms. Espionage in business is not an ethical problem; it's an established technique of business competition.

"WE DON'T MAKE THE LAWS"

Wherever we turn in business, we can perceive the sharp distinction between its ethical standards and those of the churches. Newspapers abound with sensational stories growing out of this distinction:

We read one day that Senator Philip A. Hart of Michigan has attacked food processors for deceptive packaging of numerous products.

The next day there is a Congressional to-do over Ralph Nader's book, *Unsafe at Any Speed*, which demonstrates that automobile companies for years have neglected the safety of car-owning families.

Then another Senator, Lee Metcalf of Montana, and journalist Vic Reinemer show in their book, *Overcharge*, the methods by which utility companies elude regulating government bodies to extract unduly large payments from users of electricity.

These are merely dramatic instances of a prevailing condition; there is hardly a major industry at which a similar attack could not be aimed. Critics of business regard such behavior as unethical, but the companies concerned know that they are merely playing the business game.

Among the most respected of our business institutions are the insurance companies. A group of insurance executives meeting recently in New England was startled when their guest speaker, social critic Daniel Patrick Moynihan, roundly berated them for "unethical" practices. They had been guilty, Moynihan alleged, of using outdated actuarial tables to obtain unfairly high premiums. They habitually delayed the hearings of lawsuits against them in order to tire out the plaintiffs and win cheap settlements. In their employment policies they used ingenious devices to discriminate against certain minority groups.

It was difficult for the audience to deny the validity of these charges. But these men were business game players. Their reaction to Moynihan's attack was much the same as that of the automobile manufacturers to Nader, of the utilities to Senator Metcalf, and of the food processors to Senator Hart. If the laws governing their businesses change, or if public opinion becomes clamorous, they will make the necessary adjustments. But morally they have in their view done nothing wrong. As long as they comply with the letter of the law, they are within their rights to operate their businesses as they see fit.

The small business is in the same position as the great corporation in this respect. For example:

In 1967 a key manufacturer was accused of providing master keys for automobiles to mail-order customers, although it was obvious that some of the purchasers might be automobile thieves. His defense was plain and straightforward. If there was nothing in the law to prevent him from selling his keys to anyone who ordered them, it was not up to him to inquire as to his customers' motives. Why was it any worse, he insisted, for him to sell car keys by mail, than for mail-order houses to sell guns that might be used for murder? Until the law was changed, the key manufacturer could regard himself as being just as ethical as any other businessman by the rules of the business game.

Violations of the ethical ideals of society are common in business, but they are not necessarily violations of business principles. Each year the Federal Trade Commission orders hundreds of companies, many of them of the first magnitude, to "cease and desist" from practices which, judged by ordinary standards, are of questionable morality but which are stoutly defended by the companies concerned.

In one case, a firm manufacturing a well-known mouthwash was accused of using a cheap form of alcohol possibly deleterious to health. The company's chief executive, after testifying in Washington, made this comment privately:

We broke no law. We're in a highly competitive industry. If we're going to stay in business, we have to look for profit wherever the law permits. We don't make the laws. We obey them. Then why do we have to put up with this "holier than thou" talk about ethics? It's sheer hypocrisy. We're not in business to promote ethics. Look at the cigarette companies, for God's sake! If the ethics aren't embodied in the laws by the men who made them, you can't expect businessmen to fill the lack. Why, a sudden submission to Christian ethics by businessmen would bring about the greatest economic upheaval in history!

It may be noted that the government failed to prove its case against him.

CAST ILLUSIONS ASIDE

Talking about ethics by businessmen is often a thin decorative coating over the hard realities of the game:

Once I listened to a speech by a young executive who pointed to a new industry code as proof that his company and its competitors were deeply aware of their responsi-

bilities to society. It was a code of ethics, he said. The industry was going to police itself, to dissuade constituent companies from wrongdoing. His eyes shone with conviction and enthusiasm.

The same day there was a meeting in a hotel room where the industry's top executives met with the "czar" who was to administer the new code, a man of high repute. No one who was present could doubt their common attitude. In their eyes the code was designed primarily to forestall a move by the federal government to impose stern restrictions on the industry. They felt that the code would hamper them a good deal less than new federal laws would. It was, in other words, conceived as a protection for the industry, not for the public.

The young executive accepted the surface explanation of the code; these leaders, all experienced game players, did not deceive themselves for a moment about its purpose.

The illusion that business can afford to be guided by ethics as conceived in private life is often fostered by speeches and articles containing such phrases as, "It pays to be ethical," or, "Sound ethics is good business." Actually this is not an ethical position at all; it is a self-serving calculation in disguise. The speaker is really saying that in the long run a company can make more money if it does not antagonize competitors, suppliers, employees, and customers by squeezing them too hard. He is saying that oversharp policies reduce ultimate gains. That is true, but it has nothing to do with ethics. The underlying attitude is much like that in the familiar story of the shopkeeper who finds an extra $20 bill in the cash register, debates with himself the ethical problem—should he tell his partner?—and finally decides to share the money because the gesture will give him an edge over the s.o.b. the next time they quarrel.

I think it is fair to sum up the prevailing attitude of businessmen on ethics as follows:

We live in what is probably the most competitive of the world's civilized societies. Our customs encourage a high degree of aggression in the individual's striving for success. Business is our main area of competition, and it has been ritualized into a game of strategy. The basic rules of the game have been set by the government, which attempts to detect and punish business frauds. But as long as a company does not transgress the rules of the game set by law, it has the legal right to shape its strategy without reference to anything but its profits. If it takes a long-term view of its profits, it will preserve amicable relations, so far as possible, with those with whom it deals. A wise businessman will not seek advantage to the point where he generates dangerous hostility among employees, competitors, customers, government, or the public at large. But decisions in this area are, in the final test, decisions of strategy, not of ethics.

THE INDIVIDUAL AND THE GAME

An individual within a company often finds it difficult to adjust to the requirements of the business game. He tries to preserve his private ethical standards in situations that call for game strategy. When he is obliged to carry out the company policies that challenge his conception of himself as an ethical man, he suffers.

It disturbs him when he is ordered, for instance, to deny a raise to a man who deserves it, to fire an employee of long standing, to prepare advertising that he believes to be misleading, to conceal facts that he feels customers are entitled to know, to cheapen the quality of materials used in the manufacture of an established product, to sell as new a product that he knows to be rebuilt, to exaggerate the curative powers of a medicinal preparation, or to coerce dealers.

There are some fortunate executives, who, by the nature of their work and circumstances, never have to face problems of this kind. But in one form or another the ethical dilemma is felt sooner or later by most businessmen. Possibly the dilemma is most painful not when the company forces the action on the executive but when he originates it himself—that is, when he has taken or is contemplating a step which is in his own interest but which runs counter to his early moral conditioning. To illustrate:

The manager of an export department, eager to show rising sales, is pressed by a big customer to provide invoices, which, while containing no overt falsehood that would violate a U. S. law, are so worded that the customer may be able to evade certain taxes in his homeland.

A company president finds that an aging executive, within a few years of retirement and his pension, is not as productive as formerly. Should he be kept on?

The produce manager of a supermarket debates with himself whether to get rid of a lot of half-rotten tomatoes by including one, with its good side exposed, in every tomato sixpack.

An accountant discovers that he has taken an improper deduction on his company's tax return and fears the consequences if he calls the matter to the president's attention, though he himself has done nothing illegal. Perhaps if he says nothing, no one will notice the error.

A chief executive officer is asked by his directors to comment on a rumor that he owns stock in another company with which he has placed large orders. He could deny it, for the stock is in the name of his son-in-law and he has earlier formally instructed his son-in-law to sell the holding.

Temptations of this kind constantly arise in business. If an executive allows himself to be torn between a decision based on business considerations and one based on his private ethical code, he exposes himself to a grave psychological strain.

This is not to say that sound business strategy necessarily runs counter to ethical ideals. They may frequently coincide; and when they do, everyone is gratified. But the major tests of every move in business, as in all games of strategy, are legality and profit. A man who intends to be a winner in the business game must have a game player's attitude.

The business strategist's decisions must be as impersonal as those of a surgeon performing an operation—concentrating on objective and technique, and subordinating personal feelings. If the chief executive admits that his son-in-law owns the stock, it is because he stands to lose more if the fact comes out later than if he states it boldly and at once. If the supermarket manager orders the rotten tomatoes to be discarded, he does so to avoid an increase in consumer complaints and a loss of good will. The company president decides not to fire the elderly executive in the belief that the negative reaction of other employees would in the long run cost the company more than it would lose in keeping him and paying his pension.

All sensible businessmen prefer to be truthful, but they seldom feel inclined to tell the *whole* truth. In the business game truth-telling usually has to be kept within narrow limits if trouble is to be avoided. The point was neatly made a long time ago (in 1888) by one of John D. Rockefeller's associates, Paul Babcock, to Standard Oil Company executives who were about to testify before a government investigating committee: "Parry every question with answers which, while perfectly truthful, are evasive of *bottom* facts." This was, is, and probably always will be regarded as wise and permissible business strategy.

FOR OFFICE USE ONLY

An executive's family life can easily be dislocated if he fails to make a sharp distinction between the ethical systems of the home and the office—or if his wife does not grasp that distinction. Many a businessman who has remarked to his wife "I had to let Jones go today" or "I had to admit to the boss that Jim has been goofing off lately," has been met with an indignant protest. "How could you do a thing like that? You know Jones is over 50 and will have a lot of trouble getting another job." Or, "You did that to Jim? With his wife ill and all the worry she's been having with the kids?"

If the executive insists that he had no choice because the profits of the company and his own security were involved, he may see a certain cool and ominous reappraisal in his wife's eyes. Many wives are not prepared to accept the fact that business operates with a special code of ethics. An illuminating illustration of this comes from a Southern sales executive who related a conversation he had had with his wife at a time when a hotly contested political campaign was being waged in their state:

I made the mistake of telling her that I had had lunch with Colby, who gives me about half my business. Colby mentioned that his company had a stake in the election. Then he said, "By the way, I'm treasurer of the citizens' committee for Lang. I'm collecting contributions. Can I count on you for a hundred dollars?"

Well, there I was. I was opposed to Lang, but I knew Colby. If he withdrew his business I could be in a bad spot. So I just smiled and wrote out a check then and there. He thanked me, and we started to talk about his next order. Maybe he thought I shared his political views. I wasn't going to lose any sleep over it.

I should have had sense enough not to tell Mary about it. She hit the ceiling. She said she was disappointed in me. She said I hadn't acted like a man, that I should have stood up to Colby.

I said, "Look, it was an either-or situation. I had to do it or risk losing the business."

She came back at me with, "I don't believe it. You could have been honest with him. You could have said that you didn't feel you ought to contribute to a campaign for a man you weren't going to vote for. I'm sure he would have understood."

I said, "Mary, you're a wonderful woman, but you're way off the track. Do you know what would have happened if I had said that? Colby would have smiled and said, 'Oh, I didn't realize. Forget it.' But in his eyes from that moment I would be an oddball, maybe a bit of a radical. He would have listened to me talk about his order and would have promised to give it consideration. After that I wouldn't hear from him for a week. Then I would telephone and learn from his secretary that he wasn't yet ready to place the order. And in about a month I would hear through the grapevine that he was giving his business to another company. A month after that I'd be out of a job."

She was silent for a while. Then she said, "Tom, something is wrong with business when a man is forced to choose between his family's security and his moral obligation to himself. It's easy for me to say you should have stood up to him—but if you had, you might have felt you were betraying me and the kids. I'm sorry that you did it, Tom, but I can't blame you. Something is wrong with business!"

This wife saw the problem in terms of moral obligation as conceived in private life; her husband saw it as a matter of game strategy. As a player in a weak position, he felt that he could not afford to indulge an ethical sentiment that might have cost him his seat at the table.

PLAYING TO WIN

Some men might challenge the Colbys of business—might accept serious setbacks to their business careers rather than risk a feeling of moral cowardice. They merit our respect—but as private individuals, not businessmen. When the skillful player of the business game is compelled to submit to unfair pressure, he does not castigate himself for moral weakness. Instead, he strives to put himself into a strong position where he can defend himself against such pressures in the future without loss.

If a man plans to take a seat in the business game, he owes it to himself to master the principles by which the game is played, including its special ethical outlook. He can then hardly fail to recognize that an occasional bluff may well be justified in terms of the game's ethics and warranted in terms of economic necessity. Once he clears his mind on this point, he is in a good position to match his strategy against that of the other players. He can then determine objectively whether a bluff in a given situation has a good chance of succeeding and can decide when and how to bluff, without a feeling of ethical transgression.

To be a winner, a man must play to win. This does not mean that he must be ruthless, cruel, harsh, or treacherous. On the contrary, the better his reputation for integrity, honesty, and decency, the better his chances of victory will be in the long run. But from time to time every businessman, like every poker player, is offered a choice between certain loss or bluffing within the legal rules of the game. If he is not resigned to losing, if he wants to rise in his company and industry, then in such a crisis he will bluff—and bluff hard.

Every now and then one meets a successful businessman who has conveniently forgotten the small or large deceptions that he practiced on his way to fortune. "God gave me my money," old John D. Rockefeller once piously told a Sunday school class. It would be a rare tycoon in our time who would risk the horse laugh with which such a remark would be greeted.

In the last third of the twentieth century even children are aware that if a man has become prosperous in business, he has sometimes departed from the strict truth in order to overcome obstacles or has practiced the more subtle deceptions of the half-truth or the misleading omission. Whatever the form of the bluff, it is an integral part of the game, and the executive who does not master its techniques is not likely to accumulate much money or power.

An Analysis of Carr's "Is Business Bluffing Ethical?"

When Carr's article first appeared in the *Harvard Business Review* some years ago, it created a great deal of controversy. No doubt most readers find at least some things in the article with which to disagree. But it is never enough simply to disagree. One must give reasons to support the disagreement, and a necessary precondition of this is to give Carr's article a careful and fair reading. The remainder of this chapter will analyze the views expressed in the article and attempt to show that Carr's positions are mistaken. In this way, we hope to show that the belief that ethics is irrelevant to business is wrong.

Let us review the two strategies by which this belief might be defended. The *ethically neutral* approach argues that the activities of business are somehow "special" and outside of ordinary ethical regulation. Business is governed by its own rules and, like games and etiquette, the rules of this activity are independent of the rules of ethics. The *ethical relativist* approach argues that there is no objective basis for ethical values and that this should prevent the application of ethical norms to business.

Carr argues in both of these ways. The extended analogy between business and poker is Carr's version of the ethically neutral approach to business. Like poker, business has its own rules and as long as the participants know about and follow the "rules of the game," there can be no objection from ethics. When Carr speaks of ethics as "private morality" or of "ethics as conceived in private life," or when he recommends "subordinating personal feelings," he seems to be taking an ethical relativist point of view. Implicit in these last comments is Carr's belief that ethics applies only in the private or personal sphere. He suggests that ethical norms are based upon feelings or, as he mentions elsewhere in the article, "Judeo-Christian" religious beliefs. The implication is clear: since ethics is private, personal, and based on feelings, it has no objective basis and therefore has no place in business. Let us examine each of these strategies in turn.

BUSINESS AS ETHICALLY NEUTRAL

Initially, the claim that business is independent of ethical evaluation may strike us as strange. Ordinarily, we make ethical judgements about a wide variety of human activities. It is unclear why business should be any different. Even Carr acknowledges the strong temptation to apply ethical norms to business. To understand why Carr would adopt such an initially counter-intuitive position, we need to consider what he says and what he means. Specifically, we should begin with his understanding of ethics.

Looking back at the article, we see Carr referring to the "ethics of business," the "ethics of poker," the "ethics of religion," "game ethics," and "personal ethics." In such use, the word "ethics" apparently refers to the rules or standards of proper conduct for a specific activity. Hence, the "ethics of business" refers to the rules of proper conduct in business, the "ethics of poker" refers to the rules of proper conduct in poker, and "personal ethics" refers to those rules or standards that guide our personal lives.

Given this understanding of ethics, it is not difficult to see why someone might think that business should be immune from ethical standards. Private ethics, or as Carr sometimes calls it, "morality," involves rules of an activity different from business and therefore is inappropriate when applied outside of its own context. In this view, just as it would be a mistake to apply the standards of espionage to science (imagine scientists who kept their discoveries secret!), or the rules of the legal system to baseball (imagine putting someone in jail for stealing a base!), so, too, it would be wrong to apply the rules of "religion" or "morality" to business.

As a first step in analyzing this view, we need to clarify a potential confusion. Given this understanding of "ethics," there is an ambiguity in Carr's article. If "ethics" refers to just any rules of conduct, so that there can be an ethics of business and an ethics of poker, then there is no problem in applying "ethics" to business. But Carr clearly thinks that there is a problem, and this fact shows that he has a second understanding of "ethics" operating throughout. This would be the sense of "ethics" in ordinary usage: the rules or standards of right conduct for all human activities. This is the ethics that Carr believes is irrelevant to business. To avoid the confusion of having to use the word "ethics" in two different ways, and to remain somewhat consistent with Carr's general meaning, let us refer to any rules or standards of proper conduct as "ethics," and reserve "morality" as the word for those rules that are thought to apply to all human behavior. Thus Carr's claim will be that morality is irrelevant to business because the ethics of business are independent of the rules of morality. Business has its own rules (ethics), and this special character exempts business activity from evaluation by moral standards.

This distinction is more than mere quibbling over words; it uncovers a serious confusion in Carr's position. An example may help to make the point. Think of the Mafia and the elaborate code of conduct that guides behavior within this group. Following Carr's use of "ethics," we can call such rules "Mafia ethics." Now, could an argument similar to Carr's be constructed to show that Mafia hit squads are ethical? We might write a paper on the topic and call it "Is Mafia Murder Ethical?" Within the ethics of organized crime, such activity is accepted, is well-known by the participants, and is necessary for the successful operation of organized crime. Murder is, after all, part of the "rules of the game." To paraphrase the final sentence in Carr's section on poker, "No one should think any the worse of the Mafia game because its standards of right and wrong differ from the prevailing traditions of morality in our society."

Presumably, however, we all want to say that murder is morally wrong regardless of its role in the rules of the Mafia game. In fact, we would say that the entire game is immoral. We would, in other words, insist that the standards of morality be applied to the activities of organized crime and conclude that morality overrides the rules of that game.

This example demonstrates what should happen when we remain clear about the two uses of "ethics." When "ethics" is taken to mean just any rules of conduct, it is easy to think that all "ethics" are equally valid when applied to their own activities and equally invalid when imported into other fields. However, when ethics is understood as "morality," we normally do not hesitate to make ethical (moral) judgements about any serious human activity.

What should we then conclude? Using reasoning similar to Carr's, one could argue that the activities of the Mafia are morally neutral. Since we are not ready to accept that conclusion, we must recognize that morality legitimately can be applied to activities that have their own standards, or "ethics." Thus, if Carr wants to maintain the moral neutrality of business, he must show us a relevant difference between the activities of organized crime and the activities of business that exempts one, but not the other, from moral evaluation.

But what could this relevant difference be? One suggestion might be that business activities are "good," "right," and "not harmful," while the activities of the Mafia are "bad," "wrong," and harmful." Unfortunately, this cannot serve the purpose for which it is intended because, in this context, these terms are clearly being used in a moral sense. By distinguishing business from organized crime in that way, Carr would be admitting not only that morality is relevant to business, but also that business is morally praiseworthy! But, to admit this is to contradict the claim that ethics is irrelevant to business. Carr simply has not established that there is something special about business that would make it immune from moral evaluation.

MORALITY AND THE LAW

In defense of his view, Carr might claim that it is the law that distinguishes business from the Mafia. After all, throughout the article he insists that business activities must take place within the law. As long as business operates legally, there is a relevant difference between business and the Mafia. Unfortunately, not only will the law not serve this purpose, it will help show in another way how morality *is* relevant to business.

Consider first why obeying the law should be a relevant difference between business activities and Mafia activities. Apparently, the reasoning here is that by operating within the law, business is doing what is "right," while the Mafia is doing what is "wrong." But "right" and "wrong" in what sense? If we mean *morally* right and *morally* wrong, then we must admit defeat for the business-as-morally-neutral claim. On the other hand, we could mean *legally* right and *legally* wrong. But why should this be a relevant difference between business and the Mafia? Why should obedience to the law exempt business from moral evaluation?

Imagine an entire country controlled by the Mafia. Like many small countries controlled by a military dictatorship, the laws of this country would be made to advance the interests of the ruling class. In such a country many normal business activities might be made illegal (e.g., private ownership, free trade, etc.). In this case, the Mafia would be doing what is *legally* right and business activities would be *legally* wrong. Should we therefore say that the Mafia but not business would be exempt from moral evaluation? Presumably not. In fact, most of us would argue that the Mafia would be morally wrong and business morally right, despite what the law would say. This example shows that mere obedience to the law is not sufficient to exempt one from moral evaluation. Obedience to the law would be relevant to Carr's purposes only if we already knew that the law itself was morally legitimate and that there were no moral requirements beyond what was required by the law. But, to admit this is to admit, once again, that morality is relevant to business—if only through the mediation of the law.

There are two ways in which Carr might continue to defend his views. First, he might argue that obeying the law is not a *moral* responsibility at all, but merely the prudent thing to do. In this view, we obey the law not because the law is morally justified, but out of a fear of punishment.

Ignoring that this is a rather cynical and immature understanding of the law (and one not at all consistent with our liberal, democratic political principles), this attempt to salvage Carr's position will certainly fail. In this view, the only difference between business and the Mafia is the degree to which one, but not the other, is willing to take the risks of being punished. Surely this is no reason to exempt business from moral evaluation.

Second, Carr might admit that business is not, after all, completely independent of morality. Rather, he might suggest that business should fulfill only those moral responsibilities that are legally enforced and should ignore those recommendations of morality that are not legally binding. (One reason why he might say this is because these further moral recommendations are viewed as mere subjective feelings or preferences. This relativist view will be considered in more detail below.)

The first thing to note about this strategy is that it admits defeat for the ethically neutral claim. Carr would no longer be arguing that business is independent of morality. More importantly, there are other implications of this strategy that are not very attractive.

Consider for a while what our society would be like if we followed Carr's advice to operate in business according to law but not according to our moral judgements. In such a society, we would all retain our moral beliefs, for Carr thinks that morality is acceptable in its place. Except when required by law, however, we would keep such personal beliefs apart from our business decisions. To do otherwise would jeopardize our chance to compete successfully in the business game.

In such a society, should people be free to participate in the political process and try to translate their moral beliefs into law? If we are committed to a democratic political system, we must answer "yes." Democratic systems give each member of the society the right, indeed some may say the responsibility, to participate in its lawmaking function. Like the rest of us, Carr presumably would support the democratic political process and grant to each citizen the right to try to translate his or her moral beliefs into law.

Since Carr's advice to the businessperson is to ignore moral standards except when required by law, conflicts between accepted business practices and the moral beliefs of private citizens are likely to occur quite often. (Indeed, Carr's entire article is predicated upon the existence of such conflicts.) Given the right to change the law and given the fact that business practices conflict with some deeply held moral beliefs, we should expect that some new laws and government regulations that enforce "private morality" will be passed. Should business obey such laws? If Carr wishes to maintain the claim that business should be exempt from moral standards, he would have to conclude that business should ignore these laws, otherwise business would be operating according to moral standards. But, to do this is to reject not only the democratic political system, but *any* legal system at all. On the other hand, to allow that business should obey such new laws is to allow, at least indirectly, that business legitimately can be subject to any moral standard.

But would this be a desirable society in which to live? Would we want laws to require us to do all the things that morality advises us to do? Should we have laws requiring people to be friendly, to help elderly persons across intersections, to care about others? We can see that such a society is also a threat to democratic principles because it would involve gross restrictions upon the freedom of its citizens. Individual liberty is a central value in a democratic society, and this liberty would be threatened if we legally enforced all that is morally required. Our society tries to balance a citizen's right to change the law with the right to be free from interference by others. One way in which we do this is to assume that, free from legal interference, people will generally do what is morally right. Individual moral responsibility is what allows us to grant maximum individual freedom within our society. In Carr's world, there is no place for individual moral responsibility in business.

The options, then, would appear to be: (1) many laws, less individual freedom, and no interference by private morality, or (2) fewer laws, more individual freedom, and the legitimate guiding of business by morality. Carr's view can easily lead to (1), which in a liberal, democratic society is undesirable. For this reason, we should be reluctant to accept Carr's analysis.

Another implication of this strategy is that it would make it impossible to morally criticize the law. If Carr tells us that laws should be obeyed but other moral recommendations should not, then there must be something special about those moral requirements that are legally enforced. Presumably, this specialness would be that those moral rules that have become law have passed through the democratic lawmaking process. Thus it would be the lawmaking process that confers objective legitimacy on moral rules. But if this is so, we could never legitimately criticize a law that has been democratically adopted. Carr would thus have to admit that there are no grounds for business to criticize, for example, minimum wage laws, OSHA regulations, affirmative action requirements, environmental regulations, etc. While Carr might be satisfied with this, most people in business would not. They would not be satisfied, we suggest, because like everyone else, people in business believe that their moral judgements have a legitimate role to play in shaping the activities of business.

In summary, the strategy of arguing that business deserves some special exemption from moral evaluation must be rejected. To defend this view would be to deny the obvious social reality. Business is a highly complex social activity. It has tremendous implications for all areas of society. Virtually every aspect of our lives is affected in some manner or form by decisions made in a business context. From the food we eat to the homes we live in, from the products and services we buy to the jobs we hold, our lives are affected by business. To deny that we should make moral judgements about the activities of business is to deny that we should make moral judgements at all. It is to abandon the goals, requirements, and ideals of the moral life altogether. Thus Carr cannot sustain the claim that business should have some special exemption from morality simply because it has its own "ethics," unless he is willing to tell us to abandon the moral life altogether.

THE ETHICAL RELATIVIST VIEW OF BUSINESS

This brings us to the second way in which Carr might defend the claim that moral evaluations should be kept out of business. Earlier, we called this the ethical relativist approach to business and morality; we need now to characterize this view in more detail. In general, *ethical relativism* holds that there is no objective basis for our moral beliefs. Moral beliefs are "relative to" individual people, cultures, or religions. Accordingly, it is a mistake to think that moral judgements are universally valid. One reason for thinking that there are no objective moral standards would be the belief that all of our moral judgements are reducible to personal feelings or are mere judgements of personal preferences. We can call the view that holds that moral judgements are nothing but expressions of personal feelings or preferences, *ethical subjectivism.*

It would appear that Albert Carr is an ethical subjectivist. He often identifies morality as "private," as reducible to "personal feelings," or as being based upon one's religious preferences. On the basis of this subjectivism, it appears that Carr concludes that ethical relativism is correct. Carr tells us that business decisions "must be as impersonal as those of a surgeon performing an operation." The implication is that since morality involves "personal feelings," it cannot be as impersonal or objective as medicine. Since moral judgements are subjective, ethical relativism must be true. To assess this view, we need first to sort out some of the issues involved.

The first issue about which we must be clear involves the belief of many people, including apparently Albert Carr, that when personal feelings are involved, objectivity is not. It is commonplace to hold that if one can show that "feelings" or "emotions" are involved in morality, then one has succeeded in showing that morality is non-objective and arbitrary. In other words, ethical subjectivism implies ethical relativism. It is true that in our everyday language we often use "feelings" or "emotions" to stand for those beliefs that are accepted uncritically. "I feel that nuclear weapons are immoral" is often a shorthand way of saying "I believe that nuclear weapons are immoral, but I really do not have a carefully reasoned argument to support that belief." Sometimes to say that a belief is an emotional one is simply to say that it is one to which I am firmly committed and will be unlikely to change. In short, we need to be very clear about what is meant by "feelings" or "emotions." Without detouring into an elaborate discussion of human emotions, however, we can recognize that feelings and emotions are objectively and rationally evaluated all the time. We can criticize a person's feelings, and we do make objective judgements about a person's emotions. Words like "coldhearted" and "unfeeling" point to the existence of objective standards for judging human emotions. So, even if ethical subjectivism is correct and moral beliefs are reducible to feelings or personal preferences, it would not follow that ethical relativism is also correct and that, therefore, we cannot make objective assessments about these feelings and preferences.

There can be no denying that morality involves feelings and emotions. Of course it does. Morality is concerned with the most important aspects of human life and we all have strong feelings about that. Nonetheless, from the fact that feelings and emotions are involved in morality, we should not conclude that objectivity is not. To the degree that Carr does this, he is mistaken. Business decisions that involve emotional issues or about which people have strong feelings will not necessarily be arbitrary, confused, or wrong decisions.

Next, we should distinguish the view we are calling "ethical relativism" from what is often called "cultural" or "anthropological" relativism. Ethical relativism is a *normative* position; it holds that it is illegitimate to apply one's own ethical standards to other people or cultures because there are no ethical standards that are objectively valid for all people. Cultural relativism is a *descriptive* position; it holds that, as a matter of fact, there are no moral standards that are applied by all people in all cultures. It is very easy to confuse these two positions, and in fact many people believe that ethical relativism is valid because cultural relativism is true. However, while cultural relativism may be true (although we suspect that it is less true than many people think), we will argue that ethical relativism is mistaken.

It is true that in various and diverse cultures people hold moral beliefs that are quite different from our own. This fact about the world is the essence of cultural relativism. However, it would be a mistake to conclude on the basis of this fact that there can be no moral standards objectively valid across cultures. An analogy might help to make this point. In times past various cultures held widely different beliefs about the sun and the earth. Some believed that the sun was a god who travelled across the sky. Others thought that the earth was a stable body in the center of the universe and the sun orbited the earth. Scientific *beliefs*, in this sense, are also culturally relative. In various and diverse cultures people hold scientific beliefs that are quite different from our own. Nevertheless, it would be a mistake to conclude that there is no objectively valid account of the solar system on the basis of these diverse beliefs. The *fact* that people disagree is not enough to prove that there are no objective means for determining what they should believe. So it is with morality. The facts of cultural relativism do not imply the validity of ethical relativism.

A third and final issue about which we need to remain clear concerns the importance that we place on the value of tolerance in our society. In democratic societies, which value individual liberty, people are reluctant to make judgements about or to criticize others. This follows from our strong commitment to tolerate the opinions and beliefs of others. This commitment is a central value in a free and democratic society. However, we should be careful not to confuse this reluctance to judge others—a reluctance that is, after all, based upon the strong moral value of tolerance—with the inability to judge others (ethical relativism).

If we remain clear about these three issues, we will be less likely to find the relativist view plausible. These are three common traps into which many relativists fall. We now need to consider more serious reasons for holding the relativist position.

One reason for thinking that relativism is correct is the fact that many moral debates seem to be inconclusive. People just don't agree in morality the way that they do in, for example, science. Moral disagreements go on and on without any apparent hope for resolution. As the congressman quoted in Carr's article said, "Ethics is a barrel of worms." In practice, there just do not seem to be any objective decision procedures in morality.

There can be no doubt that many moral debates are inconclusive. But should this be surprising? Whenever strongly held beliefs are involved, people are reluctant even to listen to the other side, let alone to change their views. Nevertheless, there is nothing special about morality in this respect. One need only to think about the vigorous reactions against Copernicus, Galileo, and Darwin to see that similar things happen in science. When people make strong commitments involving complex issues, simple solutions are hard to find.

Granting all of this, it is nevertheless true that there is a great deal of agreement in moral debate. Although some moral issues are "a barrel of worms," others are quite straightforward. There is a strong consensus that murder is wrong, freedom is good, lying is to be avoided, and friendships should flourish. People do not always do what is right and avoid what is wrong, but they do agree, to a surprising degree, about what should and should not be done. There is a substantial amount of objectivity in moral debates; we should not be misled by the inconclusiveness of a few examples. Just as the views of a Copernicus or Galileo came to be widely accepted over time, so, too, have many moral beliefs come to be widely accepted as objectively correct. In Copernicus's day, for example, torturing criminals was an accepted form of punishment. Today we reject such beliefs as morally wrong.

We need to distinguish between agreement on answers and agreement on methods or procedures for reaching answers. The analogy with science can help here again. Scientists disagree about the answers to scientific questions all the time. For example, many scientists believe that dinosaurs were warm-blooded, while many others believe that they were cold-blooded. Still, we all agree that science is objective. The reason for this is that scientists have a commonly accepted procedure, the "scientific method," for adjudicating disputes and reaching conclusions. It is the procedure and not the answers that allows science to avoid relativism.

We suggest that similar methods are available for morality. Even if we do not have agreement about moral answers, we do have some procedures available that can help in finding answers. The proof that morality is open to rational analysis and not completely relative to personal feelings, religious beliefs, or cultures is that, through the past few pages, we have been engaged in a rational analysis of moral beliefs. We started with a point of view which, if accepted, would have important implications for how people ought to behave in business. Through a process of clarifying facts, being consistent with our terms, drawing out the implications of what Carr had said, pointing out unacceptable conclusions and inconsistent beliefs, and giving reasons for alternative views, we have shown that objectivity can be achieved in moral debates. Indeed, the remainder of this book is testimony to the indisputable fact that business is, and can be, the proper subject of moral evaluation. If the ethical relativist view of business is correct, then we could not do what we have just done. To the degree that we have engaged in a rational and objective analysis, the ethical relativist view of business must be mistaken.

A more practical version of this argument can be developed by considering what Carr himself is attempting to do. Although part of his article is meant simply to describe how the business world "really is," much of the article is an attempt to defend the legitimacy of that description. He does that by offering numerous *arguments*, reasoned attempts to convince us that his views are valid. But, since the acceptance of his view would have important moral implications (we would be changing radically our ordinary understanding of moral responsibility, for example), Carr is arguing for a moral position. This shows that Carr himself cannot accept the very position that he defends! An ethical relativist denies that rational and objective analysis is possible in moral matters. By his actions, Carr has denied his own conclusions.

Of course, the consistent ethical relativist could claim that this sort of reasoning and argument is possible at a certain level, but that ultimately there can be no absolute resolution of moral conflicts. The problem with this answer is that it seems to be holding morality to too strong a standard. If we are looking for absolute certitude in our moral beliefs, we will be unlikely to find it. If we expect people to be fully rational and readily willing to revise their moral beliefs in the face of reasoned argumentation, we will be disappointed. If we expect people always to act in accord with their beliefs, we will often be frustrated. However, in these respects morality is not unlike science. Few scientists would ever claim that they have absolute certitude. The history of science is full of examples of scientists who refuse to revise their theories in light of new and conflicting evidence. There are many cases of scientists who, motivated by money, fame, jealousy, or laziness, failed to live up to the ideals of the scientific community. Nevertheless, we still think that science is an objective enterprise. For similar reasons, we should be reluctant to think differently about morality.

It might be responded that we achieved some semblance of objectivity in the analysis of Carr's article only because, at bottom, we share many of Carr's assumptions. For example, it was only because we share with Carr a commitment to a democratic society with a high regard for individual liberty that we were able to refute his view that the law should be the sole guide of proper business conduct. But, this response might argue, if one is free to reject those assumptions, then relativism ultimately is still possible. To prove our position fully, then, we must defend these assumptions against relativism.

At this point, philosophers typically appeal to an ethical theory to defend the values that, like democracy or individual liberty, are used in more concrete ethical debates. Historically, many different ethical theories have been advanced to supply the type of ultimate response to relativism not present in the preceding pages. Utilitarianism, Kantianism, and natural law theories are three such ethical theories. However, even when these theories are used to justify more concrete values, questions about the justification and validity of these theories themselves can still be raised. (For example, how should one decide between utilitarianism and Kantianism?) It has always been the philosopher's role to pursue these questions of justification. Typically, this pursuit leads the philosopher to the more abstract areas of epistemology and metaphysics.

Unfortunately, if we were to follow this course, we would be unlikely to return to the more practical issues of business ethics within the foreseeable future! The question of justification must end somewhere, and we shall, somewhat arbitrarily, end it at the level of those shared social and political values of our society. In this sense, the ethical relativism implicit in Carr's article is refuted not by appeal to some abstract ethical theory, but because it is inconsistent with our commitment to the objectivity of the values in our liberal, democratic society.

If the relativism implicit in Carr's approach were accepted, then we would be forced to conclude that there is no ultimate moral difference between democracy and totalitarianism. We would have to say that there are no moral reasons for preferring liberty over slavery; that there is no objective moral difference between murder and charity. We would have to say that those moral rights protected by the Bill of Rights—such things as free speech, freedom of assembly, a right to a fair trial, free press, and freedom of religious worship—are culturally relative and can legitimately be given or denied according to the interests of the local culture.

It is logically possible for Carr to pursue the defense of relativism into areas of epistemology and metaphysics. Perhaps he would want to argue that there are strong metaphysical reasons for rejecting democracy. (Plato, for example, argued that democracy was a corrupt form of government on what were essentially metaphysical grounds.) For our purposes, we shall ignore that pursuit. In the selections that follow, many analyses, defenses, and criticisms of business are made in terms of the shared social and political values of our liberal, democratic society. We accept such values as sufficient to refute relativism.

Ethical relativism can be very seductive. If we are lazy in our thinking, if we are not careful in our reading, if we are not intellectually honest, we can easily fall under its spell. On the other hand, if we hope to make any progress at all towards making our society a better place in which to live, we must move beyond relativism to the vigorous analysis and defense of our moral beliefs.

AN OVERVIEW OF CARR'S "BUSINESS BLUFFING"

We've seen that Carr cannot sustain the morally neutral approach to exempting business from moral evaluation without sacrificing some of our strongly held social and political values. On the other hand, if Carr wants to take the relativist approach to business ethics, not only must he admit that the values of democracy and individual liberty are without justification, he must himself remain silent on the issue. To write articles that argue for a moral position is to admit that ethics is open to rational analysis which, in turn, is to admit that relativism is mistaken. The fact that we have engaged in a reasoned debate with Carr refutes his relativism. Further, we must admit that even Carr acknowledges that a shared commitment to some standards (e.g., honesty and other "rules of the game"), is essential for the continued functioning of business.

If all of this is correct, what can we make of Carr's article? Is there some other interpretation of his views that would escape the criticisms raised above? With some work, perhaps we can find one.

Let us return to the opening paragraphs of this chapter. We started with a distinction between the *unethical* (or immoral) and the *non-ethical* (or, morally neutral). Presumably, Carr does not wish to suggest that business is unethical. On the other hand, we have argued that he cannot sustain the view that holds that business is non-ethical. The only alternative is to hold that business is ethical, that it deserves moral praise. But how might Carr make this claim while at the same time holding that business should be exempt from ordinary moral standards? An answer might be found in an early passage of the article.

Carr tells us that business "as practiced by individuals as well as by corporations, has the impersonal character of a game—a game that demands both special strategy and an understanding of its special ethics." This suggests not that business is exempt from morality but, perhaps, that the commands of morality when applied to business yield "special" results. Thus, Carr could salvage his view if he were to accept certain moral values as fundamental—as objectively valid for all people—but argue that when these values are applied to business activities they have special implications. In this sense, our ordinary moral standards are irrelevant to business not because they are subjective or relative, but because when fundamental values are applied to business they yield non-ordinary results. For example, Carr might argue that given the crucial role that business plays in our society, morality presents business with special moral rights and obligations. Of course, this is to admit that morality is relevant to business after all. In Chapter 2 we shall consider a more detailed version of the claim that business has a special moral role in our society and that, therefore, business should be exempt from ordinary moral evaluation.

J. D.

CHAPTER ONE
Study Questions

1. It was claimed that, like the Mafia, business cannot have its own "ethics." Yet very often we talk as if there are special "ethical codes" for doctors, lawyers, and politicians. How can this be so?

2. Carr suggests that one's moral beliefs depend in some way upon one's religious beliefs. Do you need religion in order to be moral? If there were no God, could there still be objectivity in morals?

3. Carr says that business does have its own code, or "ethics," which comprises its own "rules of the game." What are the "rules of the game" in business that are analogous to the rules of the poker game?

4. Carr advises us to keep our personal lives out of our business lives. Is such a distinction between "lives" possible? Advisable?

5. How accurate is the poker analogy? Every analogy contains both similarities and dissimilarities. Do you think that poker is similar enough to business to carry the argument? What are the similarities? Dissimilarities?

6. What are some of the "shared values" of a liberal democracy? How do these values actually function in our society? Are some democratic values more important than others?

7. This chapter gave *reasons* for avoiding relativism. For some people, even if these reasons seem plausible, reasons are not enough. How would you *motivate* such a person to avoid relativism? How, in general, can you motivate someone to do the right thing?

CHAPTER TWO

*M*ORAL THEORY
AND THE FREE MARKET

Introduction

*T*HE PRECEDING CHAPTER showed that it is difficult to hold that business has ethical standards different from and completely independent of the moral standards governing normal interpersonal relationships. That is the relativist position that sees business standards as an autonomous set of rules logically unrelated to the everyday demands of morality. Of course, one could maintain the relativist position in a sensible way, since it is not internally incoherent. However, if one maintains this view, one cannot also argue that society *ought* to allow business to function according to this independent set of rules, since that "ought" judgement itself suggests the existence of an objective moral point of view. Such a suggestion contradicts the relativist denial of moral objectivity. Thus, the relativist view that business possesses autonomous standards is a view that precludes the possibility of presenting arguments about how business ought to be treated by the society. Those who wish to convince us that we should judge business behaviors by standards different from those we use to judge other behaviors had better find another approach.

Chapter 1 also indicated that another approach is available. It is possible to claim that the specific ethical standards governing business are and ought to be different from the standards governing other activities. One can reasonably argue this claim if one agrees that (1) the same fundamental goals and principles of morality exist for all types of human behavior, and (2) there are good reasons why those basic principles and goals dictate different specific standards of behavior for different areas of human endeavor. This approach is an ordinary and familiar one; it simply recognizes that we properly judge behaviors differently when the circumstances of those behaviors are relevantly different. Thus, we allow that the set of obligations of a spouse is importantly different from the set of obligations of a nonmarried person; we hold policemen to possess different responsibilities than do physicians. One could argue for different specific standards of responsibility for business people, then, by showing that the relevantly different circumstances of business require different sorts of behavior in order to achieve more effectively the fundamental objectives of morality. Of course, one then must also specify just where the standards ought to differ and why the specific difference in circumstances supports the suggested difference in responsibilities.

This approach to business ethics is implicit in the writings of popular authors who argue that the further good of society is achieved by allowing behavior in business that we would not condone between neighbors. The approach is also evident in those who warn of dire consequences for the populace as a whole if business is forced to operate according to strict standards of moral responsibility adapted from nonbusiness contexts. The following article by Milton Friedman is a classic instance of this form of argument for a set of responsibilities for business that differs from the set of responsibilities governing other types of behavior. The difference in responsibilities for which Friedman argues is, as we shall see, quite a radical one. We shall also see that such a radical difference in responsibilities cannot be supported by the arguments found in the selection.

After a careful analysis of Friedman's article reveals this deficiency, two other traditional moral arguments for his position will be investigated. One of these is a utilitarian argument; the other, an argument based on a right to liberty. These arguments also will be found wanting. The plan of this chapter, then, is to argue that business ethics and ordinary personal morality cannot be as radically different as some would have them.

MILTON FRIEDMAN

The Social Responsibility of Business Is to Increase Its Profits

When I hear businessmen speak eloquently about the "social responsibilities of business in a free-enterprise system," I am reminded of the wonderful line about the Frenchman who discovered at the age of 70 that he had been speaking prose all his life. The businessmen believe that they are defending free enterprise when they declaim that business is not concerned "merely" with profit but also with promoting desirable "social" ends; that business has a "social conscience" and takes seriously its responsibilities for providing employment, eliminating discrimination, avoiding pollution and whatever else may be the catchwords of the contemporary crop of reformers. In fact they are—or would be if they or anyone else took them seriously—preaching pure and unadulterated socialism. Businessmen who talk this way are unwitting puppets of the intellectual forces that have been undermining the basis of a free society these past decades.

The discussions of the "social responsibilities of business" are notable for their analytical looseness and lack of rigor. What does it mean to say that "business" has responsibilities? Only people can have responsibilities. A corporation is an artificial person and in this sense may have artificial responsibilities, but "business" as a whole cannot be said to have responsibilities, even in this vague sense. The first step toward clarity in examining the doctrine of the social responsibility of business is to ask precisely what it implies for whom.

Presumably, the individuals who are to be responsible are businessmen, which means individual proprietors or corporate executives. Most of the discussion of social responsibility is directed at corporations, so in what follows I shall mostly neglect the individual proprietor and speak of corporate executives.

In a free-enterprise, private-property system a corporate executive is an employee of the owners of the business. He has direct responsibility to his employers. That responsibility is to conduct the business in accordance with their desires, which generally will be to make as much money as possible while conforming to the basic rules of the society, both those embodied in law and those embodied in ethical custom. Of course, in some cases his employers may have a different objective. A group of persons might establish a corporation for an eleemosynary purpose—for example, a hospital or a school. The manager of such a corporation will not have money profit as his objective but the rendering of certain services.

In either case, the key point is that, in his capacity as a corporate executive, the manager is the agent of the individuals who own the corporation or establish the eleemosynary institution, and his primary responsibility is to them.

Needless to say, this does not mean that it is easy to judge how well he is performing his task. But at least the criterion of performance is straightforward, and the persons among whom a voluntary contractual arrangement exists are clearly defined.

Of course, the corporate executive is also a person in his own right. As a person, he may have many other responsibilities that he recognizes or assumes voluntarily—to his family, his conscience, his feelings of charity, his church, his clubs, his city, his country. He may feel impelled by these responsibilities to devote part of his income to causes he regards as worthy, to refuse to work for particular corporations, and even to leave his job, for example, to join his country's armed forces. If we wish, we may refer to some of these responsibilities as "social responsibilities." But in these respects he is acting as a principal, not an agent; he is spending his own money or time or energy, not the money of his employers or the time or energy he has contracted to devote to their purposes. If these are "social responsibilities," they are the social responsibilities of individuals, not of business.

What does it mean to say that the corporate executive has a "social responsibility" in his capacity as businessman? If this statement is not pure rhetoric, it must mean that he is to act in some way that is not in the interest of his employers. For example, that he is to refrain from increasing the price of the product in order to contribute to the social objective of preventing inflation, even though a price increase would be in the best interests of the corporation. Or that he is to make expenditures on reducing pollution beyond the

amount that is in the best interests of the corporation or that is required by law in order to contribute to the social objective of improving the environment. Or that, at the expense of corporate profits, he is to hire "hardcore" unemployed instead of better-qualified available workmen to contribute to the social objective of reducing poverty.

In each of these cases, the corporate executive would be spending someone else's money for a general social interest. Insofar as his actions in accord with his "social responsibility" reduce returns to stockholders, he is spending their money. Insofar as his actions raise the price to customers, he is spending the customers' money. Insofar as his actions lower the wages of some employees, he is spending their money.

The stockholders or the customers or the employees could separately spend their own money on the particular action if they wished to do so. The executive is exercising a distinct "social responsibility," rather than serving as an agent of the stockholders or the customers or the employes, only if he spends the money in a different way than they would have spent it.

But if he does this, he is in effect imposing taxes, on the one hand, and deciding how the tax proceeds shall be spent, on the other.

This process raises political questions on two levels: principle and consequences. On the level of political principle, the imposition of taxes and the expenditure of tax proceeds are governmental functions. We have established elaborate constitutional, parliamentary and judicial provisions to control these functions, to assure that taxes are imposed so far as possible in accordance with the preferences and desires of the public—after all, "taxation without representation" was one of the battle cries of the American Revolution. We have a system of checks and balances to separate the legislative function of imposing taxes and enacting expenditures from the executive function of collecting taxes and administering expenditure programs and from the judicial function of mediating disputes and interpreting the law.

Here the businessman—self-selected or appointed directly or indirectly by stockholders—is to be simultaneously legislator, executive and jurist. He is to decide whom to tax by how much and for what purpose, and he is to spend the proceeds—all this guided only by general exhortations from on high to restrain inflation, improve the environment, fight poverty and so on and on.

The whole justification for permitting the corporate executive to be selected by the stockholders is that the executive is an agent serving the interests of his principal. This justification disappears when the corporate executive imposes taxes and spends the proceeds for "social" purposes. He becomes in effect a public employee, a civil servant, even though he remains in name an employee of a private enterprise. On grounds of political principle, it is intolerable that such civil servants—insofar as their actions in the name of social responsibility are real and not just window-dressing—should be selected as they are now. If they are to be civil servants, then they must be selected through a political process. If they are to impose taxes and make expenditures to foster "social" objectives, then political machinery must be set up to guide the assessment of taxes and to determine through a political process the objectives to be served.

This is the basic reason why the doctrine of "social responsibility" involves the acceptance of the socialist view that political mechanisms, not market mechanisms, are the appropriate way to determine the allocation of scarce resources to alternative uses.

On the grounds of consequences, can the corporate executive in fact discharge his alleged "social responsibilities"? On the one hand, suppose he could get away with spending the stockholders' or customers' or employees' money. How is he to know how to spend it? He is told that he must contribute to fighting inflation. How is he to know what action of his will contribute to that end? He is presumably an expert in running his company—in producing a product or selling it or financing it. But nothing about his selection makes him an expert on inflation. Will his holding down the price of his product reduce inflationary pressure? Or, by leaving more spending power in the hands of his customers, simply divert it elsewhere? Or, by forcing him to produce less because of the lower price, will it simply contribute to shortages? Even if he could answer these questions, how much cost is he justified in imposing on his stockholders, customers and employees for this social purpose? What is his appropriate share of others?

And, whether he wants to or not, can he get away with spending his stockholders', customers' or employees' money? Will not the stockholders fire him? (Either the present ones or those who take over when his actions in the name of social responsibility have reduced the corporation's profits and the price of its stock.) His customers and his employees can desert him for other producers and employers less scrupulous in exercising their social responsibilities.

This facet of "social responsibility" doctrine is brought into sharp relief when the doctrine is used to justify wage restraint by trade unions. The conflict of interest is naked and clear when union officials are asked to subordinate the interest of their members to some more general social purpose. If the union officials try to enforce wage restraint, the consequence is likely to be wildcat strikes, rank-and-file revolts and the emergence of strong competitors for their jobs. We thus have the ironic phenomenon that union leaders—at least in the U.S.—have objected to Government interference with the market far more consistently and courageously than have business leaders.

The difficulty of exercising "social responsibility" illustrates, of course, the great virtue of private competitive enterprise—it forces people to be responsible for their own actions and makes it difficult for them to "exploit" other people for either selfish or unselfish purposes. They can do good—but only at their own expense.

Many a reader who has followed the argument this far may be tempted to remonstrate that it is all well and good to speak of government's having the responsibility to impose taxes and determine expenditures for such "social" purposes as controlling pollution or training the hardcore unemployed, but that the problems are too urgent to wait on the slow course of political processes, that the exercise of social responsibility by businessmen is a quicker and surer way to solve pressing current problems.

Aside from the question of fact—I share Adam Smith's skepticism about the benefits that can be expected from "those who affected to trade for the public good"—this argument must be rejected on grounds of principle. What it amounts to is an assertion that those who favor the taxes and expenditures in question have failed to persuade a majority of their fellow citizens to be of like mind and that they are seeking to attain by undemocratic procedures what they cannot attain by democratic procedures. In a free society, it is hard for "good" people to do "good," but that is a small price to pay for making it hard for "evil" people to do "evil," especially since one man's good is another's evil.

I have, for simplicity, concentrated on the special case of the corporate executive, except only for the brief digression on trade unions. But precisely the same argument applies to the newer phenomenon of calling upon stockholders to require corporations to exercise social responsibility (the recent G.M. crusade, for example). In most of these cases, what is in effect involved is some stockholders trying to get other stockholders (or customers or employees) to contribute against their will to "social" causes favored by the activists. Insofar as they succeed, they are again imposing taxes and spending the proceeds.

The situation of the individual proprietor is somewhat different. If he acts to reduce the returns of his enterprise in order to exercise his "social responsibility," he is spending his own money, not someone else's. If he wishes to spend his money on such purposes, that is his right, and I cannot see that there is any objection to his doing so. In the process, he, too, may impose costs on employees and customers. However, because he is far less likely than a large corporation or union to have monopolistic power, any such side effects will tend to be minor.

Of course, in practice the doctrine of social responsibility is frequently a cloak for actions that are justified on other grounds rather than a reason for those actions.

To illustrate, it may well be in the long-run interest of a corporation that is a major employer in a small community to devote resources to providing amenities to that community or to improving its government. That may make it easier to attract desirable employees, it may reduce the wage bill or lessen losses from pilferage and sabotage or have other worthwhile effects. Or it may be that, given the laws about the deductibility of corporate charitable contributions, the stockholders can contribute more to charities they favor by having the corporation make the gift than by doing it themselves, since they can in that way contribute an amount that would otherwise have been paid as corporate taxes.

In each of these—and many similar—cases, there is a strong temptation to rationalize these actions as an exercise of "social responsibility." In the present climate of opinion, with its widespread aversion to "capitalism," "profits," the "soulless corporation" and so on, this is one way for a corporation to generate goodwill as a by-product of expenditures that are entirely justified in its own self-interest.

It would be inconsistent of me to call on corporate executives to refrain from this hypocritical window-dressing because it harms the foundations of a free society. That would be to call on them to exercise a "social responsibility"! If our institutions, and the attitudes of the public make it in their self-interest to cloak their actions in this way, I cannot summon much indignation to denounce them. At the same time, I can express admiration for those individual proprietors or owners of closely held corporations or stockholders of more broadly held corporations who disdain such tactics as approaching fraud.

Whether blameworthy or not, the use of the cloak of social responsibility, and the nonsense spoken in its name by influential and prestigious businessmen, does clearly harm the foundations of a free society. I have been impressed time and again by the schizophrenic character of many businessmen. They are capable of being extremely far-sighted and clear-headed in matters that are internal to their businesses. They are incredibly short-sighted and muddle-headed in matters that are outside their businesses but affect the possible survival of business in general. This short-sightedness is strikingly exemplified in the calls from many businessmen for wage and price guidelines or controls or income policies. There is nothing that could do more in a brief period to destroy a market system and replace it by a centrally controlled system than effective governmental control of prices and wages.

The short-sightedness is also exemplified in speeches by businessmen on social responsibility. This may gain them kudos in the short run. But it helps to strengthen the already too prevalent view that the pursuit of profits is wicked and immoral and must be curbed and controlled by external forces. Once this view is adopted, the external forces that curb the market will not be the social consciences, however highly developed, of the pontificating executives; it will be the iron fist of Government bureaucrats. Here, as with price and wage controls, businessmen seem to me to reveal a suicidal impulse.

The political principle that underlies the market mechanism is unanimity. In an ideal free market resting on private property, no individual can coerce any other, all cooperation is voluntary, all parties to such cooperation benefit or they need not participate. There are no "social" values, no "social" responsibilities in any sense other than the shared values and responsibilities of individuals. Society is a collection of individuals and of the various groups they voluntarily form.

The political principle that underlies the political mechanism is conformity. The individual must serve a more general social interest—whether that be determined by a church or a dictator or a majority. The individual may have a vote and a say in what is to be done, but if he is overruled, he must conform. It is appropriate for some to re-quire others to contribute to a general social purpose whether they wish to or not.

Unfortunately, unanimity is not always feasible. There are some respects in which conformity appears unavoidable, so I do not see how one can avoid the use of the political mechanism altogether.

But the doctrine of "social responsibility" taken seriously would extend the scope of the political mechanism to every human activity. It does not differ in philosophy from the most explicitly collectivist doctrine. It differs only by professing to believe that collectivist ends can be attained without collectivist means. That is why, in my book *Capitalism and Freedom*, I have called it a "fundamentally subversive doctrine" in a free society, and have said that in such a society, "there is one and only one social responsibility of business—to use its resources and engage in activities designed to increase its profits so long as it stays within the rules of the game, which is to say, engages in open and free competition without deception or fraud."

An Analysis of the Free-Market View of Responsibility

FRIEDMAN'S ARGUMENT

Certainly the first, and probably the most important, thing one must do when evaluating an article like the preceding one is to clarify the position of the author as precisely as possible. Friedman's position in this article represents a particular view of the responsibilities and rights associated with the ownership and control of productive property. His article defends what is known as the free-market or *laissez faire* economy. His precise free-market view here, as elsewhere, is implicitly composed of two parts: one dealing with the proper role of government in regulating business; the other dealing with the responsibilities that business managers have to others in the society.

First, Friedman holds that government should avoid regulating business activities except when regulation is necessary to prevent the use of force or fraud. Support for this reading of Friedman's article can be found by noting his references to "the rules of the game." His first reference is in the fourth paragraph, where the rules include those embodied in law. His final reference is in the last paragraph of the selection, where he describes the content of the rules as the demand for free and open competition without deception. This focus on free competition without deception, of course, means that the rules do not allow us to engage in force or fraud. Apparently, by limiting the rules to this prohibition, Friedman indicates his belief in the legitimacy of any other behavior. However, since the law is a subset of the rules, the law should also limit itself to proscribing the use of force and fraud and it should not attempt to regulate economic activity for other purposes. Hence, Friedman's view must be that government has the authority to prevent coercion and deception; further activity transgresses the legitimate powers of government. (The term "free market" clearly derives from the freedom of economic transactions from government interference.)

The second aspect of Friedman's view, his approach to the responsibilities of management, is similarly a reflection of his free-market position. He suggests that those in control of productive property have responsibilities to provide (maximal) return on investment for stockholders. So long as it stays within the rules (avoids coercion and fraud), management ought to do whatever it can to increase this return. By implication, management can have no responsibilities to seek the welfare of anyone other than shareholders. Management's only responsibility other than making profits, then, is to obey the rules and to avoid coercing or deceiving third parties. (Friedman, of course, allows that owners may choose to lower their returns by instructing managers to have a concern for the well-being of others, but he clearly believes that owners are under no obligation to do this.)

Friedman's Radical Position.   How does Friedman's position relate to the discussion in Chapter 1? In the text preceding his selection, Friedman was described as holding that business obligations are radically different from the ordinary moral obligations normally recognized for individuals. An example should make clear that Friedman argues for a radical distinction. Suppose you are yachting off the Cape and you come across a shipwrecked and drowning woman. You have only one life preserver and it has significant sentimental value for you. (It is silk covered and was a gift from your first love upon the achieving of your first million.) What moral obligations or responsibilities do you have to this unfortunate woman? Must you unconditionally throw her the life preserver and ruin the silken fabric in the process? Can you bargain with the woman until she agrees to a monetary compensation you consider appropriate for the loss of such a valued item? Clearly, our normal moral code would require you to provide the life preserver and would condemn you for placing conditions on its provision.

Thus, it would seem that our ordinary moral obligations on occasion include a responsibility to provide aid even when the circumstances causing the need for aid were not of our doing. Compare this, however, with the responsibilities Friedman suggests for management. He is explicit in his claim that action to aid individuals other than stockholders is not among the obligations of managers. For example, managers have no obligations to help alleviate social problems such as inflation or pollution. Here is a major difference, then, between the set of responsibilities governing management according to Friedman and the set governing nonbusiness relationships.

Other differences can be identified also. Ordinary moral norms are taken to prohibit inflicting at least some harms that are not easily classified as coercion or deception. Truthful but malicious speech aimed at destroying a person's reputation or intentionally frightening a person with heart disease are (hopefully) obvious examples. However, Friedman's set of business responsibilities includes no such obligations to avoid harms that are not caused by fraud or coercion. (Note that the concepts of "fraud" and "coercion" are usually narrowly defined by those who defend the free-market theory; thus, coercion is normally not seen by defenders of the free market when market conditions severely limit a person's real options for choice.)

To point to these differences between ordinarily accepted responsibilities and the responsibilities Friedman suggests for business managers is not sufficient reason for dismissing his position, of course. For Friedman does attempt to persuade us that a society run according to his suggestions is a morally better society than one where business is constrained by stricter responsibilities or where government attempts to increase well-being by means other than the simple prevention of force and fraud. In fact, Friedman offers a number of connected comments that might be taken as serious arguments for the superiority of his *laissez faire* approach to responsibility. Before we evaluate those arguments, however, we should note that there are two other comments that are often seen as decisive arguments for Friedman's position.

Although these comments are often rhetorically effective, on intellectual grounds they are insufficient support for the conclusion Friedman desires.

The Social Responsibility of Business.   The first of these comments concerns the "looseness" of discussions of the social responsibility of business. Friedman contends that it is senseless to speak of responsibilities in this way since "business" is a term referring to a collection of distinct corporations and these corporations are not real persons. Apparently, Friedman believes that there cannot be collective responsibility for a group and that only actual persons can possess responsibilities. If Friedman is correct in his understanding of these beliefs, it would be impossible even to raise a question concerning the extent of business responsibilities, since the very application of a notion of responsibility would be meaningless.

Despite Friedman's objections, though, we can talk of the responsibility of "business." First, we can discuss the responsibility of "business" (in general) if the types of responsibility for individual corporations exhibit some regularity. For example, if all businesses have the responsibility of seeking profits for shareholders, as Friedman suggests, then we can speak of the responsibility of "business" as a shorthand way of expressing the similar respective responsibilities of individual businesses to pursue profit. Second, Friedman's assertion that only real persons have responsibilities, while perhaps correct in some sense, cannot prevent us from applying the concept of social responsibility to a corporation as a whole. Undoubtedly, it is appropriate for a society to question itself about the sorts of institutions it wants to encourage, since even Friedman would not deny that we can ask whether a society with or without free speech is preferable. And so long as we can ask what sorts of institutions we ought to sanction in our society, we can ask how we ought to define the rights and obligations of business.

A discussion of business responsibility, then, can be coherently pursued as a discussion of the proper behavior of business institutions in relation to other institutions of the society and to the implicit objectives of the society as a whole. Thus, we can discuss whether it is better for business to singlemindedly seek profit or to attempt to contribute directly to the well-being of society. In this sense, Friedman's very article counts as admission of the meaningfulness of the concept of corporate responsibility. For while he may believe that the real responsibility of a corporation is to make profits, he cannot dismiss the other position as incoherent on the grounds that it attempts to decide how business institutions should function. He can, of course, dispute this other position, but for that he needs an argument that we have yet to see.

(Note that to discuss the social responsibility of business in this way is not to settle the difficult question of how to apportion responsibility within a corporation for purposes of punishment when the corporation fails to operate properly. Here Friedman is most likely correct, in that any sanction will have its final effect only on real persons since even the dissolution of a corporation punishes only those individuals whose welfare depends on the corporation.)

Friedman's Free Society.   The second Friedman comment that often misleads readers concerns his use of the term "free society" when describing his ideal social arrangement. Friedman seems to suggest that a free society is, by definition, the society he desires, i.e., a society where government's role is restricted to the prevention of coercion and deception and where business operates on a principle of self-interested pursuit of profit. We shall see upon analysis, however, that what we value in a free society has no logical connection to Friedman's ideal for business responsibility.

In contemporary North America the term "free society" has tremendous positive connotation. Unfortunately, its meaning is often left as a vague reference to some political and economic features of our own society. To untangle the meaning of "free society" we need to carefully define the political and economic systems at issue. Our societies are marked by *democratic* (representative) political systems and by primarily *capitalist* economic systems. A democracy is a form of political decision making where the ultimate authority for making political decisions rests in the hands of the voting population. Opposed to democracy are such nondemocratic systems of political decision making as dictatorships, oligarchies, monarchies, and totalitarian regimes, where the ruling elites are not formally accountable to the populace. As a system of political decision making, a democracy does not exclude or include by definition any particular aspect of the society as subject to majority rule; democratic decisions can be made about taxing policies, immigration quotas, or business regulations.

Capitalism, on the other hand, is an economic system whose characteristic mark is that the means and resources of production are privately owned. Under a capitalist system, factories, raw materials, and the like are privately controlled in the effort to produce profits for private owners. Opposed to capitalism, of course, is the socialist economic system, where the means and resources of production are somehow in the hands of the public. Each of these systems has variants, and any particular society may exhibit both capitalist and socialist ownership patterns. For example, public ownership can be achieved by centralized control of factories or by workers' ownership and control of their respective firms. Capitalism can be either extreme free-market capitalism, where government activity in the economy is minimal, or it can be state-regulated capitalism (such as our own), where the state places significant restrictions on how production can be carried out. Finally, in any given society, some industry groups, e.g., steel companies, might be organized on capitalist lines while other groups might be publicly owned; or, even within industry groups, some firms might be privately owned while others are publicly controlled.

The important thing to note here is that our "free society" is composed of logically distinct political and economic systems. There is no logical necessity that democratic societies be capitalist or that socialist societies be nondemocratic. For example, consider the numerous dictatorial regimes of capitalist Latin America and the significantly more socialized yet strongly democratic societies of West Germany and Israel. Nor is there any necessity that all capitalist economies allow business as free a hand as Friedman would like it to have. Unfortunately, members of our own society are too often confused about their commitments to democracy and capitalism, so that they consider socialist societies as necessarily undemocratic. Friedman's use of "free society" trades on this common confusion and, because of that confusion, some are convinced that our democratic freedom is logically tied to the existence of a Friedman *laissez faire* brand of capitalism. We can see, however, that participants in a socialist economy need not be unfree in the sense that they lack the power of political self-determination.

(It is true, of course, that among current democracies, most exist in countries that until recently had strongly capitalist economies. It would be ingenuine to pretend that the rise of modern Western democracies had nothing to do with the rise of capitalism in Western Europe. The ability of a new bourgeois class to achieve economic self-sufficiency did much to reduce the powers of the monarchs in Europe. We should not, however, confuse this particular historical sequence with a claim that democracy cannot exist without capitalism. For while it may be true that the development of democracy was influenced by the power of the new middle class to resist the monarch, the continued existence of self-determination need not depend on the power of the citizens to resist a central political authority. In fact, in circumstances with a strongly rooted democratic tradition and the absence of a nondemocratic political authority, many see the greatest threat to continued self-determination in the power of unregulated and concentrated wealth. In any case, the historical argument fails to show a strong practical connection between the existence of a *free-market* capitalist economy and the existence of a democratic political system, since it fails to note the special and unrepeated circumstances surrounding the joint rise of these political and economic systems.)

The contemporary confusion between political and economic systems on which Friedman trades can, perhaps, be traced to the fact that ours are constitutional democracies, i.e., they are the democracies where the power of majority rule is limited by explicit constitutional constraints in the form of guaranteed legal rights for all citizens. Thus, in the United States a simple majority cannot determine that women cannot vote or that citizens may be prevented from the exercise of their religion. These constitutional rights are, in effect, liberties or freedoms for all citizens. Perhaps it is the actual mix of these rights that leads to the confusion that causes some to accept Friedman's position too quickly. We should focus on these actual rights and their importance to a free society, then.

If we had to choose which rights besides the right to self-determination were most important to a free society, which would we list? Of course, the classic political liberties from the Bill of Rights would be listed: the freedom of speech, the freedom of religion, the freedom of the press, the freedom from unwarranted search and seizure, etc. A society with these freedoms and the freedom of self-determination would certainly qualify as a free society. However, our constitutional rights have been interpreted to include also a right to hold private property. In actual practice, this right to property encompasses both a right to personal property (e.g., a car) and a right to property in the means of production. We could be misled into believing that this actual set of freedoms we have is an unbreakable set. Particularly we could be misled if we think only vaguely about "freedoms" without specifying what freedoms are at issue. There is, however, no apparent logical connection between these respective rights, and it seems perfectly possible for persons to have the classic civil liberties without the right to operate business free from all but minimal government regulation.

The confusion that makes Friedman's position attractive to many, then, is one that makes a free society appear to be a society that includes the freedoms associated with a capitalist economic arrangement. Further, Friedman apparently hopes that your unconscious identification of a "free society" will include not only the freedom to hold personal and productive property but also to control that property with narrowly defined obligations and with government regulation only to ensure free and open competition. It should be clear that Friedman has given no argument for his position yet. Thus, we should be on guard against accepting too quickly the superiority of Friedman's approach because of his comments concerning the concepts of "business responsibility" and "free society." Now that we have cautioned against these potentially misleading comments, we can proceed to investigate more carefully the central and serious argument that Friedman presents.

The Tax Argument.   Friedman's only serious and explicit argument is what we might call his "tax argument." This argument claims that business managers who act against the economic interests of the firm in order to achieve some social objective such as lowering pollution are, in effect, imposing taxes. Such actions will lower profits, raise prices, and/or lower wages. Thus, the manager who decides to reduce pollution below the level allowed by law is privately levying taxes on shareholders, consumers, and/or employees in order to benefit society. Friedman suggests that the imposition of such taxes by individual decision is intolerable both in principle and because of its likely consequences.

Before we begin a careful assessment of this argument, two cautions are in order. First, the word "taxes" may be misleading since tax issues these days are emotionally charged. Some, on hearing the word "tax," have an automatic negative reaction. To avoid prejudicing the conclusion, it is better if we translate Friedman's "tax" into the more neutral word "costs." The managers' actions are not taxes in the traditional sense of government levys, but they are the imposition of costs that otherwise would not exist. So, hereafter we will speak of a manager's expenditure on pollution equipment that reduces profits as the imposition of a cost on shareholders.

The second preliminary caution concerns the extent to which the tax argument could be an argument for Friedman's dual position on management responsibility and government regulation. Note that this tax argument discusses only the range of responsibilities for management. It contains nothing that can be seen as an argument that government regulation of business should aim only at preserving free and open competition. So, even if the argument were successful, which it is not, Friedman would be justified in asserting only that half of his position that defines management responsibilities narrowly. It is needless to say that a failure to argue for fully half of one's position is a serious defect.

As it was just described above, Friedman's argument against the private imposition of costs in order to achieve social objectives has two aspects. First, he claims that on the level of political principle such social objectives and costs should be the product of joint decisions by the citizens; unilateral imposition of costs in pursuit of such objectives is contrary to accepted and morally justified democratic political principles. Second, Friedman indicates that even were such unilateral actions not objectionable in principle, the likely consequences of these private decisions would be harmful to the society. Thus, Friedman argues that there are two good moral reasons for not holding business persons to ordinary standards of moral responsibility which would require a broad concern for the welfare of society.

We can deal with the consequentialist branch of the argument first. Friedman claims that management is technically unprepared to make the complex judgements necessary for deciding what actions would produce the greatest net benefit for society. His example is that of a manager trying to pursue the social objective of reducing inflation. The ordinary manager has no procedure for making a careful estimate about the consequences of his or her pricing policy on inflationary trends in the society. The reasons for this are clear in Friedman's article.

This may be a proper description of management expertise on the complex economic problem of inflation. Friedman, however, means to convince us that management has *no* social responsibility other than avoiding fraud and coercion while staying within the law. But a single example that shows the unfortunate consequences of encouraging an additional responsibility logically cannot show that all further responsibilities have the same unhappy consequences. For example, suppose that newly available and conclusive studies proved that the discharge into a nearby stream of some by-product of a firm's production process was causing serious health damage to members of the surrounding community. Or suppose the pollution only threatened the continued availability of a popular recreation area. Suppose also that the discharge could be eliminated by expenditures that lowered profits but did not threaten the economic viability of the firm. Would management assumption of a responsibility to stop the discharge, an assumption beyond the range Friedman suggests, produce negative consequences for the society? Presumably not in the case where health was threatened. Not clearly even in the threat to the recreational area.

Thus whether management assumption of responsibilities beyond the narrow range defined by Friedman would have unhappy consequences appears to depend on the particular responsibility at issue. So, we cannot assume that management lacks the technical information and ability for reasonable action on the basis of any social responsibility simply because it lacks that information or ability in one case. In fact, sometimes management may have exactly the expertise necessary. Friedman's consequentialist argument commits the fallacy of over-generalizing from a small set of examples to a universal claim about all possible cases. The argument must be rejected as unconvincing.

Friedman's defense of his management responsibility thesis will have to rest with his argument from political principle. That argument demands that the imposition of costs in pursuit of social objectives must be the result of joint political decisions. Any position that allows the imposition of such costs by private individuals is intolerable in principle, according to Friedman.

A word about costs should begin the analysis of this argument. As any student of introductory economics who is familiar with the concept of opportunity costs will attest, a cost is a relative thing. The full cost of any purchase, policy, or decision can only be measured relative to the alternatives that one thereby forgoes. Thus, since resources are finite, to spend money on an MX missile has a cost not only in dollars but also in the inability to use those dollars for nutritional programs. Similarly, when a business executive spends for new pollution control equipment to benefit society, that spending is a cost to shareholders in that it precludes using those same dollars for greater dividends. That expenditure is also a cost to employees and consumers since it also precludes spending those dollars for higher salaries or lower prices.

This reveals a characteristic mark of costs: What is a cost to one person or group is usually a benefit to another. Providing expensive workplace safety equipment is a benefit to employees but a cost to shareholders and consumers if it means lower profits or higher prices. Costs and benefits can even be exchanged for a single individual. Increased wages can be an employee benefit won at the cost of decreased corporate pension contributions. The economic point is clear: Since costs are always relative to alternatives forgone, every business decision will involve the imposition of costs. Friedman's economic system is no exception. In that system, when a manager acts to increase profits within the rules of the game, that action carries an implicit cost for others affected by corporate policy: consumers, employees, and society at large.

As an economist, Friedman of course recognizes that the imposition of costs is unavoidable in any economy. So, presumably he is not attempting to convince us that the imposition of costs is unacceptable in principle. Perhaps he merely means to enjoin managers from imposing costs on the basis of personal moral decisions. Friedman might be contrasting his own view with the "social responsibility thesis" by suggesting that the latter allows managers to impose such costs while his own view does not. If this is his argument, however, we will see that Friedman cannot sustain an in-principle rejection of the "social responsibility thesis" while he maintains a commitment to his version of the responsibilities of business.

In Friedman's free-market view, managers have only the responsibility of seeking profits for shareholders while staying within the rules of the game. Those rules, remember, included the law and prohibited the use of force or fraud. In fact, law was legitimate only if it was an attempt to eliminate coercion or deception. Since prohibiting these behaviors is the criterion of an acceptable law, the behaviors must be identifiable independently of law or political decisions. And, undoubtedly, force and fraud are singled out for prohibition because they are seen as intrinsically evil.

The justification for the legal prohibition, then, is that the use of these is morally unacceptable. However, if uses of coercion and fraud are morally unacceptable, Friedman ought to enjoin their use even when the law does not prohibit them. It is, of course, implausible to expect that an instrument as technical and general as the law could explicitly single out every instance of coercion and deception. There will, then, be cases of coercion or deception that are not covered by the law. But business managers must refrain from such actions, in Friedman's view, if his injunction to avoid force and fraud is to be taken seriously. The decision to refrain from such actions when they are not prohibited by law, though, is a personal moral decision made by the individual manager. It is also a decision that imposes costs (most likely on shareholders who stand to reap higher profits from these actions). Moreover, whether an action not prohibited by law is coercive or deceptive is sometimes unclear. Certainly it is coercive to relieve a person of his earnings at gunpoint. Is it coercive to ask a person who has no other employment opportunities to accept hazardous work at low pay? If it is, then such wage offers are morally unacceptable. Managers must decide if this is an instance of coercion.

Thus managers, even in Friedman's view, must involve their personal moral judgement both in avoiding the use of force or fraud where not prohibited by law and in determining whether a specific action counts as either of these behavior types. It appears that if one rejects the "social responsibility view" in principle, because it allows the imposition of costs on the basis of personal moral decisions, one must reject Friedman's view as well. The presence of costs so imposed cannot serve to distinguish between the moral standing of these opposing approaches to the responsibilities of management.

Friedman might try to rescue his argument at this point by claiming that he is not against the imposition of costs or even against the imposition of costs on the basis of personal moral convictions. Rather he might claim that he only opposes in principle the imposition of costs on the basis of personal moral decision when those costs are imposed in pursuit of a social objective. For example he might distinguish pursuit of profits within the rules from pursuit of the social objectives of a lower level of inflation or pollution.

This use of "social objective" to rescue the argument will not succeed for an obvious reason. Friedman must still allow a general responsibility to avoid coercion and deception. Avoiding or eliminating coercion or deception from the economy, however, certainly seems the pursuit of a social objective. This rescue of his argument of principle can succeed, then, only if he views the absence of force and fraud as a social objective of different importance than other social objectives. But any number of these other social objectives involve the attempt to avoid seriously harmful or undesirable circumstances. Consider the following social objectives: a more equitable distribution of power, a healthier and more pollution-free environment, and a safer workforce and consumer population. The benefits of these objectives and the harms they seek to avoid are highly significant in the moral perspectives of most people. It is difficult to see how Friedman could argue that these are all objectives whose importance is less significant than the objective of avoiding coercion and deception. He has, at least in this selection, presented us with no argument for this ranking of importance.

Friedman might, of course, simply assert that force and fraud are somehow so especially repugnant that only avoiding them could constitute a serious moral obligation for managers. However, without an argument to that effect, his article is reduced to presuming the truth of the very point at issue; namely, that the only moral obligation falling upon business managers is to pursue profits while refraining from coercion and deception. It will not do, though, in defense of a belief simply to assert that it is true. Only by begging the question, then, can the Friedman selection establish a moral distinction in principle between a narrow view of business responsibilities and a broader view that finds business responsible beyond the injunction to avoid coercion and fraud. Thus, both of Friedman's arguments concerning costs must be rejected because of logical flaws.

(Interestingly, the question-begging nature of Friedman's argument of principle is underscored by the fact that nearly identical arguments are used by democratic socialists to support public control of industrial decision making. These socialist arguments claim that in capitalist economies business managers privately make decisions about public goods, e.g., the safety of the workplace or the allocation of investment capital. They find intolerable that decision-making power about such socially important goods should rest in private persons concerned with personal profit. This dispute between Friedman and the democratic socialists resides not so much in the arguments used as in a view of what social goals impose obligations on those in control of production.)

The final assessment of Friedman's article must be that it is unable to provide sufficient intellectual support for the conclusions it wishes to draw. Aside from the two misleading but rhetorically effective comments that begin the selection, Friedman's only arguments concern the harmful consequences of private imposition of costs and the rejection of such private decisions on grounds of principle. Neither of these arguments should convince the careful reader. Moreover, Friedman's position contains a view of both the proper role of government and the range of management responsibility. The arguments presented, even were they successful, would be sufficient to establish only the latter part of his theory. Thus, the selection suffers from serious under-argument and from logical flaws. These deficiencies prevent it from providing support for the claim that business, because of its special circumstances, has responsibilities radically different from those ordinarily accepted as governing interpersonal relationships.

TWO ARGUMENTS FROM FUNDAMENTAL MORAL CONCERNS

We should not make a logical error of our own by concluding that Friedman's position is unacceptable, however. For the failure of one article to provide evidence for a particular conclusion does not mean that the conclusion is unsupportable. There may be other arguments that could convince us that business responsibilities are radically different or that government should limit its regulation of business to the maintenance of free and open competition.

In fact, there are two traditional arguments for the superiority of Friedman's position on business regulation and responsibility. Both of these arguments start from goals basic to morality and attempt to show that the achieving of these goals is more probable under a Friedman-like approach. One of the arguments focuses on the consequences of Friedman's approach for the welfare of everyone in the society. It claims that people will be better off under that approach. The other argument focuses on a right to liberty, and it claims that any approach other than Friedman's will violate that right. We will investigate each of these arguments in turn, and we will see that each has crucial failings. In the final analysis, our conclusion will be that the proper approach to business allows for more government regulation and more management social responsibility than Friedman would like.

Pursuit of either of these arguments requires that we come to some understanding of the nature of morality and its basic objective. We can safely say that if there is any point to morality, it will involve (at least) the promotion of human welfare. However, for a set of rules or guides for behavior to count as a morality, it must do more than just promote human well-being, since an individual who follows rules for successful selfish behavior also aims at human well-being (his or her own). For most of us, though, morality functions to curb such selfish pursuit of one's own interests; it requires, instead, that we consider the effect of our behavior on the welfare of others. Clearly, then, a morality must not only promote well-being but it must do so without arbitrarily ranking the interests of one person as inherently more important than the interests of another. This demand for non-arbitrariness means that *morality seeks to promote human welfare impartially.* We can consider this as a rough characterization of the features that define the basic goal of morality.

A Utilitarian Argument.   One straightforward interpretation of this basic moral objective is *utilitarianism*. Utilitarianism is a classic moral theory that, roughly speaking, directs us to seek "the greatest good for the greatest number of people."

This moral theory sees a person's good as a function of the degree to which his or her interests are satisfied. A person's interests might include actual desires and/or those goods that rational persons would want. Classic human interests, then, would be health, freedom, and friendship. Thus utilitarianism promotes human well-being by seeking the satisfaction of these and other human interests.

Further, it seeks such satisfaction impartially by requiring that all persons be treated as if they were of equal worth and by demanding that the similar interests of different individuals be weighed similarly when we decide how to act. Utilitarianism will require, for instance, that your desire for health be weighted equal to my equally intense desire for health.

The utilitarian interpretation of morality's basic goal, then, tells us to consider the interests of everyone who will be affected by our choice of actions. It suggests that our moral obligation is to choose the action that appears to provide the greatest overall balance of interest satisfaction. Thus, if action *A* seems as if it will cause some harm but also cause great satisfaction, while alternative possibilities appear to cause more harm and less benefit, utilitarianism will hold that we are obligated to perform *A*.

Thus we can characterize utilitarianism as an approach to moral obligation that focuses solely on the interest-satisfying consequences of action. And we can identify the fundamental principle of utilitarianism as the directive "seek to maximize net interest satisfaction." Determining how to act under this principle involves simply a careful estimation of the probable effect of our actions on human happiness.

This approach to morality is probably the most common initial interpretation of how to promote human well-being impartially. It is also an approach from which springs the first traditional argument for Friedman's position on minimal regulation and narrow business social responsibilities. Following the early economist Adam Smith, many have seen maximal economic benefit in the operation of a free market where individuals pursue private gain. They believe that the possibility of private profit provides both the increased motivation necessary for higher levels of production and a guarantee of the most efficient use of resources.

The contemporary form of this argument claims that much government regulation and management assumption of social responsibility lead the society as a whole to be worse off. Government regulation, it is said, requires that particular businesses divert capital to satisfy regulatory requirements when that capital could otherwise be spent on increasing or improving production. It also requires the diverting of capital from the productive private economy in order to support the nonproductive machinery of a regulatory bureaucracy. Similarly, management assumption of social responsibilities to persons other than shareholders (the installation of nonmandated pollution abatement technology, for instance) diverts capital from more productive uses. On the other hand, less government regulation and a management unhindered by social responsibilities beyond legal profit-seeking will allow more efficient use of capital with the results of expanded production, more jobs, and an overall higher *per capita* GNP (the total dollar value of the goods and services produced by the economy.)

So the traditional utilitarian argument for a Friedman-like approach defends the *laissez faire* economy as producing higher levels of interest satisfaction and, hence, as the economic arrangement mandated by morality's fundamental goal of impartially promoting welfare. In today's political climate such utilitarian arguments for the moral superiority of the Friedman approach to management responsibility and government regulation should be familiar. Criticisms of these arguments should also be familiar.

The first general criticism of this utilitarian defense accepts the utilitarian mandate to maximize interest satisfaction, but doubts that the *laissez faire* economy is the maximizing alternative. (Another form of criticism will be discussed below. It rejects the utilitarian approach to morality altogether.) Any number of versions of this criticism are current. One common version admits the possibility that less government regulation or less management responsibility may increase the total wealth of the society. However, it questions whether the increase in wealth maximizes interest satisfaction because it worries that the increased wealth may lead to satisfying the luxurious desires of a few while leaving the majority worse off with respect to relative wealth and level of interest satisfaction. This criticism is offered by those who claim that conservative economic policies lead to a greater concentration of wealth in the hands of a few.

Other versions of this general criticism argue that *per capita* GNP is not an adequate measure of interest satisfaction. These versions reject the utilitarian defense of the Friedman position because they believe a person's interests involve aspects that a quantitative measure of goods and services cannot hope to include. For example, some will argue that without government regulation of minimum wage rates, workers may lose significant amounts of power in their relationship with ownership because they no longer have the protection of government-mandated baselines in their contract negotiations. Thus, if some government regulations minimize differences in economic power, the elimination of those regulations carries with it the loss of a good that is not calculated in the GNP. If these goods are important ones, their loss makes it less likely that fewer government regulations would maximize net interest satisfaction.

Others criticize the utilitarian defense of the free market by focusing on the externalities of the production process. Externalities are costs of production that are not reflected in the company ledger or in the price of the product. Thus, production might expand and more workers might be hired if business had fewer regulations or social responsibilities governing the provision of workplace safety equipment. In the years immediately following the removal of such constraints, we might see an increase in GNP. However, the long-term cost in chronic health problems of eliminating regulations would not be measured in that GNP calculation. Of course, we would not want to conclude too quickly that under these circumstances the society as a whole is better off according to utilitarian standards.

Similar points have been made already about the external costs of pollution. Without EPA regulations or without management assumption of broader social responsibilities than Friedman suggests, many cheaper waste disposal policies would be legally or socially available for corporations. Savings from these cheaper policies might be reflected in more production and more jobs but, again, the critics warn that we would not be better off even with those increases. We would have lost both the aesthetic value of a cleaner, more pristine environment and, potentially, the important good of a healthier population. Neither of these goods is easily measured by the quantitative assessment of the GNP. Thus, the critics argue that the utilitarian defense of the Friedman position on regulation and responsibility takes a too narrow view of what constitutes human interests. They claim that we could very well be worse off if government and management did not attempt to protect the welfare of all those affected by business decisions.

Given its continuing widespread support for workplace safety and environmental protections, the general population, in spite of its well-reported anti-regulatory tendencies, appears in broad agreement with critics of the utilitarian argument. People are properly suspicious that we could be worse off without either government regulation or a more active moral conscience to constrain management decisions. We can at least conclude, then, that a management unconcern about third parties has not been proven to maximize interest satisfaction. And, if we take public opinion seriously, we might even have grounds for thinking that the free-market approach to responsibility and regulation could produce less interest satisfaction than alternative approaches. Thus, this first argument from the basic goal of morality cannot convince us that business ought to have responsibilities that differ radically from the ordinary responsibility to consider consciously the welfare of everyone affected by our actions.

A second form of criticism of this defense of the free market objects to the utilitarian moral theory on which the defense is based. Thus, even in the unlikely event that the Friedman position on management responsibility were mandated on utilitarian grounds, many would remain unconvinced of its moral superiority. Many would remain unconvinced because they find the utilitarian approach to morality unacceptable, since it unrestrictedly permits the sacrifice of any interest of one person as a means towards a greater corresponding net increase in interest satisfaction for others. Utilitarianism looks only at a debit/credit balance sheet of interest satisfaction; in theory, nothing prevents a utilitarian decision from sacrificing my interest in life or health for a net increase in the summed satisfaction of other persons' desires for more wealth. Many moral theories find this aspect of utilitarianism objectionable. They hold that some central interests of the person ought not to be subject to frustration for the purpose of satisfying the interests of others. These understandings of morality that hold some interests outside the sphere of utilitarian exchange do so because they believe that there is a moral importance to the human person that can only be expressed if we occasionally preclude using the frustration of one individual's interests as a means for the satisfaction of another. Since the above defense of the Friedman position derives from this objectionable perspective on morality, that position would not be proven acceptable even if it did satisfy utilitarian demands.

We need now to discover how to correct this perceived defect in utilitarian moral theory. We shall see that a moral theory that avoids this problem of utilitarianism can lead us to a new argument for the Friedman position by protecting from frustration a human interest in liberty. This new liberty argument, however, will fare no better than did the utilitarian attempt to convince us that Friedman's *laissez faire* economy is morally preferable.

A Rights Argument.   A corrective to this perceived defect of utilitarian theory is to conceive of morality as including rules that provide some protections for the central interests of a person and to require that any frustration of those interests by humanly alterable conditions be justified by more than a simple net increase in satisfaction for others.

(This is not to say that the protections must be absolute. It only prevents a simple summative calculation of increased satisfaction from justifying a frustration of the interests protected. It remains possible for the otherwise protected interests to be frustrated if the consequences of protecting them were catastrophic and not just negative on balance. A constitutional analogue of this moral point can be found in the prohibition on government silencing of speech on the grounds that the speech in question is distasteful to a majority. Traditional First Amendment theory requires a stronger justification, e.g., a clear and present danger to the society, before speech can be outlawed.)

When some interests are protected in this way, we call them rights, i.e., more or less inviolable interests to whose nonfrustration we are entitled. To have a moral right to life, for example, is (1) to be entitled to continued satisfaction of your interest in being alive and (2) to be protected from the actions of people in society who would jeopardize that interest as a means for increasing their happiness. So, if you hold that humans have an intrinsic importance, you will most likely want to hold, in a way utilitarianism cannot, that there are basic human goods that are off-limits to interest-maximizing calculations.

(Note that these rights are moral rights, not legal rights. Legal or constitutional rights are liberties or protections granted to citizens by actual written law. Moral rights are entitlements deriving from a concern for promoting human welfare coupled with a commitment to the intrinsic value of the person. Moreover, the list of legal rights in any given nation need not include what we settle upon as moral rights, and legal rights may include entitlements that have little to do with morality, e.g., a legal right to a driver's license at age sixteen. These two types of rights should be kept distinct in our minds even if there are some rights that appear in both categories.)

It is possible, then, to avoid the defects of utilitarianism and to interpret the impartial promotion of human well-being as requiring something other than maximized interest satisfaction. In protecting some interests as rights, we are promoting welfare while we may not be achieving the greatest balance of happiness. For instance, were a circumstance to arise where a killing would make others happier to a degree just sufficient to outweigh the damage to the interests of the prospective victim, utilitarianism would condone the death. A rights-based approach to morality that included a right to life would demand a much stronger justification, perhaps self-defense, before a killing would be sanctioned.

If this second interpretation of the fundamental objective of morality is to be acceptable, however, it too must promote welfare *impartially*. For a rights-based theory of morality, this demand for impartiality must extend to those interests that are given protection. If the protections are to be provided impartially, we would appear committed to two further claims. First, those interests to be protected must be chosen in a way that does not prejudicially prefer the interests of one person or group over another. Second, the interests chosen for protection must be protected universally, for all persons. For suppose I controlled the selection of interests to be protected and I selected an interest in a position teaching philosophy at a university. We would then promote only the welfare of some, since only a few are perverse enough to have that interest! Also, such a choice procedure itself would be biased because it would not guarantee the desires of everyone a fair hearing. Alternatively, suppose we chose for protection an interest in health, but we protected only the health of Anglo-Saxons. We would again fail to be impartial, since our protections were distributed in a way that was prejudiced against the health of other ethnic groups. So, it seems that both the procedure for choosing what interests to protect and the distribution of the protections chosen must be impartial.

The second of these impartiality requirements is easy enough to satisfy: we need only to be sure that whatever rights are settled on are extended as rights for all persons. The first requirement, that the selection procedure be impartial, is more troublesome to satisfy. What procedure for selecting the protected interests would be impartial? We might settle on protection for all the interests that rational people hold in common. A problem here, however, is that some interests that rational people might hold in common could be practically impossible to protect for all persons. Consider that rational persons might all have an interest in possessing many more economic goods than they now have. As a practical matter of the facts of economic exchange, protecting everyone's interest in this might well be beyond our abilities. Of course, it would make little sense to extend protected status to an interest whose frequent frustration by others was humanly impossible to prevent. We have to restrict the class of protections, then, even though protecting the interests everyone held in common would be an impartial criterion for selecting which interests were treated as rights.

A more promising criterion would be to focus on those interests that every rational person held in common *and* that are somehow central to human existence or that are necessary for the effective enjoyment or pursuit of other more particular interests. We could then include only very important interests and arrive at a more manageable and practically possible list of protections. For example, such a criterion for selecting rights would certainly provide some protection for the most central good of life, a good without which the satisfaction of other interests would be of little concern. Just what other protections would be chosen by this procedure we will not pursue at this moment. However, something like this sketch appears to be the most plausible account of the nature and origin of rights; and, as indicated above, rights are an important component of any acceptable approach to morality's mandate to promote human welfare impartially.

Some of you are probably wondering at this point whether the publisher has mistakenly included these last pages from some other textbook! What has any of this to do with business ethics or management responsibility? Actually, this theory of rights has significant implications for business ethics, since the second argument for narrow management responsibilities arises from a concern for moral rights. In particular, the second traditional argument focuses on a moral right to liberty, and it argues that protecting a human interest in liberty entails that government intervene in business only to maintain free and open competition and that management is responsible only for making profits without using coercion or deception. That, of course, is just the view for which Friedman argued in the selection beginning this chapter. An analysis of this second traditional moral argument for the Friedman position demands that we first understand liberty and why it might be chosen for protection as an interest that is central to human life or necessary for the effective enjoyment or pursuit of other interests.

Liberty is characteristically understood as an absence of interference in one's pursuits. To have a right to liberty would be to have a right to some protection from preventable interference in one's affairs by the actions of others. Numerous reasons support the choice of this interest in non-interference as a central interest worthy of protection according to the above criteria. The most obvious reason is that an absence of interference by others makes more probable the effective pursuit of one's goals.

Thus liberty clearly meets one condition necessary for an interest to have protected status. However, it also seems to have importance on other grounds. In allowing an individual freedom from interference, we can express a belief in the dignity of the person as a deliberative agent who is capable of freely forming and acting on rational plans. This capacity is a central element in what we value about the human person; allowing its exercise allows the individual the opportunity to develop his or her human potential more fully. Liberty, then, might be seen as central to our human existence, and it would appear a prime candidate for protection as a moral right.

The use of liberty as a moral right in the second traditional argument for the free-market position apparently has solid justification, then. The argument's application of this right to non-interference in the arena of business is fairly straightforward. We can investigate first its use in deriving a moral limitation on government activity. The argument claims that if individuals have a right to an absence of interference in their affairs, then they ought to be able to engage in whatever economic transactions they wish to enter. Government regulations on the economy, except those preventing the use of force and deception, constrain business people from participating in desired transactions. Moreover, government regulation paternalistically prevents consumers from entering transactions in which they otherwise would engage. Government economic regulations, then, are interferences in the affairs of citizens and, as such, are unjust violations of their liberty. According to this second traditional argument, a just society would be one where the economic role of the government was limited to the maintenance of free and open competition.

The conclusion of this argument about the proper role of government also can be used to suggest that management responsibility extends only to avoiding coercion and fraud. If, as the preceding paragraph indicates, morality dictates that managers of businesses should not be prevented from entering certain transactions, then, presumably they are morally permitted to engage in those transactions. If we believe that morality permits those transactions, however, we cannot also believe that morality places managers under an obligation that prohibits those same transactions. This is simply a result of the logical relationship between the concepts of obligation, permission, and prohibition: failure to do what is obligatory is prohibited, what is permissible is not prohibited; thus, we are under no obligation not to do what is permissible. If managers should be permitted to act in any way that does not involve force or fraud, then they can have no obligations that require more than the avoidance of those behaviors. Both aspects of the Friedman view thus may be supported by a focus on liberty.

These arguments are attractive to those living in a society that places a high value on freedom, but they are nonetheless critically flawed. A right to non-interference cannot generate a defense of the *laissez faire* view because, first, liberty is not best protected under that economic arrangement and, second, liberty cannot be the most important or most fundamental moral right. We will pursue extensively both of these objections so that we can see that the failings of the liberty argument force us to admit the legitimacy of more extensive government regulation and management social responsibility.

The first difficulty with the above liberty argument is that it focuses on only one type of interference: government interference with the will and desires of business persons and consumers. Interference can come in many varieties, however. And, while it may be true that we should not interfere with the ideally voluntary agreements between people, in reality, market transactions often fall short of ideally voluntary status and will, instead, be interferences with what people would otherwise want to do. The first response to the preceding argument, then, is that significant interferences with people can exist under the *laissez faire* approach to regulation and responsibility. (The argument that follows has been adapted from one offered by James Sterba.[1])

To pursue this first response to the liberty argument, we need to understand both the meaning of "interference" and what makes interferences objectionable. Initially, many see the primary examples of interference as cases where a person is compelled to act in a particular way. The paradigm is that of a gunman relieving you of your money. When a gunman utters, "Your money or your life," however, there is technically no absolute compulsion, since there are alternatives to surrendering your cash. For instance, you might fight or run. So this paradigmatic interference is not a case of strict compulsion; rather, it is a case where the alternatives are highly limited. What makes this interference so particularly objectionable is that another is undesirably limiting your choices by placing important personal goods in jeopardy. Thus, in the gunman case, your choices are limited because you no longer have available the alternative of acting to keep your money without risk to your life.

We should note here that the limitation on your choices by another does not, by itself, make an interference morally objectionable. Consider that a friend asks a favor of me. I am willing to grant the favor, but only if she consents to join me for a beer on Sunday afternoon. Unfortunately, she had planned to attend a rare free concert by the Heath Brothers that day. The conditions I place on the favor interfere with her plans; the conditions limit her choices by eliminating the possibility of attending the concert without risk to the desired favor. Most of us would be willing to grant that I had interfered with what my friend would otherwise have done, but we would not see the interference as a highly objectionable one. What seems a more crucial aspect in making an interference objectionable, then, is not that another places limits on the alternative actions available for your choice, but that the limitation is highly undesirable because it threatens some central human good.[2]

That this latter aspect is more crucial than the fact of limitation alone is especially obvious when we recognize that in economic transactions choices are always limited by what the other party will agree to. This is true even of apparently acceptable transactions where the options are still dictated by how much bargaining each party is willing to allow. For instance, I might be willing to sell my car, but only if I receive $2,000 for it. The buyer's options are limited since she cannot act to buy the car for $1,800. This limiting of options is a generic feature of economic transactions and, of course, no one claims that all economic transactions are unacceptable.

An implication of this generic feature of economic agreements is that interferences, limitations on choice, will always exist. We cannot, then, avoid all interferences; rather, we ought to avoid only those interferences or limitations that are most objectionable. But we have seen that interferences are objectionable when they place important goods in jeopardy. Thus, a concern for liberty or non-interference dictates that we strive to minimize those occasions of significant interference when (1) the alternatives available for choice are highly distasteful and (2) it is humanly possible for us to extend the range of choice to include less threatening alternatives. (The latter condition is necessary for identifying morally significant interferences, since limitations we can do nothing about, while still interferences, are simply unfortunate facts of life. To say otherwise would be to require us to change what we cannot and, of course, we can have obligations only when it is realistically possible for us to discharge them.)

Are there any reasons to think that the free-market approach to regulation and responsibility allows such threatening and objectionable interferences? Certainly, there are many severe interferences possible in that economic arrangement. We know that under market conditions it is likely that some individuals will gain more market power than others. The causes of the inequality in market power are numerous. They include luck, superior cleverness, possession of greater inherited wealth, greater natural intelligence, etc. Over time, it becomes quite possible that some individuals will accumulate a power in capital resources that places their basic economic welfare beyond threat and enables them to strike agreements with others that are less than ideally voluntary.

A normal example of this occurs when the skills of a laborer are in low demand and the laborer is forced by market conditions to accept an unenviable wage offer for hazardous work. Of course, under a free market where government regulation and taxation does not provide a minimum wage, safety inspections, or unemployment compensation, the worker's options would be even more limited than they are in contemporary American economic downturns. From time to time, similar unhappy limitations on options could occur for consumers who might have to buy necessary but expensive or unsafely designed items from a single supplier or a small number of suppliers with matching interests.

A third example of a potentially threatening free-market interference exists when management with strong market power and limited social responsibilities can resist social and economic pressures (e.g., boycotts) to reduce the production of environmentally damaging wastes. Clearly, under a free-market arrangement, the real potential for unequal market power entails the possibility for objectionable interferences, interferences where the available alternatives are undesirable and where important goods are jeopardized. (Even defenders of the free market admit the existence of these temporary "dislocations" of labor, consumer, or society ability to effect change in corporate policy.)

Some might deny that these limitations on choice are violations of liberty or morally objectionable interferences for those with the undesirable alternatives. That denial is most often supported by a claim that since there is no direct intent to limit options to undesirable ones, but only an intent to increase profits, those with more market power cannot be accused of an injustice against those with less power.

Such an absence of intent to interfere is undoubtedly important for a moral judgement about the character of the interfering person or for determining if sanctions against the interferer are appropriate. However, if we are discussing the very design of social institutions, the intent of agents in institutions designed along free-market lines is irrelevant, for we had the potential of a serious commitment to liberty because of its connections with the dignity of persons as free agents, the exercise of the human capacity for choice, and the effective pursuit of other human interests. However, unintentional interference that jeopardizes important goods can limit free choice and hinder pursuit of specific goals as significantly as can intentional interference.

Thus, if we ought to design institutions to maximize the protection extended to the interest in non-interference, we should limit the possibility for both intentional and unintentional interferences. When we decide between institutional arrangements, then, what we need to look at is the severity and frequency of all possible limitations on choice. If we focus on this, we must admit that in the free market there can be serious and humanly alterable interferences, just as there can be in government-regulated markets.

So, it appears that serious interferences may exist under any economy; they are an unavoidable fact of life. We are faced, then, with a choice about which sorts of potential interference to protect against and which we will allow. Of course, as before, this choice must be made with fair weight given to the liberty interests of each person. Such a choice can only be made on the basis of a comparison between the severity of potential interferences under alternative approaches to economic institutions.

A fruitful comparison of alternatives with respect to severity of interference can be made most efficiently if we characterize types of interference in some way. One possible characterization would be to divide interference into two sorts: government interference with individuals, and private interference with individuals by other individuals or corporations. Government interference can be severe or mild. It can be severe when there are no constraints on what government might do to people, when there are no constitutional rights protecting the important interests of the populace. Government interference is milder where there are such constraints and where government respects them. Market interference by corporations or private individuals can also be severe or mild. It can be severe when the basic interests of individuals have no institutional protection but are at the mercy of changing market forces. It is milder where the market is guaranteed by law or moral convention to operate within limits that respect each person's basic desires for well-being.

Of course, the severe interferences possible by individuals under free-market conditions or by the government are to be avoided. Guaranteeing against those severe interferences and allowing only the milder interferences by government or market conditions requires us to accept a particular arrangement of political and economic institutions. That arrangement certainly would include government regulation of business transactions to prevent the severe limitations on choice caused by market forces. Hence, a concern for protecting against serious interference will not entail a commitment for Friedman's conservative *laissez faire* economy. Instead, it generates a commitment to a more liberal state where government activity aims at protecting the basic interests of all.

However, if an overriding commitment to non-interference allows such government activity, the liberty argument cannot derive narrow management responsibilities from the impropriety of government interference. (That, recall, was the structure of the liberty argument.) So, the argument fails to establish that a concern for avoiding serious interference requires a Friedman approach to either government regulation or management responsibility. In fact, the social and political institutions preferred as best protecting liberty seem quite far from those described in Friedman's free-market theory. The liberty argument fails to see this because it does not analyze the nature of objectionable interferences and because it does not consider the severity of interferences from sources other than the government.

The liberty argument has another major flaw. It implicitly supposes that non-interference is the most fundamental interest worthy of protection. That assumption exists because the argument ignores any other interest that might rival liberty for protected status. The preceding comments can show that non-interference cannot be the most fundamental right, however.

We have already seen that there cannot be a general right to liberty, since interferences are impossible to avoid and we cannot be obligated to provide the impossible. In addition, many interferences are intuitively benign and unobjectionable. Thus, if there is any serious right to liberty it can only be a right to be free from specific sorts of interference. We have identified those specific interferences against which we should be most protected as severe interferences that threaten important human goods. However, if morally objectionable interferences are identified as those that threaten certain central goods, then it would appear that what we have a right to is those goods and not some absence of interference in general. Thus, non-interference is not the fundamental concern in avoiding these objectionable interferences.[3]

Non-interference had appeared a fundamental right because it seemed connected to the human capacity for free and deliberative choice and because it allowed more effective pursuit of particular interests. However, we should see now that free choice and effective pursuit of goals can exist even where broad *laissez faire* economic liberty does not. In fact, the argument above shows that free choice and the ability to pursue one's interests are most likely greatest when one is protected from free-market threats to centrally important goods. Thus, the values supporting a commitment to liberty in the above arguments cannot demand a commitment to liberty in general. Rather, they demand that people be protected against that potential frustration of basic interests present in severe interferences. Again, it would appear that a moral right to an absence of specific interferences derives from the importance of the goods that might be threatened in those interferences.

To this point, however, we have provided no analysis of what makes some interferences more severe or some human goods more central. Once we offer such an analysis, the fact that liberty in general cannot be a fundamental right will be even more obvious. Also obvious will be the difference in importance between basic interests and the interest in *laissez faire* economic liberty.

If we consider three intuitively objectionable interferences—one that threatens an individual's life and two others that threaten, respectively, the individual's privacy or free exercise of religion—we can understand why some human goods are so central. It is obvious why the good of life is so basic and why it deserves protection from interferences that threaten it. The protection of an individual's existence is at the heart of the anti-utilitarian, rights-based approach to morality. It would be hard to understand how a morality could forsake the utilitarian approach and place an inherent value in the individual person while it allowed his or her life to be threatened merely as a means for satisfying the desires of others. So, interferences that involve threats to life are objectionable not simply as limitations on choice, but as interferences that violate the very spirit of the anti-utilitarian approach to morality. What is fundamental here is a commitment to the intrinsic importance of each person.

Violations of the above two political rights are also intuitively objectionable. Both of these political rights can be seen as liberties, since they prohibit interference with religious activity or privacy. Once again, though, these specific rights to non-interference gain their importance from the value of the goods involved and not from the value of non-interference alone. If, for example, we allowed interference with an individual's religious beliefs, we would be denying him or her the opportunity to develop and express deep-seated convictions about the meaning and significance of human existence. We would also prevent others from hearing and evaluating those beliefs. These are traditionally important human activities; the human species has long been distinguished from others precisely because it raises these basic questions. Thus, to allow interference with a person's religion presumptively indicates that we lack respect for both that individual and others as beings capable of that characteristic human speculation about the ultimate point of our lives.

Similarly, we threaten fundamental human goods if we allow interferences with a person's privacy. The ability to control the availability of information about yourself allows you the opportunity to have a private life that helps to mark yourself off as an individual. Moreover, to have control over information about yourself allows you to distinguish as more meaningful some of your relationships from others by controlling the degree of intimacy shared.[4] A society that does not protect against interferences with this ability to control personal information undermines these opportunities and lessens the significance of individuality and intimacy. And certainly, our maintaining psychic individuality and our intimate relationships are important human interests. The importance of interferences with religion and privacy, then, is that they cut to the heart of our lives as human persons. Beyond this, to allow interference with another's religion or privacy, when we so dearly value our own, expresses a disrespect for the other and a prejudice that one's own humanity is somehow more intrinsically important than that of the other. Of course, that is an attitude directly counter to the one contained in morality's requirement of impartiality.

How central in human importance is the good of unhindered, *laissez faire* economic activity (the good at issue in the specific right to non-interference defended by Friedman)? Some have argued that production (economic activity) is another characteristic human activity and, therefore, it too ought to be protected. From this we might derive a universal right to employment, to access to the means of production.[5] Of course, such a right might also demand government full-employment policies or management responsibility to hire the unemployed. On the other hand, a right to be free from government regulation or from broader management responsibilities (even when the life, health, privacy, etc. of others is jeopardized) does not seem to be required even if productivity activity is central to human life. We could, of course, engage in productive activity without also having a right to this extensive economic liberty.

Moreover, as we have seen, allowing a right to this economic liberty would place other goods at the mercy of market bargaining power and, therefore, would effectively undermine the attempt to protect some basic goods against threat. Thus, this specific economic liberty could not stand alongside health or privacy as a fundamental human interest worthy of protection; its protection would prevent significant protection of these other goods. Since we have seen no powerful reason for considering this *laissez faire* liberty centrally important, we would be unwise to choose to protect it over these other goods.

If we are cautious, then, and investigate the basis for those specific rights to non-interference that appear strongest, we find that their strength derives from the fundamental interests that would be threatened. Their strength does not derive from the inherent importance of non-interference. Liberty does not appear to be a fundamental right; rather, a right to equal respect as a person with common and humanly central interests is more fundamental. Thus, the liberty argument in favor of government regulation and management responsibility only to avoid force and fraud fails because it implicitly presumes non-interference to be morally fundamental when, in fact, it cannot be.

Of course, neither of the preceding criticisms of the liberty argument for the *laissez faire* approach suggests the propriety of arbitrary interference in economic activity when more central goods are not at stake. There is still an importance in having as much autonomy as possible beyond that which would be guaranteed when basic interests are protected from threat. This more general absence of interference, however, must have a secondary moral importance that does not jeopardize the protection extended to fundamental interests. In addition, if it is to be granted protection even as a secondary interest, it must be protected for all. Thus, if we assume a moral perspective on social institutions, we should commit ourselves to institutions that by law or convention respect equally the fundamental and common interests of each person and that then allow each person as much a guarantee against other interferences as is compatible with an equal guarantee for all. As an example, the social institution of business should operate so that interferences that place life, health, and privacy in jeopardy are prohibited before interferences that threaten only the ability to enter specific economic transactions. This clearly requires that both the law and the consciences of managers concern themselves with more than prohibiting direct coercion and outright deception. A morally acceptable approach to social and political theory, then, demands the rejection of Friedman's extreme and radical distinction between the responsibilities of business persons and ordinarily recognized moral responsibilities.

SUMMARY AND CONCLUDING COMMENTS

A summary of the chapter's argument to this point could be helpful. We began by indicating that some people believe business has no responsibility to society, consumers, or employees beyond the responsibility to avoid coercion and deception. These same people also hold that government's only proper role is to maintain free and open competition. Milton Friedman's article provided one example of an argument for this position. We saw, however, that the Friedman article had no cogent argument but instead was question-begging. So, in search of another argument for the position, we looked at two appeals to the fundamental nature of morality: the utilitarian and the liberty arguments.

The utilitarian argument was unconvincing in its claim that we would be better off on the whole with the narrow management responsibility and minimal government regulation of the free market. The argument was unconvincing for two reasons. First, it failed to account for external costs of production that were not amenable to standard quantitative economic calculations (the GNP, for example). Second, the entire utilitarian approach to morality fails to provide any basis for an inherent value of the human person.

As a corrective to the utilitarian approach, we discussed the notion of a moral right and saw reasons why liberty or non-interference might be a moral right. This potential moral right to liberty formed the basis of the second fundamental moral argument for a management responsibility much more limited than the responsibilities ordinarily recognized for individual agents. However, the liberty appeal also failed, again for two reasons. First, liberty, properly understood, is not best protected in a *laissez faire* arrangement of business institutions. Second, liberty is not the most fundamental human interest deserving protection. The implications of these criticisms of the liberty and utilitarian arguments are (1) that the Friedman approach to regulation and responsibility is without support and (2) that a clearer understanding of the moral requirements on social institutions demands a rejection of the free-market approach in favor of broader areas of management responsibility and government regulation.

To end this chapter, we need only pursue a few brief comments on the extent and focus of these broader business responsibilities. Some theorists of business accept the foregoing arguments that business has responsibilities for the welfare of those it affects that go beyond simply avoiding force and fraud. They wish, though, to limit these broader responsibilities to a duty to avoid actively causing harm. For example, they might recognize a business responsibility for marketing safe products but not a responsibility to support the arts or local public education.

It is difficult to understand the basis of this limitation. Perhaps it arises in an ancient philosophical distinction between positive duties (duties to provide assistance even when the circumstances creating the need for aid were not of your doing) and negative duties (duties to avoid inflicting injury). Many philosophers hold the latter type of duty to be more stringent. They also believe that positive duties do not exist every time there is some need for aid. Business ethicists, then, might recognize the lesser status given to positive duties and conclude that the only real and strong obligations are obligations to avoid inflicting harms.

It is a mistake, however, to appeal to this traditional philosophical distinction in order to dismiss, in principle, the existence of business duties to bring aid. For in order to dismiss positive duties in this way, we would have to draw a very sharp distinction in moral significance between actively causing a harm and simply failing to prevent it. That sharp distinction would have to limit moral responsibility to cases where an individual was an active part of the causal chain leading to the existence of some harm. For two reasons it is impossible to draw such a sharp distinction.

First, the causal chain leading to a harm is not open to description only in terms of things present in the sequence of events; sometimes the causal chain can just as well be described in terms of those things that are absent. Is a man's drowning the result of water in the lungs or an absence of air to breathe? Both descriptions are appropriate causal accounts of the drowning.

Second and more importantly, the categories of moral and causal responsibility are not identical in what they include. One can be morally responsible for a harm without being causally responsible for it in an ordinary sense; alternatively, one can be causally responsible for a harm without being morally responsible for it. Consider two cases dealing with harm to a child. In one case, you are a baby-sitter charged with the moral responsibility of looking after the child in the absence of its parents. You leave the child alone in the house while you visit friends and the child burns herself at the kitchen stove. You certainly did not cause the harm in any ordinary physical sense, but you are nonetheless morally responsible. On the other hand, suppose you are driving down a busy street at 15 miles an hour and a small child darts from between two parked cars directly into your path. You are a direct cause of the harm, but few would hold you morally responsible. Thus, the limitation of moral responsibility to cases where harm is directly caused by a person seems unreasonable. Equally unreasonable, then, would be an attempt to restrict the responsibilities of business in a similar way. We might consider business's responsibility to bring aid less strict than its duties to avoid harm, in that business need not always provide assistance when it could, but we cannot entirely dismiss the existence of that area of potential responsibility. The significance of this conclusion is that it prevents business from ignoring social problems that it did not cause but that it has the power to alleviate.

If the argument is correct so far, business has responsibilities beyond those identified by the *laissez faire* approach, and those responsibilities potentially include the discharge of both positive and negative duties. But when we identify areas of business responsibility in this way, we have not yet identified on which persons in business the responsibilities fall. Are only managers responsible for the actions of the business? Or do lower-level employees also bear some responsibility?

This question is impossible to answer in the abstract. The obligations morality imposes on persons vary with the roles of those persons and with the specific circumstances at hand. No general rule identifying the locus of responsibility is possible, then.

For example, we usually would hold management responsible for obeying pollution control laws. However, we might also find a responsibility for complaining about and changing policy in an engineer who knew of a violation. The responsibility of the engineer in this example would seem to change in intensity as the seriousness of the violation changed. The more dangerous the immediate threat to public health, for instance, the greater the responsibility of the engineer to complain publicly. Further, in judging the behavior of the engineer we might need to distinguish between having a responsibility and a person being excused for failure to discharge a responsibility he or she has. We might hold the engineer to have a responsibility to warn the public of grave dangers to its health, but we might not be willing to condemn her for failing to do this if her job and her family's welfare were seriously threatened by public criticism of her employer.

Thus, for all our theoretical discussion of business responsibility, we are unable to locate easily the specific persons within a business who are responsible for making the business act as it ought. That difficulty, however, does not prevent us from discussing the manner in which our social institutions should function. Nor should this difficulty be accepted as easy grounds for a person's denial of responsibility for a harm that occurs. (Remember Nuremberg.)

We can now, at last, end our discussion of the general theory of corporate moral responsibility. Admittedly, this has been rather heady social and political theory for a business ethics text. However, the implications of this social and political theory for a general discussion of business responsibility are clear, and without this theory no satisfactory account of the social institution of business would be possible.

The conclusion of this extended analysis is that business institutions have responsibilities beyond that narrow range often acknowledged by managers who see themselves solely as the economic agents of owner interests. If conventional moral norms fail to encourage discharge of these further responsibilities, then government might have the moral authority to design other mechanisms to encourage their discharge. What, in specific circumstances, these additional responsibilities include will depend on the vastly varying characteristics of those circumstances. Similarly, how appropriate government regulation is will depend on the specific regulation and the circumstances of its enforcement. It is for these reasons that the present chapter has not attempted to identify specific regulations or responsibilities that are acceptable.

The purposes of this chapter have been (1) to defeat a position that saw business responsibilities as radically different from ordinary moral norms and (2) to indicate potential areas where business might have moral responsibilities. Subsequent chapters will present opposing discussions of specific responsibilities and regulations. Those discussions will provide the reader with the conceptual and factual information needed to make reasonable judgements about specific cases.

J. McC.

NOTES

1. Cf. James Sterba, *The Demands of Justice* (Notre Dame, Ind.: University of Notre Dame Press, 1980), pp. 112–18.

2. Someone might object to this analysis of why certain interferences are objectionable. Instead, he or she might propose that interferences are objectionable when they are interferences with goods to which we have a right. We have no quarrel with that analysis. Note, however, that it no longer argues for a right to non-interference *per se*, but only for a right to specific goods. Note also that such an analysis would demand an account of when certain goods are goods we have a *moral* right to. Both of these points are developed later in this analysis.

3. This argument and the points that follow are developed from suggestions made by Ronald Dworkin. Cf. Ronald Dworkin, *Taking Rights Seriously* (Cambridge, Mass.: Harvard University Press, 1977), pp. 269–78.

4. Cf. Richard Wasserstrom's article on privacy reprinted in Chapter 6 of this anthology.

5. Cf. C. B. MacPherson, *Democratic Theory* (Oxford, England: Oxford University Press, 1973), pp. 120–40.

CHAPTER TWO
Study Questions

1. How does Friedman's view of management social responsibilities differ from the moral responsibilities that people ordinarily have toward each other?

2. Do you believe that Friedman's approach to management responsibility and government regulation will lead the society to be better off, all things considered, than it would be under other approaches?

3. What are the definitions of "democracy," "capitalism," "socialism," and *laissez faire* capitalism?

4. What is a right? How does it function in moral theory?

5. Why did this chapter argue that a serious concern for liberty would demand more management social responsibility and more government regulation than Friedman wishes?

6. What was the argument for the claim that liberty cannot be a fundamental right? What sorts of rights were more important? How did those rights lead to a rejection of Friedman's position?

7. What is the difference between a positive and a negative duty?

8. Why is it that a person cannot escape moral responsibility simply by showing that he or she was not causally responsible for a harm?

PART TWO

BUSINESS
AND CONSUMERS

CHAPTER THREE

*P*RODUCT LIABILITY

CASE STUDY

The Michigan Toy Box Company

Part One

The Michigan Toy Box Company of Detroit, Michigan has established a reputation of producing durable, high-quality toy chests for children. Recently, however, they have discovered that the very durability of their toy chest can pose serious threats to the children who use them. The toy chests are constructed of prime hardwoods with a thickness of three-quarters of an inch. The lids of these chests alone weigh eight pounds. Reports have returned to the company that nationally nearly one hundred children a year are either killed or seriously injured when a toy box lid falls on their heads or necks while they are reaching into the chest.

Consumer advocates have suggested a solution to the problem. It involves installing a friction-hinge on the lid which prevents the lid from falling freely. The hinge functions by providing a resistance which causes the lid to close by dropping slowly. If all toy chests had such a safety device, consumer safety experts claim, the deaths and injuries suffered by children using toy chests would decline to almost zero. The recent nature of the safety problem and the slowness of government regulatory agencies concerned with safety, however, have prevented any mandatory safety standards for toy chests from being established as law. The Michigan Toy Box Company must decide whether to voluntarily install the suggested safety device.

The production costs associated with the addition of the safety hinge are clear. The cost per unit for the hinges is rather small, under $1.50. However, the company has determined that installation of the hinge will require an additional quarter-hour of labor time in the production of each chest. Salaries of workers at the plant are higher than national averages for unskilled laborers because of the competition for labor in the Detroit area and because of the strength of unions in the local labor scene. The additional quarter hour will cost the company $1.25 for each chest produced. Although the hinges would require no major re-tooling for the production line, the installation of the hinges will also entail capital and maintenance expenditures associated with the purchase of additional tools and the creation of a new work station in the assembly process.

The company estimates that installation of the hinges will raise costs about $5.00 per chest.

Although the company's reputation and sales are strong, there is increasing competition from other manufacturers because inflation has made the Michigan Toy Box product appear high priced to parents of young children. The company doubts whether it could increase retail prices by $5.00 and retain an important segment of its consumer population. In fact, the relatively infrequent rate of injury associated with the toy chests makes it less than probable that marketing which emphasized the new safety feature could offset expected sales losses due to increased prices. The infrequent injury rate also makes less likely any major liability settlements against the company and in favor of families whose children were injured. (The expectation is that the courts will not find the product defective and that liability insurance will not increase because of large settlements.)

Management of the company has decided for the interim to forego installation of the hinges because of an impending recession which will dampen sales. They do not wish to exacerbate that decline in sales by installing the hinges, although the addition of the hinges would not threaten the continued viability of the company.

Part Two

The company's sales remained stable, though not as strong as expected, throughout the re-

cession. The result was that the company had a backlogged stock of toy chests in its storage facilities. During the recession, however, consumer advocates succeeded in having mandatory safety standards requiring the hinges passed into law. In order to sell the boxes in the United States the company would have to remove the boxes from storage, transport them to the factory, and install the hinges. The additional labor and transportation costs would add further to the list price of the chests. Rather than install the hinges, the company sold the chests to another company (which it has frequently supplied) in neighboring Windsor, Ontario. Canadian law does not require the safety hinge.

Was the company's financial judgement not to produce toy chests with safety hinges morally acceptable? What about its decision to supply the stored chests to another legal jurisdiction in order to avoid installing the hinges on the chests in stock? When should financial considerations be sufficient to override a concern for the safety of the product? Does the frequency of injury have any implications for an answer to the preceding question? Would your judgement about the morality of the management decision have been any different were the injured from the adult consumer population? Does this indicate that moral standards of product safety should differ between types of products and types of consumers who use those products?

Introduction

*I*N THIS CHAPTER we examine a number of questions involving business's responsibility for the goods and services it produces. Is a business morally responsible for a product that is defective, even if the business has not been negligent? Should a business be legally liable for all defective products it produces? Or, in the absence of negligence on the part of the producer, should we resort to a policy of *caveat emptor*—"let the buyer beware"—and say that consumers bear the risks of defective products when they make a purchase?

In addition to these questions about the responsibility for defective products, we also need to consider what would be an appropriate public policy for preventing, or at least restricting, unsafe or defective products. Should producers take the initiative and establish standards for safety and quality? Should consumers be left alone to decide for themselves about the safety of products in the marketplace? Should government step in with regulations to restrict what is produced? These and other questions of product liability will be examined in the readings that follow.

Before we can begin to answer these questions of how to assign moral and legal responsibility for what is produced, we first should consider how, in fact, liability is and has been assigned in our society. This history of product liability is provided by our first reading, which is from the *Final Report of the U. S. Interagency Task Force on Product Liability*. The task force was established by the Economic Policy Board of the White House in 1976 in response to what many in business were calling a crisis in the field of product liability. In the words of the task force:

> A number of manufacturers and business periodicals alleged that product liability insurance had become unavailable or unaffordable. The consequences of this situation included the possibilities that business might terminate because they were unable to get coverage; that injured persons would be unable to enforce product liability judgments; and that manufacturers would be hesitant to produce some products that would be useful in our society. It was also alleged that the system of private insurance in the field of product liability was breaking down. Finally, it was alleged that relatively few injured persons benefited from the system.

Clearly, the reason for the creation of the task force was that businesses often saw themselves in a dilemma: Pay greatly increasing premiums for product liability insurance or accept the risk of producing and selling goods without carrying insurance against the damages that those products might cause. In either case, a business would find itself in financial danger, either from profits disappearing into insurance premiums or from court settlements in favor of injured consumers and against the assets of the uninsured business.

The crisis for business caused by this dilemma has led many business people to call for reform of the presently liberal product-liability law. Currently, businesses can be held legally liable for compensating victims when defective products cause damage to consumers. Business persons see this "strict liability" approach as too liberal, because it allows court judgements for damages against a company even when the company was not morally negligent in its marketing of a defective product. Understandably, there is strong sentiment in the business community for a change in approach to product liability, perhaps to one where product liability insurance is underwritten by the federal government.

(However, it is interesting to note in passing that while the task force's conclusion recognized the pressure on business caused by increasing costs of insurance, it also found little evidence of greatly increased total settlements against insurance companies to warrant the size of their premium increases. Hence, the task force suggested that much of the cause of the product liability crisis lay not in the contemporary legal approach to product liability, but rather in insurance companies increasing premiums on the *expectation* of larger and more frequent judgements against them.)

Whatever the cause of the crisis perceived by business, the contemporary legal approach to product liability remains controversial. To aid in our understanding of this product liability law, we have included the task force survey of recent changes in that law.

As the task force selection indicates, product liability law has undergone drastic changes since 1960, when the precedents for the contemporary approach were set. Currently, persons who suffer damages due to defects in a product can legally reach the manufacturer of that product in an attempt to gain compensation. To have a basis for legal action, the consumer needs only to prove that the product was defective.

The extent to which this approach liberalizes the ability of injured persons to recover damages is underscored by the distance between this approach and the approach to product liability prevalent before 1916. Before that date, suits for recovery of damages by consumers were limited to parties with whom they had direct contractual relations. In actual practice, this legal doctrine, known as "privity of contract," meant that consumers in most instances were able to recover damages only from the retailers of products and not from the manufacturers of those products. In a landmark case of 1916, *MacPherson v. Buick Motor Co.*, the New York Court of Appeals extended the power of injured consumers to reach manufacturers with suits when it allowed a judgement for an injured consumer on the grounds that the manufacturer had not exercised due care in inspecting wooden automobile wheels for defective materials. The *MacPherson* case thus abandoned the privity of contract requirement in those cases where consumers could establish negligence on the part of the manufacturer. Of course, this decision, while liberalizing the product liability law somewhat, still placed a significant burden of proof on the injured consumer, since proving negligence is often difficult.

Greater changes in the legal approach to assigning liability for damages due to defective products came through two major decisions of the early 1960s. The first case, *Henningsen v. Bloomfield Motors Inc.*, decided in 1960 by the Supreme Court of New Jersey, allowed the recovery of damages without proof of negligence, on the grounds that consumers have a right to expect that purchased products carry an implied warranty that they are reasonably safe for intended use. Injured consumers, then, were able to recover damages under a new interpretation of contract law if they could show that the purchased product did not perform reasonably.

In 1963, a California court ruling in the *Greenman v. Yuba Power Products Inc.* case reached similar conclusions on the basis of tort law (that area of law concerned with suits by individuals for redress of personal injuries) rather than contract law. The *Greenman* decision heralded the arrival of what is now known as the "strict liability in tort" approach to product liability. This approach, which is the approach currently used, allows the recovery of damages if the consumer can prove that the injurious product was defective. In this decision, as in the *Henningsen* decision, it was determined that injured parties need not establish manufacturer negligence in order to win damages in court.

Naturally, these decisions place manufacturers in greater financial jeopardy than earlier decisions did. Injured parties now have the legal power to reach manufacturers for damages even when the manufacturers were not morally negligent in allowing the defective product on the market. (For example, a judgement for the recovery of damages conceivably could be won even if the manufacturer adhered to strict quality-control procedures that demanded that a high sample proportion of its products undergo safety tests.) In essence, the strict liability approach operates somewhat like a no-fault insurance policy for injuries due to product defects.

Businesses, of course, dislike this liberalized ability of injured parties to sue. Businesses are not, however, without defense, as the task force indicates. The conduct of the user, for example through misuse or contributory negligence, may be enough to prevent recovery of damages. Thus, while current law is more liberal in its treatment of consumer suits, the interests of business have not been totally ignored.

Nonetheless, there is significant debate about the merits of this contemporary approach. The second and third readings in this chapter present two perspectives on that debate. Before considering the arguments raised by those articles, however, the reader should be aware of the range of options available for dealing with damages due to product defects.

At one extreme there is the *caveat emptor* (buyer beware) approach, which places the burden of cost for injury upon the injured consumer. This option simply counsels consumers to exercise caution in use of products. Other options would be to allow consumers to recover damages when injuries are due to negligence on the part of the manufacturer (the *MacPherson* approach), or to follow the strict liability in tort theory of the *Greenman* decision. A final option would be to have public funds underwrite the cost of injuries to consumers, perhaps through tax subsidies for business product liability insurance or through a government-administered insurance program. Students are encouraged to consider the relative strengths and weaknesses of these options, as well as to consider carefully the arguments of the second and third selections of this chapter.

The first option, identified above with the phrase *caveat emptor*, would hold that consumers should be responsible for their purchases. If a consumer wishes to minimize the risk of defective products, he is free to purchase a higher quality product at, presumably, a higher price. If, on the other hand, the consumer chooses to pay a lower price, then he has freely taken on the risk that the product will prove unsatisfactory. Although this might appear to be a radical suggestion to some observers, especially when consumers are injured or killed by a defective product, there is a substantial rationale behind this answer.

The rationale for this option claims that by assigning liability to consumers, we will achieve the most efficient economic distribution of costs and benefits possible. When consumers are responsible, they will be free to decide for themselves what risks they should take, what price they should pay for what degree of safety, etc. Producers also will be free to decide for themselves the degree of quality and safety to place in their products; and the price they will charge, assuming a competitive market, will be lower, since they will not be required to pay insurance costs, costs for meeting government regulations, etc.

Such an economic situation will be the most efficient distribution of costs and benefits, since every person decides for himself how much he is willing to pay or accept for a product and how much risk he is willing to take. Assuming that individuals are the best judges of what is in their own interest, this policy approaches an optimal distribution of want satisfaction (see the description of utilitarianism in Chapter 2). More people have their wants satisfied under this policy than under any alternative. Those consumers who would rather pay a lower price and take a higher risk will be satisfied by a policy of *caveat emptor*. So, too, will those consumers who value a high degree of safety or quality more than money. Producers are satisfied by being allowed to produce whatever there is demand for at a relatively low and therefore, in a competitive market, profitable rate.

Such a policy is efficient in the sense that no one individual can be made better off (perhaps by a reduction in risks) except by making someone else worse off (perhaps by reducing his freedom to choose). Economists call such a situation a *Pareto-optimal distribution*. Even if the reader finds this rationale for the *caveat emptor* approach unsatisfactory, the question of consumer responsibility for product safety should be kept in mind. To what degree should a manufacturer be liable for damages caused to a careless or untrained consumer?

In our second reading, Roland McKean discusses the economic consequences of alternative products liability arrangements. McKean, a professor of economics, outlines in some detail the economic implications of the *caveat emptor* approach and suggests that this policy would more likely lead to economic efficiency than the alternatives of producer liability or taxpayer liability. The implication of McKean's article is that given a free and competitive market, there are strong economic reasons for preferring a policy of *caveat emptor*.

One necessary condition for the proper functioning of this free and competitive market is an equal opportunity for all individuals to participate in the competition. Indeed, part of what it means to say that the market is free, is that individuals have the opportunity to enter the bargaining that takes place in the market. In our third selection, George Brenkert argues that this aspect of the free enterprise system implies that we should adopt a policy of strict products liability. This policy would hold producers liable for products that prove to be defective, even if the defect is not the result of the producer's negligence.

Brenkert's argument appeals to our concern with compensatory justice. Compensatory justice requires that individuals who have been unfairly harmed receive compensation from the person who caused the harm. This is the sense of justice operating in slander and libel suits, for example. In the free enterprise system, individuals bargain and compete with each other in order to best satisfy their own interests. When a consumer is harmed by a defective or unsafe product, he loses the equal opportunity to participate in the bargaining and competition. This places him at an unfair competitive disadvantage (less able to earn money, shop around, bargain, etc.), and compensatory justice would seem to require that the person who caused this disadvantage, even if unintentionally, compensate for it. In short, the rationale of the free enterprise system, that it gives everyone an equal opportunity to gain benefits, provides the justification for adopting a policy of strict products liability.

Both McKean and Brenkert are concerned with the proper legal assignment of liability for damages done by defective products. Our final two selections consider the regulatory role that government standard setting should play in product liability concerns.

Since 1972, with the passage of the Consumer Products Safety Act, our government has empowered an agency, the Consumer Products Safety Commission, to set safety standards for products and to enforce those standards through economic sanctions against violators. In the fourth selection, Murray Wiedenbaum points out that the Consumer Product Safety Commission stresses establishing product standards rather than the taking of punitive action against producers. This indicates that this commission is less concerned with assigning liability for damages than it is with preventing damages in the first place. Even so, Wiedenbaum, a former member of the President's Council of Economic Advisors, suggests that consumer product regulation has undesirable effects upon both consumers and business. In part because consumers have "unequal tastes for safety," government regulation will not necessarily be the most economical and efficient way of achieving safety objectives, since it may force some people to pay for levels of safety they would not otherwise have chosen to purchase.

In addition, as Wiedenbaum points out, the regulatory standards enforced by the CPSC are costly for businesses to meet. Those costs can be reflected in higher prices or lower levels of employment. Wiedenbaum's implicit suggestion, then, is that government product-safety regulation does not now promote the greatest good of the society at large.

Apart from the economic issues raised by Wiedenbaum, there are important moral concerns about government regulation of product safety. As defenders of the free market point out, the moral legitimacy of the market comes from its enabling individuals to choose for themselves. When government becomes involved in regulating the safety of products, the freedom of individuals to choose is restricted. Of course, governments restrict our choices often and with good reason. Enforcing traffic laws, for example, justifiably restricts the freedom of individuals. What makes product liability regulation appear different is that, in this case, the government restricts our choice in the marketplace in part for the expressed reason that it is for our own good. Government regulation of consumer product safety prevents the individual from choosing a less safe product at a lower price.

This government restriction on consumer choice presents another issue about the legitimacy of product safety regulation, besides the question of its efficiency raised by Wiedenbaum. Restricting the choice of consumers for their own good raises the question of paternalism, which is the general question of whether it is ever justifiable to restrict the freedom of an individual for his or her own good. Thus, product safety regulations are open to criticisms that they are both inefficient and unjust violations of individual liberty.

In part, the success of both of these criticisms turns on the same issue: Are individuals always the best judges of their own interests? If the answer is yes, then it would seem that government regulation will be highly suspect, since even those who accept paternalistic restrictions on a person's liberty usually do so only if the person has a defect in rationality that prevents him or her from judging properly. Moreover, if the answer is yes, then it would seem that *caveat emptor* is the best means for achieving economic efficiency. If individuals are the best judges of their own interests, then allowing them to choose for themselves seems the way to guarantee that most interests will be most efficiently satisfied. On the other hand, if people can often be mistaken about what is in their best interest, then there is more room for justifying paternalistic government regulation and it becomes less likely that *caveat emptor* will lead to economic efficiency.

A related and important question arises if we believe that paternalistic legislation can be justified. If we believe that it can be, we have to ask what standards of safety or defectiveness the government should adopt when deciding how to prevent harms. Should the government try to prevent harms to all persons who might make errors in judgement? Or, should it only try to prevent harms due to those judgement errors reasonable people are likely to make?

In the final selection of this chapter, Steven Kelman examines the specific question of the relation between paternalism and government regulation of consumer product safety. Kelman believes that there are good nonpaternalistic arguments for regulation of product safety. Kelman, who once worked for the Bureau of Consumer Protection, Federal Trade Commission, argues that it is sometimes rational for individuals to relinquish their own choice-making authority in favor of some third party. When we avoid the overused examples of seatbelts and motorcycle helmets and consider instead chemicals, drugs, and the like, we see the reasonableness of allowing third parties to decide issues of consumer product safety.

When developing our own views about product liability, we would be well-advised to follow Kelman's suggestion and examine a wide range of consumer products. Considering not only motorcycle helmets and lawnmowers, but also food additives, household chemicals, children's products, medicines, etc., we will likely discover that there are few simple solutions to this issue.

Note that the questions concerning paternalism and those concerning the choice of regulatory standards arise elsewhere in this anthology. In particular, the chapters on advertising (Chapters 4 and 5) and the chapter on occupational safety (Chapter 9) will ask the reader to apply and refine the concepts used in this discussion of product safety.

THE UNITED STATES INTERAGENCY TASK FORCE ON PRODUCT LIABILITY

An Overview of Product Liability Law

INTRODUCTION

As one reviews the product liability cases from the past two decades, it is clear that courts did not intend to create a product liability problem. Rather, they were attempting to weed the law of antiquated doctrine or stumbling blocks that appeared to deprive injured plaintiffs of their right to recover against manufacturers of defective products. For many decades an injured consumer was, in theory, entitled to damages when the product that injured him was negligently manufactured. Often, how-

From the *Final Report*, U.S. Interagency Task Force on Product Liability.

ever, the plaintiff was unable to show that the defendant failed to act as a reasonable manufacturer, or he was barred because he was contributorily negligent with respect to the product. Sometimes his claim failed because he was unable to reach the manufacturer of the product by judicial process. Instead, he was only able to sue the retailer or distributor of the product and was unable to prove negligence against those parties.

An alternative approach to negligence was the law of warranty. Here plaintiff only had to show that the product was unreasonably constructed or designed in regard to its *intended* use. But in cases other than those dealing with foods or cosmetic preparations, the courts usually required that the plaintiff be in privity of contract with the defendant. Therefore, if a non-purchaser was injured, his claim had to be based on negligence. The privity requirement was so important that it was commonly referred to as a "citadel."

"The Fall of the Citadel," according to the late Dean Prosser, occurred on May 9, 1960, when the Supreme Court of New Jersey announced the decision in *Henningsen v. Bloomfield Motors, Inc.* The *Henningsen* court held the manufacturer and dealer of a defective automobile liable for a breach of implied warranty without any showing of negligence and without privity of contract. The basis of the decision was that when a seller places a defective product into the stream of commerce, the loss should fall on that seller, who is in a position to control the danger and to distribute the losses equitably, rather than on the innocent plaintiff, who cannot control the danger and who has less ability to distribute the loss.

Greenman v. Yuba Power Products, Inc., a 1963 decision of the Supreme Court of California, represents the next significant development in the evolution of a cause of action other than negligence in product liability cases. While *Henningsen* was based on the contractual theory of breach of implied warranty, the *Greenman* decision rested in tort—the cause of action was one of strict tort liability. Thus, although the rationale of the *Greenman* decision was congruent with that of *Henningsen*, the theory of recovery differed.

The court in *Greenman* recognized what had occurred in a long series of cases that ended with *Henningsen*. A doctrine that had in the twentieth century been associated with contracts (warranty)

was being utilized to create a new cause of action in tort. The *Greenman* court, by identifying the true legal basis for the cause of action, hoped to bring more rationality to the system. For example, by labeling the product liability claim one of tort rather than warranty, technical requirements (such as the commercial code's requiring that a notice to a seller be supplied within a reasonable time after the buyer discovers a defect) could be avoided when they were inappropriate.

Henningsen and *Greenman* were important building blocks in establishing a new cause of action in product liability cases. Under the reasoning of these decisions, the plaintiff was no longer required to prove negligence on the part of the manufacturer or seller in order to recover for injuries arising through the use of a defective product. Instead, the focus was shifted from the conduct of the manufacturer to the performance of its product. If the product proved to be defective, then the parties responsible for placing the product into the stream of commerce were liable to the plaintiff for the injuries caused by the product.

Over time most courts extended the rationale of these cases to both retailers and distributors. It would appear that strict liability may strike at these groups more harshly than at manufacturers: retailers and distributors are often in a situation where they have neither the ability nor the opportunity to discover or correct defects in a product. In point of fact, case law suggests that retailers and distributors are usually able to transfer the cost of a product liability judgment back on to the manufacturer. Nevertheless, it has been reported to the Task Force that these groups are still subject to substantial defense costs. Courts extended strict liability to retailers and distributors, in part, on the assumption that those groups would place pressure on the manufacturer to produce safe products. Courts also believed that retailers and distributors might be more accessible to suit than manufacturers.

Although the *Henningsen, Greenman* and other early strict product liability cases dealt with consumer goods, courts soon applied the same theory to workplace injuries. Some have argued that there was less need to have strict liability with respect to product-related workplace injuries. The basis for this argument is that the injured worker often has recovered medical costs and a percentage of his loss of earnings through Worker Compensation, whereas the consumer (unless successful in a product liability action) has often obtained no compensation whatsoever.

The protection established by *Henningsen* and *Greenman* was also extended beyond users and consumers of products to all persons who might foreseeably be injured if a product misfired.

Finally, the *Henningsen* and *Greenman* cases (which dealt with injury to the person) were extended to situations where there had been property damage. To date, most courts have drawn the line at that point and decline to apply strict liability in tort where there has been pure economic loss.

As far back as 1965 with the promulgation of Section 402A of the *Restatement (Second) of Torts*, it was hoped that reasonably uniform standards might evolve for strict product liability law. Nevertheless, these hopes have not borne fruit. To illustrate this fact we will examine some of the more important doctrinal areas where diversity of view has arisen. A common theme in each of these areas is a difference in perspective (identified in the Task Force's Briefing Report) between courts who view product liability law as a means of apportioning responsibility based on fault and those who assume that this area of law should be a compensation system for persons injured by products.

SOME MAJOR ISSUES IN PRODUCT LIABILITY LAW

A Manufacturer's Duty to Design Its Product Properly

Introduction. While most courts agree that the duty of the manufacturer is to design a product that is not "defective," no satisfactory definition of the term "defect" has been articulated. Michael Hoenig has recently remarked, in fact, that "[w]hat constitutes a defect is no clearer today than it was a decade ago when Section 402A of the *Restatement (Second) of Torts* was published." The term is particularly difficult to define in connection with cases where the alleged defect is one of design. On the one hand, in cases involving manufacturing defects, the plaintiff need merely illustrate that the performance of the product was deficient; on the other hand, in cases involving alleged design de-

fects, the plaintiff must impugn a conscious design choice of the manufacturer. Courts have had problems in both defining and applying the so-called strict liability standard where plaintiff has alleged that a design was defective.

Defectiveness and Strict Liability. In the 1963 case of *Greenman v. Yuba Power Products, Inc.,* where the underlying rationale of strict liability was set forth by Justice Traynor of the Supreme Court of California, it was held that a manufacturer is strictly liable when its product "proves to have a defect that causes injury to a human being." The *Greenman* court did not undertake, however, to define the meaning of defect. In 1965, when the *Restatement (Second) of Torts* was published, it was postulated in Section 402A that one who sells any product in a "defective condition unreasonably dangerous" is subject to liability for physical harm caused by the product, even though the seller exercised all possible care in preparing and selling the product. Thus, notwithstanding the fact that the court in the *Greenman* case held the manufacturer liable for any product which proved to have a "defect," the *Restatement* used the differently worded standard of a "defective condition unreasonably dangerous."

The term "unreasonably dangerous" generated little discussion in the years immediately after the inception of Section 402A. Those courts, including the Supreme Court of California, which applied the strict liability doctrine, often spoke of the *Greenman* standard and Section 402A as basically synonymous. It was not until the decision of the Supreme Court of California, in *Cronin v. J.B.E. Olson Corp.*, that a controversy was created. The *Cronin* case attempted to analyze the two standards and found the *Greenman* formula to be preferable because the "unreasonably dangerous" element had the effect of introducing negligence-related considerations into a strict liability case. The court held that the plaintiff need not show a product to be "unreasonably dangerous" in order to recover on a strict liability theory.

The approach advocated by the *Cronin* court—allowing the issue of defect to be decided in an "intuitive" manner—has created great confusion and has met with widespread resistance. For example, this approach has been compared to instructing the jury in a negligence case that the defendant is liable if he breached a duty owed to the plaintiff, without defining the duty as that of reasonable care. Many courts have expressed a preference for the *Restatement* formula as opposed to that adopted in California. Other courts, however, for various reasons, have rejected the "unreasonably dangerous" standard in favor of a different test. Substitutions for the "unreasonably dangerous" test include the imposition of liability in Washington if the product is "not reasonably safe" or, in Oregon, if the product is "dangerously defective." Still another view is that the term "defective" is synonymous with "unreasonably dangerous."

Many states, of course, continue to adhere to Section 402A. Others recognize Section 402A but adapt it to reflect principles established in the state law. Wisconsin, for example, purports to recognize Section 402A but holds that the Section 402A standard is the equivalent of negligence *per se*. New York has established a negligence-based cause of action entitled "strict products liability," which states the ingredients for liability and the applicable defenses in one three-pronged formula. The formula provides that the manufacturer of a defective product which causes injury is liable if (1) the product was being used for its intended purpose—this also includes foreseeable misuses; (2) the user would not, by the exercise of reasonable care, have discovered the defect and perceived its danger; and (3) the person injured could not, by the exercise of reasonable care, have averted the injury. A majority of the judges on the New York Court of Appeals have recently reaffirmed their preference for the New York rule, which recognizes the defense of contributory negligence in a strict liability action, as opposed to the standard enunciated in Section 402A.

This wide disparity surrounding both the definition of defect and the most desirable form of strict liability has led to substantial confusion and unequal treatment of products cases in state courts.

Strict Liability in Design Cases.   The process of applying strict liability in design defect cases is somewhat different from that in manufacturing defect cases. Inasmuch as strict liability was initiated to alleviate problems of the plaintiff's burden of proof, it is clear that the theory works reasonably well in manufacturing defect cases where the defect was in the construction of the product. In design defect cases, on the other hand, the alleged defective design is the result of a conscious choice of the manufacturer to design its product in a certain manner. Thus, although strict liability shifts the focus from the conduct of the manufacturer to the performance of the product, the way in which the product was designed resulted from a conscious human choice. Consequently, some courts have pointed out that the results in design cases seldom differ, whether the cause of action is one of negligence or of strict liability.

Dean Wade has pointed out that the difference between negligence and strict liability in design defect cases should be that the element of *scienter*—knowledge of the risks created by a product—is imputed to the manufacturer when strict liability is applied. Yet, even when the negligence standard of reasonable care is imposed, the manufacturer is still obligated to assume the position of an expert in the field and to keep abreast of the most recent scientific developments in the industry. Under this standard, the negligence test of whether the manufacturer knew or should have known of the dangers is only slightly less demanding than the strict liability technique of imputation of knowledge of the dangers. As Dean Keeton has observed, "strict liability as to design defects is virtually a myth," unless knowledge of scientifically unknowable risks is imputed to manufacturers when strict liability is applied. Because most courts have refused to impute knowledge of unknowable risks to manufacturers, negligence and strict liability are functional equivalents in design defect cases in most states.

To determine whether a product is defectively designed, the risks presented by the product must be weighed against its utility. A product which presents substantial risks is not necessarily defective, as it may also have great utility. In balancing the risks and utility of the product, one of the most comprehensive lists of factors to be considered has been proposed by Dean Wade, and has been adopted by courts in Oregon and Arizona as well as the Federal District Court for the Eastern District of Pennsylvania. Under this test, the factors to be considered are:

1. The usefulness and desirability of the product—its utility to the user and to the public as a whole.

2. The safety aspects of the product—the likelihood that it will cause injury, and the probable seriousness of the injury.

3. The availability of a substitute product which would meet the same need and not be as unsafe.

4. The manufacturer's ability to eliminate the unsafe character of the product without impairing its usefulness or making it too expensive to maintain its utility.

5. The user's ability to avoid danger by the exercise of care in the use of the product.

6. The user's anticipated awareness of the dangers inherent in the product and their avoidability, because of general public knowledge of the obvious condition of the product, or of the existence of suitable warnings or instructions.

7. The feasibility, on the part of the manufacturer, of spreading the loss by setting the price of the product or carrying liability insurance. . . .

Conclusion. While the balancing approach is a conceptually sound technique to apply in deciding design issues, it is by no means an easy test, whether the factors involved are weighed by the judge or by the jury. Due to the complexities involved in the process, a return to negligence law has been advocated as one means of minimizing the uncertainty in design cases. . . . With such diversity of opinion, a uniform approach to design cases does not seem close at hand. Nevertheless, the distinction between "strict liability" and "negligence" in product liability is often more one of language, than actual results. The time may have arrived to make the law clear as to what is required in regard to the manufacturer's duty to design.

The Manufacturer's Duty to Warn Users or Consumers About Hazards Connected with Its Product

Introduction. A manufacturer has a duty to warn purchasers and users of its product of the dangers associated with the use of that product. Liability for failure to give such warning may be predicated on negligence, strict liability in tort, and even breach of warranty. The doctrine has wide applicability and it has recently been observed that "almost every product liability case has a potential issue of failure to warn."

The frequency with which plaintiffs use failure to warn as a basis for asserting that manufacturers should be held liable for injuries which result from the use of their products stems from two major factors. The most important is that courts commonly require no additional showing, either of fault on the part of the manufacturer or of a defect in the product, in order to allow a plaintiff to recover for injuries which occurred because of the absence of a proper warning. As a result, plaintiffs in product litigation often rely on an alleged failure to warn in order to avoid the proof problems involved in demonstrating the existence of manufacturing or design defects.

Even in situations where other kinds of defects are alleged, plaintiffs frequently rely on manufacturers' failures to warn as an alternative ground for claiming damages. There is a particular logical nexus, for example, between a manufacturer's duty to design a product which is safe for ordinary use and its duty to warn of the dangers of a product which has not been—or even cannot be—designed to be completely safe. Where, however, the manufacturer does in fact provide an adequate warning, it will sometimes insulate him from liability for harm caused by what would otherwise be a design defect. Where the testing processes of the manufacturer are inadequate, on the other hand, courts have usually imposed liability on the failure to warn rather than on the failure to test the product adequately. . . .

Conclusion. Despite the growing reliance on the failure to warn as a basis for imposing liability on manufacturers for injuries which result from the use of their products, confusion still reigns as to the theoretical basis of this liability. While courts attempt to distinguish liability based on negligence from strict liability in the failure to warn area, the factors at play under either theory remain the same. Thus, the more serious the harm, the greater the probability of the harm and the less obvious the danger, the greater the likelihood that courts will require the manufacturer to warn of the hazards involved in the use of his product.

But there can be little doubt that strict liability has given courts latitude to shift the balance among these factors and occasionally allow juries to reach decisions that can be justified only by the application of hindsight. . . .

How Does the Conduct of the Product User or Consumer Affect His Claim?

Introduction. Product liability actions which are based on negligence have traditionally been subject to the defenses of assumption of risk and contributory negligence. These types of conduct are generally treated as affirmative defenses, and the burden of establishing them rests with the defendant. The distinction between the two is that assumption of risk concerns knowledge of the danger and acquiescence in it, while contributory negligence involves a departure from the standard of conduct of a reasonable person.

As has been indicated in the previous section, it has been held that a manufacturer may be relieved of liability for injury caused by a dangerous product if the danger it presented was patent or obvious, or should have been obvious, to the plaintiff. The rationale for the patent danger rule is that a manufacturer is under no duty to guard against injury from a source which is manifestly dangerous. Because a determination of the question of duty is usually a matter for the court, rather than the jury, a finding that the defect was an obvious one will usually result in a directed verdict for the defendant. Not all jurisdictions recognize the patent danger rule, and a trend toward its abolition may be indicated by its abandonment in New York, a jurisdiction which was formerly a leading exponent of the rule.

Another situation in which the defendant in a negligence-based product action may be excused is where the plaintiff has used the product in a manner which was unintended by the manufacturer. This type of conduct is usually characterized as misuse or abnormal use. . . .

Assumption of Risk. The elements of the defense of assumption of risk, are knowledge of the danger or defect, and a voluntary and unreasonable encounter of it. The plaintiff must have *actual* knowledge of the particular risk in order for assumption of risk to constitute a valid defense. Stated otherwise, assumption of risk requires a subjective realization by the plaintiff of the danger presented by a product. A plaintiff may not be barred from recovery merely because circumstances should have put him on notice that the product was dangerous. Nevertheless, actual knowledge may be inferred from the circumstances of the case.

There is currently a split of authority between jurisdictions as to exactly what knowledge or type of knowledge on the part of a plaintiff is required to establish assumption of risk. Some courts seem to require that a plaintiff must be aware of the specific defect which threatens him with danger. Thus, in a recent Pennsylvania case involving a helicopter crash due to an alleged defect in design, it was said that a plaintiff "is precluded from recovery only if he knows of the specific defect eventually causing his injury and voluntarily proceeds to use the product with knowledge of the danger caused by the defect."

In apparent opposition to the decisions which hold that knowledge of the specific defect is necessary for assumption of risk are those which deem the knowledge requirement satisfied by a generalized knowledge of the danger encountered without reference to the specific defect. For example, where the plaintiff's decedent was working under the bed of a dump truck, a knowledge of the danger of his position, but not of the alleged design defect which caused the bed to fall, was held to be sufficient to satisfy the knowledge requirement.

Courts will consider factors such as age, experience, and surrounding circumstances in evaluating a plaintiff's knowledge of a defect. Thus, a carpenter who was struck in the eye by a nail which shattered when he hammered was found not to have assumed the risk even though he continued to use the nails after the heads of several of them had broken off. In affirming a jury verdict for the plaintiff, the court noted that he was only 19 years old and had only been working for a short period of time. . . .

The second element of the assumption of risk defense in strict liability actions is the voluntariness of the plaintiff's action in encountering the danger presented by the defective product. In evaluating the voluntariness of the plaintiff's encounter of the risk, some decisions take into consideration the fact that the plaintiff was required to make a split-second decision. For example, where the plaintiff's defective brakes had failed and he was required to decide whether to turn into a gas station wall or to continue along the highway, his decision to turn into the gas station wall was held, as a matter of law, not to be assumption of risk because the decision was not "voluntary." Similarly, the Supreme Court of Texas has observed that "a negligent failure to choose the best escape from the throes of peril is not a voluntary encounter with the danger." It has also been recognized that in an employment situation, the economic pressure on an employee assigned to a dangerous machine may negate the element of voluntariness. . . .

Misuse.   That conduct on the part of the plaintiff which the courts categorize as "misuse" differs significantly from assumption of risk. Comment h to Section 402A recognizes that an abnormal use or misuse of a product may defeat a claim that an injury was caused by the defective or unreasonably dangerous condition of the product. Causality, of course, is a necessary element of the plaintiff's case. For example, a plaintiff who suffered a fall from an allegedly defective ladder is required to show that the ladder was being used in a normal fashion in order to recover. In another case, the manufacturer prevailed on the causation issue where a metal pin inserted in the plaintiff's leg broke when the plaintiff tried to walk on it against the specific instructions of his doctor.

Misuse by the plaintiff may indicate the absence of a defect, as well as lack of causation. In a case where the plaintiff disregarded a warning not to use a grinding wheel above certain speeds, for example, his action for damages was defeated because he failed to prove that the wheel was defective. Alteration of a product may also constitute misuse. When the plaintiff nailed wooden strips to the bottom of a ladder, the ladder was found not defective and recovery was barred.

In the situation where the plaintiff's misuse and the defective condition of a product combine to cause the injury, the plaintiff will be allowed to recover. In a Texas case where the jury found that the plaintiff was negligent in his use of the product and also that the product was defectively designed, it was held that recovery would be barred only if the plaintiff's misuse had been the sole cause of his injuries.

The test for establishing whether a plaintiff's conduct in relation to a product should bar his recovery is whether the plaintiff's manner of use was foreseeable. Foreseeability seems firmly accepted as the preferred standard for evaluating the legal consequences of a plaintiff's conduct because of the broad protection which it affords plaintiffs in comparison with other standards. Occasional decisions, however, apply a narrower, intended use test. The major distinction between foreseeability and intended use is the difference between an objective and subjective standard in evaluating the use of a product. In the automobile-crashworthiness cases where a defective or dangerous condition results in enhanced injuries, although it was not the cause of the accident, the application of an intended use standard will result in a dismissal of the plaintiff's case: accidents are not the intended use of an automobile. On the other hand, accidents are an easily foreseeable occurrence, and application of a foreseeability standard will allow recovery for injuries enhanced by a dangerous design.

A number of factors are relevant in determining whether a particular use of a product is foreseeable. Some courts compare the gravity of the potential harm with the expense of discovering and guarding against a dangerous use of a product. The frequency or unusual nature of a particular use may also be considered relevant as to whether a plaintiff's recovery should be barred. Some decisions appear to place a very great burden on manufacturers. For example, one court has indicated that in order to constitute a bar, the alleged misuse must be so unusual as to eliminate any need of the defendant to anticipate it. Other courts will look to the actual frequency of the misuse and only impose liability if it was likely to occur.

Finally, it should be noted that there is confusion in the case law as to whether a plaintiff's foreseeable, but careless, use of a product will bar recovery. For example, in some situations a manufacturer might be able to foresee that a product user will remove a safety device on a machine or fail to heed a warning. This is one more area where it is extremely difficult for a manufacturer to predict his basic responsibility for injuries caused by his products.

Contributory Negligence.   Unlike misuse, there is no question but that contributory negligence is an affirmative defense. Comment n to Section 402A, however, does not recognize the applicability of contributory negligence in its conventional form in strict liability actions. Thus, the negligent failure to discover a defective condition or failure to use reasonable care to avert injury after such discovery will not bar recovery. However, to the extent that a plaintiff proceeds negligently in the face of a known danger, his conduct will be covered by the defense of assumption of risk.

Only three jurisdictions expressly reject the *Restatement* view that failure to discover a defect or avoid injury may constitute contributory negligence. The New York Court of Appeals in *Codling v. Paglia* held that plaintiffs in strict liability actions were required to have exercised that degree of care for their own safety that a reasonably prudent person would have exercised under the same circumstances. Nevertheless, contributory negligence which plays a minor role in causing an accident will not bar recovery. The plaintiff's negligence must be a substantial factor in bringing about his injury.

In a later decision, New York abolished the patent danger rule, which formerly would have defeated the plaintiff's action. However, it was noted that the obviousness or openness of the danger is available as a defense to the defendant on the issue of whether the plaintiff had exercised the reasonable care required to protect himself under the circumstances.

New Hampshire and Wisconsin have also recognized the applicability of conventional contributory negligence to strict liability actions. In both jurisdictions, this result has been tempered by the application of comparative fault principles.

Comparative Fault. The application of comparative fault principles to actions in strict liability is regarded as having great potential for relieving some of the inequities incurred by both plaintiffs and defendants as a result of the "all or nothing" approach to recovery presently in use. A number of jurisdictions now have decisions in which the relationship between comparative fault and strict product liability is considered.

Wisconsin is the jurisdiction with the most experience in this area. Its initial decision to adopt strict liability indicated that no distinction would be made between contributory negligence in its

conventional form, and assumption of risk, in the application of Wisconsin's comparative negligence statute. The Wisconsin court also indicated that misuse of a product might relieve or limit liability. The rationale of the Wisconsin approach of applying comparative fault in strict liability cases was that the latter merely amounted to negligence *per se*, to which the plaintiff's fault could be compared. Thus, the court reasoned that the defective nature of a product could, as a causal factor of an injury, be compared with the causal contributory negligence of the plaintiff. Other courts, in applying comparative fault principles to strict liability actions, have simply concluded that such actions are imbedded in the concept of fault.

In contrast to the Wisconsin approach to comparative fault, a more limited approach has been adopted in Florida, where apportionment of fault in strict liability actions is restricted to assumption of risk, and the failure to exercise due care for one's safety *after* the discovery of the product's dangerous condition. Oklahoma has said that applying a comparative negligence statute to the defense of assumption of risk in a products case is forbidden because of specific statutory language limiting apportionment to situations where the plaintiff's conduct was formerly classified as contributory negligence.

A recent Wisconsin decision has indicated that foreseeable misuse of a product by a plaintiff would limit his recovery under the comparative fault approach, while unforeseeable misuse would bar recovery completely. Different reasoning has been adopted by a Federal District Court sitting in Idaho. The court concluded that the rationale of Idaho's comparative negligence statute required a comparison of *all* legal causes of the plaintiff's injuries. This led the court to reject the argument that unforeseeable misuse would constitute an absolute defense. Accordingly, both foreseeable and unforeseeable misuse are taken into account in the apportionment of damages.

A growing number of jurisdictions have expressed approval of the concept of applying comparative fault concepts to strict liability actions, even though strict liability applies where all possible care was exercised in the preparation of the product. Legal commentators have also pointed out the advantages to be derived from apportioning damages on the basis of fault in strict liability cases. Only one jurisdiction has departed from this trend. Thus, it seems safe to say that, although it entails certain conceptual problems, the approach of applying comparative fault principles to strict liability actions will be increasingly utilized in order to overcome the inequities currently involved in application of the "all or nothing" approach. This trend may be accelerated by the National Conference of Commissioners on Uniform State Laws' recent approval of a model Comparative Fault statute. The law encompasses both negligence and strict liability actions. Nevertheless, it would seem that for the foreseeable future uncertainty and variety of results will be part of state tort law on the subject of plaintiffs' conduct in product liability actions. . . .

ROLAND N. McKEAN

Products Liability: Implications of Some Changing Property Rights

The use of products, from tractors to glass shower doors, often results in accidents and damages, sometimes to the purchaser and sometimes to bystanders. Who should be liable for these costs has for many years been a subject of much concern. Politicians and officials have become increasingly aroused about the safety of items ranging from Corvairs to "shamburgers," leading in part to complaints about liability assignment (though mainly to advocacy of product specifications). In the legal profession, this subject of who is or should be liable has been labeled "products liability" and has caused concern, particularly because of its connection to individuals' notions of equity or fairness. In economics, since accidental damages are a special case of externalities, the subject is also of great concern, especially because of the connection between externalities—those interdependencies that are not mutually, voluntarily accepted—and economic efficiency.

The existence of any externality is related to the rules for and costs of assigning and exchanging property rights. The basic things that we exchange are not products' physical features as such but rather packages of rights to do things with those features. *If* all rights were clearly defined and assigned, *if* there were zero transaction costs, and *if* people agreed to abide by the results of voluntary exchange, there would be no externalities.

Accidental damage is no exception. Wherever it results in an externality, this is related to the rules for and costs of assigning and exchanging rights. In this instance, one of the principal rights involved[1] is the right not be liable for damages or, to look at the other side of the coin, the obligation to pay for damages. As is the case with other rights, this one exists as some sort of expectation, not as a certainty.

The right to avoid liability, like the right to resell one's land, is a feature of an asset that has value. Alternative right assignments may have different impacts on equity (as conceived of by each individual) and, since there are transaction costs, different impacts on production processes and costs, insurance carried, the allocation of resources among uses, and the options open to consumers. In this article I shall discuss some of those impacts of different right assignments pertaining to liability for damage. The coverage will not include "safety legislation," e.g., requiring that all cars be equipped with safety belts. Such legislation is a big topic in itself, and while requiring certain behavior affects right-assignment, the discussion here will be confined to requiring right-reassignments that affect behavior. First, however, I shall sketch out some of the background concerning products liability.

I. DEVELOPMENTS CONCERNING PRODUCTS LIABILITY

After the development of industrial societies, one of the most important conditions for the existence of products liability was that privity, or a direct contractual relationship, had to exist.[2] In other words, a manufacturer might be liable to the wholesaler, the wholesaler to the retailer, and the retailer to his customer, but the manufacturer was not liable to remote customers or to third parties because he had no contractual relationship with them. For the most part this requirement of privity was upheld in England and the United States throughout the nineteenth century. In one famous case, *Winterbottom v. Wright* (1842), in which a coach with a defective wheel had overturned, Lord Abinger said: "There is no privity of contract between these parties; and if the plaintiff can sue, every passenger, or even any person passing along the road, who was injured by the upsetting of the coach, might bring a similar action. Unless we confine the operation of such contracts as this to the parties who entered into them, the most absurd and outrageous consequences, to which I can see no limit, would ensue."[3]

A. Evolution of Sales Law

In connection with certain products and activities, quite a few exceptions to the privity rule developed, especially late in the nineteenth and early in the twentieth centuries.[4] There is a long history of special concern about foods and about "inherently or imminently dangerous" or "ultrahazardous" products, e.g., explosives. In developing special rules for these categories, the courts may have been groping for changes in rights that would yield more gain than cost, as gauged by the judges.[5] Concern about liability for injuries from these products rose whenever people became more impressed with the hazards. For instance, concern about foods soared after the publication of Upton Sinclair's work.[6]

The big breakthrough, however, was the decision in the famous case of the collapsing automobile, *MacPherson v. Buick Motor Company*.[7] This 1916 decision held the manufacturer liable, in the absence of privity, for injuries resulting from the use of a product, whether or not inherently

dangerous, if there is evidence of "negligence" in the manufacture or assembly of the product. Afterward, this position was adopted in case after case and state after state. The ruling was applied, not just to special categories, such as food, beverages, firearms, and explosives, but to such varied items as a sanitary napkin,[8] an inflammable celluloid comb,[9] and a defective bar stool.[10] The product usually had to pose significant danger to life and limb, and the courts sometimes refused to make awards for minor hazards, such as a defective high heel or coffee-can key.[11] Nonetheless, there was unquestionably a shift toward making producers liable in a wider range of circumstances.

Other extensions of producers' liability were brought about by means of special ad hoc devices. It is often difficult to prove negligence on the part of a manufacturer, but in some instances the courts applied the doctrine of "res ipsa loquitur": let the matter speak for itself. If a sealed bottle of soft drink was found to contain a cockroach, it seemed highly unlikely that anyone, after the bottling was done, had opened the container and inserted the insect. The courts were prepared to assume that the production process did involve negligence. Similarly, if a sealed unit in a machine caused damage, the courts often concluded that the matter spoke for itself. Another device for getting around the privity requirement was to regard the wife as an agent for her husband so that, even if he has no direct contractual relationship with the seller, the latter may be liable if the husband suffers injuries while using the product.

These devices are often criticized as being tortured or "artificial" attempts to move toward strict producer liability, but with uncertainty one might without being illogical judge these rules to be better than the alternatives. The courts were uneasy about proceeding to strict liability lest it yield more harm than good, yet they felt that these small steps with comparatively unambiguous cut-off points would yield more good than harm. Similarly one might be uneasy about permitting automobiles to proceed in the face of a red traffic light whenever drivers deem it safe, yet feel confident that allowing *right* turns on a red light would yield more good than harm.

Express warranty and especially implied warranty have been extended by recent interpretations of the law, further reflecting the shift toward "let the seller beware." There may now be an implied warranty of fitness for a particular purpose as distinct from the item's ordinary purpose. For this warranty to hold, the seller must have reason to know that purpose, but it is not necessary for the buyer to have informed the seller; the buyer must be relying on the seller's judgment in selecting *or furnishing* the goods (formerly the seller was liable only if he selected the goods); and purchase by trade name no longer means that the seller's judgment is not being relied upon. The course of dealing and trade usage may generate implied warranties, e.g., may give the seller "reason to know" the particular purpose to which goods are put in a particular locality.[12] Advertising directly to consumers can generate warranties to them. In *Baxter v. Ford Motor Co.*, the manufacturer was held to be liable because a windshield advertised as shatterproof did in fact shatter when struck by a stone.[13]

B. Shifts toward Strict Liability under Tort

Strict liability under tort can be roughly defined as liability simply because a wrong was done, not because a contract was unfulfilled. No attribution of negligence is necessary (though the presence of a "defect," which may simply substitute another word for negligence, is necessary), and no contract need be involved. To many observers it seems that products liability has been evolving rapidly toward strict liability under tort. The following are typical comments: "With privity on the wane, *caveat venditor* will be the rule, not *caveat emptor;* the time has come to hold a requiem for this . . . anachronism."[14] "It seems safe to predict that strict liability for products will soon be the established law in this country."[15]

A crucial case was that of *Henningsen v. Bloomfield Motors, Inc.* in 1960.[16] Mrs. Henningsen suffered injuries when the car suddenly turned right and ran into a wall, presumably due to a defective steering gear. Without any evidence of negligence, the court held Chrysler as well as the dealer liable, saying: "an implied warranty that it [the product] is reasonably suitable for use as such accompanies it into the hands of the ultimate purchaser. Absence of agency . . . is immaterial."[17] There had been earlier and unsuccessful attempts to put automobiles under the heading of "deadly and dangerous instrumentalities" or to apply the

rules for "ferocious animals" to the "devil wagon,"[18] but the Henningsen case appeared to eliminate the requirements for privity or negligence with respect to *all* products, and to cast doubt on the effectiveness of disclaimers. Within a few years the Henningsen precedent was applied to a wide variety of products, including a glass door, shotgun, dental chair, and hula skirt. Liability to bystanders, and other extensions of manufacturer liability, have been established more recently.[19]

Even strict tort liability, however, would still require that there be a defect in the product. The issues about proof of injury and defect, abnormal use (a manufacturer will not be held liable simply because he produces a hammer with which someone manages to hit his head), intervening conduct, and knowledge of the defect will still exist and relieve the producer of liability in many circumstances.[20] Thus the full development of strict liability under tort would simply go further to raise the probability that the producer would be held liable. It would reassign certain property rights in a probabilistic sense.

C. Moves toward Other Liability Assignments

Some writers appear to have in mind more than strict tort liability, however, for they urge or foresee more comprehensive compensation of victims than would occur under strict liability. One writer explicitly supports eliminating the requirement of a defect.[21] For some situations, compulsory accident insurance has been urged, assigning the liability to a large group of potential victims without regard to fault. Automobile accidents especially—with the high court costs and long delays, the difficulties of determining fault, and the large financial consequences—have given rise to proposals such as the Keeton-O'Connell plan.[22] Debate about these liability assignments may lead in turn to serious consideration of social accident insurance under which the taxpayers would be liable.

II. IMPLICATIONS OF ALTERNATIVE ASSIGNMENTS OF LIABILITY

I shall attempt, not to identify optimal policies, but simply to discuss some of the consequences of alternative products-liability arrangements.[23] (Indeed, while each individual can identify the policies *he* prefers, there is no criterion of optimality that *all* members of a group are compelled by logic to accept.) These consequences will be mainly certain costs generated by the alternative arrangements—costs in terms of the price tags that are implicit in a predominantly voluntary exchange system and that would help direct one toward Pareto-optimal policies. Such costs may not be relevant from the standpoint of every individual, but I believe that the value judgments of many persons would cause these costs to be pertinent to their choosing among products-liability arrangements.

Let us examine a spectrum of possibilities from customer liability without fault to taxpayer liability without fault.

A. *Caveat Emptor*

As a starter, what would be the consequences of complete *caveat emptor*—of having customers watch out for themselves and bear the losses that occur during the use of a product? As Coase has shown,[24] that arrangement would lead to economic efficiency—to the production of safety features, caution in using products, and so on, by those parties having a comparative advantage in accident prevention—*if* there were zero transaction costs, and *if* people agreed to accept the results of voluntary exchanges. Purchasers of products would hire producers to include safety features and hire themselves to be careful as long as these actions paid. What about third parties who were injured? If owners of products were liable, they would modify their choices of products and hire bystanders to be careful as long as the gains outweighed the costs. Bargaining would lead to economic efficiency in producing safety features, warnings, instructions to users, instructions to bystanders, caution in using products, caution in standing or walking nearby, and so on. (Or, another possible arrangement would be to make the third parties liable for injuries to themselves. In this case, the third parties could costlessly get together and pay as much as it would be worth to them to have safer products or more cautious use of them.)

Transaction costs, it might be noted, include the costs of negotiation, contracting, and enforcement, which therefore include the costs of acquiring information about the features of products and

about contract violations. If we are to consider products-liability issues in a world of zero transaction costs, however (and in my view it is useful to *start out* that way), that world cannot mean zero information costs in the sense of complete certainty about everything; for in those circumstances there would be no defects, carelessness, chance, accidents, or questions of liability.[25]

In actuality, of course, there are heavy transaction costs. Sometimes one may judge that alternative assignments of rights would bring roughly equivalent results, but often transaction costs vary markedly with different right assignments.[26] With customer liability, however, note that *certain* transaction costs are in fact *comparatively* low. The costs of hiring producers to make safer products and issue warnings and instructions are relatively low, for the market is a mechanism through which customers are able to bid for safer products, instructions, and so on. If one is injured, financially or physically, by defective merchandise, he feels after the event that he has been at the mercy of producers and completely without influence on the design of products. (Moreover, *caveat emptor* may strike one as being inequitable—but for the present let us confine our attention to costs and economic efficiency.) Nonetheless, as disappointments occur to thousands of customers, they turn to rival products or producers—unless upon reflection they prefer the lower price plus that risk to higher prices with reduced risks; and producers find it profitable to make a larger percentage of their products relatively safe, to issue instructions and warnings, to carry liability insurance, and to have broader warranties or more generous returned-goods policies. Hence, while disappointments and injuries never cease, users are able in the aggregate to register their preferences by turning to competitors and bidding more for the goods that they prefer.

Transaction costs become higher if they deal with producers whose profits are regulated or who are sheltered from entry (even through the purchase of existing enterprises), since such producers will be less responsive to consumers' willingness to pay. Such costs will be still higher if one buys from a government agency and tries to hire this producer to offer a safer or otherwise modified product. If a publicly owned highway or reservoir strikes you as being dangerous, the threat of your turning to competitors will not influence the design of the output. Hiring these producers to alter their products takes the comparatively expensive form of organizing pressure groups.

Customer liability would hold another kind of transaction cost in check: the cost of information about what degree of product safety in particular uses is economical. The buyer is in a better position than anyone else to know the exact use to which he plans to put a product and what alternative qualities, or degrees of safety, in the product would mean to his costs and gains. The customer, if he is liable, has an extra incentive to acquire and make appropriate use of information. To get the information, he must deal, not with thousands of individuals, but with the seller and a few other identifiable persons. Now the result will *not* be zero information cost or complete information or zero mistakes. All that is being asserted is that customer liability tends to keep *part* of the information costs relatively low.

On the other hand, *caveat emptor* may keep other types of information cost comparatively high. The manufacturers do know more than anyone else about the nature of their products, and unless they probe and offer consumers numerous alternative amounts of information, customers may never know how much information they would be willing to pay for. This could be especially serious with enterprises that do not count heavily on repeat business and customer goodwill. With any arrangement, many resources will go into acquiring and providing information about products. At present, buyers utilize consumer reports, producer brochures, telephone enquiries, conversations with friends and salesmen, advertisements that convey information, engineers' and other experts' services, and directories and the Yellow Pages to help them find out where to make enquiries. But useful information about products is very costly. How difficult it is to inspect many modern products; how little one discovers about color TV sets or psychiatric treatment or new plumbing fixtures even after investigation. With high costs, potential buyers settle for relatively little information and either forego exchanges that might be mutually advantageous or accept risks that would be rejected—*if* information costs were lower. One may judge that overall costs—information, transaction, foregone-exchange, and accident costs—could be

reduced by directing government,[27] or inducing producers, to provide additional information.

The amount of information that it is economical to generate and the costs of generating information will be different for different products. For example, producers surely provide all the information that customers are willing to pay for in the case of simple familiar products like ordinary tools and supplies. When one considers new, changing, or complex products like new drugs or power tools, however, it may take years of transactions before customers can determine what kind of extra information can be offered and how much various amounts will cost. For complex secondhand items, great effort to gather information will still leave enormous uncertainty. Information about items that one does not buy frequently—e.g., swimming pools, gas furnaces, specialized medical-care equipment, food at unknown restaurants, a house in an unfamiliar city—is also comparatively expensive per unit of the product purchased. (In addition, the consequences of a bad outcome or of nonoptimal calculations by consumers may be particularly serious for certain products, which may bring forth value judgments that consumers should be protected against themselves.) Thus different treatment, e.g., liability assignments, for different product categories (such as "ultrahazardous" or "highly complex" products) may make sense even though it might be foolish in some ideal world with zero transaction costs.

Caveat emptor would also keep another transaction cost relatively low—that of hiring the users to be careful in employing the product. For the user is most frequently the buyer of the product or an acquaintance or a member of his family. Thus if he is liable for losses, he has to obtain the cooperation, not of thousands of strangers, but of himself and a few individuals with whom he has direct personal contact, in seeing that an appropriate degree of care is exercised. This does not mean that he will be as careful as it is humanly possible to be; it merely means that he will choose by weighing the costs of extra care, such as loss of time, against the gains, such as the reduced risk of suffering uncompensated losses or injuries.

With customer liability it is costly—as it would also be with either victim or producer liability—for bystanders to register their bids. It would be very expensive for potential third-party victims to acquire information about the myriad contingencies, and then to get together and bid for safer products, better instructions, more warnings, greater care by the user, and so on. Again, one may judge that total costs could be reduced by reassigning rights so as to elicit safer products, more warnings, and more careful use from the standpoint of bystanders. (And, with regard to fairness, rather than efficiency, *most* people would probably say that product users or producers, or perhaps taxpayers, should compensate injured bystanders.)

Incidentally, when third-party effects or any externalities are large and one sees no way of reducing the costs of voluntary negotiations, one may judge that the use of compulsion would cut total costs. When people are denied options, e.g., when producers are forbidden to produce items that do not have specified safety features, there is no objective evidence about the magnitude of certain costs and gains, since there is no way to see how much people would be willing to pay for options denied or items they are forced to take. Nonetheless, one must sometimes make judgments about these costs and gains. For instance, I understand that in the early days of television, each receiving set emitted signals that interfered with the reception of other sets in the vicinity. Bargaining among set owners to hire each other to install shielding or to watch television only at designated times would have been extremely expensive. The government ordered producers to install shielding on all future sets, thus compelling even isolated set owners to buy this extra feature. Most of us would probably agree in this instance that this action was preferable to doing nothing, i.e., we would judge that the gains exceeded the costs.

On balance, customer liability probably does bring relatively low transaction costs for many product categories. Wherever this is so, bargaining under customer liability would effect additional Pareto-optimal exchanges in comparison with other liability assignments. There are nonetheless several major reasons that might make one oppose *caveat emptor*. (1) One might believe that he could negotiate through the political process for liability assignments that would yield more equitable[28] outcomes, yet that high negotiation costs preclude making tax-subsidy arrangements that would yield an equally desirable wealth distribution *and* economic efficiency. (2) One might attach value to

certain political procedures or arrangements per se (e.g., for ideological reasons) and simply not care much about costs that are relevant to Pareto-optimal steps. (3) One might attach value to preventing people from taking the risks they would voluntarily choose to take. (4) One might still believe that customer liability leads to less economic efficiency than other arrangements, since the issue is in doubt once transaction costs are recognized. It is in doubt because we do not know exactly what information, negotiation, and enforcement costs would be with some other assignment of rights (or compulsory product specifications). Since some of these costs will be in doubt, one must in the end make personal judgments in deciding what arrangement he believes would be efficient. One individual, or a majority of individuals, may judge that total costs could be reduced by departing from customer liability.

B. Producer Liability with Defect

What are the consequences of moving further toward producer liability—of reducing the chances that the purchaser will be held liable and increasing the chances that the producer will face liability? (And this, to repeat, is what seems to have happened.) In my judgment the effects would not have great quantitative significance but would be along the following lines. I would expect more court cases and court costs, since under complete customer liability, the product owner is not compensated, and there is no court determination of the extent of injury, the presence of defects, or the existence of negligence. There would now be higher costs of hiring purchasers to exercise care, for this would now require myriad special contracts with prohibitive enforcement costs, and those higher transaction costs would result in the existence of more externalities; i.e., accident rates would rise.[29] Producers would turn increasingly to liability insurance, and since it would not be economical to adjust the premiums continuously or precisely, producers might, up to certain thresholds, find it efficient to neglect safety features,[30] diluting the shift toward safer products that is noted below.

With the customer facing a lower probability of being liable, relatively hazardous designs would be less unattractive to him, and the demand curve for such products would rise relative to the demand curve for comparatively safe products. With the producer facing a higher probability of being liable and with his either carrying liability insurance or paying damages, relatively hazardous designs would be more costly, and the supply curve for such products would decrease. On the basis of this shift in liability assignment by itself, there is no presumption that the quantity of hazardous products sold would change, and while the consumer would pay a higher price to the producer, he would simply be forced to buy insurance from the producer instead of having the option of insuring himself. The only thing that would happen to the consumer's position is that he would be denied the opportunity of taking the risk. Since that option would be preferred by some consumers, especially by the poor, this would mean in effect a rise in the price of hazardous products relative to the price of "safe" products, resulting in the end in some shift toward safer products and working to the detriment of the poor.

The shift in liability assignment would decrease efficiency, however, if there was a net increase in transaction costs. (As noted above, producer liability would surely raise the costs of hiring users to be careful and raise some, though not all, information costs.) If this happened, the supply curve would decrease still further, resulting in higher prices for hazardous relative to safer products and in a net shift from hazardous to safer products.

C. Producer Liability without Defect

Let us turn now to a rather extreme arrangement that has been mentioned in recent years—producer liability *without fault or defect*. The manufacturer would simply be held liable for all injuries occurring with the use of his product, regardless of circumstances. As in the other cases, if there were zero transaction costs, producers could hire purchasers to be careful, third parties could hire users to be careful and producers to issue safer products, and purchasers could hire manufacturers to provide various safety features. Each would take these actions as long as the extra gain exceeded the extra cost, and resource use would end up at an efficient point. With transaction costs, however, manufacturer liability without fault or defect would alter resource allocation, and, unless the transactions costs could be measured, it would be uncertain which

liability assignment would lead to an efficient point.

I conjecture that costs would be affected in the following ways and that the changes would be important quantitatively. The cost of hiring thousands of purchasers or third parties to exercise care would be enormous, and therefore these persons would now find it relatively inexpensive to be careless. Accident rates would rise. Insurance premiums would become high except on relatively safe products, increasing the net price of hazardous products relative to the price of safe products. As in the preceding case, there would be a shift away from the comparatively hazardous product lines toward the safer products. The net impact on accident costs is not clear, but total costs would rise, because accident prevention would not be produced by those having a comparative advantage in doing so. Court costs per case would decline in comparison with the fault system, but the number of claims would rise; and, unlike the case of *caveat emptor*, disputes and court costs would not be nil, because even if fault did not have to be established, the fact and extent of injury would have to be determined. (Otherwise, claims would be infinitely large.) Consumers would face a narrower range of choice—a significant sacrifice, but one that is impossible to quantify in any generally valid fashion. As far as this particular sacrifice is concerned, poor people would be hardest hit, because their options would now be to buy relatively expensive safe products, or hazardous products plus high producer-insurance costs, or nothing at all.

The higher accident prevention costs would be borne largely by the customers and potential customers in each industry in the form of higher prices and restricted choice (though I would predict legislative intervention in an effort to check the rising costs). Some of the burden might be passed on to customers in other industries, as people shifted their purchases, and input rents might be reshuffled somewhat. Whether or not one regarded these changes in wealth distribution as being equitable would depend upon the precise impacts and upon one's value judgments.

D. Taxpayer Liability

Many persons believe that it would be more equitable to spread the burdens more widely, e.g., to spread the burden of aircraft accidents over owners in, and customers of, airlines or aircraft manufacturers or both. As far as equity is concerned, however, such redistributions still seem rather arbitrary. Why not put the burden on taxpayers in general?

One way to do this would be to have government compensate people for all injuries without regard to fault. Of course a claim that an injury had occurred would have to be checked; so there would still be this sort of administration cost. Note, however, that neither purchasers nor producers (nor third parties) would now have to worry about being liable, so that carelessness in design and use of products would become relatively inexpensive to these persons. With the customer not liable, hazardous products would be less unattractive. As the cost of selling unsafe or defective products went down from producers' standpoints, they would expand supplies. Thus both the demand curve and the supply curve of relatively hazardous products would increase, and, without government regulation, there would be a shift toward the use of dangerous products. As the cost of failing to inspect products or of employing products carelessly went down from purchasers' standpoints, they would take more of these actions. If officials or taxpayers thought of hiring these persons to behave differently, ordinary bargaining would be prohibitively expensive.

It is virtually certain that voters and their representatives would find this situation unsatisfactory. Costs would soar too high. Liability insurance, warnings, and disclaimers—in this extreme arrangement and without governmental regulation—would practically disappear. To make taxpayer liability workable, government would have to draw up a network of specifications for products, regulations of their use, and required instructions and warnings. Some "unavoidably unsafe products" might be banned altogether. Producers would inevitably face penalties (a kind of liability) for violating the requirements. Again, consumers would find their choice restricted, this time by law; they would be unable to buy relatively cheap, albeit relatively unsafe, products if they preferred them. Some new kind of penalties for negligence in using products, and perhaps for carelessness by bystanders, would be devised. Administrative and enforcement costs would be high. In the end there would be increased sacrifices in general, and these burdens would be shifted around according to the complex factors that determine tax incidence. One cannot say that social accident insurance would be a "bad" policy, but he can say with confidence that it would not amount to a "free lunch."

In short, as with property right assignments in general, different liability assignments would often bring about significant differences in resource use because of differential transaction costs. It is important to know more about the variation of transaction costs under alternative institutions and about the implications for wealth distribution and resource allocation of different right or liability assignments.

NOTES

1. Others would include rights to use items for various purposes and with varying degrees of care.

2. Only the high spots will be reviewed here. For more detail see such articles as Dix W. Noel, "Manufacturers of Products—The Drift Toward Strict Liability," *Tennessee Law Review*, 24 (Spring 1957), 963-1018 or William L. Prosser, "The Assault Upon the Citadel (Strict Liability to the Consumer)," *Yale Law Journal*, 69 (June 1960), 1099–1148. This section will be nonanalytical, but I hope that the background will be of interest to economists. The AEA-AALS Committee arranged for the study in the hope of stimulating interest among economists in the evolving legal framework and its analysis (and to stimulate lawyers to be more concerned with the economic implications of that framework).

3. 10 M & W 109, 152 Eng. Rep. 402 (Exch. 1842).

4. Lester W. Feezer, "Tort Liability of Manufacturers and Vendors," *Minnesota Law Review,* 10 (Dec. 1925), 1–27.

5. Ronald H. Coase, "The Problem of Social Cost," *Journal of Law and Economics*, 3 (Oct. 1960), 19–20.

6. Upton Sinclair "said later that he had aimed at the public's heart, and by accident hit it in the stomach" (C. C. Regier, "The Struggle for Federal Food and Drugs Legislation," *Law and Contemporary Problems*, 3 (1933), 9, cited by Prosser, *op. cit.*, 1106).

7. 217 N.Y. 382, 111 N.E. 1050 (1916).

8. *La Frumento v. Kotex Co.*, 131 Misc. 314, 226 N.Y. Supp. 750 (N.Y.C. City Ct. 1928).

9. *Farley v. Edward E. Tower Co.,* 271 Mass. 230. 171 N.E. 639 (1930).

10. *Okker v. Chrome Furniture Mfg. Co.,* 26 N.J. Super. 295, 97 A. 2d 699 (1953).

11. *Timpson v. Marshall, Meadows and Stewart, Inc.*, 198 Misc. 1034, 101 N.Y.S. 2d 583 (Sup. Ct. 1950); *Boyd v. American Can Co.*, 249 App. Div. 644, 291 N.Y.S. 205 (2d Dep't 1936). For a discussion and other citations see Noel, *op. cit.*

12. K. Sidney Neuman, "The Uniform Commercial Code and Greater Consumer Protection Under Warranty Law," *Kentucky Law Journal*, 49 (Winter 1960–61), 240–69.

13. 168 Wash. 456, 12 P. 2d 409.

14. Walter H. E. Jaeger, "Privity of Warranty: Has the Tocsin Sounded?" *Duquesne University Law Review* (1963), 1.

15. John W. Wade, "Strict Tort Liability of Manufacturers," *Southwestern Law Journal*, 19 (1965), 5–25.

16. 32 N.J. 358, 161 A. 2d 69 (1960). See William L. Prosser, "The Fall of the Citadel (Strict Liability to the Consumer)," *Minnesota Law Review*, 50 (1966), 791–848.

17. 32 N.J. 384, 161 A. 2d 84.

18. *Lewis v. Amorous*, 3 Ga. App. 50, 55; 59 S.E. 338, 340 (1907).

19. *Time Magazine*, May 23, 1969, p. 66.

20. Prosser, "The Fall of the Citadel," *loc. cit.*, 824–48.

21. Thomas A. Cowan, "Some Policy Bases of Products Liability," *Stanford Law Review*, 17 (July 1965), 1094.

22. Robert E. Keeton and Jeffrey O'Connell, *Basic Protection for the Traffic Victim* (Boston: Little, Brown, 1965).

23. See also Walter J. Blum and Harry Kalven, Jr., *Public Law Perspective on a Private Law Problem: Auto Compensation Plans* (Boston: Little, Brown, 1965); Guido Calabresi, "Does the Fault System Optimally Control Primary Accident Costs?" *Law and Contemporary Problems*, 33 (Summer 1968), 429–63; and Oliver E. Williamson, Douglas G. Olson, and August Ralston, "Externalities, Insurance, and Disability Analysis," *Economics*, 34 (Aug. 1967), 235–53 for other pertinent analyses.

24. Coase, *op. cit.*

25. Another condition for applying the Coase theorem, according to some, is that there be perfect competition, which may seem inconsistent with the existence of products-liability issues (since they often involve brand names, differentiated products, and warranties on such products). In the zero-transaction-cost case, however, monopolists would be hired by consumers to act like competitors. Also, homogeneity of products to customers does not necessarily imply that retailers, wholesalers, and manufacturers of particular items cannot be identified. In any event, one can discuss the implications of right assignments for costs and Pareto-optimal changes without assuming conditions that would lead to overall Pareto-optimality; "second-best" complications raise doubts, but they raise the same doubt about any partial equilibrium analysis.

26. For example, if one knew that group A would nearly always buy certain rights from group B, he could reduce transaction costs by assigning these rights to group A in the first place (see Harold Demsetz, "Some Aspects of Property Rights," *Journal of Law and Economics*, 9 (Oct. 1966), 66).

27. It should be remembered, however, that governments are often inefficient providers of useful information; the incentives of those who write government pamphlets will not reflect a premium placed on gaining customers' goodwill.

28. I.e., distributional impacts that one prefers.

29. Some people argue that removing liability from users, thus reducing the monetary cost of their having accidents, would not induce those persons to have additional painful and perhaps fatal accidents. To be sure, if more carelessness meant a 100 percent probability of having a serious accident, prospective pain would be deterrent enough, but what more carelessness really means is ordinarily a modest increase in the probability of having some sort of accident. We trade such increased chances of having an accident for a saving of money or time every day. If carelessness is made to cost less, more will be taken. (Admittedly, the costs that people associate with extremely low risk are unclear. For instance, they may treat a trivial chance, and a still lower chance, of a large loss as being equivalent. There is all the more reason, it seems to me, to expect people to respond to clearly perceived costs in money or time.)

30. Williamson, Olson, and Ralston, *op. cit.*

GEORGE G. BRENKERT

Strict Products Liability and Compensatory Justice

I

Strict products liability is the doctrine that the seller of a product has legal responsibilities to compensate the user of that product for injuries suffered due to a defective aspect of the product, even though the seller has not been negligent in permitting that defect to occur.[1] Thus, even though a manufacturer, for example, has reasonably applied the existing techniques of manufacture and has anticipated and cared for non-intended uses of the product, he may still be held liable for injuries a product user suffers if it can be shown that the product was defective when it left the manufacturer's hands.[2] To say that there is a crisis today concerning this doctrine would be to utter a commonplace observation which few in the business community would deny. The development of the doctrine of strict products liability, they say, financially threatens many businesses.[3] Further, strict products liability is said to be a morally questionable doctrine since the manufacturer or seller has not been negligent in the occurrence of the injury-causing defect in the product. On the other hand, victims of defective products complain that they deserve full compensation for injuries sustained in using a defective product whether or not the seller is at fault. Medical expenses and time lost from one's job are costs no individual should have to bear by himself. It is only fair that the seller share such burdens.

In general, discussions of this crisis focus on the limits to which a business ought to be held responsible to compensate the injured product user. Much less frequently do discussions of strict products liability consider the underlying question of whether the doctrine of strict products liability is rationally justifiable. But unless this question is answered it would seem premature to seek to determine the limits to which businesses ought to be held liable in such cases. In the following paper I discuss this underlying philosophical question and argue that there is a rational justification for strict products liability which links it to the very nature of the free enterprise system.

II

It should be noted at the outset that strict products liability is not absolute liability. To hold a manufacturer legally (and morally) responsible for any and all injuries which product users might sustain would be morally perverse. First, it would deny the product user's own responsibility to take care in his actions and to suffer the consequences when he does not. As such, it would constitute an extreme form of moral and legal paternalism. Second, if the product is not defective, there is no significant moral connection between anything that the manufacturer has done or not done and the user's injuries other than the production and sale of the product to its user. But this provides no basis to hold the manufacturer responsible for the user's injuries. If, because of my own carelessness, I cut myself with my pocket knife, the fact that I just bought my knife from Blade Manufacturing Company provides no moral reason to hold Blade Manufacturing responsible for my injury. Finally, though the manufacturer's product might be said to have harmed the person,[4] it is wholly implausible, when the product is not defective and the manufacturer not negligent, to say that the manufacturer has harmed the user. Thus, again there would seem to be no moral basis upon which to maintain that the manufacturer has any liability to the product user. Strict products liability, on the other hand, is the view that the manufacturer can be held liable when the product can be shown to be defective even though the manufacturer himself is not negligent.[5]

There are two justifications of strict products liability which are predominant in the literature. Both justifications are, I believe, untenable. They are:

a. To hold producers strictly liable for defective products will cut down on the number of accidents and injuries which occur, by forcing manufacturers to make their products safer.

b. The manufacturer is best able to distribute to others the costs of injuries which users of his defective products suffer.

There are several reasons why the first justification is unacceptable. First, it has been plausibly argued that almost everything that can be attained through the use of strict liability to force manufacturers to make their products safer can also be attained in other ways through the law.[8] Hence, to hold manufacturers strictly liable will not necessarily help reduce the number of accidents. The incentive to produce safer products already exists without invoking the doctrine of strict products liability.

Second, at least some of the accidents which have been brought under strict liability have been due to features of the products which the manufacturers could not have foreseen or controlled. At the time the product was designed and manufactured, the technological knowledge required to discover the hazard and take steps to minimize its effects was not available. It is doubtful that, in such cases, the imposition of strict liability upon the manufacturer could reduce accidents.[9] Thus, again, this justification for strict products liability fails.[10]

Third, the fact that the imposition of legal restraints and/or penalties would have a certain positive effect, viz., the reduction of accidents, does not show that the imposition of those penalties would be just. It has been pointed out before that the rate of crime might be cut significantly if the law would imprison the wives and children of men who break the law. Regardless of how correct that claim may be, to use these means in order to achieve a significant reduction in the rate of crime would be unjust. Thus, the fact, if fact it be, that strict liability would cut down on the amount of dangerous and/or defective products placed on the market, and thus reduce the amount of accidents and injuries, does not thereby justify the imposition of strict liability on manufacturers.

Finally, the above justification is essentially a utilitarian appeal which emphasizes the welfare of the product users. It is not obvious, however, that those who use this justification have ever undertaken the utilitarian analysis which would show that greater protection of the product user's safety would further the welfare of product users. If emphasis on product user safety would cut down on the number and variety of products produced, the imposition of strict liability might not, in fact, enhance product user welfare but rather lower it. Furthermore, if the safety of product users is the predominant concern, massive public and private education safety campaigns might just as well lower the level of accidents and injuries as strict products liability.

The second justification given for strict products liability is also utilitarian in nature. Among the considerations given in favor of this justification are the following:

a. "An individual harmed by his/her use of a defective product is often unable to bear the loss individually";

b. "Distribution of losses among all users of a product would minimize both individual and aggregate loss";

c. "The situation of producers and marketers in the marketplace enable them conveniently to distribute losses among all users of a product by raising prices sufficiently to compensate those harmed (which is what in fact occurs where strict liability is in force)."[11]

This justification is also defective.

First, the word "best" in the phrase "best able to distribute to others the cost" is usually understood in a non-moral sense; it is used to signify that the manufacturer can most efficiently pass on the costs of injuries to others. Once this use of "best" is recognised, then surely the question may correctly be asked: Why ought these costs be passed on to other consumers and/or users of the same product or line of products? Even if the imposition of strict liability did maximize utility, it might be the case that it was still unjust to use the producer as the distributor of losses.[12] Indeed, it has been objected that to pass along the costs of such accidents to other consumers of products of a manufacturer is unjust to them.[13] The above justification is silent to these legitimate questions.

Second, it may not be, as a matter of fact, that manufacturers are always in the best (i.e., most efficient and economical) position to pass costs on to customers. This might be possible in monopoly areas, but even there there are limitations. Further, some products are subject to an "elastic demand" and as such the manufacturer could not pass along the costs.[14] Finally, the present justification could justify far more than is plausible. If the reason for holding the manufacturer liable is that the manufacturer is the "best" administrator of costs, then one might plausibly argue that the manufacturer should pay for injuries suffered not simply when he is not negligent but also when the product is not defective. That is, theoretically this argument could be extended from cases of strict liability to absolute liability. Whether this argument could plausibly be made would depend upon contingent facts concerning the nature and frequency of injuries people suffer using products, the financial strength of businesses, and the kinds and levels of products liability insurance available to them. The argument would not depend on any morally significant elements in the producer/product user relation. Such an implication, I believe, undercuts the purported moral nature of this justification. It reveals it for what it is: an economic, not a moral justification.

Accordingly, neither of the major, current justifications for the imposition of strict liability appears to be acceptable. If this is the case, is strict products liability a groundless doctrine, willfully and unjustly imposed on manufacturers?

III

This question can be asked in two different ways. On the one hand, it can be asked within the assumptions of the free enterprise system. On the other hand, it could be raised such that the fundamental assumptions of that socio-economic system are also open to revision and change. In the following, I will discuss the question *within* the general assumptions of the free enterprise system. Since these are the assumptions which are broadly made in legal and business circles it is interesting to determine what answer might be given within these constraints. Indeed, I suggest, it is only within these general assumptions that strict products liability can be justified.

To begin with, it is crucial to remember that what we have to consider is the relation between an entity doing business and an individual.[15] The strict liability attributed to business would not be attributed to an individual who happened to sell some particular product he had made to his neighbor or a stranger. If Peter sold an article which he had made to Paul, and Paul hurt himself because the article had a defect which occurred through no negligence of Peter's, we would not normally hold Peter morally responsible to pay for Paul's injuries. Peter did not claim, we may assume, that the product was absolutely risk free. Had he kept it himself, he too might have been injured by it. Paul, on the other hand, bought it. He was not pressured, forced, or coerced to do so. Peter mounted no advertising campaign. Though Paul might not have been injured if the product had been made differently, he supposedly bought it with open eyes. Peter did not seek to deceive Paul about its qualities. The product, both its good and bad qualities, became his through his purchase of it. In short, we assume that both Peter and Paul are morally autonomous individuals capable of knowing their own interests, that such individuals can legitimately exchange their ownership of various products, that the world is not free of risks, and that not all injuries one suffers in such a world can be blamed on others. To demand that Peter protect Paul from such dangers and/or compensate him for injuries resulting from such dangers, is to demand that Peter significantly reduce the risks of the product he offers to Paul. He would have to protect Paul from encountering those risks himself. However, this smacks of paternalism, and undercuts our basic moral assumptions about such relations. Hence, in such a case, Peter is not morally responsible for Paul's injuries or, due to this transaction, obligated to aid him. Perhaps Peter owes Paul aid because Paul is an injured neighbor or person. Perhaps simply for reasons of charity Peter ought to aid Paul. But Peter has no moral obligation, stemming from the sale itself, to provide aid.

It is different in the case of businesses. They have been held to be legally and morally obliged to pay the victim for his injuries. Why? What is the difference? The difference has to do with the fact that when Paul is hurt by a defective product from corporation X, he is hurt by something produced in a socio-economic system purportedly embodying free enterprise. To say this is to say, among other things, that (a) each business and/or corporation produces articles or services which they sell for profit; (b) each member of this system competes with other members of the system in trying to do as well as he can for himself not simply in each exchange but through each exchange for his other values and desires; (c) competition is to be "open and free, without deception or fraud"; (d) exchanges are to be voluntary and undertaken when each party believes he can thereby benefit. One party provides the means for another party's ends if the other party will provide the first party the means to his ends[16]; (e) the acquisition and disposition of ownership rights, i.e., of private property, is permitted in such exchanges; (f) no market or series of markets constitutes the whole of a society; (g) law, morality, and government play a role in setting acceptable limits to the nature and kinds of exchange in which people may engage.[17]

What is it about such a system which would justify claims of strict products liability against businesses? Calabresi has suggested that the free enterprise system is essentially a system of strict liability.[18] Thus, the very nature of the free enterprise system justifies such liability claims. His argument has two parts. First, he claims that "bearing risks is both the function of, and justification for, private enterprise in a free enterprise society."[19] "Free enterprise is prized, in classical economics, precisely because it fosters the creation of entrepreneurs who will take such uninsurable risks, who will, in other words, gamble on uncertainty and demonstrate their utility by surviving—by winning more than others."[20] Accordingly, the nature of private enterprise requires that individual businesses assume the burden of risk in the production and distribution of its products. However, even if it be granted that this characterisation of who must bear the risks "in deciding what goods are worth producing and what new entrants into an industry are worth having" is correct, it would not follow that individual businesses ought to bear the burden of risk in cases of accidents. Calabresi himself recognises this. Thus, he maintains, in the

second part of his argument, that there is a close analogy which lets us move from the regular risk bearing businesses must accept in the marketplace to the bearing of risks in accidents: "although . . . (the above characterisation) has concerned *regular* entrepreneurial-product risks, not accident risks, the analogy is extremely close."[21] He proceeds, however, to draw the analogy in the following brief sentence: "As with product-accident risks, our society starts out by allocating ordinary product-production risks in ways which try to maximize the chances that incentives will be placed on those most suited to 'manage' these risks."[22] In short, he simply asserts that the imposition of strict products liability on business will be the most effective means of reducing such risks. But such a view does not really require, as we have seen in the previous section, any assumptions about the nature of the free enterprise system. It could be held independently of such assumptions. Further, this view is simply a form of the first justificatory argument we discussed and rejected in the previous section. We can hardly accept it here under the guise of being attached to the nature of free enterprise.

Nevertheless, Calabresi's initial intuitions about a connection between the assumptions of the free enterprise system and the justification of strict products liability are correct. However, they must be developed in the following, rather different, manner. In the free enterprise system, each person and/or business is obligated to follow the rules and understandings which define this socio-economic system. Following the rules is expected to channel competition among individual persons and businesses so that the results are socially positive. In providing the means to fulfill the ends of others, the means to one's own ends also get fulfilled. Though this does not happen in every case, it is supposed that, in general, this happens. Those who fail in their competition with others may be the object of charity, but not of other duties. Those who succeed, *qua* members of this socio-economic system, do not have moral duties to aid those who fail. Analogously, the team which loses the game may receive our sympathy but the winning team is not obligated to help it so that it may win the next game, or even play better the next game. Those who violate the rules, however, may be punished or penalized, whether or not the violation was intentional and whether or not it redounds to the benefit of the violator. Thus, a team may be assessed a penalty for something a team member unintentionally did to a member of the other team but which, by violating the rules, nevertheless injured the other team's chances of competition in the game.

This point may be emphasized by another instance involving a game but one which brings us closer to strict products liability. Imagine that you are playing table tennis with another person in his newly constructed table tennis room. You are both avid table tennis players and the game means a lot to both of you. Suppose that after play has begun, you are suddenly and quite obviously blinded by the light over the table—the light shade has a hole in it which, when it turned in your direction, sent a shaft of light unexpectedly into your eyes. You lose a crucial point as a result. Surely it would be unfair of your opponent to seek to maintain his point because he was faultless—i.e., he had not intended to blind you when he installed that light shade. You would correctly object that he had gained the point unfairly, that you should not have to give up the point lost, and that the light shade should be modified so that the game could continue on a fair basis. It is only fair that the point be played over.

Businesses and their customers in a free enterprise system are also engaged in competition with each other.[23] The competition here, however, is multifaceted as each tries to gain the best agreement he can from the other with regard to the buying and selling of raw materials, products, services, and labour. Such agreements, however, must be voluntary. The competition which leads to them cannot involve coercion. In addition, such competition must be fair and ultimately result in the benefit of the entire society through the operation of the proverbial "invisible hand." Crucial to the notion of fairness of competition is not simply the demands that the competition itself be open, free, and honest, but also that each person in a society be given an equal opportunity to participate in the system in order to fulfill his own particular ends. Friedman formulates this notion in the following manner: "the priority given to equality of opportunity in the hierarchy of values ... is manifested particularly in economic policy. The catchwords were free enterprise, competition, laissez-faire. Everyone was free to go into any business, follow

any occupation, buy any property, subject only to the agreement of the other parties to the transaction. Each was to have the opportunity to reap the benefits if he succeeded, to suffer the costs if he failed. There were to be no arbitrary obstacles. Performance, not birth, religion, or nationality, was the touchstone."[24]

What is obvious in Friedman's comments is that he is thinking primarily of a person as a producer. Equality of opportunity requires that one not be prevented by arbitrary obstacles from participating (by engaging in a productive role of some kind or other) in the system of free enterprise, competition, etc. in order to fulfill one's own ends ("reap the benefits"). Accordingly, monopolies are restricted, discriminatory hiring policies have been condemned, and price collusion is forbidden. However, each person participates in the system of free enterprise *both* as a worker/producer *and* as a consumer. The two roles interact; if the person could not consume he would not be able to work, and if there were no consumers there would be no work to be done. Even if a particular individual is only (what is ordinarily considered) a consumer, he too plays a theoretically significant role in the competitive free enterprise system. The fairness of the system depends upon the access to information, which is available to him, about goods and services on the market, the lack of coercion imposed on him to buy goods, as well as the lack of arbitrary restrictions imposed by the market and/or government on his behavior. In short, equality of opportunity is a doctrine with two sides which applies both to producers and to consumers. If, then, a person as a consumer or a producer is injured by a defective product, which is one way in which his activities might be arbitrarily restricted by the action of (one of the members of) the market system, surely his free and voluntary participation in the system of free enterprise will be seriously affected. Specifically, his equal opportunity to participate in the system in order to fulfill his own ends will be diminished.

It is here that strict products liability enters the picture. In cases of strict liability the manufacturer does not intend that a certain aspect of his product injures a person. Nevertheless, the person is injured. As a result, his activity both as a consumer and as a producer is disadvantaged. He cannot continue to play the role he might wish either as a producer or consumer. As such he is denied that equality of opportunity which is basic to the economic system in question just as surely as he would be if he were excluded from employment by various unintended consequences of the economic system which nevertheless had certain racially or sexually prejudicial implications. Accordingly, it is fair that the manufacturer compensate the person for his losses before proceeding with business as usual. That is, the user of a manufacturer's product may justifiably demand compensation from the manufacturer when a product of his which can be shown to be defective has injured him and harmed his chances of participation in the system of free enterprise.

Hence, strict liability finds a basis in the notion of equality of opportunity which plays a central role in the notion of a free enterprise system. This is why a business which does *not* have to pay for the injuries which an individual suffers in the use of a defective article made by that business is felt to be unfair to its customers. Its situation is analogous to a player's unintentional violation of a game rule which is intended to foster equality of competitive opportunity. A soccer player, for example, may unintentionally trip an opposing player. He did not mean to do it; perhaps he himself had stumbled and consequently tripped the other player. Still, he is to be penalized. If the referee looked the other way, the tripped player would rightfully object that he had been treated unfairly. Similarly, the manufacturer of a product may be held strictly liable for a product of his which injures a person who uses that product. Even though he be faultless, it is a causal consequence of his activities that renders the user of his product less capable of equal participation in the socio-economic system so as to fulfill his (the user's) own ends. The manufacturer too should be penalised by way of compensating the victim. Thus, the basis upon which manufacturers are held strictly liable is compensatory justice.

In a society which refuses to resort to paternalism or to central direction of the economy and which turns, instead, to competition in order to allocate scarce positions and resources, compensatory justice requires that the competition be fair and losers be protected.[25] Specifically no one who loses should be left so destitute that he cannot reenter the competition. Further, those who suffer injuries traceable to the defective results of the

activities of others which restrict their participation in the competitive system should also be compensated. As such, compensatory justice does not presuppose negligence or evil intentions on the part of those to whom the injuries might ultimately be causally traced. It is not perplexed or incapacitated by the relative innocence of all parties involved. Rather it is concerned with correcting the disadvantaged situation an individual experiences due to accidents or failures which occur in the normal working of that competitive system. It is on this basis that other compensatory programs which alleviate the disabilities of various minority groups are founded. It is also on compensatory justice that strict products liability finds its foundation.

An implication of the preceding argument is that business is not morally obliged to pay, as such, for the physical injury a person suffers. Rather, it must pay for the loss of equal competitive opportunity—even though it usually is the case that it is because of a (physical) injury that there is a loss of such equal opportunity. This, however, corresponds to actual legal cases in which the injury which prevents a person from going about his/her daily activities may be emotional or mental as well as physical. If it were the case that a person were neither mentally nor physically harmed, but still rendered less capable of competitively participating due to a defective aspect of a product, then there would still be grounds for holding the company liable. For example, suppose I purchased and used a cosmetic product guaranteed to last a month. When used by most people it is odorless. On me, however, it has a terrible smell. I can stand the smell, but my co-workers, and most other people, find it intolerable. My employer sends me home from work until it wears off. The product has not physically or mentally harmed me. Still, on the above argument, I would have reason to hold the manufacturer liable. Any cosmetic product with this result is defective. As a consequence my opportunity to participate in the socio-economic system so as to fulfill my own ends is disadvantaged. I should be compensated.

IV

There is another way of arguing to the same conclusion about the basis of strict products liability.

To speak of business or the free enterprise system, it was noted above, is to speak of the voluntary exchanges between producer and customer which take place when each party believes he has an opportunity to benefit. Now surely customers and producers may miscalculate their benefits and something which they voluntarily agreed to buy or sell turn out actually to be something which is not to their benefit. In this situation, I have noted, the successful person does not have any moral responsibilities to the unsuccessful person—at least as a member of this economic system. If, however, one person does not benefit due to fraud on the part of another person, the system is, in principle, undermined. If such fraud were universalised, the system would collapse. Accordingly, the person committing the fraud does have a responsibility to make reparations to the one mistreated.

Now consider, once again, the instance of a person who is harmed by a product, which he bought or used, and which can reasonably be said to be defective. Has the nature of the free enterprise system, as above characterised, also been undermined or corrupted in this instance? They have exchanged the product but it has not been to their mutual benefit; the manufacturer may have benefited, but the customer has suffered due to the defectiveness of the manufacturer's product. Further, if such exchanges were universalised, the system would also be undone. Suppose that whenever people bought products from manufacturers the products turned out to be defective and the customers were always injured, even though the manufacturers could not be held negligent. Though one party to such exchanges might benefit, the other party always suffered. If the rationale of this economic system—the reason why it was adopted and is defended—was that in the end both parties share the equal opportunity to gain, surely this economic system with the above consequences would collapse. Consequently, as in the case of fraud, an economic system of free enterprise would require that injuries which result from defective products be compensated. The question is: who is to pay for the compensation?

There are three possibilities. The injured party could pay for his own injuries. However, this is implausible since what is called for is compensation and not merely payment for injuries. If the injured party had simply injured himself, if he had been negligent or careless, then it is plausible that he should pay for his own injuries. No compensation is at stake here. But in the present case the injury stems from the actions of a particular manufacturer who, albeit unwittingly, placed the defective product on the market and stands to gain through its sale. The rationale of the free enterprise system would be undermined, we have seen, if such actions were universalized, for then the product user's equal opportunity to benefit from the system would be effectively denied. Accordingly, since the rationale and motivation for an individual to be part of this socio-economic system is his opportunity to gain from participation in it, justice requires that the injured product user receive compensation for his injuries. Since the individual can hardly compensate himself, he must receive compensation from some other source.

Second, some third party, e.g. the government, could compensate the injured person. This is not wholly implausible if one is prepared to modify the structure of the free enterprise system. And, indeed, in the long run this may be the most plausible course of action. However, if one accepts the structure of the free enterprise system, this alternative must be rejected because it permits the interference of government into individual affairs.[26] Thus, third, we are left with the manufacturer. Suppose a manufacturer's product, even though the manufacturer wasn't negligent, always turned out to be defective and injured those using his products. Though we might sympathize with his plight, he would either have to stop manufacturing altogether (no one would buy such products) or else compensate the victims for their losses (some people might buy and use his products under these conditions). If he forced people to buy and use his products he would corrupt the free enterprise system. If he did not compensate the injured users, they would not buy and he would not be able to sell his products. Hence, he could partake of the free enterprise system, i.e. sell his products, only if he compensated his user/victims. Accordingly, the sale of this hypothetical line of defective products would only be voluntarily accepted as just or fair only if compensation were paid the user/victims of such products by the manufacturer. The same conclusion follows even if we must consider a single defective product. The manufacturer put the defective product on the market. It is because of his actions that others who seek the opportunity to participate on an equal basis in this system in order to benefit therefrom are unable to do so. Thus, it is as a result, even though unintended, of his actions that the system's character and integrity are, in principle, undermined. Accordingly, when a person is injured in his attempt to participate in this system, he is owed compensation by the manufacturer. The seller of the defective article must not jeopardize the equal opportunity of the product user to benefit from the system. The seller need not guarantee that the buyer/user will benefit from the purchase of the product—he may miscalculate or be careless in the use of a nondefective product. But supposing that he is not careless or has not miscalculated, then his opportunity to benefit from the system is illegitimately harmed if he is injured in its use because of the product's defectiveness. He deserves compensation.

Accordingly, it follows from the argument in this and the preceding section that, opposed to what some have claimed, strict products liability is not only compatible with the system of free enterprise but were it not attributed to the manufacturer the system would be itself morally defective! And the justification, we have seen, of requiring manufacturers to pay compensation in cases in which individuals are injured by defective products is that the demands of compensatory justice are fulfilled.[27]

NOTES

1. This characterisation of strict products liability is adapted from Weinstein et al., *Products Liability and the Reasonably Safe Product*, ch. 1. I understand "the seller" to include the manufacturer, the retailer, as well as distributors and wholesalers. For convenience sake, I will generally refer simply to the manufacturer.

2. Cf. John W. Wade, "On Product 'Design Defects' and Their Actionability," 33 *Vanderbilt Law Review* 553 (1980). Weinstein, et al., *Products Liability and the Reasonably Safe Product*, pp. 8, 28–32. Reed Dickerson, "Products Liability: How Good Does a Product Have to Be?," 42 *Indiana Law Journal* 308–316 (1967). Section 402A of the Restatement (Second) of Torts characterises the seller's situation in this fashion: "the seller has exercised all possible care in the preparation and sale of his product."

3. Cf. John C. Perham, "The Dilemma in Product Liability," *Dun's Review*, 109 (1977), pp. 48–50, 76. W. Page Keeton, "Products Liability—Design Hazards and the

Meaning of Defect," 10 *Cumberland Law Review* 293–316 (1979). Alvin S. Weinstein et al., *Products Liability and the Reasonably Safe Product* (New York: John Wiley & Sons, 1978), ch. 1.

4. More properly, of course, the person's use of the manufacturer's product harmed the product user.

5. Clearly one of the central questions confronting the notion of strict liability is what is to count as "defective." With few exceptions, it is held that a product is defective if and only if it is unreasonably dangerous. There have been several different standards proposed as measures of the defectiveness or unreasonably dangerous nature of a product. However, in terms of logical priorities, it really does not matter what the particular standard for defectiveness is unless we know whether we may justifiably hold manufacturers strictly liable for defective products. It is for this reason that I concentrate in this paper on the justifiability of strict products liability.

6. Michel A. Coccio, John W. Dondanville, Thomas R. Nelson, *Products Liability: Trends and Implications* (AMA, 1970), p. 13. Keeton, "The Meaning of Defect in Products Liability Law—A Review of Basic Principles," p. 580. William L. Prosser, "The Assault Upon the Citadel (Strict Liability to the Consumer)," pp. 1119.

7. Coccio, Dondanville, Nelson, *Products Liability: Trends and Implications*, p. 13. Keeton, "The Meaning of Defect in Products Liability Law—A Review of Basic Principles," pp. 580–1. Owen, "Rethinking the Policies of Strict Products Liability," p. 686. William L. Prosser, "The Assault Upon the Citadel (Strict Liability to the Consumer)," p. 1120.

8. Marcus L. Plant, "Strict Liability of Manufacturers for Injuries Caused by Defects in Products—An Opposing View," 24 *Tennessee Law Review* 945 (1957). William L. Prosser, "The Assault Upon the Citadel (Strict Liability to the Consumer)," pp. 1114, 1115, 1119.

9. Keeton, "The Meaning of Defect in Products Liability—A Review of Basic Principles," pp. 594–5. Weinstein et al., *Products Liability and the Reasonably Safe Product*, p. 55.

10. It might be objected that such accidents ought not to fall under strict products liability and hence do not constitute a counterexample to the above justification. This objection is answered in Sections III and IV.

11. These three considerations are formulated by Michael D. Smith, "The Morality of Strict Liability in Tort," *Business and Professional Ethics Newsletter*, 3 (1979), p. 4. Smith himself, however, was drawing upon Guido Calabresi, "Some Thoughts on Risk Distribution and the Law of Torts," 70 *Yale Law Journal* 499–553 (1961).

12. Michael D. Smith, "The Morality of Strict Liability in Tort," p. 4. Cf. George P. Fletcher, "Fairness and Utility in Tort Theory," 85 *Harvard Law Review* 537–573 (1972).

13. Rev. Francis E. Lucey, S. J., "Liability Without Fault and the Natural Law," 24 *Tennessee Law Review* 952–962

(1957). Perham, "The Dilemma in Product Liability," pp. 48–9.

14. Marcus L. Plant, "Strict Liability of Manufacturers for Injuries Caused by Defects in Products—An Opposing View," pp. 946–7. By "elastic demand" is meant "a slight increase in price will cause a sharp reduction in demand or will turn consumers to a substitute product" (pp. 946–7).

15. Cf. William L. Prosser, "The Assault Upon the Citadel," 69 *Yale Law Journal* 1140–1141 (1960). Wade, "On Product 'Design Defects' and Their Actionability," p. 569. Coccio, Dondanville, Nelson, *Products Liability: Trends and Implications*, p. 19.

16. F. A. Hayek emphasizes this point in "The Moral Element in Free Enterprise," in *Studies in Philosophy, Politics, and Economics* (New York: Simon and Schuster, 1967), p. 229.

17. Several of these characteristics have been drawn from Milton Friedman and Rose Friedman, *Free to Choose* (New York: Avon Books, 1980).

18. Calabresi, "Product Liability: Curse or Bulwark of Free Enterprise," p. 325.

19. *Ibid.*, p. 321.

20. *Ibid.*

21. *Ibid.*, p. 324.

22. *Ibid.*

23. Cf. H. B. Acton, *The Morals of Markets* (London: Longman Group Limited, 1971), pp. 1–7, 33–37. Milton Friedman and Rose Friedman, *Free To Choose.*

24. Milton Friedman and Rose Friedman, *Free To Choose*, pp. 123–124.

25. I have heavily drawn, in this paragraph, on the fine article by Bernard Boxhill, "The Morality of Reparation," reprinted in *Reverse Discrimination*, ed. Barry R. Gross (Buffalo, New York: Prometheus Books, 1977), pp. 270–278.

26. Cf. Calabresi, "Product Liability: Curse or Bulwark of Free Enterprise," pp. 315–319.

27. I would like to thank the following for providing helpful comments on earlier versions of this paper: Betsy Postow, Jerry Phillips, Bruce Fisher, John Hardwig, and Sheldon Cohen.

MURRAY WEIDENBAUM

Consumer Product Regulation

The actions of numerous federal agencies relate to consumer products. Of these, the Consumer Product Safety Commission has the most direct and explicit responsibility. The Consumer Product Safety Act of 1972 created an independent regulatory agency "to protect the public against unreasonable risks of injury associated with consumer products."[1] A five-member Consumer Product Safety Commission sets safety standards for consumer products, bans products presenting undue risk of injury, and in general polices the entire consumer product marketing process from manufacture to final sale.

In creating the Commission, Congress adopted a "no-fault" view of accidental product injuries, involving a complex interaction between the consumer, the product, and the environment. Rather than stressing punitive action against the producers and distributors of unsafe products, the emphasis in the statute is on setting new product standards. Under this approach, products would be redesigned to accommodate to possible consumer misuse and ignorance of proper operation of the product.[2]

Specific functions of the Commission include aiding consumers in the evaluation of product safety, developing uniform product safety standards, gathering medical data and conducting research on product-related injuries, and coordinating federal, state, and local product safety laws and enforcement. Consumers are assured the right to participate in the Commission's activities, as "any interested person . . . may petition the Commission to commence a proceeding for the issuance, amendment, or revocation of a consumer product safety rule."[3] Safety standards cover product per-

Murray L. Weidenbaum, *Business, Government, and the Public,* © 1977, pp. 24–31. Reprinted by permission of Prentice-Hall, Inc., Englewood Cliffs, New Jersey.

formance, contents, composition, design, construction, finish, packaging, and labeling.

A provision of the Consumer Product Safety Act that became operative in November 1975 gave both business and consumers more power to force the CPSC to accelerate its standard-making process. Under Section 10(e), any private party can bring suit against the Commission if it denies a rule-making petition or if it fails to act on a petition within 120 days. No other federal agency is bound by such a deadline on its decision-making.[4]

Powers of the Commission extend to requiring manufacturers of products found to be hazardous to take corrective actions. These actions include refunds, recalls, public warnings, and reimbursements to consumers for expenses of the recall process. Any product representing an unreasonable risk of personal injury or death may, by court order, be seized and condemned. Under the Consumer Product Safety Act of 1972, the Commission's jurisdiction extends to more than 10,000 products. In addition to banning offending products and requiring expensive recalls and debates, it can charge offending executives with violations that are subject to jail sentences.[5]

THE IMPACT ON CONSUMERS—BENEFITS AND COSTS

Important benefits to the public can be expected from an agency designed to make consumers more aware of product hazards and to require the removal from the market of products likely to cause serious injuries. Simultaneously, it must be noted that such actions also can generate large costs, which will be borne ultimately by the consumer. The consumer's total welfare is therefore maximized by seeking out the most economical and efficient ways of achieving safety objectives. Thus, banning products can be seen as one of a variety of alternatives. These can range from relabeling a product (so that the consumer becomes aware of a previously hidden hazard) to recalling and modifying an existing line of products.

The Stanford Research Institute has estimated that the mandatory safety standards developed by Consumers Union for the Commission would add

$250 million to the price tag for power lawn mowers and put 25 companies out of the business. The Institute estimated that the proposed standards could raise the price of a $100 gasoline-powered rotary mower to as much as $186. Push mowers would increase in price between 30 and 74 percent. The cost of more expensive riding mowers would go up at a slower rate, between 19 and 30 percent. The largest price rises, in the range of 35 to 86 percent, would occur on manual-start push rotary motors.[6]

At times, higher consumer product prices result from the Commission's actions and are brought about by their forcing expensive complexity on the manufacturers of consumer products. Poor, and even middle income, families may thus be priced out of many markets for consumer products. A case in point is the four million electric frying pans for which the Commission has ordered formal hearings to determine if they are hazardous. What is puzzling, however, is that, out of the four million pans, not a single injury has been reported by the Commission.[7]

Professor Max Brunk of Cornell University gets to the heart of the matter: "Consumerism is aimed at the consumer ... look what it does to the consumer who pays the cost and loses the benefits that a prohibited product or service could have provided."[8] Following this line of reasoning, business can better adjust to these controls than can the consumer, because it can pass on the added costs that result.

Brunk notes that it is interesting to observe that consumer advocates sometimes have as much difficulty convincing the consumer of his or her need for protection as in convincing a regulatory body to provide the protection.[9] The truth-in-lending law is a cogent example. The compulsory requirement to show true interest costs has not slowed down the growth of consumer debt or the rise in interest rates. Since the passage of the act, the ratio of consumer debt to consumer income has reached an all-time high, and, interest rates, for many reasons, have risen sharply. The average credit purchaser still seems to be more interested in the absolute amount of the monthly payment than in the rate of interest that is included in it. Similarly, despite the justification for unit pricing as a means of helping low income families to stretch their dollars further, available surveys show that it is the high income, well-educated customers who are most aware of this information.[10]

In the area of product safety, it should be recognized that consumers have unequal tastes for safety as well as other characteristics of product performance. Particularly where the safety hazard is minor (the occasional blister on a finger), policy makers need to realize that very large cost increases may merely deprive many consumers of the use of many products. As elsewhere, there is the need to recognize trade-offs between safety and other criteria important to consumers.

For example, a power tool selling for $20 may not have the capability of being in use for more than an hour; the $500 piece of equipment may be safely used for a much longer period. Although the instructions on each tool may be very clear in this respect, some consumers may willingly buy the cheaper model and knowingly take the chance of burning it out. A policy of complete product safety would ban the cheaper item, thereby effectively depriving the low income consumer of buying a power tool.[11]

A vast majority of Americans is concerned over product safety, and this concern has risen steadily since 1971. However, 87 percent of the adult Americans participating in a Harris survey blame consumers themselves for injury from products. Many believe that "most products are safe, but a lot of people do not read the directions or misuse products, so it is unfair to put all the safety blame on manufacturers." In the same survey a distinct opposition was shown to bans on products. Of the consumers surveyed, 73 percent believed that product safety objectives should be accomplished through publicity on product risks and dangers and by health warnings such as those required on cigarettes and drugs.[12]

THE EFFECT ON BUSINESS

The recordkeeping requirements imposed by the Consumer Product Safety Commission's early actions are substantial. In its first major proposed rule in August 1973, it called on every manufacturer, distributor, or retailer—upon learning that a product it sold "creates a substantial risk of injury"—to inform and provide the Commission with a wide array of information including:

1. The number of products that present a hazard or potential hazard.
2. The number of units of each product involved.
3. The number of units of each product in the hands of consumers.
4. Specific dates when the faulty units were manufactured and distributed.
5. An accounting of when and where such products (and the number of units of each) were distributed.
6. The model and serial numbers affected.
7. A list of names and addresses of every distributor, retailer, and producer, if known.
8. A description of the effort made to notify consumers of the defect.
9. Details of corrective tests, quality controls, and engineering changes made or contemplated.[13]

The reporting requirement is not completed until the company submits a final report indicating that the "potential" product hazard has been corrected. Thus, the Commission shifts to the company the responsibility and costs of determining and remedying potential product defects with the possibility of criminal sanctions should the Commission disagree with the company's decisions. Product safety reporting by companies is a necessary input to the Commission's evaluation of potentially dangerous products. The reporting requirements are substantial and, therefore, costly. It is not, however, a question of whether or not companies should report information on product injuries, but of how much detail is needed for decision-making.

An example of prudent action on the part of the Commission was its handling of the alleged hazards involving spray adhesives. In August 1973, the Commission quickly banned these products when informed of findings by a University of Oklahoma scientist suggesting a causal relationship between the adhesives and chromosome breaks leading to birth defects.[14] The following January, however, the Commission announced that the ban was being lifted after in-depth research and independent evaluation reversed the conclusion of the initial study. In this case not only was the Commission quick to impose a ban on a product that it thought might be potentially hazardous, but it also acted expeditiously in conducting confirmatory studies and lifted the ban once evidence negated the original study.

The Commission has turned down the most extreme demands of consumer advocates. It rejected the petition of Ralph Nader's Health Research Group, which warned of the "imminent hazard to the public health" represented by lead-wick candles. The petition asserted that small children might chew or swallow the candles, taking lead into their systems, and candlelit suppers would result in "meals literally bathed in lead." In a letter to the Nader group, Commissioner Laurence M. Kushner stated that the petition "was drawn either with abysmal ignorance of elementary physical science, colossal intent to deceive the public, or both. The calculations, in the petition, of possible concentrations of lead in air which might result from burning such candles, were based on assumptions that are physically impossible . . ."[15]

THE POWER OF GOVERNMENT REGULATION

In the words of Chairman Arnold Elkind of the National Commission on Product Safety, whose recommendations led to the creation of the Consumer Product Safety Commission:

It's true that the CPSC may be the most powerful independent regulatory agency ever created . . . but it has to be. It has to have a wide choice of weapons to cope with the diverse range of situations it confronts.[16]

The Commission does have an impressive array of powers and at times uses them in a fashion that could seem arbitrary, at least to some people. For example, in promulgating its ban lists, the CPSC appears to have taken the position, perhaps unwittingly, that a company can be guilty until proved innocent. This surprising stand, which contradicts the basic notion of fairness in legal matters, seems implicit in the following statement in an issue of the CPSC's Banned Products List:

Articles not meeting the requirements of the regulation are to be considered as banned even though they have

not yet been reviewed, confirmed as banned, and added to the Banned Products List by the Consumer Product Safety Commission.[17]

Taken literally, the Commission's statement means that the responsibility for treating a product as being banned can fall entirely on the company involved, and in circumstances where the Commission is not even aware of the product's existence, much less of its supposedly hazardous characteristic.

The case of Marlin Toy Products of Horicon, Wisconsin, illustrates the dangers that can arise in the excessive use of the CPSC's great powers. Due to an "editorial error," the Commission put Marlin's major products on its new ban list in 1973. When the error was called to its attention, CPSC refused to issue a prompt retraction. As a result, Marlin was forced out of the toy business.

Although the Congress has assigned it responsibility for product safety, the Commission members have tried to extend this task to newspapers and magazines. In a session with reporters, the chairman and other members of the Commission stated their belief that publishers should attempt to verify the safety of the products advertised in their publications. Richard O. Simpson, CPSC chairman, was quoted as saying that newspapers and magazines who carry advertisements should consider hiring specialists to look over products or should farm out the task to outside consultants.[18] Thus, producers and distributors would have to satisfy not only the federally chartered Consumer Product Safety Commission but also the private safety commissioners appointed by each individual private publication.

Despite having substantial resources at its disposal and after several years of operation, the Commission has been chastized for its slowness in carrying out its principal function—the writing of safety standards for products. As of late 1975, no standards had been completed. In September 1975, the first standards—for swimming pool slides—were proposed.

In addition to difficulties in developing standards, the Commission has encountered problems in determining the boundaries of its own jurisdiction. This was displayed by its involvement in the handgun controversy. In response to a request to ban handgun ammunition as a hazardous substance, the Commission was required by statute to ask for public comments. It received more than 130,000 cards and letters, all on an issue that four of the five commissioners believed they had no business investigating.[19]

The stepped-up pace of regulation by the CPSC is resulting in "reverse distribution"—product recalls—becoming an important part of the marketing function of many companies. In addition to motor vehicles, increasing numbers of manufacturers of television sets, bicycles, ovens, and other nonautomotive products are being involved in recall situations. Product recalls in these cases are frequently justified and may well withstand the test of cost-benefit analysis.

This relatively new activity, however, is requiring a major expansion in record-keeping so that owners of the recalled product can be promptly notified. The Consumer Product Safety Commission ultimately may require manufacturers to keep records of all product complaints and to turn them over to the Commission if it so requests. This information thus could form the basis for additional product recalls. It is, therefore, likely that more of the complaint letters from consumers will be kept in company files—and perhaps acted on.

A particularly costly aspect of the newer product safety regulations is that they often contain retroactive clauses. Should a company discover a product defect several years after it begins selling a product, and if the defect requires a recall, the firm may find that the recall costs exceed the company's net worth.[20]

The cost of recalls varies with the number of products sold, the amount of time and effort required to track down the purchasers, and the percentage of products that require repair, replacement, or refund. It cost General Motors $3.5 million for postage alone to notify by certified mail, as required by law, the 6.5 million owners of cars with questionable engine mounts. The cost to Panasonic to recall and repair 280,000 television sets, as ordered by the CPSC because of possible harmful radiation emission, may total $11.2 million—the equal of the company's profits in the United States for the past several years.

Expectations, either for private or public activities, should not be set too high. Considering the importance of the problems confronting the CPSC and the difficulties involved in solving them,

perhaps the sympathetic, thoughtful comments of Paul Weaver may provide an appropriate ending note for this section:

In the end there is no such thing as a perfect safety regulation; in most cases, in fact, even a fairly good one is hard to find. Thus there's nothing surprising or dishonorable about the failure of the Commission to issue perfect regulations in wholesale lots.

But the environment within which they work—the law, the expectations of Congress, the conflicting pressures from consumerists and industry, the nature of government, the climate of public opinion, the methods and ambitions of the staff, and above all the monumental complexity of the task—makes good judgment difficult. The scarcest ingredient in this marvelously intricate and rational system is the homely virtue of common sense.[21]

· · ·

NOTES

1. Consumer Product Safety Act, Public Law 92-573.

2. Paul H. Weaver, "The Hazards of Trying to Make Consumer Products Safer," *Fortune*, July 1975, pp. 133–34.

3. Consumer Product Safety Act, Public Law 92-573.

4. "Spurring New Action on Product Safety," *Business Week*, November 10, 1975, p. 60.

5. Consumer Product Safety Act, Public Law 92-573.

6. *Reprints of Selected News Items* (Menlo Park, Cal.: Stanford Research Institute, 1975), p. 8.

7. "Some Fry Pans and Chain Saws May Be Unsafe," *St. Louis Post-Dispatch*, January 15, 1974, p. 8A.

8. Max E. Brunk, "Consumerism and Marketing," in *Issues in Business and Society*, ed. George Steiner (New York: Random House, 1972), p. 462.

9. Ibid., p. 463.

10. Ibid., p. 465.

11. J. Fred Weston, "Economic Aspects of Consumer Product Safety," in *Issues in Business and Society*, ed. George Steiner (New York: Random House, 1972), p. 499.

12. Louis Harris, "Concern over Product Safety," *Washington Post*, June 1, 1975, p. F-2.

13. *Federal Register*, August 3, 1973, vol. 38, no. 149.

14. *CPSC Bans Three Spray Adhesives—Asks Manufacturers of Others to Halt Production* (Washington, D.C.: U.S. Consumer Product Safety Commission, August 20, 1973.)

15. "Please Don't Eat the Candles," *Wall Street Journal*, January 16, 1974, p. 12.

16. William H. Miller, "Consumer Product Safety Commission," *Industry Week*, October 29, 1973, p. 41.

17. U.S. Consumer Product Safety Commission, *Banned Products*, October 1, 1973, p. 1.

18. "Consumer Agency Is Critical of Ads," *New York Times*, February 13, 1974, p. 47.

19. Burt Schoor, "Consumer Product Safety Commission Finds Deep Hazards In Just Getting Itself Rolling," *Wall Street Journal*, May 6, 1975.

20. E. Patrick McGuire, "The High Cost of Recalls," *New York Times*, March 30, 1975, p. E-1.

21. Weaver, "Trying to Make Consumer Products Safer," p. 140.

STEVEN KELMAN

Regulation and Paternalism

Opposition to paternalism plays an important role in the current national debate over the appropriate scope for government regulation, especially consumer protection regulation on behalf of safety and health. It is frequently summoned in condemning calls to ban saccharin or laetrile. It is pronounced likewise against proposals to require people to wear seatbelts or motorcycle helmets. And it appears in criticisms of safety standards for lawnmowers or autos, since such standards, although they neither ban nor mandate use of the product in question, do require that consumers pay for certain safety features if they wish to buy the product. The antipaternalistic contention is simple. If people know the risks of, say, saccharin and choose to run these risks for themselves in order to obtain the benefits they believe they will gain, who are we to interfere with that choice?

I believe that it is correct to oppose paternalism, but incorrect to tar most government consumer protection health and safety regulations with a paternalistic brush. . . .

There are, in other words, good nonpaternalistic arguments for such regulation, although these arguments are often mistaken for paternalistic ones. In the final section, I will discuss explicitly the question of whether there are ever any occasions when regulation might be justified on avowedly paternalistic grounds.

The force of the argument to be made and most of the examples selected involve regulation of consumer products for purposes of safety or health.

Some of the arguments will, however, also be applicable to other public policy domains that raise issues of paternalism, such as the use of in-kind as opposed to cash transfer payments. . . .

DECISION-MAKING COSTS AND VOLUNTARY RENUNCIATION OF CHOICE AUTHORITY

In this section, I argue that when there are costs associated with deciding what choice to make, it is rational in some situations for an individual to renounce his authority to make the choice for himself, and to hand over such authority to a third party who will make the choice in the individual's interest. Such third-party choices are not paternalistic, because they are not made against the person's wishes. They introduce a new category, separate both from choices one makes oneself and from choices made paternalistically. Much government safety regulation of consumer products, I believe, falls into this category.

The probability that one would want to renounce the authority to choose increases (1) the more that the decision-making costs for the person exceed those for the third party, and (2) the closer the choice the third party makes is to the choice the person would have made.[1]

The situation where voluntary renunciation of the authority to choose is rational may be illus-

From *Public Policy*, vol. 29, no. 2 (Spring 1981). Copyright © 1981 by the President and Fellows of Harvard College. Reprinted by permission of John Wiley & Sons, Inc.

trated by a simple example. Imagine that a person could, without bearing any decision-making costs, simply go out and choose, off the top of his head, to buy a product with certain general features. Let us say that such a choice would produce a net benefit of ten units of satisfaction for him. Imagine further that he could gain perfect information about the specific features of the different types of the product that are available. If he had this information and processed it, he would be able to make a better choice—say, one that gives him 15 units of satisfaction. But if gathering and processing the information cost him eight units of satisfaction, his net benefit from the choice, after decision-making costs are taken into account, would be only seven units. In such a case, the "off the top of the head" choice, yielding ten units of satisfaction, would be preferable to the "better" but decision-costly choice, which yields only seven units of satisfaction.

But these may not be the only two alternatives. Let us say someone else can gather and process the same information *much more cheaply than the person himself*—for two units of satisfaction (units that presumably would be billed to the person in some way). Armed with this information, the third party would make a decision for the person yielding only 13 units of satisfaction. The third party has gathered and processed the same information that the person did, but the decision he makes may not yield as much satisfaction, even though he is supposed to act in his person's best interest. This may be because he makes a faulty judgment about exactly what those interests are. It may be because he takes advantage of the opportunity and imposes his own judgment of what he thinks is best for the person, or acts in his own self-interest and imposes a decision that better satisfies his own interests. The net benefits of authorizing the third party to make the decision in this case would be 11 units (13 units for the decision minus two units of decision-making costs). Of the three alternatives—uninformed choice by consumer, informed choice by consumer, and informed choice by third party—the last yields the highest net benefits. This is so despite the fact that if one looks simply at the benefits of the choice itself and not at decision-making costs, the informed choice by the consumer himself would have appeared to be the most advantageous one.

The costs of decision-making include information-gathering costs, information-processing costs, and possibly psychological costs of choice. Information-gathering costs are the costs of determining the existence of all the relevant features across which the different types of a product can vary and the different values these variables take across the different types of a product. Information-processing costs are the costs of calculating the implication of the different values for a judgment of the benefits of the product, given one's preferences. Psychological costs are the frustration that may be felt from information overload or the trauma that may be experienced from having to make difficult choices.

An immense disservice to intelligent discussion of the safety regulation of consumer products occurs because of the tendency to base such discussions on a small number of dramatic instances—saccharin, seatbelts, laetrile. A statement such as, "People know that it's more risky to drive without seatbelts than with them, and if they choose to take that risk to avoid the discomfort of wearing the belts, that should be up to them," may be made with a straight face. People know the feature they are making a choice about (that is, they know what seatbelts are). They know what values the variable can take (the seatbelts may be worn or not worn). They know the implications of these different values for their judgments about the choice (wearing seatbelts decreases risk but may increase discomfort).

The problem is that such individual dramatic examples are unrepresentative of the universe of choices that consumers would have to make for themselves in a world where they had to make all decisions about the safety features of products they buy themselves. Statements about consumers knowing the risks of failing to use seatbelts or consuming saccharin and choosing to bear them are plausible. Statements such as the following are far less so: "People know that if the distance between the slats on the infant crib is 2⅜th inches there is little risk that an infant will strangle himself falling through the slats, while if the distance is 3¼th inches the risk is much greater, and if they choose to take this risk to get a crib that is less expensive, that should be up to them." The reader may ask himself if he would feel confident identifying which one of the four following substances that may be present in food is far more risky than the other three: calcium hexametaphosphate, methyl paraben, sodium benzoate, and trichloroethylene. Or he may ask himself how confident he would feel making decisions about what safety features to buy in order to guard against power lawnmower accidents or to protect against a radio exploding or electrocuting him. If he does know, how confident does he feel that he understands the risks associated with various levels of the substance? Is five parts per million of benzene hexachloride a lot or a little? If the bacteria count in frozen egg is one million per gram, should we be alarmed?

What these examples suggest—and they could be multiplied manyfold—is that consumers do not ordinarily have anything approaching perfect information for judging the safety of most consumer products themselves, the misleading examples from widely publicized regulatory controversies over issues such as seatbelts and saccharin to the contrary notwithstanding. Compared with their knowledge of product features such as appearance, convenience, or taste, knowledge of safety features is typically very small.

One conclusion sometimes drawn is that lack of knowledge demonstrates lack of concern. If people do not know about safety features, it is sometimes argued, that means they do not care about them. This conclusion does not follow from the premise. When information-gathering costs something, the amount of information gathered depends not only on the perceived benefits of the information but also on how costly it would be to gather. I may "care" about two product features equally, but if information on one is cheap to obtain and information on the other is expensive, I will gather more information on the first feature than on the second. Information on product features such as appearance or convenience is often relatively easy to get. Information on a product's appearance is garnered by simple observation. For a product that does not cost very much and that is frequently repurchased, experience is a cheap way to gain information about the product's convenience or taste.[2] I may buy a certain brand of orange soda or paper tissue and try it. Then I will know whether I like it.

By contrast, gathering information on safety features is often very costly. Frequently, arcane or technical facts must be understood, and the recourse to experience is not available in the same way as with many other product features. Using a risky product does not always lead to an accident. Drinking a brand of orange soda will always lead to information on its taste, but not on its additives. To go through the pain of an injury or illness is a very high cost to pay for gathering information about a product's safety. As Victor Goldberg (1974) has noted sardonically, "Learning from one's own experience is even more impractical if the injury is a very serious one. In the extreme case of a fatal accident, of course, the learning experience might be profound, but the learning curve is abruptly truncated."

The first criterion for a situation in which it would be rational for an individual to hand over decision-making authority to a third party is when the third party can gather the information more cheaply than the individual can. This criterion often applies in the case of safety features. The per consumer cost of gathering safety information is likely to be much less for an expert third party gathering it for a large group of consumers than for an individual. An expert has an easier time finding out about and evaluating different technical safety features. Since only one gathering process need occur, its cost can be divided among the large group for whom it is undertaken, rather than having to be separately borne by each individual consumer assembling similar information for himself.

The second cost associated with the act of choosing is the cost in information-processing. This involves taking information about a product feature and evaluating its significance in light of one's preferences. Memory and other cognitive limitations make it costly or simply impossible to process large amounts of information about a product, even if the information is available. Information-processing costs clearly vary across people and situations, but the more information that must be processed, the higher the processing costs. Furthermore, there is evidence that at some point "information overload" occurs, where the brain has too much information to process. Under the circumstances, one's skill at evaluating information can decrease so much that the choice reflects one's preferences worse than a choice made where less information was available, but could be processed better (see, e.g., Jacoby et al., 1974). Overload may appear not only when we must process a lot of information for a single choice, but also when we must process little information for many choices.

Choice may carry with it psychological costs as well. To be sure, there are many instances, as noted earlier, where people relish the opportunity to choose. In other instances, people might not relish the process, but believe that a choice made by a third party is likely to be so inferior to the choice they make themselves that they are willing to pay possible psychological costs. But this is not always the case. Life would be unbearable if we constantly had to make all decisions for ourselves. Information overload may produce not only evaluations poorer in quality but also feelings of frustration growing out of the realization that our brains are not processing information as well as they usually do. Furthermore, people can find some kinds of decisions very unpleasant to make. These might include choices that are complicated, ones that involve thinking about distasteful things, or ones where all the alternatives are disagreeable. Everyday experience is filled with instances where people try to avoid making unpleasant decisions—if this were not the case, Harry Truman would never have placed the sign "The buck stops here" in his office. Linus, the Peanuts comic strip character, expressed the trauma that can accompany difficult choice when he said, "No problem is so big or so complicated that it can't be run away from." Yet, as Irving Janis and Leon Mann have noted, "In the extensive writings by social scientists on decision making we find hardly any mention of this obvious aspect of human choice behavior" (Janis and Mann, 1977). (Some of the same people who argue against proposals for, say, greater employee participation in choices currently made by management in the workplace, on the grounds that most workers would prefer not to be burdened psychologically with such choices, forget about this burden when proposals for government regulation of consumer products are made.)

As with costs of information-gathering, the costs of information-processing and the psychological costs of choice are likely frequently to be lower for an expert third party, as far as safety is concerned, than for the individual. Decisions about safety, because they involve so much techni-cal information, are likely to be those where information overload makes processing costly. They are also likely to be decisions that many people find unpleasant to make. They require that one contemplate the prospect of illness, disfigurement, or even death. They also necessitate thought about tradeoffs between saving money and taking risks—thoughts that most people also find unpleasant, as can be seen by looking at how politicians, agency officials, and even business spokesmen themselves squirm when such topics are raised. In fact, I believe this uneasiness is one of the main reasons why safety decisions are handed over to government. (The argument that people do not like to think about injury is sometimes used as a justification for paternalistic interventions in the safety area, on the grounds that "people don't like to think about these things, so they won't take safety into account enough." The argument here is different. It depends on a judgment by the person *himself* that thinking about illness or injury is unpleasant and that therefore he wishes to renounce his authority to choose to a third party.) An expert third party can generally process information much more cheaply per consumer, both because of his expertise and because the cost of processing can be divided among a large group. A third party's per consumer charge for bearing any psychological costs of choice (presumably in the form of a wage premium required to attract people to such work) is also likely to be far less than the cost an individual would have to bear himself. These costs are lowered further because the third party's expertise and experience reduce possible frustration from information overload. Furthermore, the trauma of dealing with difficult choices is counterbalanced by the satisfaction that arises from power to make decisions affecting many people. Also, there may be some self-selection into such kinds of work of people who find it less traumatic to make difficult choices.

One point ought to be made about decision-making costs before proceeding. It is unrealistic to believe that many consumers consciously tote up the difference between their own and third-party decision-making costs in making a judgment about whether to renounce voluntarily the authority to choose. If a consumer does not even know about the existence of a feature along which he might judge a product, it is hard to conceive of his "de-ciding" how much it would cost him to gather information. Instead, the judgment consumers might reasonably be thought to make is of a much grosser sort, namely, that they know enough to know that they are quite ignorant about the whole area of product safety and that finding out will be costly. They might also conclude that they know they do not find thinking about illness or injury pleasant. On this basis, they know enough to make the general judgment that they want product safety choices *as a whole* to be turned over to a third party. This is why Milton Friedman's objection that government safety regulation "amounts to saying that we in our capacity as voters must protect ourselves in our capacity as consumers against our own ignorance" is unconvincing (Friedman, 1962). In our capacity as voters we need know only that we are ignorant or reluctant in our capacity as consumers about certain areas.

Another consideration was cited earlier as influencing the probability that it would be rational to renounce voluntarily the authority to choose: How similar is the choice the third party would make to the person's own fully informed choice? Insofar as safety choices are concerned, there are reasons to believe that government officials often attach a higher weight to safety than the average consumer (does in deciding what safety features to mandate). This is because the organizational mission of these agencies is to promote safety and because many agency officials are recruited from safety or health professions whose ideology stresses such protection.[3] On the other hand, there is also reason to believe that the disparity normally will not be extreme. "Safety" is a value attributed high weight whenever people discuss it consciously; indeed, environmentalists have shifted the focus of their political efforts from woods and streams to safety and health out of a conviction that this strikes the most responsive chord among large numbers of Americans. I shall return to the subject of the weight people attach to safety at the end of this section. But the possibility of large disparities between the weight many consumers attach to safety and the weight government officials attach to it is the strongest reason why consumers might not wish to renounce to the government their authority to choose the safety features of products they buy. In most cases, however, the disparity in

weights is not likely to be large enough to outweigh the benefits in lower decision-making costs.

Objections to the Information Argument for Intervention

Different objections might be made to the argument developed so far. One that is frequently heard runs something like this: if the consumer has difficulty making choices about safety features because he lacks information, then let the government see that the requisite information is provided, rather than mandating safety features or banning products. To do more, the argument goes, would be to throw out the baby of individual choice with the bathwater of imperfect information. (A more radical argument could be made as well: Market forces will see to it that consumers are provided with appropriate information and that there is thus no need even for government to provide or mandate information.)

Another objection is sometimes raised: Voluntary renunciation of consumer choice to *some* third party need not justify *government* standards or product bans. Consumers might hire a personal agent to make the choice for them. Or the government might be limited to certify that a product meets whatever safety standards the agency determines to be appropriate. All these methods, it is argued, allow voluntary renunciation of the authority to choose without mandatory government regulation.

I will first consider arguments claiming that the government's role should be limited to information provision—or even that such an information provision role is unjustified. For the government to mandate provision of information or to provide it itself does indeed lower information-gathering costs. To require its dissemination in nontechnical form lowers these costs further. And to make the information conveniently available (as part of labeling) lowers it still further. These steps sometimes do lower decision-making costs enough to make it worthwhile for consumers to retain their authority to choose. An example would be in the area of product quality, where the psychological costs of choice are low and preferences differ widely across consumers. In these cases, government should stick to such tasks. But in other situations, all these steps still would not lower decision-making costs enough to make it rational for a consumer to retain his authority to choose. Under such a regime, consumers still might be confronted frequently with columns of fine print presenting large numbers of product features and risk information about each. The information-processing costs of evaluating this information in the light of one's preferences remain unaffected by the cheaper information-gathering. Any psychological decision-making costs are unaffected as well.

A more radical argument against any government role even in information provision suggests that whenever products vary along a feature that some group of consumers would find relevant, the producers of the product with the more attractive features themselves have an incentive, if markets are competitive, to provide consumers with information about that attractive feature. With competitors whose products lack such features unable to make similar claims, consumers will become informed, through producer efforts, about whatever features a significant number of people value.[4]

The operation of such a mechanism is clearly seen sometimes. Manufacturers of low-tar cigarettes or margarines with a high polyunsaturated fat content advertise these features of their products widely. Manufacturers who have removed antioxidants from their potato chips promote them as being additive-free. But to show that this mechanism works sometimes is not to show that it is sufficient to obviate any need for a government role. It has a chance of working mainly where consumers *already know* something about the feature in question. Most consumers know that cigarettes and saturated fats are hazardous. This makes it much easier for producers to advertise their product's good performance on such dimensions. In cases where producers would need to create knowledge of the feature itself from scratch, such advertising is far less likely. This is because, in part, if one producer advertises, some of the benefits of creating such consumer awareness would be reaped by competitors whose products also perform well on the relevant dimension, without the competitors having to share the significant costs of educating consumers. Furthermore, the distrust consumers have of self-serving claims by producers might discourage them from accepting the information.

Alternatively, it may be argued that if ways exist

to make information-gathering cheaper by using experts to gather the information and sharing the costs among large numbers of people, market incentives would also exist for private firms to arise to perform such information-gathering functions, thus making a government role unnecessary. Again, this mechanism does indeed operate to an extent. *Consumer Reports* tests products and reports the results, but this information is not as accessible as, say, information on a product label, and the cost to the consumer of locating it must thus be added to the information-gathering costs the private organization bears. Also, the decreasing marginal cost of disseminating information once it is gathered means that marginal cost pricing will not meet a private firm's cost, while pricing at higher than marginal cost will mean that an inefficiently small amount will be produced. This market failure suggests the preferability of public provision.[5] There are, then, still likely to be instances where individuals would wish to renounce voluntarily to a third party their authority to choose.

Let us turn now to objections that the third party need not be the government. Consumers might choose to let decisions be made for them by friends they trust or by expert agents they hire to make the decisions in their interests (Stigler, 1975). Mandatory government regulation, the argument continues, is a poor vehicle for making decisions that a consumer chooses to renounce, because it binds not only those who choose *not* to make the choice themselves, but also those who *would* have wanted to do so.

Certainly there are instances where choice by agents that a consumer seeks out might be preferable to decisions by government. Consumers use doctors as agents, for instance, and to some limited extent retail stores act as agents as well. One advantage such choices have is that the agent can be apprised of the client's individual preferences. By contrast, a government agency must make a single choice, despite the existence of diverse preferences among citizens. But in other instances, looking for, paying, and monitoring a privately hired agent would be more expensive than having the government undertake the same tasks. This greater expense might outweigh the advantages of a choice personally tailored to the client's preferences. Furthermore, the private provision of the information-gathering aspect of the agent's job creates the same public goods problems as any private provision of information. And for a person to seek an agent in any individual instance, he must have enough knowledge of the existence of dimensions along which he wishes to judge the product in question to know that he needs an agent in the first place.

Another way for a person to renounce his authority to choose without requiring mandatory government regulation is for the government to certify the safety of products and for the consumer, who wished to renounce his authority, to choose simply to buy the certified product. In certifying a product, the government would decide on appropriate safety features. The only difference would be that it would not be mandatory that all products comply with the features. Only those that did comply, however, would be certified. If a consumer decides to buy a certified product, he in effect has let the government make his decision for him. But those who wish to decide for themselves would have the choice of buying a product without the certified safety feature package.

Choosing to buy certified products might be an appropriate form for voluntary renunciation of the authority to choose. But it might not be a consumer's preferred alternative either. Most important as a reason for preferring mandatory regulation to certification is the fear that despite one's general resolution to buy only certified products, one might be tempted in individual cases to depart from one's resolution and buy noncertified ones. The concept of "temptation"—of doing something one does not "really" want to do—is a difficult one for the standard economic paradigm where, if John has voluntarily chosen x over y, he has become better off because the choice shows a preference for x over y. Therefore, he should be glad he had the opportunity to make the choice. In fact, though, it is common for people to fear that at some future moment they might act "in a moment of weakness" in a way that under normal circumstances they would not. Even if we end up not giving in to temptation, we might wish to be spared temptation so as to avoid the anxiety costs of realizing that one might, at any time, give in. Thus, a person might well prefer mandatory regulation to certification out of fear that in many specific instances, with one lawnmower in front of him that is certified and

another that is not, he might "take a chance" and get the cheaper, noncertified one, although as a general matter of considered reflection he would wish to buy only certified products. People frequently choose to have an alternative withheld from them at later times just to avoid temptation.

If there are psychological costs to the very *thought* of choosing something that one would ordinarily shun, the most tragic aspect of temptation is that once one has been tempted, one may be better off giving in. This may well be the case in situations where one is being tempted to risk life and limb to save a few dollars. Imagine a situation where at the moment of temptation the perceived net benefits of choosing a cheaper, more dangerous product over a more expensive but safer one is one unit. But the pangs from just considering the choice cost two units. Since these pangs are experienced whether the choice is made one way or the other, once the situation is clearly in front of you, you are better off choosing the cheaper but more dangerous product, because you then "cut your losses." But you are still one unit worse off than you otherwise would have been had the possibility of choice never been presented.

A consumer may have other reasons as well to prefer regulation to certification. If he must decide in each case whether to buy a certified or noncertified brand, the decision-making costs are still significant. Even if a consumer decides that he will buy only certified brands, he still must remember to check for the certification every time he buys an unfamiliar product. Given the number of times that people buy unfamiliar products, this may add up to a not insignificant annoyance. Imagine also the situation of the consumer buying an unfamiliar product who sees no certification on the product. This may be because the product has no significant safety or health aspects that need to be regulated, and thus it has not been subject to certification. The consumer who wishes simply to trust the judgment of the government agency and buy only certified (or regulated) products need not check if the product is subject to mandatory regulation. Either the product will possess the safety features the regulation requires or it will not have been regulated because it was deemed that the product had no safety aspects that needed regulation. In either case, the consumer can proceed without further ado to buy the product. If the signal to the consumer is *only* a certification, however, absence of certification requires further investigation by the consumer who wishes to buy only certified products. He must check whether the product type has been subject to certification (in which case the particular product in question has not been certified) or whether the product type has not been subject to certification. Again, extra effort is required that a consumer may prefer not to expend. He may thus favor regulation to certification. (This might be dealt with by placing the certification on products that were not required to meet any standards in order to gain the certification, but this would probably reduce the general perceived value of the certification in the eyes of many consumers.) Lastly, a consumer who wants to see the government demonstrate a higher level of concern for his welfare might prefer regulation to certification because the former provides that demonstration.

It may be accepted that there are people who would rather have government set mandatory safety standards than hire private agents or have the government certify product safety. Yet it still might be protested that others who would prefer to make the decisions themselves (or to hire their own agents or choose with the help of government certification) should not be forced to pay for safety features they do not want.

Under the circumstances, one group or the other will end up being hurt. Either those opposed to mandatory safety standards are harmed by being forced to buy products with mandated features, or those favoring mandatory standards are hurt by having to do without the mandatory standards they seek. Whether the social decision finally made responds to the wishes of the first group or the second has, then, external effects on the group whose wishes are denied. I shall return to the question of how social determinations may be made in such situations when dealing with external effects, in a different context, in the next section. Those seeking mandatory regulation are demanding something that will help themselves and hurt those who would prefer to choose for themselves. The latter group, then, may be seen as passive victims of the acts of those demanding regulation. The *prima facie* duty to do justice suggests sympathy with passive victims against active encroachers. Nevertheless, considerations of the size of the groups seeking and wishing to avoid regulation, as well as of the nature of the interference contemplated, are relevant to such judgments. In regard to the size of the groups in the case of government safety regulation, there exist unambiguous survey data. In a 1974 poll, respondents were asked whether the government should "make sure that each packaged, canned, or frozen food is safe to eat." An overwhelming 97% agreed, a degree of unanimity hard to replicate for any government policy. In a 1976 poll, respondents were asked a similar question about government product safety standards and 85% agreed.[7] As for the extent of interference, it is not generally great. Those opposed to regulation are interfered with to the extent of having to pay some extra money for safety features they would have preferred to avoid. Their homes are not broken into. They are not restrained by physical force from moving around where they wish. Their fortunes are not decimated. My own conclusion is that it would be wrong to prevent the vast majority of Americans who prefer to turn the general run of decisions about product safety over to the government from doing so.[8]

The figures on the percentages of those who wish to turn safety decisions over to the government also shed light on the earlier brief examination of whether decisions made by government safety regulators were likely to be sufficiently similar to those that consumers would make themselves, if fully informed, to make it rational for consumers voluntarily to hand such choices over to regulators. If government agencies did make decisions frequently that wildly departed from those that consumers would make themselves, one would expect the survey results to have been dramatically different. Instead, they show a broad vote of confidence for the efforts of government agencies regulating product safety.

There remain instances of public outcry over issues such as saccharin. A wise agency official might well conclude that such outcries signify withdrawal in the specific instances of consumers' general delegation to government of the authority to choose. It is not irrational for a consumer to decide as a general matter to renounce that authority but wish to reclaim it when he feels himself sufficiently informed and/or when the agency would make a decision sufficiently different from his own.

Not to allow people the option of delegating to government agencies decisions they would prefer not to make is to do liberty a disservice. Those who oppose such an option appear to place choice on a pedestal as a supreme value. But in doing so they set it up for a fall. Erich Fromm wrote almost 40 years ago about the desire among some people to "escape from freedom" which the support for Nazi and Communist totalitarian movements showed (Fromm, 1941). People might want to escape from freedom, Fromm wrote, if they felt overwhelmed by constant demands to make choices they did not feel they could handle. If the only options perceived are either having to make too many choices they would prefer to delegate or giving up their freedom entirely, many might choose the course—horrible to all who value liberty—of giving up freedom. Ironically, those who would refuse to allow people the option of delegating choices to the government often end up themselves making paternalistic arguments—that liberty of choice is such an important value that people must be required to give it priority under all circumstances, whether they wish to or not, or that people must be protected against the long-term erosion in ability to choose that might result from choosing to give up too many choices. Those who truly value liberty of choice will be eager to allow people to delegate to the government choices they do not wish to make, so that they can better husband their choice-making resources for decisions they genuinely wish to make for themselves.

EXTERNAL EFFECTS AND THE OVERRULING OF A PERSON'S OWN CHOICE

John Stuart Mill affirmed in *On Liberty* that the restriction against interference with a person's authority to choose applied to acts that affected only the individual himself and not to those acts affecting others. Ever since Mill, however, this distinction has come under withering attack. Government intervention in people's choices may occur not out of a desire to overrule paternalistically an individual's choices insofar as they regard only himself, but out of a desire to protect others against the negative consequences of those choices. Thus,

banning saccharin or requiring people to wear seatbelts might be justified on nonpaternalistic grounds even if people did not want to hand these decisions to the government, because of the effects bladder cancer or auto accidents have, not on the individual himself, but on others. The distinction between intervention on paternalistic grounds and intervention on the grounds that others must be protected against the negative consequences of a person's behavior is often lost in the general public debate on regulation, where opposition to both kinds of intervention tends to get lumped together as complaints against "government interference." Thus, the resentment of businessmen against OSHA or EPA regulations should not be confused with resentment against a bureaucrat who believes he knows what is good for a person better than the person does himself.

The discussions of external effects, such as pollution, in introductory economics textbooks tend to obscure the issue, because they imply that most actions lack external effects. That "no man is an island" dashes any attempt to make such neat categorizations. Clearly the argument for freedom of political speech, an argument often made in terms similar to the one against paternalism, can hardly be made on the grounds that free speech affects no one else. The famous argument by Lord Devlin against allowing pornography was based on its external effects on social cohesion (Devlin, 1971).

The inevitability of external effects extends to actions in the private sphere as well. Words we speak everyday, small gestures we make, even the tone of our voices all may profoundly affect the feelings of those around us who value our friendship or our love. The clothes we wear, the opinions we express, the plays we attend, the colors we paint our houses all may give joy to or offend those around us. If I choose to patronize a new business in town, my action has an affect on other businesses that lose my patronage. Even if we are passive, our passivity affects others. Words we fail to say or gestures we fail to make can affect another person as much as words we do say or gestures we do make. Whenever we are passive, we affect others who could have benefited from our aid. The person who sees a fire starting in a building and goes on his way without calling the fire department is hardly in a position to say that his failure to act had no external effects.

If a person becomes sick or is injured or if he dies because he purchased an unsafe product, clearly his action in buying the product had external effects on friends and loved ones. If a person is insured, other policyholders ultimately foot the bills.[9] If a person is not insured and suffers great financial hardship, other members of society still end up paying. When the victim appears before us after a sad fate has befallen him, the rest of us pay cash to help the uninsured victim out—or pay in the form of the guilty feelings occasioned by turning our backs on the victim, even if we attempt the justification that the victim made his bed and now should have to lie in it. The fact that we end up either saving people from the really bad consequences of their choices or feeling guilty if we do not is an argument, based on external effects and not on paternalism, for intervening in the original choices. Consequently, we require people to provide for their old age through Social Security, give the poor in-kind rather than cash transfers, or mandate safety regulations.

None of this means that our every move should be subject to government restrictions. Almost everyone who has thought seriously about the implications of the ubiquity of external effects has come to the conclusion that society must establish which acts individuals have a right to do or refrain from doing, despite the harm the act may inflict on others, and which are too harmful to permit to go unhindered or be left undone, despite the fact that the individual would prefer to behave otherwise (Hart, 1964; Lieberman, 1977; Calabresi and Malamed, 1972).[10]

To decide in a given case whether an individual should have the right to make decisions about what risks to take, despite the harm that the bad consequences of such decisions can cause others, raises difficult questions to which answers cannot be cranked out deductively. It will not do to argue, as is sometimes done, that external effects arguments must never be used to justify restricting risks because it would be possible to use such arguments to eradicate all exercises of liberty. For the fact is that *everyone*, even libertarians, recognizes that at some point the external effects of an individual's acts become great enough to justify taking

away the individual's right to act. Thus, all agree that murder or assault are not rightful displays of liberty. We cannot escape a controversial balancing process in which the extent of the external effects that the person's actions produce, the importance of the act for the individual, and possible deontological considerations regarding *prima facie* duties, are weighed against one another.

One way of balancing these elements is to apply the utilitarian criterion of maximizing net benefits, where the right to act is assigned to a person if he values his action more highly than those bearing the costs of the act value being spared those costs. Such an approach might appear to offer scant shelter for small groups whose acts or failures to act produce even the slightest cost to a large group. But this view underestimates the scope for liberty of choice that would likely result from such a calculation. It fails, first, to consider the effects of many different, potentially discomforting or offensive acts performed by many different people, with the strong probability that across this universe of acts a person will be both perpetrator and victim. Most people usually feel more dissatisfaction in being prohibited from doing something that they wish to do than they feel happiness in stopping another's act that they find offensive. I may not like your pink polka-dot shirt, but I probably do not dislike it enough to outweigh the distaste I would feel if you could stop me from wearing my favorite motorcycle jacket. I may be unhappy seeing part of my insurance dollar go to pay for injured lawnmower users who bought mowers without any safety features, but I would be more unhappy if I were told I had to sleep between seven and eight hours a night because people who do so tend to live longer. A basis therefore exists for agreements to tolerate each other in cases where the harm one person's acts produces involves small cost, discomfort, or offense. This is the basis of the hoary doctrine of "live and let live." Furthermore, as Mill argued in *On Liberty*, the existence of many varied "experiments in living" confers external benefits on others. They can learn about a wide portfolio of possible choices they themselves might make (and something about the consequences of those choices) at a much lower cost than if they were required to try out everything for themselves. Third, if some are offended by polka-dot shirts or distasteful political views, others derive satisfaction from living in a diverse society. I may not skydive or attend the ballet, but I am happy to know that such alternatives exist around me. Or people may derive satisfaction from living in a society where the liberty to choose is valued highly and derive offense from the knowledge that the exercise of liberty is being constantly meddled with. Finally, interference with liberty of action has enforcement costs, and these costs increase with the extent of the interference.

A nonutilitarian case that people should have the liberty to choose even in some instances where the benefits to them do not outweigh the costs to others may also be made. The basis for such a right might be that it is *prima facie* wrong to violate human dignity by restricting a person's liberty. Thus we might conclude that A has a right to act a certain way, even though A's act causes B greater unhappiness than it causes A happiness, because interfering with A's liberty would violate A's human dignity.[11] Nonutilitarian judgments on rights become extremely complicated and ultimately raise the most profoundly difficult issues in moral philosophy. Thus we might conclude, contrary to the above example, that A does *not* have a right to act a certain way, even though the prohibition causes A greater unhappiness than it causes B happiness, because the harm that would have been caused B had the act been permitted would have violated B's human dignity far more than would the interference with liberty violate A's dignity. Those bearing costs through the acts of others might also be regarded as victims of injustice, because they have suffered harm without deserving it. In such cases, the *prima facie* duty to do justice may argue for not granting a person the right to act as he wishes even though such an act might provide net benefits.

One approach to the problem of external effects is to grant a person the right to act as he wishes, while charging him for the monetary costs of his behavior. Thus, smokers might be charged higher insurance rates or accident victims not wearing seatbelts might be denied a portion of insurance recovery. Although it is not possible to consider here the details of such an approach, its applicability is limited by administrative costs that may outweigh savings from them, by the nonmonetary nature of many harms, and by uneasiness

at placing an implicit price tag on certain behaviors.[12] Such approaches ought to be considered when the significant externalities are purely pecuniary and when administrative costs do not overwhelm other advantages.

The considerations that must be applied in deciding, in situations involving external effects, whether the right shall be assigned to the person wishing to act or to others bearing the costs of the act, are complex. They have occupied lawmakers and judges for centuries, and they cannot be wished away with formulas or slogans. The argument of this section has been that there are, indeed, instances where the external effects of a person's action may justify overriding his own decision. I have also tried to present both utilitarian and nonutilitarian grounds for being relatively cautious about such restrictions. Beyond that, one can only conclude that situation-by-situation determinations must be made, with attention to the concerns presented here. . . .

The purpose of this article has not been to defend or criticize any specific example of government safety regulation. Rather, I have attempted to defend the justifiability, in principle, of such regulation against the specific accusation that it inevitably involves paternalism and hence should be condemned. I have agreed with the general condemnation of paternalism, while suggesting nonpaternalistic justifications for such intervention and arguing that there are certain cases where cautious paternalistic intervention might be justified.

That government safety regulation can be justified in principle does not necessarily mean that the safety regulatory activities of the Food and Drug Administration, the Consumer Product Safety Commission, and the Federal Trade Commission on balance have been justified in practice. My own belief, though, is that they clearly have been. Establishing the case for such a proposition would require going through a representative sample of the regulatory interventions these agencies have undertaken and analyzing them in light of the conceptual criteria for intervention presented here. This does not imply that there are not individual regulations that are excessively or insufficiently protective, or that some things that have been regulated should never have been regulated while others not regulated should have been. The view that such regulation is to be condemned in principle as paternalistic has constituted a not-insignificant part of the attack on consumer product safety regulation. That bulwark of the case against such regulation thus falls.

BIBLIOGRAPHY

Brandt, Richard (1959): *Ethical Theory*, Englewood Cliffs, NJ: Prentice-Hall, Chaps. 15–17.

Calabresi, Guido and Malamed, A. Douglas, "Property Rights, Liability Rules, and Inalienability," *Harvard Law Review, 85* (April 1972).

Cornell, Nina W., et al. (1976): "Safety Regulation," in Henry Owen and Charles L. Schultze, Eds., *Setting National Priorities: The Next Ten Years*, Washington, DC: The Brookings Institution, pp. 465–466.

Cyert, Richard and March, James (1963): *A Behavioral Theory of the Firm*, Englewood Cliffs, NJ: Prentice-Hall, p. 118.

Demsetz, Howard, "Toward a Theory of Property Rights," *American Economic Review, 57* (May 1967).

Devlin, Lord Patrick (1971): "Morals and the Criminal Law," reprinted in Richard A. Wasserstrom, Ed., *Morality and the Law*, Belmont, CA: Wadsworth.

Food and Drug Administration (1976): *Consumer Nutrition Knowledge Survey, Report I*, Washington, DC: FDA, p. 39.

Friedman, Milton (1962): *Capitalism and Freedom,* Chicago, IL: Univ. Chicago P., p. 148.

Fromm, Erich (1941): *Escape from Freedom*, New York, Rinehart.

Goldberg, Victor, "The Economics of Product Safety and Imperfect Information," *The Bell Journal of Economics and Management Science, 5* (Spring 1974), 686.

Hart, H. L. A. (1964): *Law, Liberty and Morality*, Stanford, CA: Stanford U.P.

Jacoby, Jacob, et al., "Brand Choice Behavior as a Function of Information Load," *Journal of Marketing Research, 11* (February 1974), 65.

Janis, Irving L. and Mann, Leon (1977): *Decision Making: A Psychological Analysis of Conflict, Choice, and Commitment,* New York: The Free Press, p. 3.

Kelman, Steven (1979): "The Psychological Costs of Markets" (stencil).

Kelman, Steven (1981): *Regulating America, Regulating Sweden: A Comparative Study of Occupational Safety and Health Policies*, Cambridge, MA: MIT Press, Chap. 3.

Lieberman, Jethro, "The Relativity of Injury," *Philosophy and Public Affairs, 6* (Summer 1977).

Lipset, Seymour Martin and Schneider, William, "The Public View of Regulation, *Public Opinion, 2* (January 1979), 11.

Nelson, Philip, "Information and Consumer Behavior," *Journal of Political Economy, 78* (March 1970).

Posner, Richard A. (1979): "The Federal Trade Commission's Mandated Disclosure Program," in Harvey J. Goldschmid, Ed., *Business Disclosure: Government's Need to Know*, New York: McGraw-Hill.

Ross, W. D. (1930): *The Right and the Good*, London: Oxford U.P.

Stigler, George (1975): *The Citizen and the State*, Chicago, IL: Univ. Chicago P., p. 12.

Tversky, Amos, "Intransitivity of Preferences," *Psychological Review, 76* (January 1969).

Tversky, Amos and Kahneman, Daniel (1974): "Judgment under Uncertainty: Heuristics and Biases," in Richard Zeckhauser et al., Eds., *Benefit-Cost and Policy Analysis*, Chicago, IL: Aldine.

Wikler, Daniel, "Paternalism and the Mildly Retarded," *Philosophy and Public Affairs, 8* (Summer 1979).

NOTES

1. Throughout this part of the discussion I will consider the case of an individual consumer. Both decision-making costs and the gap between the fully informed decision an individual would have made and the choice a third party makes may of course vary among individuals. I discuss the aggregation question in a situation with variation across individuals at the end of this section.

2. This point is made in Nelson (1970).

3. For a discussion of these points, see Kelman (1981).

4. This argument appears in Posner (1979).

5. On this point, see Cornell et al. (1976).

6. Another alternative is possible in the case of products not subject to certification. Such products might carry a statement such as "This product not subject to certification." Note, however, that this alternative would require relearning behavior on the part of consumers whenever certification was newly introduced, either because the government finally got around to looking at the product in question or because of a change in knowledge about the product's safety that led to development of certification criteria where none had previously existed.

7. These figures are from Food and Drug Administration (1976) and Lipset and Schneider (1979).

8. A case could probably be made for allowing establishment of certain stores, with warnings prominently posted, that sell only products that do not meet regulatory standards. This would allow those who wish to buy such products the opportunity to do so without subjecting others to serious temptation problems. There would be important implementation problems with such proposals, however, especially with fraud at the manufacturer level (labeling noncomplying products as complying ones) or at the distributor level. Also, if an important part of the justification for regulation in a specific instance is the external effects of choices a person makes (to be

discussed below), then the individual's own choice might be overridden. These problems make the establishment of such outlets for noncomplying products hardly a top-priority item on the consumer protection regulation agenda.

9. That situation is only partly remedied if the policy-holder falls into an experience category with a higher premium. It is sometimes argued that only the existence of government-provided health insurance creates the external effect from accidents that may be used to justify government intervention. This contention is then used to illustrate the general view that government regulation pyramids on itself, one regulation soon requiring another, with the implication being that the process should never have started. The use of government-provided health insurance to argue for this contention is unwarranted. First, there exist important external effects from an accident other than bills paid by fellow insurance policyholders. Second, this problem exists whether insurance is governmental and mandatory or private and voluntary.

10. Also see any of the "property rights" writings by Chicago school economists, such as Demsetz (1967).

11. What is being done here is using the statement that it is *prima facie* wrong to violate human dignity to justify a social decision about rights that will favor A's good over that of B. Note that it is intuitively easier to accept the use of the moral principle that it is wrong to violate human dignity to decide that a policy should favor A's good over B's good even though B's good is greater, because doing otherwise would violate A's human dignity, than it is to accept the view, presented earlier, that a policy that produces x-1 units of good for A may be preferred over one producing x units of good for A because the first policy preserves and the second violates A's human dignity. In the former case, we are, at least, maximizing A's good (although sacrificing B's), while in the latter case we are not maximizing anyone's good.

12. On reasons for the latter, see Kelman (1979).

CHAPTER THREE
Study Questions

1. Do you believe that standards that aim at preventing dangerous products are preferable to procedures for compensating consumers for damage done? Would it make a difference if the standards or procedures were voluntarily adopted by industry rather than enforced by government regulation?

2. Do you think that strict products liability is just one of the risks that a businessperson takes when entering a competitive market? Or, should negligence be proven? By the way, what is "negligence" anyway?

3. Are there some products that just should not be produced at all because they are too dangerous? Should manufacturers of teflon-coated bullets be liable when those bullets are used to pierce a policeman's bullet-proof vest?

4. How much should the consumers' behavior (use or misuse of products) count in assessing liability? How might a business's advertising and marketing policies affect this?

5. Are individual consumers always the best judges of their own interests? If not, where do you draw the line?

CHAPTER FOUR

ADVERTISING: DECEPTION AND UNFAIRNESS

In 1970, the FTC began an investigation of *Reader's Digest's* direct mail marketing campaigns. Typically, the campaigns involved mass mailings of sweepstakes which promised money or merchandise to a small percentage of those who returned the sweepstakes entry forms. At the conclusion of its investigation one year later, the FTC concluded that these sweepstakes promotions were unfair and deceptive.

In November 1971 the FTC issued a formal complaint and reached an agreement with the *Digest*. The agreement involved acceptance of a cease and desist order by the *Digest* with no admission that the *Digest* had violated any law.

One of the allegations of the FTC complaint stated that the *Digest* represented that "simulated checks, money, and other negotiated instruments and simulated 'New Car Certificates'" were "valuable and [could] be cashed, redeemed, or exchanged for United States Currency or a new car." In fact the items were not valuable and could not be cashed, redeemed, or exchanged. These items merely accompanied entry forms for the sweepstakes. The consent order prohibited the use or distribution of "simulated checks, currency, 'new car certificates' or any confusingly simulated item of value."

In early 1973, the *Digest* initiated a new sweepstakes promotion. The *Digest* mailed millions of "travel checks" which purported to pay a grand prize winner "one hundred thousand dollars a month for life." In April 1973, the FTC informed the *Digest* that the travel check clearly violated the consent order. On May 2, the *Digest* informed the FTC that "while not admitting that the 'travel check' in any way violates" the order, it would discontinue its use after June 30, 1973. Between May 7 and June 30, the *Digest* completed its mailings, sending out over four million checks during that time.

In September and November 1974 the *Digest* distributed approximately two million "cash-convertible bonds" as part of a new sweepstakes campaign. The bonds purported to award to a grand prize winner "one hundred dollars a month for life." The FTC did not contact the *Digest* at the time of that mailing.

On July 7, 1975, the government filed a complaint in district court against *Reader's*

Digest. The complaint charged that the *Digest* had continued to violate the consent order and sought legal penalties for these actions. *Reader's Digest* responded by claiming that the new mailings were sufficiently different from the ones prohibited by the consent order. They also claimed that the FTC had to prove that the travel checks and cash convertible bonds had actually deceived consumers.

The district court concluded, and the appeals court upheld, that the new mailings had the same tendency to deceive as the original checks and were therefore indistinguishable from them in terms of the consent order. The courts also ruled that the FTC did not have to prove that the mailings had actually deceived anyone. Having the "same capacity to mislead consumers" meant the new mailings were similar enough to the ones which the

Digest had already agreed to stop. The courts did not rule on whether or not, had the *Digest* not earlier agreed to the consent order, the FTC would have had to establish actual deception. Finally, the courts ruled that each letter mailed during the promotions, exactly 17,940,521, was a separate violation of the consent order. As a result, the courts assessed a penalty of $1,750,000 and issued a permanent injunction against further violations of the consent order.

What, if anything, do you find deceptive and unfair about these sweepstakes? Do you think many people are deceived by these mailings? Who might be most susceptible to being deceived by these promotions? Should the FTC be required to prove actual deception before prohibiting any advertising or promotional methods?

Introduction

BUSINESS INTERACTS WITH consumers not only through the goods and services which it produces, but also through various advertising and marketing practices. Two of the most common moral criticisms of these practices, that they are deceptive or unfair, will be examined in this chapter. Such criticisms have led the FTC to adopt deception and unfairness as the two major standards by which it regulates advertising. Much of this chapter's analysis of deception and unfairness will take place within a context of evaluating government regulation of advertising.

In the previous chapter we considered some of the standard objections to government regulation. Besides these objections, government regulation of advertising has been criticized on other grounds. The United States Constitution explicitly prohibits the regulation of free speech, and critics charge that regulating commercial speech violates the right of free speech. This issue is examined in the first selection of this chapter. After reviewing justifications of free speech in general, we examine both legal and moral arguments for exempting commercial speech from constitutional protection. Under normal circumstances, an individual's speech cannot be regulated on the grounds that it is deceptive or unfair. Consequently, some relevant difference between commercial speech and individual speech must be established before government regulation of commercial speech can be justified. Our first selection examines some of these differences.

As we have seen before, a helpful step in any analysis is to come to a clear understanding of the central concepts. As we have also seen, it is not unusual to find some dispute at this point. For although even the most vigorous defenders of a free-market economy believe that avoiding deception is one of the legitimate goals of government regulation, there is little overall agreement about what exactly constitutes a deceptive practice. Indeed, much of the criticism of the FTC in this regard claims that there has been no clear understanding of the concepts of deception and unfairness. Some claim that the standards are too vague, that they can be extended to include almost any advertising practice the regulators dislike. Others claim that the concepts overlap, that they are different versions of the same problem.

For example, some years ago Miller Brewing Company began to market Lowenbrau beer. Miller had purchased the rights to use this German brand name in the United States. The German Lowenbrau beer would no longer be sold in the United States; instead, a beer brewed by Miller would be sold as "Lowenbrau." Many people believed that Miller was guilty of deceptive advertising. For consumers who were accustomed to drinking the German beer, the ads probably were initially deceptive. However, the complaint that the FTC received was not from consumers who felt deceived, but from a competitor who considered the advertising and marketing of this product unfair competition. An advertising practice that might be deceptive to consumers may be unfair to Anheuser-Busch. As in the case of product safety, the appropriateness of regulatory standards in advertising will depend somewhat upon the audience addressed.

Our next selection begins the analysis of deception. Joseph Kupfer offers an account of the wrongs, or "disvalues," inherent in lying. In general, deception is wrong because it is a form of lying, and lying, Kupfer tells us, has at least two inherent negative components: All lies involve a restriction upon the deceived person's freedom and a threat to the integration of the liar's own personality.

The freedom of the deceived is restricted because the deceived person is prevented from making rational and informed decisions about how to act. In the attempt to "mug the intellect" of another, the liar expresses disrespect for his or her victim by denying that victim the status of an autonomous and self-determining individual. A consumer who has been victimized by a deceptive practice has been coerced into making a decision he otherwise would not have made. Moreover, that denial presumably indicates that the liar unfairly considers his own interests to be more important than the interests of others. Lying, then, conflicts with fundamental moral demands that every person be treated with equal respect as a human individual and that conflicting interests be weighed impartially. It would be interesting to compare Kupfer's discussion concerning the danger that lying presents to the liar's own character with Carr's recommendation in Chapter 1 that we keep our personal lives separate from our business lives.

We should note that Kupfer's arguments will ultimately locate the immorality of deception in the intent of the liar. In his analysis, a lie remains wrong even when no one is actually deceived by it. If one accepts that analysis, there is a moral presumption against any attempt to deceive another. Does this presumption against the intent to deceive generate a presumption in favor of regulating any market practice that Kupfer's view would brand as immoral? Should or could the law attempt to ensure conformity to clear moral standards?

Obviously, if government attempted to ensure such conformity with respect to deception, it would have to determine the actual intent of advertisers. This is a task for which government is ill-suited. A more reasonable approach to government regulation of marketing practices would concern not the intent of advertisements, but their effect on an audience. A practice that is morally unacceptable is not always a practice that could reasonably be subject to regulation. It may also be that some practices with unintentionally deceptive effects should be regulated even though they may not be immoral.

Next, we turn more directly to the debate over the FTC's use of deception and unfairness as standards for regulating advertising with deceptive effects. The first issue we consider has been mentioned before (and will be raised again in the next chapter). Part of our judgements about business will depend upon the nature of the audience interacting with business. As Albert Carr claimed, "A falsehood ceases to be a falsehood when it is understood on all sides that the truth is not expected." We have also seen in Chapter 3 that a safe product for an adult is not necessarily a safe product when used by children. In this chapter, we recognize that an advertisement that deceives one person might not deceive another. Accordingly, the FTC must decide what audience it represents when regulating deceptive advertising.

Our third selection traces the evolution of various standards employed by the FTC in making this decision. Ivan Preston describes two standards, the "ignorant man" and "reasonable man" standards. At various times the FTC has used each of these standards, with only moderate overall success. The ignorant man standard attempts to protect virtually all consumers from deception. By this standard, an ad is deceptive if it would deceive even the most naive, gullible, or ignorant consumer. An ad violates the reasonable man standard only if it would deceive reasonably careful consumers. After detailing the benefits and shortcomings of each standard, Preston describes a movement towards a modified reasonable man standard which is concerned more with typical consumers than in the past.

James Miller, an FTC commissioner in the Reagan Administration, argues that the deception standard needs to be restricted. Miller believes that the jurisdiction of his own commission is too broad. He outlines numerous problems that he sees as plaguing the current standard. Miller believes that too much has been left to the interpretation of the FTC and too little attention has been paid to actual cases where consumers are deceived. When FTC employees apply these ideal standards they are in reality engaging in nothing more than armchair speculation about how many consumers will be deceived by an advertisement. As a partial solution to these problems, Miller urges the commission to use research evidence in order to restrict its activities to actual cases of deceptive effect only.

A problem with this approach to deciding when to regulate, however, is that it allows harm to a significant number of consumers before regulation can correct the deceptive practice. Some would criticize this reliance on market studies, then, as an attempt to close the barn door after the horse has escaped. We can see a tension between the benefits of a review of advertisements on the basis of expected effect and a reliance on studies of actual consumer effects. The reader must decide what approach to regulation is preferable.

Ralph Winter next argues that the regulation of advertising must consider overall costs to consumers. Winter believes that numerous consumer benefits follow from advertising, including the more efficient functioning of the market, and that these facts shift the burden of proof to those who call for regulation. One of Winter's most serious claims is that "the premises of a democratic society" imply consumer autonomy in the marketplace. Unless we opt for paternalistic intervention, we should leave consumers free to make their own decisions. Another implication of these premises, which he does not mention but which we shall consider in the first reading, is the right of free speech.

The rest of Winter's argument is based upon the workings of a free and competitive market. Like Albert Carr and Milton Friedman in earlier chapters, Winter believes that government does have a role to play in restricting fraud and deception in the marketplace. These practices frustrate the very goals at which competitive markets aim. However, to avoid the costs, ambiguities, and mistakes that happen when government bureaucrats are left free to interpret deception, Winter thinks that regulation should be limited to cases of fraud. Fraud "should be narrowly defined to mean a demonstrated false statement," and all fraudulent advertising that can be costlessly eliminated should be.

Our final selection examines unfairness in advertising, the second standard that the FTC uses to regulate advertising. Dorothy Cohen traces the history of the unfairness standard and describes how the FTC has made increased use of unfairness since 1972. After characterizing the current status of the unfairness standard, Cohen evaluates the argument in defense and in criticism of unfairness. After careful analysis, Cohen concludes that use of this standard is advantageous for both public policy and competitive market reasons. Overall, then, she believes that the FTC should continue to use unfairness as a criterion for advertising regulation.

JOSEPH R. DES JARDINS AND JOHN J. McCALL
Advertising and Free Speech

I

Commercial speech is significantly constrained by a wide variety of Federal Trade Commission regulations. When compared with the relative absence of constraints placed on other forms of speech, this fact reveals that our political institutions apply widely different standards for determining the constitutional limits of government interference with speech. There are a number of reasons why the different treatments given to commercial speech and, for example, that given to political speech, should concern marketers and ordinary citizens alike.

First, and most generally, understanding this difference and the reasons offered in its support will force any citizen to examine the basis of our society's belief that free speech is important enough to warrant constitutional protection.

Second, when any speech is subjected to constraints, there is always the danger that precedents set in the restraint of that form of speech might evolve into a justification for future restraints on other, perhaps more important, forms of speech. Reasons offered to regulate commercial speech today might be offered tomorrow for regulating journalistic or religious speech.

Finally, understanding the basis for treating commercial speech differently from other forms of speech might provide us with a guide for deciding future social policy with respect to regulating corporate political advertising.

These three reasons for being concerned with the special constitutional status of commercial speech will provide the framework for our discussion of advertising regulation. In the next section, we sketch reasons why a right of free speech is an important component of any acceptable political structure. We then explain the precise differences between the treatment given to commercial speech and that given to other forms of speech. We will outline and reject certain justifications offered for this dissimilarity. However, we will defend the

different treatment by explaining how the general justification for a right of free speech can allow for the regulation of advertising in ways that are unacceptable for other forms of speech. In addition, we use that defense of free speech to underscore some constitutional limitations on regulating advertisements. In the final section, we note some implications that our analysis has for corporate political advertising and sketch some potential solutions to the practical political problems raised by that analysis.

II

Freedom of speech is important both because of the specific values it promotes and because of the general moral attitude towards persons that the promotion of these values encourages. Historically, political and constitutional theory have recognized a practical connection between the existence of free speech on the one hand, and the values of political autonomy, individual development, and the discovery of truth on the other.[1]

Free speech clearly is a means towards greater political autonomy for the citizens of a society. Where institutions allow freedom of speech, citizens are able to raise critical questions concerning the policies of their government. Open discussions of political questions provide citizens with a powerful opportunity for influencing the direction of those policies. Alternatively, where speech is suppressed, government authorities have greater power to set the public agenda, to indoctrinate the populace by promoting only approved opinions, and to stifle public criticisms of their actions. Collective self-rule by the citizens is thus furthered when those citizens are provided a constitutional guarantee of free speech.

Persons living in a society with such guarantees also possess an opportunity for individual self-development not possessed by other persons. The capacity for rational and deliberative choice is an important component of adult human existence. In fact, the capacity for deliberative choice is often offered as one characteristic that distinguishes persons from mere animals. This important human capacity certainly has a much higher chance of being realized when individuals are able to freely speak their minds. In circumstances allowing freedom of speech, speakers have an opportunity through discussions with others for refining the ideas they express. (We all recognize the improvement in our own deliberations that is provided by criticisms received from others.) In addition, listeners are presented an opportunity for receiving and evaluating new points of view when others are able to express their opinions freely. Even from the perspective of the listener, then, freedom of speech provides an opportunity for improving the human capacity for informed and critical deliberation. Thus, free speech has an important instrumental value in that it promotes political autonomy and the development of central human capacities.

Freedom of speech also has been defended as an effective means for the discovery of truth. John Stuart Mill, for example, claimed that a long-term competition in the marketplace of ideas will be won by those ideas that are most true. Since true ideas are understood as a benefit to society and as a necessary component in reasonable deliberations by individuals, the value of free speech would be increased if it led to greater discovery.

Finally, these three values (political autonomy, self-development, and the discovery of truth) which have played a significant role in First Amendment theory, all exhibit a particular attitude towards human beings. A concern with promoting each of these values can be seen as an outgrowth of the attempt to treat each person with respect, since each of these values expresses a belief in persons as rational autonomous agents capable of directing the courses of their own lives. Thus, we move towards respect for persons when we allow them to govern themselves. The defense of freedom of speech based upon these three historically important values, then, expresses as a fundamental tenet of our political morality that all persons are to be treated with equal respect.

First Amendment rights to free speech are thus important political rights whose interpretation should be a matter of concern for all. Moreover,

the fact that one form of speech, commercial speech, is significantly regulated should be of special concern, since the precedents for regulation in that area are potentially available as justifications for new restriction on speech in other areas. We need, then, to understand the precise way in which commercial speech is accorded different treatment, as well as to understand the potential justifications for that different treatment.

III

Until quite recently, commercial speech was provided with little or no constitutional protection under the First Amendment. The source of modern constitutional theory on this issue is found in the 1942 Supreme Court decision in *Valentine v. Christensen*, where the Court decided that commercial speech was undeserving of protected status.[2] The basis of that decision was that the presence of an economic motive was sufficient to disqualify an expression from having protected status. More recent decisions have moderated this position somewhat, but commercial speech is still without full protected status. For instance, in the 1976 *Virginia State Board of Pharmacy v. Virginia Citizens Consumer Council, Inc.* decision, the Supreme Court expressly asserted that commercial speech is entitled to a lesser degree of protection. The same comment occurs in a landmark case in 1978, *Ohralik v. Ohio State Bar Association*, which freed regulators to prohibit broad classes of commercial speech.[3] Thus, while the Supreme Court has recently expanded the protections offered to commercial speech, it still has steadfastly refused to judge the regulation of such speech by the same strict standards applied to regulation of, for example, political speech.[4] The following specific differences in the extent of allowable regulation are instructive.

Ordinarily, other forms of speech, such as political speech, are provided protection regardless of their truth; commercial speech, however, must be true in order to gain even its limited protected status. We prosecute advertisers for false claims made within their advertisements. On the other hand, we all recognize that even intentionally false statements made by political candidates are ordinarily beyond prosecution. But constitutionally acceptable differences in treatment extend well beyond this. Commercial speech that is not strictly false is subject to broad regulation if government regulatory agencies deem it to possess a significant tendency to deceive. Thus, regulation can include even cases of harmless speech if regulating those cases is an effective means for eliminating other potentially deceptive instances of commercial speech.

This court-sanctioned regulation applies a significantly different standard than is applied to other forms of speech. Regulation in other areas is subject to a relatively strict requirement that the regulation not be "overbroad"—that it not discourage speech beyond the extent necessary to solve a particular difficulty. This "overbreadth" or "least restrictive means" doctrine has not been applied with the same rigor in commercial speech cases.[5]

Moreover, advertisements are subject to compliance with regulatory standards that set requirements of unfair language in order to avoid possible deception and misunderstanding.[6] Government regulatory agencies also can impose requirements of affirmative disclosure by requiring advertisers to include health warnings or by requiring them to correct misleading impressions that may have been created by previous advertisements.[7] Further, the Federal Trade Commission, through cease and desist orders for classes of advertisements, also has a further court-recognized power of prior restraint over advertising speech. None of these regulatory powers ordinarily are acceptable for limiting other forms of speech in advance of their utterance.

More recent Supreme Court decisions have carried the current doctrine requiring a lesser burden of proof in order to justify restricting commercial speech even further. In *Friedman v. Rogers* (1979), the Court allowed regulation prohibiting even true information (about manufacturers' trade names) from being used in ads because of the possibility that such information *might* mislead and because trade names have little intrinsic meaning.[8] The *Central Hudson Gas and Electric v. Public Service Commission* (1980) decision even recognized the legitimacy of a state action suppressing nondeceptive commercial speech in order to promote a state interest in lessening a demand for a legally available product (electricity).[9]

Thus commercial speech, unlike other forms of speech, must be true to have constitutional protection. However, even nondeceptive commercial speech is subject to significant regulation. The dissimilarity in constitutional treatment for commercial speech and other forms of speech is striking.

IV

Any number of explanations and justifications for this different treatment have been offered, some by the Supreme Court in its own rulings, and others by legal theorists. Not all of these justifications are sufficiently convincing. For instance, the previously cited basis of the *Christensen* doctrine (that economic motive disqualifies speech from constitutional protection) seems overbroad in itself, since paid political speakers and newspapers have economic motive for their speech.[10] Similarly, the Court in the *Virginia Board* decision argued that commercial speech is, because of its economic motivation, more "hardy" (less likely to be totally discouraged) than other forms of speech and, hence, can withstand greater restraints. The difficulty with this justification, however, is that it seems clear that threats of government regulation do in fact deter advertisers.[11] In addition, since some accepted regulations actually *prohibit* some types of commercial speech, it seems inappropriate to claim that such speech is "hardier" and can resist such regulation.

The *Virginia Board* decision also justifies government regulation of commercial speech because such speech is factually more verifiable than political or religious speech and, thus, the possibility of government bias does not arise as easily in the area of advertising regulation. However, this justification exhibits a naive understanding of advertisements. Certainly many advertisements are at least as unverifiable or open to dispute as are statements in the area of politics or religion. In fact, political speech is often more verifiable than statements in commercials, and yet no Supreme Court Justice would argue that similar regulation of political speech is therefore justifiable.[12]

Serious problems also exist in a number of other potential justifications for this special treatment accorded commercial speech. Some have argued that this dissimilar treatment is justified because advertisers possess an unequal power to influence, because advertisements involve emotional appeals, or because advertising is not a truth-seeking or self-correcting process.[13] Since each of these beliefs can equally as well describe certain political debates, it would appear inappropriate to use them as justification for a difference in treatment between the two classes of speech. There is a difficulty, then, in constructing an explanation for why commercial speech ought to be treated differently. The difficulty lies in the possibility that the proposed explanations would also justify restrictions on forms of speech that we would not want to regulate.

Another plausible explanation for the different treatment accorded commercial speech lies in the state interest in regulating commerce and contracts. As implicit contract offers, advertisements might justifiably be regulated in ways that all contracts are. Unfortunately, this explanation also is insufficient to explain completely the different treatment accorded religious and commercial speech because it presupposes that the state has a legitimate interest in regulating commerce for the welfare of its citizens, and it implicitly denies that the state has an equal interest in regulating religious expression for the welfare of its citizens.

But, of course, a citizen's welfare might well be endangered by certain religious practices just as it could be by certain advertising or contract practices that are now subject to regulation. What needs explaining, then, is why commerce and commercial speech are accorded a status of lesser importance. Presupposing that status fails to carry the explanation far enough.

V

A more plausible, if controversial, explanation can be found by appealing to the values cited in traditional defenses of free speech and in the attitude of respect towards persons evidenced by those values. For example, it seems unlikely that free commercial speech is as practically necessary for promoting political autonomy as is free political speech. Certainly there is an obvious danger in allowing a government regulatory body to regulate the very political speech that concerns the evaluation of government policy. The open debate necessary for real political autonomy appears less than likely unless there is a strong presumption against government interference with political speech.

The absence of such an equally strong presumption against government regulation of commercial speech would not similarly threaten the existence of political autonomy. Hence, one of the traditional values provides a substantial reason for treating regulation of commercial speech according to standards different from those used for regulating political speech. We should note, however, that this reason does not claim that commercial speech should be without protection. It only argues for a status of lesser protection.

Nevertheless, this reason fails to explain why the speech of advertisers ought to be treated differently than, say, speech about religious or moral matters, which is protected in a manner similar to political speech. Free religious or moral speech seems no more practically required for political autonomy than does free commercial speech. (There *may* be a reason for treating moral speech in a manner similar to political speech, in that one of the legitimate interests of the government is to promote the welfare of its citizens, and moral speech often is about what constitutes that welfare. Thus, there may be a threat to political autonomy in allowing government control over moral speech.) Accordingly, if we grant religious and moral speech a protected status equal to political speech and greater than commercial speech, and if serving the value of political autonomy is not a relevant difference between religious or moral speech and commercial speech, then we must defend the special status given religious and moral speech by appeal to some other value.

It also appears that, without some amending, the other traditional values cannot offer a reason for treating either moral or religious speech differently than commercial speech. One cannot, for example, argue that commercial speech leads to less development of rational capacities for choice, since much moral and religious speech makes the same use of emotional appeals and has the same paucity of reasoned or factual analysis as is found in many advertisements. Of course, emotionally based religious or moral speech is protected to a greater extent than is commercial speech.

Why, then, do moral and religious speech deserve special constitutional protection? It seems that the greater protection depends upon a particular view concerning the sorts of discussions that are most central to human experience. Some types of speech might be more valuable to human life than others. No doubt, any such view contains significant bias in its judgement that certain issues are of more momentous human concern. However, that need not imply that the bias is unreasonable or unacceptable.

The elevation of discussions of moral and religious issues to full constitutional protection indicates that investigations into those issues are more valuable than other investigations. Religious and moral questioning is part of what provides human life with its special status. Religious and moral speech contribute to the pursuit of meaning and value in human existence. Freedom of expression in offering an item for sale, in comparison, appears a rather mundane concern. (The Court implicitly adopted this view in the *Christensen* decision.[14])

Thus, while freedom for commercial speech might promote the development of a human capacity for deliberative choice, the manner in which it promotes this development differs markedly from the manner in which human development might be promoted by deliberation about other choices that are seen as more central to human existence. On the one hand, commercial speech promotes the capacity for rational choice by encouraging us to deliberate about various and competing consumer choices. Religious and moral speech, on the other hand, promotes this capacity by encouraging us to deliberate about the very meaning and value of human life. Thus, on the basis of this idea of what makes a human life valuable, a respect for the humanity of each person might dictate a stronger presumption against restrictions on moral or religious speech than against restrictions on commercial speech.

None of this, however, is to say that commercial speech is without significant value. Inasmuch as it promotes, to some degree, important values, it too deserves a measure of protection. The preceding analysis offers only an explanation of why the protection for it ought to be less.

In its recent decisions the Supreme Court seems to agree with the conclusion that commercial speech deserves increasing protection. The Court has overturned government prohibitions on certain particular types of factual advertising by

lawyers, pharmacists, and abortion services, arguing that there is no legitimate state interest that would justify preventing the public from having such information available.[15] In addition, the strong presumption in favor of free political speech would be consistent with the Court's decision in the 1980 *First National Bank of Boston v. Bellotti* case, where the Court ruled against state prohibition of corporate advocacy advertisements on current political issues. If we wish to prevent government from controlling political debate, from setting the public agenda, or from stifling political criticism, then there seems no good reason to allow it to prohibit outright any political expression.

This last Court decision raises a number of new and potentially significant problems for future government policy, however. By granting strong protection to corporate political advertising, this decision presents the problem of distinguishing between corporate "image" advertising (which apparently deserves only the limited protection accorded commercial speech) and more mainstream political advocacy advertisements (which deserve stronger constitutional protection). It also raises an important question concerning the ability of powerful and monied interests to influence inordinately the political agenda and debate by heavy promotional campaigns. A comment about each of these potential problems is in order.

VI

Most observers of television and radio advertising trends have recognized that large corporations have begun to advertise more frequently in ways that do not directly present any specific products for sale but which, rather, present a positive image of the corporation as a loyal and concerned member of the community. Since such image advertisements do not provide consumers with the factual information necessary for informed consumer choice, it is not clear in which direction recent precedents will move the Court. As was noted above, some of the recent Court decisions have expanded protection for commercial speech. As also noted above, however, in its *Friedman* decision the Court found the use of trade names to be undeserving of protection, since trade names were thought to have little intrinsic significance of their own. Likewise, image advertising seems to lack the intrinsic significance of informative product advertising. The *Friedman* decision, then, might provide some grounds for government regulation of non–product-related and non-informational image advertising. Thus, there seem to be opposing tendencies in the Court's recent history that make its direction regarding cases of image advertising ambiguous.

Of course, it may turn out that the Court need not decide whether the constitutional status of image advertising would preclude certain forms of government regulation. However, there is a significant possibility that cases dealing with image advertising might come before the Court in conjunction with cases dealing with corporate political advertising. This possibility becomes increasingly probable when corporate image advertising not only presents positive images of the corporation but when it also, by implication, suggests that certain political positions are more appropriate than others. Instances of this might be seen in image ads that argue, at least implicitly, for a free enterprise economy with less government regulation. Other instances can be found in recent ads by energy companies that promote the virtues of expanding production of untapped oil reserves or the positive features of nuclear electric power plants. Since these are important contemporary political issues as well as issues of economic concern to the corporate world, there is some sense in which corporate image advertising can be seen as increasingly political in nature. Thus, whatever might give rise to Court deliberation on corporate political advertising might also give the Court reasons for ruling on corporate image advertising. We ought to consider what responses to political advocacy advertising by corporations would be appropriate.

In the *Bellotti* decision referred to above, the Supreme Court has already issued a ruling that prevents the state from *prohibiting* corporate political advertising. The Court's ruling in *Bellotti* seems particularly appropriate when we recognize the grave dangers to political autonomy present when the state is able to determine the direction or content of political debates. However, we should not misread the *Bellotti* decision as one which prevents state *regulation* of political advocacy advertisements by corporations. (Prohibition and

regulation, of course, are not identical.) In fact, there are strong reasons for suggesting that the recognition of the value of political autonomy should encourage state regulation of such corporate advertising.

If promoting political autonomy is tied to maintaining a free and open system of expression in which opposing points of view can be offered and received, then there might be a danger to political autonomy other than that presented when the government can control political debate. The ability of citizens to autonomously determine the direction of their political institutions could also be threatened if powerful private interests were capable of dominating media discussions of political issues. In fact, with the increasing influence and cost of advertising, in the electronic media especially, there is a very real danger that unregulated political advertising by corporations might render meaningless the right of free expression of opinion for ordinary citizens or unmonied groups.[16] Thus, if traditional constitutional theory supports the right to free speech by connecting it to the value of political autonomy, the Court ought to recognize the legitimacy and potential need for some regulation of corporate political advocacy advertising.

In fact, there are already precedents for such limitations on corporate speech in the Court's sanctioning of FCC fairness rulings requiring equal time for presentation of opposing views after presidential broadcasts on television and radio. Thus, possible regulations requiring equal time (perhaps with public financing) and/or limiting the frequency of political advocacy advertising might be both needed and appropriate if citizens are to have fair value for their rights to freedom of speech.

In summary, consistent with traditional justifications for freedom of speech, recent Supreme Court decisions have expanded the rights of commercial speakers to disseminate factual product information. However, also consistent with appropriate approaches to free speech, these same decisions have made clear that commercial speech deserves less constitutional protection than that provided political or religious speech. On the basis of the appropriateness of these decisions, any future Court decisions ought also to reaffirm the government's right to apply a fairness doctrine to corporate political advertising. Hence, corporate rights to commercial speech should not preclude government activity necessary to ensure both that a fair value for the right to free speech is available to all citizens and that corporate monied interests are unable to set the agenda for public discussion.

NOTES

1. See John Stuart Mill, *On Liberty* (New York: Bobbs-Merrill, 1956); D.A.J. Richards, *The Moral Criticism of Law* (Belmont, CA: Wadsworth, 1977); Thomas Scanlon, "A Theory of Freedom of Expression," *Philosophy and Public Affairs* 1 (1972); Jonathan Weinberg, "Constitutional Protection of Commercial Speech," 82 *Columbia Law Review* 720, (1982).

2. Daniel Farber, "Commercial Speech and First Amendment Theory," 74 *Northwestern University Law Review* 377 (1979).

3. Weinberg, p. 726.

4. Tracy Westen, "The First Amendment: Barrier or Impetus to FTC Advertising Remedies?" 46 *Brooklyn Law Review* 501.

5. Weinberg, pp. 727 and 747; Westen, p. 503; Farber, p. 390.

6. Westen, p. 505.

7. *Ibid.,* p. 506.

8. Farber, p. 397; Westen, p. 496.

9. Weinberg, p. 728.

10. *Ibid.,* p. 720; Michael Davis, "Should Commercial Speech Have First Amendment Protection?" *Social Theory and Practice* 6:2 (Summer, 1980) 127; Farber, p. 382.

11. Farber, p. 385.

12. *Ibid.,* p. 386; Davis, p. 128.

13. Westen, p. 493–98.

14. Weinberg, p. 722–23.

15. The *Ohlarik, Virginia Board*, and *Bigelow* decisions, respectively.

16. Westen, 508–12; Thomas Emerson, "The Affirmative Promotion of Freedom of Expression: Radio and Television," in *Freedom of Expression*, Fred Berger, ed. (Belmont, CA: Wadsworth, 1980) 163–77.

JOSEPH KUPFER

The Moral Presumption Against Lying

I

Most of us feel an aversion to lying and believe that it always stands in need of justification. One expression of this is to say that there is a prima facie duty not to lie. Another is Sissela Bok's "Principle of Veracity"[1] which holds that lying has an "initial negative weight" so that there is always a presumption against telling a particular lie. Still a third variation can be found in Arnold Isenberg's "constancy principle"[2] which holds that what is inherently bad in any lie is the same for all, constant from one lie to the next. While these sorts of view are plausible, the literature on lying provides little in the way of a specific account for the negative weight inherent in all lies—their common disvalue. What follows is proposed as such an account, one which should also help clarify why some lies are worse than others, why some are excusable and others justifiable. Without presuming to be exhaustive, the view offered maintains that there are at least two inherent negative components of all lies; further, each of these inherent disvalues disposes the liar toward a particular, contingent harm. The inherent disvalues and the harms they threaten collectively constitute sufficient grounds for the presumption against lying.

The first inherent disvalue is the immediate restriction of the deceived's freedom. This, subsequently, inclines the liar in the direction of disrespect for people. The second inherent disvalue found in lying is the self-opposition or internal conflict involved in speaking what one disbelieves. This, in turn, contingently threatens the integration

Originally published in *The Review of Metaphysics*, Vol. 36, (1982), reprinted with permission.

of the liar's personality. In both cases, the harm contingently risked pertains to the liar. The inherent disvalue is a "force for" the evil, "disposing" or "inclining" the liar in this harmful direction. This is the sense in which the inherent disvalues contain further "risks" for the liar; they jeopardize his character or personality. While the realization of these risks is contingent, dependent upon variables in the liar's and deceived's lives, the inherent disvalues are not. The way the disvalues are "necessary to" or "embedded" in all lying depends upon language and human psychology and will be explained in the course of the discussion. Before proceeding to it, some preliminary clarification about lying itself is called for.

It should be noted first that lying is a species of linguistic deception. Thus, non-linguistic and non-lying linguistic deception are distinct from lying. It is not obvious what follows from differentiating lying from these other sorts of deception, however, the discussion of disrespect (section 3) raises some germane considerations. The motivation for drawing out the significance of this distinction is simply the fact that we seem to single lying out for special opprobrium.

A person lies when he asserts something to another which he believes to be false with the intention of getting the other to believe it to be true. More precise definitions can be honed,[3] but this should capture the common sense of the concept while allowing for the following sort of important fine point: a person can assert a true statement and still be lying. In such a case, of course, he simply could not believe that it is true.

The following analysis, however, applies primarily to "successful" lies: statements which are indeed false and believed true by the deceived. This may seem unduly restrictive, so that whatever is established is too limited in scope, not bearing on all lies. However, this is not the case because the presumption against lying turns upon the inherent negative weight of successful lies. They are the paradigmatic case for our intuition concerning the justificatory burden all lies bear. "Unsuccessful" lies (statements which are either indeed true or false statements not believed by the would-be deceived) are derivatively discredited by being failed attempts at successful lies.[4] (In a similar way do we demand justification for failed attempts to do bodily harm to another.)

That lying can and often does have a wide range of harmful effects either in particular actions or as widespread practice seems obvious. Because Smith is lied to, for example, he fails to do what is needed for him to secure this or that good thing. Or, again, because lying is rampant in this sector of society, great inefficiency is produced as people must check information and so forth. Such harmful consequences may or may not be produced by any particular lie or practice of lying. But the presumption against lying has a deeper base than this very general danger. Lying always includes the two inherent disvalues of freedom restriction and self-opposition. Their weight must always be added to the lie's purely contingent bad consequences in our deliberations and evaluation of particular lies. The lie's contingent good consequences must, therefore, overshadow not only contingent bad consequences, but the inherent disvalues and the specific respective harms they dispose us to: the habit of disrespect and personality disintegration.

II

Immediate restriction of the deceived's freedom is inherent in all (successful) lies because they limit the practical exercise of his reason: reasoning about possible courses of action. Believing true what is false or vice versa, the deceived's perspective on the world and his possible futures in it are distorted. As a result, his choices of action concerning that future are circumscribed. By limiting the horizon or content of his practical reasoning, the lie restricts the choosing and subsequent acting of the deceived. He reasons within a more or less false view of the world; misinformed, his practical conclusions and the actions they motivate are misdirected.

The lie misdirects the deceived's reasoning about future conduct in two complementary ways: it may suggest choices that are not available or eliminate from consideration live options. Both the illusion and elimination of choice limit the deceived's freedom. The first makes this reasoning practically fruitless, thereby retarding or postponing the deliberations necessary to the exercise of freedom. The latter excludes options from the scope of his volition; they are "shielded" from his view. In this respect, lying establishes "conditions of unfreedom . . . [which] restrict choice by making alternatives unavailable or ineligible."[5]

Both the illusion and elimination of choice have the net effect of deflecting the deceived's reasoning. Unwarranted inferences are drawn; barren plans of action laid; irrelevant course of inquiry opened. The lie not only determines what the deceived thinks about, but it skews *how* he thinks of things, e.g., whether he sees something as a threat or a boon. Misinformed and misdirected, the deceived's practical reasoning and thereby his freedom are restricted.

In lying, the deceived's thinking is channelled through a distorted view of the world as lying always aims to misrepresent the way things really are. But the more we see things the way they really are the more free our choices and subsequent actions. In offering a criterion for freedom as autonomy, Benn and Weinstein speak to the issue of one individual controlling the thinking of another. Though not specifically about lying, what they say is clearly germane to it: "it [criticism, choice, eventually freedom] . . . requires that B's sources of information shall not be controlled by A, for then B's view of reality is what A chooses to make it."[6] Lying is clearly a way of choosing another's view of reality for him.

It is important to underscore the significance of the deceived's reasoning and the liar's motivation in all this. Lying presupposes that the deceived has enough reason and memory to be affected by what people tell him, whether true or false. *Attempting* to get another to believe a false proposition true requires that that person have the capacity to understand, believe, and so forth. As for the liar, his speech is purposeful—aiming at an end beyond mere deception or constraint of freedom (this is to be developed shortly). The deceived's rational competency together with the liar's purposefulness explain the sense in which restricting reason (and freedom) is "inherent" in or "necessary to" lies. Lies being what they are, the restriction is "practically" necessary—necessarily part of the practice. Lies being purposeful endeavors at getting someone capable of reasoning to hold a false belief, restricting that person's reasoning is simply how lies "work." And since restricting reasoning necessarily restricts freedom, restriction of freedom is inherent in lying.

In all cases of lying, the liar[7] is trying to channel the thinking and subsequent choosing of the other by his utterance, though this is rarely the *only* thing he is trying to accomplish. The restriction is usually thought to serve some further purpose. As Isenberg points out, "it is impossible to understand why, without ulterior purpose, anyone should wish another to believe a proposition, P, when he himself thinks that P is false."[8] It is a rare liar who seeks simply to deceive. But regardless of ulterior or ultimate purpose, the lie always *immediately* limits the particular deliberations and choosing of the deceived. "Immediately" is important here, since it is possible to enhance the other's freedom in the *long run* by lying. Similarly, lying may benefit the deceived in other ways as well, such as prompting him to think and choose intelligently for himself. These and considerations like them are what enable us to excuse or justify some lies[9]

Even excused or justified lies however immediately restrict the deceived's freedom by circumscribing the exercise of his reason (the general *ability* to reason is not usually impaired, rather its particular exercise is limited).[10] What enables us to excuse or justify a lie are its "material conditions": the *content* of the lie and the *situation* in which it occurs. These material conditions provide a basis for excusing and justifying lies because of their bearing on the way lying restricts the deceived's freedom. Either the content or the situation in which the lie is offered are so related to his loss of freedom that we excuse or justify the lie. Let us consider the paradigm cases of the excused "white" lie and the justified "defensive" lie. These should reveal the centrality of freedom in the relationship between liar and deceived.

The reason we are usually so quick to forgive or excuse white lies[11] is that as a group they usually do not restrict the deceived's freedom very much. Because of their content, typical situation, or both, lies considered "white" tend to be innocuous, not limiting the deceived's freedom seriously or for long. One reason for this is somewhat trivial: the deceived is familiar with the social convention (standard responses to questions such as "Do you like my new tie?") and so does not take the speech as straight-forward assertion.

On the analysis offered by Chisholm and Feehan, because of the implicit conventions governing linguistic practice, such an assertion might not even count as a lie. More important is the fact that we categorize a lie as "white" precisely because it does not limit freedom very much—not just *any* good, such as the securing of pleasure or the like, but *freedom*. The deceived's reasoning and subsequent choices are not seriously limited by the white lie. Conversely, knowing the truth in that situation or about that subject (material conditions) simply would not immediately enhance his freedom. It seems similar to borrowing a friend's possession without his permission: borrowing his pencil typically limits his choices less than borrowing his car does. But perhaps more refinement is needed.

Perhaps we really ought to distinguish between non-white lies which just do not *happen* to limit the deceived's freedom much and white lies which could, through unforeseen and untoward events, restrict his freedom quite a bit. The difference is a matter of probabilities—probabilities determined by the material conditions of content and situation. The probabilities are that a white lie will not have a serious impact on the deceived's freedom. Pebbles have less capacity for serious harm than guns even though in a particular instance the former may in fact do more damage. So, a lie is properly classified as "white" because its impact on freedom is expected to be minimal due to its content or situation.

White lies, as a class, tend to be about matters that are not very serious or to be situated as not to speak seriously to important matters. The restriction of freedom should vary proportionately with the seriousness of the lie's content or situation. By focusing on freedom, we are able to see clearly one way the material conditions of lies provide for variation in their severity. This is necessary in order to account for excusing lies. However, one more aspect needs mention.

When excusing a lie we actually excuse the *liar*; his state or circumstance mitigates the blame. We excuse the "white liar," therefore, for lack of imagination or linguistic facility in being kind, generous, or simply evasive. White lies might not be needed if we could express ourselves more gracefully on the spur of the moment. Or, if we had sufficient foresight to plan more imaginatively, for example, a surprise party. Combined with the mildness of the lie's content or situation, we excuse the white liar for common human deficiencies. Yet what of the case when we *justify* a lie under serious material conditions?

Consider, as a paradigm of justified lying, the "defensive" lie: a lie which aims to defend one's (or another's) freedom. The material conditions of a lie may justify it because we are sometimes justified in restricting another's freedom: in particular, when an individual tries to constrain our freedom as in the use or threatened use of force. When this occurs, practices that are otherwise questionable come to be candidates for morally permissible response. The usual regard we ought to have for another's freedom is altered, perhaps enough and in such ways to permit (or even require) lying.

The limitation or attempted limitation of our freedom changes the moral boundaries which usually confine lying precisely because lying itself is anti-freedom. The content of the lie may provide an appropriate response to a coercive situation. The unjustified restraint of our freedom may "free" us to lie even as it may justify the use of force, intimidation, or otherwise prohibited behavior. This is not to suggest that we are thereby freed of our moral responsibility, only that we may be freed of moral constraints that usually obtain. The restriction of another's freedom through lying may in fact be justified because of his threat to our freedom. It cannot, of course, be said a priori or in what degree the moral boundaries shift, but simply that threat of or actual limitation of freedom is always a relevant consideration in assessing the permissibility (or even obligatoriness) of lying.[12] The invasion of freedom inherent in lying is morally defendable, then, as a response to such an invasion by another.[13]

The cases of white and defensive lies are clarified by this account. Excusing the former and justifying the latter are thoroughly understood only if we appreciate the freedom restriction inherent in lies. Our understanding of excuses for some lies and justifications of others is broadened, moreover, by considering how the lie's restriction of another's freedom poses a contingent threat to the liar's character.

III

By limiting the deceived's freedom, lying does not respect it. In addition, lying immediately alters the relationship between the liar and the deceived. The liar's freedom increases vis-à-vis the deceived's with regard to the subject matter of the lie. Lying enhances the liar's position relative to the deceived by limiting the latter's options (even though, in the long run, the liar's options and his reasoning about them may well be more limited than the deceived's. Relative advantage is itself usually in need of justification regardless of who or what is causally responsible. (Imagine, for example, a teacher giving only one student suggestions on what to study for an examination.) But the fact that one of the two involved parties brings about the alteration in relative freedom is morally germane. It is one thing unwittingly to receive advantage which may not be deserved (the fortunate student above); it is another to initiate it. Responsibility for the change in the relationship endangers the liar's character. Specifically, altering the relationship by lying disposes the liar toward the general habit of disrespect.

Two things need clarification here: the sense in which both inherent disvalues "dispose" the liar toward a harmful condition, and the sort of habit which presently concerns us.

Each inherent disvalue moves the liar in a harmful direction. Here we are concerned with the way in which restricting the deceived's freedom disposes the liar toward disrespect. . . . But the relationship between the inherent disvalue and the contingent harm is the same in each pair: the inherent disvalue disposes the liar to harm in the same way improper rest disposes us to mental error or irascibility. The harm is more than "accidentally" produced by the inherent disvalue, but does not *necessarily* follow from it. The inherent disvalue—restricting the deceived's freedom, here—is *always a force* in the direction of the respective harm. Human nature being what it is, the fact that lying restricts freedom moves the liar in a definite direction, even though he may not arrive at the destination.

This notion of contributing cause or disposing factor is exemplified daily. Treating a child with suspicion, for example, tends to generate in him furtive, duplicitous behavior. Giving reasons for our actions disposes others toward reasonableness in a way that arbitrary use of superior force does not. While this is hardly a complete account of either habit or personality development, it should

clarify the sort of claim made when we say that lying endangers the liar's character or personality by means of its inherent disvalues. How does the first disvalue, restriction of the deceived's freedom, promote the habit of disrespect? And what sort of habit is it?

This sort of habit is a character defect or vice. The relationship established through the lie, altered freedom with regard to the subject at hand, always invites in us the general disposition to place ourselves above others in either thought or action. The deceived is immediately less free relative to us because of our action. The propensity toward this sort of relationship involves regarding the other as less worthy or capable of wielding freedom than ourselves. We are thereby encouraged by the lie to see ourselves as superior to others. This involves loss of proper perspective on ourselves as we esteem ourselves too highly, becoming arrogant. For lying is to arrogate to oneself the truth about the matter at hand as well as the truth about *oneself*, what the liar really believes. Such loss of perspective and denigration of others is a character failing.

"Character" refers to sets of habits and dispositions; of special moral significance are those of interpersonal prominence such as courage or honesty rather than technical varieties such as those making up driving competency. In discussing the implications of lying for the liar's character we are considering one kind of contingent consequence. But it is not obviously of the utilitarian stripe, not a matter of calculating satisfactions or other transitively ordered mental states. Character is not a momentary plus or minus to be weighed against other moments of positive or negative interest. Rather, considerations of character illuminate what we are as people; they penetrate to the level of identity. We might say that they unite the ontological and moral realms by taking a stand on what way of being is itself good.

It is interesting to notice how this claim of contingent danger to the liar's character bears on the "white" lie excuse and the "defensive" lie justification. White lies arise out of concern for the other's welfare. We are trying to avoid embarrassing someone or are trying to bring some pleasure into his or her life. The impetus toward disrespect is therefore mitigated by our concern for the other's well-being (though it is possible to have little respect for those you try to help). More importantly, the tendency toward disrespect is dampened by the fact that there is little gain in freedom vis-à-vis the deceived as a result of white lies. Because white lies typically do not involve serious restriction of the deceived's freedom, therefore, they do not move us greatly toward disrespect.

Neither are we in danger of becoming disrespectful as a result of lying in defense of our freedom. When justified, someone else either already has or is trying to constrain our freedom. Being put at a relative disadvantage is either actual or in the offing. Unjustified constraint of our freedom mitigates the danger lying poses to our character by altering the usual context in which virtue (and vice) is displayed or nurtured. It is not disrespectful to prevent another from unwarranted incursion on our freedom; he has already shown disrespect for us. Respecting others hardly demands conspiring in treating ourselves with disrespect. On the contrary, there is considerable strength in the argument that self-respect demands defending one's freedom, perhaps by means of a lie.

. . . It is instructive to note how the lack of respect shown in lying suggests several ways in which lying is distinct from and perhaps distinctively worse than other forms of deception. It may be that lying demonstrates greater disrespect than these sorts of deception or demonstrates it in a particularly insulting way.

First of all, the lie addresses another as a language user and then abuses that capacity. Lying *must* immediately abuse a dimension of human beings that is decisive to their humanity. Charles Fried points out that language is shared and communal in nature. Lying can succeed (as Kant's universalization procedure reveals) only against a backdrop of widespread truthfulness. The disrespect, then, is not merely for the deceived but for mankind in general since the lie trades upon a communal practice and human interdependence. In explicating Kant's claim that a lie "does wrong to men in general," and "injures humanity," Fried states: "Every lie violates the basic commitment to truth which stands behind the social fact of language."[14] This seems to be true and to help account for our repugnance at lying, but it is not enough to distinguish lying from non-lying linguistic deception.[15]

The social nature of language, however, may provide grounds for such differentiation. Lying is disrespectful to the deceived by being a kind of "treachery." Fried suggests that lying not only attacks the deceived but does so with an *instrument* (language) *that belongs to him:* the indignity of being struck with one's own property! But this is also true of linguistic deception in general. In lying, however, the treachery is greater because the deceived is attacked directly and completely with the shared linguistic instrument. Lying offers a complete falsification; the deceived is required simply to accept it passively. In both non-linguistic and non-lying linguistic deception, the deceived must actively make an inference from some outward behavior. At least some deference is paid to the deceived's reason as he is given some "reasoning room" in which to complete the attack on him; he must be somewhat of an accomplice to the deception process. In lying, however, we abuse language more flagrantly, using it to produce completely the opposite of what we believe true. Perhaps it is the flagrance with which we disrespect the deceived as language user that gives indignation to the phrase "boldfaced lie." Lying requires a boldness and coldness of purpose in order that we confront the other with a falsehood "complete-in-itself."

In a more pointed consideration of disrespect, Chisholm and Feehan return us to the particular relation between the liar and the deceived. They offer a quick suggestion as to why lying is thought worse than other kinds of deception. The deceived has a right to expect that the liar himself believes what he asserts.

If a person L *asserts* a proposition p to another person D, then D has the *right to expect* that L himself believes p. And it is assumed that L knows, or at least that he ought to know, that, if he asserts p to D, while believing himself that p is not true, then he violates this right of D's. But analogous assumptions are not made with respect to all other types of intended deception. . . . Lying, unlike the other types of intended deception, is essentially a breach of faith.[16]

Violating any right of another's exhibits lack of respect. But if Chisholm and Feehan are correct and lying involves a right with regard to expectation about the *liar himself*, then the disrespect seems heightened. The liar trades upon a trust placed in him as a speaker. The deceived is encouraged to believe that the liar is revealing his self and this aspect of falsely leading another "into" one's self amplifies the element of disrespect in cases of lying. . . .[17]

NOTES

1. Sissela Bok, *Lying: Moral Choice in Public and Private Life* (New York: Random House, 1978), p. 32.

2. Arnold Isenberg, "Deontology and the Ethics of Lying," in *Aesthetics and the Theory of Criticism; Selected Essays of Arnold Isenberg*, ed. William Callahan (Chicago: University of Chicago Press, 1973).

3. Roderick Chisholm and Thomas D. Feehan (in "The Intent to Deceive," *Journal of Philosophy*, 74, 3 [March 1977]: 143–159) offer a helpful albeit technically elaborate definition, a summary of which follows.

An individual *lies* when he *asserts* a proposition to another which he believes to be not true or false; he *asserts* a proposition when he *states* it under conditions which he believes justify the other in believing that he (the liar) intends to contribute causally to the other's believing that he (the liar) accepts the proposition; he *states* a proposition when he believes that the expression he utters has the standard use in the language of expressing this proposition and he thereby intends the other to believe that he (the liar) intends to utter the expression in this way.

The authors also fruitfully distinguish between deception by commission and deception by omission.

4. It is interesting to see what happens to my position in the case of unsuccessful lies, but we should keep in mind the specific bases of failure. If the failure is due to the would-be deceived not believing the false statement, then the first inherent disvalue (restriction on the deceived's freedom) is reversed. The attempted lie backfires on the liar and *he* loses freedom due to lack of trust just as he would when an initially successful lie is eventually "uncovered." The second inherent disvalue (self-opposition) still obtains, but briefly. Because the would-be deceived does not believe the statement, the opposition between what the liar says and believes dissipates, to be replaced, perhaps, by negative self-appraisal such as shame.

If the failure is due to the statement being true, again, the first inherent disvalue is reversed. The would-be deceived carries on believing a true statement. The "liar" however has two false beliefs: concerning the content of the statement *and* the would-be deceived's beliefs. Now, of course, the liar is no worse off after the lie with regard to the content of the conveyed belief; he thought it false before the lie and still does. But, believing that the would-be deceived now possesses a false belief could

rather easily restrict the liar's freedom. The liar has become his own deceived due to the truthfulness of the statement. The second inherent disvalue obtains since there is still opposition between what the liar believes and what he says.

Whether the contingent dangers are still risked is, of course, another question. If the "deceived" is not taken in by the lie, perhaps the liar risks self-loathing or resentment of the deceived (for not being an easy mark) rather than lose the respect for the deceived. If the statement is indeed true, perhaps the liar risks personality rift. He will still conceal his real beliefs; insulated from open discussion (in a way different from one who simply holds a false belief), the liar still has opposed himself in speech. The details of this discussion should be clarified by the subsequent examination of the two inherent disvalues and their risks to the liar.

5. S. I. Benn and W. L. Weinstein, "Being Free to Act and Being a Free Man," *Mind*, 80, 318 (April 1971), p. 197.

6. Ibid., p. 210.

7. I am using the word simply to distinguish the one who lies from the deceived or other parties. Strictly speaking, only those habituated to lying are properly considered "liars."

8. Isenberg, "Deontology and the Ethics of Lying," p. 260.

9. Contrary to some philosophers, e.g., Bok, we see an important difference between excusing and justifying actions (including lies). We excuse the *person* for committing the act; he is exonerated because of circumstances or some state he is in. Being misinformed about a danger, for example, might excuse someone for lying. But the fact that the lie occurred is nevertheless lamentable or unfortunate. The *act* is still wrong and is excused *after* the fact.

On the other hand, we *justify* an *action*: after *and* before its performance. Circumstances or relationships make morally permissible what might otherwise be prohibited. Lying might be justified, for example, by an individual's manifest intentions to do harm. The act is not wrong, though we might decry the circumstances which permit it.

The distinction between excuses and justifications will be developed specifically in connection with the way lying restricts freedom.

10. The ability to reason might well be impaired in the extreme sort of case: a lie *about* the reasoning process itself. Thus, a seemingly far-fetched lie about the harmfulness of inductive reasoning (in deference, perhaps, to divination) would likely undermine the deceived's reasoning capacity itself.

11. I do not mean to suggest that white lies are the only or main cases of excused lies. But their frequency and demarcated "classification" makes them compelling examples. A *serious* lie could, of course, be excused, e.g., because of an excusable error on the part of the liar.

12. It is because Kant has an abstract view of freedom, unindividuated and unaffected by concrete conditions, that his strictures on lying (among other practices) cannot take coercion into account. Yet coercion provides just the sort of cases which make his moral conclusions seem counter-intuitive.

13. In deontological language: the unjustified threat to my freedom mitigates my "prima facie" duty not to lie or the presumption of such a duty. Prima facie or presumptive duties are the deontologist's formulations of prohibitions which may be overridden in particular cases. The deontologist, however, bases duty on the concept of freedom. Freedom is the ground of duty. Therefore, the jeopardization of freedom is not on a par with other considerations of duty. Freedom reaches "deeper" than any particular duty, such as not to lie, since it grounds them all. Thus, defending my freedom is not on the same moral level with my particular duty not to lie. It takes precedence over such particular duties.

14. Charles Fried, *Right and Wrong* (Cambridge, Mass.: Harvard University Press, 1978), p. 68.

15. An example of non-lying linguistic deception might be helpful. Suppose that I am asked whether I expect to attend a meeting tomorrow and I reply, "No, I'm leaving for Chicago tomorrow." Although I *am* leaving for Chicago tomorrow, my departure in no way interferes with attending the meeting: I could easily do both. The ques-

tioner quite reasonably and simply "fills in" that the departure would interfere with attending the meeting and infers the false belief that attendance is impossible *because* I am leaving town. He takes me to be offering a *reason* when I have literally only laid the statement about leaving town *alongside* my negative response.

It might be, however, that this and all other non-lying linguistic deception can plausibly be analyzed as an implicit or elliptical lie in which the deceived reasonably fills in the false belief (which the liar never explicitly states). Thus, in the above example, the deceived questioner infers that I won't be attending the meeting *because* I will be on my way to Chicago. On this analysis of non-lying linguistic deception, it escapes the label "lie" on a "mere technicality"—a difference without much difference. If cogent, we should not chafe at the lack of a strong basis for differentiating the sub-species of lies from linguistic deception as a whole.

16. Chisholm and Feehan, "The Intent to Deceive," p. 153.

17. If lying shows greater disrespect than other forms of deception (including non-lying linguistic deception), then it should follow from my position that lying has a greater tendency to engender disrespect as a character trait, or a tendency to engender a greater degree of disrespect.

IVAN PRESTON

*R*easonable Consumer or Ignorant Consumer? How the FTC Decided

Is the Federal Trade Commission obligated to protect only reasonable, sensible, intelligent consumers who conduct themselves carefully in the marketplace? Or must it also protect ignorant consumers who conduct themselves carelessly?

Since its origin in 1914 the Commission has varied its answer to these questions. It has committed itself at all times to prohibit seller's claims which would deceive reasonable people, but has undergone changes of direction on whether to ban claims which would deceive only ignorant people. At times it has acted on behalf of the latter by

invoking the "ignorant man standard."[1] At other times it has been ordered by courts to ignore these people and invoke the "reasonable man standard." In still other cases it has chosen to protect certain ignorant persons but not others.

The significance of the issue is that the FTC will rule against the fewest types of seller's claims under the reasonable man standard, and against the most under the ignorant man standard. The latter guideline therefore means, in the eyes of many, the greatest protection for the consuming public. Consumerists may feel, in fact, that such a

From *The Great American Blow-Up*, by Ivan Preston, 1975, The University of Wisconsin Press. Reprinted by permission of The University of Wisconsin Press.

standard should be mandatory on the grounds that a flat prohibition is needed against all seller's deceptions which would deceive anyone at all.

The FTC, however, works under a constraint which makes it necessary to temper its allegiance to the ignorant man standard. The constraint is that the Commission may proceed legally only in response to substantial public interest.[2] Over the years the Commissioners have been sensitive to the argument that there is no public interest in prohibiting messages which would deceive only a small number of terribly careless, stupid, or naive people. To explain the compelling nature of this argument, I would like to describe a deception of that sort.

In my hometown of Pittsburgh, Pennsylvania, there appears each Christmastime a brand of beer called Olde Frothingslosh. This quaint item is nothing but Pittsburgh Brewing Company's regular Iron City Beer in its holiday costume, decked out with a specially designed label to provide a few laughs. The label identifies the product as "the pale stale ale for the pale stale male," and there is similar wit appended, all strictly nonsense. One of the best is a line saying that Olde Frothingslosh is the only beer in which the foam is on the bottom.

My old friend at Pittsburgh Brewing, John deCoux, the ad manager there, once told me about a woman who bought some Olde Frothingslosh to amuse friends at a party, and was embarrassed to find the claim was nothing but a *big lie:* the foam was right up there on top where it was on every other brand of beer she'd ever seen! She wanted her money back from the beer distributor (another quaint Pennsylvania custom), but he told her Hell, no, so she went to her lawyer with the intention of bringing suit. The story (and it's true) ended right there; the lawyer told her to forget it. She would have had less chance than poor Herbert Williams,[3] because air conditioners have been known to exist on automobiles but nobody in earth's history ever saw a beer with the foam on the bottom. The reasonable man (woman! person!) standard would be applied to her suit, her reliance on the belief about the foam would be judged unreasonable, and that would be the end of that.

Had the ignorant man standard applied she would possibly have succeeded, which illustrates the difference the choice of standards makes. It also illustrates the essential weakness (in conjunc-

tion with definite strengths) possessed by a legal standard which sets out to protect everybody from everything. Many of the prohibitions it produces would eliminate only infinitesimal amounts of deception.

There are other reasons, too, for the FTC's cautious attitude toward the ignorant man standard. One problem is that the Commission does not have the resources to prosecute all cases;[4] therefore those which are investigated might better be ones which endanger greater numbers of people. Another problem is that an extreme concern for the ignorant could lead to repression of much communication content useful to consumers, and could lead as well to possible violation of the First Amendment's freedom of speech guarantee.[5]

Probably the most important objection to the ignorant man standard is that the reasonable man standard was traditional in the common law which preceded the development of the FTC in 1914. The common law held that to avoid being negligent a person must act as a reasonable person would act under like circumstances.[6] Mention of the reasonable or prudent person first appeared in an English case of 1837[7] and has been in widespread use since.

I have described the concept of negligence in discussing misrepresentation law,[8] but am using it here in a different sense. The earlier use involved whether the seller (defendant) was negligent: did he state a misrepresentation which he didn't know but ought to have known was false, and which deceived and damaged the recipient (plaintiff)? Here, however, the question is whether something called contributory negligence may be charged against the plaintiff, the person deceived. He brings a suit against the deceiver, and the rules require him to assert and show that he relied upon the misrepresentation, and that the damages suffered were a result of such reliance. In addition, he must show that his reliance was justified—that is, his reliance must pass the test of the conduct of a reasonable person. He may not claim to have relied on a statement which sensible and prudent people would recognize as preposterous. If he does, he is guilty of contributory negligence which the deceiver may use as a defense which can result in having the suit dismissed.[9]

This rule usually does not apply in the case of a

fraudulent misrepresentation, where the deceiver consciously knows it was false and intentionally seeks to deceive with it. If that is shown, the person deceived is entitled to rely without having to justify his reliance as reasonable.[10] But an exception to the exception comes with puffery and the other false but legally nondeceptive claims which are the topic of this book. The law states that people know and understand they are not to rely on such misrepresentations, even when stated fraudulently.[11] Therefore with these kinds of statements the reasonable man standard, when it is the prevailing standard, applies.

At the time the FTC was created, the only specific law on these matters was the common law just described. The FTC Act said nothing explicitly about what persons the Commission was authorized to protect; it said only that proceedings must "be in the interest of the public."[12] The most obvious way of pursuing this mandate would have been to follow the common law precedents and embrace the reasonable man standard. Instead, the FTC did the unexpected and flaunted the reasonable man standard in many of its early cases. Neither that concept nor a replacement standard were discussed explicitly, but numerous cases show that the Commission was applying an ignorant man standard or a close approximation of it. In 1919 it ordered a manufacturer to stop advertising that its automobile batteries would "last forever."[13] One might assume that no reasonable person even in that year would have relied upon the claim literally, especially when the same ads offered a service by which "the purchaser pays 50 cents per month and is entitled to a new battery as soon as the old one is worn out." The FTC saw the latter phrase, however, as confirming the falsity and deceptiveness rather than the sheer frivolousness of "last forever." The case indicates the Commission was developing a deliberate policy of stopping deceptions which would deceive only a minority.[14]

This switch to the ignorant man standard appeared questionable legally; precedent did not support it. But before we describe the eventual court considerations of this matter, we should acknowledge that there was much argument against the reasonable man standard in common sense if not in law. The legal conception of the buyer who failed to be reasonable in the marketplace was that of a person who made a stupid purchase through his own fault—he should have known better.[15] It was this conception with which common sense could disagree. Some so-called stupid choices may be made not through carelessness but through the impossibility of obtaining and assessing information even when great caution and intelligence are applied. The world of goods and services was once simple, but has become terribly technical. Many poor choices are made by persons who *couldn't* know better.

These problems might have been incorporated into the reasonable man standard by adjusting that standard to the realities of the market. Consider a store scene in which a product is available at six cans for a dollar while one can is sixteen cents. In considering whether a reasonable person would be deceived, the law might have taken into account that many people are slow at arithmetic, and that the bustle of a market and the need to make many other choices in the same few minutes render it unlikely they would fully use the mathematical capacity they possess. The competence assumed of a "reasonable person" might have been reduced accordingly, and the traditional standard, altered in this way, might still have been applied.

What actually occurred in legal actions was something bordering on the opposite. The reasonable person came to be regarded as a *better* than average person, as someone who was never negligent and who therefore was entirely fictitious outside the courtroom.[16] He was "an ideal creature. . . . The factor controlling the judgment of [his] conduct is not what *is*, but *what ought to be*."[17] The law, apparently, had created an unreasonable conception of the reasonable person.

It was this problem the FTC sought to correct. We do not know, because the point was not discussed as such, whether the Commission regarded its new conception as a move to the ignorant man standard or as a redefinition of the reasonable man standard by the method described above. But the practical effect was the same either way—the Commission moved toward protecting the public from deceptions which regulators previously had ignored because they did not harm the fictitiously reasonable person.

Considerations of the reasonable and ignorant man standards eventually were made explicit through the intervention of appeals court decisions into FTC affairs. In *John C. Winston* of 1924,[18] the Commission outlawed a sales method which offered an encyclopedia "free" provided a purchaser paid $49 for two supplementary updating services. The seller appealed and won a reversal on the grounds that no deception was involved: "It is conceivable that a very stupid person might be misled by this method of selling books, yet measured by ordinary standards of trade and by ordinary standards of the intelligence of traders, we cannot discover that it amounts to an unfair method of competition. . . ."[19]

The FTC did not adopt the reasonable man standard as a result of this ruling; its subsequent activities reflected instead a posture of resistance.[20] When it stubbornly invoked a similar restraint against a different encyclopedia company, Standard Education Society, in 1931,[21] it was again reversed by an appeals court.[22] Circuit Judge Learned Hand was most adamant in declaring that "a community which sells for profit must not be ridden on so short a rein that it can only move at a walk. We cannot take seriously the suggestion that a man who is buying a set of books and a ten year's 'extension service,' will be fatuous enough to be misled by the mere statement that the first are given away, and that he is paying only for the second. Nor can we conceive how he could be damaged were he to suppose that that was true. Such trivial niceties are too impalpable for practical affairs, they are will-o'-the-wisps which divert attention from substantial evils."

This time, however, the FTC took the case to the Supreme Court, where a new justice delivering his first opinion told Learned Hand that the encyclopedia decision *was* a substantial evil. Hugo Black's opinion in *FTC v. Standard Education* of 1937[23] restored the Commission's use of the ignorant man standard: "The fact that a false statement may be obviously false to those who are trained and experienced does not change its character, nor take away its power to deceive others less experienced. There is no duty resting upon a citizen to suspect the honesty of those with whom he transacts business. Laws are made to protect the trusting as well as the suspicious. The best element of business has long since decided that honesty should govern competitive enterprises, and that the rule of caveat emptor should not be relied upon to reward fraud and deception."

Though Black mentioned the name of neither standard, his words suggest he was rejecting the reasonable man standard rather than proposing merely to adjust it. Black's words, above all, led to the concept of an "ignorant man standard" for the FTC in place of what went before.

Just how *Standard Education* was supported by precedent is a curious question. Justice Black's opinion cited none. It affirmed that the sales method not merely had deceptive capacity but clearly deceived many persons, and it also stated that the deception was committed knowingly and deliberately.[24] This suggests that the Supreme Court was invoking the common law notion that the reasonable man standard should not apply in case of deliberate deception. Something left unclarified, however, is what significance such a ruling should have for an agency such as the FTC which routinely did not make findings of deliberate deception. Deliberate intent to deceive undoubtedly occurs in many cases where no one can prove it. The whole advantage of FTC procedure, in comparison with what went before, was that it could rule seller's messages out of the marketplace *without* bothering with the traditional requirement of proving intent. What was the advantage, then, of obtaining the right to use the ignorant man standard only in conjunction with proving intent to deceive?

The result, strangely, was that the FTC, on the basis of *Standard Education*, began applying the ignorant man standard liberally without regard for determining intent, and in some cases without regard for the fact that intent to deceive was almost surely absent. The appeals courts, also via *Standard Education*, approved this procedure. The trend was thoroughly questionable but was pursued decisively, particularly by the Second Circuit Court of Appeals, the court which *Standard Education* had reversed. In *General Motors v. FTC* of 1940,[25] a case involving a "6% time payment plan" which actually charged 11.5 percent interest, the Second Circuit's Judge Augustus Hand concluded: "It may be that there was no intention to mislead and that only the careless or the incompetent could have been misled. But if the Commission, having discretion to deal with these matters, thinks it best to insist upon a form of advertising clear enough so that, in the words of the prophet Isaiah, 'wayfaring men, though fools, shall not err therein,' it is not for the courts to revise their judgment."

The influence of the *Standard Education* reversal was unmistakable on the one Hand—and on the other Hand as well. When Judge Learned Hand considered an appeal to the Second Circuit of the Commission's finding of deception in an admittedly untrue claim that "one Moretrench wellpoint is as good as any five others,"[26] he said: "It is extremely hard to believe that any buyers of such machinery could be misled by anything which was patently no more than the exuberant enthusiasm of a satisfied customer, but in such matters we understand that we are to insist upon the most literal truthfulness. Federal Trade Commission v. Standard Education Society. . . ."

Turning to another literally untrue Moretrench claim, that its product had an advantage to which "contractors all over the world testify," Hand stated: "It is again hard to imagine how anyone reading it could have understood it as more than puffing; yet for the reasons we have just given, if the Commission saw fit to take notice of it, we may not interfere."

It was clear that the Second Circuit's Hands were tied. Substitution of the ignorant man standard for the reasonable man standard proceeded in additional Second Circuit cases,[27] and in others as well.[28] Under these liberal interpretations the FTC appeared during most of the 1940s to be knocking down right and left every advertising claim it thought had the slightest chance of deceiving even the most ignorant person. There was a good bit of unchecked exuberance in this spree, including the action against Charles of the Ritz's use of "Rejuvenescence" as a name for its face cream.[29] The FTC outlawed the term on the grounds that it referred literally to the restoration of youth and the appearance of youth. The company protested that it was merely a "boastful and fanciful word" used nondeceptively, but the Second Circuit agreed with the Commission. I find it amusing that Charles of the Ritz has been using the trade name "Revenescence" ever since, avoiding the literal meaning but apparently retaining some of the persuasive value it once received from "Rejuvenescence."

The Second Circuit's thoughtfulness toward the ignorant man reached an extreme when it agreed with the FTC in forbidding Clairol to say that its dye will "color hair permanently."[30] The FTC thought the public would take that as a claim that all the hair a person grows for the rest of her life will emerge in the Clairol color. That expectation was based on the testimony of a single witness who said she thought somebody might think that—although she added that *she* wouldn't.

On Clairol's appeal one judge of the Second Circuit, Clark, agreed fully with the FTC: "Petitioner's [Clairol's] actual defense is that no one should be fooled—a defense repudiated every time it has been offered on appellate review, so far as I know, since it is well settled that the Commission does not act for the sophisticated alone."

The majority of judges, Swan and Augustus Hand, disagreed with this reasoning. They said they couldn't imagine *anybody* believing the Clairol claim: "There is no dispute that it imparts a permanent coloration to the hair to which it is applied, but the commission found that it has 'no effect upon new hair,' and hence concluded that the representation as to permanence was misleading. It seems scarcely possible that any user of the preparation could be so credulous as to suppose that hair not yet grown out would be colored by an application of the preparation to the head. But the commission has construed the advertisement as so representing it. . . ."

Nonetheless, the majority said, they had to support the FTC position no matter what they personally thought: "Since the Act is for the protection of the trusting as well as the suspicious, as stated in Federal Trade Commission v. Standard Education Society . . . we think the order must be sustained on this point."

In basing the decision on *Standard Education*, the Second Circuit offered no judgment that the Clairol claim was used with intent to deceive, and made no acknowledgment that *Standard Education* might have been intended by the Supreme Court to apply only where such intent was evident. The inclination to apply the ignorant man standard appears to have overridden any other consideration. We may speculate that if the Olde Frothingslosh matter had been appealed to the Second Circuit in the same year as the Clairol case, 1944, the purchaser might have recovered damages because the beer's foam wasn't on the bottom!

This [selection] thus far has discussed the development of a strong emphasis on the ignorant man standard. The next task is to describe how this emphasis came to be diluted, a matter which involved additional curious events. One of the arbitrary facts of life in American law is that the various circuit courts of appeal are sometimes inconsistent in their rulings. They need not take each other's decisions into account, so a case may be decided differently in one than in another. The Second Circuit was the one reversed by *Standard Education*, and we have seen that this court in subsequent cases applied the ignorant man standard assiduously. This included the prohibition of puffery in *Moretrench*, even though puffery had traditionally been called nondeceptive. With its long-standing immunity, puffery might have been expected to resist the courts even if nothing else did, but under the ignorant man standard the Second Circuit moved to eliminate this kind of falsity along with everything else.

But the time came, in 1946, when a puffery case was appealed to the Seventh Circuit rather than the Second, and the difference was significant. *Carlay*[31] involved a claim that Ayds candy mints make weight-reducing easy, which the FTC said was false. On appeal the Seventh Circuit,[32] which had tended earlier to object to the ignorant man standard,[33] decided, "What was said was clearly justifiable ... under those cases recognizing that such words as 'easy,' 'perfect,' 'amazing,' 'prime,' 'wonderful,' 'excellent,' are regarded in law as mere puffing or dealer's talk upon which no charge of misrepresentation can be based." The court cited previous non-FTC cases which allowed puffery,[34] and completely ignored the cases stemming from Justice Black and the Second Circuit, which would have supported the FTC's outlawing of "easy."

As a result the FTC had a contradiction on its hands. The Second Circuit told it to protect the ignorant man; the Seventh Circuit told it to permit puffery which could deceive the ignorant man. The contradiction might have been resolved by the Supreme Court, but was never considered there. The FTC's resolution was to allow puffery thereafter, which tended to dilute the ignorant man standard.

The trend away from the extreme ignorant man standard had begun, but only slightly. Cases followed in which the FTC retained a strong protective stance on behalf of ignorant consumers.[35] But in 1963 the Commission finally commented that the standard could be carried too far. *Heinz W. Kirchner*[36] was a case about an inflatable device to

help a person stay afloat and learn to swim. Called Swim-Ezy, it was worn under the swimming suit and advertised as being invisible. It was not invisible, but the FTC found it to be "inconspicuous," and ruled that that was all the claim of invisibility would mean to the public: "The possibility that some person might believe Swim-Ezy is, not merely inconspicuous, but wholly invisible or bodiless, seems to us too far-fetched to warrant intervention."

What about the few persons who would accept this "far-fetched" belief? The Commission made clear it no longer intended to protect such ignorant persons:

True ... the Commission's responsibility is to prevent deception of the gullible and credulous, as well as the cautious and knowledgeable. ... This principle loses its validity, however, if it is applied uncritically or pushed to an absurd extreme. An advertiser cannot be charged with liability in respect of every conceivable misconception, however outlandish, to which his representations might be subject among the foolish or feeble-minded. ... A representation does not become "false and deceptive" merely because it will be unreasonably misunderstood by an insignificant and unrepresentative segment of the class of persons to whom the representation is addressed.

That is the position the FTC has followed since. It holds no longer to the strict ignorant man standard by which it would protect everyone from everything which may deceive them.[37] It would reject consideration, for example, of the Olde Frothingslosh claim which apparently fooled only one stray individual. Perhaps we may call the new stance a modified ignorant man standard which protects only those cases of foolishness which are committed by significant numbers of people.

Some readers may protest that any behaviors which are customary for a substantial portion of the population shouldn't be called "ignorant." They might rather call the new stance a modified reasonable man standard in which what is reasonable has been equated more closely than before with what is average or typical.[38] Whatever the name, however, the FTC's present position appears to remain closer to the spirit and practice of the strict ignorant man standard of the 1940s than to the reasonable man standard of tradition.[39]

NOTES

1. "Ignorant man standard" is my own term, which I feel is correctly blunt. The terms "credulous man standard" and "lowest standard of intelligence," which lack semantic punch, have been used elsewhere; see *Truth in Advertising: A Symposium of the Toronto School of Theology*, 2–3, 30–34 (1972); Ira M. Millstein, "The Federal Trade Commission and false advertising," 64 *Columbia Law Rev.* 439, 458–62 (1964).

2. FTC Act, § 5(b); see chapter 9, note 1; Millstein, "False advertising," 483–87; "Developments in the law—deceptive advertising," 80 *Harvard Law Rev.* 1005, 1023–25 (1967).

3. See chapter 2, at note 13.

4. "Deceptive advertising," 1082; Millstein, "False advertising," 494; Edward F. Cox, Robert C. Fellmuth, and John E. Schulz, *Nader's Raiders: Report on the Federal Trade Commission* (1969).

5. Millstein, "False advertising," 462–65; "Deceptive advertising," 1027–38; Peter B. Turk, "Justice Hugo Black and advertising: the stepchild of the First Amendment," in *For Freedom of Expression: Essays in Honor of Hugo L. Black*, ed. Dwight L. Teeter and David Grey (in press).

6. *Restatement of the Law of Torts (Second)*, § 283 (1965). Section 283A adds that a child must act as would a reasonable person of like age, intelligence, and experience under like circumstances.

7. *Vaughan v. Menlove*, 3 Bing. N.C. 468, 132 Eng. Rep. 490 (1837). For other cases and references see Reporter's Notes to § 283 of *Restatement of Torts (Second)*.

8. See chapter 6, following note 10.

9. The term *contributory negligence* is not always used, but the idea of denying recovery for unreasonable reliance on misrepresentations is based on that concept; William L. Prosser, *Handbook of the Law of Torts*, 4th ed., 717 (1971).

10. Prosser, ibid., 716.

11. See extended discussions in chapters 3, 7, 11.

12. FTC Act, § 5(b); see chapter 9, note 1.

13. *FTC v. Universal Battery*, 2 FTC 95 (1919).

14. See also *FTC v. A. A. Berry*, 2 FTC 427 (1920); *FTC v. Alben-Harley*, 4 FTC 31 (1921); *FTC v. Williams Soap*, 6 FTC 107 (1923); *Alfred Peats*, 8 FTC 366 (1925).

15. See discussion above at note 6 ff.

16. *Restatement of Torts (Second)*, § 283, comment c.

17. Francis H. Bohlen, "Mixed questions of law and fact," 72 *Univ. of Pennsylvania Law Rev.* 111, 113 (1923).

18. 8 FTC 177 (1924).

19. *John C. Winston v. FTC*, 3 F.2d 961 (3rd Cir., 1925).

20. *Nugrape*, 9 FTC 20 (1925); *Ostermoor*, 10 FTC 45 (1926), but set aside in *Ostermoor v. FTC*, 16 F.2d 962 (2d Cir., 1927); *William F. Schied*, 10 FTC 85 (1926); *Good Grape*, 10 FTC 99 (1926); *Hobart Bradstreet*, 11 FTC 174 (1927); *Frank P. Snyder*, 11 FTC 390 (1927); *Dr. Eagan*, 11 FTC 436 (1927); *Berkey & Gay Furniture*, 12 FTC 227 (1928), but set aside in *Berkey & Gay Furniture v. FTC*, 42 F.2d 427 (6th Cir., 1930); *Northam-Warren*, 15 FTC 389 (1931), but set aside in *Northam-Warren v. FTC*, 59 F.2d 196 (2d Cir., 1932); *Fairyfoot Products* 20 FTC 40 (1934), affirmed in *Fairyfoot v. FTC*, 80 F.2d 684 (7th Cir., 1935).

21. *Standard Education Society*, 16 FTC 1 (1931).

22. *FTC v. Standard Education Society*, 86 F.2d 692 (2d Cir., 1936).

23. 302 U.S. 112, 58 S.C. 113 (1937).

24. Ibid., 116: "It was clearly the practice of respondents through their agents, in accordance with a well matured plan, to mislead customers. . . ."

25. 114 F.2d 33 (2d Cir., 1940).

26. *Moretrench v. FTC* 127, F.2d (2d Cir., 1942). This was the same judge who once had rejected similar claims on the grounds that "there are some kinds of talk which no man takes seriously . . ."; *Vulcan Metals v. Simmons*; see chapter 7, note 24.

27. See notes 29 and 30 below.

28. *D.D.D. v. FTC* (1942); see chapter 9, note 26; *Aronberg v. FTC* (1942), see chapter 9, note 34; *Gulf Oil v. FTC*, 150 F.2d 106 (5th Cir., 1945); *Parker Pen v. FTC*, 159 F.2d 509 (7th Cir., 1946). In the latter case the FTC's role was said to be to "protect the casual, one might say the negligent, reader, as well as the vigilant and more intelligent. . . ." A much-used quotation, cited in *Aronberg, Gulf Oil*, and *Gelb* (see note 30 below), stated, "The law is not made for the protection of experts, but for the public—that vast multitude which includes the ignorant, the unthinking, and the credulous, who, in making purchases, do not stop to analyze, but are governed by appearances and general impressions"; *Florence v. Dowd*, 178 F. 73 (2d. Cir., 1910). This was a pre-FTC case with evidence of deliberate deception.

29. *Charles of the Ritz v. FTC*, 143 F.2d 676 (2d Cir., 1944), following *Charles of the Ritz*, 34 FTC 1203 (1942).

30. *Gelb v. FTC*, 144 F.2d 580 (2d Cir., 1944), following *Gelb*, 33 FTC 1450 (1941).

31. 39 FTC 357 (1944).

32. *Carlay v. FTC*, 153 F.2d 493 (1946).

33. *Allen B. Wrisley v. FTC*, 113 F.2d 437 (7th Cir., 1940); also later in *Buchsbaum v. FTC*, 160 F.2d 121 (7th Cir., 1947).

34. See detailed discussion of such cases in chapter 7.

35. *Lorillard v. FTC* (1950), see chapter 9, note 35; *Independent Directory*, 47 FTC 13 (1950) (but see dissent by Commissioner Mason); *Goodman v. FTC*, 244 F.2d 584 (9th Cir., 1957); *FTC v. Sewell*, 353 U.S. 969, 77 S.C. 1055 (1957) (see chapter 11, at note 32); *Bantam Books v. FTC*, 275 F.2d 680 (2d Cir., 1960) (but see questions raised by Judge Moore); *Exposition Press v. FTC*, 295 F.2d 869 (2d

Cir., 1961); *Giant Food v. FTC*, 322 F.2d 977 (D.C. Cir., 1963); *FTC v. Colgate*, 380 U.S. 374, 85 S.C. 1035 (1965) (see chapter 15, at notes 38–42).

36. 63 FTC 1282 (1963).

37. In *Papercraft*, 63 FTC 1965, 1997 (1963), Commissioner MacIntyre protested that the retreat from the extreme ignorant man position was unfortunate. The majority opinion had withdrawn from protecting the "foolish or feeble-minded," and MacIntyre dissented: "Should this observation be construed as a retreat from our long-held position that the public as a whole is entitled to protection, including even 'the ignorant, the unthinking, and the credulous,' then the result may well be confusion."

38. *Truth in Advertising*, 31.

39. "It might be said that the test of consumer competence generally employed by the Commission appears to approximate the least sophisticated level of understanding possessed by any substantial portion of the class of persons to whom the advertisement is addressed." Personal correspondence to Peter B. Turk from Gale T. Miller, law clerk, Bureau of Consumer Protection, Federal Trade Commission, December 6, 1971. The "class of persons" assumed generally consists of adults. Special consideration for representations made to children (see note 6) was recognized in *FTC v. Keppel*, 291 U.S. 304, 54 S.C. 423 (1934). As for other groups, Miller wrote: "It is the position of the staff that advertising geared towards other special audiences, such as the ghetto dweller, the elderly, and the handicapped, might also be subjected to a more rigorous test than is applied to advertisements addressed to the public at large."

JAMES C. MILLER
Why FTC Curbs Are Needed

When the Federal Trade Commission began its children's advertising rule making, the advertising community moved to eliminate the FTC's jurisdiction over unfair advertising. The "kidvid" experience revealed that the only limit on the commission's powers under the unfairness standard was the imagination of those in charge.

It is time to describe, that is, to specify the FTC's basic mission. It is time Congress set limits on what is now virtually unlimited authority. Broad power in the hands of a few nonelected officials is neither in the public's interest nor, paradoxically, in the agency's interest. Indeed, I believe that one reason the agency has been under so much fire recently is that under Section 5 of the FTC Act three commissioners could just as easily wreak havoc as pursue the interest of the public.

The commission's authority needs to be narrowed and redefined. That, in my view, is the right approach, not exempting special interest groups. A more directed FTC would mean a clearer focus on real problems and more benefits for individual consumers, for providers of goods and services and for the advertising industry.

Should advertisers achieve their goal—the elimination of our unfairness jurisdiction over commercial speech—they would discover they had won a battle but lost the war. Unfairness is only half the critical phrase of our statute. The other half is deception. It too, needs attention as a legal concept. Indeed, with respect to advertising, almost anything the agency has ever done, or proposed to do under its fairness jurisdiction, could have been addressed under a deception theory.

The very proceeding that demonstrated the breadth of the commission's unfairness doctrine—children's advertising—might well have been based on a deception theory. Indeed, the initial staff report proposed the rule making on the basis of *both* unfairness and deception.

The report argued that advertising to young children is inherently deceptive because children can't distinguish between ads and programs. Based on this alleged deception, as well as upon unfairness, commission lawyers asserted that the ads should be banned. As for sugared products, the staff argued that the ads' failure to mention the adverse health effects of sugar was deceptive.

In sum, the staff believed that the commission could proceed with the children's advertising rule under either the deception standard or under an unfairness theory. (When the staff recommended ending "kidvid," it was because of the difficulties in defining which ads would be covered, not because they thought the legal basis was inadequate.)

Another example of the breadth of the commission's deception jurisdiction involves the staff's proposal for rotational warnings to advise consumers on the specific health hazards of smoking. The proposed legal basis for commission action is that if some consumers do not know that smoking causes heart attacks, then it is deceptive to advertise cigarets without disclosing that fact.

No one argues that current advertisements imply that cigarets *don't* cause heart attacks. Instead, they argue that some consumers do not have the requisite information linking cigarets with heart attacks. Let me make clear that I'm not addressing whether Congress should impose a rotational warning scheme. My point is that if the commission can require cigaret health warnings under a deception theory, what couldn't it do in other areas of advertising?

Deception seems to be a concrete word, one independent of the perceptions of individual commissioners. Perhaps it is because the meaning of the word seems obvious that the central element of the current definition is circular—that an ad is deceptive if it has a "tendency or capacity to deceive." Within this broad definition, the commission's law of deception has few limits. For example, the commission need not interpret an ad's claim as would a reasonable consumer.

Consider the case against Ford. The company produced an ad describing a mileage test. The test covered how the cars were broken in, how fast they were driven and so forth. The ads also said, "You yourself might actually average less, or for that matter more. Because mileage varies according to maintenance, equipment, total weight, driving habits and road conditions. And no two drivers, or even cars, are exactly the same." Nevertheless, the FTC read this carefully qualified claim to mean that the *average* driver would get the advertised mileage and demanded substantiation. Quick-on-the-trigger action of this type may keep valuable information from being disseminated.

The Ford case illustrates an additional problem. The commission can evaluate claims with only its own "expertise." Sometimes how a reasonable consumer will interpret an ad is obvious. I believe that the commission should be bound to consult research evidence, such as surveys of consumer responses.

Of course it is occasionally inappropriate to base deception only on whether reasonable consumers are misled. Certain groups are particularly vulnerable. An example would be a miracle cure aimed at the terminally ill.

There is another major problem with the commission's discretion with respect to deception. The commission doesn't have to consider if consumers have actually been harmed. The Poli-Grip denture cream case is illustrative. The ad claimed users could eat "problem" foods. Although this product was inexpensive, frequently purchased and, by its nature, something each consumer could easily evaluate, the commission took issue with the ads. As then-commissioner Thompson put it: "It is inconceivable to me that any denture wearer who applied Poli-Grip or Super Poli-Grip and bit into a red apple and then saw his dentures smiling back at him would ever purchase the gripper again."

Finally, under current law the commission can find an ad deceptive not only for what it says but for what it does not say. For example, the commission has required sellers of salt substitutes to state that the products are not appropriate for those on potassium-restricted diets. The commission found the ads to be deceptive and required this disclosure even though the ads made no claims regarding potassium.

As I've argued elsewhere, the commission needs new legislation defining the term "unfair." I've tried to show here the need for a similar clarification of our deceptive jurisdiction.

Legislation is needed to provide a clear mission for the FTC now and in the future. If Congress acts, the commission will be able to give more specific guidance to its staff. Advertisers will have a better indication of what is permitted and what is prohibited. And consumers will receive more accurate information on which to base their purchasing decisions.

RALPH K. WINTER, JR.

Advertising and Legal Theory

ADVERTISING AND THE LAW

No commentator seriously contends that advertising should be regulated regardless of the cost imposed on consumers. Nor should anyone seriously contend that the regulation of advertising be undertaken for any reason except the protection of consumers.

The issue thus is whether or not the costs of a particular regulation are greater or less than the benefits to consumers gained thereby. Estimating costs and measuring them against the estimated benefits invariably lead to a substantial measure of disagreement, although much of that disagreement can be resolved by locating a burden of proof in the proper way. The burden of demonstrating the cost-benefit judgment ought to be placed on those calling for the regulation of advertising rather than on those who object to it. This is so for three reasons.

First, the benefits derived from advertising are more verifiable than the costs of deceptive or other harmful advertising practices. The latter are in many ways avoidable on the consumer's part and claims about the extent of damage from them are almost always impressionistic. What we do know is that the suppression of advertising impairs competition. It is difficult to see what could replace advertising as a means of informing the consumer if its role is diminished.

Second, because law schools and economics departments are so often fully engaged in their assigned task of discovering market failure, all too little has been done in the way of examining the costs of regulation and the incidence of regulation failure. Not only the bureaucratic budget and the overt costs incurred by those regulated, in the way of lawyers' fees and the like, are involved. Every mistake an agency makes in the regulation of advertising is as harmful to the consumer as fraud.

The consumer who does not buy a product he would have enjoyed because advertising is suppressed or because the product is not produced because of the disincentives created by FTC rules is also injured. Injury to consumers is thus as easily accomplished by regulation failure as market failure.

Third, the premises of a democratic society compel us to view the consumer as having powers of discernment and the ability to maintain a level of resistance to advocacy. We cannot consistently call for the vigorous straining of all commercial information received by the public while trusting the very same public to separate the wheat from the chaff in a robust open political debate. Unless we are to decide for the consumer what is best for him—a far cry from democracy—we ought to be as reliant on the marketplace of ideas in the commercial world as in the world of politics.[1]

The Regulation of Deceptive Advertising

As a threshold proposition all would agree that government ought somehow to provide a suitable remedy for fraud. This remedy might well be administrative if suits by consumers are thought to be too unwieldy procedurally or if it is believed that intervention is necessary because false advertisers are getting a "free ride" on the reputation of those who advertise truthfully and thus are diminishing the overall incentive to advertise.

Fraud should be narrowly defined to mean a demonstrated false statement. Government agencies should not be responsible for determining whether a statement is simply misleading or deceptive, rather than false, since perception of the meaning of an ad varies so widely from individual to individual. To ask an agency to act on *its* perception is to ask it to engage in intuitive and highly subjective behavior that can never be reliably pro-consumer.

Fraud so defined cannot in any sense benefit the consumer, and there would be no reason to permit it to exist *if* it could be eliminated costlessly. The suppression of fraud is costly, however, both in an administrative sense and in the "chilling effect," that is, the disincentive to engage in any advertising, that some kinds of antifraud rules may have on truthful advertisers. A first step in reducing these costs is the identification of the kinds of fraud that are clearly damaging and unlikely to be corrected by market forces and thus may be targets for regulation. As Richard Posner has noted, fraud is more likely in circumstances in which the performance of the product, for example, patent medicine, is uncertain or where the seller can leave the business easily, for example, a "fly by night" operation. In either case, market forces may insufficiently deter fraud. Similarly, where all brands of a product suffer from a common undesirable characteristic, for example, the effect of cigarettes on health, there is no incentive on the part of any seller to expose that characteristic. In contrast, where the costs to the buyer in discovering fraud are low or where competitors have an incentive to expose the fraud, more reliance ought to be placed upon the market.

To reduce the costs of enforcement, this kind of analysis should be the basis of the antifraud strategy. Not only will the more serious cases of fraud be detected but the number of cases uncovered will give us an idea of the probable level of fraud in other kinds of markets. If, for example, a relatively small number of cases of fraud are detected in markets peculiarly susceptible to it, we may rest easier as to the workings of other markets.

A general rule requiring that advertisers substantiate claims made on behalf of their products goes much too far. By its very terms it may suppress truthful claims that the Federal Trade Commission (FTC) decides have not been properly substantiated—and this is as harmful to consumers as failing to suppress fraudulent claims. As an adjunct to the rule against fraud, this rule seems far too costly unless restricted to markets in which a likelihood of damage through fraud exists and the costs of substantiation are moderate. Such a rule, broadly applied, would necessarily reduce the advertiser's power to engage in advocacy and thus

reduce his incentive to provide even undisputed information to consumers. Proving a claim may be very costly—the lawyers' fees alone could be staggering—and substantiation would surely decrease the volume of advertising and the volume of new products introduced because of the increased difficulties in advertising them. Such reasoning was the basis of the decision in *The New York Times v. Sullivan*, which forbade defamation judgments against the media in cases involving public officials unless knowing falsity was proven.[2] The Court there specifically relied upon the fact that closer scrutiny of news stories by the judiciary would reduce the volume of news because of the higher costs of reporting stories that might be difficult to substantiate fully.

A requirement that manufacturers disclose particular information about their products can also be justified only in carefully defined circumstances. Where the information is such that some manufacturers of the product would have an incentive to disclose if consumers were sufficiently interested, the cost-benefit judgment should be left to those manufacturers. Where, however, the information is such that none of the competitors has an interest in disclosure—health information about cigarettes—required disclosure makes more sense provided the information is of importance.

The FTC has undertaken a program of requiring corrective advertising in cases in which a history of deception has supposedly been found. Since we know so little about the actual impact of deceptive advertising, I have grave doubts as to the worthiness of this program. The FTC's remedial powers may be inadequate as deterrents, but adoption of a remedy that may further injure consumers does not seem appropriate.

It has often been noted that one impact of rigorous administrative scrutiny of advertising may be to instill an unwarranted confidence in consumers, who believe that every ad meets government approval. I cannot help but note that among the most misleading ads currently in use today are the Environmental Protection Agency (EPA) estimated mileage figures for new cars. As I understand it, these figures are wildly inaccurate as a practical matter but come with a government stamp of authenticity and are thus constantly used.

One wonders whether the reverse impact of

FTC vigor may not be of considerable importance, particularly since the scope of actual policing of advertising is so small. It has been suggested that government forgo a compulsory substantiation rule and, instead, invite advertisers to submit their claims voluntarily for authentication. The consumer then would be exposed to both authenticated and unauthenticated advertising claims and could use his own judgment. This, along with proper antifraud rules, seems to me a far more intelligent approach to the problem of advertising regulation than either substantiation or a requirement of product information disclosure.

Advertising as a Barrier to Entry

Of all the claims about the harmful effect of advertising, the most baseless are the allegations about its anticompetitive effect. It may well be that those who see in advertising a barrier to entry are like Mr. Nader and his associates, who recently declared that managerial talent and production techniques that give a firm a cost advantage are barriers to entry about which antitrust ought to concern itself. To be sure, superior managerial talent or production techniques are "barriers to entry," but antitrust ought not concern itself about such barriers since they work to the consumers' advantage. The purpose of antitrust is not to protect the least efficient producer but to insure that producers compete so that efficiency is maximized.

It is not enough, therefore, to show that advertising by one firm hampers entry by another. It must be also shown that this is anticompetitive. The advertiser who creates goodwill for himself has in fact created and paid for a capital asset like any other capital asset owned by a firm, and there is no reason for antitrust to be concerned about the fact that others cannot enter effectively without acquiring similar capital assets. Those who reject this argument are again simply demonstrating their distrust of the consumer, since it is his loyalty developed through experience with the product that makes entry difficult.

Nor can product differentiation be viewed as anticonsumer. What firm in its right mind would incur the costs of differentiation unless some consumers preferred its variant of the product? Indeed, I would think that product differentiation on its face should be treated as presumptive evidence of rampant competition. Advertising and product differentiation may in fact help rather than hamper entry. For example, heavy advertising of ready-to-eat cereals and a proliferation of brands make it easier rather than harder for new brands to enter since consumers are accustomed to a variety of choice and it is the brand name rather than the manufacturer's name that the consumer knows. People may also be more inclined to eat ready-to-eat cereals than if there had been no advertising, since brand advertising is advocacy of a product type—cereal as against bacon and eggs—and is thus a help to competing brands.

Those who criticize advertising for its anticompetitive effect have the matter exactly backwards. Advertising is an important weapon of competition. Its suppression, as in the case of prescription drugs, will almost invariably restrict competition.

NOTES

1. See Ronald Coase, "The Market for Goods and the Market for Ideas," *American Economic Review*, vol. 64, no. 2 (May 1974), p. 385; also Reprint no. 28 (Washington, D.C.: American Enterprise Institute, 1975). Recently, constitutional protection has been extended to certain kinds of commercial speech. See Virginia State Board of Pharmacy v. Virginia Citizens Council, U.S. 48 L. Ed. 2d 346 (1976) in which the Supreme Court struck down certain state restrictions on the advertising of prescription drug prices. See also below, pp. 24–26.

2. The New York Times v. Sullivan, 376 U.S. 254, 266 (1964).

DOROTHY COHEN

Unfairness in Advertising Revisited

A 1972 Supreme Court decision (*FTC v. Sperry & Hutchinson Co.*), encouraging the FTC to apply unfairness in protecting consumers, added a new dimension to advertising regulation and control (Cohen 1974). Recent criticisms from various sources of the FTC's use of unfairness in determining the presence of unfair acts or practices led to the passage of an FTC Improvements Act (Federal Trade Commission 1980), which places a number of limitations and restraints on the Commission's activities. In specific reference to unfairness the Act forbids the promulgation of any rule by the FTC which "prohibits or otherwise regulates any commercial advertising on the basis that such commercial advertising constitutes an unfair act or practice in or affecting commerce" for the fiscal years 1980, 1981, and 1982.

In the interim, Congress will hold hearings to determine if unfairness can be adequately defined and implemented and if it should be fully returned to the FTC statute. In an effort to provide clarification on the issues, this article examines the evolution of the unfairness doctrine, the FTC's use of unfairness, the challenges and defenses to this concept, its current status, and the significance of this statutory provision to marketers and public policy makers.

EVOLUTION OF THE "UNFAIRNESS DOCTRINE"

Congress noted the difficulty in establishing standards for unfairness when, in 1914, it granted the FTC power to proceed against "unfair methods of competition," declaring that it "is impossible to frame definitions which embrace all unfair practices" (House Report, 1914, at 18).

Earlier attempts to define unfair related to unfair methods of competition, which was interpreted to mean its purpose was to protect competitors only and not consumers. In 1937 the Wheeler-Lea Amendments extended the FTC's regulatory powers beyond the prohibition of "unfair methods of competition" and authorized the Commission to forbid "unfair or deceptive acts or practices." The addition of this phrase was designed to indicate that the consumer was to be protected from "an unfair trade practice," just as the merchant or manufacturer was to be protected from the unfair methods of a "dishonest competitor" (House Report 1937).

The Act also specified that the dissemination of a false advertisement was an unfair or deceptive act or practice. While the FTC subsequently used deception as the basis for its advertising complaints concerning consumers, the term unfair did not become the focus of attention until 1972. In *FTC v. Sperry & Hutchinson Co.* (1972), the Supreme Court noted that the consumer as well as the merchant and manufacturer must be protected from unfair trade practices. The Court, however, did not define unfairness and in fact designated the "congressionally mandated standard of unfairness" as "elusive."

In a footnote in *Sperry & Hutchinson*, the Court cited, with apparent approval, criteria for unfairness the FTC had expressed in an earlier proposed cigarette rule. These criteria, which have been characterized by the Supreme Court as sufficient but not necessary factors in determining unfairness, are (FTC Trade Reg. Rule, ... Cigarettes, 1964):

☐ Whether the practice, without necessarily having been previously considered unlawful, offends public policy as it has been established by statutes.

☐ Whether it is immoral, unethical, oppressive, or unscrupulous.

☐ Whether it causes substantial injury to consumers (or competitors or other business people).

In 1975 the Magnuson-Moss Act provided the Commission with rulemaking authority, permitting the FTC to establish trade regulation rules that specify unfair or deceptive acts or practices that are prohibited. This Act neither defined nor clarified the concept of unfairness.

THE FTC USE OF UNFAIRNESS

Prior to the *Sperry & Hutchinson* decision in 1972, the FTC made limited use of unfairness in advertising complaints. The FTC's advertising substantiation program (established around this time) initially was based on unfairness (Cohen 1980). In "In re Pfizer" (1972), the benchmark case for the advertising substantiation program, the FTC's opinion quoted the cigarette criteria but did not utilize these criteria in applying the unfairness standard to unsubstantiated advertising. Instead the Commission declared that it was unfair to make an advertising claim without a reasonable basis since "economically, it is more rational and imposes far less cost on society to require a manufacturer to confirm his affirmative product claims rather than impose a burden on each individual consumer to test, investigate or experiment for himself" ("In re Pfizer," at 62).

In other advertising complaints, the FTC has generally used unfairness in conjunction with deception. Where advertisements were directed at adults, the Commission relied primarily on the deceptiveness theory. The FTC has complained of unfairness in advertising to children in several recent cases, expressing its concern for ads that may have the tendency or capacity to influence children to engage in unsafe behavior. The term deception, however, was also included in the complaints. Several companies have agreed to FTC consent orders prohibiting them from engaging in such practices.

The use by a company of "Spider Man" vitamin advertising to children was considered an unfair and deceptive practice because such advertising can induce children to take excessive amounts of vitamins, which can be dangerous to their health. Hudson signed a consent order limiting the use of "Spider Man" and other hero figures in certain ads and at certain times ("In re Hudson Pharmaceu-

tical Corp." 1976). General Foods agreed not to depict Euell Gibbons picking and eating or pointing to certain wild plants and stating that the particular plant indicated is edible or good tasting, since some plants may be harmful if eaten ("In re General Foods Corp." 1975).

A commercial for Mego's "Cher" doll depicted a very young girl seated on a stool next to a bathroom sink filled with water as she washed the doll's long black hair. The girl's mother entered and gave the girl a hand-held electric hairdryer. The mother then left the scene and the young girl dried the doll's hair with the appliance. Mego agreed to discontinue this type of ad ("In re Mego International Inc." 1978). Similarly, AMF agreed not to depict unsafe bicycle and tricycle riding behavior in its ads ("In re AMF Inc." 1979).

Trade Regulation Rules

While the FTC made limited use of unfairness in its case by case approach, it applied this concept in a number of trade regulation rules issued or proposed in recent years. Many of these do not deal specifically with advertising.

Unfairness in advertising was examined in the first trade regulation rule issued under the expanded authority granted to the FTC by the 1975 Magnuson-Moss Act. Briefly, the ophthalmic rule (FTC Trade Reg. Rule, Advertising of Ophthalmic Goods, 1978) preempted state laws restricting advertising of eyeglasses and eye examinations and prohibited advertising restraints such as those found in professional codes.

In promulgating the rule, the Commission argued that the term unfair cannot be narrowly defined nor is it static. The agency repeated the three criteria for unfairness cited in the cigarette rule—public policy, immorality, and substantial injury—and decided that the eyeglass rule was justified on the basis of the first and third of these factors. Nondisclosure of prices offends public policy, since Supreme Court decisions have held that the consumer's right to receive price advertising is protected by the First Amendment. Moreover, according to the Commission such nondisclosure creates substantial harm.

Subsequently, FTC Trade Reg. Rule, ... Vocational ... Schools (1978) rule, which also focused on unfair practices, was promulgated. Briefly, it required vocational schools to disclose enrollment and job placement statistics in their promotional material.

A number of proposed rules were included in the FTC's 1979 agenda involving, for example, funeral industry practices, credit practices, used motor vehicle sales, standards and certification, mobile home sales and services, appliance labeling, and hearing aids. Several others dealt with the advertising of protein supplements, thermal insulation material, food, over the counter antacids, food advertising options, and children's television advertising. A number of these were subject to criticism, and the proposed children's rule generated the greatest public outcry.

In preparing the proposed children's ad rule, the FTC staff did note that television advertising of sugared products to children was deceptive. However, much of the thrust of their arguments related to unfairness (FTC Staff Report on Television Advertising to Children 1978). The three cigarette rule criteria were cited to denote children's advertising as unfair:

□ Such acts were offensive to public policy in terms of protecting children and protecting parental authority. The staff cited, for example, the attractive nuisance doctrine, voidability of minors' contracts, and prohibitions against minors' purchases of dangerous products.

□ In determining immorality, unethicality, oppressiveness, and unscrupulousness, they noted that advertising to children enticed them to gamble with their health. They also used the term unconscionable that the courts apply to certain contracts arrived at by parties of highly disparate bargaining power, which excessively favor the more powerful and injure the weaker.

□ There was substantial injury to children themselves, to parents, to parent-child relationships, and to competitors.

In general, the staff declared if it is unfair or deceptive to bypass defenses that adults are presumed to have, then a fortiori it is unfair or deceptive to address television advertising to children in whom these defenses do not even exist (FTC Staff Report 1978, p. 224).

Current Status of FTC Rules

As of this writing, the eyeglass and vocational school rules have been set aside by the courts and remanded to the FTC for reconsideration. A court of appeals suspended most portions of the eyeglass rule and questioned whether the Commission had not exceeded its authority to preempt state laws and gratuitously intruded on the exercise of the police power of the states. It found there was insufficient evidence to support the FTC's conclusions as to the need for a rule in light of recent Supreme Court decisions striking down state prohibitions on professional advertising (*American Optometric Association* 1980).

The court did uphold a portion of the rule requiring that persons undergoing eye examinations immediately be given a copy of their eyeglass prescription and banning the use of disclaimer of liability statements by ophthalmologists. These provisions of the rule would remain unaffected by any changes in state statutes following the Supreme Court's decision.

The vocational school rule was also set aside by a court of appeals, which declared the rule was illegal in that it contained procedural and substantive errors (*Katherine Gibbs School v. FTC* 1980). In remanding the rule to the FTC, the court directed the agency specifically to define the unfair practices that the rule was designed to remedy.

The court did uphold provisions of the rule requiring schools to disclose the number and percentage of enrolled students in each course who graduate, and a provision requiring schools to afford a 14-day cooling off period in which enrollment contracts can be cancelled ("In the matter of . . ." 1980, p. 6).

The 1980 Federal Trade Commission Improvement Act imposes a number of procedural restrictions on the FTC's rulemaking. At six-month intervals the Commission must list the trade regulation rules it intends to propose, the legal justifications for the proposals, and the date when each is likely to happen. Each rule must be supported by statements analyzing the projected costs and benefits and the reasons for choosing the particular alternatives rather than others. If the rule is adopted, six months after its adoption the Commission must begin a detailed audit to determine if the rule is working. The Act also placed a major restraint on the FTC's rulemaking powers by subjecting such rules to a congressional veto.

In reference to the FTC's proposed rules, the Act indicates that the Commission does not have the power under the Magnuson-Moss Act to develop a rule with regard to standards and certification. It did not completely prohibit the funeral rule but limited such a rule to mandating price disclosure, banning deceptive or coercive practices, and prohibiting unlawful practices such as boycotts or threats. It prohibited the FTC from promulgating a children's advertising rule on the basis of unfairness in commercial advertising, but permitted the establishment of future proceedings in children's advertising if it meets the requirements of advance notice of such proposals and is based on deception.

UNFAIRNESS: CHALLENGES AND DEFENSES

The complaints against unfairness were mostly in anticipation of its future application by the FTC (*Unfairness . . .* 1980); in actual practice, its use by the Commission in advertising regulation has been limited. As a consequence of the 1980 FTC Act, its use will no doubt continue to be limited, at least until further clarification emerges, either through legislative action or through the development of an unfairness standard considered acceptable by various parties. Future decisions in this area require an examination of the challenges and defenses to the unfairness doctrine.

The Commission's unfairness doctrine appears to raise issues in three constitutional areas: 1) First Amendment considerations, 2) the delegation of legislative power, and 3) due process right to a "reasonable opportunity to know what is prohibited" (Bork and Bickel 1980, p. 20). Furthermore, there is concern over a lack of precise criteria for determining unfairness.

First Amendment Considerations

Criticisms of Unfairness as a Standard.   While the recent Supreme Court decisions do not fore-

close the regulation of false, deceptive, and misleading information, they do not discuss unfair. No empirical test exists for unfairness, and such a test may be impossible for this vague concept. Its elusiveness causes advertisers to steer away from its uncertain boundaries, and thus it inhibits the free flow of truthful, legitimate commercial information protected by the First Amendment (Morgan 1980, p. 145).

Defenses of Unfairness.   Although First Amendment protection has recently been extended to commercial speech, according to recent Supreme Court decisions there are certain kinds of advertising that may be subject to control (Cohen 1978).

Constitutional protection for commercial speech is relatively new in judicial history, and the limits of such protection are still evolving from court decisions. At this writing there is no decision that specifically eliminates restrictions against unfair advertising. It is, therefore, possible that the boundaries of permissible control of commercial speech expressed in some of the Court's decisions may encompass unfair advertising.

Delegation of Legislative Power

Criticisms.   The unfairness doctrine improperly involves the Commission in basic policy matters, without even minimal statutory guidance (Bork and Bickel 1980, p. 21). It delegates legislative power to the FTC, which may force advertisers to promote the Commission's view on any social, economic, or political issue (Committee Report on S1991, 1979).

Defenses.   The FTC, as an administrative agency, is required to develop standards for defining its administrative authority. Such standards help structure administrative decisions and provide safeguards against careless or arbitrary actions by administrative officers (Carney 1972, p. 1086).

Standards devised by the FTC are not immutable and in fact are subject to court review. The courts have the authority to approve or disapprove of the standards employed by an administrative agency in reaching its conclusions (*FCC v. RCA Communications, Inc.* 1953). Furthermore, legislators are free to revise agency activities or, as in the recent Act, temporarily suspend them if they are deemed excessive and require redirection.

Due Process

Criticisms. The unfairness standard fails to conform to the basic constitutional requirement of fair notice (National Association of Broadcasters 1980, p. 86). It does not provide a standard for advertisers against which to measure advertising, nor does it convey a reasonably definite warning as to what conduct is proscribed and what is not. Unlike the term false, it conveys no popular referrent by which affected parties may judge their conduct. Accordingly, the unfairness doctrine is contrary to the "basic principle of due process that an enactment is void for vagueness if its prohibitions are not clearly defined" (*Grayned v. City of Rockford* 1972, at 108).

Defenses. While at one time the due process of law clause was severely restrictive in regulating business, the Supreme Court has provided a much more permissive interpretation (Smead 1969, p. 11). Both FTC procedure and the ability to appeal FTC decisions to the court provide for due process under this interpretation.

Lack of Criteria for Unfairness

Criticisms. The only expressed criteria (public policy, immorality, injury) are lacking analytical content. Public policy is unacceptable since some manifestation of public policy can be found in support of, or against, almost any proposition one can name (Hobbs 1980, p. 33).

Immoral, unscrupulous, oppressive and *unethical* are words that add only "emotional coloration" (Hobbs 1980, p. 33) and are extremely susceptible to contrasting definitions, depending upon one's politics and values (Rice 1980, p. 110).

Substantial injury to consumers as a criterion may afford objective analysis. However, such a test requires more refinement and focus than the Commission has given it in the past (Hobbs 1980, p. 34).

Defenses. While unfairness is a broad and even vague standard, the Supreme Court has upheld legislation involving similarly vague standards such as "just and reasonable," "public interest," "public convenience, interest or necessity," "reasonable variations," "unduly or unnecessarily complicate the structure," and "inequitably distribute voting power among security holders" (Carney 1972, p. 1085). The lack of specific criteria for unfairness should be no bar to its use. In fact, in suggesting that the FTC concern itself with unfairness to consumers, the Supreme Court encouraged the FTC to measure "a practice against the *elusive*, but Congressionally mandated standard of unfairness" (*FTC v. Sperry & Hutchinson Co.* 1972).

THE CURRENT MEANING OF "UNFAIR OR DECEPTIVE ACTS OR PRACTICES"

An understanding of the current status of the phrase "unfair or deceptive acts or practices" is important for marketers and public policy makers. Its clarification is necessary both for devising efficient advertising practices that are not subject to challenge, and for developing a regulatory framework consistent with marketers' needs and appropriate for public policy goals. For proper understanding and analysis, it is necessary to examine both "deceptive" and "unfair" and their implications for advertising regulation.

DECEPTION

The 1980 FTC Act does not place any limitations on FTC efforts to eliminate deceptive advertising. These can be pursued through the development of a trade regulation rule or through case by case litigation.

It is doubtful that there will be serious efforts in the future to limit control over deception in advertising. Recent Supreme Court decisions noting that First Amendment protection does not extend to deceptive speech provides further support for efforts to control deception. As a consequence of the 1980 Act, the FTC may expand its use of deception and in fact has indicated it will follow this approach in its concern relevant to children's advertising.

While it is clear that deception in advertising

can be regulated, there is no precise listing of criteria for a finding of deception, nor clear guidelines for its determination.

In legal terminology, the word "deceptive" is most commonly defined as "having the capacity or tendency to deceive" (*Trade Regulation Reporter 1980, 1, #7536*). In its regulation of deception in advertising, the FTC has primarily focused on the claims or representations made in the ads. More recently, there have been suggestions that such an approach is inadequate and that deception cannot be correctly understood without an understanding of the interaction of the advertisement and the consumer (Gardner 1975).

In recent years lawyers, social scientists, marketers, and others have attempted to provide guidelines for a determination of deception (Barry 1980, Brandt and Preston 1977, Kuehl and Dyer 1978). While an in-depth analysis of these suggestions is beyond the scope of this paper, in the current context the need for precise guidelines becomes more significant. The extent to which the parameters of deception are broadened limits the need for regulating unfairness, and conversely, a narrow definition of deception may suggest that unfairness should be regulated.

UNFAIRNESS

The 1980 FTC Act does not completely eliminate the FTC's ability to control unfair advertising practices. Although the FTC cannot use unfairness as a basis for developing trade regulation rules concerning advertising, under the new Act the Commission remains free to impose its unfairness theory upon individuals or groups of advertisers in case by case adjudications.

Furthermore, although the FTC cannot use unfairness as a basis for developing an industry-wide trade regulation rule against advertising, it can achieve industry-wide adherence to its orders by notifying industry members that they could be sued for civil penalties if they engage in conduct that the Commission has held unfair in issuing an order against someone else. The FTC derives this ability, which covers both unfair or deceptive advertising, from its case law authority provided under Section 5(m) of the FTC Act (Section 205(a)

of the 1975 Magnuson-Moss Act). Under this authority, if, in a litigated case, the FTC determines that a type of advertising is unfair, it may send copies of its complaint and order to other advertisers who were not parties in the original case. If the other advertisers engage in similar practices in the future, the Commission can sue them for penalties without holding an administrative trial to determine that they broke agency laws, but on the basis that the companies violated agency rules developed in litigation against other firms.

An example of such agency-made law involving deception occurred recently when the FTC notified the General Mills Fun Group of previous cases on toy performance advertising, together with notice of its power to sue in court for penalties. Subsequently, General Mills Fun Group agreed to pay $90,000 in civil penalties in settlement for a television advertisement that showed a toy horse standing when it could not, and another $10,000 for slack filled (lightly filled) areoplane kit boxes ("In re Toy Firm Settles Penalty ..." 1979). Although the FTC has not yet used this authority in unfairness cases, it retains the ability to do so under the 1980 FTC Act.

Current Unfairness Standards

Subsequent to the passage of the 1980 FTC Amendments Act, the FTC issued a policy statement concerning the "scope of its consumer unfairness jurisdiction" and providing a more "detailed sense of the definition and limits" of criteria for unfairness (FTC letter to the ... Consumer Subcommittee ... 1980).

The Commission declared that two of the three cigarette criteria (consumer injury and public policy) were factors to be considered in applying prohibitions against consumer unfairness. The standard of unethical, oppressive, or unscrupulous conduct was considered largely duplicative and unnecessary since, according to the Commission, conduct that is truly unethical or unscrupulous will injure consumers or violate public policy. The FTC indicated the limits of the other two criteria as follows:

Consumer Injury. The most important criterion and the primary focus of the FTC Act is unjustified consumer injury. Every consumer injury by itself is not sufficient to warrant a finding of unfairness. To justify unfairness the injury must satisfy three tests:

1. It must be substantial. Examples of substantial injury involve monetary harm, coercing consumers into purchasing unwanted goods or services, or unwarranted health and safety risks (as when a company distributed free sample razor blades in such a way that they could come into the hands of small children).

2. It must not be outweighed by any countervailing benefits to consumers or competition that the practice produces. For example, when a seller fails to present technical data on his/her product and thus lessens a consumer's ability to choose, this may also result in a reduction in the initial price the consumer must pay for the article and, therefore, is not considered unfair.

   On the other hand, although the FTC's holder-in-due-course rule increased costs to creditors and sellers, the FTC anticipated an overall lowering of economic costs to society because the rule gave creditors the incentive to police sellers, thus increasing the likelihood that those selling defective goods or services would either leave the marketplace or improve their practices.

3. The injury must be one that consumers could not reasonably have avoided. Examples are withholding or failing to generate critical price or performance data, engaging in overt coercion (as by dismantling a home appliance for inspection and refusing to assemble it until a service contract is signed), and promoting fraudulent cures to seriously ill cancer patients.

Violation of Public Policy. According to the Commission this criterion may be applied in two different ways. Most frequently, it will be used not as a separate consideration but as additional evidence on the degree of consumer injury caused by a specific practice.

Occasionally the Commission will examine outside statutory policies and established judicial principles. As an example, in its eyeglass rule the agency referred to First Amendment decisions upholding consumers' rights to receive information

to confirm that restrictions on advertising tend unfairly to hinder the informed exercise of consumer choice.

Sometimes public policy will independently support a Commission action. For example, the Commission has applied the statutory policies of the Uniform Commercial Code to require automobile manufacturers and their distributors to refund to their customers any surplus money that was realized after they repossessed and resold their customers' cars.

DISCUSSION

Unfairness is an evolving concept and future investigations may provide sufficient input for more informed decisions concerning its application to advertising regulation.

The constitutionality of unfairness has not yet been tested; however, recent first amendment decisions do not preclude government regulation of commercial speech. Nor does the unfairness doctrine provide excessive delegation of legislative powers to an administrative agency, since the FTC has always been subjected to judicial review, and as a result of the new Act, is now subject to legislative review. It does not impede due process as a number of procedural requirements have been established for the development of trade regulation rules. Moreover, if the term unfairness were to be considered too vague for use, innumerable statutes might fall under the same condemnation, such as those that predicate rights and prohibitions upon "unsound mind," "undue influence," "unfaithfulness," "unfair use," "unfit for cultivation," "unreasonable rate," "unjust discrimination" (*Sears, Roebuck & Co. v. FTC* 1919).

There is justification for the criticisms that the FTC has failed to articulate criteria and consistently apply them in enforcement of its statute (Hobbs 1980, p. 36). However, this can be remedied, and recently the FTC has recommended a number of specific criteria. Moreover, an analysis of congressional intent and judicial review indicates there is no intention to require the FTC to articulate precise standards, but rather to develop these to meet emerging situations.

Public Policy Considerations

From a public policy viewpoint, the term unfair or deceptive acts or practices was added to the FTC Act in order to ensure that consumers as well as competitors would be protected from such practices. In addition, the unfairness doctrine provides a mechanism for dealing with an issue that is likely to be increasingly significant in the future—the need for consumer information disclosures.

Protecting Consumers. Unfairness supplements rather than duplicates the deceptive aspects of the FTC Act. A ban on unfairness may leave the Commission unable to deal with some unacceptable acts and practices they have prohibited, such as ads that encourage children to engage in unsafe behavior or bringing suits in forums unreasonably distant from a consumer's place of residence (*Spiegel, Inc. v. FTC* 1977).

Unfairness may be present when an imbalance in bargaining power exists between merchant and consumer and the merchant has abused his/her superior position to the detriment of consumers (Carney 1972, p. 891). The courts have approved of Commission activities aimed at correcting abuses resulting from a merchant's superior product knowledge by affirming Commission orders requiring affirmative disclosures of product information (*Williams Co. v. FTC* 1967).

Providing Consumer Information. Accurate and valid information in advertising is socially useful because it minimizes the search costs for consumers who otherwise would be required to gather this information. Recent Supreme Court decisions relevant to the First Amendment rights of commercial speech suggest that there may be a right to require information disclosure. The growth of the right to know in the First Amendment doctrine may mean the right of the public to obtain information to participate intelligently in decision making (Emerson 1980).

We are entering an era of communication when technology and innovations abound for message delivery as well as sophisticated techniques for their design. This is not the time to limit the FTC's ability to ensure that innovations in information presentation operate in the consumer's interest.

It is true that nondisclosure of information, under certain circumstances, is considered a deceptive practice. Thus, if a specific representation is made without information necessary to qualify the advertising claim, it may be considered deceptive, and under such circumstances, the FTC can require affirmative disclosure.

However, product information disclosures may also be necessary, regardless of the particular representation made, in order to sell a particular product in a fair manner. Examples are the cigarette advertising warning and the octane rating requirement; however, both of these have been imposed by Congressional legislation. The Commission has used deception by silence in its early cases and found that, in light of express claims in the ad or the nature of the product, failure to disclose pertinent information would be misleading. Nonetheless, in *Alberty v. FTC* (1950), where the Commission failed to make any findings of deception or of other special circumstances, the Court of Appeals reversed, noting that the FTC lacked the power simply to require advertisers to be more informative. Unfairness may be used to indicate the circumstances where additional information is required.

Designating nondisclosures of information as unfair is consistent with a "Less-Restrictive-Alternative Principle" (Struve 1967). Hobbs cited this principle, noting: "To the extent that reasonably tailored disclosure remedies are chosen to correct unfairness, any concern about governmental overreacting is diminished. Indeed considerations of this nature may push the FTC toward a 'least drastic means' type of analysis in its regulation of unfairness" (1980, p. 35, footnote 46).

Disclosure requirements are also consistent with economic market analysis, since they "help restore the competitive market model to its proper working order" (Rice 1980, p. 107). The market model, among other assumptions, presupposes that consumers will have sufficient information with which to make rational purchase decisions. Rice declares, "(to) the extent that the market provides disincentives for sellers to supply that information, they will refuse to do so." He describes disincentives as existing for sellers marketing products with negative attributes, such as in the case of cigarettes with high levels of tar and nicotine. Similarly, to foster brand loyalty in the marketing of analgesic compounds, manufacturers advertise insignificant product differences, rather than reveal that "all aspirins are alike." Imposing a greater countervailing incentive for such disclosures may rectify this situation.

Unfairness would permit the FTC to require sellers to make additional information available to consumers for use in marketplace decisions. To measure unfairness in nondisclosure the FTC can apply its recently expressed criteria.

Marketer's Needs

Restrictions on unfairness may have a salutary effect on the marketer. The original prohibition of unfair methods of competition in the 1914 FTC Act was designed to protect merchants from competitors. While the additional prohibition of unfair or deceptive acts or practices was primarily directed at consumers, it should be noted that to the extent unfairness is permitted, it puts the more moral business person at a disadvantage with some competitors.

Nor are restrictions on unfairness inconsistent with the current movement toward deregulation. Deregulation does not mean no regulation; instead it focuses on eliminating excessive business restrictions and encouraging self-regulation. A ban on unfair acts or practices accompanied by criteria for determining unfairness, as well as legislative and judicial oversight on unfairness standards, would not be restrictive. The promulgation of unfairness guidelines would familiarize practitioners with the acceptable standards and establish parameters for the development of marketing practices that are not subject to regulatory challenge.

REFERENCES

Alberty v. FTC (1950), 182 F.2d 36 (D.C. Cir.), *cert. denied*, 340 U.S. 818.

American Optometric Association v. FTC (1980), 5 Trade Reg. Rep. #63165.

Barry, Thomas (1980), "Ascertaining Deception in Children's Advertising," *Journal of Advertising*, 9 (Winter), 11–18.

Bork, Robert H. and Alexander M. Bickel (1980), in *Unfairness: Views on Unfair Acts and Practices . . .* (April), 17–22.

Brandt, Michael T. and Ivan L. Preston (1977), "The Federal Trade Commission's Use of Evidence to Determine Deception," *Journal of Marketing*, 41 (January), 55–62.

Carney, James A. (1972), "Section 5 of the Federal Trade Commission Act: Unfairness to Consumers," *Wisconsin Law Review*, V. 1972 (no. 4), 1071–1096.

Cohen, Dorothy (1974), "The Concept of Unfairness As It Relates to Advertising Legislation," *Journal of Marketing*, 38 (July), 8–13.

——— (1978), "Advertising and the First Amendment," *Journal of Marketing*, 42 (July), 59–68.

——— (1980), "The FTC's Advertising Substantiation Program," *Journal of Marketing*, 44 (Winter), 26–35.

Committee Report on S1991, S. Rep. No. 96-500, 96th Cong., 1st Sess. (1979), Consumer Information Remedies, Policy Session (1979). Washington, DC: U.S. Government Printing Office (June).

Emerson, Thomas I. (1980), "First Amendment Doctrine and the Burger Court," *California Law Review*, 50 (May), 422–481.

FCC v. RCA Communications, Inc. (1953), 346 U.S. 86.

FTC v. Sperry & Hutchinson Co. (1972), 405 U.S. 233.

Federal Trade Commission (1980), *Improvements Act of 1980,* Public Law No. 96-2532.

FTC letter to the Honorable Wendell H. Ford and the Honorable John C. Danforth of the Consumer Subcommittee of the Committee on Commerce, Science and Transportation (Dec. 17, 1980).

FTC Staff Report on Television Advertising to Children (1978), submitted to the Federal Trade Commission (February).

FTC Trade Regulation Rule, Advertising of Ophthalmic Goods and Services (1978), BAN ATTR No. 865 (May).

FTC Trade Regulation Rule for the Prevention of Unfair or Deceptive Acts or Practices in the Sale of Cigarettes (1964), 29 Fed. Reg. 8325, 8355.

FTC Trade Regulation Rule, Proprietary Vocational and Home Study Schools (1978), 43 Fed. Reg. 60796, 60800.

Gardner, David M. (1975), "Deception in Advertising: A Conceptual Approach," *Journal of Marketing*, 39 (January), 40–46.

Grayned v. City of Rockford (1972), 408 U.S. 104, 108.

Hobbs, Caswell O. (1980), "Unfairness at the FTC—The Legacy of *S & H*," in *Unfairness: Views on Unfair Acts and Practices . . .* (April), 27–38.

House Report No. 1142 (1914), 63rd Cong., 2d Sess., 18–19.

House Report No. 1613 (1937), 75th Cong., 1st Sess., 3.

"In re AMF, Inc.," (1979), 3 Trade Reg. Rep. #21,589.

"In re General Foods Corp.," (1975), 3 Trade Reg. Rep. #20,928.

"In re Hudson Pharmaceutical Corp.," (1976), 3 Trade Reg. Rep. #21,191.

"In re Mego Int'l Inc.," (1978), 3 Trade Reg. Rep. #21,399.

"In re Pfizer, Inc.," (1972), 81 FTC 23.

"In re Toy Firm Settles Penalty-Without-Trial Advertising Case," (1979), Trade Reg. Reports #387.

"In the Matter of Proposed Trade Regulation Rule on Standards and Certifications," (1980), FTC #21,711.

Katherine Gibbs School v. FTC (1980), 48 U.S. W. 2427 (2d Cir.).

Kuehl, Philip C. and Robert F. Dyer (1978), "An Experimental Examination of Deception in Labeling: Consumer Research and Public Policymaking," in *Advances in Consumer Research*, 5, H. Keith Hunt, ed., Ann Arbor: Association for Consumer Research, 206–212.

Morgan, Charles, Jr. (1980), in *Unfairness: Views on Unfair Acts and Practices* . . . (April), 140–149.

National Association of Broadcasters (1980), in *Unfairness: Views on Unfair Acts and Practices* . . . (April), 82–89.

Rice, David A. (1980), "Market Place Unfairness: An Objective Basis for Restricting Commercial Speech to Children Within the Boundaries of the First Amendment," in *Unfairness: Views on Unfair Acts and Practices* . . . (April), 97–112.

Sears, Roebuck & Co. v. FTC (1919), 258 F. 307.

Smead, Elenor E. (1969), *Governmental Promotion and Regulation of Business*. New York: Meredith Corp.

Spiegel, Inc. v. FTC (1977), 540 F.2d 289 (7th Cir.).

Struve, Guy Miller (1967), "The Less-Restrictive-Alternative Principle and Economic Due Process," *Harvard Law Review*, 80 (March-June), 1463.

Trade Regulation Reporter (1980), Chicago, IL: Commerce Clearing House, Inc.

Unfairness: Views on Unfair Acts and Practices in Violation of the Federal Trade Commission Act (1980), prepared at the request of Howard W. Cannon, Chairman, Committee on Commerce, Science, and Transportation, United States Senate, Washington, DC: U.S. Government Printing Office, April.

Williams Company v. FTC (1967), 381 F. 2d 884 (6th Cir.).

CHAPTER FOUR
Study Questions

1. What, if anything, is the difference between a false statement, a lie, and a deceptive statement?

2. How many different types of "non-literally true" advertisements can you think of? Can you put them on a continuum from least to most offensive?

3. How would you define "fairness"? How would you decide if some practice is fair? Think of "fairness" in sports and other competitive activities. How should a teacher assign grades if he or she wanted to be fair?

4. How much responsibility should be carried by consumers when they are deceived? Is your answer consistent with your views on consumer responsibility for product liability?

5. Should corporations have the same legal right of free speech as individual citizens? In Chapter 2, Milton Friedman suggested that it makes little sense to attribute *responsibilities* to business. Does it make sense to attribute *rights* to business?

CHAPTER FIVE

ADVERTISING: AUTONOMY AND PRODUCTION

CASE STUDY
Subliminal Advertising

On May 18, 1978, the New York *Times* reported on an FTC-sanctioned use of a subliminal message on television. After broadcasting a story about a local murder, a mid-western television station was contacted by the murderer. Police were advised by a psychiatrist that this call might indicate a subconscious desire to give himself up. Police requested, and the FTC approved, that the station insert a subliminal message within future reports of the murder. The subliminal message, "Contact the Chief" was embedded within these news stories.

Subliminal techniques also have been used to prevent crime. Some Canadian department stores embedded "Don't steal" messages within the Muzak which they broadcast throughout their stores. Unlike the first case, where authorities hoped a subliminal message would cause a particular person to do a particular thing, these department store messages were not aimed at anyone in particular or at bringing about a particular result. Instead, the department store only hoped for a general reduction in the incidence of shoplifting. Success in the first case could be measured by the occurrence of a specific act. Success in the second case was measured by a statistical reduction in shoplifting.

Research on the effectiveness of subliminal messages is inconclusive. There is little empirical evidence to suggest that you could control a specific person's behavior with subliminal techniques. However, if like the department store you were interested in overall results, subliminal techniques might be more attractive. Managers of shopping malls, for example, were quite interested in the results of the Canadian experiment.

Consider these issues from the point of view of a manager of a shopping mall. Her job is to promote sales not at any particular store or of any particular item. Rather, success of the manager's job is measured by an overall growth in sales throughout the mall. Would you recommend that this manager use subliminal techniques to deter shoplifting? The manager might be tempted to extend these techniques from preventing theft to promoting sales. Rather than embedding "Don't steal," she might embed "Buy" within the background Muzak. Would you recommend this extension?

Introduction

ADVERTISING AND MARKETING activities involve moral concerns other than the issues of deception and unfairness which were discussed in the previous chapter. The effects that even the most truthful advertisements have upon the consumer raise far-reaching moral questions. It is clear that most advertisements aim not only at providing information to consumers, but also aim at influencing consumers, to persuade them to purchase the products advertised.

Morally speaking, the attempt to persuade someone seems permissible enough. Indeed, it would be difficult to deny this without undermining free speech, freedom of press, and the very nature of democracy itself. On the other hand, controlling someone's behavior is, *prima facie*, morally illegitimate. Control of another's behavior strikes at the very heart of a free and democratic society. Critics claim that some advertising and marketing techniques involve more control than persuasion and accordingly are morally unacceptable. According to these critics, consumers are controlled not in any overt way, but in more subtle, yet still effective, ways. Consumers are controlled when the interests, wants, and desires that motivate them in the marketplace are unduly controlled or created through advertising. Although advertising doesn't directly cause us to purchase a product, the critics claim it does so indirectly by creating the desire which in turn motivates us to make the purchase.

To understand why this criticism is important, consider the role that "consumer interest" or "consumer demand" has played in just the few issues we have examined in the first four chapters. That business is "giving the consumer what he/she wants" has been used as moral support for a number of positions. Milton Friedman, for example, argues that free-market capitalism is morally justified because it is the most efficient economic arrangement for "giving people what they want." Critics of government regulations who charge that regulating the market is a paternalistic infringement upon free choice base their criticism upon the belief that individual consumers are the best judges of their own interests. Critics of strict products liability argue that consumers should be allowed to take greater risks concerning product quality or safety in exchange for lower prices, if they so want.

If business can use advertising to create or control the wants and interests of consumers, then none of these arguments will succeed. Friedman's connection of the free market with democracy, his critiques of government regulation as paternalistic, and his criticisms of strict products liability will be unacceptable if the consumer interests are indirectly controlled by business.

Of course, to say that consumers can be easily controlled by advertising is also to cast doubt on other important values. This would seem to suggest that individuals are not the best judges of their own interest, which, in turn, challenges the values of autonomy and self-determination. To say that a great deal depends upon this issue is an understatement.

Ultimately, to resolve this problem one would be required to distinguish precisely between free and unfree acts. Unfortunately, the problem of freedom and determinism is one of the oldest and most difficult philosophical issues. Good reasons can be given in support of both sides. Who can deny that some human behavior can be controlled by others? Behaviorist psychology testifies to that fact. On the other hand, is it even coherent to defend this alternative? If determinism is true, then such words as "persuade," "convince," "reason," and "decide" are at best confused, at worst incoherent.

Nevertheless, some questions should be kept in mind as one reads through the following selections. For example, need this be an either/or debate? Could some human acts be autonomous while others are not? Are some people more free and autonomous than others? How are interests and desires acquired? What is the difference between education and indoctrination? How do you distinguish between *causing, controlling, influencing,* and *modifying* someone's behavior? How have your own desires for consumer goods been influenced by advertising and marketing techniques?

Economist John Kenneth Galbraith has been perhaps the most vocal critic of business's attempt to control consumer behavior. Galbraith identifies this issue as the "dependence effect," the process by which consumer demand depends upon the very process of production, which in turn seeks to satisfy this demand. The economic benefits from such practices are clear. If consumer purchasing is a function of consumer demand, and if that demand can be created by producers, then producers would be able to control how consumers spend their money. Besides this obvious and significant economic incentive for attempting to control consumer behavior, Galbraith suggests a second explanation in the following selection.

Sociologists have described how large bureaucracies tend towards self-perpetuation. The institutional structure works to encourage individuals within it to take the preservation of the institution itself as their continual, if not primary, goal. Zero-based budgeting is a contemporary attempt to control this tendency in government bureaucracies. Galbraith suggests that in corporate bureaucracies this tendency manifests itself in the attempt to control consumer behavior. In this view, changing consumer demands are a serious threat to the preservation of the corporate bureaucracy. To be free of consumer whims and therefore to stabilize its own existence, a corporation will seek to control consumer behavior. We thus have two major explanations, one economic and one sociological, for corporate attempts to "manage consumers."

Two major concerns follow from such activities. We can call these concerns issues of *production* and *autonomy*. According to Galbraith, the dependence effect reverses, and therefore invalidates, the so-called "law" of supply and demand. Rather than goods and services being produced in response to consumer demand, the sequence is reversed and consumer demand becomes a function of production.

Consider an example from the fashion industry. Each year as new fashion seasons approach, new styles are introduced to replace the previous season's styles. Major marketing campaigns accompany the change in styles. Fashion shows, magazine advertisements and supplements, and appearances by celebrities wearing the new styles are just some of the methods used to promote the new fashions. Given the relatively short fashion season, it is necessary that many decisions about production be made well before consumers have any knowledge of the new styles. In order for the new clothes to be available in retail stores as the season begins, manufacturers must have already produced the clothing, and buyers for the retail stores must have already decided to stock it. The entire marketing campaign aims to create a demand for specific products already produced and, more generally, aims to create a previously nonexisting desire for new styles each season. In this way, the supply of goods creates both specific and general demands, rather than the demand creating the supply. Classical economic assumptions about production are thus seriously flawed. Galbraith concludes that as a result, the production of public goods (e.g., education, health care, food for the poor, roads and bridges, etc.) is sacrificed in order to satisfy the demand for more private consumer goods (e.g., designer jeans and video games).

The dependence effect also involves a direct attack upon the autonomy of consumers. From the moral point of view, practices that attempt to bypass the decision-making ability of the individual are wrong. The dependence effect represents an attempt to subvert the moral commitment to self-determination. While Galbraith would claim that this is true of advertisements directed towards the average consumer, there are other practices even more suspect. Subliminal advertising, for example, is explicitly intended to bypass individual autonomy. While other advertisers can claim that the dependence effect is an unintended consequence of their work, this claim cannot be made by subliminal advertisers. Also, it seems clear that some people are more susceptible than others to having their wants and desires controlled. Advertisements directed at children and the elderly deserve special attention in this regard. A child who cannot distinguish between programming and commercials is an easy target for unscrupulous advertisers. A retired person living on a fixed income might be especially susceptible to advertisements for medical insurance, especially when the salesman is a well-known, kindly, and reassuring elderly actor.

Of course, all of this is not to say that Galbraith's description of the dependence effect, let alone his characterization of its undesirable consequences, is correct. Numerous critics have challenged the very existence of the dependence effect, while others have argued that while something like it occurs, the implications are not as bad as Galbraith would have us believe.

In our second selection, G. William Trivoli argues that it is undeniable that consumers freely choose for themselves in the marketplace. Trivoli argues that changes in consumer behavior that accompany advertisements can be better attributed to a greater knowledge of the many choices available than to a change in tastes or interests brought about by the advertisements. In this view, wants and interests are general and advertising simply supplies information about specific means available for satisfying these wants and interests. (Of course, opponents would respond that it is these general wants, e.g., the desire for new clothing styles, and not specific behaviors, e.g., buying a new wardrobe, that are created by advertising and marketing.)

Two further points should be mentioned. Trivoli argues that if Galbraith is correct, then large firms should always, or usually, have successful products. Studies show, however, that between 30% and 80% of new products fail. Accordingly, Galbraith's views must be mistaken. Further, if Galbraith is correct, then there should be a positive relationship between advertising and product acceptance. While there obviously is some relationship, Trivoli suggests that it is not as significant as one would expect.

In our third selection, Ralph K. Winter, Jr. continues the critique of Galbraith. Winter argues on both empirical and moral grounds. Empirically, he claims that there is no evidence to establish the manipulative power Galbraith attributes to advertising. Among other things, Winter points out that there are no guarantees that consumers will even pay attention to ads, let alone be persuaded by them. We also should recognize that many ads compete with one another and that this prevents all of them from being successful. Finally, we know that the success of advertising varies greatly depending upon who sees it and the conditions of the exposure. (Again, the reader should be careful here to distinguish the claim that advertising can control behavior from the claim that advertising creates general wants and desires.)

Winter also raises some important moral concerns. If our democratic values commit us to assuming that citizens are capable of making their own political decisions, we should assume that these same people are capable of making their own economic decisions. Winter finds Galbraith's view "profoundly antidemocratic," and he warns us that critics of advertising are often ready to substitute their own choices for the choices of other consumers.

Alan Goldman takes up this issue within the context of a more general examination of the free market. Goldman believes that the pursuit of profit can be an efficient means for maximizing utility only if certain moral constraints are obeyed. Among these would be the avoidance of creating and exploiting consumer desires. Against critics of Galbraith, Goldman points out that not all wants deserve to be satisfied. Advertising and production that is aimed at irrational wants, for example those of an alcoholic, should be limited in the name of overall social good. Also, while it is true that individuals can resist specific advertising influences, it is not clear that the entire consumer "lifestyle" depicted in advertisements can be resisted. For example, while it is true that individual consumers are free to choose whether or not to purchase a certain product, in general we are not free to choose the society into which we are born. If that society places a high regard (through status or peer acceptance, for example) on the acquisition of consumer goods, then it is less clear that individual consumers are as autonomous as we might think. The desire for a certain style of life can, in turn, lead to specific consumer behaviors. Goldman claims that such factors make it less likely that a free-market approach to advertising and production will achieve the overall social good at which it, presumably, aims.

In the next selection, Gerald Dworkin offers an analysis of autonomy that develops some of the issues raised by Goldman. Dworkin tells us that no one is autonomous in the sense of being absolutely free from any external influences. We are all born into an environment that shapes us socially and psychologically, we all have a biological endowment, and we all are heavily influenced by parents, family, and friends. True autonomy can be achieved only when the individual steps back from these influences and makes a decision to accept or reject them as his or her own. In this view, advertising does not violate autonomy simply by creating consumer demand. Our wants and demands are influenced by myriad environmental factors. Our autonomy is violated when, in some way, there is an interference with the ability to step back from these factors and make a judgement about them. In today's society, Dworkin sees many different techniques that threaten autonomy, including, but not limited to, operant conditioning, psychotropic drugs, and psychosurgery. The reader is challenged to apply Dworkin's analysis to advertising and marketing techniques, especially to subliminal advertising and advertising to children and the elderly.

In our next reading, Robert Arrington presents a more detailed analysis of the relationship between advertising and autonomy. After considering several arguments for and against the anti-autonomy view of advertising, Arrington examines the notions of autonomous desire, rational desire, free choice, and control. He concludes that, in general, advertising does not violate the autonomy of consumers.

Even granting this, we must also admit that autonomy is a relative concept. Some people have greater autonomy than others. Individual persons can gain or lose autonomy over time. Given this, the degree to which advertising threatens autonomy will depend a great deal upon the audience addressed.

Arrington's analysis basically assumes an adult audience. Suppose that an advertisement was not aimed at that adult's conscious, decision-making mind, but instead at his or her subconscious. Subliminal advertising aims at the subconscious desires and preferences of individuals and seeks to influence consumer behavior in this hidden way. If effective, subliminal advertising seems to be a clear violation of a person's autonomy, since it prevents that individual from reflecting upon the factors influencing his or her wants and desires.

In our next selection, Timothy Moore argues that a large body of empirical evidence contradicts the belief that subliminal advertising can be an effective marketing tool. Psychological research indicates that subliminal processes "have no apparent relevance to the goals of advertising."

On the other hand, Dan Rochowiak argues that Moore's conclusions do not follow from his evidence. Rochowiak claims that there is empirical support for the effectiveness of subliminal advertising techniques, especially when the goals of advertising are clearly understood. Against Moore's view that in order to be effective subliminal advertising must result in a specific behavior, i.e., purchase of a product, Rochowiak points out that quite often advertisers are happy merely with name recognition or an increased general desire (e.g., increased thirst rather than purchase of a soft drink).

Both of these articles are concerned primarily with the question of whether or not subliminal advertising is effective. Readers should be alert to the moral issue of the intent of subliminal advertisers. Moore suggests that there is no major moral issue once the ineffectiveness of subliminal advertising is demonstrated. We should recognize, of course, that the intent to control behavior with this technique is itself a moral concern, regardless of its success or failure.

Furthermore, we again should be careful to distinguish creating wants from controlling behavior. The moral evil involved in subliminal advertising, the violation of autonomy, follows from the attempt to persuade someone in a way that cannot be resisted. Autonomy is violated when wants are created in ways in which the consumer is prevented from stepping back and reflecting upon the nature and origins of the want, regardless of whether or not the consumer then acts upon that want.

In our final selections, John Culkin and Carol Levine consider the morality of advertising to children. Culkin argues that children are especially vulnerable to advertising and that all interested parties, including parents, teachers, business, and government, have the responsibility of protecting children in this area. Levine reviews for us some recent research on the effects of advertising on children.

Consider, for example, Saturday morning television shows. Many of these shows are based upon characters first developed for commercial purposes (e.g., Smurfs, Pac-man, etc.). Critics have charged that these television shows are little more than thirty-minute commercials. Children typically have trouble distinguishing programs from commercials as it is, and these shows seem to exacerbate the problem. A child exposed to these shows over a period of time might well be socialized to the point where he or she will unreflectively accept the consumer "lifestyle." As a result, the child may uncritically place a disproportionate amount of value on those items found only in toy stores and video arcades.

A standard response to this criticism cites the parents' ability to veto the child's choice in the marketplace. Since parents can prevent children from irresponsible buying, the child's autonomy remains protected. Besides the fact that children do spend a significant amount of money independently of their parents, this objection misses the point. The type of persuasion that concerns critics of advertising to children does not attempt to control children's behavior directly, but involves implanting the desire for a certain lifestyle at a very early age. This type of persuasion aims at an audience unable to take a step back from its wants and desires and reflect upon them. On Dworkin's account, it would seem to violate autonomy, regardless of whether or not specific purchases resulted from these wants.

While adults usually can reflect upon advertisements and decide for themselves what is in their own interests, children typically cannot. In this regard, it would be interesting to extend the discussion of paternalism and government regulation from Chapter 3 to these issues. Should advertising to children be regulated by government action? Are other groups, e.g., the elderly, similarly unlikely to be capable of stepping back and reflecting upon their own interests? Should advertisements aimed at selling life or medical insurance to the elderly be regulated?

JOHN KENNETH GALBRAITH

Persuasion—and Power

Mr. Hill wanted more women to smoke Lucky Strikes: research showed that sales to them were down because the green-packaged cigarettes clashed with their costumes. "Change the color of the package," I suggested. Mr. Hill was outraged. I then suggested we try to make green the dominant color of women's fashions . . . For a year we worked . . . Green became fashion's color.

Edward L. Bernays
The Business History Review
Autumn 1971

1

We come now to a decisive point in the development of a modern view of the economic system. The neoclassical model concedes that producers in many industries have a substantial measure of control over prices and costs. Such is the nature of monopoly and oligopoly. So long as this is to maximize profits, and is not part of any more comprehensive exercise of power, the firm remains subordinate to the ultimate will of the user of the goods. As the tastes and needs of the user change, so does the amount he will take and the price he will pay. In responding to these changes, as it must if it is to keep its profits at a maximum, the firm responds to the user's authority. Although the response is imperfect, the sovereignty of the user remains unimpaired.

This admirable vision of the ultimate power of the user cannot be sustained, however, if his tastes and needs fall under the authority of the producer. This does not require much explanation. The consumer is not sovereign if he or she is subordinate, or partly subordinate, to the will of the producer. That the economy is ultimately in the service of the consumer cannot be believed if the producer can manage the consumer—can bend him to his needs. And once it is agreed that the producer has a measure of authority over the consumer or other

user of his goods, the way is open for a further and massive breach in the dike. For then it can be argued that the control of prices, costs, consumer demand and the state is all part of a single deployment of power—one that serves the purposes of the technostructure in particular and the planning system in general. Exponents of the neoclassical system unite, not without a certain scholarly fervor, in denying that the producer has effective power over the users of his products. Once again their instinct, viewed in the light not of truth but of self-preservation, does not serve them badly.

Yet no myth, however serviceable to particular interest, is wholly satisfactory if it taxes belief. In the exercise of monopoly power there is control of prices and, where possible, of costs. The existence of this power is accepted in the traditional or neoclassical view. But the profit maximization of the monopoly would be most negligently served, as almost all must agree, if, the initial power over prices having been secured, no effort were made to affect the demand for the product—if the firm then relaxed and contented itself with the whimsical acceptance or rejection of its product by the consumer. The obvious counterpart of the control of prices is an effort to control the response of buyers to those prices. A strategy for protecting established belief which seeks to confine corporate power to the control of prices and costs, however great its service to intellectual vested interest, is also absurd.

2

The final users of goods and services are private consumers and the government. Efforts to influence demand extend comprehensively to both. The management of the private consumer has two dimensions: There is the preference or nonpreference of the consumer for the producer's product or service. This must be favorably influenced. And there is the equally poignant question, given that preference, of whether the consumer has the income to buy the product or service. Not much is gained by persuading customers to a product if they cannot afford it. An effective strategy for ensuring the desired response of the private consumer must be concerned therefore both with influencing his attitude toward the particular product or service and ensuring, insofar as may be possible, that he—and consumers generally—have the wherewithal or effective demand to buy the product.

The management of the private consumer of goods is inextricably associated with the management of the public demand for goods. The corporation seeks to manage the choices of the private consumer. It seeks also to manage the purchases of the state. The techniques are radically different in the two cases; the purpose is the same. And there are further interrelationships. The public expenditures that are the product of the influence of the technostructure on public procurement are also important for sustaining the flow of public expenditure that stabilizes the purchasing power of the private consumer. Military expenditures in particular both buy the products of the supplying firms and sustain demand in the economy as a whole. It is thus seen that what economists compartmentalize as macroeconomics and microeconomics are parts of a larger whole, one that is formed by the power of the planning system.

The management of demand requires management of the state for yet other reasons. Some kinds of private demand are only possible if there is complementary action by the state—the demand for automobiles requires facilitating public expenditure for highways; demand for air travel and aircraft requires public expenditure for terminals and airways. And broad patterns of consumption are established by public policy. People go to work by automobile in the United States partly, no doubt, because of preference but partly because no alternatives exist. The use of public resources for alternative modes of travel has been powerfully discouraged by automotive interests.[1]

Although we are here concerned with tightly interrelated phenomena, it will be convenient to look first at the way in which the planning system brings its power to bear on the private consumer.

Then we shall see how it influences public purchases of its products and otherwise arranges needed public action. The problem of stabilizing demand in general, though a part of the same process, will be postponed to a later chapter [not included in this anthology], where its bearing on the market system can also be seen.

3

The management of the private consumer is a task of no slight sophistication; the cost is considerable, and it uses some of the most expert and specialized talent to be found anywhere in the planning system. Its most obvious instrument is advertising. And the uniquely powerful instrument of advertising is television which allows persuasive communication with virtually every user of goods and services and with no minimum requirement in effort, literacy or intelligence. But the management also involves the deployment of sales and merchandising staffs and of sales and dealer organizations. It makes extensive use of market research and testing to ascertain to what the consumer can be persuaded and by what means and at what cost. It extends deeply into the choice and design of goods to ensure that they incorporate features that lend themselves to persuasion—that have good selling points. It makes extensive use of innovation which, as we shall presently see, differs sharply from the classical purposes of invention, which were to serve some need the inventor had perceived and sought to fill. Modern innovation is more often to create a need that no one had previously perceived. Or it exploits the close association that exists in the public mind between innovation and improvement. To the peculiarities of modern technical innovation we return in the next chapter [not included in this anthology].

A special word is required on market research. This, it has occasionally been argued, is to ascertain what consumers want. In consequence its existence affirms the ultimate power of the consumer and ensures that production is more efficiently subordinated to that power. As often or more often it is to ascertain the effectiveness of different kinds of persuasion or how well different products, brands or packages lend themselves to such persuasion. From this the firm learns how money for persuasion can be most efficiently spent—what sales effort gets the best results and what products lend themselves best to persuasion and how much. Such effort hardly affirms the sovereignty of the consumer.

Much of what is called market research, it may also be noted, is imprecise. Subjective, random or fraudulent judgments are offered in impressive pseudosociometric tables to suggest a precise relationship between outlay on different kinds of persuasion and the resulting sales. This will not be surprising. And industry that employs much carefully tempered mendacity will not be sensitive to its application to itself.

The power to influence the individual consumer is not, of course, plenary. It operates within limits of cost. The winning of customers or custom will generally be at increasing cost; the shape of this function (the curve showing the cost of obtaining each added increment of sales) will depend on the nature of the product and the quality of the persuasion, and it will be subject to sharp variation over time. Both the position and stability of this function will depend on past outlays for persuasion. What will have to be spent to win a given amount of custom for a particular soap will depend on what has been spent on that soap in the past and also on what has been spent by all soap manufacturers to establish the imperatives of a clean and odorless personality.

That the power to manage the individual consumer is imperfect must be emphasized. Scholars who, for traditional and instrumental reasons, argue that the sovereignty of the consumer is unimpaired normally hold that the alternative to total independence of consumer choice is total subordination of that choice to the will of the producer. The consumer, not being wholly sovereign, is wholly a puppet of the producer. It is necessary only to outline this dialectic to indicate its tendentious design.

4

The protective purpose of going beyond prices to influence consumer response is to prevent the defection of consumers which thus would plunge the firm into loss. The affirmative purpose is, of course, to recruit new customers and thus to expand sales—to serve the goal of growth. As sufficiently remarked, the typical industry of the planning system consists of a few large firms. This means that sales can be expanded both by recruiting new users and by persuading customers of other firms to switch. Other firms, for their part, will be engaged in the same effort. The management of the consumer is thus an intricate complex of efforts to recruit new users, win the customers of other firms and hold existing customers in face of the corresponding efforts of the other firms. Since the gain of customers by one firm means their loss by another, the affirmative and protective purposes of consumer management, as they are actually pursued in any consumer industry, are in some degree in conflict.

This, however, is only partially so. For firms that have the scale and resources to participate fully in the persuasion[2]—in the automobile industry, General Motors, Ford and perhaps Chrysler as distinct from American Motors or such earlier casualties as Studebaker and Packard; in the soap and detergents industry, Procter & Gamble, Lever Brothers, Colgate-Palmolive—the aggressive and defensive operations of the participating firms come eventually into a rough equilibrium. The company that is gaining rests with its existing system of persuasion; the company that is doing less well seeks more effective means of persuasion as to existing products or searches for products or designs that lend themselves more effectively to persuasion. Sooner or later it succeeds, and this returns the play to its previously more successful rivals. The result is a control of consumer reactions which, though imperfect and greatly complicated by the rivalry, is still far more secure than would be the ungoverned responses of consumers in the absence of such effort.

Meanwhile the aggregate result of the effort is solidly beneficial to all the participants in the planning system. It recruits new customers for all firms in the particular industry, associates existing customers more firmly with the products of the industry and powerfully advances the larger purposes and values of the planning system. These are vital services and deserve a special word of summary.

The advertising of the individual automobile company seeks to win consumers from other makes. But the advertising of all together contributes to the conviction that happiness is associated with automobile ownership. Additionally, make and model apart, it persuades people that the contemporary tendencies in automobile physiognomy and decoration are desirable, that those of the past are obsolete, eccentric or otherwise unworthy. Thus it encourages the general discarding of old vehicles and the purchase of new. Similarly, if one soap manufacturer can establish that white sheets are an index of womanly virtue, this virtue is rewarding to all soap and detergent manufacturers. If one manufacturer can make modest intoxication a mark of suave respectability, so it becomes for all makers of intoxicants. If one hairdressing contributes to successful seduction, then so may all.

More important still, the aggregate of all such persuasion affirms in the most powerful possible manner that happiness is the result of the possession and use of goods and that, pro tanto, happiness will be enhanced in proportion as more goods are produced and consumed. Thus the persuasion proclaims and extends the values of the planning system in general and its commitment to growth in particular. This helps also to support its claim for assistance from the state on behalf of its needs. One branch of neoclassical economics has long held that the advertising and persuasion in the typically oligopolistic industry is a purely wasteful exercise in aggression and defense—"a form of nonprice competition ... of a mutually neutralizing, standoff sort, with no technical or social benefits at all."[3] The only consequence is higher prices to the public or lower earnings for the participants.

Were this the case, steps would long ago have been taken to limit advertising outlays by common agreement. No law would have stood against this effort, for the cost to the industry and the waste for the public would have been solemnly and influentially cited and policy would thus have been accommodated to the needs of the planning system. In fact, competitive persuasion serves the common purposes of the planning system. Accordingly no important effort has ever been made to limit it.

5

The technostructure also extensively influences the purchase of public goods in accordance with

its needs. Here, however, there is general recognition that the orthodox economic view, though ceremonially presented to the young as a conventional characteristic of democracy, has little relation to the reality.

In the orthodox or traditional view the choice between private and public goods and services and between different public goods and services is expressed, indirectly, in the choice of candidates and party for public office—in the choice between those avowing an interest in more or less taxation and, given the level of public expenditure, between those urging greater or less emphasis on education, welfare, public works or other public goods and services. Among the latter services are weapons and weapons development, but they are singled out for no special attention.[4] The candidates so chosen relate the public will to the executive through their power over legislative authorization and appropriations. The executive—the bureaucracy—is the passive servant of the legislature and thus, ultimately, of the citizen. In the United States the election of the Chief Executive, who exposes his position on these matters to the voters, further reinforces the citizen control.

Few who teach this doctrine would be willing to admit personal belief; to do so would be to damage one's reputation for a minimally reputable skepticism. In the case of weapons—missile systems and missile defenses, nuclear aircraft carriers, fighter aircraft, manned bombers—the process, it would be agreed, almost exactly reverses the orthodox formula. The initiating decision is taken by the weapons firm and by the particular service for which the item is intended. The action is ratified by the President who, though not without power, is extensively a captive of the bureaucracy he heads. The Armed Services Committees of the Congress, staffed with reliable sycophants of the weapons firms and the services, accept all but automatically the decision so taken. The role of the rest of the Congress is minimal; that of the public is nil.

The foregoing as distinct from the doctrinal view accords with what would be expected from the present analysis, given our knowledge of where power is located and how it is used. Some would assign a special primacy to the weapons firm. This derives from a view of capitalism which automatically accords a commanding role to the capitalist firm. However two sets of bureaucracies, the technostructures of the weapons firms and that of the Pentagon, are involved. It cannot be assumed that the one kind of organization is less powerful than the other.

Rather they jointly pursue common interests in growth and technical innovation—they have the same relationship as that between private technostructures described in the last chapter [not included]. Members of both the public and private bureaucracies are served by growth and the consequent promotions, pay, perquisites, prestige and power, and what expands one bureaucracy expands the other. Technical development, as the next chapter [not included] will show, is particularly important both for the autonomy and growth of the public bureaucracy and for the supplying technostructure. Here, accordingly, the reciprocal support is especially great. The service, often with the help of the weapons firm, defines the need for the product; the firm then undertakes the development. Both gain.

There will be a similar tendency to reciprocal support whenever a technostructure and a public bureaucracy are closely juxtaposed. Such is the relation between the Atomic Energy Commission and its supplying industries. Such is the relation, as regards roads, between the Department of Transportation and the automobile industry. Even where there is a presumptively adversary relationship between a public and a private bureaucracy, as between the Federal Communications Commission and the television and broadcasting networks, reciprocal support is possible. This tendency for the public and private organizations to find and pursue a common purpose is of sufficient importance to justify a name. It may be called Bureaucratic Symbiosis.

In the United States bureaucratic symbiosis reaches its highest state of development in the relation between the weapons firms and the Department of Defense and its constituent elements. Lockheed, Boeing, Grumman or General Dynamics can develop and build military aircraft. This serves their affirmative goal of growth with the concurrent reward to their technostructures. The public bureaucracy that is associated with research and development, contracting, contract supervision, operations and command is similarly rewarded by the development and possession of a new generation of planes. But bureaucratic symbiosis also works at a more elementary level. The technostructure of the weapons firm is a natural source of employment for those who have completed a career in (or otherwise exhausted the possibilities of) the public bureaucracy. Leadership in the Department of Defense, by the same token, is extensively in the hands of men recruited temporarily from senior positions in the technostructures of the weapons firms. Not only is this exchange rewarding to individuals, but it serves, more than incidentally, to cement the symbiotic relationship.

In the symbiotic relationship between the public and private bureaucracies, it may be stressed once more, no conclusion can or should be reached as to where the initiative lies. Certainly no one can say with assurance that it is with either the public bureaucracy or the firm. What is clear is that the initiative does not come from the citizen. More completely even than in the case of the consumer, effective power has passed to the producers— either to the producer of the weapons or the producer of the military service that employs the weapons. And, as noted, even pretense to the contrary is no longer quite respectable.

6

Obviously the power of different producers in relation to the consumer or citizen varies greatly. It is greatest where the development is most advanced—where the firm is largest and its technostructure is most fully developed. In the private sector of the economy it is greater for the automobile, soap, tobacco and manufactured-food industries than in, say, housing, medical care or the arts. In the market system the power of the producer becomes minimal or disappears. In the public sector the power of the producer will be greatest, that of the citizen least, where there is bureaucratic symbiosis—where a large aerospace firm works symbiotically with the Air Force. It will be least where small construction firms build low-cost housing for a local housing authority or funds are supplied to a local school district.

Thus the conclusion, already suggested and now becoming firm. How economic resources— capital, manpower, materials—are allocated to production, both in the private and public sectors of the economy, depends, and heavily though of course not exclusively, on producer power. And, with the development of the economy, it depends increasingly on that power. This is a basic tendency of the economic system.

In the neoclassical model production is controlled by consumer and citizen choice. The ultimate equilibrium corresponds to their need as interpreted by themselves and made effective by their income. In the modern reality the equilibrium reflects the power of the producer. This, not "need" in any exclusive or dominant sense, controls what the economy does. Production is great not necessarily where there is great need; it may be great where there is great capacity for managing the behavior of the individual consumer or for sharing symbiotically in the control of the procurement of public goods and services, all in the interest of bureaucratic growth. This is in sharp contrast with the neoclassical view of power which holds that power restricts output in the manner of the classical monopoly. But a moment's thought directed to the areas of abundance in the economy—automobiles, weapons, soaps, deodorants and detergents—will suggest that the present analysis is not in conflict with common observation and common sense.

Discussion of the practical issues associated with this overproduction—and the underproduction of other things—can only be avoided if it is agreed that the consumer and citizen are resistant to the power of the producer; if advertising and salesmanship are the froth and not the substance of economics; if, as an expression of oligopolistic rivalry, they cancel out; and if the great weapons firms, though admittedly powerful, are a flaw, sui generis, left over from the Cold War. If economics helps with such belief, it is, from the viewpoint of those who exercise power, a most benign thing. If it insists on identifying the exercise of power that explains the reality, it is less benign. Questions as to the legitimacy of power follow. So do questions as to the effects of its use. The need for remedial

action to align the use of power with the public interest can no longer be escaped. And such remedial action ceases to be exceptional but becomes, instead, an intrinsic need.

NOTES

1. The extent to which consumer choice is affected by such denial of alternatives has been brought to my attention by Paul Sweezy, who has taxed me, I think rightly, for neglecting it in earlier work. See his "Comment," *The Quarterly Journal of Economics*, Vol. 86, No. 4 (November 1972), p. 661 et seq.

2. See William S. Comanor and Thomas A. Wilson, "Advertising and the Advantages of Size," *The American Economic Review*, Papers and Proceedings, Vol. 59, No. 2 (May 1969), p. 87 et seq. The authors conclude that the large firm enjoys significant advantages in the use of advertising. In an earlier article ("Advertising Market Structure and Performance," *The Review of Economics and Statistics*, Vol. 419, No. 4 [November 1967], pp. 423 ff.) the same authors also found a general association between advertising expenditure and profits. Roughly the same conclusion is reached by Leonard W. Weiss in "Advertising, Profits and Corporate Taxes," *The Review of Economics and Statistics*, Vol. 51, No. 4 (November 1969), pp. 421 ff. There are various possible explanations for this; the most obvious is that aggressive demand management serves effectively to protect and enhance returns. The notion of an equilibrium as here outlined follows the argument advanced in *The New Industrial State*, 2d ed., rev. (Boston: Houghton Mifflin, 1971), p. 204 et seq.

3. William G. Shepherd, *Market Power and Economic Welfare* (New York: Random House, 1970), p. 53. I do not imply that Professor Shepherd, to whose competent work all who are concerned with these matters are indebted, is by any means a captive of the stereotypes.

4. "Introductory courses in economics, as reflected in principal textbooks used in American colleges and universities, usually do not recognize the existence of the military-industrial firm or a war economy. In these texts the magnitude and the characteristics of military economic activity in the United States since the Second World War either are not mentioned at all, or are dealt with in a few sentences or paragraphs." Seymour Melman, "The Peaceful World of Economics I," *The Journal of Economic Issues*, Vol. 6, No. 1 (March 1972), p. 1.

G. WILLIAM TRIVOLI

Has the Consumer Really Lost His Sovereignty?

John Kenneth Galbraith has eloquently stated in *The New Industrial State*[7], and other places, that the consumer has lost his sovereignty. Embarrassing? Yes, quite, for economists, anyway. This contention, if true, strikes at the very heart of the science of economics, which is based upon rational choice by a free and discerning consumer. This contention has obvious important implications for all the other social sciences as well. For, if true, all the study of man's behavior is irrelevant. What should be studied, then, are the institutions molding his wants, especially the large corporation.

According to Galbraith, so that the giant corporation may effectively plan its output it must be free from the whims of consumer sovereignty. This is supposed to be achieved by the corporation managing consumer demand largely through advertising and other subtle selling techniques.

This paper reviews briefly the theoretical arguments involved in the contention that consumers' wants are controlled by producers. An important implication is that if large firms are able to manipulate consumers' product desires, then most new products introduced by large firms should be successful. A further implication is that there should be a positive relationship between advertising and product acceptance by consumers.

Galbraith develops what he calls the "revised sequence" meaning that, instead of catering to the consumer's wishes, large firms attempt to eliminate uncertainties of the market by managing consumer demand. In Galbraith's own words:

> The mature corporation has readily at hand the means ... for managing what the consumer buys at the prices which it controls. This control and management is required by its planning.[7]

Galbraith sees advertising in particular and salesmanship in general as the major methods by which the corporate behemoths manipulate consumers' wants. In fact, he seems to equate these tasks with controlling the consumer when he states "Advertising and salesmanship—the management of consumer demand—are vital for planning in the industrial system."[7]

This argument by Galbraith has been popular in one form or another for quite some time, not only in economics, but also in sociology and psychology. There has been a growing literature that has posited that advertisers are able to manipulate consumers. Recent developments in the science of psychology, and the publicity given some of its more sensational applications, such as subliminal advertising or brainwashing, have strengthened this belief.[2] Galbraith's argument thus falls upon receptive ears when he maintains that giant firms are now in a position to organize their research and marketing in such a way that they can impose upon the consumer the products they make. Yet, the hard evidence on this particular argument of the industrial system hypothesis is difficult to find.

The underlying theory of Galbraith's revised sequence is dealt with in greater detail in *The Affluent Society*[6] under the name of the dependence effect. Galbraith asserts that the marginal increments in consumer satisfaction from added production are low and declining. As the wealth of a society increases, the importance of economic goals is somehow lessened and private production consequently becomes less important.

The key contention of Galbraith's argument is that if the individual's wants are to be urgent they must be original with the individual. They cannot be urgent, he feels, if they must be contrived. Above all, wants must not be contrived by the process of production by which wants are satisfied. Thus, Galbraith maintains

© 1970 *Akron Business and Economic Review*, vol. 1, no. 4 (Winter 1970). Reprinted by permission.

One cannot defend production as satisfying wants if that production creates the wants ... If production creates the wants, it seeks to satisfy, or if the wants emerge pari passu with the production, the urgency of the wants can no longer be used to defend the urgency of production. Production only fills a void that it has itself created.[6]

Galbraith asserts that those wants of man that remain unsatisfied in modern society would not be experienced spontaneously by the individual if left to himself, leading to the conclusion that wants are increasingly created by the process by which they are satisfied.

Following the criticism of Friedrich Hayek,[7] the revised sequence of dependence effect is found to be a non sequitur. Galbraith asserts that most consumer wants in a modern society would not be experienced by the individual in a primitive society; these acquired or learned wants, which are supposed to be generated by the producers themselves, are represented as not urgent and therefore unimportant. The first part of Galbraith's argument is probably true; that is, one would not desire any of the amenities of civilization if others in the economy did not provide them. The innate human wants are probably confined to a very few things such as food, shelter and sex.[8] The desire for food, for instance, may be satisfied crudely and simply or lavishly. Galbraith apparently would prefer that people choose the simpler satisfactions.

"To say a desire is not important," states Professor Hayek, "because it is not innate, is to say that the whole cultural achievement of man is not important."[9] In some contexts, Hayek states, it perhaps would be legitimate to say production generates wants. This clearly would not justify the contention that particular producers can determine the wants of individual consumers. The joint but uncorrelated efforts of producers create but a single element in the environment by which wants of consumers are shaped.[9] However, no producer can in any real sense determine the individual wants or desires of consumers. Yet this is the implication of such statements by Galbraith that wants are "both passively and deliberately the fruits of the process by which they are satisfied."[6]

Galbraith views the process of the revised sequence first from the production side, with the corporate form of business enterprise as an instru-

ment for the accumulation of capital, the practical application of technical progress and the planning of future output. Next he views the consumption side, with the affluent consumer, whose standard of living is already above that which may be related to basic needs for food, clothing and shelter and is being raised continuously higher through the creation of new and more demanding wants. The link between the two sides, and the institutional manifestation of want creation driving the system to greater heights of production and consumption, is advertising.[10]

GALBRAITH ON ADVERTISING

Galbraith's position on advertising may be interpreted as maintaining that advertising changes consumers' tastes. An opposing view is that consumers' changed behavior can be attributed not to a change in tastes but rather to a widened knowledge of choices available for the better satisfaction of wants.[3] Aligned with Galbraith are numerous sociologists and several economists, including Robin Marris. Although Marris claims that his theory places less emphasis on the effects of advertising as such, he still maintains that he sees

... the process by which consumer tastes develop as a complicated interaction of personal influence (meaning the influence of consumers on other consumers), greatly helped at critical points by advertising and marketing efforts generally.[12]

The contention raised by Galbraith is that, increasingly, the wants satisfied by additional production are themselves created by the production process itself; thus, the satisfaction of these wants cannot be regarded as a true increase in satisfaction. Harry G. Johnson has pointed out that Galbraith's contention, if correct, strikes at the heart of liberal economics, which is posited on the independence of consumer wants.[10] Galbraith is raising the fundamental question of the validity of economics science itself in both its positive and normative aspects.

For discussion, the above contention is separable into two parts: first, the observation that the growth of affluence is characterized by the creation and satisfaction of new wants by means of social and commercial pressures on consumers and second, the judgment that the wants so created are valueless or even contemptible.

The notion that progress essentially involves the creation of new wants is not new to economic literature. Alfred Marshall was drawing on a long tradition of economic thought when, in introducing his analysis of demand, he stated

Speaking broadly therefore, although it is man's wants in the earliest stages of his development that give rise to his activities, yet afterwards each new step upwards is to be regarded as the development of new activities giving rise to new wants, rather than of new wants giving rise to new activities.[13]

Marshall fully recognized the desire for distinction as an influence on wants; thus he stressed the desire for excellence as a stronger motive than the inborn basic wants. Furthermore, Marshall left no doubt of his belief that the trend of wants was upward and not simply sideways.

To maintain a hierarchy of wants is to argue that changes in taste are governed ultimately by accepted standards of good and better taste, standards which are capable of being learned and applied by a consumer. The consumer learns standards of taste and applies them in response to both his own maximizing behavior and influences of fellow-consumers (the "Joneses"), advertising and the entire socio-economic environment.[10] It is toward influencing these standards as well as informing that advertising and marketing in general must ultimately appeal. Harry G. Johnson, in a discussion of this question of definable standards for recognizing improvements in the consumption function, states

The notion of standards for recognizing improvements in the consumption function is admittedly much more hazy and imprecise than the notion of standards for recognizing improvements in the production function; nevertheless, their existence is I think, undeniable.[10]

Neil H. Borden, in a study of a number of products conducted to determine the economic effects of advertising, concluded that the basic trends of demand for products are determined mainly by underlying social and environmental conditions rather than by advertising.[5] In addition to demonstrating the inability of advertising alone

to shape consumer demand, Borden found (1) that advertising is profitably used only when product demand in a particular area is comparatively new and hence demand is expandable and, conversely, (2) for certain products advertising over a period of years has tended to make new products more responsive to price competition.[5]

To illustrate the first finding, Borden discusses dentifrices as a product for which advertising plays an important part in determining consumer values. Yet, following the Civil War there was a tremendous public education program to augment the basic desire for attractiveness in promoting awareness of the relationship of the teeth to health and the importance of care of the teeth in preventing oral ills. Borden concludes that although advertising was an important factor in stimulating the practice of brushing teeth, it had no appreciable effect on per capita consumption during the postwar decade; nor was advertising able to stem a marked decline in consumption during the Great Depression.[5]

As an illustration of the second point, Borden cites the case of mechanical refrigerators as an example of a product whose elasticity of demand was increased by advertising and aggressive selling. The increased interest generated by advertising helped build public acceptance; thus the product became more responsive to lowered prices and price competition. Other products he mentions as having become more responsive to price competition as a result of advertising are automobiles, radios, oil burners and numerous electrical appliances.

An important distinction must be made regarding the meaning of the term "create." Whether the firm is considered to create the consumer demand, or respond to it, depends on the interpretation of the word create. Maurice Zinkin, in a discussion of Galbraith and consumer sovereignty, states that if, by create

. . . one means produce a demand which was not there before in that form, then firms, big and small, very often do create demands. One could not want the latest style of the hairdresser round the corner before he had conceived it. . . . In that limited sense, the demand for any invention is a creation of its inventor . . . if it is implied that the new want is "created" in the sense of being artificial, then this is normally not true. The new want is nearly always an old want but satisfied in a new way.[16]

Galbraith would choose the latter definition; thus he sees giant producers somehow creating artificial wants, wants that would not be present if the consumer were left to his innate wants for food, shelter and clothing. This is brought out most clearly in Galbraith's famous quote:

The fact that wants can be synthesized by advertising, catalyzed by salesmanship, and shaped by the discreet manipulation of the persuaders shows they are not very urgent. A man who is hungry need never be told of his need for food.[6]

The fact that consumers may occasionally be persuaded to spend some of their income unwisely, at least from Galbraith's point of view, does not prove that the dollars spent in this manner yield negative or zero utility. One may regard unwise expenditures as misguided effort, but it would not deny consumers sovereignty.[9]

Galbraith, it seems, is confused by the fact that consumers willingly allow the manufacturer to take the risks of predicting their future demand and producing the commodities that possibly will satisfy that demand. Frank Knight reaches the core of the problem in his discussion of the uncertainty problem in economics. Knight points out that two elements of uncertainty are introduced in the process of production of goods over time, corresponding to two different kinds of foresight that must be exercised:

First, the end of productive operations must be estimated from the beginning. It is . . . impossible to tell accurately when entering upon productive activity what will be its results in physical terms, what (a) quantities and (b) qualities of goods will result. . . . Second, the wants which the goods are to satisfy are also, of course, in the future to the same extent, and their prediction involves uncertainty in the same way. The producer, then, must *estimate* (1) the future demand which he is striving to satisfy and (2) the future results of his operations in attempting to satisfy that demand.[11]

The consumer is rationally and intelligently shifting these uncertainties of production and prediction of his future wants. The consumer willingly allows the producer to take the risks of choosing and estimating future consumer wants, but the consumer maintains his veto power if the resulting product in some manner fails to meet his tastes. In short, the important aspect neglected by Galbraith

is the informational role advertising plays in a modern mass consumption economy. Thus, even the Soviets have discovered that production of vast amounts of goods and services requires huge amounts of information for factories to operate with efficiency and flexibility. George Stigler points out that

Advertising plays a large role in providing this information, but Mr. Galbraith implies that most advertising is nonrational in method and persuasive in purpose. And he offers no support for this implicit measurement beyond caustic remarks on an evening at home with television.[15]

THE EMPIRICAL EVIDENCE OF THE SUCCESS OF NEW PRODUCTS

It is Galbraith's contention that failure of a new product introduced by a large firm is a rarity, thus establishing his supposition that corporations are able to control consumer wants. If it can be shown that new product failures are not a rare occurrence but instead quite common, the argument becomes suspect. An empirical test of new product success is suggested by Stephen A. Greyser, a leading authority in the field of marketing. He suggests

New product introductions particularly represent a "test" of fit with consumers' wants. New product failures are very high; percentage estimates vary from 80% to 30% failures.[8]

Galbraith as much as concedes that such a test of his hypothesis may be proper when he states, regarding the failure of the Edsel, "Its notoriety owes much to its being exceptional."[7] His hypothesis concerning the ability of large corporations to control consumers' demand seems to imply the following: (1) new products of large corporations should not fail; in fact, most new products would be expected to succeed and (2) since advertising is the major device by which consumers' demand is manipulated, those who spend the most on advertising should have greatest success.

In a summary of extensive research and experience in the introduction of new products, Booz, Allen & Hamilton discusses the significant body of information on new product success gathered in over 800 client assignments conducted over the past several years. In addition, their management research department has made confidential studies of new product activities of 200 firms noted for their product development programs. The two basic conclusions of their experience are as follows:

Most manufacturers cannot live without new products. It is commonplace for major companies to have 50% or more of current sales in products new in the past 10 years. In the next three years alone, about 75% of the nation's growth in sales volume can be expected to come from new products. . . .

Most new products are failures. Even among the most important and effective United States companies, 1964 research shows that for about every three products emerging from research and development departments as technical successes, there is an average of only one commercial success.[4]

Management judgment in the new product development process meets its final test at the last state—commercialization. At that point, the firm must pronounce its product worthy and introduce it at great expense. Despite the lengthy screening process, analysis, development and testing, the ratio of successful to unsuccessful new products for prominent companies is two to one.

The failure rate of new products varies surprisingly little among the industries studied by Booz, Allen & Hamilton. There is, however, great variation in failure rates among individual firms, apparently as a reflection of differences in management effectiveness. The average product performance rate for several industries is shown in Table 1. The actual success rate for new product ideas for all industry groups studied was 1.7 percent. Successes for products once they reached the product development stage, which is turning the design into a product-in-hand, for all industry groups was 14.5 percent. Finally, the success of products actually introduced in the market (commercialization stage) rose to 62.5 percent for all industry groups studied, which is still only slightly better than half of all products marketed by leading corporations.

Jules Backman reports a study made of the experiences of the 125 companies which were the largest advertisers in terms of dollars in 1964 and in 1965:[1] *Advertising Age* published a list of 125 companies with the largest dollar expenditures for advertising, and, as part of this tabulation, the domestic sales for these companies and their expenditures as a percentage of these sales were reported. Profit data were available for 111 companies in 1965 and 114 in 1964. The advertising-to-sales ratios for these firms were related to their return on invested capital by Backman in order to determine to what extent more intensive advertising was accompanied by larger rates of profits. The average return on net assets for the 102 manufacturing companies included in this study was 14.7 percent in 1965 as compared with 13.8 percent for 2,298 leading manufacturers reported by the First National City Bank of New York. Even if the entire difference in profit returns were attributable to the effects of advertising, the most that could be said is that manufacturing companies with large dollar advertising expenditures reported profits that were 0.9 percent higher than the average of leading manufacturing companies. The relationship for 1964 gave the heavy advertisers a one percent margin over the average for leading manufacturers reported by the First National City Bank of New York. Backman concludes from this study that ". . . companies with large dollar expenditures for advertising have not earned much more on invested capital than leading manufacturing corporations generally."[1]

In the general range of manufactured goods, it is possible to find numerous cases of failures of products introduced by firms that Galbraith would consider large mature corporations. In an article describing several new product failures, Burt Schorr referred to studies of overall product performance. He mentions a study by Lippincott and Margulies, a New York industrial design firm, which indicates that of every 26 products introduced by industry, 23 fail. Also, McCann-Erickson, Inc., a large advertising agency, reported that of every 25 products test marketed, only one succeeds.[14] Some notable market failures discussed by Schorr in a survey of new product introductions by large firms include the following:

The Predicta line of television sets of advanced design was introduced in 1959 by Philco Corporation. Philco had exceeded development and retooling budgets by 25 percent as well as sponsored an extensive promotion and advertising campaign. Profits on the new Predicta line were negligible; it was regarded as a clear failure.

TABLE ONE

Rate of Commercial Success

| | **Success Percentages** | | |
	New Product Ideas	Product Development Projects	New Products Introduced
All industry groups	1.7	14.5	62.5
Chemical	2	18	59
Consumer packaged goods	2	11	63
Electrical machinery	1	13	63
Metal fabricators	3	11	71
Non-electrical machinery	2	21	59
Raw material processors	5	14	59

Source: Booz, Allen & Hamilton, *Management of New Products*, 1968.

The Bristol-Myers Company introduced a new product called Analoze, a combination pain killer and antacid. The failure of Analoze indicates not only that a large producer was unable to shape consumers' wants, but in addition extensive consumer research could not even predict what the consumer wanted. The executives who conceived of the product were impressed by the fact that Americans were consuming record amounts of aspirin; thus they felt a combination analgesic and antacid that could be taken without water would have a ready market. Backed by heavy advertising outlays, Analoze moved into test markets: dealers were enthusiastic and prospects appeared bright. Then the sales figures indicated that, despite all the careful preparations, the public was buying only small quantities of the new product. After weeks of test marketing, Bristol-Myers finally withdrew Analoze.[14]

Schorr goes on to list failures of such giants as General Mills, Inc. (a meringue mix in the fall of 1958) and General Foods (a line of gourmet foods that included imported biscuits and Swedish lingonberries) and, finally, to the failure of a heavily advertised cigarette by a leading cigarette manufacturer, the American Tobacco Company. The failure of American's Hit Parade cigarettes is significant since the cigarette manufacturers are regarded as the nation's most extensive advertisers. In his discussion about the American Tobacco Company's first entry in the filter tip cigarette market Burt Schorr states

According to a survey conducted by Brown & Williamson Tobacco Co., a competitor, American poured $40 million into Hit Parade advertising and promotion during the three years following the introduction of the cigarette in late 1956. While American labels this estimate "much too high," it's known the company paid over $17 million for air time and publication space alone during those three years.[14]

CONCLUDING REMARKS

The basic error of Galbraith and others in asserting the loss of consumer sovereignty is the assumption that producers somehow create wants that never before existed. The assumption is not warranted on the basis of existing evidence. One might legitimately question on normative grounds whether man should satisfy his wants in ever more affluent and ostentatious ways, but that man himself chooses, in a free market economy, from among a multitude of means to satisfy his wants is undeniable.

REFERENCES

1. Jules Backman, *Advertising and Competition.* New York 1967.

2. Raymond A. Bauer, "Limits of Persuasion." *Harvard Business Review*, XXXVI No. 5 (1958).

3. Robert L. Bishop, "Monopolistic Competition and Welfare Economics" in Robert E. Kuenne, ed., *Monopolistic Competition Theory: Studies in Impact.* New York 1967.

4. Booz, Allen & Hamilton, Management Consultants, *Management of New Products.* 1968.

5. Neil H. Borden, *Advertising in Our Economy.* Chicago 1945.

6. J. K. Galbraith, *The Affluent Society.* Boston 1958.

7. J. K. Galbraith, *The New Industrial State.* Boston 1967.

8. Stephen A. Greyser, Assistant Professor, Harvard University Graduate School of Business Administration, letter dated June 25, 1968.

9. Friedrich A. Hayek, "The Non Sequitur of the Dependence Effect." *Southern Economic Journal.* April 1961.

10. Harry G. Johnson, "The Consumer and Madison Avenue" in Lee E. Preston, ed., *Social Issues in Marketing: Readings for Analysis.* Glenview 1968.

11. Frank H. Knight, *Risk, Uncertainty and Profit.* New York 1965.

12. Robin Marris, "Galbraith, Solow, and the Truth about Corporations." *The Public Interest.* Spring 1968.

13. Alfred Marshall, *Principles of Economics*, 8th ed. New York 1948.

14. Burt Schorr, "Many New Products Fizzle Despite Careful Planning, Publicity." *Contemporary American Marketing: Readings on the Changing Market Structure.* Homewood 1962.

15. George Stigler, "Galbraith's New Book: A Few Problems." *Wall Street Journal.* June 26, 1967.

16. Maurice Zinkin, "Galbraith and Consumer Sovereignty." *Journal of Industrial Economics*, XV No. 1 (1967).

RALPH K. WINTER, JR.

Advertising and Legal Theory

ADVERTISING AND ITS CRITICS

Integral to many critiques of the private sector and particularly of American business are allegations that advertising inflicts injuries on consumers and that its overall role is harmful. Such charges are generally of three kinds.

The first allegation plays on what an American Bar Association study of the Federal Trade Commission called "a general conviction that marketing frauds against consumers are widespread in this country and constitute a problem of major national concern."[1] Central to this charge is the view that advertising is by nature peculiarly useful if not essential to carrying out frauds, and is thus a prime source of consumer deception.

A second allegation is that advertising is a device by which "artificial" tastes are created. Consumers, it is argued, would be better off employing their income according to their own preferences,

and would enjoy more leisure once released from the pressure of having to earn and buy more than they need. Professor John Kenneth Galbraith has stated that "advertising and salesmanship" are simply "the management of consumer demand" and are "vital for planning in the industrial system."[2] His point is that, without advertising, persons would find a terminal satisfactory income and not continue on the treadmill of earning more and more income in order to purchase more and more presumably superfluous goods. He thus argues that the link between production and consumer desires is almost the opposite of that described in classical economics. Instead of production following consumer wants, the producer must create the want to justify the production. Galbraith argues:

Modern advertising and salesmanship . . . cannot be reconciled with . . . independently determined desire. . . . A new consumer product must be introduced with a suitable advertising campaign to arouse an interest in it. The path for an expansion of output must be paved by a suitable expansion in the advertising budget. Outlays for the manufacturing of a product are not more important . . . than outlays for the manufacturing of demand for the product.[3]

A final allegation is that advertising is anticompetitive; that is, large advertising expenditures create a "barrier to entry" that reduces competition. Those who hold this conviction have even suggested that legal measures be taken to restrict advertising expenditures.

THE LIMITS OF ADVERTISING

Advertising's critics attribute to it a power that even the most immodest dweller of Madison Avenue would hesitate to claim. Widespread deception and fraud, the endless creation of artificial tastes, and the erection of barriers to competitor entry would be possible only if the advertising industry were able to manipulate consumers virtually at will and to evoke the desired response with Pavlovian regularity.

I make no claim to exhaustive research of the literature of psychology and social psychology relevant to these matters. I do have some familiarity with it, however, and students of mine have from time to time undertaken studies of various aspects of it. The conclusion invariably reached is that the alleged manipulative powers of advertising are simply not established in the literature and that even subliminal advertising is a very limited tool. To be sure, all agree that advertising is a useful and often indispensable tool to sellers. But all also agree that it can never guarantee undivided public attention, much less commercial success, and that deceptive advertisers cannot freely engage in extensive fraud by reducing the hapless buyer to an endlessly willing victim.

These conclusions are merely consistent with common observation. Advertising is one of numerous elements (level of education, views of peers, views of family, previous experience with the product, individual judgment, and so on) that influence a consumer's spending decisions. Because advertising is available to all who would sell a product or service, no single message can possibly dominate our attention. This applies as much to decisions

between kinds of products as to different brands of a particular product. The advertisement for a Caribbean vacation competes not only with other vacation ads, but also with reminders from a bank or investment broker about providing for one's future. If common observation reveals anything, it is that the market share of a particular brand is remarkably unstable, as is the relative market share of particular products. Studies indicate that most consumers experiment with a variety of brands and are in no sense wedded by advertising to any given product.[4] The history of political repression strongly suggests that the ability to silence competitors' advertising is a far more effective manipulative device than issuing one's own advertising.

Advertisers face an exceedingly complex task in seeking to persuade, much less manipulate, the public. Individual perceptions vary widely, and the impact of an ad on one person is generally different from its impact on another. In addition, consumers are aware of the self-interest of the commercial advertiser and are naturally skeptical of his advertised claims. Much of mass advertising is, as a consequence, little more than an attention-getting device seeking to increase brand name recognition. Nor is there any evidence that advertising can, in any but exceptional cases, offset a previous bad experience with a product. There is a strong temptation for advertisers to exaggerate the benefits of their products but much less of a temptation to employ outright lies, which tend to be self-defeating. The goal of most advertisers is to entice the consumer to purchase the product and then to satisfy him through experience.

One may well question, therefore, whether allegations of widespread fraud are in fact accurate. Not only would the seller have to construct an effective deception to begin with, but he would also have to be, somehow, immune to consumer retaliation and loss of patronage in the market afterwards. To be sure, plenty of examples of fraud exist, but they constitute a tiny fraction of commercial transactions. The Federal Trade Commission prosecutes only a couple of hundred deceptive practices cases a year, of which almost half are in the protectionist textile and fur mislabeling areas. One suspects similar agencies in the states have a comparably small caseload. Given the size of the American economy, the claims of widespread fraud seem more exaggerated than the advertising they deplore.

Mr. Galbraith's allegations about the creation of artificial consumer wants seem equally shaky and surely imply a very bleak view of democracy. As a genre, commercial advertising is anything but unique. The tools of persuasion employed by advertising are used by everyone who engages in mass persuasion. My colleague Arthur Leff once noted, for example, that the "Nader Reports" were a form of franchising similar in merchandising technique to Colonel Sanders' Kentucky Fried Chicken.

Every segment of society in fact employs such techniques. In the 1960s, for example, a major topic among the campus intelligentsia was "the urban crisis." It was not enough to study economics, sociology, history, political science, or law. If a course did not bear the brand label "urban," it was irrelevant; if it did, a sizable enrollment was guaranteed, no matter what the content. The lack of urban studies was regarded as a sure sign that a university was on the way to obscurity. A decade later "urban" studies still draw interest but on a very reduced scale, even though the "crisis" has assumed a more tangible form and its existence is less subject to doubt. As another example, political advertising employs techniques indistinguishable from those employed in commercial advertising. Name recognition is of critical importance, and sloganeering, hyperbole, and symbols are used pervasively.

The point is that virtually every aspect of our lives is affected by attempts at persuasion and that the techniques of advertising are common to every form of persuasion. Either we believe that citizens are capable of independent and balanced judgment or we do not. If in fact consumers are endlessly manipulated by advertising, then the same consumers are no better able to avoid manipulation in their political judgments. The case for fearing "artificial" desires for more and more government regulation is as good as the case for deploring "artificial" wants for more and more consumer goods. It is for this reason that I find Mr. Galbraith's view profoundly antidemocratic.

THE BENEFITS OF ADVERTISING

A wholesale legal assault on advertising would entail great costs. It would predictably diminish the flow of goods, reduce the diversity of products and brands, decrease consumer satisfaction, and increase poverty because of the general decline in the level of commercial activity.

This is so because advertising performs the critical function of informing consumers about the availability of certain goods at certain places and at certain prices. Critics of advertising frequently slip over this point by arguing that in an academic model of "perfect competition," no advertising would exist because the flow of information would be perfect; therefore, according to this argument, the existence of advertising illustrates the lack of competition. In any case, the issue is not perfect or imperfect competition in an academic model but the maximization of consumer satisfaction in everyday life. Perfect competition is nothing but an abstraction useful for analytic or pedagogic purposes, and a departure from its assumptions in no sense implies a net injury to consumers. For example, when economies of scale invalidate the model's assumption of an atomistic market, industrial concentration may benefit consumers since the price effects of the reductions in cost may exceed the price effects of the restrictions in output. Similarly, because the collection and transmittal of product information consumes resources, the attainment of perfect information, even if possible, would be prohibitively expensive for consumers. Information is a commodity that itself should be allocated by a price system that reflects its costs. Advertising does just that, as the cost of providing information about a product becomes part of the price of the product.

Many dispute this view of advertising on the grounds that the information provided in mass advertising seems inadequate to inform consumers about much more than the existence of a product. But is this so? One would be hard put to find examples of advertising that did not also inform us what the product is for, the advantage of using it, where to get it, and so on. Advertising may well be the least costly method of introducing the basic features of the product to the consumer. Should more information be desired, interested consumers may thereafter seek out further details from dealers or from people who already own the product. This is far less costly than attempting to transmit every conceivable detail on a mass basis.

To be sure, ads of a general nature are sometimes accompanied by hyperbole that may overstate the merits of the product or simply fail to inform. Claims that a product is "unique" or the "best buy" do not give the consumer hard information, but what evidence is there that consumers take them seriously? If they did, they would either be paralyzed by indecision or go sleepless trying to purchase every advertised product. Compared to the rhetoric of others engaged in mass persuasion, like political candidates or some so-called consumer advocates, commercial advertising is a model of restraint. Hyperbole in commercial advertising is part and parcel of the advocacy necessary to attract attention to the name and kind of product. Without the advocacy, the incentive to advertise would be greatly reduced.

Similarly, many criticize advertising for creating product images that they believe are not consistent with the actual physical qualities of the product. To the extent that consumers disagree and find psychic pleasure in a product in addition to "practical" utility, this is not an illegitimate function. If advertising enables purchasers of certain beer to suppose themselves more rugged and manly, or purchasers of cosmetics to think that they are more beautiful as a result, that attribute of advertising itself seems a good worth paying for. The critics are merely substituting their judgment for the consumers'.

Advertising also provides a benefit in that it facilitates competitive behavior. A businessman who wishes to cut price, for example, will think twice if news of the price cut cannot be quickly transmitted to his competitors' customers. And it is surely the case that established firms wishing to bar entry by newcomers would find a prohibition on advertising a means well tailored to that end. Indeed, prohibitions on advertising almost always have the suppression of competition as their goal.

Many of the benefits gained through advertising are denied by the critics. They contend that in the absence of regulation, the octane content of gasoline usually would not be revealed to the consumer and the practice of unit pricing would not exist. My suspicion again is that this criticism is second guessing the consumer. In reading some of the literature in preparation for this conference, I learned for the first time about the disclosure of octane readings. Now I remain puzzled over what I am to do with them, particularly since my purchase of gasoline is for the most part governed by my desire for a reliable repairman. Similarly, I have never mastered the art of deciphering the hieroglyphics underneath products in supermarkets. One's personal view of whether the information produced by advertising is adequate is rarely relevant to the issue of whether consumers in general are receiving the optimal amount of product information, given the cost of producing it. Tastes for information are as varied as tastes for the performing arts, and it is not enough for the critics to argue that all the information that might be relevant in lawyers' terms is not disclosed by advertising.

NOTES

1. Report of the American Bar Association Committee to Study the Federal Trade Commission, 1969, p. 36.

2. John K. Galbraith, *The New Industrial State* (New York: Signet, 1967), p. 281.

3. John K. Galbraith, *The Affluent Society* (New York: Mentor, 1969), p. 141.

4. James M. Ferguson, "Advertising and Liquor," *Journal of Business*, vol. 40 (October 1967), pp. 414–434.

ALAN H. GOLDMAN

*B*usiness Ethics:
Profits, Utilities, and Moral Rights

... There is the problem of the relation of consumer preferences to true interests and needs. In Section I [not included in this anthology], I argued that opposing preferences expressed through the market to a different conception of interests is often as problematic and objectionable as unwarranted paternalism. But, as Galbraith has argued, when honoring preferences does not seem to lead to long-range satisfaction or happiness, they become suspect as being largely created by those who benefit from satisfying them.[1] The satisfaction of wants is utility-maximizing when the wants are given and represent disutilities when unsatisfied. But if the process in question includes creation of the wants themselves, and if their satisfaction results in greater wants or in other harmful side effects, then the whole process may be objectionable from a utilitarian point of view. As the ancient Greeks realized, contentment may be easier to achieve by eliminating superfluous desires than by creating and attempting to satisfy them.

Certainly for many businesses the goal of profit maximization requires the creation of demand as much as its satisfaction. Advertising and salesmanship are not merely informative. The fact that a certain set of desires is created by those who then attempt to satisfy them is not in itself grounds for condemning the desires or the process that creates them. Such cycles are as characteristic of desires for the most exalted aesthetic experience—appreciation of fine opera, for example—as they are of desires for electric gadgets or tobacco.[2] But this shows only that Galbraith's argument is incomplete, not that it is enthymemically unsound. When we have an independent criterion for wants worth fulfilling, then processes can be condemned which create those that fail to satisfy this criterion. One weak criterion that can be adopted from a want-regarding or utilitarian moral theory relates to whether satisfaction of the desires in question in-

creases overall satisfaction in the long run, whether it contributes to a fulfilled or worthwhile life. Desires are irrational when their satisfaction is incompatible with more fundamental or long-range preferences, either because of harmful side-effects or because of the creation of more unsatisfied desires. Alcoholism is an example of such irrational desire, the satisfaction of which is harmful overall. Processes that create and feed such desires are not utility-maximizing, since even the satisfaction of these desires lowers the subject's general level of utility. The pursuit of profit might well encourage the creation of such wants, especially desires for quickly consumable products. When this occurs, the appearance of efficiency masks a deeper utilitarian inefficiency. The profit motive contributes more to negative than positive utility, creating more unsatisfied than satisfied wants.

It has been argued also against Galbraith that most people are not so influenced by advertisement. They learn to be distrustful of claims made in ads and take them with a grain of salt. But while it is true that consumers become resistant to specific product claims of advertisers, it is not at all so clear that they can easily resist the total life style that bombards them constantly in subtle and not so subtle ways in ads for beer, cars, perfume, clothes, and whatever else can be conspicuously consumed.[3] The desire for this life style may in turn influence particular desires for products or features of products that are irrational and would not arise without this continuous programming. Consumers may desire flashy and fast automobiles more strongly than safe ones; but this may be only because safety cannot be conspicuously consumed or because it does not provide the kind of dashing sexual allure that car advertisers attempt to project onto their products. If this preference is suspect in itself, it certainly appears more so when we recognize its source. In some industries there is a natural lack of rational restraint on the part of consumers of which those out for maximum profits can take advantage, for example in the funeral or health-care industries. In others, consumers can be influenced to view certain products as symbols of a glamorous life style and desire them on those grounds. Furthermore, the encouragement of a life style of super consumption by numerous advertisers probably results in overproduction of consumable products and underutilization of resources for public goods that are not advertised, not conspicuously consumed, and less immediately enjoyed—for example clean air, water, and soil, quality schools, and so on. The congruence between free-market outcome and aggregate utility or social good is once more suspect.

Thus the pursuit of profit is efficient to the public only if it operates under certain moral constraints. It is not efficient or utility-maximizing if it results in elimination of competition and hence of alternatives for consumers, in deception regarding product defects, imposition of neighborhood social costs, the creation and exploitation of irrational desires, or the neglect of needs and wants of those unable to express demand from lack of wealth. And it is likely to result in all of these if maximization of profits is accepted as the principal norm of business ethics. . . .

NOTES

1. See John Kenneth Galbraith, *The Affluent Society* (Boston, 1958), chap. II.

2. For this reply to Galbraith, see F. A. von Hayek, "The Non Sequitur of the 'Dependence Effect,'" *Ethical Theory and Business*, ed. Tom Beauchamp and Norman Bowie (Englewood Cliffs, NJ, 1979), pp. 508–512.

3. Compare John I. Coppett, "Consumerism from a Behavioral Perspective," in *Social Issues in Business*, pp. 444–454.

GERALD DWORKIN

Autonomy and Behavior Control

Autonomy = Authenticity + Independence

The advent of new modes of behavioral technology raises important issues for our understanding of human nature and our moral views about how people ought to influence one another. On the theoretical level we find claims that an adequate explanatory scheme for understanding human behavior can dispense with notions of free will, dignity, and autonomy. On the practical level we are faced with claims of effectiveness, efficiency, and moral legitimacy for methods of influencing people such as operant conditioning, psychotropic drugs, electrical stimulation of the brain, and psychosurgery. The theoretical and practical issues are, of course, linked. Our views as to what it is permissible to do to people reflect our views about the existence and desirability of various conditions. If autonomy is neither desirable nor possible then the question whether different methods affect autonomy in different ways will hardly be an interesting one. If, on the other hand, autonomy is both possible and desirable, then the possibility that various techniques of controlling behavior affect autonomy in distinctive ways, and to different degrees, may play a crucial role in our normative debates about such matters.

Are there significant differences, in terms of their impact on autonomy, among the various ways of influencing people? The ways of influence may be as varied as: offers of money, threats, hypnotism, argument, electrodes, providing information, lying, education, subliminal stimulation, psychotherapy, operant conditioning, and psychosurgery. Answering such a question would obviously require a good deal of very specific factual information about each technique, so my answer will be of the form: What would we want to know about such techniques in order to decide the issue? What information about their effects, our attitudes towards them, the causal mechanisms that explain their effects, and so forth, would we have to know to make reasonable judgments about their impact on autonomy? To answer this we must have a clearer understanding of the concept of autonomy.

AUTONOMY

There is a recurring theme that runs through most attempts to clarify the notion of autonomy. It is indicated by the etymology of the term: *autos* (self) and *nomos* (rule or law). The word was first applied to the Greek city-state. A city had *autonomia* when its citizens made their own laws, as opposed to being under the control of some conquering power. To leap two thousand years of intellectual history, we find the same basic notion expressed by Kant:

The will is therefore not merely subject to the law, but is so subject that it must be considered as also making the law for itself and precisely on this account as first of all subject to the law (of which it can regard itself as the author).[1]

For Kant the forces that contrasted with self-rule were not merely external forces (in the sense of other agents) but those of one's own phenomenal self, in particular one's empirical inclinations. The principles one adopted could not be accounted for by any contingent facts about the individual or his social and biological circumstances. Only by reference to one's nature as a rational being could their selection be explained.

Extending the Kantian notion to the political realm, Robert Wolff defines the autonomous man as follows: "The autonomous man, insofar as he is autonomous, is not subject to the will of another. He may do what another tells him, but not because he has been told to do it. ... For the autonomous man, there is no such thing, strictly speaking, as a command."[2]

We find the same basic conception of self-rule or independence in all these formulations. It is clear then that some investigation of the notion of

the self and that of rule or law is required to advance our understanding beyond that of what is essentially a metaphor.

Let us start with what appears to be the simpler of the two concepts, that of rule or law. In the political and moral context it is clear what one is being autonomous with respect to. As Wolff indicates, the problem is how a citizen relates to the commands of authority. The relation in question is one of compliance or non-compliance with an authoritative order or command (in its legal form a law or injunction or notice or rule). But it is more than just a matter of what the agent does; it is also a matter of why he does it. Only certain kinds of reasons for complying will preserve autonomy. Autonomous behavior is related to a particular explanation of why the person obeys a given command. Similarly, in the moral context the Kantian notion concerns the moral principles on which a person acts and the reasons which explain their adoption. In his *Moral Judgment of the Child*, Piaget comments upon the relationship between the rules of a game and the child's acceptance of the rules. "Autonomy follows upon heteronomy; the rule of a game appears to the child no longer as an external law, sacred insofar as it has been laid down by adults; but as the outcome of a free decision and worthy of respect in the measure that it has enlisted mutual consent."[3]

All these cases share the feature that what the self is acting on is some regulative device which can be represented propositionally. "Each player takes a turn." "Pay your taxes." "Keep one's promises." But this does not seem to be the same problem that we are concerned about. Those worried about whether drugs interfere with autonomy are not worried about the rules or commands or principles which the agent is obeying or adopting. They are concerned about a more general relationship between the way people behave and their motivational structure. True, they are also concerned with what explains people's specific behavior, but that explanation can (and usually does) refer to a much broader set of mental elements—beliefs, wishes, choices, judgments, desires, emotions, reasons, habits, compulsions, and so forth. We may explain behavior via upbringing, social class, culture, glands, genes, religion, etc. Autonomous behavior concerns the relationship between the "self" and these explanatory factors.

Moral and political autonomy are special cases in which the behavior is to be explained by reference to explicitly formulated rules or commands.

I would argue that once the problem is viewed in this broader fashion, the traditional notion of autonomy I have outlined is inadequate and leads to paradoxes and other difficulties—chief among them that it makes autonomy impossible.

Consider this last point first. We all know that persons have a history. They develop socially and psychologically in a given environment with a given set of biological endowments. They mature slowly and are heavily influenced by their parents, siblings, peers, and culture. What sense does it make to speak of their convictions, motivations, principles, and so forth as "self-selected"? This presupposes a notion of the self as isolated from the influences just enumerated and, what is almost as foolish, that the self which chooses does so arbitrarily. For to the extent that the self uses canons of reason, principles of induction, judgments of probability, etc., these also have either been acquired from others or, what is no better from the standpoint of this position, are innate. We can no more choose *ab initio* than we can jump out of our skins. To insist upon this as a condition is to make autonomy impossible.

The same view leads to a paradox in the relationship between autonomy and moral goodness. Autonomy, on this view, demands that the agent choose his moral principles independently of external constraints. But for many moral philosophers the principles of morality are such that their correctness or truth is independent of whether they are chosen or not. So we have a conflict between being subject to the constraints of a correct set of principles and the notion of choosing whatever the self decides upon. This is more than a theoretical paradox since one of the tasks of education is to achieve both ends. Following the advice dictated by the view in question, educators are left with the frustrating task of urging their pupils both to "think for themselves" and to "think, thusly."

Both of these difficulties can be avoided by facing squarely the fact that in most cases we cannot be said to have adopted or chosen or selected our beliefs, desires, emotions, principles, and so forth. In some cases this idea doesn't even make sense. In other cases it is simply a contingent fact that we find ourselves moved in certain ways. Autonomy cannot be located on the level of first-order considerations, but in the second-order judgments we make concerning first-order considerations. If the autonomous man cannot adopt his motivations *de novo*, he can still judge them after the fact. The autonomous individual is able to step back and formulate an attitude towards the factors that influence his behavior.

AUTHENTICITY

Let me present a theory which may be characterized, in desperate brevity, by the formula autonomy = authenticity + independence. The autonomous person is one who does *his own* thing. So we need characterizations of what it is for a motivation to be *his*, and what it is for it to be his *own*. The first is what I shall call authenticity; the second, independence.

It is characteristic of persons that they are able to reflect on their decisions, motives, desires, habits, and so forth. In doing so they may form preferences concerning these. Thus a person may not only desire to smoke. He can also desire that he desire to smoke. He may not simply be motivated by jealousy or anger. He can also desire that his motivations be different (or the same).

A person may want to break the habit of smoking and prefer to stop smoking because he recognizes its harmful character and because that recognition alone is effective in changing his behavior. But if he sees that causal path closed he may, all things considered, prefer to have a causal structure introduced which brings him to be nauseated by the taste or odor of tobacco. Even though his behavior is not then under his voluntary control, he may wish to be motivated in this way in order to stop smoking. When this is true he views the causal influences as "his." The part of him that wishes to stop smoking is recognized as his true self, the one whose wishes he wants to see carried out.

To give another example, a person might desire to learn to ski. He might believe he has no further motivation than this straightforward and simple desire, or he might believe that what causes the desire is the wish to test his courage in a mildly dangerous sport. Suppose he is now led to see (correctly) that he desires to ski because he is envious of a brother who has always excelled in sports. Having recognized the source of his desire, he can now either wish he were not motivated in this way or reaffirm the desire. If the latter, then he is acting authentically in that he identifies himself as the kind of person who wants to be motivated by envy.

Similarly, to return to the problem of moral autonomy, if one affirms one's moral principles, no matter how first acquired, because of their conformity with what one believes to be a correct moral theory, then this is an expression of the fact that they are indeed one's moral principles. For Thrasymachus, on the other hand, who views moral principles as inculcated by the powerful to enforce their rule, and who does not regard such considerations as ones he wishes to act in accordance with, to continue to act in accordance with such principles would be inauthentic.[4]

It is the attitude a person takes towards the influences motivating him which determines whether or not they are to be considered "his." Does he identify with them, assimilate them to himself, view himself as the kind of person who wishes to be motivated in these particular ways? If, on the contrary, a man resents his being motivated in certain ways, is alienated from those influences, resents acting in accordance with them, would prefer to be the kind of person who is motivated in different ways, then those influences, even though they may be causally effective, are not viewed as "his."[5]

So far I have not mentioned an obvious question—whether one can change the determinants affecting one's behavior. It might be objected that approval of a way of being moved to action which could not be changed, even indirectly, puts the agent in the position of the willing slave. Such an individual may approve of his master's orders, and indeed of the fact that he is ruled by a master, yet if he disapproved there might be nothing he could do about it. It is certainly true that the slave is not free. What about the man who is a drug addict, who cannot give up his physiological cravings for the drug, and yet who wants to be in the grip of his compulsion? On my view the agent is autonomous. He, like the slave, is not free since he will take the drug independently of whether he wishes to be motivated in this way. But important as that fact is, there is another fact which is also true and which is

also important. Namely he identifies with his addiction. And it is this identification that I am designating as authenticity.

This view of authenticity is opposed to the traditional existentialist position with its emphasis on choice and decision. Given that we are born into societies at a particular stage of development, with given social roles which provide a framework for participation, with a body of knowledge built up over time, with moral and other assumptions built into the social framework, the notion of decision or choice is implausible as a description of how we acquire our motivational structures.

We simply find ourselves motivated in certain ways and the notion of choosing, from ground zero, makes no sense. Sooner or later we find ourselves, as in Neurath's metaphor of the ship in mid-ocean being reconstructed while sailing, in mid-history. But we always retain the possibility of stepping back and judging where we are and where we want to be.

INDEPENDENCE

Authenticity, while necessary for autonomy, is not sufficient. A person's motivational structure may be *his*, without being his *own*. This may occur in either of two ways. First, the identification with his motivations, or the choice of the type of person he wants to be, may have been produced by manipulation, deception, the withholding of relevant information, and so on. It may have been influenced in decisive ways by others in such a fashion that we are not prepared to think of it as his own choice. I shall call this a lack of procedural independence.

Concern about such procedural failures is not simply an expression of general worries about determinism. Even if some strong thesis of determinism is correct, we will still want to make a distinction between those forms of influence which contribute to the agent making his own decisions and those which make those decisions and choices in some sense that of others.

Another way of seeing this point is that the notion of authentic behavior leaves no room for "false consciousness." An individual may identify or approve of his motivational structure because of an inability to view in a critical and rational manner his situation.

Suppose, however, that the identifications and approvals are influenced in such a way that they are procedurally independent. Still, a person may decide to renounce his independence of action or thought because he wants (genuinely) to be that sort of person. A person may want to do whatever his mother, or his government, tells him to do, and do so in a procedurally independent manner. By giving up what I call substantive independence he has authentically abandoned something we are inclined to think of as an important part of autonomy.

We now have two distinct problems: to characterize procedural independence and to characterize substantive independence.

The problem of analyzing procedural independence is the task of characterizing those influences which in some way prevent the individual's decisions from being his own. It may be helpful to think of procedural independence as a generalization of the notion of liberty. The paradigm cases of interference with liberty have been those of coercion, and the analytical task is to offer an account of why certain ways of getting a person to do something other than he originally intended (incentives, information, argument) do not count as interferences, whereas others (threats, physical force) do infringe freedom. With respect to autonomy, conceived of as authenticity under conditions of procedural independence, the paradigms of interference are manipulation and deception, and the analytic task is to distinguish these ways of influencing people's higher order judgments from those (education, requirements of logical thinking, provision of role-models) which do not negate procedural independence. This is a difficult problem, but it looks as if a solution is possible.

With respect to autonomy conceived as authenticity plus substantive independence I believe matters are different. The problem here is to characterize when a person is giving up independence (perhaps authentically) and when he retains it. I cannot, however, think of a hypothesis which will at the same time classify obvious examples of non-autonomy correctly (the servile lackey, the conformer to group pressures) and yet not also classify the compassionate or loyal or moral man as nonautonomous. For the compassionate or loyal or moral man is one whose actions are to some extent determined by the needs and predicaments of others. He is not independent or self-determining.

Again, any notion of commitment (to a lover, a goal, a group) seems to be a denial of substantive independence and hence of autonomy. There seems to be no way of conceptualizing substantive independence which avoids this classification.

One can adopt various conclusions at this point. The first, and most reasonable, is that we should keep looking for an adequate account. The second is that we should be prepared to accept the idea that the compassionate man is less autonomous than the selfish one. This would indicate that any account of autonomy describes a value possibly in direct conflict with other crucial values and desirable traits. To discover that a person cannot be moral and autonomous at the same time would certainly be an unsatisfactory outcome to our quest for a theory of autonomy. A third view is that the notion of autonomy is not simply descriptive; that we are only prepared to designate a particular kind of independence as autonomy when we value *that kind* of independence. The main drawback of this last position is that it makes the concept useless in trying to evaluate various methods of behavior control in terms of their effect on autonomy. For we would already have had to answer the question whether a given form of influence is desirable or not in order to decide the question of whether autonomy is affected or not.

My view at this point is that autonomy can be conceived as authenticity + independence (procedural and substantive). But since it is unlikely that the notion of substantive independence is a genuinely desirable one, the notion of autonomy which should play a role in the evaluation of various methods of behavior control is that which requires authenticity and procedural independence.

One reason for reluctance to abandon substantive independence is the fear that the link with moral responsibility may be broken. As Wolff argues, if men are to be responsible agents and to assume responsibility for their actions, it is necessary for them to ascertain what is right. So far, so good. But there is no reason to suppose that by considering autonomy as authenticity plus procedural independence men are able to avoid responsibility. The man who does what his mother tells him is no more nor less responsible for what he does than the man who thinks through each issue for himself. He cannot evade responsibility by saying, "She told me to do it," precisely because, on our account of autonomy, he affirmed his own desire to be motivated by her desires—and hence bears the responsibility for that determination of his will.

GUIDELINES FOR THE PRESERVATION OF AUTONOMY

Given the second-order nature of autonomy as I have considered it, there is an immediate consequence concerning the kinds of methods it is legitimate to use to influence people. If one values autonomy (and though I shall not argue why we should, I believe such reasons can be given), then methods which interfere with the ability of the individual to reflect on his first-order motivations should not be used. There are various ways, in principle, that such interference might take place. There might be methods which keep the agent in ignorance of the true determinants of his behavior. Methods which rely on causal influences of which the agent is not conscious are of this nature. Subliminal motivation, if such were indeed possible, would be a primary example. Since the agent does not know the real reasons for his actions, he cannot reflect on such reasons and make a favorable or adverse judgment concerning them. Another example of this type would be those methods of changing people's attitude and conduct which rely on the theory of cognitive dissonance. Consider the following experiment.

Children are asked to rank a number of toys in order of preference. The adult then leaves the room and warns them not to play with the most preferred toy. He then returns, and the children are asked again to order their preferences. It turns out, as predicted by the theory, that the children shift downward their previous first choice. The theory predicts this on the basis of a conflict between preference and action inconsistent with preference. The conflict is resolved by shifting preference. But the agent is not aware of this as the cause of his change in attitude, and hence cannot make an independent judgment of whether he wishes to be motivated in this fashion.

Obviously, methods of influence which destroy the ability of the agent to reflect critically and

intelligently on his motivations violate autonomy. The processes by which this might be accomplished can vary from those which destroy parts of the brain necessary for such reflective tasks to processes which make the psychic costs of such examination so painful that something analogous to coercion takes place. In general, however, I think autonomy is in greater danger from manipulative methods of influence than from those outright assaults on the individual associated with the notions of brainwashing and psychosurgery.

It follows from this analysis that there will be only a small number of methods of influence which are in themselves denials of autonomy. It remains true, nevertheless, that we have certain broad preferences concerning ways in which we would like to be motivated, and though a contingent fact, it may be decisive in generalizing about autonomy. There are, I believe, certain general categories of influence whose link to second-order attitudes can be understood in light of the causal mechanisms by which the techniques work.

One of the things we know about ourselves is that we have varied interests and ideals, varied tastes and preferences, varied desires and wishes. There are various life plans that individuals may have, and there is no choosing between most of them in terms of some over-all ideal or principle of rationality. The good for humans is irreducibly multiple and variegated. Given this knowledge, are there considerations which make it preferable for rational agents either to encourage and adopt, or to discourage and reject, certain techniques of influence on the ground that the former facilitate, and the latter make more difficult, our tasks of forming rational plans for our own lives?

Given these general considerations, what more specific guidelines can be deduced or, perhaps more accurately, be harmonized with the preceding? I say "more accurately" because it seems to me that, although some of the specific guidelines might be made deductions by the introduction of various premises, the relation will often be one of "expressing an ideal" or "reflecting a general conception."

1. We have favorable attitudes towards those methods of influence which support the self-respect and dignity of those who are being influenced. Ideally such methods should constitute a public expression of agents as equal and sovereign individuals.

Obviously at this level of abstraction not much guidance is provided concerning specific techniques. All depends on how the techniques work and what their effect on dignity is supposed to be. But it is important to be clear about the distinction between expressing and supporting self-respect, and being causally connected with producing a state of affairs which might be called increased self-respect or dignity. For example, it is often argued that certain drastic techniques such as psychosurgery or aversive conditioning may result in the agent's being able to leave an institution, or to no longer "act out" in various ways. Hence such techniques are promoting dignity. Be that as it may, it may still be the case that the methods used are not expressive of the dignity of the agent. They may treat him as an object rather than a subject. Though leading to increased self-respect they are not expressive of it. Of course it might be that methods which are expressive of self-respect or dignity are not causally effective in producing it.

2. Methods of influence which are destructive of the ability of individuals to reflect rationally on their interests should not be used.

This approximation seems fairly uncontroversial. At one time I thought that a stronger principle might be reasonable—that ideally methods should be used which appeal to the reasoning capacities of individuals. I was persuaded that this represented a rather parochial view, one perhaps endemic to philosophers, of the role of reasons in determining action. Is it really preferable to appeal to an individual's ability to think that what he is doing is just rather than to his love of justice?

3. Methods should not be used which affect in fundamental ways the personal identity of individuals. To the extent that the effects of certain modes of influence are such as to raise questions about whether the individual is the same person, or in a less extreme version, whether the discontinuities between the person at two close points of time are sufficiently sharp, we would not agree to their use.

We need to maintain a coherent and unified conception of our own identity. Notions of personal responsibility, long-range plans, a connec-

tion with our past, all depend on our being sufficiently similar at various time-stages to be thought of as the same person. We may welcome change, but within a framework of continuity.

4. Methods which rely essentially on deception, on keeping the agent in ignorance of relevant facts, are to be avoided.

This is not to assert that more knowledge is always better than less. Sometimes knowledge does increaseth sorrow. There are times when we really "don't want to know." But we do resent being manipulated even in our own interest.

5. Modes of influence which are not physically intrusive are preferable to those which are. By physically intrusive is meant roughly those methods which penetrate the body. Hence drugs, psychosurgery, electric shock treatment, monitoring devices, etc.

The argument for this condition relies on psychological assertions concerning the necessity of some realm of physical integrity which cannot be violated. This is related to notions of dignity and privacy. It is possible that these feelings may be primitive (not capable of being reduced to other kinds of considerations) or it may be the case that this is not an independent condition but may be derived from some other conditions.

6. There will be some restrictions on the time in which the changes take place and the ability of the agent to resist the effects of various modes of influence.

Given our knowledge of the possibility of changing tastes, desires, new knowledge and so forth, we wish to maintain some options for reversing our behavior. Thus changes which are reversible are preferable to those which are not. We wish to guard against error and mistake in our current judgments. Of course, in some cases, the possibility of error is so slight that we may not care very much about this condition. It *is* better to be rich and healthy than poor and sick.

Similarly we are concerned about the rapidity with which the effects take place, and the duration of the change. Both of these are connected with the notion of reversibility, with the question of whether the agent can bring about the initial status unaided or requires the aid of another party. With respect to duration, even if the effect eventually wears off it makes a difference whether its duration is five minutes or five years.

7. We prefer methods of influence which work through the cognitive and affective structure of the agent, which require the active participation of the agent in producing the change, to those which short-circuit the desires and beliefs of the agent and make him a passive recipient of the changes.

This preference is partly explicable in terms of the previous condition—the ability of the agent to resist the changes—but is also a distinct condition. In the first place the two are not tightly linked. Very powerful incentives (you offer me a Mercedes-Benz for a nickel) may be almost impossible to resist, but there is no question of short-circuiting the motivational apparatus of the agent. I accept the offer because I want to. On the other hand, I may be able to resist the effects of so-called truth serums although their influence is of the short-circuiting kind.

But even if the two were contingently related in a very strong fashion I believe our reasons for resenting them are distinguishable. To the extent that my participation is required to bring about the change I can identify with my changed self. To the extent that the changes are brought about via purely physiological mechanisms, or even psychological ones which bypass my normal reflective processes (perhaps hypnotism might serve as an example), I view my new self as less continuous with the old.

The matter is, however, complicated. It is plausible in some circumstances to regard the more rational parts of ourselves as obstacles to a genuine part of ourselves which is suppressed and waits to be released. So various drug induced states are thought of as no less "me" although (or

even because) they are brought about by a short-circuiting process.

IN CONCLUSION

There are, it should be noted, two parts to my argument which, at least theoretically, are independent of one another. One can accept my analysis of autonomy while rejecting the claims concerning considerations relevant to the preference for some means of influencing behavior over others; or one can reject the analysis while accepting the considerations, and then try to find another theory to explain their choice.

Such a theory may either be one which analyzes autonomy in a different manner or one which does not make use of autonomy at all. It may be that quite different factors such as liberty, privacy, dignity, or notions of capacity or power are adequate to explain our reasoned judgments about the legitimacy of various methods of behavior control.

NOTES

1. Immanuel Kant, *Groundwork of the Metaphysic of Morals* (London: Hutchinson University Library, 1961), p. 98.

2. Robert Wolff, *In Defense of Anarchism* (New York: Harper & Row, 1970), p. 14.

3. Jean Piaget, *The Moral Judgment of the Child* (London: Routledge & Kegan Paul, 1932), p. 57.

4. This shows that one cannot identify as "his" motivations the ones which in fact explain a person's actions. That is necessary but not sufficient.

5. This notion is more fully worked out in my "Acting Freely," *Nous* 4, no. 4 (1970). See also H. Frankfort, "Freedom of the Will and the Concept of a Person," *Journal of Philosophy* 68, no. 1 (1971).

ROBERT L. ARRINGTON
Advertising and Behavior Control

Consider the following advertisements:

1. "A woman in *Distinction Foundations* is so beautiful that all other women want to kill her."

2. Pongo Peach color for Revlon comes "from east of the sun . . . west of the moon where each tomorrow dawns". It is "succulent on your lips" and "sizzling on your finger tips (And on your toes goodness knows)". Let it be your "adventure in paradise".

3. "Musk by English Leather—The Civilized Way to Roar."

4. "Increase the value of your holdings. Old Charter Bourbon Whiskey—The Final Step Up."

5. Last Call Smirnoff Style: "They'd never really miss us, and it's kind of late already, and it's quite a long way, and I could build a fire, and you're looking very beautiful, and we could have another martini, and it's awfully nice just being home . . . you think?"

6. A Christmas Prayer. "Let us pray that the blessings of peace be ours—the peace to build and grow, to live in harmony and sympathy with others, and to plan for the future with confidence." New York Life Insurance Company.

These are instances of what is called puffery—the practice by a seller of making exaggerated, highly fanciful or suggestive claims about a product or service. Puffery, within ill-defined limits, is legal. It is considered a legitimate, necessary, and very successful tool of the advertising industry. Puffery is not just bragging; it is bragging carefully designed to achieve a very definite effect. Using the techniques of so-called motivational research, advertising firms first identify our often hidden needs (for security, conformity, oral stimulation) and our desires (for power, sexual dominance and dalliance, adventure) and then they design ads which respond to these needs and desires. By

associating a product, for which we may have little or no direct need or desire, with symbols reflecting the fulfillment of these other, often subterranean interests, the advertisement can quickly generate large numbers of consumers eager to purchase the product advertised. What woman in the sexual race of life could resist a foundation which would turn other women envious to the point of homicide? Who can turn down an adventure in paradise, east of the sun where tomorrow dawns? Who doesn't want to be civilized and thoroughly libidinous at the same time? Be at the pinnacle of success—drink Old Charter. Or stay at home and dally a bit—with Smirnoff. And let us pray for a secure and predictable future, provided for by New York Life, God willing. It doesn't take very much motivational research to see the point of these sales pitches. Others are perhaps a little less obvious. The need to feel secure in one's home at night can be used to sell window air conditioners, which drown out small noises and provide a friendly, dependable companion. The fact that baking a cake is symbolic of giving birth to a baby used to prompt advertisements for cake mixes which glamorized the 'creative' housewife. And other strategies, for example involving cigar symbolism, are a bit too crude to mention, but are nevertheless very effective.

Don't such uses of puffery amount to manipulation, exploitation, or downright control? In his very popular book *The Hidden Persuaders*, Vance Packard points out that a number of people in the advertising world have frankly admitted as much:

As early as 1941 Dr. Dichter (an influential advertising consultant) was exhorting ad agencies to recognize themselves for what they actually were—"one of the most advanced laboratories in psychology". He said the successful ad agency "manipulates human motivations and desires and develops a need for goods with which the public has at one time been unfamiliar—perhaps even undesirous of purchasing". The following year *Advertis-*

From *Journal of Business Ethics* 1 (1982) 3–12. Copyright © 1982 by D. Reidel Publishing Co., Dordrecht, Holland. Reprinted by permission.

ing Agency carried an ad man's statement that psychology not only holds promise for understanding people but "ultimately for controlling their behavior".[1]

Such statements lead Packard to remark: "With all this interest in manipulating the customer's subconscious, the old slogan 'let the buyer beware' began taking on a new and more profound meaning".[2]

B. F. Skinner, the high priest of behaviorism, has expressed a similar assessment of advertising and related marketing techniques. Why, he asks, do we buy a certain kind of car?

Perhaps our favorite TV program is sponsored by the manufacturer of that car. Perhaps we have seen pictures of many beautiful or prestigeful persons driving it—in pleasant or glamorous places. Perhaps the car has been designed with respect to our motivational patterns: the device on the hood is a phallic symbol; or the horsepower has been stepped up to please our competitive spirit in enabling us to pass other cars swiftly (or, as the advertisements say, 'safely'). The concept of freedom that has emerged as part of the cultural practice of our group makes little or no provision for recognizing or dealing with these kinds of control.[3]

In purchasing a car we may think we are free, Skinner is claiming, when in fact our act is completely controlled by factors in our environment and in our history of reinforcement. Advertising is one such factor.

A look at some other advertising techniques may reinforce the suspicion that Madison Avenue controls us like so many puppets. T.V. watchers surely have noticed that some of the more repugnant ads are shown over and over again, *ad nauseum*. My favorite, or most hated, is the one about A-1 Steak Sauce which goes something like this: Now, ladies and gentlemen, what *is* hamburger? It has succeeded in destroying my taste for hamburger, but it has surely drilled the name of A-1 Sauce into my head. And that is the point of it. Its very repetitiousness has generated what ad theorists call *information*. In this case it is indirect information, information derived not from the content of what is said but from the fact that it is said so often and so vividly that it sticks in one's mind—i.e., the information yield has increased. And not only do I always remember A-1 Sauce when I go to the grocers, I tend to assume that any

product advertised so often has to be good—and so I usually buy a bottle of the stuff.

Still another technique: On a recent show of the television program 'Hard Choices' it was demonstrated how subliminal suggestion can be used to control customers. In a New Orleans department store, messages to the effect that shoplifting is wrong, illegal, and subject to punishment were blended into the Muzak background music and masked so as not to be consciously audible. The store reported a dramatic drop in shoplifting. The program host conjectured whether a logical extension of this technique would be to broadcast subliminal advertising messages to the effect that the store's $15.99 sweater special is the "bargain of a lifetime". Actually, this application of subliminal suggestion to advertising has already taken place. Years ago in New Jersey a cinema was reported to have flashed subthreshold ice cream ads onto the screen during regular showings of the film—and, yes, the concession stand did a landslide business.[4]

Puffery, indirect information transfer, subliminal advertising—are these techniques of manipulation and control whose success shows that many of us have forfeited our autonomy and become a community, or herd, of packaged souls?[5] The business world and the advertising industry certainly reject this interpretation of their efforts. *Business Week*, for example, dismissed the charge that the science of behavior, as utilized by advertising, is engaged in human engineering and manipulation. It editorialized to the effect that "it is hard to find anything very sinister about a science whose principle conclusion is that you get along with people by giving them what they want".[6] The theme is familiar: businesses just give the consumer what he/she wants; if they didn't they wouldn't stay in business very long. Proof that the consumer wants the products advertised is given by the fact that he buys them, and indeed often returns to buy them again and again.

The techniques of advertising we are discussing have had their more intellectual defenders as well. For example, Theodore Levitt, Professor of Business Administration at the Harvard Business School, has defended the practice of puffery and the use of techniques depending on motivational research.[7] What would be the consequences, he asks us, of deleting all exaggerated claims and fanciful associations from advertisements? We would be left with literal descriptions of the empirical characteristics of products and their functions. Cosmetics would be presented as facial and bodily lotions—and powders which produce certain odor and color changes; they would no longer offer hope or adventure. In addition to the fact that these products would not then sell as well, they would not, according to Levitt, please us as much either. For it is hope and adventure we want when we buy them. We want automobiles not just for transportation, but for the feelings of power and status they give us. Quoting T. S. Eliot to the effect that "Human kind cannot bear very much reality", Levitt argues that advertising is an effort to "transcend nature in the raw", to "augment what nature has so crudely fashioned". He maintains that "everybody everywhere wants to modify, transform, embellish, enrich and reconstruct the world around him". Commerce takes the same liberty with reality as the artist and the priest—in all three instances the purpose is "to influence the audience by creating illusions, symbols, and implications that promise more than pure functionality". For example, "to amplify the temple in men's eyes, (men of cloth) have, very realistically, systematically sanctioned the embellishment of the houses of the gods with the same kind of luxurious design and expensive decoration that Detroit puts into a Cadillac". A poem, a temple, a Cadillac—they all elevate our spirits, offering imaginative promises and symbolic interpretations of our mundane activities. Seen in this light, Levitt claims, "Embellishment and distortion are among advertising's legitimate and socially desirable purposes." To reject these techniques of advertising would be "to deny man's honest needs and values".

Philip Nelson, a Professor of Economics at SUNY-Binghamton, has developed an interesting defense of indirect information advertising.[8] He argues that even when the message (the direct information) is not credible, the fact that the brand is advertised, and advertised frequently, is valuable indirect information for the consumer. The reason for this is that the brands advertised most are more likely to be better buys—losers won't be advertised a lot, for it simply wouldn't pay to do so. Thus even if the advertising claims made for a widely advertised product are empty, the consumer reaps the benefit of the indirect information which shows the product to be a good buy. Nelson goes

so far as to say that advertising, seen as information and especially as indirect information, does not require an intelligent human response. If the indirect information has been received and has had its impact, the consumer will purchase the better buy even if his explicit reason for doing so is silly, e.g., he naively believes an endorsement of the product by a celebrity. Even though his behavior is overtly irrational, by acting on the indirect information he is nevertheless doing what he ought to do, i.e., getting his money's worth. " 'Irrationality' is rational", Nelson writes, "if it is cost-free".

I don't know of any attempt to defend the use of subliminal suggestion in advertising, but I can imagine one form such an attempt might take. Advertising information, even if perceived below the level of conscious awareness, must appeal to some desire on the part of the audience if it is to trigger a purchasing response. Just as the admonition not to shoplift speaks directly to the superego, the sexual virtues of TR-7's, Pongo Peach, and Betty Crocker cake mix present themselves directly to the id, bypassing the pesky reality principle of the ego. With a little help from our advertising friends, we may remove a few of the discontents of civilization and perhaps even enter into the paradise of polymorphous perversity.[9]

The defense of advertising which suggests that advertising simply is information which allows us to purchase what we want, has in turn been challenged. Does business, largely through its advertising efforts, really make available to the consumer what he/she desires and demands? John Kenneth Galbraith has denied that the matter is as straightforward as this.[10] In his opinion the desires to which business is supposed to respond, far from being original to the consumer, are often themselves created by business. The producers make both the product and the desire for it, and the "central function" of advertising is "to create desires". Galbraith coins the term 'The Dependence Effect' to designate the way wants depend on the same process by which they are satisfied.

David Braybrooke has argued in similar and related ways.[11] Even though the consumer is, in a sense, the final authority concerning what he wants, he may come to see, according to Braybrooke, that he was mistaken in wanting what he did. The statement 'I want x', he tells us, is not incorrigible but is "ripe for revision". If the consumer had more objective information than he is provided by product puffing, if his values had not been mixed up by motivational research strategies (e.g., the confusion of sexual and automotive values), and if he had an expanded set of choices instead of the limited set offered by profit-hungry corporations, then he might want something quite different from what he presently wants. This shows, Braybrooke thinks, the extent to which the consumer's wants are a function of advertising and not necessarily representative of his real or true wants.

The central issue which emerges between the above critics and defenders of advertising is this: do the advertising techniques we have discussed involve a violation of human autonomy and a manipulation and control of consumer behavior, *or* do they simply provide an efficient and cost-effective means of giving the consumer information on the basis of which he or she makes a free choice. Is advertising information, or creation of desire?

To answer this question we need a better conceptual grasp of what is involved in the notion of autonomy. This is a complex, multifaceted concept, and we need to approach it through the more determinate notions of (a) autonomous desire, (b) rational desire and choice, (c) free choice, and (d) control or manipulation. In what follows I shall offer some tentative and very incomplete analyses of these concepts and apply the results to the case of advertising.

(a) Autonomous Desire. Imagine that I am watching T.V. and see an ad for Grecian Formula 16. The thought occurs to me that if I purchase some and apply it to my beard, I will soon look younger—in fact I might even be myself again. Suddenly I want to be myself! I want to be young again! So I rush out and buy a bottle. This is our question: was the desire to be younger manufactured by the commercial, or was it 'original to me' and truly mine? Was it autonomous or not?

F. A. von Hayek has argued plausibly that we should not equate nonautonomous desires, desires which are not original to me or truly mine, with those which are culturally induced.[12] If we did equate the two, he points out, then the desires for music, art, and knowledge could not properly be

attributed to a person as original to him, for these are surely induced culturally. The only desires a person would really have as his own in this case would be the purely physical ones for food, shelter, sex, etc. But if we reject the equation of the nonautonomous and the culturally induced, as von Hayek would have us do, then the mere fact that my desire to be young again is caused by the T.V. commercial—surely an instrument of popular culture transmission—does not in and of itself show that this is not my own, autonomous desire. Moreover, even if I never before felt the need to look young, it doesn't follow that this new desire is any less mine. I haven't always liked 1969 Aloxe Corton Burgundy or the music of Satie, but when the desires for these things first hit me, they were truly mine.

This shows that there is something wrong in setting up the issue over advertising and behavior control as a question whether our desires are truly ours *or* are created in us by advertisements. Induced and autonomous desires do not separate into two mutually exclusive classes. To obtain a better understanding of autonomous and nonautonomous desires, let us consider some cases of a desire which a person does not *acknowledge* to be his own even though he *feels* it. The kleptomaniac has a desire to steal which in many instances he repudiates, seeking by treatment to rid himself of it. And if I were suddenly overtaken by a desire to attend an REO concert, I would immediately disown this desire, claiming possession or momentary madness. These are examples of desires which one might have but with which one would not identify. They are experienced as foreign to one's character or personality. Often a person will have what Harry Frankfurt calls a second-order desire, that is to say, a desire *not* to have another desire.[13] In such cases, the first-order desire is thought of as being nonautonomous, imposed on one. When on the contrary a person has a second-order desire to maintain and fulfill a first-order desire, then the first-order desire is truly his own, autonomous, original to him. So there is in fact a distinction between desires which are the agent's own and those which are not, but this is not the same as the distinction between desires which are innate to the agent and those which are externally induced.

If we apply the autonomous/nonautonomous

distinction derived from Frankfurt to the desires brought about by advertising, does this show that advertising is responsible for creating desires which are not truly the agent's own? Not necessarily, and indeed not often. There may be some desires I feel which I have picked up from advertising and which I disown—for instance, my desire for A-1 Steak Sauce. If I act on these desires it can be said that I have been led by advertising to act in a way foreign to my nature. In these cases my autonomy has been violated. But most of the desires induced by advertising I fully accept, and hence most of these desires are autonomous. The most vivid demonstration of this is that I often return to purchase the same product over and over again, without regret or remorse. And when I don't, it is more likely that the desire has just faded than that I have repudiated it. Hence, while advertising may violate my autonomy by leading me to act on desires which are not truly mine, this seems to be the exceptional case.

Note that this conclusion applies equally well to the case of subliminal advertising. This may generate subconscious desires which lead to purchases, and the act of purchasing these goods may be inconsistent with other conscious desires I have, in which case I might repudiate my behavior and by implication the subconscious cause of it. But my subconscious desires may not be inconsistent in this way with my conscious ones; my id may be cooperative and benign rather than hostile and malign.[14] Here again, then, advertising may or may not produce desires which are 'not truly mine'.

What are we to say in response to Braybrooke's argument that insofar as we might choose differently if advertisers gave us better information and more options, it follows that the desires we have are to be attributed more to advertising than to our own real inclinations? This claim seems empty. It amounts to saying that if the world we lived in, and we ourselves, were different, then we would want different things. This is surely true, but it is equally true of our desire for shelter as of our desire for Grecian Formula 16. If we lived in a tropical paradise we would not need or desire shelter. If we were immortal, we would not desire youth. What is true of all desires can hardly be used as a basis for criticizing some desires by claiming that they are nonautonomous.

(b) Rational Desire and Choice. Braybrooke might be interpreted as claiming that the desires induced by advertising are often irrational ones in the sense that they are not expressed by an agent who is in full possession of the facts about the products advertised or about the alternative products which might be offered him. Following this line of thought, a possible criticism of advertising is that it leads us to act on irrational desires or to make irrational choices. It might be said that our autonomy has been violated by the fact that we are prevented from following our rational wills or that we have been denied the 'positive freedom' to develop our true, rational selves. It might be claimed that the desires induced in us by advertising are false desires in that they do not reflect our essential, i.e., rational, essence.

The problem faced by this line of criticism is that of determining what is to count as rational desire or rational choice. If we require that the desire or choice be the product of an awareness of *all* the facts about the product, then surely every one of us is always moved by irrational desires and makes nothing but irrational choices. How could we know all the facts about a product? If it be required only that we possess all of the *available* knowledge about the product advertised, then we still have to face the problem that not all available knowledge is *relevant* to a rational choice. If I am purchasing a car, certain engineering features will be, and others won't be, relevant, *given what I want in a car*. My prior desires determine the relevance of information. Normally a rational desire or choice is thought to be one based upon relevant information, and information is relevant if it shows how other, prior desires may be satisfied. It can plausibly be claimed that it is such prior desires that advertising agencies acknowledge, and that the agencies often provide the type of information that is relevant in light of these desires. To the extent that this is true, advertising does not inhibit our rational wills or our autonomy as rational creatures.

It may be urged that much of the puffery engaged in by advertising does not provide relevant information at all but rather makes claims which are not factually true. If someone buys Pongo Peach in anticipation of an adventure in paradise, or Old Charter in expectation of increasing the value of his holdings, then he/she is expecting purely imaginary benefits. In no literal sense will the one product provide adventure and the other increased capital. A purchasing decision based on anticipation of imaginary benefits is not, it might be said, a rational decision, and a desire for imaginary benefits is not a rational desire.

In rejoinder it needs to be pointed out that we often wish to purchase subjective effects which in being subjective are nevertheless real enough. The feeling of adventure or of enhanced social prestige and value are examples of subjective effects promised by advertising. Surely many (most?) advertisements directly promise subjective effects which their patrons actually desire (and obtain when they purchase the product), and thus the ads provide relevant information for rational choice. Moreover, advertisements often provide accurate indirect information on the basis of which a person who wants a certain subjective effect rationally chooses a product. The mechanism involved here is as follows.

To the extent that a consumer takes an advertised product to offer a subjective effect and the product does not, it is unlikely that it will be purchased again. If this happens in a number of cases, the product will be taken off the market. So here the market regulates itself, providing the mechanism whereby misleading advertisements are withdrawn and misled customers are no longer misled. At the same time, a successful bit of puffery, being one which leads to large and repeated sales, produces satisfied customers and more advertising of the product. The indirect information provided by such large-scale advertising efforts provides a measure of verification to the consumer who is looking for certain kinds of subjective effect. For example, if I want to feel well dressed and in fashion, and I consider buying an Izod Alligator shirt which is advertised in all of the magazines and newspapers, then the fact that other people buy it and that this leads to repeated advertisements shows me that the desired subjective effect is real enough and that I indeed will be well dressed and in fashion if I purchase the shirt. The indirect information may lead to a rational decision to purchase a product because the information testifies to the subjective effect that the product brings about.[15]

Some philosophers will be unhappy with the

conclusion of this section, largely because they have a concept of true, rational, or ideal desire which is not the same as the one used here. A Marxist, for instance, may urge that any desire felt by alienated man in a capitalistic society is foreign to his true nature. Or an existentialist may claim that the desires of inauthentic men are themselves inauthentic. Such concepts are based upon general theories of human nature which are unsubstantiated and perhaps incapable of substantiation. Moreover, each of these theories is committed to a concept of an ideal desire which is normatively debatable and which is distinct from the ordinary concept of a rational desire as one based upon relevant information. But it is in the terms of the ordinary concept that we express our concern that advertising may limit our autonomy in the sense of leading us to act on irrational desires, and if we operate with this concept we are driven again to the conclusion that advertising may lead, but probably most often does not lead, to an infringement of autonomy.

(c) Free Choice. It might be said that some desires are so strong or so covert that a person cannot resist them, and that when he acts on such desires he is not acting freely or voluntarily but is rather the victim of irresistible impulse or an unconscious drive. Perhaps those who condemn advertising feel that it produces this kind of desire in us and consequently reduces our autonomy.

This raises a very difficult issue. How do we distinguish between an impulse we *do* not resist and one we *could* not resist, between freely giving in to a desire and succumbing to one? I have argued elsewhere that the way to get at this issue is in terms of the notion of acting for a reason.[16] A person acts or chooses freely if he does so for a reason, that is, if he can adduce considerations which justify in his mind the act in question. Many of our actions are in fact free because this condition frequently holds. Often, however, a person will act from habit, or whim, or impulse, and on these occasions he does not have a reason in mind. Nevertheless he often acts voluntarily in these instances, i.e., he could have acted otherwise. And this is because if there *had been* a reason for acting otherwise of which he was aware, he would in fact have done so. Thus acting from habit or impulse is not necessarily to act in an involuntary manner. If, however, a person is aware of a good reason to do *x* and still follows his impulse to do *y*, then he can be said to be impelled by irresistible impulse and hence to act involuntarily. Many kleptomaniacs can be said to act involuntarily, for in spite of their knowledge that they likely will be caught and their awareness that the goods they steal have little utilitarian value to them, they nevertheless steal. Here their 'out of character' desires have the upper hand, and we have a case of compulsive behavior.

Applying these notions of voluntary and compulsive behavior to the case of behavior prompted by advertising, can we say that consumers influenced by advertising act compulsively? The unexciting answer is: sometimes they do, sometimes not. I may have an overwhelming, T.V. induced urge to own a Mazda Rx-7 and all the while realize that I can't afford one without severely reducing my family's caloric intake to a dangerous level. If, aware of this good reason not to purchase the car, I nevertheless do so, this shows that I have been the victim of T.V. compulsion. But if I have the urge, as I assure you I do, and don't act on it, or if in some other possible world I could afford an Rx-7, then I have not been the subject of undue influence by Mazda advertising. Some Mazda Rx-7 purchasers act compulsively; others do not. The Mazda advertising effort *in general* cannot be condemned, then, for impairing its customers' autonomy in the sense of limiting free or voluntary choice. Of course the question remains what should be done about the fact that advertising may and does *occasionally* limit free choice. We shall return to this question later.

In the case of subliminal advertising we may find an individual whose subconscious desires are activated by advertising into doing something his calculating, reasoning ego does not approve. This would be a case of compulsion. But most of us have a benevolent subconsciousness which does not overwhelm our ego and its reasons for action. And therefore most of us can respond to subliminal advertising without thereby risking our autonomy. To be sure, if some advertising firm developed a subliminal technique which drove all of us to purchase Lear jets, thereby reducing our caloric intake to the zero point, then we would have a case of advertising which could properly be censured for infringing our right to autonomy. We should acknowledge that this is possible, but at the same time we should recognize that it is not an inherent result of subliminal advertising.

(d) Control or Manipulation. Briefly let us consider the matter of control and manipulation. Under what conditions do these activities occur? In a recent paper on 'Forms and Limits of Control' I suggested the following criteria:[17]

A person *C* controls the behavior of another person *P iff*

1. *C* intends *P* to act in a certain way *A*;
2. *C*'s intention is causally effective in bringing about *A*; and
3. *C* intends to ensure that all of the necessary conditions of *A* are satisfied.

These criteria may be elaborated as follows. To control another person it is not enough that one's actions produce certain behavior on the part of that person; additionally one must intend that this happen. Hence control is the intentional production of behavior. Moreover, it is not enough just to have the intention; the intention must give rise to the conditions which bring about the intended effect. Finally, the controller must intend to establish by his actions any otherwise unsatisfied necessary conditions for the production of the intended effect. The controller is not just influencing the outcome, not just having input; he is as it were guaranteeing that the sufficient conditions for the intended effect are satisfied.

Let us apply these criteria of control to the case of advertising and see what happens. Conditions (1) and (3) are crucial. Does the Mazda manufacturing company or its advertising agency intend that I buy an Rx-7? Do they intend that a certain number of people buy the car? *Prima facie* it seems more appropriate to say that they *hope* a certain number of people will buy it, and hoping and intending are not the same. But the difficult term here is 'intend'. Some philosophers have argued that to intend *A* it is necessary only to desire that *A* happen and to believe that it will. If this is correct, and if marketing analysis gives the Mazda agency a reasonable belief that a certain segment of the population will buy its product, then, assuming on its part the desire that this happen, we have the conditions necessary for saying that the agency intends that a certain segment purchase the car. If I am a member of this segment of the population, would it then follow that the agency intends that I purchase an Rx-7? Or is control referentially opaque? Obviously we have some questions here which need further exploration.

Let us turn to the third condition of control, the requirement that the controller intend to activate or bring about any otherwise unsatisfied necessary conditions for the production of the intended effect. It is in terms of this condition that we are able to distinguish brainwashing from liberal education. The brainwasher arranges all of the necessary conditions for belief. On the other hand, teachers (at least those of liberal persuasion) seek only to influence their students—to provide them with information and enlightenment which they may absorb *if they wish*. We do not normally think of teachers as controlling their students, for the students' performances depend as well on their own interests and inclinations.

Now the advertiser—does he control, or merely influence, his audience? Does he intend to ensure that all of the necessary conditions for purchasing behavior are met, or does he offer information and symbols which are intended to have an effect only *if* the potential purchaser has certain desires? Undeniably advertising induces some desires, and it does this intentionally, but more often than not it intends to induce a desire for a particular object, *given* that the purchaser already has other desires. Given a desire for youth, or power, or adventure, or ravishing beauty, we are led to desire Grecian Formula 16, Mazda Rx-7's, Pongo Peach, and Distinctive Foundations. In this light, the advertiser is influencing us by appealing to independent desires we already have. He is not creating those basic desires. Hence it seems appropriate to deny that he intends to produce all of the necessary conditions for our purchases, and appropriate to deny that he controls us.[18]

Let me summarize my argument. The critics of advertising see it as having a pernicious effect on the autonomy of consumers, as controlling their lives and manufacturing their very souls. The defense claims that advertising only offers information and in effect allows industry to provide consumers with what they want. After developing

some of the philosophical dimensions of this dispute, I have come down tentatively in favor of the advertisers. Advertising may, but certainly does not always or even frequently, control behavior, produce compulsive behavior, or create wants which are not rational or are not truly those of the consumer. Admittedly it may in individual cases do all of these things, but it is innocent of the charge of intrinsically or necessarily doing them or even, I think, of often doing so. This limited potentiality, to be sure, leads to the question whether advertising should be abolished or severely curtailed or regulated because of its potential to harm a few poor souls in the above ways. This is a very difficult question, and I do not pretend to have the answer. I only hope that the above discussion, in showing some of the kinds of harm that can be done by advertising and by indicating the likely limits of this harm, will put us in a better position to grapple with the question.

NOTES

1. Vance Packard, *The Hidden Persuaders* (Pocket Books, New York, 1958), pp. 20–21.

2. *Ibid.*, p. 21.

3. B. F. Skinner, 'Some Issues Concerning the Control of Human Behavior: A Symposium', in Karlins and Andrews (eds.), *Man Controlled* (The Free Press, New York, 1972).

4. For provocative discussions of subliminal advertising, see W. B. Key, *Subliminal Seduction* (The New American Library, New York, 1973), and W. B. Key, *Media Sexploitation* (Prentice-Hall, Inc., Englewood Cliffs, N.J., 1976).

5. I would like to emphasize that in what follows I am discussing these techniques of advertising from the standpoint of the issue of control and not from that of deception. For a good and recent discussion of the many dimensions of possible deception in advertising, see Alex C. Michalos, 'Advertising: Its Logic, Ethics, and Economics' in J. A. Blair and R. H. Johnson (eds.), *Informal Logic: The First International Symposium* (Edgepress, Pt. Reyes, Calif., 1980).

6. Quoted by Packard, *op. cit.*, p. 220.

7. Theodore Levitt, 'The Morality (?) of Advertising', *Harvard Business Review* 48 (1970), 84–92.

8. Phillip Nelson, 'Advertising and Ethics', in Richard T. De George and Joseph A. Pichler (eds.), *Ethics, Free Enterprise, and Public Policy* (Oxford University Press, New York, 1978), pp. 187–198.

9. For a discussion of polymorphous perversity, see Norman O. Brown, *Life Against Death* (Random House, New York, 1969), Chapter III.

10. John Kenneth Galbraith, *The Affluent Society*; reprinted in Tom L. Beauchamp and Norman E. Bowie (eds.), *Ethical Theory and Business* (Prentice-Hall, Englewood Cliffs, 1979), pp. 496–501.

11. David Braybrooke, 'Skepticism of Wants, and Certain Subversive Effects of Corporations on American Values', in Sidney Hook (ed.), *Human Values and Economic Policy* (New York University Press, New York, 1967); reprinted in Beauchamp and Bowie (eds.), *op. cit.*, pp. 502–508.

12. F. A. von Hayek, 'The *Non Sequitur* of the "Dependence Effect"', *Southern Economic Journal* (1961); reprinted in Beauchamp and Bowie (eds.), *op. cit.*, pp. 508–512.

13. Harry Frankfurt, 'Freedom of the Will and the Concept of a Person', *Journal of Philosophy* LXVIII (1971), 5–20.

14. For a discussion of the difference between a malign and a benign subconscious mind, see P. H. Nowell-Smith, 'Psycho-analysis and Moral Language', *The Rationalist Annual* (1954); reprinted in P. Edwards and A. Pap (eds.), *A Modern Introduction to Philosophy*, Revised Edition (The Free Press, New York, 1965), pp. 86–93.

15. Michalos argues that in emphasizing a brand name—such as Bayer Aspirin—advertisers are illogically attempting to distinguish the indistinguishable by casting a trivial feature of a product as a significant one which separates it from other brands of the same product. The brand name is said to be trivial or unimportant "from the point of view of the effectiveness of the product or that for the sake of which the product is purchased" (*op. cit.*, p. 107). This claim ignores the role of indirect information in advertising. For example, consumers want an aspirin *they* can trust (trustworthiness being part of "that for the sake of which the product is purchased"), and the indirect information conveyed by the widespread advertising effort for Bayer aspirin shows that this product is judged trustworthy by many other purchasers. Hence the emphasis on the name is not at all irrelevant but rather is a significant feature of the product from the consumer's standpoint, and attending to the name is not at all an illogical or irrational response on the part of the consumer.

16. Robert L. Arrington, 'Practical Reason, Responsibility and the Psychopath', *Journal for the Theory of Social Behavior* 9 (1979), 71–89.

17. Robert L. Arrington, 'Forms and Limits of Control', delivered at the annual meeting of the Southern Society for Philosophy and Psychology, Birmingham, Alabama, 1980.

18. Michalos distinguishes between appealing to people's tastes and molding those tastes (*op. cit.*, p. 104), and he seems to agree with my claim that it is morally permissible for advertisers to persuade us to consume some article *if* it suits our tastes (p. 105). However, he also implies that advertisers mold tastes as well as appeal to them. It is unclear what evidence is given for this claim, and it is unclear what is meant by *tastes*. If the latter are thought of as basic desires and wants, then I would agree that advertisers are controlling their customers to the extent that they intentionally mold tastes. But if by molding tastes is meant generating a desire for the particular object they promote, advertisers in doing so may well be appealing to more basic desires, in which case they should not be thought of as controlling the consumer.

TIMOTHY E. MOORE

Subliminal Advertising:
What You See Is What You Get

In September 1957 some unwitting theatre audiences in New Jersey were invited to "drink Coca-Cola" and "eat popcorn" in briefly presented messages that were superimposed on the movie in progress. Exposure times were so short that viewers were unaware of any message. The marketing firm responsible reported a dramatic increase in Coke and popcorn sales, although they provided no documentation of these alleged effects. Public reaction was, nevertheless, immediate and widespread:

From *Journal of Marketing*, Vol. 46, Spring 1982. Reprinted by permission.

"... the most alarming and outrageous discovery since Mr. Gatling invented his gun." (*Nation*, 1957 p. 206)

"... take this invention and everything connected with it and attach it to the center of the next nuclear explosive scheduled for testing." (Cousins 1957, p. 20)

Opponents were indignant that unforgiveable psychological manipulations would be visited upon innocent and unknowing consumers. Minds had been "broken and entered" according to the *New Yorker* (1957, p. 33). There was much talk of *Brave New World* and *1984*. But even while laws were being drafted prohibiting the use of subliminal advertising on television, Hollywood was incorporating the idea into two new movies, and a Seattle radio station started broadcasting 'subaudible' messages such as "TV's a bore."

In May 1978 police investigators in an unnamed midwestern city attempted to apprehend a murderer by interspersing subliminal messages among frames of TV news film describing the murder (*New York Times* 1978, p. c22). Later that year some department stores in Toronto began broadcasting subliminal auditory messages whose intent was to deter shoplifters. The "sinister implications" of such practices worried the *Globe and Mail*. Could unscrupulous prime ministers deliver political propaganda subliminally? (*Globe and Mail* 1978, p. 6). In British Columbia the following year, a Ministry of Human Resources policy manual on child abuse was denied inclusion in a government-commissioned publication because the manual's cover contained "sickening and obscene" sexual imagery imbedded in an apparently innocuous photograph of an adult's hand clasping a child's.

Reports of various forms of subliminal manipulation are fairly common. Evidently the practice is still with us, although a few twists have been added since 1957. Given its covert nature and the ethical considerations involved, the prevalence of subliminal advertising is very likely underestimated by reliance upon published reports. At any rate, such techniques are believed to be widespread by a great many people who can hardly be faulted for vigorously protesting against their use. John Q. Public has his hands full trying to cope with forms of exploitation of which he is fully aware. Should he also be worried that Madison Avenue is sneaking directives into his sub-

conscious through the back door? Such a possibility has pervasive ramifications (Brown 1960). The potential importance of the topic has not escaped those in marketing (Hawkins 1970, Kelly 1979, Saegert 1979); however, all lament the dearth of empirical research.

There are at least three identifiable means of subliminal stimulation for which strong behavioral effects have been claimed. The first of these involves very briefly presented visual stimuli. Presentation is usually by means of a tachistoscope, a device for carefully controlling the exposure duration of a visual stimulus. Directives or instructions are flashed so quickly that the viewer is unaware of their presence. Such stimulation purportedly registers subconsciously and allegedly affects subsequent behavior. This method of stimulus presentation has been used frequently by investigators interested in subliminal perception, although their purposes have usually been quite different. As a result, a body of research literature exists that bears on the claims being made for some kinds of subliminal advertising. Some examples from this literature will be described and some studies analyzed in detail. It should be emphasized that stimulation below the level of conscious awareness *can* be shown to have measurable effects upon some aspects of behavior. The point at issue is whether these effects are sufficient to warrant the conclusion that goal-directed behavior can be manipulated by such stimulation.

Another means by which behavior control is attempted is through the use of accelerated speech in low volume auditory messages. Here too, the claim is that while the message may be unintelligible and unnoticed at a conscious level, it is nevertheless processed subconsciously and imparts direction to the receiver's behavior.

The third procedure consists of embedding or hiding sexual imagery (or sometimes words) in pictorial advertisements. These are concealed in such a way that they are not available to conscious perusal. They have, however, a subconscious effect or so it is argued.

The effects attributed to these procedures may consist of either (1) general, nonspecific, affective consequences that are assumed to have some positive but unspecified persuasive influence, or (2) a highly specific, direct impact upon some particular motive or behavior. In what follows, the evidence and arguments put forth in defense of the effectiveness of these procedures will be reviewed and critiqued.

SUBLIMINAL PERCEPTION

Measurable responses of one kind or another can sometimes be shown to be contingent upon stimulation that the perceiver is unaware of. Pierce and Jastrow (1884) demonstrated that subjects could make reliable discriminations among stimuli differing in weight, even though they reported that the stimuli were *not* discriminably different. In this classic study, subjects indicated the degree of confidence in their judgments concerning very slight differences in pressure applied to the subjects' fingers. In those instances where no confidence at all in perceived variation of pressure was reported, subjects were nevertheless obliged to say which of the two pressures was greater. Their judgments were correct 60% of the time.

The Threshold Concept

Today, the notion that people can respond to stimuli without being able to report on their existence is accepted and well documented (Bevan 1964a, 1964b; Dixon 1971; Erdelyi 1974). Taken literally, subliminal means "below threshold." However, there exists no absolute cut-off point for stimulus intensity below which stimulation is imperceptible and above which it is always detected. When stimuli of varying intensities are presented over several trials, the minimum signal strength that is always detected is much higher than the one that is almost never detected. If some absolute threshold existed, then there ought to be a determinable stimulus intensity above which the receiver always responds and below which there is no response. Instead, a particular stimulus is sometimes detected and sometimes goes unnoticed. As a result, an individual's perceptual threshold is usually defined as that stimulus value that is correctly detected 50% of the time. The threshold, or limen, is, therefore, a statistical abstraction.

For a given individual, this threshold may vary from day to day or from minute to minute. More-over, thresholds differ rather widely between individuals. Many studies of subliminal perception are flawed because the investigators assumed that some specific exposure duration or stimulus intensity automatically guaranteed that the stimulus would be sufficiently below threshold that its presence would be undetected for all the experimental subjects on all the trials. Often this assumption is unwarranted. Stimuli below the statistical limen (which itself fluctuates) may be noticed as much as 49% of the time. As a result, studies that make little or no effort to determine a threshold for individual subjects are at risk because stimuli are presented that are effectively *supra*liminal for some subjects on some trials. The results may thus be due to the effects of weak (but not subliminal) stimulation.

Obviously the notion of a perceptual limen is of limited usefulness. For present purposes we may use the term subliminal perception to refer to the following situations (Dixon 1971, p. 12):

a. The subject responds to stimulation the energy or duration of which falls below that at which he *ever* reported awareness of the stimulus in some previous threshold determination.

b. He responds to a stimulus of which he pleads total unawareness.

c. He reports that he is being stimulated but denies any awareness of what the stimulus was.

In these instances the subject cannot recognize the stimulus. "These situations define subliminal perception, and are to be distinguished from those where the individual, though unaware of the stimulus response contingency, is either not necessarily unaware of the stimulus, or, alternatively, could be *made aware* of the stimulus if his attention were drawn to it" (Dixon 1971, p. 13). People are often unaware of stimulation or of the processes mediating the effects of a stimulus on a response (Nisbett and Wilson 1977). This is a separate issue from subliminal stimulation, wherein the subject *cannot* identify the stimulus.

Some Illustrations of Subliminal Perception

There is ample evidence that weak stimuli that are not reportable *can* be demonstrated to influence behavior. For example, a number of studies by

Bevan and his associates (Bevan 1964b) have shown that subliminal stimuli can alter judgments of perceived intensity of supraliminal stimuli when the former are interpolated into the presentation series. In one of these studies subjects were asked to judge the intensity of weak electric shocks delivered to their wrists. Between trials subliminal levels of shock were also administered. Careful control procedures ensured that these stimuli were not detected. The effect of these interpolated stimuli was to elevate the judged intensities of the detectable shocks. A control group that received no subliminal stimulation routinely estimated their shocks to be less intense than the experimental group. A similar effect was found for judgments of the perceived loudness of tones. Apparently the subliminal stimuli trigger physiological activity that affects the perception of similar supraliminal stimuli.

Signal detection research provides another example. In a signal detection task, weak stimuli are presented; some are detectable, some are not. If subjects are asked to provide confidence ratings of their judgments about the presence or absence of a signal, their ratings are highly correlated with the stimulus intensity. This is true even for signals that were reportedly not detected (Green and Swets 1966, Swets 1961).

Perceptual defense literature provides yet another sort of illustration. Many studies have shown that taboo or emotionally loaded words have higher recognition thresholds than do neutral words. That is, it takes a longer exposure duration for *whore* to be identified than for *shore*. At first this may appear illogical. How can something taboo be defended against unless it is first recognized as being taboo? The paradox is resolved if it is assumed that "perception" is by no means a discrete experiential event that is automatically determined by some particular stimulus pattern. Rather, perception is treated as a multiprocess chain of events that begins with stimulus input and terminates (subjectively) with conscious recognition of an object or event. However, not all input is subjected to the same sequence of mental processing. Stimuli are selectively filtered, transformed and attended to according to a variety of factors that are independent of the particular input. These include memory, expectations, attention, affect and

other variables. Perception then, as we conventionally use the term, represents "... the conscious terminus of a sequence of nonconscious prior processes" (Erdelyi 1974). Conscious recognition need not be and often is not the end point for many sorts of input. Some stimuli may initiate mental activity of one sort or another without being available to conscious reflection or report. This is what is typically meant by the term subliminal perception. In the case of taboo items, some kind of defensive selectivity operates to bias the processing of emotionally charged input—such selectivity having its impact *prior* to a conscious recognition of the input.

Recently Zajonc (1980) has reviewed evidence from several studies showing that under some circumstances, unattended stimuli can be processed to a degree that is sufficient to elicit a subsequent affective reaction (i.e., like/dislike) *without* their being recognized as having been previously encountered. "Affective reactions can occur without extensive perceptual cognitive encoding. Reliable affective discriminations (like/dislike ratings) can be made in the total absence of recognition memory (old-new judgments)" (Zajonc 1980, p. 151). While unattended stimuli are not necessarily subliminal, one study purports to show that affect can be influenced by stimuli that *are* truly subliminal (Kunst-Wilson and Zajonc 1980). That some behavioral processes may be influenced by stimuli whose presence is not consciously noticeable by the receiver is not at issue here. The preceding examples testify to the validity of subliminal perception as a phenomenon. The important question is whether the subliminal effects obtained justify the claims made for subliminal advertising. This question is critical because what must be posited in order to support such a proposition is not merely *an* effect, but specific, (relatively) powerful and enduring effects on the buying preferences of the public.

SUBLIMINAL ADVERTISING

Could subliminally presented stimuli have a marketing application? Can advertising effectiveness be enhanced through subliminal stimulation? Before reviewing the few laboratory studies that have addressed this question directly, it will be useful to consider what sorts of subliminal influences would be necessary in order to obtain some marketing relevance. At a minimum, we might hypothesize that a subliminal stimulus produces (or increases) some positive affective reaction to that stimulus. Whether or not such an affective response, if obtained, could have any relevant motivating influence is another question. It is probably safe to assume that positive affect would not do any harm and could conceivably influence a product's attractiveness. A much stronger prediction for subliminal effects would be one that hypothesizes some direct behavioral consequence (i.e., purchasing). Since the former prediction does not *necessarily* entail any interesting marketing implications, and the latter prediction clearly does, these hypotheses will be referred to as weak and strong claims respectively.

Practical Difficulties

Regardless of which claim is under investigation, there are some profound if not insurmountable operational constraints associated with presenting subliminal stimuli in a typical marketing context. One problem has to do with individual differences in threshold. There is no particular stimulus intensity or duration that can guarantee subliminality for all viewers. In order to preclude detection by those with relatively low thresholds, the stimulus would have to be so weak that it would not reach viewers with higher thresholds at all. Lack of control over position and distance from the screen would further complicate matters. Finally, without elaborate precautions, supraliminal material (i.e., the film or commercial in progress) would almost certainly wash out any potential effects of a subliminal stimulus. In order to duplicate the results of laboratory studies that have shown subliminal effects, it is crucial to duplicate the conditions under which the effects were obtained. From a practical standpoint, this is virtually impossible. Nevertheless, it could be argued that if 1% of 10 million viewers are influenced by a subliminal ad that completely misses the other 99%, the subsequent behavior of that 1% might make the exercise cost effective.

Does the relevant research indicate that some positive affect could become associated with a particular product through the use of subliminally presented stimuli? The evidence is not strong. The Kunst-Wilson and Zajonc (1980) study referred to earlier used irregular, randomly constructed octagons as stimuli. The stimuli themselves were first presented at one-millisecond durations and filtered so that recognition was at chance level. Subjects were instructed to pay close attention to the screen, even if nothing was distinguishable. The same stimuli were subsequently presented for one-second intervals, paired with new stimuli. Subjects' recognition of old versus new stimuli was reported to be at chance; however, the old stimuli were judged to be preferable to the new ones 60% of the time. The effect was subtle but statistically reliable ($p < .01$, 2-tail).

It is tempting to speculate that repeated subliminal exposures could bring about an increasingly stronger affective reaction, with the stimuli themselves remaining unrecognized. A study by Shevrin and Fritzler (1968) does not support such a notion. These authors demonstrated a differential effect of two different subliminal stimuli upon evoked potentials (EEG) and free word associations in the absence of a conscious discrimination between the stimuli. The effect was a fleeting one, however: "the subliminal verbal effects appeared only in the first .001-second condition, suggesting that, beyond a certain point, multiple exposures of stimuli work against subliminal influences" (Shevrin and Fritzler 1968, p. 298). Two points about the Kunst-Wilson and Zajonc study are worth emphasizing.

First, the stimuli themselves, consisting of (relatively) meaningless geometric shapes, were subjected to subliminal exposure levels; this exposure seems to have had a subsequent effect upon preference. Second, the experimental subjects were actively attending to the stimuli throughout the subliminal viewing condition; during this time, no other stimulation was present that could distract attention or mask the subliminal stimuli.

Could this procedure be utilized in an advertising context? It is possible that a display's attractiveness could be subliminally enhanced by having that same display exposed for subliminal durations prior to its supraliminal presentation. Whether the magnitude of the resultant effect could have any practical importance is not known. Moreover, it is not obvious how the subliminal exposure could be accomplished. Superimposing the subliminal display on top of supraliminal material is not a good bet:

... Ongoing supraliminal stimulation to which attention may be directed almost certainly will swamp any effect by a simultaneous stimulus below the awareness threshold ... at a peripheral level, lateral inhibition and contour suppressing mechanisms could well block any neural transmission from the weaker of two stimulus arrays ... a similar effect of restricted channel capacity would almost certainly operate centrally as well. The potential effects of one stimulus may be completely negated by the presence of another (Dixon 1971, p. 175–76).

Splicing or somehow integrating the subliminal stimulus into ongoing supraliminal material (even if technologically possible) is not too promising either, because unless a sufficient blank interval is included before and after the insert, supraliminal material will mask the subliminal stimulus (Kahneman 1968). If such intervals are provided, the viewer will most probably be aware of an interruption, even though the stimulus itself may not be detectable. At least 100 milliseconds of "clean" background on either side of the target stimulus would be necessary to preclude a masking effect. As a result, subjects could infer the presence of a stimulus. If complete unobtrusiveness is a priority, the stimulus and surrounding interval would have to be carefully located at naturally occurring breaks or cut points. Even then, completely disguising the fact of stimulation may not be possible.

Evidence Involving the Weak Claim

In addition to Kunst-Wilson and Zajonc (1980), two other studies report subliminal effects relevant to the weak claim. Byrne (1959) flashed the word "beef" for successive five millisecond intervals during a sixteen-minute movie. Experimental and control subjects did not differ in their verbal references to beef, as measured by word association tests. Nor did experimental subjects report a higher preference for beef sandwiches, when given a list of five alternatives. Experimental subjects did, however, rate themselves as hungrier than control subjects. This difference held up when ratings were co-varied with hours of food deprivation. Byrne offered no explanation for this finding. It is not obvious why the word "beef" should induce hunger particularly when it failed to influence semantic associates. Moreover, the method of presentation involved superimposing the stimulus on the movie. For reasons outlined earlier, such a procedure is likely to interfere with rather than enhance any potential subliminal affects.

In a similar study, Hawkins (1970) flashed the word "Coke" for 2.7 millisecond-intervals during the presentation of other supraliminal material. Subjective thirst ratings were higher for the "Coke" group than for a control group that received a subliminal nonsense syllable. Hawkins concludes that "a simple subliminal stimulus can serve to arouse a basic drive such as thirst" (p. 324). As Saegert (1979) has pointed out, "Hawkin's results may simply be a Type I error, especially in view of the fact that other tries have been made" (p. 55). The fact that Hawkins performed five independent 1-tail statistical tests where one analysis would have sufficed lends support to Saegert's position. There are methodological shortcomings in both of these studies. Even if the results are taken at face value, their relevance to advertising is minimal.

Evidence Involving the Strong Claim

The strong claim for subliminal advertising posits specific behavioral consequences as a result of a subliminal directive. A study by Zuckerman (1960) requiring student nurses to write stories describing the contents of a series of pictures that were projected onto a screen in front of them is pertinent to this issue. Unknown to the subjects, the instructions "write more" and "don't write" were tachistoscopically superimposed on the pictures at successive points during the presentations. A control group was treated in a similar fashion but received blank slides in place of those containing the subliminal directives.

The study was composed of three successive conditions: (1) baseline, during which no subliminal messages were presented, (2) "write more," during which subjects in the experimental group received a "write more" instruction for .02 seconds, concurrently with the picture they were asked to describe, and (3) "don't write," during which the experimental subjects received a "don't write" directive, again superimposed for .02 seconds on the picture being projected. During each condition, pictures were presented for 10 trials each. After each trial, subjects wrote a description of what they had seen. Zuckerman found that nurses in the experimental group wrote more during condition 2 ("write more") than they had during baseline. Furthermore, he noted a slight drop in output between condition 3 ("don't write") and condition 2, and interpreted this as evidence that the subliminal instructions were effective.

Unfortunately, there is a strong possibility that these results were due to a methodological artifact which psychologists call a "ceiling effect." This occurs when performance reaches an asymptote and cannot be further improved upon. The slight drop that Zuckerman observed may not have been a real decrease in performance but rather, a levelling off. This interpretation is supported by a comparison of the performances of experimental and control subjects. For some reason the students in the experimental group were enthusiastic writers. They wrote much more during baseline than did the controls. They wrote still more during condition 2 ("write more"), and the controls increased their output as well. By condition 3 the experimental subjects may have reached asymptote. They were all "written out," and a slight drop was observed in the number of words written.

Because of time constraints (and possibly writer's cramp), experimental subjects may already have been writing as much as could reasonably be expected by the end of condition 2. The slight drop during condition 3 may be due to statistical artifact. When variability is possible in only one direction (in this case down), a slight decrease in performance is predictable. Controls were still increasing their output during condition 3 and by the end, their output had barely surpassed that of the experimental subjects' performance during baseline. When differences between groups are large prior to any experimental manipulation, it is risky to attribute some subsequently observed differences to that manipulation. In this study, the preexisting differences between experimental and control subjects was as great or greater than any other subsequently observed difference between or within groups. Zuckerman has little to say by way

of explaining the finding, but submits that "the subject's operant behavior is supposedly brought under control by suggestive cues of which he is not aware" (p. 404). This is not an explanation but rather a description of the outcome couched in operant terminology.

Dixon (1971), commenting on Zuckerman's results, speculates that "it may be impossible to resist instructions which are not consciously experienced" (p. 177). Again, this is more an assertion than an explanation, but it does reflect an apparently prevalent (although not articulated) notion that instructions, directives and/or slogans are intrinsically compelling. When the instruction is delivered supraliminally the receiver can counter-argue or derogate the source, thereby diminishing the stimulus' influence. However, if the instruction is presented subliminally, the recipient is unaware of its presence and is consequently unable to counter-argue.

Several researchers have investigated and described some of the cognitive processes that may mediate acceptance of advertising claims (Harris et al. 1979, Wright 1973). Wright analyzed the responses of 160 women who were exposed to a target ad embedded in other surrounding material, and subsequently queried about their reactions to the arguments contained in the advertising message. Counter-arguing by the receiver was identified as an important processing strategy. Neither the reliability nor validity of this finding is being disputed. However, it would be a mistake to assume that "resistive cognitions" are an inevitable consequence of advertising. Such a position is reminiscent of a behavioristic view of people as passive receivers of inputs to which they respond in automatic and stereotyped ways.

Perhaps the single most important lesson to be learned from cognitive psychology in the last decade is that the meaning of a stimulus does not reside in the stimulus itself. Meaning is constructed by the receiver in active, complex and often specialized ways. With respect to advertising the selectivity of attention and the active control over subsequent processing of the input means that stimulation is not a sufficient condition for any response at all, let alone some particular response. We are constantly subjected to a barrage of external and internal stimuli, of which only a fraction acquire phenomenal representation. Some neural activity is no doubt provoked by stimuli that are not consciously processed. But to attribute to a subliminal stimulus a strong influence, which it cannot be shown to have when supraliminal, is not justified by any theoretical rationale. For this reason it is appropriate to insist on especially clear well-replicated empirical evidence before accepting such a proposition. To the author's knowledge, Zuckerman's (1960) finding has *not* been replicated, and the study itself is vulnerable to an important methodological criticism.

There is an additional problem with procedures that attempt subliminal persuasion through the use of written directives. In order for a subliminal message to exert a behavioral effect (the "strong" claim), the full and precise meaning of the message would have to be extracted from it. Dixon (1971) has reviewed many subliminal perception studies showing that when words are used as stimuli, "the stimulus tends to elicit responses from the same sphere of meaning" (p. 102). Since competitors' products may well be contained in this sphere, it would be essential that the full meaning of the stimulus words be identified. An effusion of mere semantic associates would be insufficient. There are no published studies that demonstrate that people educe the full meaning of a subliminal word stimulus, and there are at least two studies casting some doubt on the possibility (Heilbrun 1980, Severance and Dyer 1973). For this reason, it is difficult to construe a subliminal directive as an argument that cannot be consciously resisted.

Summary

Before turning to other methods that attempt subliminal persuasion, it will be useful to summarize the evidence reviewed. Research supporting the null hypothesis is much less likely to find its way into print than that which demonstrates some potential influence. The paucity of evidence may simply be a reflection of its lack of availability. On the basis of what little data are available, one could tentatively conclude that subliminal presentation of a stimulus may produce a positive affective response to that stimulus (Kunst-Wilson and Zajonc 1980). This positive affective response was obtained with subjects who were attending only to

the subliminal stimuli. Whether this finding could be utilized successfully in a marketing context remains to be seen. Apart from the question of the magnitude of the effect, not to mention its validity (Birnbaum 1981, Mellers 1981), there are some practical difficulties associated with achieving a realworld application.

The evidence that subliminal directives can exert any control over behavior is much less compelling (Zuckerman 1960), although there has been ample opportunity for replication. Moreover, this strong claim for subliminal influence is not accompanied by a coherent explanatory rationale. Previous reviews of the strong claim have reached similar conclusions. One of the first rigorous scrutinies of this issue was described by McConnell et al. (1958), no doubt precipitated by the furor generated by the popcorn ad in New Jersey. These authors were sceptical that any but the simplest forms of behavior could be affected by stimulation below the level of conscious awareness. Bevan (1964a) concluded that the "influences of subliminal stimulation upon preference and choice, if they occur at all, are highly subtle, and the possibility that they could constitute an effective means of controlling consumer behavior or political opinion is highly unlikely" (p. 91). Equally strong misgivings were expressed by Goldiamond (1966) and Anastasi (1964). Empirical documentation has remained elusive: "all things considered . . . secret attempts to manipulate people's minds have yielded results as subliminal as the stimuli used" (McConnell 1977, p. 231).

SUBAUDIBLE MESSAGES

The eye is capable of receiving far more information in a short period of time than is the ear. Thus most studies of subliminal perception have involved visual stimulation because the investigator can attempt to determine what particular features of a display are responsible for various sorts of neural activity that may occur below the level of conscious awareness. In contrast, studies addressing auditory reception have been concerned primarily with signal detection—determining the presence versus absence of a weak signal. Because auditory information is, perforce, temporally extended, it is particularly vulnerable to loss through lack of attention or auditory masking.

This probably accounts for the total absence of published studies investigating possible effects of subaudible messages. While the eye is sensitive primarily to spatial information, the ear is basically a processor of temporal information, especially in the case of speech perception. The difference is an important one. A great deal of information can be presented simultaneously in a visual display. An auditory stimulus is more extended in time; information arrives in consecutive bits. A speech stimulus may be thought of as a sound pattern whose acoustic features fluctuate over time. Consequently, there is no procedure for creating tachistoscopic-like auditory stimuli. Controlling the exposure duration of a visual stimulus does not change the stimulus itself; it merely limits the time available for processing it.

If speech is compressed or telescoped in time, the signal itself is altered. While the speech stream can be subjected to a surprising amount of mutilation without intelligibility being affected (Licklider and Miller 1951), there is a limit to the amount of distortion that can be tolerated without a loss in comprehension. Information is transmitted at the rate of about 150 words per minute in normal speech. Studies have shown (Foulke and Sticht 1969) that comprehension declines fairly rapidly at rates beyond 300 words per minute. There are two reasons for this. The first involves signal degradation. When playback speed is increased, component frequencies and pitch are both altered. The intelligibility of the signal consequently suffers. Secondly, channel capacity is taxed when a critical word rate is reached. Speech comprehension requires the continuous registration, encoding and storage of information. These operations take time. When the word rate is too fast, not all the input can be processed as it is received. The result is that some speech information is lost. Reducing the volume of accelerated speech will only compound these difficulties. Mass media accounts of subaudible messages report presentation rates of greater than 2,300 words per minute (*Toronto Star* 1978, p. c1; *Washington Post* 1979, p. c4; *Time* 1979, p. 63). The message is simply repeated 8- or 9,000 times an hour. Because of the fast rate, what may once have been a message is rendered an unintel-

ligible scratching sound. That such stimuli could have any influence on behavior (except to annoy) is a claim totally lacking empirical support. Since the stimulus has no apparent meaning, presenting it at a supposedly subaudible level does not thereby confer any added significance.

The accelerated nature of subaudible messages is perhaps a tangential issue. Could such messages have an influence if the presentation rate were normal, but the volume at a subthreshold level? Relevant evidence mitigates against such a notion. Weak auditory stimuli are very susceptible to auditory masking. Moreover, there is some experimental evidence that attentional focus can effectively prevent weak auditory stimuli from receiving any processing at all (Broadbent 1958, Eriksen and Johnson 1964, Peterson and Kroener 1964). Studies in dichotic listening reveal that very little of the content of an unattended message is processed when attention is focussed on another concurrent message (Kahneman 1973, Moray 1969, Treisman and Geffen 1967). Moreover the unattended stimuli used in these investigations are by no means subliminal in strength.

Speech sounds are different in principle from other auditory inputs (Liberman et al. 1967). Because of speech's temporal dimension, a certain minimal amount of attention may be essential for comprehension. This would make subliminal presentation of auditory messages not just difficult but impossible. In fact, it is difficult to conceive of a means by which speech could be rendered subliminal according to the conventional definition outlined earlier (see Dixon 1971, 1981). Neither accelerating the message nor reducing its volume seems to provide appropriate analogs to the methods used in the visual modality. At any rate, the procedures tried to date do not appear promising.

Whether or not subliminal effects could be obtained from auditory messages under more carefully controlled conditions remains to be seen. At the present time there is no evidence that such influence is possible, let alone any practical application. It should also be emphasized that a change in modality does not provide a defense against some of the objections raised earlier regarding the subliminal effects of visual stimuli. The assumption that behavior can be automatically triggered by the presentation of some particular stimulus is as unwarranted for auditory messages as it is for visual ones.

EMBEDDED STIMULI

A different kind of procedure for achieving subliminal effects has been described by Key (1973, 1976, 1980). In these books the author alleges that various erotic images or words have been surreptitiously concealed in magazine, newspaper and television advertisements. High-speed photography and airbrushing are among the techniques whereby subtle appeals to subconscious sex drives are hidden. Their use is ubiquitous. Ritz crackers have the word *sex* baked into them; a Gilbey's Gin ad is full of microscopic erotica. None of these are visible to the naked eye. In fact, it apparently requires weeks of analysis for many of them to be discovered, and sometimes they are embedded upside down.

According to Key, ". . . humans can be assumed to have at least two sensory input systems, one encoding data at the conscious level and a second operating at a level below conscious awareness" (Key 1973). A concealed word or symbol, ". . . usually invisible to consciousness appears instantly perceivable at the unconscious level" (Key 1976). He goes on to claim that visual or auditory stimulation whose speed and/or intensity are beyond the range for normal sensory reception can nevertheless be transmitted directly into the unconscious, whence subsequent behavior is manipulated. Precisely how these implanted cues affect a given product's desireability is not too clear, but Key assures us that they are very effective. The Ritz crackers, in fact, are reported to taste better because they have the word *sex* stamped onto them. Key provides no documentation for the effects that he attributes to embedded stimuli. For this reason, his assertions should be regarded as hypotheses awaiting empirical investigation. Key also describes some psychological mechanisms through which embedded stimuli purportedly operate. These latter claims involving perception, memory and the subconscious have probably rendered his speculations quite unpalatable to research psychologists. Man's sensory apparatus has been studied extensively for many years. There is no evidence

for more than one class of sensory input systems, as Key claims, nor is there evidence of unconscious perception of stimuli that fall outside the functional range of our receptor organs. Key appears to invent whatever features of perception and memory would be necessary to achieve the results imputed to embedded stimuli. The notion of a separate super-powerful sensory system serving the subconscious (exclusively) cannot be accommodated by any theory of perception, past or present. It is not surprising that Key's books have not been favorably reviewed by the scientific community (Schulman 1981). They are mentioned here because while they contain the least scientific substance, these books are probably largely responsible for the promulgation of a belief in the power of subliminal manipulation.

Whether or not erotic imagery has been deliberately planted is not relevant to a consideration of the imagery's alleged effects. A diligent search for a phallic symbol will probably be successful. How its presence and relationship to an advertised product might be interpreted is another matter, but the consequence is by no means predictable. The amount of information available from a purposeful scrutiny of a display is limited only by the viewer's imagination. Holding advertisers responsible for one's erotic musings is analogous to accusing Rorschach of insinuating particular themes into the inkblots. A cursory glance yields far less information than a careful inspection. Under typical circumstances, the ad's most salient characteristics will receive the lion's share of perceptual activity (Hochberg 1978), if they receive any attention at all. Completely ignoring a stimulus is an option that people frequently exercise. If you do not actively search for hidden extras, what you see is what you get, and there is nothing subliminal about such perusal. The fine print near the bottom of an ad is likely to be far more important than any concealed genitalia could be.

While Key appears to have misjudged the efficacy of embedded stimuli, it would be a mistake to dismiss out of hand all of his remarks concerning the latent effects of advertising. Ads may influence us in some ways which have nothing to do with consumer behavior per se. For example, ads help to transmit various cultural stereotypes. If women are consistently portrayed in insignificant or demeaning roles, the viewer may develop an attitude towards them that is ultimately prejudicial and harmful to women as a group. Moreover, these attitudes are not consciously formed. The rich literature on observational learning investigates how such learning takes place (Comstock et al. 1978). While the acquisition of such attitudes may occur subconsciously, there is nothing subliminal about the presentation of the role models. On the contrary, they are distressingly conspicuous. This kind of implicit learning can have important and pervasive consequences (Poe 1976; Rush 1980; Walstedt, Geis and Brown 1980).

CONCLUSION

A century of psychological research substantiates the general principle that more intense stimuli have a greater influence on people's behavior than weaker ones. While subliminal perception is a bona fide phenomenon, the effects obtained are subtle and obtaining them typically requires a carefully structured context. Subliminal stimuli are usually so weak that the recipient is not just unaware of the stimulus but is also oblivious to the fact that he/she is being stimulated. As a result, the potential effects of subliminal stimuli are easily nullified by other ongoing stimulation in the same sensory channel or by attention being focussed on another modality. These factors pose serious difficulties for any possible marketing application.

A second major problem pertains to the psychological mechanism through which a subliminal stimulus could in principle influence behavior. The proposition is appropriate only if one characterizes a person as a static organism who processes stimulus input passively and responds in automatic predictable ways. In fact, psychological research has generated a large body of evidence that such a characterization would be false. There is substantial evidence for the importance of centralized control and mediating processes and good reason to believe that humans have highly mobile selective attention. The sheer volume of constant sensory stimulation implicates a constructive, synthetic model of focal attention and perception rather than a purely receptive one. As Broadbent (1973) said, "... the brain is made of unreliable components, so that it is very unlikely that any particular impulses in any particular nerve cells

will occur predictably and consistently whenever a particular stimulus strikes our senses. In addition, we are being bombarded all the time by a very large quantity of information; and in relation to this large quantity of information we are all, like Winnie the Pooh, bears of very little brain" (p. 31).

Empirical support for subliminal influences of a pragmatic nature is neither plentiful nor compelling. On the basis of research evidence accumulated to date, the most one could hope for, in terms of marketing application, would be a potential positive affective response to a subliminal stimulus. Whether such an effect could actually be obtained in a realistic viewing situation, and whether the magnitude of the effect would make the exercise worthwhile is still an empirical question. There is no empirical documentation for stronger subliminal effects, such as inducing particular behaviors or changing motivation. Moreover, such a notion is contradicted by a substantial amount of research and is incompatible with experimentally based conceptions of information processing, learning and motivation.

None of this is to deny the existence of motives of which one may be unaware, nor to deny that subliminal stimulation can be used to investigate differences between unconscious and conscious processes (Carr and Bacharach 1976, McCauley et al. 1980, Shevrin and Dickman 1980). The point is simply that subliminal directives have not been shown to have the power ascribed to them by advocates of subliminal advertising. In general, the literature on subliminal perception shows that the most clearly documented effects are obtained only in highly contrived and artificial situations. These effects, when present, are brief and of small magnitude. The result is perhaps best construed as an epiphenomenon—a subtle and fleeting by-product of the complexities of human cognitive activity. These processes have no apparent relevance to the goals of advertising.

REFERENCES

Anastasi, A. (1964), "Subliminal Perception," in *Fields of Applied Psychology*, A. Anastasi, New York: McGraw-Hill.

Bevan, W. (1964a), "Subliminal Stimulation: A Pervasive Problem for Psychology," *Psychological Bulletin*, 61 (no. 2), 89–99.

———— (1964b), "Contemporary Problems in Adaptation Level Theory," *Psychological Bulletin*, 61 (no. 3), 161–187.

Birnbaum, M. (1981), "Thinking and Feeling: A Skeptical Review," *American Psychologist*, 36 (no. 1), 99–101.

Broadbent, D. E. (1958), *Perception and Communication*, New York: Pergamon.

———— (1973), *In Defence of Empirical Psychology*, London: Camelot Press.

Brown, K. C. (1960), "Hemlock for the Critic: A Problem in Evaluation," *Journal of Aesthetics and Art Criticism*, 18 (no. 3), 316–19.

Byrne, D. (1959), "The Effect of a Subliminal Food Stimulus on Verbal Responses," *Journal of Applied Psychology*, 43 (no. 4), 249–251.

Carr, T. and V. Bacharach (1976), "Perceptual Tuning and Conscious Attention," *Cognition*, 4 (no. 3), 281–302.

Comstock, G., S. Chaffer, N. Katzman, M. McCombe and D. Roberts (1978), *Television and Human Behavior*, New York: Columbia University Press.

Cousins, N. (1957), "Smudging the Subconscious," *Saturday Review*, 40 (October 5).

Dixon, N. F. (1971), *Subliminal Perception: The Nature of a Controversy*, London: McGraw-Hill.

———— (1981), *Preconscious Processing*, London: Wiley.

Erdelyi, M. H. (1974), "A New Look at the New Look: Perceptual Defense and Vigilance," *Psychological Review*, 81 (no. 1), 1–25.

Eriksen, C. W. and H. J. Johnson (1964), "Storage and Decay Characteristics of Nonattended Auditory Stimuli," *Journal of Experimental Psychology*, 68 (no. 1), 28–36.

Foulke, E. and I. G. Sticht (1969), "Review of Research on the Intelligibility and Comprehension of Accelerated Speech," *Psychological Bulletin*, 72 (no. 1), 50–62.

Globe & Mail (1978) (October 13), 5.

Goldiamond, I. (1966), "Statement on Subliminal Advertising," in *Control of Human Behavior*, Volume 1, R. Ulrich, T. Stachnik and J. Mabry, eds., Glenview, IL: Scott, Foresman.

Green, D. M. and J. A. Swets (1966), *Signal Detection Theory and Psychophysics*, New York: Wiley.

Harris, R. J., T. M. Dubitsky and S. Thompson (1979), "Learning to Identify Deceptive Truth in Advertising," in *Current Issues and Research in Advertising*, J. H. Leigh and C. R. Martin, eds., Ann Arbor: U. of Michigan Graduate School of Business Administration, Division of Research.

Hawkins, D. (1970), "The Effects of Subliminal Stimulation on Drive Level and Brand Preference," *Journal of Marketing Research*, 8 (August), 322–26.

Heilbrun, K. S. (1980), "Silverman's Subliminal Psychodynamic Activation: A Failure to Replicate," *Journal of Abnormal Psychology*, 89 (no. 4), 560–566.

Hochberg, J. (1978), *Perception*, 2nd ed., Englewood Cliffs, NJ: Prentice-Hall.

Kahneman, D. (1968), "Method, Findings and Theory in Studies of Visual Masking," *Psychological Bulletin*, 70 (no. 6), 404–425.

———— (1973), *Attention and Effort*, Englewood Cliffs, NJ: Prentice-Hall.

Kelly, J. S. (1979), "Subliminal Embeds in Print Advertising: A Challenge to Advertising Ethics," *Journal of Advertising*, 8 (no. 3), 20–24.

Key, W. B. (1973), *Subliminal Seduction*, Englewood Cliffs, NJ: Signet.

———— (1976), *Media Sexploitation*, Englewood Cliffs, NJ: Prentice-Hall.

———— (1980), *The Clamplate Orgy*, Englewood Cliffs, NJ: Prentice-Hall.

Kunst-Wilson, W. and R. Zajonc (1980), "Affective Discrimination of Stimuli That Cannot Be Recognized," *Science*, 207 (no. 1), 557–558.

Liberman, A. M., F. S. Cooper, D. P. Shankweiler and M. Studdert-Kennedy (1967), "Perception of the Speech Code," *Psychological Review*, 74 (no. 6), 431–461.

Licklider, J. and G. Miller (1951), "The Perception of Speech," in S. Stevens, ed., *Handbook of Experimental Psychology*, New York: Wiley.

McCauley, C., C. Parmelee, R. Sperber and T. Carr (1980), "Early Extraction of Meaning From Pictures and Its Relation to Conscious Identification," *Journal of Experimental Psychology: Human Perception and Performance*, 6 (no. 2), 265–76.

McConnell, J. V. (1977), *Understanding Human Behavior*, 2nd ed., New York: Holt, Rinehart & Winston.

————, R. Cutter and E. McNeil (1958), "Subliminal Stimulation: An Overview," *American Psychologist*, 13 (no. 3), 229–42.

Mellers, B. (1981), "Feeling More Than Thinking," *American Psychologist*, 36 (no. 7), 802–803.

Moray, N. (1969), *Attention: Selective Processes in Vision and Hearing*, London: Hutchinson Ltd.

Nation (1957), "Diddling the Subconscious: Subliminal Advertising," 185 (October 5), 206.

New York Times (1978) (May 18), c22.

New Yorker (1957), 33 (September 21), 33.

Nisbett, R. E. and T. O. Wilson (1972), "Telling More Than We Can Know: Verbal Reports on Mental Processes," *Psychological Review*, 84 (no. 3), 231–59.

Peterson, L. R. and S. Kroener (1964), "Dichotic Stimulation and Retention," *Journal of Experimental Psychology*, 68 (no. 2), 125–130.

Pierce, C. S. and J. Jastrow (1884), "On Small Differences of Sensation," *Memoirs of the National Academy of Sciences*, 3, 73–84.

Poe, A. (1976), "Active Women in Ads," *Journal of Communication*, 26 (no. 4), 185–92.

Rush, F. (1980), "Child Pornography," in *Take Back the Night: Women on Pornography*, L. Lederer, ed., New York: Morrow.

Saegert, J. (1979), "Another Look at Subliminal Perception," *Journal of Advertising Research*, 19 (no. 1), 55–57.

Schulman, M. (1981), "The Great Conspiracy," *Journal of Communications*, 31 (no. 2), 209.

Severance, L. J. and F. N. Dyer (1973), "Failure of Subliminal Word Presentations to Generate Interference to Colornaming," *Journal of Experimental Psychology*, 101 (no. 1), 186–89.

Shevrin, H. and S. Dickman (1980), "The Psychological Unconscious: A Necessary Assumption for All Psychological Theory?" *American Psychologist*, 35, 421–34.

———— and D. Fritzler (1968), "Visual Evoked Response Correlates of Unconscious Mental Processes," *Science*, 161 (no. 19), 295–298.

Swets, J. A. (1961), "Is There a Sensory Threshold?" *Science*, 134 (no. 3473), 168–177.

Time (1979), 114 (September 10), 63.

Toronto Star (1978) (October 23), c1.

Treisman, A. M. and G. Geffen (1967), "Selective Attention: Perception or Response?" *Quarterly Journal of Experimental Psychology*, 19 (no. 1), 1–17.

Walstedt, J. J., F. Geis and V. Brown (1980), "Influence of Television Commercials on Women's Self-Confidence and Independent Judgment," *Journal of Personality and Social Psychology*, 38 (no. 2), 203–210.

Washington Post (1979) (May 27), c4.

Wright, R. (1973), "The Cognitive Processes Mediating Acceptance of Advertising," *Journal of Marketing Research*, 10 (February), 53–62.

Zajonc, R. B. (1980), "Feeling and Thinking: Preferences Need No Inferences," *American Psychologist*, 35 (no. 2), 151–175.

Zuckerman, M. (1960), "The Effects of Subliminal and Supraliminal Suggestions on Verbal Productivity," *Journal of Abnormal and Social Personality*, 60 (no. 3), 404–11.

DANIEL ROCHOWIAK

Subliminal Advertising: An Open Question

Subliminal persuasion.[1] Does it exist? Is it effective? Opinions are markedly divergent.

In 1981 *Omni* announced that "subliminal persuasion is back as scientists research new ways to influence people without their knowing it."[2] A 1983 survey by Zanot *et al.* showed that respondents believed that subliminal advertising "is widely and frequently used and that it is successful in selling products." The survey further noted that the individual "most likely to have heard of subliminal advertising is white, well-educated (at least some college), with a relatively high income (over $20,000 per year)."[3]

These opinions stand in stark contrast to more academic reviews of the available literature. Timothy Moore's article is representative.[4] Moore allows that there is psychological evidence that subliminal perception does exist, but he doubts its relevance to the business world. In particular he claims that there is only marginal evidence that subliminal stimuli influence feelings or attitudes (affective reactions), and that there is either no evidence or contradicting evidence that subliminal stimuli influence behavior or action.

Should one trust the academic or expert opinion in this matter? Should the public's mind be put at ease? One can begin to formulate answers to these questions by carefully appraising the experts' opinion.

AN APPRAISAL

Moore distinguishes between two claims about subliminal stimulation relevant to the business world.[5] The claims are distinguished by the immediacy of their effect on behavior. The weak thesis maintains that subliminal stimuli produce or increase positive affective reactions. The strong thesis maintains that subliminal stimuli produce direct behavioral consequences, such as purchasing. If either of these theses is true, then subliminal stimuli could be relevant to marketing, although only the latter would entail interesting marketing applications. The issue, therefore, is one of determining whether there is strong empirical or theoretical support for either thesis.

Moore finds that there is only weak empirical support for the weak thesis. Thus, although there appears to be an effect, the validity of the research can be challenged and there would be "some practical difficulties associated with real-world applications."[6] Empirical evidence for the strong thesis is even less compelling, since results have not been replicated, might be a methodological artifact, and could be the result of a bad sample.[7]

In terms of theoretical support Moore contends that evidence is not just lacking but seems to contradict both theses. Moore believes that both theses are based on the claim that subliminal stimuli can passively produce automatic, predictable responses. Moore contends that on the basis of psychological research and theorizing this claim is false.[8] Therefore, theoretical evidence contradicts the two theses.

Moore's case seems logically cogent. His argument is valid. But is it sound? Are his premises true or likely to be true?

In order to better appraise the soundness of Moore's argument an outline of its essential features will be helpful.

MOORE'S ARGUMENT

1. If subliminal stimuli are relevant to marketing, then either the weak or the strong thesis must be well supported.

2. A thesis is well supported if and only if there is either strong empirical or theoretical evidence for its truth.

3. There is not strong empirical evidence for either the weak or the strong thesis.

4. Both theses entail that the person passively processes stimuli and reacts in an automatic, predictable way.

5. Theoretical evidence contradicts the claim that the person acts in this passive, automatic way.

6. Thus there is at best weak evidence for either the weak or strong thesis.

7. Therefore, subliminal stimulation is not relevant to marketing.

Statements 1 through 5 are the premises of the argument, 6 is a consequence of 2 through 5, and 7 is the conclusion.

Premise 2 can be treated as a stipulative definition and it seems to be a reasonable stipulation, although in practice it would be difficult to clearly specify what constitutes strong evidence.

Premise 3 seems to be accurate. An independent survey of the relevant material by McDaniel, Hart and McNeal comes to a similar but more specific conclusion.[9] McDaniel *et al.* claim that empirical research does not support the assertion that brand preference, ad recall, or buying behavior can be influenced by subliminal stimuli.

One should, however, be careful not to overstate the case for premise 3. The evidence does not support the claim that subliminal stimuli cannot be effective in the areas of concern.

There are several reasons for this. First, the research on subliminal stimuli in a marketing or advertising context is not as plentiful as it is in the psychological context. This paucity of research argues for conservatism in stating the findings of research. Second, the psychological research on subliminal stimuli indicate that it does have an effect on memory, perception, and verbal behavior.[10] This suggests, if only weakly, that subliminal stimuli *could* have a role in a marketing context. Third, new technologies or strategies could lead to a revised assessment of the empirical findings. If subliminal stimuli does have an effect upon those cognitive facilities which are related to marketing interests, then new technologies or strategies might be devised to present the stimuli and achieve a greater result. Tachistoscopes could give way to videodiscs and computer generated graphics. Advertising material might be distributed by video monitors in shopping centers. I will return to some of these possibilities. The point of these comments, however, should be clear. Even if there is now little empirical support for the two theses, this is not the same as, nor does it entail that the theses are false or that subliminal effects cannot have marketing relevance.

Premises 4 and 5 can be considered together. Premise 4 claims that the two theses have a particular theoretical consequence. Premise 5 claims that this consequence is unacceptable in terms of theoretical considerations. Thus, there is no theoretical evidence to support the theses.

Premise 4 is most curious. It is not at all clear why hypothesizing "some direct behavioral consequence (i.e., purchasing)" should entail anything about the passivity and predictability of the person. Why should a proponent of subliminal advertising need to claim that stimulation is a sufficient condition for a particular response?[11] Or that a person passively processes stimulus input? Or that a person acts in automatic predictable ways?[12]

Suppose that subliminal advertising does have an effect on purchasing behavior. Further, suppose that attention is selective and that the person processes stimuli in an active way and that behavior is not automatic and predictable. Does a contradiction follow? Moore would seem to think that it does, but this is not clear. It would seem at least possible that the purchasing behavior of a group of subjects be altered to some degree by subliminal advertising. The degree could be a function of several variables including attention, and active construction of a meaning for the stimulus, and entail no prediction about an *individual's* purchasing behavior. This would allow for the strong thesis to be true and the purportedly entailed thesis to be false. This is enough to show that the purported entailment relation does not hold. If it does not, then whether or not the passive model is true or false is not relevant.[13]

Perhaps this objection does not do justice to Moore's more general point. Let us replace 4 and 5 by 4*.

4.* There is no strong theoretical evidence for either the weak or the strong thesis.

The new premise 4* would allow the argument to maintain its validity; thus, the issue now is one of determining whether 4* is true or likely to be true.

Moore's evidence regarding 4* is that subliminal stimuli are weak and that psychological research has substantiated the general or theoretical principle that "more intense stimuli have a greater influence on people's behavior than weaker ones."[14] Thus, intense supraliminal stimuli will generate a greater effect than subliminal stimuli. This does not entail that subliminal stimuli have no effect, but Moore notes that its effects are "subtle and obtaining them typically requires a carefully structured context." Therefore, there is little theoretical evidence for the two theses.

Moore's account hangs on the truth of the general principle, but it is not clear that as stated it is true.

Suppose that a person wanted to advertise a particular product and that he acted on the belief that the general principle was true. What kind of ad would he create? Recognizing that he wanted to have as great as possible an effect on behavior, he would select the strongest possible stimuli. The advertisement most desirable would have the most intense colors with the most garish coordination accompanied by the most pounding music and the loudest voice. Bad taste? Perhaps. Intense stimuli? Yes. This choice for an advertising campaign might not be the best, but it certainly seems to be the best choice according to the general principle.

There are many advertisements that do not seem to conform to this interpretation, but have been successful. Minute Maid orange juice with Bing Crosby, the Pillsbury "Doughboy," and Polaroid cameras with James Garner and "wife" certainly do not seem to be constructed from intense stimuli. These advertisements do seem, however, to be effective.[15]

Intense stimuli are effective at gaining attention, but it is not clear that they are as effective in generating interest, desire, and action. Indeed, as Moore notes, our psychological defenses may be raised by strong stimuli.[16] "Whore" is a strong term. It is emotionally loaded. It is an intense verbal stimulus. It is, however, a word with a high recognition threshold. Perhaps there are similar high recognition thresholds that allow us to "tune out" the intense stimuli of advertising. If so, then it is not clear that a stronger stimulus will always generate a stronger influence than a weaker one.

Perhaps this interpretation is not the one that Moore intends. At various places in his review Moore indicates that the relation between stimulus and effect is mediated by many kinds of cognitive processes and that there is no simple automatic connection between stimulus and effect. Indeed, this is one of the grounds on which he launches his attack on subliminal advertising. Thus, it would be quite odd to interpret his general principle as committing him to a thesis that he would reject.

Other interpretations of the general principle are possible, but they are not congenial to Moore's overall argument.

Moore might mean that if stimulus A produces

strong effect a and stimulus B produces weak effect b, then stimulus A was more intense than B. This might be a nice way of deciding which of the two stimuli are more intense, but this is neither what Moore claims nor would it help his case if it were. What Moore claims is that if stimulus A is more intense than B, then effect a will be stronger than b. The rephrased principle is not equivalent to it nor does it follow from his claim.

Even if one were to allow that the rephrased principle is the one that should have been used, his case is not helped. Indeed, the question might be posed in terms of the rephrased principle as whether or not subliminal stimuli should be called strong. Given a comparison of stimuli, do subliminal stimuli have a stronger effect or a weaker effect? Here Moore might claim that empirical research has so far shown that there is no strong effect, but he would have to allow that future empirical research might show it to have a strong effect. If this path is followed, then it is not true that theoretical evidence does not support the strong or weak thesis. The theory is neutral; empirical evidence is the source of corroboration or disconfirmation.

Again Moore might be claiming that the general principle means that in most ordinary cases the stronger stimulus produces the stronger effect. This will not help either. It allows that subliminal stimulation could have a strong effect in special cases. If this were so, then a business person might wish to construct that set of circumstances in which the strong effect is produced.[17] On this interpretation the result would be the same. According to the principle subliminal stimuli might have a strong effect. The theoretical principle is neutral and only further empirical research can decide the issue.

SUMMARY

Moore's argument that subliminal stimuli are not relevant to marketing is valid, but it has not been shown to be sound. The empirical evidence does not show that either the weak or strong thesis is false. At best one could claim only that current research does not strongly or unequivocally support the two theses. The theoretical evidence does not clearly show that either the weak or strong thesis is false. Nor under careful analysis does it seem that the general principle contradicts the claims of the advocates of subliminal advertising. Thus, there is not sufficient reason to believe that either premise 3 or 4 is true or likely to be true.

So far the account has been largely skeptical. Are there any positive reasons for thinking that subliminal stimuli might be relevant to business?

POSSIBILITIES FOR SUBLIMINAL TECHNOLOGY IN BUSINESS

Perhaps the most commercial application of subliminal stimulation is a device called "Dr. Becker's Black Box."[18] The device embeds subliminal messages in background music. It has been put to use in a supermarket chain in an attempt to reduce theft, and in a real estate firm to make salesmen feel better. In both cases positive effects have been claimed. Theft was reduced in the supermarket chain and revenues went up in the real estate firm. There has been, so far, little scientific research on the issue, and Dr. Becker claims this lack of research is not important: "They [scientists] may worry about those things in their ivory towers, but when I talk to the president of a company, he doesn't care. He wants results. I show him results."[19]

While these applications are not marketing applications, one could think of ways in which they could become marketing applications. Consider the fact that subliminal stimulation does seem to affect drives. In a closed environment such as a department store, supermarket or shopping center, where the particular object purchased may not be as important as the act of purchasing, "Dr. Becker's Black Box" may have an application. Messages like "Buy, buy, buy" or "I love this store" may serve to increase the sales of the store. This is possible even if subliminal messages cannot aid in specific tasks such as brand recall.

A further way in which subliminal stimulation could have a marketing relevance is by concentrating on a particular segment of the population. Consider advertising on television. It hits a broad range of consumers, some of which have no interest in the product or are not even interested in that general kind of product. The whole populace watching a sporting event is not interested in a home computer. The whole populace watching a given television show is not interested in floor wax, furniture polish, detergents, etc. Perhaps subliminal advertising could have an effect upon a particular segment of that range.

How might this be done? It might be done indirectly. Saegert suggests that subliminal stimuli might be effective if it concentrates upon unconscious wishes. He suggests that "the reason a subliminal perception effect has not been demonstrated in a marketing context is that studies have not attempted to use stimuli that would appeal to special groups of individuals who may be more receptive to certain kinds of commercial appeal."[20] If the attempt to show the effect concentrated on an unconscious wish of a portion of the individuals who receive the message, then a positive effect might be found. Thus, subliminal stimulation might be effective in presenting stimuli to a specific group of persons within a context which supraliminally affects many.

Although these are only suggestions, they do illustrate that subliminal stimulation could have a relevance to marketing. However, in each case the effect is not direct and requires the use of a variety of techniques other than the presentation of the subliminal stimulus itself. This is consistent with Moore's general position that there is no simple relation between the stimulus and the resulting behavior. However, the previous arguments about the soundness of Moore's position and the possibility of business applications suggest that the conclusion that subliminal stimulation has no relevance to the goals of advertising or marketing is far too strong. McDaniel *et al.* suggest an alternative perspective. They contend that "no one aspect alone (be it the illustration, the body copy, the layout or the subliminal message) can become a controlling factor in the effectiveness of an advertisement. How this one factor of subliminal stimulation does relate to the overall advertisement will require further investigation. A similar conclusion appears to be warranted about its use in related applications, such as a subliminal message 'don't steal' directed to consumers in a retail store. Here, further investigation is required to understand how the subliminal message works in tandem with other measures to reduce shoplifting."[21]

CONCLUDING COMMENTS

Should the general public be worried about subliminal persuasion? Have the experts demonstrated that subliminal stimulation does not have a marketing relevance? The answers to both questions must be highly qualified. There is no clear-cut conclusion that can be drawn from the available evidence. Subliminal persuasion *might* become an effective marketing instrument, although there is now little positive evidence of the kind that would satisfy the academic scientific community. It is clear, however, that the public should be concerned about the topic.

The public concern rests on the belief that subliminal perception is currently effective and widely used. The reviews and arguments of Moore and McDaniel *et al.* cast doubt upon this belief. Currently, there is not strong evidence that subliminal stimulation is effective. This does not mean, however, that subliminal persuasion cannot become a widely used and effective instrument of the business world.

The development of subliminal techniques could occur outside of the academic scientific community. Dr. Becker is a clear example of the technological entrepreneur. In this context normal scientific requirements are not as relevant as demonstrations of practical effectiveness. If this becomes the normal path for the development of subliminal technology, then the expert appraisal of the scientific community might be less relevant than one would expect. The scientist might worry about controls, sample size, the mechanism for the effect, the exact theoretical description of the effect, and much else besides. The technological entrepreneur needs only to produce the effect and show the cases in which it occurred. Further, the details of the process of subliminal stimulation, the devices used, and the exact data obtained would not be made generally available by the entrepreneur. He would wish to protect his technology. Thus, although the scientific community is a potential expert critic of subliminal persuasion, it might not be the most effective actual critic.

The most effective actual critic of the technology of subliminal persuasion might be the general public. In the survey by Zanot *et al.*, the authors noted that the respondents believed that subliminal advertising "is an unacceptable, unethical and harmful advertising technique," and that "these beliefs would affect their buying behavior if they thought a particular advertiser were using subliminal techniques." Thus, given that "people act on their perceptions of reality rather than on objective reality itself [the above beliefs] must give pause to those in the trade."[22]

The public's beliefs can be a much more effective critic of the technology of subliminal persuasion than the expert opinions of the academic scientific community. This is particularly important given that this technology could develop with some degree of independence from the scientific community. Further, if the business sector realizes that there can be a negative behavioral effect, if the public believes that a given company is advertising subliminally, then this may induce the business sector not to develop or use subliminal technology.

In conclusion, it seems as though subliminal stimuli can affect our thinking and behavior, and that it is at least possible to use this in a business context. However, there is not *now* strong evidence of the kind acceptable to the academic scientific community that interesting marketing effects are being produced with current techniques and procedures. Future research could change that verdict, and the scientific community might not be the most effective critic of the development of new technology. The public's perception of subliminal advertising as wrong may be a more potent force, even when the public's assessment of the efficiency of subliminal techniques is faulty.

NOTES

1. By subliminal persuasion I mean the use of subliminal stimuli to effect a change in behavior either directly or indirectly. Subliminal stimuli are stimuli which fall below the level at which the subject has ever reported being aware. The thresholds for subliminal stimuli vary over individuals. For a more detailed account of some of the strictures which might be placed on the concept of subliminal stimuli see: Timothy Moore, "Subliminal advertis-

ing: what you see is what you get," *Journal of Marketing*, 46(1982), pp. 39–40. [The Timothy Moore article to which Rochowiak refers is found in this anthology on pp. 175–87. Bracketed pages numbers below refer to the page in this anthology. Note 1 refers to p. 177.]

2. Eric Lander, "In through the out door," *Omni*, Vol. 3 No. 5 (Feb., 1981), p. 45.

3. Eric Zanot, J. David Pincus, E. Joseph Lamp, "Public perceptions of subliminal advertising," *Journal of Advertising*, 12(1983), p. 43.

4. In addition to Moore there are two other survey articles of interest. Joel Saegert, "Another look at subliminal perception," *Journal of Advertising Research*, 19(1979), pp. 55–57 and Stephen McDaniel, Sandra Hart, and James McNeal, "Subliminal stimulation as a marketing tool," *The Mid-Atlantic Journal of Business*, 20(1983), pp. 41–48.

5. Moore, p. 41. [p. 179]

6. Moore, p. 43. [p. 182]

7. Moore, pp. 42–3. [p. 181]

8. Moore, p. 42 and p. 46. [pp. 181, 185]

9. McDaniel *et al.*, p. 46.

10. McDaniel *et al.*, p. 42. Moore admits that the subliminal effect exists. "It should be emphasized that stimulation below the level of conscious awareness can be shown to have measurable effects upon some aspects of behavior. The point at issue is whether these effects are sufficient to warrant the conclusion that goal directed behavior can be manipulated by such stimulation." Moore, p. 39. "Manipulation" is a strong term; I would prefer "influenced."

11. Moore, p. 43. [p. 182]

12. Moore, p. 46. [p. 185]

13. For a more detailed account of the passive conception of man see: Martin Hollis, *Models of Man*, (Cambridge: Cambridge University Press) 1977.

14. Moore, p. 46. [p. 185]

15. Harry McMahon, "The 7 factors of creative success," *Advertising Age*, Dec. 17, 1972, p. 42, and Carl McDaniel, *Marketing (2nd ed.)* (New York: Harper & Row) 1982, p. 554.

16. Moore, p. 40. [p. 178]

17. This could be done by augmenting and extending the ideas in the "Coke" and "beef" examples. See: Moore, p. 42, McDaniel *et al.*, p. 43; Saegert, p. 57.

18. McDaniel *et al.*, p. 46; Lander, pp. 46–47.

19. Lander, p. 47.

20. Saegert, p. 56.

21. McDaniel *et al.*, p. 47.

22. Zanot *et al.*, p. 43.

JOHN CULKIN

Selling to Children: Fair Play in TV Commercials

Does the 1st Amendment Protect Frankenberry?

A recent ad in *Broadcasting* magazine invited sponsors to buy time on a new television station in Boston.

Kid Power Is Coming to Boston
If you're selling, Charlie's Mom is buying. But you've got to sell Charlie first.

His allowance is only 50¢ a week but his buying power is an American phenomenon. He's not only tight with his Mom, but he has a way with his Dad, his Grandma and Aunt Harriet, too.

When Charlie sees something he likes, he usually gets it.

Charlie and Charlene, the kids in the two- to twelve-year-old range, attract a half billion dollars of TV advertising annually. Most of the commercials directed at them are for food and toys. These TV spots generate billions of dollars in sales. The question now before the Federal Trade Commission is whether or not the advertisers are acting fairly in their dealings with children. Rules proposed in February by the Commission staff include:

1. The prohibition of all television advertising directed at children under eight, because such children are "too young to understand" the purpose of the ad.

2. A ban on advertising highly sugared products to children under twelve since such products pose "serious dental health risks."

3. A requirement that advertisers fund health and nutrition messages to be broadcast during children's viewing times.

The Commission has asked for public comment on these proposed rules, but the hearings it plans to hold in Washington and San Francisco are

unlikely to produce any surprises. The public interest and health groups will favor some restrictions on current practices; the broadcasters and advertisers will oppose any rule-making. The arguments for both sides are also fairly predictable— the health and well-being of children versus the free enterprise system and the First Amendment rights of the advertisers.

THE ADVERTISING PROCESS

Like most adults, I have become inured to the commercial-saturated world of television; but, apart from the usual moments of pique, I have never considered seriously what is involved in the whole process of advertising aimed directly at children.

Let's return to the ad quoted at the outset. It represents the whole process in microcosm: sell to the parents by convincing the children. The sophisticated techniques of advertising are put in the service of psychologically enticing children to want something so much that they will persuade their parents to buy it. Quite apart from the question of the real value of the advertised product, what is the propriety of the sponsor contesting the parent for control of the child? When the products are harmful to the child's well-being, the process is insidious. Very young children are gullible and unsophisticated; they cannot make sound judgments about the quality of what is being sold to them.

The advertisers challenge this charge by arguing that parents have ultimate control at the point of purchase. This is hardly an adequate justification for enticing children into wanting things that are bad for them. And even with products that may be good for them, it seems like an unwarranted intrusion. Parents have enough difficulty in helping their children to make wise choices without skewing the process by 500 million dollars worth of counter-persuasion.

Where does the responsibility lie for regulating children's exposure to television commercials? Advertisers, regulatory agencies, and consumers all should bear some of the burden.

ADVERTISERS AND BROADCASTERS

William La Mothe, the president of Kellogg Foods, states the argument for the advertisers: "Once we start deciding which group can be advertised to and which group cannot, advertising as an efficient and economic method will be on its way to oblivion."

Peggy Charren of Action for Children's Television (ACT) counters with an attack on the quality of what is being advertised: "The two things sold to children most on TV are toys and food, and we've found that 98 percent of the food advertising is for products children don't have to eat, non-nutritive things. Now in fact they're designing foods that would never be on the market if it weren't for television and its ability to sell them. They actually design junk cereals like Frankenberry and Cocoa Pebbles and Cookie Crisps because they can push them to kids on television."

Jean Mayer, the well-known nutritionist and president of Tufts University, advances as a rough rule of thumb: the nutritional value of a food varies inversely with the amount of money spent to advertise it. Research confirms that the most heavily advertised foods are the ones asked for most often. One study concludes that parents accede to these requests 87 percent of the time. And this all takes place in an environment where the average child sees five hours of commercials per week and a total of 25,000 commercials per year. Richard Feinbloom of Harvard Medical School finds this an unfair use of selling techniques. "An advertisement to a child has the quality of an order, not a suggestion. The child lacks the ability to set priorities, to determine relative importance and to reject some directions as inappropriate."

The industry contends that advertisements are protected by the First Amendment. And if appeals to freedom of speech will not settle the argument, they remind us that ad revenues pay for the programs. Their cries of constitutional rights ignore the ample precedents for limiting free speech when the issue affects children. It is true the ads support the programs, but some people argue that it would be just fine if most of those shows went away; others urge more public funding for children's programming; others contend that if the junk were eliminated from the ad content, there would still be enough good products to meet program budgets.

REGULATORY AGENCIES

While the advertisers have $500,000,000 in their budget for children's advertising, the public interest groups have difficulty in getting their combined budgets up to $500,000. The battle is so unequal that federal regulatory agencies have a responsibility to act on behalf of the interests of children and parents. The self-regulation favored by the broadcasters and the advertisers does not work. They have had to be forced to accept almost all the limitations put on their activities up to this point. Right now they are organizing a massive campaign to oppose the FTC proposals.

No other country in the world allows such blatant exploitation of its children for commercial purposes. Australia, Canada, and the United Kingdom are in the process of further limiting and refining their already strict standards and practices for children's advertising. If, as we often are reminded, children are our most important natural resources, then it is perfectly legitimate for the appropriate federal agencies to protect that resource from any harm. The process which is now beginning at the FTC will provide a visible forum for the public discussion of these issues over the next year. The staff recommendations on the public comments must be submitted to the Commission members by April 1979.

PARENTS AND TEACHERS

Most of the debate before the FTC will legitimately focus on the rights and obligations of the broadcasters and advertisers. But parents and the schools also have responsibilities, which are not fully discharged by merely cataloging and taking action against the abuses of the producers. Even the best of all possible programming does not justify the four hours a day spent by the average American in front of the TV set. In our less-than-perfect world, the uncomfortable fact is that we have to reform ourselves as well as the networks.

Action for Children's Television has been the most persistent and persuasive advocacy group in the field. ACT filed one of two petitions to which the FTC formally responded in its recommendations; the other was filed by the Center for Science in the Public Interest. In addition to its effort to keep the issue of children and television before the FCC and the FTC, ACT has also encouraged parents to become more involved in controlling their children's viewing and in discussing television with them. ACT is currently distributing a red tag to be affixed to the family television set. It reads, "REMINDER: Too much television can be harmful to your child." The FCC and the FTC can only help to remove the abuses. Parents, teachers, and other adults have the responsibility to help children develop informed and disciplined choices about what images go into their heads and what foods go into their stomachs.

It has always made good sense for people who live on water to learn how to swim. Despite the recent suggestions of authors like Marie Winn in *The PlugIn Drug* and Jerry Mander in *Four Arguments for the Elimination of Television* arguing that TV should be banished from children's lives, television programs and commercials are not going to go away. And the so-called children's programs constitute only 15 percent of the average child's viewing diet. Cleaning up the Saturday morning "kid-vid ghetto" is only a small part of the enterprise. All television watched by children becomes children's television.

Early in May a House appropriations subcommittee voted five to four to bar the FTC from spending money to develop trade rules that would limit advertising for any food product whose ingredients have been designated as safe by the FDA. This provision, if approved by the full Appropriations Committee, would prevent the FTC from carrying out its planned inquiry on children's television advertising. The provision was sponsored by Mark Andrews (R.-N.D.), whose constituents include many corn, wheat, and sugar-beet growers.

In the media environment, it is no longer possible to protect children from the outside. We must provide them with habits of judgment, taste, and selectivity which will enable them to be their own TV critics and consumer guides. This is already being done in many schools where teachers discuss programs and commercials which are part of the child's ordinary viewing experience. The process helps to unpack the glut of vicarious experiences which builds up within the child.

By stimulating and informing the students' responses to television the schools can induce a critical and knowledgeable attitude toward future viewing. In many schools students also actually work with TV, film, and photographic equipment to make their own images and personal statements. This process initiates them to the myriad choices and critical judgments involved in establishing the mood, pace, and tone of any media production. The goals for the student in such programs of media criticism and production can be stated quite simply:

Smart is better than stupid.

Active is better than passive.

THE FUTURE

Winston Churchill has said: "We shape our buildings and thereafter they shape us." So with our television system. During the 1940s the United States opted for a limited-spectrum, commercially supported TV system. Once such a system is in place, it takes massive efforts to produce minimal reforms; the attempt to regulate children's advertising is a good example.

The technology of the future is now being set in place. There will be multiple (up to 100) channel systems, with recording and playback capacity, with dial-access potential allowing consumers to request specific programs, with large screens and direct or indirect satellite linkups.

The new television system will make it possible to serve the television needs of audiences in numbers far less than the 20 to 30 million people now required by network television. The new system will give us a way to let people pay for what they want. It will provide television with a turnstile and allow consumers to make direct choices as they do for books, films, and plays.

Two areas of reform that we can think about now, which cost nothing, and which make everything possible, are: (1) both cable and satellite systems should be required to allocate several channels and/or percentages of time for quality children's programming, and (2) a percentage of the taxes collected from television revenues should be earmarked for these same purposes.

Even "ideal" television, however does not guarantee an ideal world. We often overestimate the medium's power for good as well for harm. There is life after (and before) television, and it is the quality of that life that probably most determines the impact of television on children. Those who are alert and alive to their own bodies, emotions, and minds and whose lives are caught up in activities with others won't make the networks and the sponsors rich. Living well is still the best revenge and the best protection.

CAROL LEVINE

Research on Young Viewers: The Policy Implications

Is television advertising good or bad for children? Opinions are firm on both sides of the question, but what evidence exists to support either view? Academic research on the effects of television advertising on children is relatively recent, and few investigators have been specifically concerned with the field. Still, according to a recent report by the RANN (Research Applied to National Needs) Program of the National Science Foundation, the current state of knowledge, though inadequate in many areas, is "sufficient in others to provide meaningful guidance to policymakers."

The report, *Research on the Effects of Television Advertising on Children* (Washington: National Science Foundation, 1977) is a review of the literature and gives recommendations for future research. Two major conclusions emerge from the review. First, "It is clear from the available evidence that television advertising *does* influence children." Children can and do learn from commercials, and advertising is at least moderately successful in creating positive attitudes toward and a desire for certain products. The most significant variable that determines the child's perception of television advertising is age. Numerous studies have demonstrated that as children grow older,

they become more skillful in discriminating among commercial messages and are less easily persuaded by the sponsor's sales pitch. One study of fourth through seventh-graders in Michigan showed that less than one-quarter think that commercials always tell the truth. Most of the children were also irritated by the commercial interruptions.

The second conclusion is that "From a policy standpoint, the most immediately relevant research is that which either documents the effects of specific advertising practices alleged to be misleading or unfair to children's perceptions, or which tests the efficacy of regulatory provisions in preventing such abuses." Several recent studies have shown, for example, that the way in which a disclaimer is worded and presented ("some assembly required" or "batteries not included") affects the child's ability to understand and remember the message.

In reviewing the research, the report focused on ten issues that seemed to be of greatest interest to the parties involved, were amenable to empirical testing, and offered some prospects of concrete policy action based on empirical findings. These included:

1. Children's ability to distinguish television commercials from program material;
2. The influence of format and audiovisual techniques on children's perceptions of commercial messages;
3. Self-concept appeals in advertising;
4. The effects of advertising containing premium offers;
5. The effects of violence or unsafe acts in commercials;
6. The impact of proprietary medicine advertising;
7. The effects of television food advertising;
8. The effects of volume and repetition of commercials;
9. The impact of advertising on consumer socialization; and
10. The effect on parent-child relations.

In most of these areas the research findings are only suggestive. For instance, there is evidence that television food advertising to children is generally effective. However, there is no evidence directly linking food commercials to the nutritional status of children, nor to the claim that food advertising messages encourage children to use nutritionally irrelevant criteria in making food choices. An even broader value question is whether food advertisers should be responsible for communicating nutritional information beyond that pertaining to their own products.

In the future, the report concludes, research must be directed more closely to policy needs. Nevertheless, research is only one element in determining policy and practice. Ethical, legal, economic, and political considerations must all play a part. Adequate safeguards for young viewers must be based on both a solid understanding of what television does and does not do and a basic conception of what kind of consumers and citizens we want to encourage children to become.

CHAPTER FIVE
Study Questions

1. How great an influence do you believe advertising has been upon consumer demand for the following products: designer jeans, fast cars, cigarettes, diet drinks, supplemental Medicare insurance for the elderly, chocolate-flavored breakfast cereal?

2. At the end of Chapter 3, we asked if individual consumers were the best judges of their own interests. Have your views changed?

3. In general, do you think that advertisements that are directed at children are fair? What of advertising that is directed at the elderly?

4. Many of the previous readings suggest that there is a continuum between rational persuasion and controlling someone's behavior. Where along that continuum would you place the following: advertising on children's T.V. shows, college teaching, grammar school teaching, political campaigns, commercials featuring endorsements by famous people?

5. How much of your own consumer behavior is shaped by peer pressure? How do you think peer pressure arises in the first place?

6. Is there a difference between completely controlling and manipulating a person's behavior? If there is a difference, does it have any consequence for the validity of Arrington's conclusion that advertising does not generally threaten autonomy?

PART THREE

BUSINESS AND EMPLOYEES

CHAPTER SIX

PRIVACY IN EMPLOYMENT

CASE STUDY

Privacy in Employment

As the personnel director of a manufacturing firm with about 500 employees, you have the responsibility for establishing all company policies concerning personnel files. The company is in the process of computerizing all its past and present files, and this will be a convenient time to review your company's privacy policies.

The first issue you confront concerns the older files. How long should you retain information after a person has left the firm? (For that matter, is there some information about present employees which you no longer should keep?) In the past you have used these older files to supply information to landlords and banks in order to verify the individual's credit worthiness. One time you also were required to supply information for a lawsuit against your company. Although in general you would prefer not to be bothered by the extra work, computer technology has greatly reduced the trouble of long-term storage.

You also would prefer not to be bothered by credit checks on present employees. You have always verified information to landlords and credit grantors as a courtesy to employees.

After all, if they did not want this information released they could have withheld it originally. Since it is a burden to you, and since you see it as a favor to the employee, you have never thought it necessary to get the employee's consent before releasing this information. Besides, often enough you need to verify information about a potential employee and you recognize the necessity and benefits of this practice.

Recently, however, you have received an offer from a credit agency which causes you some concern. This agency, which you often have used to do background checks on potential employees (especially those in the security office), has made a new policy available to clients who have computerized personnel files. Rather than charge a fee for their service, this agency will now accept information as payment. Specifically, for each report it compiles for you, it requests access to information in your personnel files. Since this agency is in the information collection business, this practice makes sense to them.

What makes this offer particularly attractive is the ease of the entire process. With your new computerized system, the exchange of information is as easy as one telephone call. When the agency has the information which you have requested, they call up your computer and, using the access code which you supplied, simply transfer the relevant information into your files. Next, using another access code number, the agency types in the social security number of an individual about whom they seek information, and that employee's file is transferred into their own computer files. In the more likely case that they are not looking for a specific employee at the present, they have the option to choose a file at random or save the access permission for future use. Of course, you can easily program a limit to the number of times they can access your files.

Although this firm has promised to respect whatever standards of confidentiality you set, you are worried by this practice. On the other hand, it seems to be no more than an extension of present practices and it will likely save you money.

What policies should you establish for the privacy of the personnel files in your keeping?

Introduction

ALTHOUGH IT IS among the most commonly invoked rights in today's increasingly populated and technological society, privacy is one of the least understood of all civil rights. As more people come to populate the same area and as work advances in the fields of computer and information technology, many people perceive a growing threat to their privacy. Yet there is little consensus regarding the definition, nature, and justification of privacy.

Statutory protection of privacy is a relatively recent development in American legal history. The U. S. Constitution, for example, makes no explicit mention of a citizen's right of privacy. The legal discussion of privacy typically is traced to an 1890 *Harvard Law Review* article by Samuel Warren and Louis Brandeis and the 1965 Supreme Court decision in *Griswold v. Connecticut.* Indeed, it was not until this 1965 decision that the Supreme Court recognized a constitutional basis for privacy. Further, the very meaning of privacy is so confused that in 1977 the congressionally established Privacy Protection Study Commission reported that after two years of study, its members could not reach a consensus on a definition of privacy.

Before we can evaluate the nature and limits of privacy in the workplace, therefore, we need to think about privacy in general. One common understanding of privacy centers around the notion of being "let alone." Beginning with the Warren and Brandeis *Harvard Law Review* article and the decision in *Griswold v. Connecticut,* this is the sense of privacy that tends to dominate legal discussions. Privacy as the right "to be let alone" is also the understanding that we would likely find in ordinary linguistic usage. Since this is such a common understanding of privacy, and since we will suggest that it is an inadequate understanding, it will be useful to consider this view in some detail.

In their article, Warren and Brandeis were concerned that certain technological advances and business practices, in particular the practice of some newspapers of printing stories and photographs of private parties, were causing an increasing threat to the solitude of individual citizens. They defended the right of privacy as "the next step which must be taken for the protection of the person, and for securing to the individual . . . the right 'to be let alone.' "

It was not until 1965, however, that the Supreme Court recognized constitutional protection of this right of privacy. In *Griswold v. Connecticut,* the Court ruled that the Constitution guaranteed citizens a "zone of privacy" around their persons, which could not be violated by government. This particular decision invalidated a Connecticut law that prohibited use of contraceptives by married couples.

Despite the fact that there is no explicit constitutional recognition of a right of privacy, various sections of the Constitution were cited as supporting this right. For example, the First Amendment's guarantee of free speech and assembly can be extended to include the freedom to control information about oneself and the freedom to choose with whom one does or does not associate. The Third Amendment prevents the housing of soldiers in private homes "without the consent of the owner." This can be interpreted as implying the right of citizens "to be let alone" in their homes. The Fourth Amendment's protection from unreasonable searches and seizures also indicates that a citizen's privacy ought not to be invaded without probable cause. Finally, the Fifth Amendment's right to remain silent may suggest that individuals ought to retain control over personal information. Accordingly, even without an explicit constitutional guarantee, the Supreme Court found privacy within the "penumbra" of rights established by the First, Third, Fourth, and Fifth Amendments.

Much of the discussion concerning the right of privacy in employment begins with this definition of privacy. The aim of some employee-rights advocates is to preserve the integrity of this zone within the workplace. According to this view, a citizen's right "to be let alone" should not be lost when he or she enters into an employment agreement. Some defenders of employee rights seem to use this understanding in developing rather extensive lists of privacy concerns in employment. These lists include not only such issues as privacy of personnel records and files, and freedom from polygraph and psychological testing and surveillance at work, but also freedom from restrictions upon after-hours activities of employees, peace and quiet in the workplace, employee lounges, privacy of personal property at work, and employee grooming, dress, manners, etc.

Unfortunately, there are problems with this definition of privacy. Phrases like "right to be let alone" and "zone of privacy" are quite vague, and their application tends to be much broader than is appropriate. It is difficult to see how a legitimate claim to be let alone within a zone of privacy can be consistently maintained at the same time that one wishes to participate in an essentially social and cooperative activity like work. It can be argued that these and other problems result from the inadequate definition of privacy developed from Warren and Brandeis and from *Griswold v. Connecticut.*

A more satisfactory understanding of privacy is what Richard Wasserstrom, in a reading that follows, calls "informational privacy." This view understands privacy as involving information about oneself and the right of privacy as the right to control that personal information. In its analysis of privacy in the workplace, this chapter will focus upon "informational privacy."

To understand this view of privacy, let us return to the concerns of Warren and Brandeis. It seems that Samuel Warren's wife was troubled by the publicity that inevitably followed her social gatherings and parties. No doubt Mrs. Warren wanted to be "let alone," and Warren and Brandeis certainly were correct to identify her concern as involving privacy. But surely her objections were to the publication of personal information and not to interference with her liberty. Her privacy was violated when she lost control over information that was essentially personal. More precisely, her privacy was violated when people who had no legitimate claim to this information, i.e., news reporters and newspaper readers, came to know about her parties. Her privacy was not violated when invited guests, for example, came to know about the party.

As George Brenkert will suggest in a reading that follows, this fact indicates that the right of privacy involves a three-place relation between a person A, some information X, and another person Z. The right of privacy is violated only when Z comes to possess information X, *and* no relationship between A and Z exists that would justify Z's coming to know X. Following Brenkert, we shall say that the right of privacy is "the right of individuals, groups, or institutions that access to and information about themselves is limited in certain ways by the relationships in which they exist to others."

But understanding what privacy is will not be sufficient for a complete evaluation of privacy in employment. We need also to understand why privacy is valuable. Why should privacy be a desirable state of affairs rather than undesirable? Even if it is desirable, is it so important that it should be a legal and moral *right*?

Richard Wasserstrom examines the value of privacy in the first reading of this chapter. Wasserstrom reasons that there are numerous beneficial consequences of privacy. Privacy can protect people from harms, it ensures many important social and interpersonal relationships, it even contributes to the make-up and stability of one's own personality. Against those who might argue that, were we socialized differently, privacy would be socially detrimental, rather than beneficial, Wasserstrom offers some suggestions for why a society that values privacy is more desirable than one that does not.

After this initial examination of the nature and value of privacy in general, we turn to privacy in employment. Our second reading is from the congressionally established Privacy Protection Study Commission. This commission was established with passage of the Privacy Act of 1974 and spent two years (1975–77) studying the issue. Our reading is from a chapter of its 1977 Report to Congress, "Personal Privacy in an Information Society," which is concerned with privacy in employment. Leaving the philosophical analysis of Wasserstrom's article, the commission's report provides a wealth of empirical information about privacy in employment, in addition to offering numerous recommendations to ensure the protection of employee privacy.

Two issues should be noted about the commission's report. First, early in its report the commission identified three major public policy objectives served by an effective privacy protection policy: (1) to minimize intrusiveness; (2) to maximize fairness; and (3) to legitimize expectations of confidentiality. In effect, these are the social values that the commission believes are served by privacy. It would be interesting to compare and contrast these values with those presented by Wasserstrom.

A second issue to be noted is that the commission recommends mostly voluntary means for implementing a privacy protection policy in employment. Government regulation to ensure compliance with the recommendations was thought unnecessary or undesirable. In our third reading, the former chairman of the commission, David Linowes, cites survey results that suggest that corporate voluntarism has not succeeded in providing adequate protection for employee privacy. Linowes concludes that it may be time for "new incentives for action," presumably including statutory and regulatory enforcement of privacy rights in employment.

Turning from these more empirically based articles, our fourth selection, by Joseph Des Jardins, presents a general philosophical examination of employee privacy. Settling upon the informational meaning of privacy, Des Jardins adopts the three-place relationship understanding of privacy sketched above. With this, and by taking the employment relationship to be fundamentally a contractual one, Des Jardins outlines the implications that this contractual model would have for employee privacy.

In our final selection, George Brenkert focuses more specifically on the issue of polygraph examinations. Brenkert presents a strong criticism of polygraph testing. He argues that polygraphs do violate employee privacy and that, further, this fact outweighs considerations of employer interests. Brenkert presumably would agree with the Privacy Protection Study Commission's recommendation "that Federal law be enacted or amended to forbid an employer from using the polygraph or other truth-verification equipment to gather information from an applicant or employee."

RICHARD A. WASSERSTROM

Privacy

I

One thing that is true of privacy is that there are several different phenomena that have been and that can be discussed under the heading of "privacy." Almost all of the discussion is of comparatively recent vintage. In legal scholarship, the classic reference to a right of privacy is the article by Brandeis and Warren entitled, "The Right of Privacy," which appeared in *The Harvard Law Review* in 1890.[1] The first enunciation by the United States Supreme Court of an explicit constitutional right of privacy occurred in 1965 in the case of *Griswold v. Connecticut*.[2] And almost all philosophical and public policy examinations of privacy have appeared within the past fifteen years. However, while the topic of privacy is very much in the air and in the news, part of the problem in thinking about privacy is that the same thing is not always meant at all by the term, "privacy." More specifically, there are at least three distinct kinds of interests or claims that may be involved when commentators, the courts, legislatures, and ordinary citizens talk about privacy and its importance.

The kind of thing that Brandeis and Warren were concerned with was the unconsented-to use by an individual of another's identity in order to secure some special advantage. The central focus here is upon the improper use of a person's name or likeness for commercial purposes, as, for example, when a person's name and picture are included in the advertising for a product in order to enhance the sale of the product. But included within this category are cases in which true facts of a certain sort about an individual are made public, as for instance when there is an unconsented-to public showing of a film of a woman giving birth to a child.

The United States Supreme Court was concerned with a rather different sense of "privacy" in

the Griswold case. That case involved the constitutionality of a Connecticut statute, which made it a crime for any person to use any drug, medicinal article, or instrument for the purpose of preventing conception. One reason some of the members of the Court gave for holding the statute unconstitutional was that the statute intruded improperly into a constitutionally protected zone of privacy. That zone of privacy existed, apparently, in virtue of the fact that the behavior covered by the statute included that of married persons in respect to their own sexual relationship. This idea—that certain relationships and certain behaviors were immune from governmental regulation—was also utilized by the Court in the abortion decision[3] and in a case involving an individual's right to possess and read pornographic literature in his home.[4]

The third sense of "privacy" is reflected in the concern over the wrong, if any, that was done by the members of the "Plumber's Squad" who broke into the office of Daniel Ellsberg's psychiatrist to see what they could learn about Ellsberg from the notes of his psychiatrist. It is reflected, as well, in the worry many persons have over the development and use of sophisticated spying devices that make it possible surreptitiously to overhear another's conversations or observe another's behavior. And it is reflected, too, in the concern expressed by many over the large-scale accumulation of data that now exists about each one of us and which is capable of being stored in and retrieved from large-scale data banks. Here, the root issue captured by this idea of privacy is that of the kind and degree of control that an individual will be able to maintain over information about himself or herself.

It is this third sense of "privacy" that I concentrate upon in this essay. The question I want to consider is that of the type of control a person ought to be able to exercise in respect to knowledge of or the disclosure of information about himself or herself. In this essay I attempt to do three things. First, I consider what this kind of privacy is. More specifically, I examine the different types of information and situations that might be thought to be private. Second, I consider the arguments that might be given for the value of certain types of informational privacy, and the reasons why persons might worry about various types of information gathering practices and procedures. And finally, I examine fairly briefly some of the assumptions of these arguments in an endeavor to raise more explicitly the question of how important or essential this concern for privacy is.

II

As I have indicated, there are a number of different claims that can be and are made in the name of privacy. What a number of them, but by no means all, have in common is that they involve the question of the kind and degree of control that a person ought to be able to exercise in respect to the access by others to information about himself or herself. But even when the focus is upon information, it is evident that information about oneself is not all of the same type; control over some kinds may be thought to be of more importance than control over others. For this reason, the first thing that must be done is to identify some of the different types of information about themselves over which persons might desire to retain substantial access and control, and to describe the situations in which this information comes into being. One way to do this is to consider three situations and look at the ways they resemble each other and differ from one another.

There is first of all the fact that one can, if one wishes to, look "inward" and become aware of the ideas that are running through one's mind, the various emotions one is experiencing, and the variety of bodily sensations one is having—an itch on one's scalp or a pain in one's side. One thing that is significant about one's mental states—about one's dreams, conscious thoughts, hopes, fears and desires is that the most direct, the best, and often the only evidence for another of what they are consists in the individual deliberately revealing them to another. The only way to obtain very detailed and accurate information about what a person is thinking, fearing, imagining, desiring, or hating and how he or she is experiencing it is for that person to tell or show another. If one does not, the ideas and feeling remain within the person and in some sense, at least, known only to him or her. To be sure, nonverbal behavior may give an observer a clue as to what is going on in another's mind. If, for example, a person has a faraway look in her eyes another may infer that she is daydreaming about something and not paying very much attention. In addition there is, perhaps, a more intimate and even conceptual connection, between observable behavior and certain states of feeling. If someone is blushing that may mean that he is embarrassed. If she is talking very fast that may lead another to infer correctly that she is excited or nervous. It is even sometimes the case that one will not know very clearly one's own thoughts and feelings, and that by saying what one thinks they are, a skilled observer can, by listening and watching, tell better than can the speaker what is really being thought or felt.

Nonetheless, even taking all of the qualifications into account, it still remains the case that the only way to obtain much detailed and accurate information about what an individual is thinking, fearing, imagining, desiring, or hating and how it is being experienced is for the person to disclose it to another. Because people cannot read other people's minds, many of these things about a person are known only to him or her in a way in which other things are not, unless there is a deliberate decision to disclose them. They occupy, for the most part, a unique place in respect to the possibility of knowledge by others.

In some ways the situation in respect to what is going on within one's body is similar to that of mental events and in some respects different. There are things that are going on in one's body that are like one's thoughts, fears and fantasies. If, for example, a person has a slight twinge of pain in his toe, there is no way for anyone else to know that unless the person having the pain chooses to disclose it. There are, however, other things about one's body concerning which this privileged position does not obtain. Even though they are one's ribs, one cannot tell very well what they look like; even though it is one's semen, one cannot tell in virtue of that fact also whether it contains sperm.

These kinds of facts about a person's body can be known at least as well by another as by the individual.

So there are some facts about one's body that can be known in a way others logically cannot know them, that can be known to others only if they are deliberately disclosed. And there are other kinds of facts about one's body that a person does not know in this special way and that can be learned quite as well by someone or something outside of the individual.

In the second place, there is some information that is private only in virtue of the *setting* in which the information is disclosed or communicated. For example, suppose that a person has broken an arm and that the person is in a room with the door closed, alone with the doctor while he or she sets the break. Here it is the setting that makes the behavior distinctive and relevant. If no one is in a position to see the patient and the doctor then no one is in a position at that time to know about the broken arm. This kind of case can usefully be described as a case of things being done in private—meaning by that only that they are done in a setting in which there did not appear to be anyone other than the person to whom one was talking, etc., who was in a position to hear what was being said or to see what was being done. This is, of course, an extremely weak sense of privacy, and for at least two reasons. To begin with, the information is less within the individual's control than is information about his or her mental states, not yet revealed to anyone, because the other person can if he or she chooses reveal what he or she has learned. And in addition, there is nothing about *the character* of the information which seems to make further revelation a source of concern.

It is this last point which leads to the third kind of case. Suppose that instead of having a broken arm set by a doctor, a person consults a therapist in the therapist's office, where the doors are closed, etc., in order to discuss what the patient regards as a very loathsome sexual fantasy. Such a conversation takes place in private in the same sense in which the treatment of the broken arm was private, i.e., no one else could see or hear. But this also has an additional quality not possessed by the other example. When a person such as this one consults a therapist he or she typically expects that what is said will not be overheard by anyone else and will

be kept in confidence by the recipient of the information. It is what might be called a private *kind* of communication. And that is not the case with other information about oneself. Absent a further specification of the circumstances, there is no way to tell to what degree individuals have a particular interest in retaining control over the disclosure of facts about themselves.

All of what has been said so far is reasonably obvious. What is also rather apparent is that the most important connection between the idea of doing something in private and doing a private kind of thing is that persons typically do private things only in situations where they reasonably believe that they are doing them in private, i.e., in situations where they believe confidentiality or its equivalent obtains in respect to what is being disclosed. That they believe they are doing something in private in this sense is, often, a condition that has to be satisfied before they are willing to disclose an intimate fact about themselves or to engage in the doing of an intimate act.

It should be evident, too, that there are important similarities, as well as some differences, between the first and third cases—between knowledge of one's own mental states and the disclosure of intimate information to those to whom one chooses to disclose it. A thought-experiment can illuminate much of what is involved in the special concerns persons have that information of certain sorts not become known, without their consent, to others.

Suppose existing technology made it possible for an outsider in some way to look into or monitor another's mind. What, if anything, would be especially disturbing or objectionable about that?

To begin with, there is a real sense in which persons have far less control over when they shall have certain thoughts and what their content will be, than they have over, for example, to whom they shall reveal them and to what degree. Because one's inner thoughts, feelings and bodily sensations are so largely beyond one's control, persons would, no doubt, feel appreciably more insecure in their social environment than they do at present were it possible for others to "look in" without consent to see what was going on in their heads.

This is so at least in part because many, although by no means all, of one's uncommunicated thoughts and feelings are about very intimate matters. One's fantasies and one's fears often concern just those matters that in our culture we would least choose to reveal to anyone else. At a minimum persons might suffer great anxiety and feelings of shame were the decisions as to where, when and to whom to disclose, not to be wholly theirs. Were access to thoughts possible in this way persons would see themselves as creatures who are far more vulnerable at the hands of other persons than they are now.

In addition, there is always the more straightforward worry about accountability for one's thoughts and feelings. As has been mentioned, they are often not within one's control. For all of the reasons that it is wrong to hold people accountable for behavior not within their control, individuals would not want the possibility of accountability to extend to uncommunicated thoughts and feelings.

A third reason why control over intimate facts and behaviors might be of appreciable importance to individuals is this. Our *social* universe would be altered in fundamental and deleterious ways were that control to be surrendered or lost. And this is so because one way in which we mark off and distinguish our most important interpersonal relationships from other ones is in terms of the kind of intimate information and behavior that we are willing to share with other persons. One way in which we make someone a close friend rather than an aquaintance is by revealing things about ourselves to that person that we do not reveal to the world at large. One way in which persons often enter into a special relationship with another is by engaging in sexual behavior not engaged in with the world at large. Knowledge about ourselves is what has been called "moral capital" which is exchanged and otherwise used to create and maintain relationships of intimacy and closeness. On this view privacy is a logically necessary condition for the existence of many of our most meaningful social relationships.[5]

Finally, one rather plausible conception of what it is to be a person carried with it the idea of the existence of a core of thoughts and feelings that are the person's alone. If anyone else could know all that one was thinking or perceive all that one was feeling except in the form one chose to filter and reveal what one was and how one saw oneself—if anyone could, so to speak, be aware of all this at will, individuals might cease to have as complete a

sense of themselves as distinct and separate persons as they have now. For a significant, if not fundamental, part of what it is to be an individual person is to be an entity that is capable of being exclusively aware of at least some of its own thoughts and feelings.

Considerations such as these—and particularly the last one—may help to unravel some of the puzzles concerning the privilege against self-incrimination, as well as some of the worries about coercive therapies. Because of the significance of exclusive control over a person's own thoughts and feelings, the privilege against self-incrimination could be seen to rest, at least in part, upon a concern that confessions not be coerced or required by the state. On this view, the point of the privilege is not primarily that the privilege should exist as the means by which to induce the state not to torture individuals in order to extract information from them. Nor is the point even essentially that the topics of confession will necessarily (or even typically) be of the type that persons would be most unwilling to disclose because of the unfavorable nature of what this would reveal about them. Rather, the fundamental point would be that required disclosure of one's thoughts by itself diminishes the significance or role of the concept of individual personhood within the society.[6]

Similarly, non-consensual drug therapies which reduce if not destroy the patient's resistance to disclosing the things that he or she is thinking are subject to the same kind of criticism. The objection to such therapies is not merely that the individuals involved will be led to say things which they would have not otherwise said, because they regarded such disclosures as shameful or otherwise reflecting badly on themselves (although this is certainly a substantial if not decisive consideration against this kind of a practice). The additional objection to such therapies is that they take away from the individual control over that one area which is for others exclusively within their control and by which they are helped to maintain a clear sense of their own selfhood and individuality.

The more prominent worry today does not, however, concern intrusion into the domain of one's uncommunicated thoughts and feelings, but rather concerns the degree to which communications between persons about intimate things should remain exclusively within their control.

What, for example, would be the wrong that was done to a patient were another to have eavesdropped upon a conversation between the patient and a therapist, or if the therapist had told other persons what had been told to her by the patient? Or what would have been the injury that would have been done to a couple if, unknown to them, they had been observed engaged in sexual intercourse by others?

What comes first to mind is that because of social attitudes toward the disclosure of intimate facts and behavior, most persons would be extremely pained were they to learn that these had become known to persons other than those to whom they chose to disclose them. It is important to see that the pain can come about in several different ways. If one does something private with another and they believe that they are doing it in private, they may very well be hurt or embarrassed if they learn subsequently that they were observed but did not know it. Thus if they learn after the fact that they were observed while they were having intercourse, the knowledge that they were observed will cause them distress both because their expectations of privacy were incorrect and because they do not like the idea that there was an observer present during this kind of intimate act. People have the right, perhaps, simply to have the world be what it appears to be precisely in those cases in which they regard privacy as essential to the diminution of their own vulnerability.

Reasoning such as this lies behind, I think, a case that arose some years ago in California. A department store had complained to the police that homosexuals were using its men's room as a meeting place. The police responded by drilling a small hole in the ceiling over the enclosed stalls. A policeman then stationed himself on the floor above and peered down through the hole observing the persons using the stall for eliminatory purposes. Eventually the policeman discovered and apprehended two homosexuals who used the stall as a place to engage in forbidden sexual behavior. The California Supreme Court held the observations of the policeman to have been the result of an illegal search and ordered the conviction reversed. What made the search objectionably illegal, I believe, was that it occurred in the course of this practice which deceived all of the persons who used the stall and who believed that they were

doing in private something that was socially regarded as a private kind of thing. They were entitled, especially for this kind of activity, both to be free from observation and to have their expectations of privacy honored by the state.[7]

There is an additional reason why the observation or disclosure of certain sorts of activity is objectionable. That is because the kind of spontaneity and openness that is essential to them disappears with the presence of an observer or the lack of a guarantee of confidentiality. To see that this is so, consider a different case. Suppose people know in advance that they will be observed during intercourse. Here there is no problem of defeated reasonable expectations. But there may be injury nonetheless. For one thing, they may be unwilling or unable to communicate an intimate fact or engage in intimate behavior in the presence of an observer. In this sense they will be quite directly prevented from going forward. For another thing, even if they do go ahead the character of the experience may very well be altered. Knowing that someone is watching or listening may render what would have been an enjoyable experience unenjoyable. Or, having someone watch or listen may so alter the character of the activity that it is simply not the same kind of activity it was before. The presence of the observer may make spontaneity impossible. Aware of the observer, individuals will be engaged in part in viewing or imagining what is going on from his or her perspective. They thus cannot "lose" themselves as completely in the activity. And for some kinds of activities—for example, sexual intercourse—that may be an essential feature.

Nor is this the only problem presented by a nondeceptive absence of privacy. Suppose that one is in a setting in which one can be certain that there will never be privacy, that virtually everything one does and virtually everything that happens to one will be recorded and known to others. Even if nothing particularly embarrassing, incriminating, or intimate goes on (or is apt to go on) there is, perhaps, something else that is troublesome and objectionable about such an environment. To see whether this would be so, it is necessary to consider a different kind of case, that of data banks. Is there anything to worry about if a society possesses and utilizes its technological capacity to store an enormous amount of information about each of the individual members of the society in such a way that the information can be retrieved in a rapid, efficient, and relatively inexpensive fashion?

Consider a society in which the kinds of data collected about an individual are not very different from the kinds and quantity already collected in some fashion or other in our own society. It is surprising what a large number of interactions are deemed sufficiently important to record in some way. Thus, there are, for example, records of the traffic accidents one has been in, the applications one has made for life insurance, the purchases that one has made with a Mastercharge Card, the C.O.D. packages that have been signed for, the schools one's children are enrolled in, the telephone numbers that have been called from one's telephone, and so on. Now suppose all of that information, which is presently recorded in some written fashion, were to be stored in some way so that all of it that concerns a person could be extracted on demand. What would result?

It is apparent that at least two different kinds of pictures of the individual would emerge. First, some sort of a qualitative picture of the person would emerge. A number of nontemporal facts would be made available—what kind of driver the person is, how many children the person has, what sorts of purchases have been made, how often the telephone is used, how many times the person has been arrested and for what offenses, what diseases the person has had, how much life insurance, and so on.

Second, it would also be possible to reconstruct a rough, temporal picture of how an individual had been living his or her life and what the person had been doing with his or her time. Thus, there might for any given day be evidence that two or three stores were visited and purchases made, that a check had been cashed at the bank, that lunch had been eaten at a particular restaurant, and so on. There might well, however, be whole days for which there were no entries and there might be many days for which the entries would give a very sketchy and incomplete picture of how one had been spending one's time. Still, it would be a picture that is much more detailed, accurate, and complete than the one most persons could supply from their own memory, or from their own memory as it was augmented by that of their friends. One would have to spend a substantial amount of

time each day writing in a diary in order to begin to produce as complete and accurate a picture as the one that might be rendered by the storage and retrieval system envisaged—and even then it is doubtful that the diary would be as accurate or as complete, unless one made it a major life task to keep accurate and detailed records of everything that was done.

If we ask would there be anything troublesome about living in such a society, the first thing to recognize is that there are several different things that might be objectionable.

In the first place, such a scheme might make less confidential communications that were about intimate kinds of things. In order to receive welfare, life insurance, or psychiatric counseling, persons may be required to supply information of a personal or confidential nature. If so, they might reasonably expect that the material revealed will be known only to the recipient. If, however, the information is stored in a data bank, it now becomes possible for the information to be disclosed to persons other than those to whom disclosure was intended. Even if access to the data is controlled in all sorts of ways so as to avoid the risks of improper access, storage of the confidential information in the data bank necessarily makes the information less confidential than it was before it was so stored.

In the second place information that does not concern intimate things can get distorted in one way or another through storage. The clearest contemporary case of this kind of information is a person's arrest record. Now the fact that someone has been arrested is probably not the kind of fact that the arrestee can insist ought to be kept secret. But he or she can legitimately make two other demands about it. The person can insist that incorrect inferences not be drawn from the information. The person can, that is, legitimately point out that many individuals who are arrested are never prosecuted for the alleged offense nor are they in any sense guilty of the offense for which they were arrested. He or she can, therefore, quite appropriately complain about any practice which, for instance, routinely and without more being known denies employment to persons with arrest records. And if such a practice exists, then a person can legitimately complain about the increased dissemination and availability of arrest records just because of the systematic misuse of that information. The storage of arrest records in a data bank becomes objectionable not because the arrest record is intrinsically private but because the information is so regularly misused that the unavailability of the information is less of an evil than its general availability.

This does not, however, end the matter, although this is where the discussion of data banks often ends. Suppose that the information is appropriately derogatory in respect to the individual. Suppose that it is, for instance, a record of arrest and conviction in circumstances, moreover, that in no way suggest that the conviction was unfairly or improperly obtained. Does the individual have any sort of a claim that information of this sort not be put into the data bank? One might, of course, complain on the grounds that there was a practice of putting too much weight on the conviction. Here the argument would be similar to that just discussed. In addition, though, it might also be maintained that there are important gains that come from living in a society in which certain kinds of derogatory information about an individual are permitted to disappear from view after a certain amount of time. What is involved is the creation of a kind of social environment that holds out to the members of the society the possibility of self-renewal and change, which is often dependent upon the individual's belief that a fresh start is in fact an option that is still open. A society that is concerned to encourage persons to believe in the possibility of genuine individual redemption and that is concerned not to make the process of redemption unduly onerous or interminable, might, therefore, actively discourage the development of institutions that impose *permanent* marks of disapprobation upon any of the individuals in the society.

In addition, and related to some of the things already mentioned, there are independent worries about the storage of vast quantities of ostensibly innocuous material about the individual in the data bank. Suppose nothing intrinsically private is stored in the data bank; suppose nothing potentially or improperly derogatory is included; and suppose what does get stored is an enormous quantity of information about the individual—information about the person and the public, largely

commercial, transactions which were entered into. One can imagine lots of useful, efficient uses to which such a data bank might be put. Can there be any serious objections?

One thing is apparent. With such a data bank it would be possible to reconstruct a person's movements and activities more accurately and completely than could the individual—or any group of individuals—do simply from memory. As has been indicated, there would, of course, still be gaps in the picture; no one would be able to tell in detail what the individual had been doing a lot of the time. But still, as has been suggested, it would be a surprisingly rich and comprehensive sketch that is exceeded in detail in our society only by the keeping of a careful, thorough personal diary, or by having someone under the surveillance of a corps of private detectives.

What distinguishes this scheme is the fact that it would make it possible to render an account of the movements and habits of every member of the society and in so doing it might transform the society in several notable respects.

In part what is involved is the fact that every transaction in which one engages would now take on additional significance. In such a society one would be both buying a tank of gas and leaving part of a systematic record of where one was on that particular date. One would not just be applying for life insurance; one would also be recording in a permanent way one's health on that date and a variety of other facts about oneself. No matter how innocent one's intentions and actions at any given moment, a likely if not inevitable consequence of such a practice of data collection would be that persons would think more carefully before they did things that would become part of the record. Life would to this degree become less spontaneous and more measured than it is today.

More significant are the consequences of such a practice upon attitudes toward privacy in the society. If it became routine to record and have readily accessible vast quantities of information about every individual we might come to hold the belief that the detailed inspection of any individual's behavior is a perfectly appropriate societal undertaking. We might tend to take less seriously than we do at present the idea that there are ever occasions upon which an individual can plausibly claim to be left alone and unobserved. We might in addition become so used to being objects of public scrutiny that we would cease to deem important privacy in any of our social relationships. Thus as observers we might become insensitive to the legitimate claims of an individual to a sphere of life in which the individual is at present autonomous and around which he or she can erect whatever shield is wished. And as the subjects of continual observation we might become forgetful of the degree to which many of the most important relationships within which we now enter depend for their existence upon the possibility of privacy.

On the other hand, if we do continue to have a high regard for privacy both because of what it permits us to be as individuals and because of the kinds of relationships and activities it makes possible and promotes, the maintenance of a scheme of systematic data collection would necessarily get in the way. This is so for the same reason discussed earlier. Much of the value and significance of being able to do intimate things in private is impaired whenever there is a serious lack of confidence about the privacy of the situation. No one could rationally believe that the establishment of data banks—no matter how pure the motives of those who maintain and have access to them—is calculated to enhance the confidentiality of much that is now known about each one of us. And even if only apparently innocuous material is to be stored, we could never be sure that it all was innocuous as it seemed at the time. It is very likely, therefore, that we would go through life alert to these new, indelible consequences of everyday interactions and transactions. Just as our lives would be different from what they are now if we believed that every telephone conversation was being overheard, so our lives would be similarly affected if we believed that every transaction and application was being stored. In both cases we would almost surely go through life encumbered by a wariness and deliberateness that would make it less easy to live a kind of life often associated with that of a free person.

III

Many of the arguments presented in Part II may not be arguments for, one might say, the intrinsic de-sirability of privacy and confidentiality in respect to matters of intimate behavior and belief. For most of the arguments already discussed may turn only on the true but contingent fact that persons in our (and most cultures) are socialized in certain ways in respect to intimate matters of different sorts. As I have tried to indicate, given this socialization, an array of arguments and considerations can then be advanced to show why privacy and confidentiality in respect to these matters will be of great importance to individuals and how they may be specially injured and threatened by any loss of control over who, if anyone, will have access to any information concerning their intimate behavior or their thoughts, attitudes and beliefs. And, as has been suggested, in some cases the character of the experience may itself be altered when others are permitted to enter into the participant's ideational and experiential world.

Conceding all of this, however, it is also worth asking whether it would be desirable were individuals to be socialized differently. It might be that different attitudes and practices would be more desirable than those which happen to exist in our society. An alternative view is possible, and it is worth taking seriously. One problem is that it is seldom made explicit or argued for very extensively. But a reconstruction of such a view is possible. It is one which depends at least in part, upon a less individualistic, more collectivist conception of social life and social relationships. The alternative view to that which has been assumed so far might go something like this.

We have made ourselves vulnerable—or at least far more vulnerable than we need be—by accepting the notion that there are thoughts and actions concerning which we ought to feel ashamed or embarrassed. When we realize that everyone has fantasies, desires, worries about all sorts of supposedly terrible, wicked, and shameful things, we ought to see that they really are not things to be ashamed of at all. We regard ourselves as vulnerable because in part we think we are different, if not unique. We have sexual feelings toward our parents and no one else has ever had such wicked feelings. But if everyone does, then the fact that others know of this fantasy is less threatening—one is less vulnerable to their disapproval and contempt.

We have made ourselves excessively vulnerable, so this alternative point of view might continue, because we have accepted the idea that many things are shameful unless done in private. And there is no reason to accept that convention. Of course we are embarrassed if others watch us having sexual intercourse—just as we are embarrassed if others see us unclothed. But that is because the culture has taught us to have these attitudes and not because they are intrinsically fitting. Indeed, our culture would be a healthier, happier culture if we diminished substantially the kinds of actions that we now feel comfortable only doing in private, or the kind of thoughts we now feel comfortable disclosing only to those with whom we have special relationships. This is so for at least three reasons. In the first place, there is simply no good reason why privacy is essential to these things. Sexual intercourse could be just as pleasurable in public (if we grew up unashamed) as is eating a good dinner in a good restaurant. Sexual intercourse is better in private only because society has told us so.

In the second place, it is clear that a change in our attitudes will make us more secure and at ease in the world. If we would be as indifferent to whether we are being watched when we have intercourse as we are to when we eat a meal then we cannot be injured by the fact that we know others are watching us, and we cannot be injured nearly as much by even unknown observations.

In the third place, it might be argued, interpersonal relationships will in fact be better if there is less of a concern for privacy. After all, forthrightness, honesty, and candor are, for the most part virtues, while hypocrisy and deceit are not. Yet this emphasis upon the maintenance of a private side to life tends to encourage hypocritical and deceitful ways of behavior. Individuals see themselves as leading dual lives—public ones and private ones. They present one view of themselves to the public—to casual friends, acquaintances and strangers; and a different view of themselves to themselves and a few intimate associates. This way of living is hypocritical because it is, in essence, a life devoted to camouflaging the real, private self from public scrutiny. It is a dualistic, unintegrated life which renders the individuals who live it needlessly vulnerable, shameridden and lacking in a clear

sense of self. It is to be contrasted with the more open, less guarded life of the person who has so little to fear from disclosures of self because he or she has nothing that requires hiding.

This is a start toward an alternative view that deserves to be taken seriously. Any attempt to do so, moreover, should begin by considering more precisely the respects in which it departs from the more conventional view of the role of privacy maintained in the body of this essay and the respects in which it does not. In particular, there are at least three issues which must be examined in detail before an intelligent decision can be made. The first is the question of the value that this alternative view attaches to those characteristics of spontaneity and individuality that play such an important role in the more traditional view—as I have described it. On at least one interpretation both views prize spontaneity and individuality equally highly, with this alternative account seeing openness in interpersonal relationships as a better way of achieving just those ends. On another interpretation, however, autonomy, spontaneity and individuality are replaced as values by the satisfactions that attend the recognition of the likeness of all human experience and the sameness that characterizes all interpersonal relationships. Which way of living gives one more options concerning the kind of life that one will fashion for oneself is one of the central issues to be settled.

Still another issue that would have to be explored is the question of what would be gained and what would be lost in respect to the character of interpersonal relationship. For one of the important arguments for the view put forward earlier is that the sharing of one's intimate thoughts and behaviors is one of the primary media through which close, meaningful interpersonal relationships are created, nourished and confirmed. One thing that goes to define a relationship of close friendship is that the friends are willing to share truths about themselves with each other that they are unprepared to reveal to the world at large. One thing that helps to define and sustain a sexual. love relationship is the willingness of the parties to share sexual intimacies with each other that they are unprepared to share with the world at large. If this makes sense, either as a conceptual or as an empirical truth, then perhaps acceptance of this alternative view would mean that these kinds of relationships were either no longer possible or less likely. Or perhaps the conventional view is equally unsatisfactory here, too. Perhaps friendship and love both can and ought to depend upon some other, less proprietary, commercial conception of the exchange of commodities. Perhaps this view of intimate interpersonal relationships is as badly in need of alteration as is the attendant conception of the self.

Finally, related to what has just been said, one would want, I think, to examine more closely some other features of the other view. For example, even if it was no longer thought important to mark off and distinguish one's close friends from strangers (or even if it could still be done, but in some other way) perhaps the alternative conception of openness and honesty in all interpersonal relationships would make ordinary social interactions vastly more complex and time-consuming than they are now. So much so, in fact, that these interactions, rather than the other tasks of living, would become the focus of one's waking hours.

Still another example concerns the character of sexuality and sexual relationships. For most persons in our culture, matters relating to sex are paradigmatically private in all of the senses described in Part II. This is probably so for a variety of reasons. To begin with, during sexual behavior with another one is extremely vulnerable in two, quite straightforward, physical senses. The participants are vulnerable in the sense that they are fully engaged in the activity. They are vulnerable to attack in the same primitive respect in which persons who are asleep are vulnerable. And the participants are also vulnerable vis-a-vis one another. Sexual behavior brings persons in close, physical contact with each other. Trust in the security of the physical environment and in each other may, therefore, be a simple dictate of prudence.

In addition, sex and vulnerability are linked psychically in the culture. The culture appears, for instance, to teach individuals to attach great significance to their sexual competency—to their ability to achieve and bestow sexual satisfaction. Hence, many persons come to see their success or failure as individuals bound up in all sorts of ways with their sexual abilities or problems. Hence, they plausibly regard information about their sexual

behavior as relating directly to an area of great vulnerability and as potentially very damaging.

The culture also teaches many individuals that all matters pertaining to sex are shameful. One strain of the culture teaches that it is wrong to have any interest in sex for its own sake or for the pleasure it provides. Another strain of the culture teaches that there is a sharp and important difference between sexual activity that is normal and appropriate, e.g., heterosexual intercourse between persons who are married to each other, and other sexual activity that is abnormal, unnatural, or perverse. Although there will be disagreement as to where and how to draw the line precisely between these two kinds of sexual activity, it will be thought wrong to have the sorts of sexual fantasies, desires, etc.—or to engage in the kinds of sexual conduct—falling outside of the bounds of the normal and appropriate. As a result, individuals who have been socialized in these ways will regard virtually all disclosure about their own sexual beliefs and life as reflecting discreditably upon them. And finally, of course, the culture also teaches almost everyone that matters pertaining to sexual thoughts and behavior should be done in private—even if there is nothing wrong or shameful about the content of the thoughts or behavior in question. For this reason persons will be rendered uncomfortable, caused pain and discomfort, whenever the environment is altered so as to contain observers to acts of sexual intimacy or after-the-fact confidants to whom are disclosed descriptions of past sexual behavior.

What requires development and examination are theories of sexuality and eroticism so that it is possible to disentangle the distinguishable biological, psychological, social and normative components of these phenomena in order to assess the roles they can and should play in human sexual activity. For only then would one be in a position to have a well-founded opinion concerning the connection that ought to obtain between privacy and sexual behavior and attitudes. Perhaps, for instance, less privacy in respect to sexual matters would reduce the sense of vulnerability individuals now feel, but that a weakening of the connection between sex and privacy would also produce a diminished sense of the erotic.

These are some, but by no means all, of the

central issues that require continued exploration. They are certainly among the issues that the fully developed theory of privacy, its value and its place within society must confront and examine, and not settle by way of assumption or presupposition.

NOTES

1. Brandeis, Louis D. and Warren, Charles. "The Right to Privacy," 4 *Harvard Law Review* 193 (1890).

2. *Griswold v. State of Connecticut*, 381 U.S. 479, 85 S. Ct. 1678 (1965).

3. *Roe v. Wade*, 410 U.S. 113, 93 S.Ct. 705 (1973).

4. *Stanley v. Georgia*, 394 U.S. 557, 89 S.Ct. 1243 (1969).

5. This argument is advanced by Charles Fried in "Privacy," 77 *Yale Law Journal* 475 (1968) and in *An Anatomy of Values: Problems of Personal and Social Choice* (Cambridge, Mass.: Harvard University Press, 1970) Chapter IX.

6. A somewhat similar analysis is presented by Robert Gerstein in "Privacy and Self-Incrimination," *Ethics*, Vol. 80 (1970) 87. Gerstein observes that historically the privilege against self-incrimination was viewed as especially important in respect to offenses related to religious belief and freedom. He goes on to argue that a contemporary justification for the privilege—on grounds of privacy—can be developed through an account of what might be especially objectionable about requiring an individual to admit and confess to his or her own serious wrongdoing.

"It is not the disclosure of the facts of the crime, but the '*mea culpa*,' the public admission of the private judgment of self-condemnation, that seems to be of real concern." (Gerstein, "Privacy and Self-Incrimination," *Ethics*, Vol. 80 (1970) p. 91.)

Both Gerstein's analysis and my own have implications for the way in which the privilege against self-incrimination should be interpreted. Thus, in *Schmerber v. California*, 384 U.S. 757, 86 St.Ct. 1826 (1966), the Supreme Court held that it did not violate the privilege to extract a blood sample from a defendant without his consent. On my analysis, this makes sense because an individual is in no special position in respect to knowledge about the composition of his or her blood. In Gerstein's view, this makes sense because the extraction of the blood sample in no way involves the individual in a public confession of any sort.

On the other hand, immunity statutes may be more troublesome than the Supreme Court has supposed. The Supreme Court has thought that as long as immunity from the use of that testimony by the prosecution is given to an individual there can be no serious worry about the privilege. See, e.g., *Kastigar v. United States*, 406 U.S. 441, 92 S.Ct. 1653 (1972). However, since at least some of the privacy arguments for the privilege do not depend upon the possibility of subsequent prosecution of the person who is required to give evidence as to his or her own wrongdoing, these arguments are left unmet by a grant of immunity from prosecution, no matter how extensive the grant of immunity may be.

7. The case is *Bielicki v. Superior Court*, 57 Cal. 2d 600, 371 P.2d 288 (1962).

THE PRIVACY PROTECTION STUDY COMMISSION
Privacy in the Employment Relationship

A comprehensive study of the effects of record keeping on personal privacy must include records generated in the context of the relationship between employer and employee. The employment relationship affects most people over the greater part of their adult lives, and is basic to the economic and social well-being of our society. Loss of work is for most people a considerable hardship. Its consequences for an individual and for his family can be disastrous.

When an individual applies for work today, it is

not unusual for the employer to ask him to divulge a considerable amount of information about himself, and to allow the employer to verify and supplement it. In addition, the individual may be examined by the company physician, given a battery of psychological tests, interviewed extensively, and subjected to a background investigation. After hiring, the records the employer keeps about him will again expand to accommodate attendance and payroll data, records concerning various types of benefits, performance evaluations, and much other information. All of this creates a broad base of recorded information about the employee which various entities unrelated to the employee-employer relationship will view as a valuable resource.

It is the creation, maintenance, use and disclosure of these employee records which concern the Commission. At what point do inquiries about applicants and employees become unduly intrusive? What does fairness demand with respect to the uses and disclosures of records that support an employment decision? What expectation of confidentiality can an individual legitimately have with respect to the records his employer makes and keeps about him?

The analysis and recommendations that follow have focused on records generated in relationships between individuals and large, private-sector employers. The Commission does, however, believe that the limited amount of work it was able to do on the personnel record-keeping practices of small organizations warrants more general application of the principles underlying its recommendations.

GENERAL RECOMMENDATIONS

As elsewhere, the Commission has formulated its recommendations on records generated by the employment relationship in the light of three broad public-policy objectives: (1) to minimize intrusiveness; (2) to maximize fairness; and (3) to create a legitimate, enforceable expectation of confidentiality. In contrast to other areas, however, the Commission envisages adoption of most of its employment-related recommendations by voluntary action. The exceptions are all instances in which statutory or regulatory action appears to be both necessary and feasible. . . . The Commission believes that flexibility in decisions about which job an employee is best suited to perform is essential to good management and should be constrained by public policy only to the extent that employers show themselves unable or unwilling to respond to concerns about the protection of employee privacy. Nonetheless, the enforcement problem is the primary reason why the Commission does not believe that many of the privacy protection issues

the private-sector employee-employer relationship raises can be resolved by legislated record-keeping requirements.

Recommendation 1. That an employer periodically and systematically examine its employment and personnel record-keeping practices, including a review of: (a) the number and types of records it maintains on individual employees, former employees, and applicants; (b) the items of information contained in each type of employment record it maintains; (c) the uses made of the items of information in each type of record; (d) the uses made of such records within the employing organization; (e) the disclosures made of such records to parties outside the employing organization; (f) the extent to which individual employees, former employees, and applicants are both aware and systematically informed of the uses and disclosures that are made of information in the records made about them. . . .

Recommendation 2. That an employer articulate, communicate, and implement fair information practice policies for employment records which should include: (a) limiting the collection of information on individual employees, former employees, and applicants to that which is relevant to specific decisions; (b) informing employees, applicants, and former employees who maintain a continuing relationship with the employer of the uses to be made of such information; (c) informing employees of the types of records that are being maintained on them; (d) adopting reasonable procedures to assure the accuracy, timeliness, and completeness of information collected, maintained, used or disclosed about individual employees, former employees, and applicants; (e) permitting individual employees, former employees, and applicants to see, copy, correct, or amend records maintained about them; (f) limiting the internal use of records maintained on individual employees, former employees, and applicants; (g) limiting external disclosures of information in records kept on individual employees, former employees, and applicants, including disclosures made without the employee's authorization in response to specific inquiries or requests to verify information about him; (h) providing for regular review of compliance with articulated fair information practice policies. . . .

SPECIFIC RECOMMENDATIONS

With a few important exceptions, the Commission's specific recommendations on record keeping in the employee-employer relationship also embody a voluntary scheme for resolving questions of fairness in the collection, use and dissemination of employee records.

Intrusiveness

Some of the information an employer uses in making hiring and placement decisions is acquired from sources other than the individual applicant or employee. In addition to former employers and references named by the individual, such third-party sources may include physicians, creditors, teachers, neighbors, and law enforcement authorities.

One way to keep an employer's inquiries within reasonable bounds is to limit the outside sources it may contact without the individual's knowledge or authorization, as well as what the employer may seek from the individual himself. . . .

Truth Verification Devices.   The polygraph examination, often called the lie-detector test, is one technique the Commission believes should be proscribed on intrusiveness grounds. The polygraph is used by employers to assess the honesty of job applicants and to gather evidence about employees suspected of illegal activity on the job. An estimated 100,000 individuals submitted to this procedure in 1974.

The main objections to the use of the polygraph in the employment context are (1) that it deprives the individuals of any control over divulging information about themselves; and (2) that it is unreliable. Although the latter is the focal point of much of the continuing debate about polygraph testing, the former is the paramount concern from a privacy protection viewpoint.

Other truth-verification devices now on the market, such as the Psychological Stress Evaluator (PSE), now pose an even greater challenge to the notion that an individual should not be arbitrarily deprived of control over the divulgence of information about himself. . . . The use of such devices in the employment context, and the practices

associated with their use, are, in the Commission's view, unreasonable invasions of personal privacy that should be summarily proscribed.

Recommendation 3.   That Federal law be enacted or amended to forbid an employer from using the polygraph or other truth-verification equipment to gather information from an applicant or employee.

The Commission further recommends that the Congress implement this recommendation by a statute which bans the manufacture and sale of these truth-verification devices and prohibits their use by employers engaged in interstate commerce. A clear, strong Federal statute would preempt existing State laws with less stringent requirements and make it impossible for employers to subvert the spirit of the law by sending applicants and employees across state lines for polygraph examinations. . . .

Pretext Interviews.   The Commission also finds unreasonably intrusive the practices of investigators who misrepresent who they are, on whose behalf they are making an inquiry, or the purpose of the inquiry.

Because background checks in connection with the selection of an applicant or the promotion or reassignment of an employee are not criminal investigations, they do not justify undercover techniques.

Recommendation 4.   That the Federal Fair Credit Reporting Act be amended to provide that no employer or investigative firm conducting an investigation for an employer . . . may attempt to obtain information about the individual through pretext interviews or other false or misleading representations that seek to conceal the actual purpose(s) of the inquiry or investigation, or the identity or representative capacity of the employer or investigator. . . .

Reasonable Care in the Use of Support Organizations.   An employer should not be totally unaccountable for the activities of others who perform services for it. The Commission believes that an employer should have an affirmative obligation to check into the modus operandi of any investigative firm it uses or proposes to use, and that if an employer does not use reasonable care in selecting or using such an organization, it should not be wholly absolved of responsibility for the organization's actions.

Recommendation 5. That the Federal Fair Credit Reporting Act be amended to provide that each employer and agent of an employer must exercise reasonable care in the selection and use of investigative organizations, so as to assure that the collection, maintenance, use and disclosure practices of such organizations comply with the Commission's recommendations.

Fairness

Unfair practices can enter into employment record keeping in four main ways: (1) in the kinds of information collected for use in making decisions about individuals; (2) in the procedures used to gather such information; (3) in the procedures used to keep records about individuals accurate, timely, and complete; and (4) in the sharing of information across the variety of record-generating relationships that may be subsumed by the employment relationship. . . .

Recommendation 6. That except as specifically required by Federal or State statute or regulation, or by municipal ordinance or regulation, an employer should not seek or use a record of arrest pertaining to an individual applicant or employee.

Recommendation 7. That unless otherwise required by law, an employer should seek or use a conviction record pertaining to an individual applicant or employee only when the record is directly relevant to a specific employment decision affecting the individual. . . .

Notice Regarding Collection from Third Parties. The background check is the most common means of certifying or supplementing information an employer collects directly from an applicant or employee. Some employers have their own background investigators, but many hire an outside firm. . . . A background check may do no more than verify information provided by an applicant. It may, however, seek out additional information on previous employment, criminal history, life style, and personal reputation. The scope of such a background check depends on what the employer asks for, how much it is willing to pay, and the

character of the firm hired to conduct the investigation. . . .

Authorization Statements. In many instances an employer must have an applicant or employee's permission before it can get personal information about him from other persons or institutions. Testimony before the Commission indicates that employers themselves are becoming reluctant to disclose information about their former employees to other employers.

Nonetheless many employers' job application forms still include a release which the applicant must sign, authorizing the employer to acquire information from organizations or individuals that have a confidential relationship with the applicant. . . .

When any authorization or waiver of confidentiality is sought from an applicant or employee, fairness demands that it be limited both in scope and period of validity. It should bear the date of signature and expire no more than one year from that date. It should be worded so that the individual who is asked to sign it can understand it, and should specify the persons and institutions to whom it will be presented and the information that each will be asked for, together with the reasons for seeking the information.

Recommendation 8. That no employer or consumer-reporting agency (as defined by the Fair Credit Reporting Act) acting on behalf of an employer ask, require, or otherwise induce an applicant or employee to sign any statement authorizing any individual or institution to disclose information about him, or about any other individual, unless the statement is:

a. in plain language;

b. dated;

c. specific as to the individuals and institutions he is authorizing to disclose information about him who are known at the time the authorization is signed, and general as to others whose specific identity is not known as the authorization is signed;

d. specific as to the nature of the information he is authorizing to be disclosed;

e. specific as to the individuals or institutions to

whom he is authorizing information to be disclosed;

f. specific as to the purpose(s) for which the information may be used by any of the parties named in (e) at the time of the disclosure; and

g. specific as to its expiration date which should be for a reasonable period of time not to exceed one year.

Fairness in Use

Access to Records. Fairness demands that an applicant or employee be permitted to see and copy records an employer maintains about him. Allowing an employee to see and copy his records can be as advantageous to the employer as to the employee. As discussed earlier, employment records in the private sector are generally regarded as the property of management. Except where limited by State statute, ... or where controlled by collective-bargaining agreements, all the rights of ownership in employment records vest in the employer. Although many firms permit, and some even encourage, employees to review at least some of the records kept about them, there is no generally accepted rule. ...

Recommendation 9. That as a matter of policy an employer should

a. designate clearly:
   i. those records about an employee, former employee, or applicant for employment (including any individual who is being considered for employment but who has not formally applied) which the employer will allow such employee, former employee, or applicant to see and copy on request; and
   ii. those records about an employee, former employee, or applicant which the employer will not make available to the employee, former employee, or applicant ...

b. assure that its employees are informed as to which records are included in categories (a)(i) and (ii) above; and

c. upon request by an individual applicant, employee, or former employee:
   i. inform the individual, after verifying his identity, whether it has any recorded information pertaining to him that is designated as records he may see and copy; and

   ii. permit the individual to see and copy any such record(s), either in person or by mail; or
   iii. apprise the individual of the nature and substance of any such record(s) by telephone; and
   iv. permit the individual to use one or the other of the methods of access provided in (c)(ii) and (iii), or both if he prefers.

Access to Medical Records. The medical records an employer maintains differ significantly in character and use from the other records created in the employee-employer relationship. Responsibility for giving physical examinations to determine possible work restrictions and for serving as primary medical-care providers is falling ever more heavily on employers, giving them increasingly extensive medical files on their employees. ...

Recommendation 10. That, upon request, an individual who is the subject of a medical record maintained by an employer, or another responsible person designated by the individual, be allowed to have access to that medical record, including an opportunity to see and copy it. ...

However, when the employer's relationship to an applicant, employee, or former employee is not that of a medical-care provider, the Commission recommends:

Recommendation 11. That, upon request, an individual who is the subject of medical-record information maintained by an employer be allowed to have access to that information either directly or through a licensed medical professional designated by the individual.

Correction of Records. Any employee who has reason to question the accuracy, timeliness, or completeness of records his employer keeps about him should be able to correct or amend those records. ... When the employer rejects the requested correction or amendment, fairness demands that the employer incorporate the employee's statement of dispute into the record and pass it along to those to whom the employer subsequently discloses the disputed information, as well as to those who need to know the information is disputed in order to protect the individual from unfair decisions being made on the basis of it.

Moreover, if an employer attempts to verify allegedly erroneous, obsolete, or incomplete information in a record, it should limit its investigation to the particular items in dispute. . . .

Personnel and Payroll Records. As personnel planning and management systems have become more elaborate, so have the personnel file and payroll records an employer keeps on its employees. That is not to say that all employees expect personnel and payroll records to be as held in confidence within the employing organization. Some may not; but out of consideration for those who do, the Commission believes that an employer should limit the use of personnel and payroll record information to whatever is necessary to fulfill particular functions. Therefore, the Commission recommends:

Recommendation 12. That an employer assure that the personnel and payroll records it maintains are available internally only to authorized users and on a need-to-know basis. . . .

Expectation of Confidentiality

Employers have regular access to more information about employees than do credit, depository, or insurance institutions; yet there are no legal controls on the disclosure of employment information. The confidentiality of these records is maintained today solely at the discretion of the employer and can be transgressed at any time with no obligation to the individual record subject.

Evidence before the Commission indicates that, although there is no legal requirement for them to do so, private-sector employers tend to protect information about employees against disclosure. In part, this is because answering requests for such information can be a substantial administrative burden with no compensating advantage to the employer. In part, it is because employers fear common law actions brought for defamation or invasion of privacy. Such restraints, however, are uneven at best; and there are circumstances under which almost any employer routinely discloses the information in its employee records, as for example, in response to inquiries from law enforcement authorities. . . .

Recommendation 13. That an employer clearly inform all its applicants upon request, and all employees automatically, of the types of disclosures it may make of information in the records it maintains on them, including disclosures of directory information, and of its procedures for involving the individual in particular disclosures.

The Employer's Duty of Confidentiality. As the first premise of a responsible confidentiality policy, disclosures to any outside entity without the employee's authorization should be prohibited. Exceptions can then be made for directory information, subpoenas, specific statutory requirements, and disclosures made pursuant to collective-bargaining agreements. . . .

The Commission's recommendations assign employers an important task: to adopt policies and practices regarding the collection, use, and disclosure of information on applicants, employees, and former employees without being forced to do so by government. Unless each employer has a conscientious program on which applicants and employees can rely to safeguard the records the employer keeps about them, the voluntary approach recommended in this chapter will prove unsuccessful. Thus, a future commission or legislative bodies may have to consider compulsory measures, with all the disadvantages for the employee-employer relationship that would entail.

When asked how he thought industry would respond to guidelines for voluntary compliance in developing policies and procedures on employment record keeping, a witness representing the Ford Motor Company said:

> Certainly it has the merit of allowing various corporations to develop guidelines that are appropriate to their situations . . . there is a wide diversity of situations and there are numerous ways by which the principles of privacy could be implemented . . . I would simply want to take a hold on determining whether at some later date legislation is necessary. The suggestion is that we start with the voluntary and determine to what extent the compulsory may be necessary based on experience.

The Commission shares that view.

Finally, the Commission also believes that its recommendations with respect to employment relationship, or at least the concepts on which they are based, apply equally to Federal, State, and local governments and their employees.

DAVID F. LINOWES

Is Business Giving Employees Privacy?

It is more than two years since the U.S. Privacy Protection Study Commission submitted its recommendations urging business to adopt voluntarily privacy safeguards for its employment-related records. But a number of the nation's largest industrial corporations apparently still do not have adequate policies to protect sensitive confidential employee data from possible abuse. This was revealed by a survey of 145 of the nation's largest corporations. The seventy-four companies that responded to the survey, conducted by the Survey Research Laboratory at the University of Illinois, employ over 2.5 million workers. .

In one of its basic recommendations, the Privacy Commission had urged employers to examine periodically and systematically their employment and personnel record-keeping practices. Only by such a systematic examination can executives determine the extent of vulnerability to abuse of their employment records. Yet, in response to the question, "Does your organization have a policy for conducting periodic evaluations of its personnel record-keeping system," almost two-thirds of the corporations (64 percent) responded that they do not have such a policy.

It should be noted, however, that even without such a policy, over one-half (58 percent) of the companies did conduct a systematic evaluation of its existing personnel record-keeping practices within the past two years with particular attention to confidentiality safeguards. Also, almost four out of five corporations (78 percent) have designated an executive-level person to be responsible for maintaining privacy safeguards in employment record-keeping practices. This is an encouraging indication of the growing awareness of employee privacy rights.

Government's ever-increasing intrusion into the information privacy rights of the average citizen has been a concern of business executives and civil libertarians alike. An important source of confidential personal data about individuals is the files and data banks of employers. To attempt to control the easy access to employment records by overzealous governmental administrators, it is necessary for employers to have a policy concerning which records will be routinely disclosed to inquiries from governmental agencies. Yet in response to the query whether corporations had such a policy, two out of five (41 percent) said they do not. When no such policy exists, the person in charge—whether he be executive or record clerk—decides for himself what and when sensitive personal information is routinely released to any governmental agency representative.

When it comes to nongovernmental inquirers, 85 percent of the companies disclose such information to credit grantors without subpoena, as compared to 49 percent to landlords and 22 percent to charitable organizations. With such a large disparity in favor of credit grantors, can it be that there is developing a kind of "old boy network" for the credit granting community? Perhaps this is as it should be in a credit-hungry society where extenders of credit are increasingly hard pressed to evaluate creditworthiness. However, if this kind of liberal cooperation for credit grantors is to prevail, the subject individual should be informed.

In response to the question, "Does your organization have a policy to inform personnel of the organization's routine disclosure practices to nongovernmental inquirers," only 31 percent indicated that they had such a policy. That is, over two-thirds of the respondents do not inform the individual as a matter of policy that they give personal information to credit grantors. (It should be noted that in a recent Louis Harris Survey 83 percent of the people surveyed feel it is very important to notify employees before releasing any personal information from their employment files.)

Among the recommendations of the Privacy Commission, employers were urged to allow employees to see and copy their personnel records, and to make corrections, when appropriate. The survey revealed that 76 percent of the companies allowed the individual access to their personnel records, and 46 percent gave them the right to copy the record. For supervisor's records, only 16 percent gave access and 9 percent allowed copying. (In the Harris Survey, 86 percent of the people want employees to have access to their supervisor's records.) Overall, 79 percent of the companies permitted employees to place corrections in the record.

In response to the question, "Does your organization have a policy to forward these corrections to anyone who received the incorrect information from you within the past two years," only one-fourth said they took such action. With information being transmitted across the country at the speed of light, an error in one record can be propagated a hundredfold instantaneously. If no effort is made to forward a correction, as apparently is the case in three out of four companies, decisions are being made based on incorrect information—to the detriment of both the recipient organization and the individual. It should be noted that during the hearings of the Privacy Commission the one area most frequently cited for concern was errors in the records of individuals.

Apparently, most employees still are not being told much about their own records. Over two-thirds of the companies responding do not inform their personnel of the types of records maintained on them, how they are used, what they have access to, and what the companies' routine disclosure practices are. While 83 percent of the companies verify or supplement background information collected directly from their personnel, only 25 per-

cent of these companies let the individual see this supplemental information. Fairer information practices would considerably open communications between the corporate recordkeeper and the individual.

Largely because medical information can be misunderstood by an uninformed layman, the Privacy Commission urged that when an employer maintains an employment-related medical record about an individual, that record not be used for an employment decision. Nevertheless, 77 percent of the companies surveyed do use such medical information in making employment-related decisions. And 83 percent of the organizations do not allow their personnel access to their own records.

REACTION TO INACTION

The foregoing sampling of survey readings indicates that much remains to be done to accomplish the objectives set forth in our report to President Carter and the Congress, Personal Privacy in an Information Society. In that report we urged that business be given a reasonable opportunity to adopt voluntarily basic information practices of unintrusiveness, fairness, and confidentiality into their employment policies. At that time, we indicated that mandating such action by legislation was premature and might cause unnecessary hardships. We recommended that business executives be allowed time to act on their own. Subsequently, the President endorsed that recommendation. In view of the survey results, however, it might be argued that inasmuch as business has had the opportunity, new incentives for action should be considered.

JOSEPH R. DES JARDINS
An Employee's Right to Privacy

I would like to consider the nature, extent, and justification of an employee's right to privacy. After a preliminary consideration of the concept of privacy and the nature of the employment relationship, I will examine the following issues:

a. What type of information an employer can legitimately come to know about an employee before and after the hiring decision

b. What access to that information should be

allowed to the employee, to others within the business organization, and to third parties

c. The uses to which such information can justifiably be put

d. What means are permissible for acquiring information about an employee

I

Although much has been written about it, only quite recently has there been a growing consensus about the meaning of "privacy." The right to privacy is a relatively recent development in American legal history. Most discussions trace the legal understanding of privacy to the famous 1890 article by Samuel Warren and Louis Brandeis in the *Harvard Law Review*. The Supreme Court only first recognized a constitutional basis of this right in the 1965 *Griswold v. Connecticut* case.

However, the meaning of "privacy" in these cases has been somewhat confused. Warren and Brandeis referred to privacy as the right "to be let alone," and the Supreme Court settled upon a similar understanding in the *Griswold* case. Upon closer reflection, we can see why such an understanding is unsatisfactory. Being "let alone" is neither necessary nor sufficient for maintaining one's privacy. Consider the case of someone who listens in on a conversation across a room. Such a case would violate privacy but not interfere with a person's right "to be let alone." On the other hand, subliminal advertising, if effective, would violate the right to be "let alone" while explicitly not violating privacy. What has gone wrong is that privacy has been confused with a more general right of liberty or autonomy, and neither captures precisely what seems to be at issue with privacy.[1]

More recently, some writers have focused upon privacy as involving the control of information about oneself. Some think that privacy is simply the right to control personal information. For example, Alan Westin defines privacy as "the right of the individual to determine when, how, and to what extent there should be disclosure of information about himself."[2] However, there are good reasons for being even more precise than this. A bridegroom, for example, could not be said to have a right to withhold all personal information from his prospective bride. A bride coming to know that her future husband has a genetically transmittable disease, for example, would not be a violation of the groom's privacy. Conversely, it can be argued that a person, perhaps weak-willed or gossipy, who freely divulges personal information to strangers has lost his own privacy. These examples suggest that more is involved with privacy than the simple control of personal information by an individual.[3]

In an important and insightful article, George Brenkert has argued that privacy involves a three-place relationship between a person A, some information X, and another person Z.[4] The right of privacy is violated only when Z comes to possess information X *and* no relationship exists between A and Z that would justify Z's coming to know X. Thus, in our earlier example, a bride's coming to know her groom's medical history does not violate the groom's privacy because of the special relationship that exists between brides and grooms. Following Brenkert, I will say that the right of privacy is "the right of individuals, groups, or institutions that access to and information about themselves is limited in certain ways by the relationships in which they exist to others."[5]

II

With this understanding of privacy, we need next to consider the nature of the employment relationship before we can understand the nature and limits of an employee's right of privacy. Traditionally, the employment relationship was conceived in terms of an agent-principal model. In this common-law model, employees were the agents of employers and as such owed to the employer certain obligations. Among these were duties of loyalty, obedience, and confidentiality.[6] This model also granted the employer the right to terminate the employment relationship "at will." It is important to note that the employee's obligations of loyalty, obedience, and confidentiality were *conditions upon* the employment agreement and not themselves contained within that agreement. The distinction is crucial.

As conditions upon the agreement, every employment agreement was subject to them. Employers had no reason to bargain over these obvious benefits. Anyone who desired to work was subject to these duties. The effective result of this was that the only choice open to an employee who disagreed with these duties was to leave his or her job. Given the relationship between employer and employee as an agent-principal relationship, employees can have no right to privacy. Loyalty and obedience apparently would require employees to provide any information requested (under the threat of loss of job), and confidentiality was one-directional—owed to, but not by, the employer. If employees are to claim a right of privacy, a different model of the employer-employee relationship is needed.

It might be argued that given the freedom to leave the job, employees wouldn't lose the right of privacy. Thus, it is not that employees have no privacy rights under the agent-principal model, but rather that upon entering the employment relationship employees voluntarily relinquish this right.

A response to this requires a more precise account of the notion of an employee right. In general, let us say that a right is a morally justified claim either to some good and/or to protection from some harm. Employee rights, therefore, would be morally justified claims made within the employment context. To say that they are morally justified is to say that, *prima facie*, they override claims of expedience and economic efficiency. Thus employees morally cannot be placed in the fundamentally coercive position of having to choose between losing their jobs or relinquishing the good protected by their rights. This would be analogous to a government offering a citizen the choice between losing his citizenship or relinquishing, say, his freedom of religious worship. In such a situation we would say that the citizen was denied his right, not that he had been given a choice to relinquish it voluntarily. This is not to say that, analogous to a right of citizenship, employees have a right to a job, but that being employed, like being a citizen, entails certain presumptive moral claims that cannot be bargained away in return for employment (or citizenship). In this sense, employee rights are to be thought of as conditions upon the employment agreement, and not as elements of that agreement.

If this is correct, then we should not be sur-

prised that the growing interest in employee rights has paralleled a growing dissatisfaction with the agent-principal model of employment. Indeed, this common-law model seems to be giving way to a more straightforward contractual model. Courts, for example, are beginning to understand employment as contractual even when no explicit contract exists.[7] The implications of this for employee rights are significant.

As a way of finding an acceptable model for employment contracts, consider some of the necessary conditions of any valid contract. First, a valid contract must be between free and rational adults. When consent to a contract has been coerced, we say that the contract is invalid (legally, a contract of adhesion). Children and mentally handicapped adults cannot enter into valid contracts, since they cannot fully understand their obligations. Second, contracts must be free from fraud and deception. One cannot be bound by an agreement given under false or misleading circumstances. Third, contracts presuppose a legal system. Unenforceable contracts are not valid contracts.

If I have given my voluntary consent to an agreement that I fully understand, which is free from fraud and deception and which occurs within a legitimate legal context that ensures compliance, I have entered a valid contractual agreement. In the remainder of this paper I examine the implications that viewing the employment relationship as a contract will have for an employee's right of privacy.

III

Stated generally, an employee's right of privacy is violated whenever personal information is collected, stored, or used by an employer in any way or for any purpose irrelevant to or in violation of the contractual relationship that exists between employer and employee. The remainder of this paper attempts to specify this general statement.

What Can Be Known?

Since the contract presupposes the existence of a legal framework, the conditions in the contract should conform to the requirements of the legal system. In particular, obedience to tax, social security, equal opportunity, and health and safety laws will require an employer to collect and store certain information about all employees. The collection, storage, and use of personal information by an employer will not violate an employee's right of privacy when this is done in order to comply with legal requirements, provided (a) this information is used only for those purposes required by the law, and (b) the information is collected only at the time when it is needed (for example, there is no need to require social security numbers until after the hiring decision is made).

There is much other information an employer can come to know about an employee without violating that employee's privacy. Certainly, information necessary to ensure that the contract is voluntary and free from fraud or deception can be required. Accordingly, prior to the contract an employer can require, under the threat of not hiring the potential employee, information about job qualifications, work experience, education background, and other information relevant to the hiring decision. However, there is no reason to request information concerning marital status, arrest records (as opposed to conviction records), credit or other financial data, military records (unless required by law), or such things as religious convictions or sexual and political preferences. This information is irrelevant for deciding whether or not the employee is capable of fulfilling his or her part of the contract.

Only after the employment agreement has been reached does other information about the employee become relevant. Health and insurance plans, for example, may require information about the employee. However, since the contract is already in force, since, in other words, the relationship is grounded upon mutual consent, such information can only be requested with the consent of the employee. Thus, if an employee can choose not to participate in health or insurance packages, the medical examination required for participation cannot be required (although, of course, there may be other reasons to require a medical examination). After the employment agreement has been reached, and the employer has been satisfied with the employee's qualifications for the job, there is a *prima facie* prohibition against collecting evaluative information without the employee's consent. Since most employees will be seeking promotions and pay raises, this consent will likely be given readily. However, as we shall see below, this consent will not legitimize just any means of collecting this information. For example, it may rule out such things as electronic or other covert surveillance, polygraphs, psychological tests, and the unconsented search of an employee's desk, files, or locker.

Access to Employee Information

Since numerous decisions affecting the employment relationship—decisions ranging from hiring and firing to transfers, promotions, discipline, and pay raises—depend upon the information an employer has, fairness dictates that the employee have access to all personal information the employer possesses. Withholding access to this information amounts to binding the employee to a contract that he or she does not fully understand and which, therefore, does not have his or her informed consent. Further, to ensure that the contract is free from fraud and deception, employees should have the right to copy information found in personnel records. They must be allowed to delete information that can be proven incorrect and to answer information that is disputed.

To guarantee further that the employment contract is free from fraud and deception, employees must be informed of the extent of the personal information that the employer possesses. Access rights to information will prove empty unless an employee knows what information exists. For example, many businesses keep personnel files separate from medical files. Granting employees access to personnel records without informing them of the existence of the medical files would be a deceptive practice.

Of course, there can be exceptions to this rule. Files that involve information about other employees, e.g., comparative evaluations, can be excepted from this rule. So, too, access to some medical files might be restricted in some ways. (IBM, for example, grants an employee access to certain medical files only at the discretion of the medical department, due to the sensitive nature of the information involved. However, employees can inspect these files only in the presence of a medical doctor; this rather paternalistic restriction strikes me as unjustified.)

Nevertheless, an employee's right to see, copy, challenge, respond to, and know about personal information possessed by an employer is very strong. Since numerous decisions involving an employee's life prospects are made on the basis of information collected by an employer, fairness requires that the information be accurate, complete, and relevant. To guarantee this, employees must have access to this information, they must be able to respond to and challenge it, and they must be able to correct it when it is mistaken.

Access to information about employees within a firm should be strictly regulated. Not every manager or supervisor is a party to the contractual relationship with every employee. Accordingly, not every manager and supervisor has a right to have access to all employee records. The rule here should be on a "need to know" basis. For example, a supervisor from another department would have no need to know information about employees not in her department. Further, even within departments, the type of information available to supervisors should be limited. While my supervisor has a legitimate right to inspect my performance records or work history, he would presumably have no need to see my medical records.

A more serious issue involves third-party access to employee records. Since the employment contract does not include third parties, generally there should be no third-party access to employee information without the explicit consent of the employee.

Employers often are requested to supply or verify information about an employee's work record and salary for banks, mortgage companies, other credit grantors, and landlords. Release of this information without the employee's consent would be a *prima facie* violation of the employee's right of privacy. Given our definition of privacy, credit grantors or landlords might well be entitled to certain information about an employee. A mortgage company coming to know my salary typically would not involve a violation of my right of privacy. Nevertheless, having a right to the information does not justify all means of acquiring it. The relationship between a person and a mortgage company does not override the relationship between that individual and his or her employer. Accord-

ingly, employers should require an employee's consent before granting third parties access to that employee's files.

There are exceptions to this general rule. There are numerous examples in which a law enforcement agency should have access to an employee's file. However, a law enforcement agency cannot expect an employer to enforce the law or make legal decisions. For this reason, it would be better if warrants were required before a law enforcement agency is given access without consent.

Use of Employee Information

Given the important function that consent plays in the employment contract, we can say that, in general, employers should use personal information about employees only in that use for which consent was granted. For example, social security numbers, which are given to comply with legal requirements, should not be used as employee identification numbers. Medical information released for an insurance claim should not be used during an evaluation for promotion. Information relevant for evaluations should not become the object of office gossip.

More importantly, the information an employer collects about an employee is not a commodity that can be exchanged, sold, or released in the marketplace. For example, some agencies that do background searches for businesses will require as a fee for this service access to that business's employee files. Since they are in the business of buying and selling information, such access can be more valuable than money. Further, in today's world of computerized files, this access can amount to little more than a business granting the agency a set number of uses of its computer access code number. When the agency desires information in the future, all it need do is dial up the business's computer and key in the access code followed by the social security number of the person whose background it desires, and it will have access to all of the information an employer has about an employee without anyone ever leaving his office desk. Releasing information about an employee to any third party, either in response to a credit check or in exchange for money or services, without the explicit consent of the employee is a clear violation of that employee's right of privacy.

Means for Collecting Employee Information

As mentioned earlier, the fact that someone is entitled to information about another person is not sufficient justification to use just any means for acquiring that information. What sorts of limits ought to be placed upon the means used to collect information that an employer is entitled to know?

Again, since consent is crucial for the employment contract, there is a *prima facie* prohibition against any means that bypasses the employee's consent. Specifically, polygraph tests and various psychological tests that seek information in ways that disregard an employee's explicit, conscious answers in favor of some second-level interpretation of those answers should be avoided. Brenkert makes a convincing case for prohibiting polygraph tests totally.[8]

More important, perhaps, is the issue of use of third parties to acquire or confirm information about an employee. Just as employees should be free to do background checks on an employer, so, it might be argued, should employers be allowed to do the same. Since it is impractical for an employer to verify every bit of information about every employee, the use of credit agencies or private investigators are the only reasonable means available for gathering and confirming information.

It is certainly legitimate for a business to verify with a college, for example, the educational background of an employee. (Although this is most reasonable before the hiring decision is made.) On the other hand, interviewing neighbors and landlords and covert surveillance would be more questionable means to acquire information. Since the possible means for acquiring information are numerous and varied, as a general rule employers ought to seek employee consent before using a third party to obtain or verify information. Further, this consent should be specific as to the party doing the investigation and the information being sought or verified. The employee's right to know about and have access to personal information held by such investigators would require that employees be informed of the identity of third parties.

Further, the potential for abuse of privacy rights by third parties (who, after all, have no relationship with the employee) would seem to require that employers be responsible for the actions of such investigators. Employers should be responsible for monitoring the methods of their agents to ensure that an employee's privacy is not violated in the collection or verification of information.

Finally, covert surveillance methods at work should be restricted. Retail clerks and cashiers, for example, are often monitored via cameras or through one-way glass. Certainly employers have a right to protect themselves against theft or abuse of their property. Nevertheless, the innocent clerk also has a right to be protected from such intrusive methods. As a general rule, I would suggest that all employees must be informed of such surveillance procedures and that use of these procedures be restricted to those cases where a just cause for the observation exists. That is, blanket surveillance of all employees would be too intrusive, but observation of a particular department or cash register that has had problems would be reasonable. Since it will be the employer who generally will determine "just cause," prior notification that surveillance might take place would be suggested. It is better to prevent a theft than to catch a thief, if catching involves violating the privacy of innocent people.

Before concluding, something should be said about the numerous consensual exemptions mentioned above. In a number of cases I have suggested that some generally prohibited collection or use of employee information can be overridden with the employee's consent. Given the definition of employee rights sketched above, however, we must recognize that failure to give consent cannot be morally permissible grounds for punitive action (i.e., discipline or firing). Only when the consent is fully voluntary and free from any coercion can an employee's consent justify such exemptions.

Of course, more needs to be done to specify the exact extent of privacy rights in employment. Different employment situations may require different privacy rights. Department store employees likely will have different specific privacy rights than employees of the CIA, for example. Government employees might have more extensive rights than employees in the private sector. But this is just to say that in different jobs, different specific information, access, and use will be relevant. This paper has attempted only to sketch a framework into which the details of particular employment situations can be fit.

NOTES

1. See, for example, Hyman Gross, "Privacy and Autonomy," in *Privacy; Nomos XIII*, edited by J. R. Pennock and J. W. Chapman (New York: Atherton, 1971); and H. J. McCloskey, "Privacy and the Right to Privacy," *Philosophy*, vol. 55, no. 211, (1980), pp. 17–38.

2. See Alan Westin, *Privacy and Freedom*. New York: Atheneum, (1976), p. 7.

3. To see this claim developed, see Richard Wasserstrom, "Privacy," in *Today's Moral Problems*, 2nd ed. Macmillan, 1979, pp. 392–408; and George Brenkert, "Privacy, Poly-graphs and Work," in *Business and Professional Ethics Journal* vol. 1, no. 1 (1982) pp. 19–35.

4. Brenkert, *op. cit.*

5. *Ibid.*, p. 23.

6. For a good discussion of this model, see Phillip Blumberg, "Corporate Responsibility and the Employee's Duty of Loyalty and Obedience: A Preliminary Inquiry," in *Oklahoma Law Review*, vol. 24, no. 3, August 1971.

7. See David Ewing, "Your Right to Fire," in the *Harvard Business Review*, vol. 61, no. 2, (March-April 1983) pp. 32–42.

8. Brenkert, *op. cit.*

GEORGE G. BRENKERT

Privacy, Polygraphs, and Work

The rights of prospective employees have been the subject of considerable dispute, both past and present. In recent years, this dispute has focused on the use of polygraphs to verify the claims which prospective employees make on employment application forms. With employee theft supposedly amounting to approximately ten billion dollars a year, with numerous businesses suffering sizeable losses and even being forced into bankruptcy by employee theft, significant and increasing numbers of employers have turned to the use of polygraphs.[1] Their right to protect their property is in danger, they insist, and the use of the polygraph to detect and weed out the untrustworthy prospective employee is a painless, quick, economical, and legitimate way to defend this right. Critics, however, have questioned both the reliability and validity of polygraphs, as well as objected to the use of polygraphs as demeaning, affronts to human dignity, violations of self-incrimination prohibitions, expressions of employers' mistrust, and violations of privacy.[2] Though there has been a great deal of discussion of the reliability and validity of polygraphs, there has been precious little discussion of the central moral issues at stake. Usually terms such as "dignity," "privacy," and "property rights" are simply bandied about with the hope that some favorable response will be evoked. The present paper seeks to redress this situation by discussing one important aspect of the above dispute—the supposed violation of personal privacy. Indeed, the violation of "a right to privacy" often appears to be the central moral objection to the use of polygraphs. However, the nature and basis of this claim have not yet been clearly established.[3] If they could be, there would be a serious reason to oppose the use of polygraphs on prospective employees.

I

There are three questions which must be faced in the determination of this issue. First, is the nature of the information which polygraphing seeks to verify, information which can be said to violate, or involve the violation of, a person's privacy? Second, does the use of the polygraph itself as the means to corroborate the responses of the job applicant violate the applicant's privacy? Third, even if—for either of the two preceding reasons—the polygraph does violate a person's privacy, might this violation still be justified by the appeal to more weighty reasons, e.g., the defense of property rights?

It might be maintained that only the last two questions are meaningful since "there is no such thing as violating a man's right to privacy by simply knowing something about him"[4]; rather, a violation of one's right to privacy may occur because "we have a right that certain steps shall not be taken to find out facts, and because we have a right that certain uses shall not be made of facts."[5] Thus, it is said that to torture, to extort information by threat, to spy, etc. are all illegitimate ways to obtain information. If one obtains information in these ways one violates various rights of a person—and thereby also one's right to privacy.

If this view is correct, then an employer who knows, or comes to know, certain facts about a prospective employee would not as such violate the prospective employee's right to privacy. Only the use of certain means (e.g., spying or perhaps the polygraph) or the use of these facts in certain ways would violate this privacy. Thus, there could be no violation of rights of privacy by knowing certain information (the first question), only in the manner of obtaining it and the use of it (the second and third questions).

This view is, I believe, implausible when the (private) information concerned is intentionally sought, as it is in the case of polygraphs. In this case, it would seem, there are certain things which people (in their various roles as employers, government officials, physicians, etc.) and institutions (governments and businesses, etc.) ought not to know about individuals, however they might come to know these facts. Indeed, since they ought not to know such facts, those individuals who are the ultimate object of this knowledge may legitimately object to a violation of their rights and demand that steps should be taken to make sure that others do not come to know this information. For example, it would be wrong, however they went about it, for government officials to make it their business to know the details of the sexual practices of each particular citizen. It would be wrong, it has been claimed, for a physician to know by what means a patient intends to pay for the health care administered.[6] Finally, the following case suggests that there is information which an employer ought not

to know about an employee. A warehouse manager had an employee who had confessed to a theft on the job take a polygraph test in order to determine whether others had helped him steal some of the missing goods. The employee answered "no" to each person he was asked about—and the polygraph bore him out, except in the case of one person. Each time he was asked about this person the employee would deny that he had helped him, but each time the polygraph reported a reaction indicative of lying. At last they asked him why each time they raised this person's name there was such a great physiological response. After some hesitation, the thief "took a deep breath and explained that one day a few weeks before, he had walked into the company bathroom and found the fellow in a stall masturbating." The employer's reaction suggests that such information he considered to be information he ought not to know—however he found it out:

I fired the thief, but I never said a word to the other guy. He was a good worker, and that's what counts. But I'll have to tell you this: Every time I saw him for months after that, I'd think about what the thief had told me, and I'd say to myself, "God, I don't have any right to know that."[7]

It is not implausible then that there are various kinds of information which people and institutions ought not to know about individuals.[8] Surely to torture a person to get information or to extort information by threat is to violate a person's right not to be threatened or tortured as well as his right to privacy. But one may do the latter without resorting to such exotic means. One might simply ask the person about the matter which is rightfully private. Some people are weak, gullible, easily persuaded, desirous of pleasing, overly trusting, etc., etc. They might not even know that they need not disclose certain information to this person or that institution. Thus, to hold that our right to privacy of information is violated only when other rights are violated (e.g., rights not to be threatened, or tortured) is to hold an overly positive and optimistic view of the actual condition of the people.

Is it possible then to characterize the nature of privacy such that one might know what kinds of information are rightfully private? If an employer had or sought access to that information he would be said to violate the person's right to privacy. Quite often one suspects that people take the view that information about a person is private in the above sense, if that person does not want it known by others.[9] Thus, the determination of which information is protected by a right to privacy is subjectively, individually, based—it is whatever an individual does not want to be known.

There are, however, good reasons to reject this view. Though we may intelligibly talk about the privacy a person seeks and equate this with a state of affairs he wants or seeks in which he does not share himself and/or information about himself with others, we are not thereby talking about that person's right to privacy. A person might not want passers-by to know that he is bald; he may not want his doctor to know exactly which aches and pains he has; he may not want his neighbors to know about the toxic chemicals he is burying on his land. It does not follow, however, that passers-by, one's doctor, and neighbors violate a person's right to privacy in acquiring such information. It is indeed true that control of information about oneself is important in the formation of the kinds of relationships one wants to have with other people.[10] But it does not follow from this that, just because one wants—or does not want—to have a certain relationship with another person or institution, a certain piece of information which one does not want revealed to that person or institution is therefore private—that others in acquiring it would violate one's right to privacy. In this sense, privacy is not like property which is itself merely a cluster of rights. We may, on the contrary, speak intelligibly of the privacy a person seeks apart from any right to privacy to which a person may be entitled.

On the other hand, one may want some things to be public, to be exposed to the view of all, but this may also be unjustified. The person who exposes his sexual organs at mid-day on a busy downtown street or makes a practice of revealing his most intimate thoughts and feelings to unconcerned strangers may be condemned not simply for the offense he causes others but also for his refusal to treat such matters as private rather than public. Perhaps the latter sounds strange. But one should recall that it was not simply the violation of the rights of others which shocked and disturbed non-members of the late 60's and early 70's youth revolt, but the apparent lack of any sense by those

who partook of that revolt that, with regard to themselves, they ought to treat certain matters as private rather than public.[11] When they were not condemned for not treating certain (personal) matters as private, excuses and explanations were found for their behavior. They were said to be ethically immature or morally blind.[12] My purpose, however, is not to discuss this or any other particular instance in which privacy has been rejected, but to indicate that both an obligation to privacy and a right to privacy constitute the social institution surrounding privacy.

Accordingly, privacy must be seen as part of a complex social practice within which we must distinguish (a) privacy itself, (b) privacy as a value, (c) the right to privacy, and (d) the obligation to privacy which this social institution imposes upon individuals. Consequently, we cannot simply identify "A does not want X to be known" with "Knowledge of X violates A's right to privacy," although the former may be identical with "X is private to A." Similarly, "A wants (or does not care if) X (is) to be made public" is not to be equated with "Knowledge or exposure of X does not violate A's (obligation to) privacy." "X is private to A," "Knowledge or exposure of X violates A's right to privacy," and "Knowledge or exposure of X ought to be kept private by A" are not, therefore, the same, even though on occasion and by extension we may so treat them. To distinguish these notions I will speak of X being "simply private," X being "rightfully private," and X being "obligatorily private."

Upon what basis then, if it is not simply a personal determination, do we maintain that certain information is rightfully private, that the knowledge of it by others constitutes a violation of one's right to privacy? There are two points to make here. First, there is no piece of information about a person which is by itself rightfully private. Information about one's financial concerns may be rightfully private vis-a-vis a stranger or a neighbor, but not vis-a-vis one's banker. The nature of one's sex life may be rightfully private with regard to most people, including future employers, but not to one's psychiatrist, sex therapist, or mate. Accordingly, the right to privacy involves a three-place relation. To say that something is rightfully private is to say that A may withhold from or not share something, X, with Z. Thus to know whether some information, X, about a person or institution, A, is, or ought to be, treated as rightfully private, we must ask about the relationship in which A stands to Z, another person or institution. Because the threefold nature of this relation is not recognized, the view which we have argued is implausible, viz., that "none of us has a right over any fact to the effect that that fact shall not be known by others,"[13] is confused with the view which is plausible, viz., that there is no piece of information about people or institutions which is in itself private. It does not follow from this latter truth that the knowing of a piece of information by some particular person or institution may not be a violation of one's right to privacy—it may or may not be depending upon who or what knows it.

Second, then, to speak of the right to privacy is to speak of the right which individuals, groups, or institutions have that access to and information about themselves is limited in certain ways by the relationships in which they exist to others. In general, the information and access to which a person or institution is entitled with regard to another person and/or institution is that information and access which will enable the former to fulfill, perform, or execute the role the person or institution plays in the particular relationship. All other access and information about the latter is beyond the pale. Thus one cannot be a friend of another unless one knows more about another and has a special access to that person. Similarly, one cannot be a person's lawyer, physician, or barber unless one is entitled to other kinds of knowledge and access. It follows that to speak of one's right to privacy is not simply to speak of one's ability to control information and access to him, since one may be unable to control such access or information acquisition and still be said to have a right to such. Similarly, to speak of one's privacy is not to speak of a claim one makes, since one may not claim or demand that others limit their access to oneself and still have a right that they do so.[14] Such a situation might occur when one is dominated or oppressed by others such that one does not insist on—or claim—the rights one is entitled to. On the other hand, one might also, in certain situations, decide not to invoke one's right to privacy and thus allow others access to oneself which the present relationship might not otherwise permit. It is in this sense that individuals can determine for themselves which others and when others have access to them and to information about them.

II

In order to determine what information might be legitimately private to an individual who seeks employment we must consider the nature of the employer/(prospective) employee relationship. The nature of this relationship depends upon the customs, conventions and rules of the society. These, of course, are in flux at any time—and particularly so in the present case. They may also need revision. Further, the nature of this relationship will depend upon its particular instances—e.g., that of the employer of five workers or of five thousand workers, the kind of work involved, etc. In essence, however, we have a complex relationship in which an employer theoretically contracts with a person(s) to perform certain services from which the employer expects to derive a certain gain for himself. In the course of the employee's performance of these services, the employer entrusts him with certain goods, money, etc.; in return for such services he delivers to the employee a certain remuneration and (perhaps) benefits. The goals of the employer and the employee are not at all, on this account, necessarily the same. The employee expects his remuneration (and benefits) even if the services, though adequately performed, do not result in the end the employer expected. Analogously, the employer expects to derive a certain gain for the services the employee has performed even if the employee is not (fully) satisfied with his work or remuneration. On the other hand, if the employer is significantly unable to achieve the ends sought through the contract with the employee, the latter may not receive his full remuneration (should the employer go bankrupt) and may even lose his job. There is, in short, a complicated mixture of trust and antagonism, connectedness and disparity of ends in the relation between employer and employee.

Given this (brief) characterization of the relationship between employer and employee, the information to which the employer qua employer is entitled about the (prospective) employee is that information which regards his possible acceptable performance of the services for which he might be hired. Without such information the employer could not fulfill the role which present society sanctions. There are two aspects of the information to which the employer is entitled given the employer/employee relationship. On the one hand, this information will relate to and vary in accordance with the services for which the person is to be hired. But in any case, it will be limited by those services and what they require. In short, one aspect of the information to which the employer is entitled is "job relevant" information. Admittedly the criterion of job relevancy is rather vague. Certainly there are few aspects of a person which might not affect his job performance—aspects including his sex life, etc. How then does the "job relevancy" criterion limit the questions asked or the information sought? It does so by limiting the information sought to that which is directly connected with the job description. If a typist is sought, it is job relevant to know whether or not a person can type—typing tests are legitimate. If a store manager is sought, it is relevant to know about his abilities to manage employees, stock, etc. That is, the description of the job is what determines the relevancy of the information to be sought. It is what gives the employer a right to know certain things about the person seeking employment. Accordingly, if a piece of information is not "job relevant" then the employer is not entitled qua employer to know it. Consequently, since sexual practices, political beliefs, associational activities, etc. are not part of the description of most jobs, that is, since they do not directly affect one's job performance, they are not legitimate information for an employer to know in the determination of the hiring of a job applicant.[15]

However, there is a second aspect to this matter. A person must be able not simply to perform a certain activity, or provide a service, but he must also be able to do it in an acceptable manner—i.e., in a manner which is approximately as efficient as others, in an honest manner, and in a manner compatible with others who seek to provide the services for which they were hired. Thus, not simply one's abilities to do a certain job are relevant, but also aspects of one's social and moral character are pertinent. A number of qualifications are needed for the purport of this claim to be clear. First, that a person must be able to work in an acceptable manner is not intended to legitimize the consideration of the prejudices of other employees. It is not legitimate to give weight in moral deliberations to the immoral and/or morally irrelevant beliefs which people hold concerning the characteristics of others. That one's present employees can work at a certain (perhaps exceptional) rate is a legitimate consideration in hiring

other workers. That one's present employees have prejudices against certain religions, sexes, races, political views, etc. is not a morally legitimate consideration. Second, it is not, or should not be, the motives, beliefs, or attitudes underlying the job relevant character traits, e.g., honest, efficient, which are pertinent, but rather the fact that a person does or does not perform according to these desirable character traits. This is not to say, it should be noted, that a person's beliefs and attitudes about the job itself, e.g., how it is best to be done, what one knows or believes about the job, etc., are irrelevant. Rather it is those beliefs, attitudes and motives underlying one's desired character traits which are not relevant. The contract of the employer with the employee is for the latter to perform acceptably certain services—it is not for the employee to have certain underlying beliefs, motives, or attitudes. If I want to buy something from someone, this commercial relation does not entitle me to probe the attitudes, motives, and beliefs of the person beyond his own statements, record of past actions, and the observations of others. Even the used car salesman would correctly object that his right to privacy was being violated if he was required to submit to Rorschach tests, an attitude survey test, truth serums, and/or the polygraph in order to determine his real beliefs about selling cars. Accordingly, why the person acts the way in which he acts ought not to be the concern of the employer. Whether a person is a good working colleague simply because he is congenial, because his ego needs the approval of others, or because he has an oppressive superego is, in this instance, morally irrelevant. What is relevant is whether this person has, by his past actions, given some indication that he may work in a manner compatible with others.

Consequently, a great deal of the information which has been sought in preemployment screening through the use of polygraph tests has violated the privacy of individuals. Instances in which the sex lives, for example, of applicants have been probed are not difficult to find. However, privacy violations have occurred not simply in such generally atypical instances but also in standard situations. To illustrate the range of questions asked prospective employees and the violations of privacy which have occurred we need merely consider a list of some questions which one of the more prominent polygraph firms includes in its current tests:

☐ Have you ever taken any of the following without the advice of a doctor? If Yes, please check: Barbiturates, Speed, LSD, Tranquilizers, Amphetamines, Marijuana, Others.

☐ In the past five years about how many times, if any, have you bet on horse races at the race track?

☐ Do you think that policemen are honest?

☐ Do you ever think about committing a robbery?

☐ Have you been refused credit or a loan in the past five years?

☐ Have you ever consulted a doctor about a mental condition?

☐ Do you think that it is okay to get around the law if you don't actually break it?

☐ Do you enjoy stories of successful crimes and swindles?[16]

Such questions, it follows from the above argument, are for any standard employment violations of one's right to privacy. An employer might ask if a person regularly takes certain narcotic drugs, if he is considering him for a job which requires handling narcotics. An employer might ask if a person has been convicted of a larceny, etc. But whether the person enjoys stories about successful larcenists, whether a person has ever taken any prescription drugs without the advice of a doctor, or whether a person bets on the horses should be considered violations of one's rightful privacy.

The upshot of the argument in the first two sections is, then, that some information can be considered rightfully private to an individual. Such information is rightfully private or not depending on the relationship in which a person stands to another person or institution. In the case of the employer/employee relationship, I have argued that information is rightfully private which does not relate to the acceptable performance of the activities as characterized in the job description. This excludes a good many questions which are presently asked in polygraph tests, but does not, by any means, exclude all such questions. There still remain many questions which an employer might conceivably wish to have verified by the use of the polygraph. Accordingly, I turn in the next section to the question whether the verification of the answers to legitimate questions by the use of the polygraph may be considered a violation

of a person's right to privacy. If it is, then the violation obviously does not stem from the questions themselves but from the procedure, the polygraph test, whereby the answers to those questions are verified.

III

A first reason to believe that use of the polygraph occasions a violation of one's right to privacy is that, even though the questions to be answered are job relevant, some of them will occasion positive, lying reactions which are not necessarily related to any past misdeeds. Rather, the lying reaction indicated by the polygraph may be triggered because of unconscious conflicts, fears and hostilities a person has. It may be occasioned by conscious anxieties over other past activities and observations. Thus, the lying reaction indicated by the polygraph need not positively identify actual lying or the commission of illegal activities. The point, however, is not to question the validity of the polygraph. Rather, the point is that the validity of the polygraph can only be maintained by seeking to clarify whether or not such reactions really indicate lying and the commission of past misdeeds. But this can be done only by the polygraphist further probing into the person's background and inner thoughts. However, inasmuch as the questions can no longer be restrained in this situation by job relevancy considerations, but must explore other areas to which an employer is not necessarily entitled knowledge, to do this will violate a person's right to privacy.

It has been suggested by some polygraphists that if a person has "Something Else" on his mind other than the direct answer to the questions asked, a "something else" which might lead the polygraph to indicate a deceptive answer, the person might, if he so feels inclined,

tell the examiner about this "outside troubling matter" ... but as a special precaution obtain the examiner's promise that the disclosure of this information is secret and ... request that the matter be held in strict confidence. The examiner will comply with your wishes. The examiner does not wish to enter into your personal problems since they tend to complicate the polygraph examination.[17]

What this suggests, however, is that a person go ahead, under the threat of the polygraph indicating that one is lying, and tell the polygraphist matters that are rightfully private. This is supposedly acceptable since one "requests" that it be held in strict confidence. But it surely does not follow that a violation of one's right to privacy does not occur simply because the recipient promises not to pass the information on. If, under some threat, I tell another person something which he has no right to know about me, but I then get his promise that he will treat the information confidentially and that it will not be misused in any way, my right to privacy has still been violated.[18] Accordingly, whether the polygraphist attempts to prevent job applicants from producing misleading deceptive reactions by allowing them to reveal what else is on their minds or probes deceptive reactions once they have occurred to ascertain whether they might not be produced by job irrelevant considerations, he violates the right to privacy of the job applicant.

A second reason why the polygraph must be said to violate a job applicant's right to privacy relates to the monitoring of a person's physiological responses to the questions posed to him. By measuring these responses, the polygraph can supposedly reveal one's mental processes. Now even though the questions posed are legitimate questions, surely a violation of one's right to privacy occurs. Just because I have something which you are entitled to see or know, it does not follow that you can use any means to fulfill that entitlement and not violate my privacy. Consider the instance of two good friends, one of whom has had some dental work done which puts him in a situation such that he can tune in the thoughts and feelings of his friend. Certain facts about, and emotional responses of, his friend—aspects which his friend (we will assume) would usually want to share with him—simply now stream into his head. Even though the friendship relation generally entitles its members to know personal information about the other person, the friend with the dental work is not entitled to such information in this direct and immediate way. This manner of gaining this information simply eliminates any private reserves of the person; it wholly opens his consciousness to the consciousness of another. Surely this would be a violation of his friend's right to privacy, and his

friend would rightfully ask that such dental work be modified. Even friends do not have a right to learn in this manner of each other's inner thoughts and feelings.

Such fancy dental work may, correctly, be said to be rather different from polygraphs. Still the point is that though one is entitled to some information about another, one is not entitled to use any means to get it. But why should the monitoring by an employer or his agent of one's physiological responses to legitimate questions be an invasion of privacy—especially if one has agreed to take the test? There are several reasons.

First, the claim that one freely agrees or consents to take the test is surely, in many cases, disingenuous.[19] Certainly a job applicant who takes the polygraph test is not physically forced or coerced into taking the exam. However, it is quite apparent that if he did not take the test and cooperate during the test, his application for employment would either not be considered at all or would be considered to have a significant negative aspect to it. This is surely but a more subtle form of coercion. And if this be the case, then one cannot say that the person has willingly allowed his reactions to the questions to be monitored. He has consented to do so, but he has consented under coercion. Had he a truly free choice, he would not have done so.

Now the whole point of the polygraph test is, of course, not simply to monitor physiological reactions but to use these responses as clues, indications, or revelations of one's mental processes and acts. The polygraph seeks to make manifest to others one's thoughts and ideas. However, unless we freely consent, we are entitled to the privacy of our thoughts, that is, we have a prima facie right not to have our thoughts exposed by others, even when the information sought is legitimate. Consider such analogous cases as a husband reading his wife's diary, a person going through a friend's desk drawers, a stranger reading personal papers on one's desk, an F.B.I. agent going through one's files. In each of these cases, a person attempts to determine the nature of someone else's thoughts by the use of clues and indications which those thoughts left behind. And, in each of these cases, though we may suppose that the person seeks to confirm answers to legitimate questions, we may also say that, if the affected person's uncoerced consent is not forthcoming, his or her right to privacy is violated. Morally, however, there is no difference between ascertaining the nature of one's thoughts by the use of a polygraph, or reading notes left in a drawer, going through one's diary, etc. Hence, unless there are overriding considerations to consent to such revelations of one's thoughts, the use of the polygraph is a violation of one's right to privacy.[20]

Second, it should be noted that even if a person voluntarily agreed to the polygraph test, it need not follow that there is not a violation of his privacy. It was argued in Section I that there are certain aspects of oneself which are obligatorily private, that is, which one ought to keep private. Accordingly, it may be wrong for one voluntarily to reveal various aspects of oneself to others, even though in so doing one would be responding to legitimate demands. For example, consider a person being interviewed by a health officer who is legitimately seeking information from the person about venereal diseases. Suppose that the person does not simply admit to having such a disease but also—instead of providing a corroborative statement from a physician—reveals the diseased organs. Further, suppose that the health officer is not shocked or offended in any way. The person has been asked legitimate questions, he has acted voluntarily, but still he has violated his own privacy. This is not the kind of access to oneself one ought to afford a bureaucrat. Now it may well be that, analogously, one ought not to allow employers access to one's physiological reactions to legitimate questions, for the reason that such access also violates one's obligatory privacy. To act in this way sets a bad precedent, it signifies that those with power and authority may disregard the privacy of an individual in order to achieve aims of their own. Thus, even if a job applicant readily agreed to reveal certain aspects of himself in a polygraph test, it would not follow without more argument that he was not violating his own privacy.

Finally, if we value privacy not simply as a barrier to the intrusion of others but also as the way by which we define ourselves as separate, autonomous persons, individuals with an integrity which lies at least in part in the ability to make decisions, to give or withhold information and access, then the polygraph strikes at this fundamental value.[21] The polygraph operates by turning part of us over which we have little or no control against the rest of us. If a person were an accomplished yogi, the polygraph would supposedly be useless—since that person's physiological reactions would be fully under his control. The polygraph works because most of us do not have that control. Thus, the polygraph is used to probe people's reactions which they would otherwise protect, not expose to others. It uses part of us to reveal the rest of us. It takes the "shadows" consciousness throws off within us and reproduces them for other people. As such, the use of the polygraph undercuts the decision-making aspect of a person. It circumvents the person. The person says such and such, but his uncontrolled reactions may say something different. He does not know— even when honest—what his reactions might say. Thus it undercuts and demeans that way by which we define ourselves as autonomous persons—in short, it violates our privacy. Suppose one said something to another—but his Siamese and undetached twin, who was given to absolute truth and who correctly knew every thought, past action, and feeling of the person said, "No, he does not really believe that." I think the person would rightfully complain that his twin had better remain silent. Just so, I have a right to complain when my feelings are turned on me. This subtle form of self-incrimination is a form of invading one's privacy. An employer is entitled to know certain facts about one's background, but this relationship does not entitle him—or his agents—to probe one's emotional responses, feelings, and thoughts.

Thus, it follows that even if the only questions asked in a polygraph test are legitimate ones, the use of the polygraph for the screening of job applicants still violates one's privacy. In this case, the violation of privacy stems from the procedure itself, and not the questions. Accordingly, one can see the lameness of the defense of polygraphing which maintains that if a person has nothing to hide, he should not object to the polygraph tests. Such a defense is mistaken at least on two counts. First, just because someone believes something to be private does not mean that he believes that what is private is wrong, something to be ashamed about or to be hidden. Second, the polygraph test has been shown to violate a person's privacy, whether one person has really something to hide or not—whether he is dishonest or not. Consequently, if the question is simply whether polygraphing of prospective employees violates their privacy the answer must be affirmative.

IV

There remains one possible defense of the use of polygraphs for screening prospective employees. This is to admit that such tests violate the applicant's privacy but to maintain that other considerations outweigh this fact. Specifically, in light of the great amount of merchandise and money stolen, the right of the employers to defend their property outweighs the privacy of the applicant. This defense is specious, I believe, and the following arguments seek to show why.

First, surely it would be better if people who steal or are dishonest were not placed in positions of trust. And if the polygraphs were used in only these cases, one might well maintain that the use of the polygraph, though it violates one's privacy, is legitimate and justified. However, the polygraph cannot be so used, obviously, only in these cases—it must be used more broadly on both honest and dishonest applicants. Further, if a polygraph has a 90% validity then out of 1,000 interviewees, a full 100 will be misidentified.[22] Now if 10% of the interviewees are thieves, then 10 out of the 100 will steal, but 90 would not; in addition 90 out of the 900 would be thieves, and supposedly correctly identified. This means that 90 thieves would be correctly identified, 10 thieves would be missed, and 90 honest people would be said not to have cleared the test. Thus, for every thief "caught," one honest person would also be "caught"—the former would be correctly identified as one who would steal, while the latter could not be cleared of the suspicion that he too would steal. The point, then, is that this means of defending property rights is one that excludes not simply thieves but honest people as well—and potentially in equal numbers. Such a procedure certainly appears to constitute not simply a violation of privacy rights, but also, and more gravely, an injustice to those honest people stigmatized as not beyond suspicion and hobbled in their competition with others to get employment. If then using polygraph tests to defend property rights is not simply like preventing a thief from breaking into the safe, but more like keeping a thief from the safe plus binding the leg of an innocent bystander in his competition with others to gain employment, then one may legitimately doubt that this procedure to protect property rights is indeed defensible.[23]

Second, it has been claimed that just as the use of blood tests on suspected drunken drivers and the use of baggage searches at the airport are legitimate, so too is the polygraphing of prospective employees. Both of the former kinds of searches may also be said to violate a person's privacy; still they are taken to be justified whether the appeal is to the general good they produce or to the protection of the rights of other drivers or passengers and airline employees. However, neither the blood test nor the baggage search is really analogous to the use of the polygraph on job applicants. Blood tests are only administered to those drivers who have given police officers reason to believe that they (the drivers) are driving while under the influence of alcohol. The polygraph, however, is not applied only to those suspected of past thefts; it is applied to others as well. Further, the connection between driving while drunk and car accidents is quite direct; it immediately endangers both the safety and lives of others. The connection between polygraph tests of a diverse group of applicants (some honest and some dishonest) and future theft is not nearly so direct nor do the thefts endanger the lives of others. Baggage searches are a different matter. They are similar to polygraphing in that they are required of everyone. They are dissimilar in that they are made because of fears concerning the safety of other people. Further, surely there is a dissimilarity between officials searching one's baggage for lethal objects which one is presently trying to sneak on board, and employers searching one's mind for the true nature of one's past behavior which may or may not lead to future criminal intentions. Finally, there are signs at airports warning people, before they are searched, against carrying weapons on airplanes; such weapons could at that time be declared and sent, without prejudice, with the regular baggage. There is no similar aspect to polygraph tests. Thus, the analogies suggested do not hold. Indeed, they suggest that we allow for a violation of privacy only in very different circumstances than those surrounding the polygraphing of job applicants.

Third, the corporate defense of polygraphs

seems one-sided in the sense that employers would not really desire the universalization of their demands. Suppose that the businesses in a certain industry are trying to get a new government contract. The government, however, has had difficulties with other corporations breaking the rules of other contracts. As a result it has lost large sums of money. In order to prevent this in the present case it says that it is going to set up devices to monitor the reactions of board members and top managers when a questionnaire is sent to them which they must answer. Any business, of course, need not agree to this procedure but if it does then it will be noted in their file regarding this and future government contracts. The questionnaire will include questions about the corporations' past fulfillment of contracts, competency to fulfill the present contract, loopholes used in past contracts, collusion with other companies, etc. The reactions of the managers and board members, as they respond to these questions, will be monitored and a decision on the worthiness of that corporation to receive the contract will be made in part on this basis.

There can be little doubt, I think, that the management and directors of the affected corporations would object to the proposal even though the right of the government to defend itself from the violation of its contracts and serious financial losses is at stake. It would be said to be an unjustified violation of the privacy of the decision-making process in a business; an illegitimate encroachment of the government on free enterprise. But surely if this is the legitimate response for the corporate job applicant, the same kind of response would be legitimate in the case of the individual job applicant.

Finally, it is simply false that there are not other measures which could be taken which could not help resolve the problem of theft. The fact that eighty percent of industry does not use the polygraph is itself suggestive that business does not find itself absolutely forced into the use of polygraphs. It might be objected that that does not indicate that certain industries might need polygraphs more than others—e.g., banks and drug companies more than auto plants and shipyards. But even granting this point there are other measures which businesses can use to avoid the problem of theft. Stricter inventory controls, different kinds of cash registers, educational programs, hot lines, incentives, etc. could all be used. The ques-

tion is whether the employer, management, can be imaginative and innovative enough to move in these directions.

In conclusion, it has been argued that the use of the polygraph to screen job applicants does indeed violate a prospective employee's privacy. First, it is plausible that the privacy of (prospective) employees may be violated by the employer acquiring certain kinds of information about them. Second, using a polygraph an employer may violate an employee's privacy even when the employer seeks the answers to legitimate questions. Third, other moral considerations employers have raised do not appear to outweigh the employee's right to privacy. Accordingly, on balance, a violation of the privacy of a job applicant occurs in the use of the polygraph. This constitutes a serious reason to oppose the use of the polygraph for such purposes.[24]

NOTES

1. Cf. Harlow Unger, "Lie Detectors: Business Needs Them to Avoid Costly Employee Rip-Offs," *Canadian Business*, Vol. 51 (April, 1978), p. 30. Other estimates may be found in "Outlaw Lie-Detector Tests?", *U.S. News & World Report*, Vol. 84, No. 4, (January 1978), p. 45, and Victor Lipman, "New Hiring Tool: Truth Tests," *Parade* (October 7, 1979), p. 19.

2. Both the AFL-CIO and the ACLU have raised these objections to the use of the polygraph for screening job applicants; cf. *AFL-CIO Executive Council Statements and Reports: 1956–1975* (Westport, Conn.: Greenwood Press, 1977), p. 1422. See also ACLU Policy #248.

3. See, for example, Alan F. Westin, *Privacy and Freedom* (New York: Atheneum, 1967), p. 238.

4. Judith Jarvis Thomson, "The Right to Privacy," *Philosophy and Public Affairs*, Vol. IV (Summer, 1975), p. 307.

5. *Ibid.*

6. Cf. "A Model Patient's Bill of Rights," from George J. Annas, *The Rights of Hospital Patients* (New York: Avon Books, 1975), p. 233.

7. Frye Gaillard, "Polygraphs and Privacy," *The Progressive*, Vol. 38 (September, 1974), p. 46.

8. Cf. James Rachels' comment on the importance of the privacy of medical records in "Why Privacy Is Important," *Philosophy and Public Affairs*, Vol. IV (Summer, 1975), p. 324.

9. Alan Westin's definition of privacy suggests this view; cf. Alan F. Westin, *Privacy and Freedom*, p. 7. Also, Rachels' account of privacy suggests this view at times; cf. "Why Privacy Is Important," *Philosophy and Public Affairs*, pp. 326, 329.

10. Rachels emphasizes this point in his article; cf. "Why Privacy Is Important."

11. John W. Chapman discusses the "deadly danger" which "the moral psychology of the young" poses for privacy in his essay "Personality and Privacy." I take it that one of the major theses of his article is that, morally considered, the young ought to treat certain aspects of themselves and their relations to others as private. Cf. John W. Chapman, "Personality and Privacy," in *Privacy*, eds. J. Roland Pennock and John W. Chapman (New York: Atherton Press, 1971).

12. *Ibid.*, pp. 239, 240.

13. Judith Jarvis Thomson, "The Right to Privacy," p. 307.

14. Alan Westin characterizes privacy in terms of the "claim" which people make; cf. *Privacy and Freedom*, p. 7.

15. This would have to be qualified for security jobs and the like.

16. John E. Reid and Associates, *Reid Report* (Chicago: By the author, 1978), passim.

17. John E. Reid and Associates, *The Polygraph Examination* (Chicago: By the author, n.d.), p. 7.

18. It should be further pointed out that the polygraphist/job-applicant relation is not legally or morally a privileged relation. What one tells one's physician one can expect to be treated confidentially. There is no similar expectation that one may entertain in the present case. At most one may hope that as another human being he will keep his promise. On the other hand, the polygraphist is an agent of the employer and responsible to him. There is and can be then no guarantee that the promise of the polygraphist will be kept.

19. The reasons why people do not submit to the polygraph are many and various. Some might have something to hide; others may be scared of the questions, supposing that some of them will not be legitimate; some may feel that they are being treated like criminals; others may fear the jaundiced response of the employer to the applicant's honest answers to legitimate questions; finally some may even object to the polygraph on moral grounds, e.g., it violates one's right to privacy.

20. See Section IV below.

21. Cf. Jeffrey H. Reiman, "Privacy, Intimacy, and Personhood," *Philosophy and Public Affairs*, Vol. VI (Fall, 1976).

22. Estimates of the validity of the polygraph range widely. Professor David Lykken has been reported as maintaining that the most prevalent polygraph test is correct only two-thirds of the time (cf. Bennett H. Beach, "Blood, Sweat and Fears," *Time*, September 8, 1980, p. 44). A similar figure of seventy percent is reported by Richard S. Sternbach et al., "Don't Trust the Lie Detector," *Harvard Business Review*, Vol. XL (Nov.-Dec., 1962), p. 130. Operators of polygraphs, however, report figures as high as 95% accuracy; cf. Sternbach, p. 129.

23. This argument is suggested by a similar argument in David T. Lykken, "Guilty-Knowledge Test: The Right Way to Use a Lie Detector," *Psychology Today*, (March, 1975), p. 60.

24. I wish to thank the following for their helpful comments on earlier versions of the present paper: Tom Donaldson, Norman Gillespie, Ken Goodpaster, Betsy Postow, William Tolhurst, and the editors of the *Business & Professional Ethics Journal.*

CHAPTER SIX
Study Questions

1. Some people claim that an emphasis upon privacy will reinforce individualism and selfishness and work against cooperative community values. Do you think that too much privacy can be a bad thing?

2. Do you think that it is legitimate to use social security numbers as identification numbers? What sort of considerations would count against this?

3. Should a file that contains evaluations of an employee by supervisors be open to inspection? Why or why not? Should letters of recommendation be kept confidential—even kept from the person being recommended?

4. What information do you believe your employer actually knows about you? What is known by your school? Your bank?

5. Do you believe that computer technology represents an increased threat to your privacy, or greater security? How so, exactly?

6. Do you believe that an employer can legitimately know about an employee's after-hours activities? Do your views change if the employee is salaried rather than on an hourly wage?

CHAPTER SEVEN

*P*ARTICIPATION

CASE STUDY

Participation at General Foods Topeka Plant
Daniel Zwerdling

The first thing you notice when you visit the General Foods Gravy Train plant, set against a backdrop of grain elevators on the outskirts of Topeka, is not the modern decor, not the carpeting, not the single entrance for production workers and managers alike—but the smell. The odor of tallow, cooked and extruded into tons of Gravy Train at a pressure of 120 pounds per square inch, permeates the building, even the workers' skin. But many workers at the General Foods plant say the stink of tallow has been a small price to pay for the benefits of working in one of the first, and most widely publicized "humanized" factories in the nation.

General Foods calls it a "sociotechnical system," a "total system"—more specifically, "the Topeka System." The factory, which started operating in 1971, was designed on the drawing boards to allow employees a considerable degree of freedom in operating the production process. Teams of workers manage the production process day to day, with minimal supervision by management. The teams participate in hiring fellow workers and firing them, and in resolving workplace grievances. Workers at Topeka aren't paid according to their seniority or by a single job they were hired to perform—they're paid according to how many different jobs they learn. The Topeka workers can rotate from unloading a boxcar one day to testing the dog food in the quality control laboratory the next. By traditional corporate measures, the workers have been an unusually productive and satisfied group. "Our data . . . show high levels of satisfaction and involvement in all parts of the organization," a University of Michigan researcher has reported. "In fact they show the highest levels we have found in any organization we have sampled."

The General Foods Topeka System raises important questions about the possibilities and limits of a "humanized" plant in which management unilaterally imposes a "participation" structure on the workers. The workers at Topeka do not own the plant, as the miners at the Vermont Asbestos Group do, and so they have no ultimate control over the structure and direction of the operation. Yet the workers at Topeka have more day-to-day freedom and control over their jobs than the asbestos miners do.

In the long run, the Topeka System is generating potentially serious conflicts. Since the management created the system of workers' freedom and participation, the management can take it away. Observers report that new managers who are not committed to the "system" have been taking charge of the operation, and pursuing profits and production to the detriment of the "quality of work life." The Topeka System, some observers report, is eroding. More and more workers are becoming resentful toward management and dissatisfied with their jobs; the team spirit is breaking down. The entire plant may revert to a traditional autocratic managerial workstyle, observers say, unless management reverses the tide.

Curing Labor Ills. The Topeka System was created as an antidote to mounting labor and production troubles which had plagued other General Foods plants. In 1969, researcher Michael Brimm writes, General Foods was riding "the crest of a pet food business." National demand exceeded the corporation's capacity to produce. Yet its only pet food plant, in Kankakee, Illinois, was fraught with union-management conflict.

The factory suffered racial conflicts, episodes of worker violence toward supervisors, frequent worker grievances and even sabotage (an entire day's production had to be scrapped after an employee threw green dye into the dog food vat). The manager of the plant, Lyman Ketchum, was assigned by the corporation to a special team of managers to design a new dog food plant. The goal, as Ketchum wrote in December 1969, was to find "a better way to utilize the full potential of the workers and managers." The planners would "erase all

the 'givens' and begin anew to devise a management system most applicable to today's and tomorrow's environment."

At International Group Plans, the president revamped the traditional management structure upside down to accomplish political and philosophical goals. At Harman International Industries, the management and union devised the joint workplace participation program to improve the "quality of work life"—and emphasized that increasing productivity was NOT a goal. But the General Foods official planning document, Topeka Organization Systems and Development, suggested that increasing profits was a major objective of the new work system. The new system of management, encouraging more worker participation, was more a strategy toward achieving more efficient production than it was a goal in itself. "If business conditions are favorable, then human potential combined with system characteristics will yield cost and quality benefits," the corporate document said. The "objective" of the new system would be "Lowest possible cost of goods with no sacrifice of product quality, service to the trade, or marketing flexibility."

"To more fully utilize human resources is morally and ethically the right thing to do," the document noted; it also pointed out that "Yesterday's employees that were depersonalized by organizations merely became apathetic, but generally compliant workers or supervisors or managers. But today's employees who become alienated by the organization are more likely to actively challenge or even attack the organization." The corporate document continued: "Humans will best respond (be productive) when there exists a high feeling of self-worth by employee, and employee identification with success of the total organization ... an organization which more fully utilizes human potential of employees can pay off in dollars and cents."

The General Foods team selected Topeka as home for the new plant, Brimm writes, because the town gave the factory easy access to rail transportation and grain elevators, plenty of room for plant expansion, and a good supply of labor. The executive planners noted that the rural Topeka area was "free of the racial strife and urban-industrial decay" which plagued the Kankakee factory. "No power groups"—meaning no unions—"will exist within the organization that creates an anti-management posture," the planning document said. Furthermore, the Topeka location would provide "relatively high physical isolation between Topeka and the other parts of the firm." This isolation, the planners felt, would permit the unorthodox new work system to take root and grow, unfettered by the skeptical scrutiny of traditional-style executives in the White Plains, New York headquarters.

Satisfying Ego Needs. With all this in mind, the planners went about designing their new Topeka System. The layout, the equipment, even the decor would be aimed at satisfying human needs. "People have 'ego' needs," the planners wrote. "They want self-esteem, sense of accomplishment, autonomy, increasing knowledge and skill . . . People have 'social' needs. They enjoy team membership and teamwork . . . People have certain security needs. They want reasonable income and employment security, and want to be assured against arbitrary and unfair treatment." In addition, "People want to be able to identify with products they produce and firms that employ them."

Workers in the new plant, the planners decided, would have "power/voice . . . in things affecting them," such as pay and benefits, hiring and firing, disciplining and counseling fellow workers, training and promotion, job assignments, scheduling production, solving workplace problems, selecting and modifying equipment. In the new plant there would be "fair pay and benefits . . . normal status differentials minimized . . . opportunity to learn, contribute and grow . . . good working conditions . . . pay based on knowledge rather than a special job assignment . . . minimum threat of layoff . . . honest/supportive management . . . elimination of some and sharing of remaining

distasteful work . . . willingness to examine anything and change it if it doesn't fit."

The corporate planners took great care selecting employees who they felt could make the system work. Applicants for team leaders—whom the planners intended to become "*not* a foreman or supervisor . . . (but) a kind of coach"—had to pass an intensive regimen of interviews, tests, "role playing exercises" and "criticism-self-criticism" sessions. These psychological exercises, says Brimm, were designed to test the applicants' team spirit, resourcefulness, flexibility, and emotional openness. Once the six team leaders were selected, they spent four months training. More than 600 persons who applied to work on the production lines in the plant were also screened by intensive testing; finalists passed through the same kinds of role-playing techniques used to select the team leaders. The final group of 63 employees "reflected scores on general intelligence, manual dexterity, mechanical and electrical aptitude which placed them above average workers for Kansas industry and other Topeka manufacturing operations," researcher Brimm reports. Twenty percent of the new production workers had held supervisory or higher paying positions at their previous jobs; they had been attracted to General Foods by the promise of a more satisfying work life. The new employees, Brimm reports, considered themselves to be a worker "elite."

Life in the Plant. The Topeka System begins at the factory parking lot. The traditional "reserved" parking spaces which gave managers status were eliminated; workers and managers share the same spaces, and enter the plant through the same front door. The carpeting in the workers' locker rooms is the same as the carpeting in the managerial offices. The plant manager's office isn't hidden from the workers, but looks out onto the production floor through large windows—to convey the sense that he works *with* the rank and file employees in the plant, rather than *over* them.

The workers in the factory are divided into two teams of seven to 14 members, on each of three shifts. One team handles the dog food processing: the workers unload the grains, meat by-products, chemical nutrients and organic tallows from the railroad cars, premix chemical dyes and nutrients in large hoppers, transform the ingredients into dog food in enormous high-pressure cookers, and then test it for moisture, density and color in a sophisticated lab. The second team packages the dog food: the workers weigh the proper amount into individual sacks, tie the sacks into large bales, hoist the bales onto pallets, and load the pallets onto boxcars ready for shipping across the country.

When participants at the Third International Conference on Self-Management asked workers from the Topeka factory, "Who really runs the plant?" one employee answered, "As far as operation and running of the plant, the people do. The day-to-day decisions are made by the people in the plant." The corporate planners designed the factory to give workers control over production processes which could actually have been automated. For instance, the factory could have been designed so that engineers could control the mixing and cooking process from a central command center. Instead, individual operators who have never had formal training operate enormous and complex machines, varying moisture, fat content, density, heat and other critical variables on their own initiative.

The factory could have hired special lab technicians to perform quality control evaluations. Instead, rank and file workers are trained to work in the "large, well-equipped modern laboratory, dazzling in its sophistication," as Brimm describes it. Workers weigh dog food samples, titrate solutions, extract and measure moisture, and determine on their own, without a supervisor's direction, whether the day's production of dog food is good enough to be shipped to market. Rank and file workers have the power to condemn whole batches of the dog food. "The team leader said to ship the product like this," one worker told Brimm, pointing to what he and fellow workers had analyzed to be inferior product. "I just

waited till he left and scrapped until we got a good product." In a conventional factory, workers would be classified as process operators, mechanics, quality control technicians, cleaners, boiler operators, grain unloaders—but the Topeka plant workers rotate from job to job as they wish, with their fellow team members' approval. "One day I came in and worked the 10-pound line," bagging 10-pound sacks of dog food, a worker told Brimm. "The next day I worked in the lab." Workers are hired at a base starting rate, regardless of their previous job experience or expertise; once they master their first job, usually the most grueling and boring, such as hoisting bales on wooden pallets, they earn the "first-job" rate. When a worker wants to learn a new job, he or she applies to the fellow teammates. If the team members feel the member is ready to move on—the worker is judged not only by technical proficiency but by whether he or she is "willing to assist others and work hard toward the improvement of his team," according to the plant manual—they vote to "promote" the applicant to a new job. Each job takes about four to seven months to master. When a worker learns all the jobs within a team, he or she earns the "team" rate.

Workers who wish can learn all the jobs in the plant, and earn the "plant rate," about 50 percent more money per hour than the base pay. No matter what the job, workers perform most of their own maintenance work—in fact, workers can shut down the entire production line on their own initiative, if they feel the machines need work. The workers start up production on their own, too. One observer reported arriving at the factory one night at midnight. The graveyard shift was starting production—there were no managers, not even a team leader, in the plant.

Hiring and Firing.   The workers also play an important role in hiring fellow workers. When a team has a job opening—which occurs seldom according to employees, since the turnover has remained at 10 percent per year or lower—the entire team, or perhaps a subcommittee of the team, interviews and screens the applicants and votes on a final choice. Technically, the team leaders have the final say, but workers at Topeka say the team's vote usually stands. "Team elections of individuals were normally made on the criterion, 'Would you want to have a beer with this guy?' " Brimm reports. Applicants who didn't meet the test were considered "a bad system fit."

The teams also have handled discipline, including firing fellow employees. In some cases, observers report, the teams try to resolve disciplinary problems outside the team meetings, through informal talks with "problem" workers or through other kinds of peer pressure. If a worker arrived late to work, Brimm reports, "The unstated question, 'Where were you?' followed the offender until he had exonerated himself." Or, when workers feel one of their teammates has not been performing well, they may bring it up at the meeting before or after the shift.

"We have a regularly scheduled team meeting once a week," employee Karen Cooper told the Third International Conference on Self-Management. "Most of the time we just express the fact that we think it's a concern, to the person, and see what his reaction is. That makes a big difference on where you go. If his reaction is 'So what?' then the response might be, 'We think you need to take some time off [without pay] to think about your attitude.' "

The General Foods employees at the Third International Conference stressed that the teams, not the team leaders, usually impose the disciplinary sanctions on the workers. "What really works the best," Karen Cooper told the conference, "is when we ask a person what *he* thinks we should do with him. You'd be surprised how strict they are on themselves. We had one guy who was very, very bad about coming in late. The problem with coming in late is that we work with a minimum amount of people, and if we're one person short that doubles the work of the people working with him. We had a couple of meetings with him and we finally had all we could take, and

we asked him what he would do in our situation. He said, 'If it was me, one more time and that would be it.' He set that restriction on himself." Another worker who chronically came to work late, the employees at the conference said, told his team members they should demand him to bring a doctor's excuse next time he was late to work—or fire him.

Few workers have been fired; the first two employees who were fired were also black, which generated considerable tension in the plant and charges of racism. Although the system of discipline by peers is democratic at the team level, the system gives workers no structural appeal—no grievance process, no hearing by peers. Workers at the conference said that fellow employees who feel they have been unfairly disciplined can complain informally to their team leader and then to the manufacturing operations manager: "If that doesn't make you feel any better you can go to the plant manager," one employee told the conference, "and if that doesn't satisfy you, well, you can go get a lawyer." The Topeka employees at the conference dismissed the possibility that a team punishment might not be justified. "Chances are if you get punished or fired, you deserve it," one worker said.

According to Brimm, production workers not only focus their energies on disciplining each other, but also are bold in hashing out dissatisfactions with their team leaders. "Team members saw the most pressing disciplinary issues as those concerning team leaders," Brimm writes. "Over a two-week period, three team leaders were confronted by their groups regarding the frenzied competition which had developed within the management group" over which team could produce more dog food. One worker, says Brimm, reprimanded his team leader, "We don't make any more dog food when you pace up and down."

Although worker powers at Topeka have been limited mainly to the day-to-day production process, workers have been given some input in *plant*-level decisions. For instance, when equipment salesmen visit the plant they don't do business with the plant manager but with the workers who will actually be using the machines. The workers have access to production information such as sales, output, and communications from product receivers. Each year the management asks the worker teams what level production they think they can achieve, and what equipment they might need to achieve it. The workers draft proposals for pay raises from year to year, although as one worker told the Third International Conference on Self-Management, "the final say is with the corporate people in White Plains."

Getting Satisfaction.   Most observers agree that the Topeka System has had positive effects, both on the workers and on plant profits. According to General Foods consultant Richard Walton, who helped design the factory, the factory operated for almost four years without a single lost-time accident; only 70 workers have been producing the levels of output which corporate engineers had expected 110 workers would be needed to produce. Absenteeism has remained below 1.5 percent, and the factory has achieved unit costs about 5 percent less than at General Foods' conventional plants, saving about $1 million per year.

Many observers say the economical achievements stem from the fact that Topeka System workers are "satisfied"—at least, considerably more satisfied than workers at most General Foods plants. When Ford Foundation researcher Robert Schrank visited the factory in 1973 he found "high levels of worker participation, freedom to communicate, expressions of warmth, minimization of status distinction, human dignity, commitment and individual self-esteem."

One effect of the plant structure, many workers say, is increased worker cooperation and comraderie. When a boxcar of heavy sacks rolled in, Brimm reports, all the members of the processing team including team leader pitched in to help with the exhausting chore. Employees walking by the packaging line would usually help out tying some bales before moving on to their own jobs. When a worker accidentally spilled dog food or raw

ingredients, Brimm says, the mess was "seldom cleaned up without the development of an ad hoc team of volunteers."

Workers at Topeka, observers say, seem to care about each other. Since there is no formal job training program, for example, a worker who wants to learn a new job must be trained by a more experienced worker. "I have encountered few teachers and colleagues," says Harvard-educated Brimm, "who exhibit the patience, skill and sensitivity which I observed and experienced among this work force." Brimm and other researchers have noted there is a high level of emotional interaction among workers at the plant: workers counsel each other, or confront each other openly, in the lunchroom, at the lounge pool table, or perhaps in a team meeting. Occasionally, Brimm reports, team meetings developed into intense, emotional sessions "which paralleled the most intense encounters which I have seen emerge from training [T] groups."

Outside Lives.   This atmosphere has reportedly affected the workers' personal lives outside the factory door. "Something is wrong," one worker told Brimm, "when I can talk openly here at work in front of 14 other people and I get home and can't be open with my wife." "I began to be more open at home talking about my feelings and things like that," another employee told Brimm. "My wife would look at me like I was crazy."

Under the Topeka System, observers report, workers who had been tied to a single machine most of their work lives, at another factory, began learning new skills as they rotated from one job to another. It elevated their expectations, and enabled them to look at their work with a broader perspective. "Individuals who now complain openly about the content of a job design are those who passively accepted a more narrow, repetitive task in previous employment," according to Brimm.

The rotation and cross-training among jobs also has helped to break down the hierarchy of seniority and job ratings which separates one worker from another at conventional plants. In this atmosphere, Brimm observes, the workers talk about "my machine" and "our plant" with a sense of pride. "Ninety-five percent of the employees are sold on the system," employee Jim Weaver told researcher David Jenkins. "We've had our problems, but we can sit down and work them out. I like General Foods. It's the only job I ever had where I felt I was part of the company. General Foods put responsibility on me and I accept it . . . I feel wanted." Before the Topeka System came along, Weaver said, "I wouldn't have thought it possible to find this many people who took such pride in their job."

A Good Thing Goes Bad. For the first several years, according to most accounts, the Topeka System flourished. Team decision-making was an important focus of the plant's operation, workers exercised a high degree of autonomy on their jobs, and the vast majority of workers enthusiastically supported the system, their jobs and the corporation.

In the past several years, however, the plant operations and the employees' mood have started to change. The "positive work culture," reports Richard Walton, describing a November 1976 visit, "had declined. Not a steep decline, rather a moderate erosion. By general agreement it is still a very productive plant, and a superior place to work, but the 'quality of work life' had slipped. And while the majority still supported—by their own behavior— the unique strengths of the 'Topeka System,' an increasing minority did not."

Walton reports that some of the important qualities of the Topeka System—including openness and candor among workers and managers; team decision-making and team cooperation; the workers' perceived influence on plant policy; confidence in the corporation and cooperation among shifts—have begun to crumble.

One of the most important changes, both Walton and Brimm have reported, is that worker teams are controlling and influencing fewer and fewer decisions as the plant is becoming more conventionally hierarchical. During the first few years the teams usually met at least once per week, sometimes several times a week, to discuss issues ranging from hiring new members to confronting interpersonal conflicts, to voting on changes in the production line. Although General Foods workers at the Third International Conference on Self-Management reported that some teams still meet weekly, often the meetings are "as simple as to say what we're expected to be doing next week or the fact there's going to be a company picnic," one employee told the conference— management says they don't have time to spend in the luxury of meetings. The major reason: the corporate headquarters launched a "prolonged push for maximum production," says Walton, which "had a dramatically negative effect." The teams increasingly suppress discussions of controversial and emotion-laden issues, in order to "get to work."

According to Brimm, "decisions were surrendered less frequently to equipment operators and some previous decentralization was reversed. . . . Shifts which had once begun with 'Who's going to work the 25-pound (bagging) line?' were now hastened along with 'Why don't John, Fred and Bill start up the 25-pound line?' " Brimm reports that team leaders have assumed an increasingly autocratic, managerial role—cancelling workers' coffee breaks, docking a worker's pay when he returned late from a company softball game, ordering workers in the quality control lab to approve dog food which they believed was not good enough quality to be shipped—all in the name of increased production. Quality has sometimes suffered, Walton agrees, "undermining one source of (workers') pride."

Observers report that other important changes have soured the "quality of work life" at the Topeka plant. For instance, between 1973 and 1976, according to Walton, three of the four managers who had been most responsible for launching the Topeka System left General Foods. One of them was the popular plant manager, whom workers trusted and felt would "go to bat" for them, as Walton describes it; he was replaced by a manager "seen as philosophically unsympathetic to Topeka, raising doubts about the hierarchy's understanding or commitment to the Topeka innovation."

Another development which soured worker attitudes was the construction of a new canned dog food plant next door. During the first year, the canned product sold far worse than corporate planners had expected, and there were two large layoffs. In 1976, sales zoomed, however, and in an effort to maximize production, Walton writes, "management chose to defer the introduction of many aspects of the work structure." Management's seemingly harsh and conventional methods of handling the new plant convinced many workers in the dry food plant that the management commitment to the "Topeka System" was quickly waning. This deepened the workers' already growing insecurity and mistrust.

"They have a very tight schedule producing nationwide," team leader Warren Lynch told the Third International Conference on Self-Management. "So business gets in the way of taking time to stop and deal with things."

Sources

Ian Michael Brimm, *Analytical Perspectives in Organizational Behavior: A Study of an Organizational Innovation*, 1975 Dissertation, Xerox University Microfilms, Ann Arbor, Michigan.

Richard Walton, "Work Innovations at Topeka: Six Years After," draft manuscript for the *Journal of Applied Behavioral Science*, dated December 12, 1976.

"Topeka Organization and Systems Development," document by the General Foods Corporation, December 30, 1969. Quoted in Brimm.

Lyman Ketchum, paper presented at "Humanizing of Work Symposium," American Association for the Advancement of Science Annual Meeting, December 27, 1971.

Ketchum, statement before the Senate Subcommittee on Employment, Manpower and Poverty, July 26, 1972.

"Workers Share Helm," by Alta Huff, *Topeka Capital-Journal*, August 6, 1972.

David Jenkins, *Job Power*, 1973, Doubleday.

"'Worker Freedom' Experiments Appear Successful," by Jack Houston, *Chicago Tribune*, October 21, 1973.

"Stonewalling Plant Democracy," *Business Week*, March 28, 1977.

Personal interviews by Daniel Zwerdling with employees of the General Foods Topeka plant, at the Third International Conference on Self-Management.

Introduction

WORKER PARTICIPATION IN industrial decision making is a topic about which there is much misunderstanding. For example, discussions of employee participation often confuse participation with broad programs aimed at improving the quality of working life. While it is true that worker participation can improve the lot of the worker, quality of work life programs also include such "improvements" as brightly colored work environments, noise reduction, recreational facilities, and the like. Employee participation programs, however, have much more social and political significance for the character of employment because they often involve changes in the power structures of corporate governance.

Because it does concern the distribution of power in the workplace, worker participation is a very controversial issue for both management and nonmanagement employees alike. This chapter will present discussions of worker participation, in order to help the reader analyze that controversy and arrive at a reasonable position for himself or herself.

Notice that this chapter differs from many of the others because there is no explicit discussion here of government regulation of industry. The absence of issues dealing with government activity does not mean that regulation is not germane to this topic. (Government can become involved in worker participation, for example, by mandating that corporations allow employee representatives to sit on the company boards of directors, as is the case in Sweden and West Germany.) Instead, the absence of readings concerning the role of government indicates that in North America the debate over employee participation is at a very early stage. An analysis of that debate, then, is served better by a focus on issues other than those dealing with the proper sphere of government activity. Thus the readings in this chapter focus on three not always distinct issues: the meaning, the justification, and the feasibility of employee participation in the shaping of corporate policy.

Employee participation, in general, refers to the ability of all employees to influence corporate policy decisions. The possible ways in which such influence can be exercised vary widely, however. The opening case material from Daniel Zwerdling's *Workplace Democracy* presents one detailed example of how ordinary employees can participate in policy matters. The articles by Edward Greenberg and Paul Blumberg also present the reader with actual instances of employee participation. A more general description of the varieties of participation is provided by John McCall, who suggests that the variations are functions both of differences in the institutional authority of the mechanisms for participation and differences in the kinds of issues addressed by those mechanisms. The reader should attempt to understand the differences between the various approaches to participation on the basis of these articles, since that understanding is crucial for discussions of the justification and the feasibility of worker participation.

Questions about the justification of rights for all employees to participate in corporate policy involve arguments both for and against such rights. The article by Edward Greenberg implicitly supports a worker right to participate, because he sees workers suffering severe negative consequences when they lack control over their working lives. The article by John McCall is more explicit in its argument that there are five moral reasons that provide presumptive support for worker rights to participate. All of these reasons derive from a need to protect centrally important human goods; the arguments suggest that, in practice, protection for these goods is most effective when there are strong forms of employee participation.

McCall also considers some traditional arguments against participation. These opposing arguments derive from management or owner interests that are seen to be in conflict with employee participation in corporate decisions. McCall suggests, however, that these interests cannot possess the moral weight necessary to override the presumptive support for participation.

Since common opinion apparently holds that owners and managers have a moral right to decide how the corporation should be run, the reader should assess the cogency of those arguments carefully. Such an assessment of the arguments supporting participation depends in part on the practicality of employee participation. The reader should consider the feasibility of employee participation by raising the following questions: How does the economic performance of firms with participation programs compare with the performance of firms without such programs? Are workers competent to make intelligent and informed policy decisions? Will employees have any desire to participate in board-level decisions? In the process of answering these questions, readers should consider Daniel Zwerdling's analysis (in the first text selection of this chapter) concerning what went wrong with the General Foods Topeka experiment.

Since society seems committed to union collective bargaining as an effective way of protecting the economic interests of nonmanagement employees, the feasibility of participation will also depend on the relationship between participation programs and union activities; can unions alone adequately represent worker interests? Do participation programs threaten or strengthen the power of unions?

Edward Greenberg's article provides careful empirical support for a view that increased worker satisfaction is a function of the employee's ability to control his or her work life. Presumably, workers with higher job satisfaction will be more highly motivated and will be more productive. Greenberg's article, then, provides some of the research needed for answering questions about the economic efficiency of cooperative decision making. Greenberg's research also shows that participation may prevent seriously damaging psychological conditions for workers.

Herbert Northrup and G. David Garson engage the reader in a debate over the need for and the advisability of worker participation as a means for representing employees' interests. Northrup argues that in the United States, unions alone can provide workers with enough voice in the running of the corporation, and he suggests that unionized employees have little desire to become involved in direct management of the corporation. Moreover, Northrup believes that worker co-determination is often economically inefficient, and that it unjustifiably interferes with the right of shareholders to control policy. Northrup apparently would argue that this shareholder right to control policy exists because it is the shareholders' money that is at risk in the corporation. The reader should compare this defense of the owners' right to control property with McCall's argument that ownership control needs to be limited by a concern for the basic well-being of employees.

G. David Garson disputes Northrup's claim that unions can adequately represent workers through collective bargaining. Garson clearly identifies eight reasons for his disagreement with Northrup. However, Garson does not claim that union representation of employees is totally ineffectual; in fact, he believes that both internal participation and union representation are necessary for protecting employees.

The final article by Paul Blumberg discusses the possibility of simultaneous union power and employee participation. Many union supporters are favorably disposed towards labor's participation in lower-level decision making. However, union activists often worry that labor's participation at the upper levels of corporate authority will threaten the powers of the union as an adversary to management's interests. For example, some would fear that union members on corporate boards will assume the perspective of management. Thus, employee participation through such union representatives on the board might undermine the power of unions in collective bargaining. Interestingly, this fear is exactly the opposite of Northrup's fear that participation on corporate boards would enhance union power.

Paul Blumberg presents an argument that offers suggestions for how unions and internal mechanisms of participation can function smoothly and efficiently together. Blumberg's analysis derives from his criticism of Hugh Clegg, a renowned British industrial relations specialist. Clegg believed that industrial democracy where worker interests have effective representation is best achieved when unions operate outside of the corporation. He criticized schemes that involve unions directly in the internal management of the firm because he felt that such schemes destroyed the most effective forms of worker representation. Blumberg disputes Clegg's understanding of democracy, and he argues that internal worker participation can operate effectively if the adversarial functions of the union are isolated from the union's role in corporate management. Note that if this separation of functions is possible, Blumberg may have provided some response to Northrup's worry that union representation on internal management bodies will lead to inefficiency and inordinate union power.

DANIEL ZWERDLING

Participation at General Foods Topeka Plant: What Went Wrong?

WHAT'S TO BLAME?

Some of the changes in the Topeka System have been the product of personality changes: new managers, new team leaders and new employees who don't share the enthusiasm of the original "pioneers" have moved into the plant, dampening the system's spirit. Other changes which are souring the climate, according to some observers, seem to be rooted in the very nature of the General Foods experiment.

From the beginning, Brimm argues, it was a unilateral *management* experiment: management granted to the employees certain carefully planned and limited freedoms and powers. These freedoms and powers gave the employees more autonomy while performing their jobs from day-to-day, but they did not change the fundamental nature of the management-worker relationship. When workers have exercised the power to make decisions, Brimm argues, the kinds of decisions they make are often "meaningless." "The manager who asks 'How will we divide the work today to reach our goals of 100 tons of output?' yields a meaningless choice to the team," argues Brimm. "The question has not opened meaningful choices as to quantity of product, nature of product or possible technology." Furthermore, workers have enjoyed the power to make their own decisions, Brimm points out, only as long as those decisions mimic what management would have decided on its own. Warren Lynch, team leader at Topeka, told the Third International Conference on Self-Management: "If any time in my judgement I feel the team is not handling an issue correctly, I can make the decision over and above the team." In one instance, one employee told the Conference, "A guy [on the team] was up for a higher [pay] rate and the team

voted to give it to him. But Warren overruled us and said 'no way'. We got together again and decided Warren was correct."

"You get right down to the fact that they [management] can do whatever they want," said employee Tom Zappa. "They run it. They own it. What's to stop them? They can do whatever they want. I can't stop them. What right do I have? I mean, they didn't even have to let us do this whole thing [the experiment] in the first place," Zappa told the conference. "That plant is there for one reason—to make money."

The gap between what many workers expected the Topeka System to be, and the reality of what the System actually is, had caused some of the tensions, according to Brimm. The organization was misleadingly defined as 'self-management,' Brimm says: "The concept of self-management was ... developed in the promise of a future without team leaders. A later epoch was envisioned, where the total and responsible assumption of supervisory roles by team members would make their former leaders obsolete." Yet workers began to feel, according to Brimm, that they were "free to make decisions [only] so long as these yielded the same outcomes that the higher level authority would have chosen." Topeka employees unrealistically began to expect that a system which encourages rotation and training in all the jobs in the plant would never become dull or routine; when the system became not a novelty but a way of life, the vision crashed. "One individual faced the challenge of operating a fork-lift truck ... one worker achieves the autonomy of choosing among activities in the bulk unloading areas," says Brimm. "Another worker, the autonomy of moving from his job as 'humper' [hoisting bales onto pallets] after two hours." "We were all in the clouds for a long time," one employee told Brimm. "But 300 tons of dog food a day, every day, can bring you down to earth in a hurry."

These limitations have been aggravated by the fact that the job training and rotation system no longer function as well as they did during the first few years the factory was operating. "The prolonged push for maximum production," Walton writes, "also caused a deferral of the movement from one team to another which could occur after an operator had earned 'team rate.' This delay in opportunity to learn jobs on the other team postponed the date at which one could earn 'plant rate.' This tended to undermine commitment."

Some of the growing problems at Topeka stem from the way production employees interact with each other on the teams. While team decision-making has in many ways helped bring workers together in a new cooperative spirit, in some ways it has pulled workers apart. Under the pressure of increased production, teams which once went out of their way to help each other now compete for the "glory" of the highest output.

Probably the most divisive issue in the plant, according to observers, is pay. For one thing, workers who have applied to their teams for—but been denied—the plant rate, resent workers who *have* received it. They also resent the teammates who voted against them. Knowing that fellow workers will help decide their future in the plant, many employees are afraid to be open and honest, one of the original tenets of the Topeka System. "One worker explained that the tenuous basis of his security makes him continuously mindful of his relations with the many people who could help or hurt him in the future," Walton writes.

WORKER FEARS

Some workers, according to Brimm, feel that the Topeka System exploits them in the long run. For instance, while pay rates in the plant are far higher than the average rates which semiskilled or unskilled workers earn at other companies in the Topeka area, they are far lower—perhaps two thirds lower—than the rates which skilled maintenance workers or industrial mechanics earn at other plants. The General Foods workers are not

classified as mechanics or maintenance workers, yet many of them have learned and performed those tasks, and they feel they should receive higher pay. Furthermore, since they have not been classified as "maintenance" workers under the General Foods scheme, they may not even be able to take their new skills with them if they move to a new company.

This dilemma leads some workers to charge that working under the Topeka System is not a passport to a better job, but a sentence to remain in the General Foods corporation forever. "What do you say to a worker who has only a high school education but whose resume says he can run a [quality control] chemistry lab?" one researcher asked rhetorically at the Third International Conference on Self-Management. "That doesn't cut it in the outside world. You've got to have a chemistry degree." The Topeka System, the critics charge, enables General Foods to run a plant with many highly trained and skilled workers, while paying only a fraction of the wages they deserve.

Some workers at the Topeka plant have become discontent because they say the system has not been working well enough. But to some extent, the Topeka System is in trouble precisely because it was working too well—as far as some corporate executives were concerned. They think workers were exercising *too much* power. "It became a power struggle," one former employee told *Business Week*. "It was too threatening to too many people." Personnel managers objected to workers guiding decisions about firing and hiring. Quality control managers in the corporation resented the fact that rank and file workers were controlling quality control decisions in the plant lab. Engineers felt disturbed by production employees handling machine maintenance and other engineering work. The corporation has recently added seven new management positions to the plant, according to *Business Week*. The management says the new managers are necessary to handle plant expansion, but many workers feel they have arrived to scuttle worker powers and shore up the once minimal management autocracy.

In some ways, observers say, one of the early strengths of the experiment—its isolation from the corporate headquarters—became one of its most important handicaps. Planners of the Topeka System deliberately isolated the plant so that skeptical corporate executives could not tamper with the system so easily, and attempt to thwart the unorthodox methods of team decision-making and other worker powers. The fact that the executives at headquarters did not heartily support the project was not a good omen to begin with; the fact that Topeka managers tried to remain so distant from them—arousing resentments and suspicions at White Plains—made the situation even worse. Corporate evaluations, according to Brimm, gave Topeka managers low marks, and "condemned" hiring practices at the Topeka plant.

At the Topeka plant, "managers themselves," according to Walton, "felt that as a result of their pioneering work they had lost rather than gained in career progression within GF." Their feelings seemed confirmed: almost none of the top managers or team leaders at the Topeka plant were promoted inside the General Foods system. Instead, "Openings in the chain of command which linked Topeka to White Plains had been filled by managers viewed as 'hard-liners' opposed to advocates of more humanistic managerial programs of the Topeka type," according to Brimm.

WHITHER TOPEKA?

Today, some observers say, the Topeka System struggles against a combination of indifference and outright hostility from General Foods headquarters. As *Business Week* notes, "General Foods, which once encouraged publicity about the Topeka plant, now refuses to let reporters inside."

The former plant manager who helped plan and give birth to the Topeka System used to say that the system must "diffuse or die": that is, the system must spread throughout the entire corporation or, isolated and adrift, it will wither. If he is right, the prognosis for the Topeka System seems grim.

The "negative drift of the work culture" at Topeka has been important, Walton wrote after his November 1976 visit, but "more significant . . . was the absence of potent corrective devices, of a self-renewal capacity." While the work teams have not grappled effectively enough or often enough with issues at the team level, there has been virtually no system at all to grapple with issues at the PLANT level. "There have been no regular plant-wide forums in which issues can be raised and addressed," Walton writes. So while more and more employees have been feeling dissatisfied about the drift of the Topeka System, there is no structure to flush out this dissatisfaction in a constructive way—no structure which enables production workers and managers to work together to hammer out some solutions and improvements. This forbids workers and managers "to continually assess the work system and take initiatives to evolve its form," writes Walton.

Despite the growing problems at the General Foods plant in Topeka, observers and employees there agree, work under the Topeka System has been more satisfying and enriching than work at other area factories. Compared to an ideal of worker self-management, the System may not have achieved that much for its employees. Compared to a conventional, highly structured factory, however, the System has made some important advances. The major question which confronts the Topeka System is whether the corporate management will permit it to continue and to evolve—and whether any workplace participation project, controlled unilaterally by management, can survive for long.

JOHN J. McCALL
Participation in Employment

Until recently, worker participation in corporate decision making was a topic largely ignored in American management training and practice. Even in recent years, the attention usually given to worker participation by management theory has been confined to small-scale experiments aimed at increasing labor productivity. Little, if any, attention has been given to the possibility that there is a moral basis for extending a right to participation to all workers.

Numerous explanations for this lack of attention are possible. One is that management sees worker participation as a threat to its power and status. Another explanation may be found in a pervasive ideology underlying our patterns of industrial organization. The ruling theory of corporate property distinguishes sharply between the decision-making rights of ownership and its management representatives on the one hand, and employee duties of loyalty and obedience on the other. The justification for that distinction lies partly in a view of the rights of property owners to control their goods and partly in a perception that nonmanagement employees are technically unequipped to make intelligent policy decisions. The perceived threat to power and this dominant ideology of employment provide for strong resistance even to a discussion of broad worker participation in corporate decisions. But perhaps as strong a source of this resistance comes from a confusion about the possible meanings of and moral justifications for worker participation. The primary aim of this essay is to clarify those meanings and justifications. If the essay is successful, it might also suggest that the above sources of resistance to participation should be abandoned.

What people refer to when they use the term "participation" varies widely. We can get a better grasp of that variation in meaning if we recognize that it is a function of variety in both the potential issues available for participatory decisions and the potential mechanisms for that decision making. The potential issues for participation can be divided into three broad and not perfectly distinct categories. First, employees could participate in decisions involving shop-floor operations. Characteristic shop-floor issues are the schedule of employee work hours, assembly line speed, and the distribution of work assignments. Second, employees could participate in decisions that have been the traditional prerogative of middle management. Issues here are hiring or discharge decisions, grievance procedures, evaluations of workers or supervisors, the distribution of merit wage increases, etc. Finally, employees might participate in traditional board-level decisions about investment, product diversification, pricing or output levels, and the like. Simply put, employee partici-

pation might refer to participation in decision making over issues that arise at any or all levels of corporate policy.

The mechanisms for participation vary as widely as do the potential issues. These participatory mechanisms vary both in terms of their location within or outside the corporation and in terms of the actual power they possess. For instance, some see employees participating in the shaping of corporate policy by individual acceptance or rejection of employment offers and by collective bargaining through union membership. These mechanisms are essentially external to the particular business institution. Internal mechanisms for participation in corporate policy making include employee stock ownership plans, "quality circle" consulting groups, and bodies that extend employees partial or total effective control of the enterprise. Employee participation through stock ownership might exist either through union pension fund holdings or through individual employee profit sharing plans.

Internal participation can also exist in ways more directly related to the day-to-day functioning of the corporation. For example, quality circle participation is a recent adaptation of some Japanese approaches to the management of human resources. Employees in these quality circles are invited to participate in round-table discussions of corporate concerns such as improving productivity. It is important to note that these quality circle groups are advisory only; their function within the corporation is consultative and they have no actual authority to implement decisions.

Distinct from these advisory bodies are those mechanisms by which employees share in the actual power to make corporate policy. Among the mechanisms for such partial effective control are worker committees with authority to govern selected aspects of the work environment or worker representatives on the traditional organs of authority. An example of the former would be an employee-run grievance board; an example of the latter received significant notice in the United States when United Auto Workers' President Douglas Fraser assumed a seat on Chrysler's Board of Directors. Either of these mechanisms provides for only partial control, since one has a highly defined area of responsibility and the other provides employees with only one voice among many.

A final form of participation provides employees with full control of the operations of the corporation. Examples of this extensive participation are rare in North America, although some midwest farm and northwest lumber cooperatives are organized in this way.

Note that these varied mechanisms combine with the potential issues for participation in numerous ways. We might see union collective bargaining influence merit wage increases or working schedules; worker committee mechanisms of participation might deal with flexible work assignments or with evaluation of supervisors. This brief survey should indicate that discussions of employee participation must be pursued with care, since arguments criticizing or supporting participation might be sufficient grounds for drawing conclusions about one form of participation but not sufficient grounds for conclusions about other forms. That caution brings us to the second major aim of this essay—the clarification of moral arguments in favor of broad extensions of worker rights to participate in corporate decisions. Five justifications, or arguments, for participation will be sketched. Comments about the issues or mechanisms required by each justification will follow each argument sketch.

ARGUMENT 1

The first two moral justifications for employee participation are applications of points developed in Chapter 2 of this anthology. The first takes its cue from the fundamental objective of any morality— the impartial promotion of human welfare. That requirement of impartiality can be understood as a requirement that we try to guarantee a fair hearing for the interests of every person in decisions concerning policies that centrally affect their lives. Certainly, many decisions at work can have a great impact on the lives of employees. For instance, an employee's privacy and health, both mental and physical, can easily be threatened in his or her working life. Morality, then, requires that there be some attempt to guarantee fair treatment for workers and their interests. We might attempt to institutionalize that guarantee through government regulation of business practices. However, regulation, while helpful to some degree, is often an insuf-

ficient guarantee of fair treatment. It is insufficient for the following reasons:

1. Regulation, when it does represent the interests of workers, often does so imprecisely because it is by nature indirect and paternalistic.
2. Business can frequently circumvent the intent of regulations by accepting fines for violations or by judicious use of regulatory appeal mechanisms.
3. Perhaps most importantly, corporate interests can emasculate the content of proposed legislation or regulation through powerful lobbying efforts.

So it seems that an effective guarantee that worker interests are represented fairly requires at least some mechanisms additional to regulation.

We might avoid many of the difficulties of legislation and regulation if workers were allowed to represent their interests more directly whenever crucial corporate decisions are made. Thus, a fair hearing for workers' interests might have a more effective institutional guarantee where workers have available some mechanisms for participation in those decisions. In practice, then, morality's demand for impartiality presumptively may require worker input in the shaping of corporate policies. (This requirement is presumptive since we have not yet investigated what countervailing moral arguments might be offered by opponents of participation.) We have already seen, though, that there are numerous issues and mechanisms for such participation. We need to decide what participatory mechanisms dealing with what issues could satisfy the requirement of fairness.

Clearly, if worker interests are to be guaranteed as much fair treatment as possible, the participatory mechanisms must have actual power to influence corporate decisions. For while workers might receive fair treatment even where they lack such power, possession of real power more effectively institutionalizes a *guarantee* of fairness. Thus, internal participatory mechanisms that serve in a purely advisory capacity (e.g., quality circle groups) are obviously insufficient vehicles for meeting the fairness demands of morality.

Less obvious are the weaknesses of individual contract negotiations, union membership, and stock ownership as devices for guaranteeing fairness. None of these devices, in practice, can provide enough power to protect fair treatment for workers. Individual contract decisions often find the prospective employee in a very poor bargaining position. The amount of effective power possessed through union membership varies with the changing state of the economy and with changes in particular industrial technologies. In addition, the majority of workers are not unionized; the declining proportion of union membership in the total workforce now stands at about one-fifth. Stock ownership plans provide employees very little leverage on corporate decisions because, commonly, only small percentages of stock are held by workers. Moreover, all three of these participation mechanisms most often have little direct power over the important operating decisions which affect worker interests. Those decisions are usually made and implemented for long periods before contract negotiations, union bargaining or stockholder meetings could have any chance at altering corporate policy.

Thus, a serious moral concern for fairness, a concern central to any moral perspective, presumptively requires that mechanisms for employee participation provide workers with at least partial effective control of the enterprise. And since decisions that have important consequences for the welfare of workers are made at every level of the corporation, employees ought to participate on issues from the shop floor to the board room. Moreover, since a balanced and impartial consideration of all interests is more probable when opposing parties have roughly equal institutional power, employees deserve more than token representation in the firm's decision-making structure. Rather, they should possess an amount of authority that realistically enables them to resist policies that unfairly damage their interests. This first moral argument, then, provides strong presumptive support for the right of employees to co-determine corporate policy.

ARGUMENT 2

The second moral argument also derives from points that were made in Chapter 2, and its conclusions are similar to those of the preceding argument. Any acceptable moral theory must recognize the inherent value and dignity of the human person. One traditional basis for that belief in the dignity of the person derives from the fact that persons are agents capable of free and rational deliberation. We move towards respect for the dignity of the person when we protect individuals from humanly alterable interferences that jeopardize important human goods and when we allow them, equally, as much freedom from other interferences as possible. Persons with this freedom from interference are able to direct the courses of their own lives without threat of external control or coercion. (Such a view of persons provides for the moral superiority of self-determining, democratic systems of government over oppressive or totalitarian regimes.)

This moral commitment to the dignity of persons as autonomous agents has significant implications for corporate organization. Most of our adult lives are spent at our places of employment. If we possess no real control over that portion of our lives because we are denied the power to participate in forming corporate policy, then at work we are not autonomous agents. Instead we are merely anonymous and replaceable elements in the production process, elements with a moral standing little different from that of the inanimate machinery we operate. This remains true of our lives *at* work even if we have the opportunity to change employers. (Many workers do not have even that opportunity, and if they did it would be of little consequence for this issue, since most workplaces are similarly organized.) The moral importance of autonomy in respecting the dignity of persons should make us critical of these traditional patterns of work and should move us in the direction of more employee participation. However, since autonomy is understood as an ability to control one's activities, the preferred mechanisms of participation should allow employees real control at work. Thus, a commitment to the autonomy and the dignity of persons, just as a commitment to fairness, appears to require that workers have the ability to co-determine any policy that directs important corporate activity.

ARGUMENT 3

These first two arguments for broad worker participation rights have ended in an explicit requirement that workers have real and actual power over corporate policy. The final three arguments focus not on actual power but on the worker's *perception* of his or her ability to influence policy. All of these last arguments concern the potential for negative consequences created when workers see themselves as having little control over their working lives.

The third argument warns that workers who believe themselves powerless will lose the important psychological good of self-respect.[1] Moral philosophers have contended that since all persons should be treated with dignity, all persons consequently deserve the conditions that generally contribute to a sense of their own dignity or self-worth. Psychologists tell us that a person's sense of self is to a large degree conditioned by the institutional relationships she has and the responses from others that she receives in those relationships. A person will have a stronger sense of her own worth and will develop a deeper sense of self-respect when her social interactions allow her to exercise her capacities in complex and interesting activities and when they reflect her status as an autonomous human being. Of course, in contemporary America the development of the division of labor and of hierarchical authority structures leaves little room for the recognition of the worker's autonomy or for the ordinary worker to exercise capacities in complex ways. The consequence of such work organization is the well-documented worker burn-out and alienation; workers disassociate themselves from a major portion of their lives, often with the psychological consequence of a sense of their own unimportance. Contemporary American patterns of work, then, often fail to provide individuals with those conditions that foster a strong sense of self-respect; instead, they more often undermine self-respect. Numerous studies have indicated that a reversal of these trends is possible where workers are provided greater opportunities for exercising judgement and for influencing workplace activities.[2]

If we take seriously a demand for the universal provision of the conditions of self-respect, we ought to increase opportunities for satisfying work by allowing workers to participate in corporate policy decisions. It would seem, however, that this argument for worker participation need not conclude that workers be given actual power. All that the argument requires is that a worker's *sense* of

self-respect be strengthened, and that is at least a possible consequence of participation in an advisory capacity. In fact, worker satisfaction has been shown to increase somewhat when employees are involved in Japanese-style quality circles that offer suggestions for improving production. Nor does it appear that the self-respect argument requires that workers be able to influence all aspects of corporate activity, since an increased sense of one's own significance could be had through participation only on immediate shop-floor issues.

However, we must be careful to estimate the long-range effects on worker alienation and self-respect of these less extensive forms of participation. Some evidence indicates that, over time, workers can grow more dissatisfied and alienated than ever if they perceive the participatory program as without real power or as simply a management attempt to manipulate workers for increased productivity.[3] We should consider, then, that a concern for long-run and substantial increases in self-respect might require workers to exercise some actual authority, of a more than token amount, over the workplace.

ARGUMENT 4

The fourth argument supporting participation also takes its cue from the studies that show repetitive work without control over one's activities causes worker alienation. The specific consequence that this argument focuses on, however, is not a lessening of self-respect but a potential threat to the mental and physical health of workers. Certainly, everyone is now aware that alienated individuals suffer from more mental disturbances and more stress-related physical illnesses. Workers who are satisfied because they feel able to contribute to corporate policy are held to suffer from less alienation. Since mental and physical health are undoubtedly very central human goods, there seems strong presumptive moral reason for minimizing any negative effects on them that institutional organizations might have. Since broader powers apparently help to minimize such effects, we again have an argument for an expansion of worker rights to participate in corporate decisions.

As with the self-respect argument, however, the issues and mechanisms of participation that this requires are unclear. It could be that negative health effects are minimized in the short run through advisory bodies of participation. On the other hand, minimizing threats to mental or physical well-being in the long run might require more actual authority. Which sorts of mechanisms help most is a question only further empirical research can answer. However, since we have already seen presumptive reasons for actual power to co-determine policy from the first two arguments and since that power can have positive effects on self-respect and health, we perhaps have reasons for preferring the stronger forms of participation if we are presented with a choice between alternatives.

ARGUMENT 5

The fifth argument for worker participation also derives from the purported negative consequences of hierarchical and authoritarian organizations of work. This argument, however, focuses on broader social consequences—the danger to our democratic political structures if workers are not allowed to participate in corporate decisions.[4]

Many political theorists are alarmed by contemporary voter apathy. They worry that with that apathy the political process will be democratic in name only, and that the actual business of government will be controlled by powerful and private economic interests. To reverse this trend that threatens democratic government demands that individual citizens become more involved in the political process. However, increased individual involvement is seen as unlikely unless citizens believe themselves to have political power. But an initial increased sense of one's own political power does not seem possible from involvement in the large macroscopic political institutions of contemporary government. Rather, involvement in smaller, more local and immediate social activities will nurture a sense of political efficacy. Since so much time and attention is devoted to one's work life, the place of employment appears a prime candidate for that training in democracy necessary for development of civic involvement. In fact, powerless and alienated workers can bring their sense of powerlessness home and offer their children lessons in the futility of involvement. Allowing those lessons to

continue would only exacerbate the threat to vital democratic institutions. This fifth argument, then, sees participation at work as a necessary condition for the existence of a healthy and lasting system of democracy where citizens have the confidence to engage in self-determining political activities.

Again, since this argument focuses on the worker's perception of his or her own power, it provides presumptive support for those mechanisms that would increase both that sense of power and the tendency for political activity. Just what mechanisms these are can be open to argument. However, as before, if workers feel that their participatory mechanisms lack power, there is the danger that they will become even more cynical about their ability to influence political decisions. And since we have already seen arguments supporting participation with actual power to co-determine policy, there should be a presumption in favor of using mechanisms with real power.

SOURCES OF RESISTANCE

We have, then, five significant reasons for extending to workers a broad right to co-determine corporate policy. Now, in order to determine whether the presumption in favor of worker participation can be overridden, we need only to consider some of the common reasons for resisting this employee right to participate. Common sources of resistance to worker participation are that managers perceive it as a threat to their own status or power, that owners feel entitled to the sole control of their property, and that ordinary employees are believed incompetent to make corporate decisions. We shall consider briefly each of these sources of resistance in turn. Our evaluation of these claims will show them to be unacceptable sources of resistance when measured against the above moral reasons in favor of broad participation.

First, in order for management's perception that participation threatens its power to count as an acceptable moral reason for resistance, management power must have some moral basis of its own. According to even traditional conservative theories of corporate property, management has no basic moral right of its own to control the corporation. Rather, management's authority stems from its position as an agent of the economic interests of shareholders, who are seen as the ultimate bearers of a right to use, control, or dispose of property. On the traditional theory, then, management can find a legitimate moral reason for resisting participation only if it can show that schemes of employee participation are real threats to the economic interests of shareholders. Presently, we shall refer to evidence that this case against participation cannot be supported by the available data.

(Management, of course, might still resist even without a moral reason. However, such resistance can have no claim to our support; it is merely an obstacle to be overcome if there are moral reasons to support participation.)

Does participation damage the interests of ownership in a morally unacceptable way? To answer that question, we need to consider what interests ownership has and to what benefits property ownership should entitle one. In the process of confronting these issues, we will also see reasons for suspicion about claims that workers are not capable of participating in the intelligent setting of corporate policy.

In legally incorporated businesses, shareholders commonly have a monetary return on their investment as their principal desire.[5] Moreover, corporate property owners generally have surrendered their interest in day-to-day control of the corporation.[6] The usual owner interest, then, concerns the profitability of the business. Worker participation does not pose a serious threat to this interest in monetary return. Evidence shows that worker participation schemes often improve the economic condition of the business by increasing the interest, motivation, and productivity of employees.[7] In addition, corporations seeking qualified and motivated workers in the future might, out of self-interest, have to construct mechanisms for participation to satisfy the demands of a more slowly growing but more highly educated entry-level labor force.[8] And even in those cases where experiments at worker participation have not succeeded, the failures can often be explained by shortcomings of the particular program that are not generic to all forms of participation.[9] In fact, some of those with experience in constructing participatory work schemes believe that employees can be trained to operate most efficiently

with expanded responsibilities.[10] When programs are designed carefully and when time is invested in training both former managers and employees, the competence of workers has not been seen as a crucial reason behind examples of participation's lack of success. Thus, in light of both the marked economic successes of broader worker participation programs and the apparent absence of any *generic* threats to profitability (such as employee incompetence), the economic interests of owners do not appear to provide a substantial basis for a justified resistance to an employee right to participate in corporate decision making.

Some might object, however, that corporate property owners have other interests at stake. Many see a right to control one's goods as fundamental to the concept of property ownership, for example. Thus, they might claim that shareholders have, because of their property ownership, rights to retain control of the business enterprise even if they fail to exercise those rights on a day-to-day basis. This right to control one's property would effectively eliminate the possibility of an employee right to co-determine policy.

There are two reasons, however, to question whether a right to control property can provide a moral basis for denying workers a right to participate in corporate decisions. First, corporate property owners have been granted by society a limit on their legal liability for their property. If a legally incorporated business is sued, owners stand to lose only the value of their investment; an owner of an unincorporated business can lose personal property beyond the value of the business. Part of the motivation behind making this legal limit on liability available was that society would thereby encourage investment activity that would increase the welfare of its members.[11] It is not unreasonable to suggest that this justification for the special legal privilege requires that corporations concern themselves with the welfare of persons within the society in exchange for limited liability. Society, then, places limits on the extent to which owners can direct the uses of their corporate property. For example, society can require that corporations concern themselves with the environmental health effects of their waste disposal policies. Failure to require such concern is tantamount to allowing some to profit from harms to others while preventing those others from obtaining reasonable compensation for grievous harms. However, if the legal limitation on liability requires corporations to have some moral concern for the welfare of others, it can also require corporations to protect the welfare of its employees. We have already seen, though, that morally serious goods are at stake when employees are unable to participate significantly in corporate decisions. Thus, if in exchange for limited liability the control of the corporation is to be limited by a concern for others, then the shareholders' interest in controlling corporate property could be limited to allow for an employee right to participate.

A second reason for rejecting the claim that an ownership right to control prohibits employee participation looks not on the legal privileges associated with corporate property but on the very concept of property itself. This argument makes points similar to ones made in the preceding paragraph, but the points apply to property whether it is incorporated or not. It is certainly true that property ownership is meaningless without some rights to control the goods owned. It is equally true, however, that no morally acceptable system of property rights can allow unlimited rights to control the goods owned. You, for example, are not allowed to do just anything you please with your car; you cannot have a right to drive it through my front porch. We accept similar restrictions on the control of business property; we prohibit people from selling untested and potentially dangerous drugs that they produce. The point of these examples is to illustrate that control of property, corporate or not, has to be limited by weighing the constraints on owners against the significance of the human goods that would be jeopardized in the absence of the constraints. Acceptable institutions of property rights, then, must mesh with a society's moral concern for protecting the fundamental human goods of all its members.

We have seen in the first part of this essay that there are significant reasons for thinking that important moral values are linked to a worker's ability to participate in corporate decision making. If control of property, personal or corporate, is to override these moral concerns, we need to be presented with an argument showing what more central goods would be jeopardized if employees were granted strong participation rights. The burden of proof, then, is on those who want to deny an

employee right to co-determine corporate policy. They must show that an owner's interest in broad control of corporate policy can stand as an interest worthy of protection as a moral right even when such protection would threaten the dignity, fair treatment, self-respect, and health of workers, as well as the continued viability of a democratic polity with an actively self-determining citizenship.

SUMMARY

To summarize: We have seen that there are various understandings of worker participation. The difference between these various understandings is a function of the workplace issues addressed and the participatory mechanisms that address them. We have also seen sketches of five arguments that purport to show a moral presumption in favor of strong worker participation in the form of an ability to actually co-determine policy. We have seen, further, that some traditional sources of resistance to worker participation (a threat to management or owner prerogatives of control, a belief in the incompetence of workers, a fear that profits will suffer) are either not supported by the evidence or are incapable of sustaining a moral basis for rejecting participation. The provisional conclusion we should draw, then, is that our society ought to move vigorously in the direction of a broader authority for all workers in their places of employment.

NOTES

1. This argument has been made by Joe Grcic in "Rawls and Socialism," *Philosophy and Social Criticism* 8:1 (1980), and in "Rawls' Difference Principle, Marx's Alienation and the Japanese Economy," a paper presented at the Ninth Plenary Session of Amintaphil, 1983. It is also suggested by John Cotter in "Ethics and Justice in the World of Work: Improving the Quality of Working Life," *Review of Social Economy* 40:3 (1982).

2. Cf. the selection in this chapter by Edward Greenberg.

3. Cf. Daniel Zwerdling, *Workplace Democracy* (New York: Harper and Row, 1980).

4. This argument is made forcefully by Carole Pateman, *Participation and Democratic Theory* (Cambridge: Cambridge University Press, 1970).

5. Of course, the matter is more complex than this simple statement indicates. Some investors might even have interests in losing money if they are attempting to avoid taxes. Others might want to guarantee that their company does not produce immoral goods (as some Dow Chemical investors claimed was the case with Dow's napalm production). Still, in most cases the primary motivation for investment is a monetary return.

6. It is, of course, not always true that shareholders surrender their interest in day-to-day control, since some corporations are headed by their principal stockholders.

7. Cf. the articles by Greenberg and Zwerdling in this section. Additional evidence is found in the experiences of the small but highly publicized Volvo experiments and of Donnelly Mirrors, Inc. Interviews with heads of both Volvo and Donnelly can be found in *Harvard Business Review*, 55:4 (1977) and 55:1 (1977), respectively. In West Germany, co-determination is mandated by law in some major industries that have been highly competitive with their American counterparts.

8. John Cotter, *op cit.*

9. Cf. Zwerdling's analysis of the problems with the General Foods plan in the first selection of this chapter. He argues, in part, that difficulties arose because workers saw the plan as merely an experiment instituted by management in the attempt to increase productivity.

10. The Donnelly interview, *op cit.*, and Nancy Foy and Herman Gadon, "Worker Participation: Contrasts in Three Countries," *Harvard Business Review*, v. 54, no. 3, (1976).

11. Cf. W. Michael Hoffman and James Fisher, "Corporate Responsibility: Property and Liability," in *Ethical Theory and Business,* 1st ed., T. Beauchamp and N. Bowie, eds. (Englewood Cliffs, N.J.: Prentice-Hall, 1979), pp. 187–96.

EDWARD S. GREENBERG

Participation in Industrial Decision Making and Work Satisfaction: The Case of Producer Cooperatives[1]

There is considerable reason to believe that work that is organized into hierarchies of uneven power is damaging to those persons who are located near the bottom end of such hierarchies. There is reason to believe that the damage to persons caused by the experience of productive labor in settings characterized by powerlessness and the absence of autonomy is manifested in a wide range of problematic behavior, attitudinal and psychological developments. The archtypical form of such work organization, of course, is that of the *assembly line*, where evidence continues to accumulate that points to the deleterious effects of the minute division of labor, close supervision and monotonous repetition of tasks. Kornhauser's (1965) study of the auto industry has demonstrated how work fails to offer opportunities for the development of abilities, interest, sense of accomplishment and self-respect is central to the development of a broad range of negative mental health effects. Kohn's (1969) analysis of working-class socialization shows how the lack of autonomy in the work process represents the central motif in the broad lessons adults transmit to their children in several countries. In more recent work, Kohn (1976) has demonstrated the powerful linkages that exist between alienation and the routinization, closeness of supervision and lack of substantive complexity at work. Several scholars have undertaken the important task of gathering together the scattered bits and pieces of evidence concerning actual experiments in work reorganization in industry in several countries that lend strong support to the existence of a powerful relationship between the nature of

From *Social Science Quarterly*, Vol. 60, No. 4, (March 1980). © 1980 by The University of Texas Press. Reprinted by permission.

the work environment, particularly as it relates to autonomy and authority structures, and the development of a broad range of personality traits and attitudes (Blumberg, 1969; Pateman, 1970). Other, more popular treatments of the world of work powerfully convey similar impressions about the negative consequences of powerless work experiences (Sheppard and Herrick, 1972; Terkel, 1972; U.S. Department of Health, Education and Welfare, 1972).

Despite some scholarly speculation about the gradual disappearance of assembly-line forms of work in modern society (Bell, 1973; Blauner, 1964; Shepard, 1971) and despite much talk about job enrichment and other forms of workplace reforms in both the professional literature and the popular media, what must strike the careful observer is the extent to which work life in all industrialized societies (capitalist and socialist alike) continues to be characterized by a general lack of autonomy, to more closely approximate authoritarian forms than democratic ones. The paradox of enterprise authoritarianism operating within a formally democratic political system is especially striking in the United States, where the fewest advances have been made towards practical experiments in "industrial democracy" (in sharp contrast to the lively activity in this sphere in western Europe [Garson, 1975; Jenkins, 1973; Vanek, 1975]) and where the distribution and practice of formal democratic rights and liberties are theoretically the most widespread. This raises the prospect that the damaging relationship between personality and attitude development and authoritarian work settings might be a more general phenomenon than one might suspect, especially if recent research demonstrating the advance of the division of labor in American life as white-collar and service occupations rapidly take on the attributes conventionally attributed to the blue-collar factory (Braverman, 1974) is confirmed.

THE RESEARCH PROBLEM

It is thus generally accepted that certain aspects of contemporary occupational life, most importantly its lack of autonomy and its encouragement of powerlessness in the work force, are strong contributors to a wide range of problem behaviors and mental health problems and that little evidence exists to suggest that these effects might be diminishing. Powerlessness and the lack of autonomy at work, however, can be generally derived from two sources. One source, and it is here that one finds the greater part of scholarly work, is connected to the technical aspects of work itself—namely, the minute division of labor as exemplified in the assembly line (Katz and Van Maanen, 1977; Kohn, 1969, 1976; Kornhauser, 1965). The other source, one that is generally assumed to be part and parcel of the first, though we would argue otherwise, is connected to hierarchies of power in the social organization of production. While much research has focused on the effects of various forms and styles of supervision, there has been little focus on broader issues involving the organization of power and influence in the workplace.[2]

Are hierarchy and powerlessness for the vast majority inherent in modern forms of industry and organization? Is powerlessness an inescapable concomitant of modern life? While many scholars would respond affirmatively to these questions, I would submit that there exist bits and pieces in the research literature that demonstrate how even small-scale efforts to transcend traditional workplace power hierarchies by involving the work force in decision making in the production process have dramatically positive effects in counterbalancing the "normal" effects of work, even of assembly-line work, on damaging attitudes and behavior (Blumberg, 1969; Pateman, 1970).[3] As Blumberg (1969:123) points out in his summary of this large research literature:

There is hardly a study in the entire literature which fails to demonstrate that satisfaction in work is enhanced or that other generally acknowledged beneficial consequences accrue from a genuine increase in worker's decision-making power. Such consistency of findings, I submit, is rare in social research.

Given the relationship that seems to exist between powerlessness in occupational settings and behavioral and mental health problems, as well as the powerful countervailing effects that worker participation in decision making seems to have, we are led to raise the following general question for consideration: *What would be the effect of a dramatically different form of work organization such that power relationships were trans-*

formed so that the formerly powerless actors in work life gained a significant role in enterprise decision making? Do transformations of power relationship significantly alter the meaning of work even when the technical division of labor is well advanced? It is to these issues that this article is addressed.

Such broad concerns, however, must be made more specific in any careful empirical analysis. While the effects of powerlessness seem to be evident in a wide range of attitudes, personality developments and behaviors, this article will focus on a single dependent variable, work satisfaction, in order to isolate more carefully the role of power relationships at the workplace. Work satisfaction, while not necessarily a surrogate for all possible workplace effects, has been selected; first, because of the broad attention it has received from scholars, business leaders and government officials concerned with the implications of work organization (Sheppard and Herrick, 1972; U.S. Department of Health, Education and Welfare, 1972); second, because of its intrinsic interest to working people; and third and finally, because of its very close association with other important possible effects—namely, work morale, productivity, absenteeism and a variety of personality attributes (Blumberg, 1969; Kalleberg, 1977; Katz and Van Maanen, 1977; Pateman, 1970; Taylor, 1975).

Having said that, this article will attempt to assess the general impact of various forms of industrial organization by comparing the levels of expressed work satisfaction in industrial plants that vary only with respect to the degree of worker participation in decision making. By so isolating participation in decision making from additional confounding variables and by observing its effects on a specific set of responses (work satisfaction), I hope to focus the consideration of participation more sharply.

THE RESEARCH POPULATION

For purposes of shedding light on these questions, we turn to a small set of companies that are organized along radically different lines than the norm, enterprises in which the people who work within them possess *full* power of determination over the

general directions of production and distribution, as well as the particular procedures and arrangements whereby production and distribution are planned, executed and monitored. We are referring to a handful of producer cooperatives in the Pacific-Northwest plywood industry that are owned, operated and managed by the people who work in them. These cooperatives have been in continuous existence for over 20 years, and are, by every indicator, impressively prosperous and productive when compared to the plywood industry in general (Bellas, 1972; Berman, 1967; Bernstein, 1974). As a rule, responsibility for the formulation of overall production and sales policy ultimately resides in the worker-owners (customarily called shareholders). Technical and managerial specialists are hired personnel and are subject to the direction and bidding of the shareholders.

The data for this study were generated over a two-year period in three ways. First, overall descriptions and assessments of the operations of producer cooperatives and conventional plywood plants were gathered by means of interviews with people familiar with the industry and/or particular companies. Second, in-depth interviews were conducted over a 4-month period with 22 worker-owners in three producer cooperatives; with 5 hired workers in these same companies; and with 11 workers in a neighboring, conventional, non-producer-cooperative plywood company, all with an eye toward gaining a richly textured sense of the particulars of the work experience, the social dynamics internal to the plants and the felt effects of such an experience. Finally, data were gathered from 551 people (worker-owners in four cooperatives, hired workers in these same companies and workers in a single large, conventional, unionized plant)[4] by means of a lengthy mail questionnaire.[5] All of the companies involved are in close geographical proximity to one other, are identical in terms of the technical organization of production and are practically indistinguishable in terms of work force demographic characteristics (Table 1). That being the case, these firms provide an unusually well-defined scientific sample in which enterprises vary primarily with respect to the central variable or set of variables—the nature of the participatory experience—and on no others of major consequence. Such a sample of companies serves to isolate the effects of participation in decision

TABLE ONE

*D*emographic Characteristics of Work Force in Producer-Cooperative and Union Plywood Plants

	Cooperatives	Union
Sex (percent male)	97.1	91.6
Median age	43.5	42.3
Homeowners (percent)	77.8	72.5
Median education level (highest grade)	12.3	11.9
Ethnicity (percent white)	97.1	91.6
Armed service experience (percent)	59.9	52.9
Married (percent)	79.1	75.2
Unemployment experience (percent experiencing over one month)	47.3	45.8

making by diminishing the possibility that observed variations between the companies might be explained by differences in industrial processes, work routines, geographically specific cultures, work force demographics and the like.

COOPERATIVES AND CONVENTIONAL PLANTS: AN OVERVIEW

The plywood cooperatives vest ultimate decision authority and responsibility in the general membership of the cooperative. This authority finds concrete expression in the annual or semiannual general membership meeting of all shareholders. Responsible as it is for the total governance of the enterprise, the formal purview of these meetings is unlimited. In practice this means that meetings generally focus on issues that pertain to the performance of the hired general manager, the financial situation of the firm, the establishment of hourly wage rates and the division of the annual enterprise income between investment (capital equipment, buildings, timber resources, etc.) and distribution to working members. Each shareholder is entitled to a single vote in such meetings. These meetings also periodically elect a Board of Directors from among the shareholders, a body for which all members are eligible. This Board is charged with general policy making in the interim between general membership meetings, though all

of the firms require the Board to gain permission from the general membership for any expenditure beyond some specified maximum figure.

As to the general tone or mood of these cooperatives, one generally finds that no matter what the initial reasons for joining,[6] co-op members over time come to appreciate deeply the unique environment that these enterprises provide for those who own and work in them. A recurring theme in the interviews with shareholders is the sense that they run the enterprise, that they are responsible for what goes on in it and that they have the opportunity, within certain boundaries, to make of their environment what they will.

Well . . . the stockholders have absolute rule down there. In fact it has happened in this mill before . . . if things get too bad, the stockholders can just break down and say, "Wait a minute . . . we are going to change this." And if they have enough of them, they can do it, if enough guys get together. I think that's great because there's a lot of companies that . . . take advantage of the workers . . . and there's nothing that can be done about it.

The contrast to the mood in conventionally run mills, where workers are essentially apart from the decision-making process, could not be more marked. Within them, people feel that they are beings who are acted upon by distant and inaccessible decision makers.

But we never see any high-level guys that would let us know what's going on. So I don't know where the major decisions come from . . .

This sense of distance from decision making, this sense of being an object rather than a subject in the workplace is a familiar theme in noncooperative companies.

Not surprisingly, while there remains a great deal of variation among shareholders in their rates of actual participation in governance, the pervasive participatory environment of these places fosters an extremely strong sense of collective responsibility and mutuality.

... It's altogether different here [compared to his former job]. It took me a little while to get used to this because where I worked over there, there was a union and you did your job and you didn't go out and do something else. Here you get in and do anything to help ... Everybody pitches in and helps ... The people stick together, that's the reason we've gone so far and production is so high, cuz everybody works together.[7]

I have suggested that the differences in collective mood between the plants might be traced to differences in the organization of power and authority within them, one set characterized by self-governance, the other by hierarchical authority and superordinate-subordinate relations. This discussion has been fairly general, however, and it is necessary to look at these governing processes in more detail.

Shop Floor Governance

In some respects, the actual day-to-day governance of the work process is not much different in the plywood cooperatives than in the conventional firms. This is especially the case with respect to the pace and manner by which raw logs are transformed into finished plywood panels. This can be traced to the simple fact that the technical processes, the nature of the machinery, the optimal level of operation of that machinery and the division of labor are virtually identical in all of the plywood plants, cooperative and conventional. One cannot easily tell the difference in the actual production process between cooperative and conventional firms. To all outward appearances, they are the same.

Nevertheless, many significant differences do exist between the plants in virtually all of those matters that surround the technical work process, all of which point to some degree of self-

governance in the co-ops. As one might expect within firms where workers own and are responsible for the entire enterprise, there is a greater tendency to cooperate on production problems among shareholders than there is among workers in a conventional plant. Indeed, the latter are likely to stick to an assigned job, not to meddle in what is considered the business of other workers or the responsibility of some other production unit in the plant. In the cooperatives, the job boundaries, while there to be sure, are less rigid and more permeable when, in the opinion of the people actually involved in production, the situation demands it.

It took me a little while to get used to this because where I worked before ... there was a union and you did your job and you didn't go out and do something else. Here you get in and do anything to help ... I see somebody needs help, why you just go help them ...

This spontaneous cooperation in the production process extends also to the informal rotation and sharing of jobs, something that is notable for its absence in the conventional plant where jobs are assigned through precise and formal agreements made between management and the union. Once assigned, these workers do not generally make their own informal and alternative arrangements. While job assignments are made in a similar fashion in the plywood cooperatives (a bidding system based almost exclusively on seniority), there is a greater tendency, when the occasion arises, to share and rotate jobs.

I'm on a three-man crew that edge glues stock ... and we rotate positions. I have insisted on this. We have a feeder and a jointer and an off bearer. And we each one of the three rotate.

Given both the commitment to the success of the overall enterprise and the relative freedom to institute informal work arrangements (that is, within the boundaries set by the technical process), it is not surprising to learn, moreover, that shareholders in cooperatives seem much more likely to suggest and to initiate various innovations in work procedures.

The greatest differences are noted between producer cooperatives and conventional plants in terms of shop floor governance, however, in the area of supervision. Most striking is the vast difference in the number of supervisors and foremen found in conventional plants as compared to the plywood cooperatives. While the latter are able to manage production with no more than *two* per shift, and often with only *one*, the former often requires *six* or *seven*. Such a disparity is not uncommon. We discovered in one mill that had recently been converted from a worker-owned to a conventional privately owned firm that the very first action taken by the new management team was to *quadruple* the number of line supervisors and foremen.

Themes of close supervision and intense control were also common in our interviews with workers in the conventional plants.

... on day shift you never know when they're going to pop through there ... They might stand there and watch you for awhile and they'll move on. Very seldom that they'll ever speak to any of us ... [when they're watching you] you kind of tense up and wonder, geez, am I doing this right, am I doing that right?

In such a hierarchical system of supervision, workers are treated not as autonomous, rational and responsible people, but as persons to be watched, carefully managed and compelled to work. Indeed, workers in such settings often say that they are treated like children.

The contrast with the producer cooperatives could not be more marked. In the first place, since there are significantly fewer of them, supervisors are not "on the backs" of the production workers, but are forced to be concerned with broader, plant-wide issues having to do with the flow of materials and machine usage. In the second place, even when there is some direct contact between them, the nature of the relationship between workers and supervisors is different than in the conventional mill. The words that shareholders use to describe these relationships stand in sharp contrast to those of workers in conventional mills who see supervision as close, intense and omnipresent.

They're there to help us. They're there to make our job easier. They're not there as bosses ... They're just hired help. [If he wants us to do something] he says, would you please? Would you mind?

Cooperative and conventional mills are different in the direction of interaction between supervisor and worker. In the conventional plant, communication is hierarchical and one-way, with orders coming from the top, and compliance (whether willing or unwilling, enthusiastic or begrudging) coming from the bottom. In the producer cooperatives, communication is two-way, open and relatively freewheeling, characteristic of communications between equals.

How free do I feel to make suggestions? Just as free as I would to be talking to you. No hesitation at all.

How is it possible, then, to operate a mill in which upwards of 150 people work on a shift without close supervision? How does this complex production process, using a variety of woods and glues, and manufacturing a wide range of grades of finished panel, get coordinated? The answer is startlingly obvious, one that crops up in every one of our interviews in one form or another, yet so divergent from "normal" industrial organization assumptions that it gives pause. The shareholders individually manage themselves and each other. That is to say, on the one hand, filled with a sense of responsibility for the enterprise as a whole, they work in a manner that is sufficiently diligent and responsible so as to require little outside supervision. On the other hand, where coordination becomes necessary, or where some members are not contributing in a way that is considered appropriate by other members, groups of shareholders will tend to act as collective supervisors on the job.

And if somebody ... is goofing off ... you can holler over there and tell him, "Let's get going here." You know, frankly, we're all watching each other so that nobody else is goofing off too much.

Enterprise Level Decision Making

The first thing that one would want to know about decision making at this level is the degree to which shareholders are actually informed, interested and involved in the mechanism by which general policy is formulated. When we began to talk with shareholders about this issue, the first thing that became evident was the impressively widespread availability of information necessary to informed judgment, and the rather high level of continuous discussion about this information and the policy decisions for which it is appropriate. While only a small percentage of shareholders actually make it a regular practice to examine the company books, to read all of the minutes or to interrogate the manager as is their right, information flow is maximized by the fact that Board members continue to hold their regular jobs in the mill and are continually required to discuss policy matters with the shareholders working with them.

Like I say, sometimes, they jump us the first thing we come in and they want to know why we did this or why we done that. And I don't know how they learn about it before the day's over in the Board meeting.

What is also immediately evident to an outsider studying the cooperatives is the degree to which matters of company policy are part of the normal, everyday discussions in the plant among the shareholders.[8]

As to the shareholder meetings themselves, our interviews suggest that no particular single description serves to characterize the prevalent mood. Some meetings are generally routine, with the manager and other officers reading reports and responding to questions. At other times, discussions can be lively and intense. What we do know for sure about them, however, is that attendance is very high (92% of our sample reported *regular* attendance), and that involvement in discussions at the meetings are quite significant. In our shareholder sample, 31% reported that they "often" or "always" participated in discussions at these sessions.

In many respects, the key institution of democratic life in the plywood cooperative is the Board of Directors, an elected representative institution that is more actively engaged in making policy, formulating alternatives and monitoring the performance of the hired management team than is the general shareholder meeting. What we need to know with respect to such a representative institution is the degree to which the Board is responsive and responsible to its constituency.

Most significantly with respect to this issue, while only a minority of the shareholders has actually served on them, the Boards of Directors of the plywood cooperatives are universally characterized by regular and significant membership

turnover. As far as we have been able to determine, no tight-knit group of people regularly dominates these positions and imposes its views on the remainder of the membership.

Shareholder contact with the Board is continuous and takes various forms. We have already pointed out, for instance, the relatively high degree of information held by the shareholders relative to company policy, the degree to which they demonstrate a continuing interest in the activities of the Board and the level of continuous discussion that goes on in the mill about these matters. Another way to gain a sense of the level of participation is to note that 31.5% of all shareholders reported to us that they had, at one time or another, actively run for a Board position, and that 17.5% of all shareholders had, in fact, been elected and served. The Board, most importantly, does not become a distant and separate institution because of the inescapable fact that Board members continue to hold jobs in the mill during their tenure and are completely accessible to the shareholders. We might add that such access is not simply theoretical but is a fact of everyday life in the mill.

If I have a gripe? Well, I generally go over and talk to the president of the Board. Most people do . . . and you can find out what the scoop is most of the time.

If somebody's got a gripe, they come to me; I like to hear them. And I tell them what I think and I say, by golly . . . Let's go after so-and-so, he's on the Board and sometimes we'll go together and ask . . . We'll get the answer and the guy's happy.

From all of the above indications, it is probably safe to conclude that the Board does not succumb to the problems of rigidity, distance and professionalization so common to representative institutions. The tendency for shareholders to be actively participant in and well informed about all aspects of the business of the Board of Directors serves as a powerful guard against such developments.

As to managers, while shareholders tend to give them a free hand, what keeps the position from becoming too distant, too independent and too out-of-tune with the membership is the simple fact that the occupant of the position is a hired hand and is universally so defined. This structural relationship is critical, for it not only leaves the shareholders psychologically free to approach managers about any business matter whatsoever, but free as well both to criticize them and to fire them when the company is not performing as the members believed it should.

> We own it lock, stock and barrel ... I'm not working for that turkey in the office; he's working for me. And when I go into that office and want some information, I demand it and get it!

While few of the respondents put matters as vehemently, this sense that the general manager is a hired person, without tenure, and subject to the desires of the shareholders is powerful and pervasive but, most importantly, regularly acted upon. Average tenure for managers in producer cooperatives is, in fact, quite low.

DATA ANALYSIS: PARTICIPATION AND WORK SATISFACTION

Equipped now with some sense of the internal social dynamics of cooperative and conventional plants in the plywood industry, let us turn to the main business at hand: an analysis of the implications of these alternative work settings. More specifically, in the pages that follow I shall explicate the relationship between participation in decision making in industrial settings and expressed work satisfaction. Work satisfaction is, to be sure, a rather ambiguous concept that has been defined in a wide variety of ways in the research literature (Taylor, 1975). I understand work satisfaction to be, following Kalleberg (1977:126), "an overall affective orientation ... toward presently occupied work roles"—and it is to be distinguished from expressed satisfaction with specific aspects of those same work roles. It is a broadly conceived orientation toward the total job situation. Using this approach, our measure of work satisfaction is constructed from four Likert-type questions that ask respondents how satisfied they are with their jobs as a whole:[9]

1. If I had it to do over again, I'd probably go to work here again.
2. When I start off for work in the morning, I'm generally enthusiastic about going.

3. This place is not as good a place to work as most other plants around here.
4. I get a great feeling of satisfaction from the work I am doing.

An Index was constructed. ... Individual item correlations with the Index of Work Satisfaction provided to be quite strong.

The Index is first used to examine the effects of contrasting work settings. Much as expected from the previous discussion, significant variation in work satisfaction is evident between work settings that differ in their modes of participation.[10]

Several things are worth noting about these figures. First, while the differences between work settings on the Index are perhaps not dramatic, even small differences in populations so closely matched must be interpreted as theoretically significant. Recall the description of these plants set out above. The producer cooperatives and the conventional plant are almost uniformly matched with the only significant difference between the cooperatives and the conventional plant being the nature of their internal organization. This would tentatively suggest a powerful role for worker participation in decision making as a critical factor in explaining the differences between work settings in patterns of work satisfaction.

Second, and more importantly, much of the literature on work satisfaction strongly suggests that the decisive factor in the determination of satisfaction is the technical nature of the work itself. More pointedly, low work satisfaction seems to be most closely tied to work characterized by the extreme specialization and repetition characteristic of the minute division of labor (Gartil, 1977; Kohn, 1969; Kornhauser, 1965; Terkel, 1972). In the cases here under consideration, the technical division of labor is not only well advanced but does not vary in any perceptible manner across plants. One would expect to find, given the powerful influence of the division of labor, uniformly low levels of work satisfaction across all of the plywood plants. Significant variation on this measure, then, suggests that participation might be a powerful independent factor in the reaction to the work experience. Other possibilities remain, however.

The interpretation that work satisfaction is closely tied to factory type is given added emphasis by the analysis of the effects of other possible explanatory variables. Since the analysis is confined to white males, the possibly confounding effects of race and sex have already been controlled for. Furthermore, level of education shows no statistically significant relationship to the Index of Work Satisfaction, nor does the length of employment/service in the plant. Two additional variables show significant relationships, however, and are worth further discussion.

Income is related to the Index of Work Satisfaction, but there is some reason to believe that the relationship might be an artifact of the overall differences between cooperative and conventional plants, and not significant in its own right. The average annual income in the cooperatives *as a group* is about 30% higher than it is in the conventional plant. In noting the relationship between income and satisfaction, therefore, we may well be simply seeing the effects of organizational type. On the other hand, in noting the relationship between factory type and work satisfaction, we may well be simply seeing the effects of higher income in the cooperatives. Unfortunately, there is no way to directly examine this issue because there exists almost no variation in income *within* each of the categories. That is to say, in each of the individual plants, shareholders all receive closely similar annual remuneration, as do workers in conventional plants. To control for income within plants, therefore, is impossible. There is some indirect evidence, however, that speaks to this point. If one looks at the producer cooperatives, one notes very wide variations in their income positions and economic health. Share values range from a low $17,000 to well over $50,000. Nevertheless, despite these wide variations in the economic situation of the cooperatives (and, thus, of the income of shareholders in each of the cooperatives), one finds no significant difference in the average scores on the Index between them. If income was a powerful factor in the development of work satisfaction, one would have expected to find significant differences of the Index between producer cooperatives that varied widely in their economic performance and shareholder remuneration. There is some reason to believe, then, that the relationship between income and satisfaction is an artifact of work setting rather than a significant independent contributor. Our evidence is only indirect, however, so we are able to reach only tentative conclusions.

Age also shows a significant relationship to the Index with older people showing higher scores than younger ones. Once we control for factory type, however, the relationship washes out in the participatory settings. That is to say, the relationship between age and work satisfaction is almost entirely accounted for by works in conventional plants. Among shareholders in the cooperatives, no relationship exists between age and work satisfaction. Or to put it another way, scores on the Index of Work Satisfaction are uniformly higher across all age categories in the cooperatives.

Another possible contributor to the observed relationship is that of *plant size*. Could it not be the case that the higher satisfaction scores among shareholders is an artifact of the smaller sizes of the producer cooperatives? In the plants used in this study, the cooperatives ranged in size from 90 members up to 189, while the conventional union plant employed a production work force of 212. Nevertheless, there are reasons to discount the effects of size on satisfaction. First, comparative research has not found the size factor to be importantly related to satisfaction (Tannenbaum, 1974). Second, and far more importantly, much as was the case with income considered above, no variation is evident among the producer cooperatives in the sample on the Index of Work Satisfaction even though they vary among themselves in work force size. While this is an indirect and somewhat unsatisfactory approach to this question, it remains all that is possible given the limitations of the data.

Age, income, education, time of service, work force size, race and sex, then, do not seem to appreciably undermine the relationship between type of work setting and work satisfaction. That is, to be a worker-owner in a producer cooperative increases the probability of scoring well on the Index of Work Satisfaction as compared to work in conventional enterprises. What is it about these work settings that best explains the persistence of this relationship? We have only assumed up to this point that the relationship is explained by participation in decision making, based on the observation that these differences in internal power relationships between plants seem to be the only discernible differences between them. More direct evidence helps to establish the veracity of this posited relationship.

In the first place, the variables with which the Index of Work Satisfaction is most strongly correlated are those that can be logically derived from the descriptions already presented in the above pages about the participatory milieu of the cooperatives.

Significantly, two major dimensions of life within cooperative settings prove to be strongly related to the Index when we take the entire sample into consideration: namely, a felt sense of collective responsibility for the success of the production process, and a relatively egalitarian relationship between supervisors and workers.

In the second place, and more pointedly, we can isolate the role of participation on work satisfaction. We can do this because of a set of questions that ask shareholders about their degree of involvement in the various governing activities of their enterprises. Five questions were asked:

1. Do you attend almost all shareholder meetings?
2. Do you participate in discussions at shareholder meetings?
3. Do you talk about decisions of the Board of Directors with other shareholders in the plant?
4. Have you ever run for the Board of Directors?
5. Have you ever served on the Board of Directors?

An *Index of Participation* was constructed by summing the responses on each of the individual items. The Index represents a fairly straightforward measure of the degree of actual participation in governing activities. While it is prone to all of the standard problems of self-reported behavior, it is, nonetheless, a measure of actual activities (as opposed to subjective feelings about such activities) which are quite close to the everyday experiences of shareholders.

When we run the Index of Work Satisfaction against the Index of Participation we find a correlation. That is to say, those shareholders who are highly participant in enterprise governance tend to be the shareholders who are most likely to score towards the upper end of the Work Satisfaction Index. More significantly, when we enter a wide range of control variables, the relationship between participation and satisfaction is virtually unaffected, suggesting the power of the linkage between the two. Of particular note are those items which have been previously demonstrated to have had a significant independent effect on work satisfaction—namely, the sense of group responsibility and egalitarian relationships in supervision.

Given the strength of the relationship between the two indices and its relative immunity to the effects of additional variables, as well as other data presented above, it seems that the experience of direct participation in enterprise governance is a significant factor in explaining the differences in work satisfaction between producer cooperatives and conventional firms. One additional piece of information helps cement this relationship, for it demonstrates that it is participation in *direct enterprise governance* that is the key factor here, and not some generalized participation in other institutional spheres. More specifically, if we build an *Index of Participation in Union Affairs*[11] for those persons who work in the conventional factory setting, we do *not* find a relationship between such participation and work satisfaction. It appears, then, that only a particular kind of participation is decisive, namely, participation within the work setting itself.

SUMMARY

The main finding reported in these pages is reasonably straightforward: that participation in the governance of industrial enterprises significantly enhances the sense of satisfaction at work. To be sure, several alternative explanations remain possibilities, given the indirect ways they have been considered here, but, in our view, they seem remote. Income, for instance, might yet prove important, though the absence of variation in satisfaction between cooperatives that vary in income would seem to make that unlikely. Similarly, work force size might be a factor, though the congruity of scores on the Index of Satisfaction between the cooperatives, despite their varying sizes, would seem to diminish the explanatory centrality of this variable. Finally, the possibility that the producer cooperatives might simply be recruiting people with a propensity to participate who might then show greater satisfaction in these settings is made less tenable both by the data demonstrating the reasons why people join these enterprises and by the data that show the absence of a significant relationship between participatory types (as shown by union activities) in the conventional plant and satisfaction. While none of these alternative explanations may be conclusively rejected, they do not seem powerful enough to undermine the strong relationship that exists between industrial self-governance and satisfaction. In that relationship is, perhaps, a lesson for the more reasonable organization of work in other industries.

NOTES

1. Research for this paper was supported by grant #SOC 76–11897 from the National Science Foundation. The author wishes to acknowledge the assistance of Thaddeus Tecza at all stages of this research project.

2. An exception to this generalization is the broadly comparative work of Arnold Tannenbaum (1974).

3. Tannenbaum (1974) reports mixed results in his comparative study. On his measure of "alienation," workers in conventionally organized industrial plants in the United States scored lower than those in worker-managed plants in Yugoslavia. On his measure of the incidence of peptic ulcers, however, the condition of American workers is considerably more negative than that of Yugoslav workers.

4. The union (control) plant that was selected is characterized by excellent union-management relations and relatively high morale as indicated by the absence of strikes over the past decade and the very high average tenure of its work force (equal to that of the cooperatives).

5. The return rate on the mail questionnaire was a surprisingly high 63%. Preliminary analysis of data gathered during the summer of 1978 from a sample of the remaining 37% shows no systematic variation on major variables in comparison with those in the main data set.

6. While it is generally the subject of another paper, let us note the fact that almost everybody who joins these cooperatives does so for reasons of job security. Not a single respondent selected either the nature of the work environment or the political organization of the enterprise as the main reason for joining. What this suggests to us, relative to the subject matter of this article, is that the cooperatives do not necessarily attract people with a predisposition toward participation.

7. When respondents were asked about the degree to which they felt responsible for the success of the enterprise, and the degree to which they were willing to do extra work to bring about that success, shareholders in the cooperatives scored significantly higher than workers in the conventional plant on both measures.

8. Almost 65% of the shareholders report that they are very often involved in discussions with other shareholders about company production, finance, sales and investment policies.

9. Using the Kalleberg (1977) approach, the job satisfaction measure to be used in these pages is a composite of two surface forms of satisfaction: job and place of employment. Nevertheless, we feel justified in doing so because of their empirical unidimensionality as discovered through factor analysis procedures (prinicpal factor with iteration, varimax rotation).

10. The plants used in this survey were almost universally comprised of white males. Since nonwhite males were too few to allow for comparative analysis but were numerous enough possibly to contaminate the results if not properly accounted for, data analysis was confined to white males. This reduced the sample size by 69.

11. The following items were used to construct the Index:
(1) Do you attend almost all union meetings?
(2) Have you ever run for union office?
(3) Have you ever served as a union officer?
(4) Have you ever served as a union shop steward?
(5) Do you participate in discussions at union meetings?

BIBLIOGRAPHY

Bell, Daniel. 1973. *The Coming of Post-Industrial Society* (New York: Basic Books).

Bellas, Carl. 1972. *Industrial Democracy and the Worker Owned Firm* (New York: Praeger).

Berman, Katrina. 1967. *Worker Owned Companies* (Pullman, Wash.: State University Press).

Bernstein, Paul. 1974. "Run Your Own Business: Worker Owned Plywood Firms," *Working Papers*, 2: 24–34.

Blauner, Robert. 1964. *Alienation and Freedom: The Factory Worker and His Industry* (Chicago: University of Chicago Press).

Blumberg, Paul. 1969. *Industrial Democracy* (New York: Schocken Books).

Braverman, Harry. 1974. *Labor and Monopoly Capital* (New York: Monthly Review Press).

Crozier, Michel et al. 1975. *The Crisis of Democracy* (New York: New York University Press).

Garson, C. David. 1975. "Recent Developments in Worker's Participation in Europe," in J. Vanek, ed., *Self-Management* (Baltimore: Penguin Books).

Gartil, Bertil. 1977. "Autonomy and Participation at Work," *Human Relations*, 30 (6): 515–33.

Greenberg, Edward S. "The Governing of Producer Cooperatives." (Palo Alto, Calif.: Center for Economic Studies) (forthcoming).

Jenkins, David. 1974. *Job Power* (Baltimore: Penguin Books).

Kalleberg, Arne L. 1977. "Work Values and Job Rewards: A Theory of Job Satisfaction," *American Sociological Review*, 40 (February): 124–43.

Katz, Ralph and John Van Maanen. 1977. "The Loci of Work Satisfaction: Job, Interaction, and Policy," *Human Relations*, 30 (5): 469–86.

Kohn, Melvin L. 1969. *Class and Conformity.* (Homewood, Ill.: Dorsey Press).

———. 1976. "Occupational Structure and Alienation," *Journal of Sociology*, 83 (July):111–30.

Kornhauser, Arthur. 1965. *The Mental Health of the Industrial Worker* (New York: John Wiley and Sons).

Pateman, Carole. 1970. *Participation and Democratic Theory* (London: University Press).

Shepard, Jon M. 1971. *Automation and Alienation* (Cambridge, Mass.: MIT Press).

Sheppard, N. L. and N. O. Herrick. 1972. *Where Have All the Robots Gone: Worker Dissatisfaction in the Seventies* (New York: Free Press).

Tannenbaum, Arnold S. 1974. *Hierarchy in Organization* (San Francisco: Jossey-Bass).

Terkel, Studs. 1972. *Working* (New York: Pantheon Press).

Vanek, Jaroslav. 1975. "The Worker-Managed Enterprise as an Institution," in J. Vanek, ed., *Self-Management* (Baltimore: Penguin Books).

HERBERT R. NORTHRUP

Worker Participation: Industrial Democracy or Union Power Enhancement?

THE MEANING OF PARTICIPATION

According to Webster, participation is "the art . . . of sharing in common with others." There is no connotation that this sharing should be confined to any one type of organization or method. The success and strength of the German economy, however, had centered attention on its system and tended in the minds of many to make that system synonymous with participation. This has been done either despite, or in complete ignorance of, the German heritage and the characteristics of its system, which are not replicated outside of Europe, and which are even fundamentally different in other European countries.

Foremost among these differences is works council representation at the local level. This is common in Europe, but nonexistent, and probably illegal, in the United States. The works council system has a long and honorable European history, and in Germany the duties of, and obligations to, the works council are set forth in great detail by the Shop Constitution Act of 1972. In the broadest sense, participation of German workers is very great with the works council. Yet although employee works council members are usually union members, the existence of works councils as separate and distinct organizations from unions results in what to Americans seems to be a curiously divided employee representation. For along with the presence of the works council in various European countries is the absence of local unions. Con-

Excerpted from speech delivered at the 64th National Foreign Trade Convention, November 1977, reproduced with permission of the author, Dr. Herbert R. Northrup, Professor of Industry and Director of Industrial Research Unit, The Wharton School, University of Pennsylvania.

tracts are regionally or nationally negotiated between unions and companies, but local conditions
are negotiated with the councils, or in Britain with
shop stewards. Works councils and unions are in
conflict in many ways. This shows up clearly in
union demands for changes in participation legislation. I refer, of course, to the already successful
drive of the German unions to have union appointees, rather than employee-elected personnel, on
the Supervisory Board and to the Dutch union
push for greater union control of works councils.

Two other basic differences, again between the
German system particularly, but also European
ones in general, and the United States one, are the
presence of a two-tier board system in the former,
and Germany's inflation and war experiences. Until now, at least, except in the coal, iron, and steel
industries, and at Volkswagen, the German two-tier
system has tended to separate policy making and
management and keep the labor members, who
were a board minority, out of management decision making. In addition, memories of the ravages
of inflation and wars have led to restraint on the
part of German employee and union participants
and willingness to forego present demands for
future needs. Those who would generalize from
the German system would do well to hold themselves in check for a few years in order to see how
the new rules providing for greater employee and
union representation work in practice, and
whether a new generation will heed the lessons of
inflation and war. They might also carefully study
the coal, iron, and steel experience and that of
Volkswagen, both of which I shall briefly return to
later.

In sum, then, the word "participation" has been
transposed from its proper, basic meaning to one
that connotes employee and/or union (and it is
rarely made clear which or both) representation
on the board of directors of a company along the
lines of the German model. Moreover, this is typically done without due regard to the special characteristics of the German system, environment, and
background, and with a presumption that, despite
very fundamental changes in the German law of
co-determination, and the coming to power of a
new generation raised in prosperity and without
experience in the ravages of war and inflation, past
in Germany will be prologue.

PARTICIPATION IN THE UNITED STATES

It is common for writers to state that participation
does not exist for employees or trade unions in the
United States. Unless this refers to the German
model, it is totally incorrect. Participation in the
United States actually is widespread in areas in
which it is the most meaningful. In the United
States, as I believe in Canada, also, local unions are
directly affiliated with, and subordinate in varying
degrees to, national unions. Collective bargaining
may be national, regional, or local, but in any case,
much is left to local union-management determination.

Under United States law and practice, companies must bargain over "terms and conditions of
employment," and this phrase has been most
generously interpreted by the National Labor Relations Board and the courts. Thus, besides wages
and fringe benefits, the employer must discuss and
bargain about such matters as hours of work, starting and quitting time, shift practices, layoff and
rehiring procedures, premium pay for overtime,
supervisors' rights to do journeyman work, contracting out work, automation, plant relocation,
partial and complete plant closings, and a host of
other matters. In addition, if disputes regarding
these or other matters arise during the life of the
labor agreement, the issue is generally settled by
binding, third-party arbitration, from which there
is no appeal.

New products or processes usually involve new
methods of work. Their success can be assured or
thwarted by the degree of union cooperation in
their installation and manufacture. The point is, of
course, that the union, and employees through the
union, do indeed participate in such decisions, or
in some cases even have a veto over whether matters go forward. Moreover, they participate where
it counts—on the shop floor or in the negotiation
process, which continues throughout the life of the
contract.

Nor is this all. Unions in the United States have
participated in a host of decisions affecting company management in a variety of ways. Unions
energetically lobby for tariffs and quotas, usually in
cooperation with management; like managements,
unions also seek special legislative favors in order

to bolster companies' abilities to pay higher wages; they promote products through advertising or use of the union label; and they influence the demand or supply of products in numerous ways. In short, by a variety of means and activities, unions participate in management decision making.

To the employee, however, participation on the shop floor remains the most significant. This affords him protection against arbitrary action of his supervisors, sees to it that such matters of grave importance to his future as hours of work, layoffs, rehiring, upgrading, training, transfers, choice of shifts, extra compensation for difficult work or hours, protection against the risks of old age, unemployment, accident, and health, and, of course, compensation are all co-determined. This is where the action is.

The United States worker, accustomed to the co-determination of what is important to him, is likely to find European-type participation not to his liking. The six U.S. automobile workers who were sent to Sweden by the Ford Foundation with the hope that they would be living proof that socialized Sweden is a heavenly spot, undoubtedly reacted as most other United States workers would:

The American reaction was indifferent or negative to the worker participation schemes. They observed that the works council meeting seemed more like a mixture of shareholders and general sales meeting, and that the members of the works council did not seem to be a representative sample of workers throughout the plant. The production and development group meetings seemed an adjunct of the works council meeting. There were discussions of problems with little attention directed at possible solutions. *In general, all six workers viewed the production and development groups as inadequate in handling disputes at the workplace* [emphasis added].

The official union position in the United States is no different. Despite a tongue-in-cheek suggestion at Chrysler which excited some *New York Times* reporters, and other pseudo-avant-garde types, and publicity seekers, the United Automobile Workers aimed directly at the pocketbook, rather than detouring toward the board of directors in the recent labor negotiations. If the UAW

officials had exchanged some cents per hour for a place on Chrysler's board, I suspect that they would soon be among the unemployed.

Meanwhile, George Meany was electing a president of the United States, has been telling Congress what to write in labor laws, and not worrying about representation on anything as insignificant as a company board of directors. His executive assistant, Thomas R. Donahue, previously summed it all up by declaring that moves of unions to join a board of directors "offer little to American unions" on the job. "We do not want to blur in any way the distinctions between the respective roles of management and labor in the plant," he said. If unions were to become a "partner in management," he suggested that they would "be, most likely, the junior partner in success and the senior partner in failure." Unions, he noted, "currently bargain on more issues than the number we might have any impact on as members of a board of directors." . . .

"WORKER" PARTICIPATION AS A UNION POWER VEHICLE

We could go from country to country and find that participation exists in various facets of industrial relations in many ways that reflect the history and institutions of the land involved. Why then a push for the German model, such as received support in the United Kingdom from the so-called Bullock Committee, or the new Swedish law, or the interest generated by co-determination in Canada? Certainly, no one has been able to discern any significant rank-and-file interest, or to contend seriously that the men in the shop would be better off financially or emotionally if a designated worker sat on the company board.

The answer, of course, is that both the German model and its emulation abroad are power issues, not industrial relations issues. The Labour Party–dominated Bullock Committee in Britain recommended *union official board members*, not worker board members, with the former appointed, not elected. A brief review of the evolvement of the German systems further underscores the power element involved.

CHANGING CHARACTER OF THE GERMAN SYSTEM

Participation at the supervisory board level in Germany was designed in part to insure that unfettered managerial control of industry would not again lead to cooperation with fascism. It provided for one-third of the supervisory board members to be elected from the worker group. The system, which still applies to companies with less than two thousand employees, seems to have worked well in the German environment. In most situations, where the employee board members had no political allies on the board, it did not seemingly interfere with economic decision making and sometimes aided effective personnel management by bringing operating managements' attention to people's problems that required correcting. Of course, there was wide diversity in results from company to company.

Unions, were, however, quite dissatisfied with the results. They wanted "true" co-determination—equal supervisory board membership, control over the "labor-director," and union appointment, rather than worker election, of "worker" directors. All these they had in the steel and coal industries by special legislation and at Volkswagen by de facto arrangements. They received somewhat less, but they have obtained, for companies with more than two thousand employees, some union-appointed directors and near equity between worker and shareholder supervisory board members. Where union board members are able to dominate other worker directors—and it is reasonable to expect that over time this will be increasingly the situation—the unions may force management to make many concessions in order to be able to operate the business. Control of the labor director, not mandated by the new law, is a key union objective, and it is not impossible that other members of management may decide to become beholden to the unions in order to advance their careers.

From a libertarian point of view, union control of industry must be regarded most gravely. In effect, it makes the social partners a single institution, thus negating checks and countervailing power. Like other forms of power, participation advocates talk in favor of democracy while stepping toward tyranny. The idea that workers will be in a superior position because their union leaders are also their bosses is extraordinary on its face. The United States was compelled to enact special legislation as early as 1959 because of union leadership malpractices in regard to their members. To enhance that power over employees and to term it "democratic" is to delude ourselves and to pervert the meaning of democracy. There is nothing in the union official—or any of us—that provides exemption from the dictum that power corrupts, and absolute power corrupts absolutely.

In terms of social well-being, worker participation has equally unappetizing aspects if carried toward the goal advocated by European trade unionists. Equal participation, as already noted, means that the worker board members, who may be expected to be union dominated, have a veto over managerial action. This inevitably means that key decisions are made on an internal political basis rather than on an enterprise economic basis. Previous studies of German co-determination have tended to ignore how much postwar growth and prosperity have covered up the contradiction inherent in having representatives of different constituencies on a board of directors. Now more realistic studies are appearing.

For example, little has been written about the experience of the coal and steel companies. In fact, however, Germany's largest union, Industriegewerkschaft Metall (IG Metall) exerts considerable control over these companies. Recently, the worker representatives at one major company, Stahlwerke Roechling-Burbach GmbH (SRB), persuaded the neutral chairman to vote with them to override management's decision not to make a DM 400 million investment in a new plant in the Saar. The union wanted it because of unemployment among its members; the management, noting that the company is already losing money and that the steel industry is very depressed, obviously is concerned about such an uneconomic proposition and the fact that the shareholders, not the workers, take the commercial and financial risks.

Dr. Alfred L. Thimm's careful study of the Volkswagen experience affords another preview of what can happen when unions achieve a dominant position on boards of directors. Volkswagen is 40 percent owned by the German Federal Republic and the State of Lower Saxony. Alone of major German industries, it bargains directly with IG Metall, largest and strongest of German unions. On its Supervisory Board sit representatives of these governments, the president of IG Metall, a representative of a union-controlled bank which owns Volkswagen stock, plus employee directors. Private shareholders, therefore, have only a minority representation. A review of Volkswagen's Supervisory Board decisions, including the long fight over a United States plant, show a costly political tug of war, as economic decisions were vetoed or modified by union-political control. The whole story is a somber one in terms of economic efficiency and social well-being; yet it is a likely preview of the future if we march to the tune of the German-model participation siren.

Such equal or union-controlled participation puts the entire management structure in jeopardy. A union-controlled corporation forces management personnel to form a protective organization and to bargain for their income and status. This in turn ends what individual initiative that they have left. The difference between this result and the dead hand of socialism is difficult to discern.

G. DAVID GARSON

Beyond Collective Bargaining

The diminishing returns of collective bargaining are everywhere apparent. Far from representing some imagined "post-modern" resolution of the economic problem, the bargaining system is now yielding fewer and fewer real gains. Unions find themselves on an economic treadmill, forced to run ever faster simply to protect gains already won. Labor economists have long agreed that the collective bargaining system has left the share of labor in the national income quite unchanged in this century. More recently, real wages have approached a standstill while profits continued to mount. The American Federation of Labor–Congress of Industrial Organizations, for example, recently reported that in real wages a worker with three dependents earned a dollar less in July 1970 than he had five years earlier. As James O'Connor noted, real income of state employees has actually been declining since 1965, in spite of the great increase in unionism in the public sector. It may be objected that these trends injurious to the workingman are not due to collective bargaining per se, but to government policy, the War, economic conditions—in short, to the state of the capitalist order. Such an objection, of course, misses the central point: it is precisely because collective bargaining

has been unable to advance the share of the worker against the tendencies of the prevailing political economic system that discontent abounds!

Although remuneration is at the heart of the established system of business unionism, the failure in this area is not the fundamental cancer devitalizing collective bargaining. Here one must consider the failure of collective bargaining to alter the basic social relations of production and the consequent continuing assault on the mental health and opportunity for self-fulfillment of the worker. That to talk of such objectives seems lofty and remote from current forms of unionism is indicative of the limited nature of the dominant bargaining system.

In July 1970, *Fortune* magazine ran an article titled "Blue-Collar Blues on the Assembly Line," analyzing how "young auto workers find job disciplines harsh and uninspiring," venting "their feelings through absenteeism, high turnover, shoddy work, and even sabotage." From the union point of view, dissatisfaction is shown in the increase in wildcat strikes and the diminution of union loyalty of members, particularly among young workers. Perhaps of more importance, psychological studies compiled by Charles Hamden-Turner in a recent

From *Workers' Control* by Gerry Hunnius, G. David Garson, and John Case, eds. Reprinted by permission of G. David Garson.

*W*ages of Unionized Workers Compared With Unorganized Workers in Selected
Occupational Groups, 1966

	Organized	Unorganized
Construction craftsmen	$8,580	$5,955
Mechanics and repairmen	7,954	5,943
Metal craftsmen	8,240	7,526
Assemblers, checkers, examiners, and inspectors in mfg.	5,929	4,821
Drivers and deliverymen	7,843	5,518
Clerical workers	5,867	4,572
Male service workers	5,183	4,149
Female nonhousehold service workers	3,913	2,603

report for the Center for Community Economic Development (Cambridge, June 1970) show that mental ill health and dissatisfaction become prevalent as one descends the ladder of industrial occupations. Matthew Dumont has documented in his recent article on "The Changing Face of Professionalism" how discontent with traditional forms of worker association and with bureaucratic work organization is leading to the formation of new insurgent coalitions in medicine, social work, education, and other fields.

The failure to change the social relations of work is evident in many ways. In his recent study, *Blue-Collar Life*, Arthur Shostak has examined these issues, concluding that reform is essential: 1) reforms to help workers deal more effectively with problems of health, housing, education; 2) reforms which would "grapple with the workingman's sense of powerlessness in confrontation with anonymous and authoritarian bureaucracies"; 3) reforms "addressed to the workingman's loss of the meaning of work." Shostak notes, "Increasingly technology undermines the conviction that it is through his labor that a man establishes his identity and his relationships both to his neighbor and to God." The problem is not that the collective bargaining labor system causes the problems that beset the worker; it is rather, of course, that it is inadequate to deal with them. In fact, these problems have become so severe that an important Republican advisory group has urged President

Nixon to exploit for the traditional enemies of unionism the opportunity created by just this inadequacy.

THE ADVANTAGES AND LIMITS OF BARGAINING

This is not to say that unionism is merely form without content, of no real advantage to workers. Nothing could be further from the truth. Consider, for example, the data released in 1970 by the United States Bureau of Census (see table). The clear advantage in wages of union workers is due to organization, even after such factors as lack of unionism in small, traditionally poor-paying firms is taken into account. Striking examples abound as, for instance, the recent accomplishment of the new New York City hospital workers union in raising wages thirty percent to fifty percent above previous rates (and above rates in cities such as Boston) in a few short years.

Nor has the bargaining system been limited to wages: one could cite extensive programs achieved through collective negotiations for pensions, health and welfare benefits, unemployment compensation and job retraining, and job security, as well as union-initiated housing, recreation, and social service projects. Thus George Meany could hold, at the 1965 convention of the AFL-CIO, that "Far from being obsolete or on its way out—as some of our 'way-out' friends on the sidelines predict—[collective bargaining] is being extended and expanded into new and broader areas of employment and in the resolution of new issues confronting workers in their relations with their employers." One could cite, for example, the 1970 campaign of the auto workers for extremely progressive health care benefits, forcing companies to favor national health insurance as a way of transferring costs to the public sector.

In spite of these gains, there are certain limits to the bargaining system. To be sure, one can imagine and even find historical examples of American unions under the collective bargaining system which have transcended customary limits, managing to act as if they were also workers' councils, preempting managerial decisions. Worker self-management is not a matter of replacing one form (unions) by another (councils); it makes no essential difference if existing unions take on new functions and structures or if alternative associations arise to fill new needs. In fact, the European record suggests that government-established workers' councils ordinarily come to work closely with existing unions, often augmenting their effectiveness and acting as a catalyst for the spread of labor organization to unorganized plants.

To say the bargaining system has limits is not at all to say that it is obsolete. On the contrary, most advocates of worker self-management have stressed the necessity of preserving free, independent unions to protect worker interests even when these are antagonistic to those of government or industry. But after this is duly noted, it is still possible to observe tendencies in the prevailing bargaining system that restrict labor interests and prevent effective dealing with the basic problems of workers suggested at the outset:

1. Collective bargaining generally neglects involvement of the shop-level worker. Apart from occasional crises the union is remote from the rank-and-file worker, even when it is valued. Low attendance at union meetings occurs even in democratic, responsive unions not because workers aren't organizationally minded or because union leaders are unfamiliar with the techniques of making participation attractive, but because the bargaining system itself makes the selection of the bargaining team leadership the only essential deci-

sion apart from strike votes. Nor, from the leadership point of view, is there much real need to contact members apart from referenda on contract offers (even here, many unionists feel they know member interests and have no real need to consult). While attempts to reinvigorate union democracy are commendable and may at times succeed, the tendency of the present labor system is to make participation seem irrelevant. Needless to say, this neglect of the shop-level worker undermines the extent to which the union can mobilize his support.

2. Collective bargaining cannot significantly alter the distribution of the economic surplus accruing to the working class. As innumerable liberal (Galbraith) and radical (Baran) economists have shown, the increasing concentration of industrial control has so severely undercut the "free competition" capitalist model that labor cost increases are generally passed on to the consumer (that is, back to the worker). Under these conditions it has been impossible for the union movement, as effective as it has been in particular cases, to increase the share of wages in national income. Only as worker organizations begin to acquire power over price decisions, with or without coordinate government planning, can the vicious cycle that has trapped the labor movement for the last century be broken and the consumer interest protected. Again, price control could conceivably be effected through bargaining, but the tendency of the collective bargaining system is against this possibility: 1) because of the present "legal rights" of capital under the existing labor relations system; 2) because in any given instance the union will find it preferable to trade price control demands for more direct economic gains; and 3) because the highly uneven development of American unionism prevents price control from even being attempted on a national basis through voluntary, concerted efforts of unions.

3. Collective bargaining serves only a minor section of those who work. There is a modern liberal equivalent to the old ideology of rugged individualism which places on social movements the burden of remedying the systematic evils of prevailing institutions, rather than also insisting on the change of those institutions themselves. There is no reasonable and realistic ground for expecting the spread of strong and effective unions to encompass the bulk of workers, regrettable as that is, without serious alteration of the system of labor relations itself. Even the establishment of weak co-determination schemes, as in Germany, would be a far stronger impetus to worker organization than is continued reliance on traditional union organizing drives alone. Most workers are not organized and most unions themselves are struggling parts of what Sidney Lens has labeled "little labor." Just as supportive government legislation was essential to the spread of trade unionism in the 1930s, so government action will be required again to assure organized protection for all workers; the European example, whether of the moderate capitalist type or of the more radical socialist variety, suggests that the most likely form of such government action would be the required establishment of worker participation bodies in all sizable firms. For unions, this change in the system of labor relations could provide a realistic opportunity for the spread of independent unionism to most workers. For government, it would promise more peaceful labor relations, a factor now becoming acute in relation to state workers as well as those in leading industries.

4. Collective bargaining involves serious problems of organizational control from the union and worker points of view.

The American collective bargaining contract is a relatively unique document among Western industrial nations, legally binding for a specified period and often incredibly detailed in content. These characteristics give certain advantages, of course, but the limits involved again raise the question of whether additional channels of worker organization are not also desirable. It is difficult, for example, to use a contract to specify general rules once every three years that can adequately meet the constantly changing work situation of modern industry. In the absence of a continuing works council with any power, the union's shop steward is reduced to reliance on relatively informal powers to meet changing needs and may often find himself restricted by an inflexible contract. It is this situation which underlies the increase in "wildcat" strikes that has disturbed union, management, and government leaders in recent years: workers, boxed in

by the legal framework of the bargaining system, turn to illegal walkouts in the absence of any decision-making labor body capable of acting between contract expiration periods.

An equally serious problem of organizational control inherent in the bargaining system, from the union and worker points of view, is the necessity for reliance on management to implement contract provisions. It is an elementary principle of administration that it is an organizational defect to place program implementation in the hands of unsympathetic managers and bureaucrats. A union frequently finds that the provisions it thought it won at the bargaining table are administered away in practice, the theoretic legal enforceability of the contract notwithstanding. One of the causes of the Boston teachers' strike of 1970, for instance, was the failure of public management to implement a provision in the previous contract specifying a maximum class size, and this example is not exceptional. Only the development of an alternative labor body with managerial functions will assure that contracts will be sympathetically and effectively enforced.

5. Collective bargaining is excessively bureaucratic.

Even apart from the tendencies against participation in bargaining itself, discussed above, the grievance procedures meant to allow for adjustment of particular problems on a day-to-day basis are becoming unnecessarily top-heavy. Because such grievances, if not settled informally by the shop steward, must be sent up the union and management hierarchies rather than being adjudicated through decentralized self-management bodies, it is commonplace to find that bureaucratic delay often renders an original grievance irrelevant by the time it can be settled. Needless to say, this characteristic of the bargaining system works to the systematic disadvantage of the worker: the bureaucratic organization of work is far more in the interests of management than of labor. A prominent arbitrator, David Cole, has detailed the deterioration of the grievance function in large American companies in his book, *The Quest for Industrial Peace*, concluding that traditional grievance procedures "have been surrounded with so many safeguards that they have become almost self-defeating . . . they tend to enlarge rather than resolve problems." For this reason companies such as International Harvester have made token moves toward decentralized joint management in the form of floating union-management grievance teams with power.

6. Collective bargaining reinforces a regressive expectation system. Related to the problems of participation mentioned earlier, the present labor relations system entails low expectations about the shop-level worker: neither the union nor the management expect him to feel responsible for work process or to concern himself with raising productivity or coordinating his work with that of other departments—these are managerial responsibilities. Given the collective bargaining system this is a virtually universal phenomenon, wishful management rhetoric to the contrary, because 1) the ideological underpinnings of the hierarchic organization of work demand low leadership expectations about worker capacity for self-management; 2) the absence of self-management bodies denies the worker a structure through which to exercise his responsibilities, and also denies him 3) the power to assure himself that the benefits of his innovation or exercise of responsibility will actually accrue to him and his peers; and 4) bargaining tends to involve conflict over division of the economic surplus and only rarely cooperation over its expansion. Yet if social psychologists have discovered anything it is that negative expectations tend to become self-fulfilling. In contrast, the relatively recent Scanlon Plans in dozens of American firms have shown that surprising productivity increases can be gained by a system of higher expectations and incentives to match, workers in some Scanlon plants being routinely placed in charge of introduction of the innovations they propose—another successful, if token, step toward self-management.

7. Collective bargaining has even failed to secure for workers control over the essential information needed for negotiations, let alone self-management. The demand for "opening of the books" is an ancient and honorable—and unrealized—one, in spite of the great difficulty of workers' representatives to act effectively for their members and responsibly for the public without access to "managerial" information about profits, costs, inventories, price policies, and

the like. This is true even of strong unions like the United Auto Workers, who find that the books are "opened" only when it is to the advantage of management to do so. This failure of management is, of course, rooted in the conflict model of the collective bargaining system, and has led to additional token steps toward self-management: 1) larger unions' research departments have tended, in effect, to duplicate managerial recordkeeping, replete with accountants and economists; 2) even smaller unions, as the United Electrical Workers in Lynn, Massachusetts, have recently found it desirable to duplicate management information systems for health claims. These steps are directly related to the problem cited earlier of the unreliability of unsympathetic management from the labor point of view, and may be the beginning recognition of the need to transform the bargaining system itself.

8. The collective bargaining structure is inappropriate for relating labor interests to those of the larger democratic community. Under the present labor relations system even if a union's resources are not consumed by the bargaining process itself, the most to be expected is that the union will become one more interest group affiliated with some progressive coalition for change. When this is done on a conscious and systematic basis, as in the Community Action Programs of the United Auto Workers, governmentlike bodies are created within the union dealing with health, education, etc., potential parts of a future self-management system. While under the present system, for example, a union may join with parents to help elect a new school board, an institutionalized system of community participation in which labor played a major role as a matter of course would require teachers' councils (already extant in some unionized areas) meeting jointly with community representatives (from parents' groups, community school paraprofessionals, etc.) to determine local variations of general school policy. Unionism plus some form of self-management makes possible a far firmer basis for labor-related community participation than does unionism alone. (In fact, without a self-management structure union conflict with community participation-oriented forces is likely.) Similarly, with regard to comprehensive city planning, only a strong self-management structure can enable a rational, highly progressive local taxation and employment policy without the blackmail of entrepreneurial emigration. Without such a structure, unions and workers will always be manipulated as pawns in the conflict between the interests of management and the public interest.

BEYOND COLLECTIVE BARGAINING

This is far from constituting a comprehensive list of the restrictive tendencies of the prevailing labor system, yet it suggests the reasons for the growing movement to reconsider the American bargaining system. This reappraisal is further motivated by growing antagonism toward national strikes, which constitute the one real power on which collective negotiations are based. The acceptance of the American labor system is part and parcel of acceptance of more intense and protracted labor conflict than prevails where even token steps have been taken toward self-management, conflict as restrictive in form on workers as it is costly to management and government.

Self-management is based on the principle that organizational health can be achieved only if those who actually do the work are given due weight in decision making. As the General Secretary-elect of Great Britain's one-and-a-quarter-million-member Transport and General Workers' Union recently stated, "those who invest their lives in a business have a bigger right to a say than those who merely invest their cash." Thus the question of self-management is at once a question of morality, of administration, and of labor strategy.

This is not to say that self-management is not without its own problems. Indeed, in a system dominated only by workers' councils, an equally strong argument could be made for the necessity of trade unionism as a coordinate form of worker organization. In such a system there would be several forces encouraging the self-management councils to adopt unionlike forms, just as American unions have reason to move toward self-management. First, unions are better able than councils alone to represent those interests of workers which are antagonistic to management (even self-management) interest in maximizing the economic surplus generated by the firm. In a free society, even the democratic organization of work would not justify suppression of the right of organized opposition to collectively determined interests. Second, the organization of production under monopolistic and oligopolistic management, private or public, requires the union of workers on an industry basis. While it is possible to envision an alliance of worker councils performing this function, the more centralized and professional structure of unions seems more appropriate. Third, unions would be needed to assure the independence of the self-management councils themselves. While independent councils have existed apart from strong unions, this existence has derived from sympathy of management or government, unreliable in the American context.

Thus, the crisis of collective bargaining need not suggest the demise of unions or even of bargaining, but it does lay the basis for a reevaluation in which the role of workers' self-management councils may emerge as central.

PAUL BLUMBERG

The Case against Workers' Management: Hugh Clegg's World of Industrial Democracy

The recent discussions of industrial democracy by Hugh Clegg—one of Britain's leading industrial relations experts—are extremely important for the entire subject of workers' management. In essence, Clegg's views represent the culmination of an ideological and political retreat from the idea of workers' control, an idea which reached the peak of its influence in Britain in the period between 1910 and 1922 with the influence of syndicalism in British unions, the rise of guild socialism, and the development of the shop stewards' movement. What Clegg offers is the latest, most contemporary, and most sociologically sophisticated refutation of workers' management, a refutation which has been embraced by the Centre and Right of the British Labour party and used as a justification for opposing any extension of workers' management in the nationalised sector.[1] Clegg directs his theses both at and beyond the British industrial scene and stresses that his arguments against workers' management have near-universal applicability. It is therefore crucial to assess these arguments here.

Before offering a critical appraisal of Clegg's theory of industrial democracy, I should like to sketch out his argument as it has developed in two books which he has written since 1951. The theories I shall discuss here were developed in his *Industrial Democracy and Nationalisation* (1951)[2] and were later repeated and elaborated in *A New Approach to Industrial Democracy* (1960).[3]

Underpinning this new view of *industrial* democracy, according to Clegg, is a changed definition of *political* democracy, especially among socialists. Clegg argues that the conception of political democracy held by nineteenth-century social democrats was both naïve and fallacious. For the most part they believed that socialism would abolish not only class conflict but political conflict as

well. Once the opportunity for economic exploitation was removed, then political exploitation arising out of the class struggle would also disappear. In the new society checks on political power would be unnecessary because a workers' government would naturally rule in the interests of the workers.

However, under the impact of twentieth-century totalitarian socialism, democratic socialists have had to revise their previous views drastically. Now it is recognised that it is indeed possible for political exploitation to be superimposed upon a socialist economic base, as in the Communist world. Democratic socialists, according to Clegg, have come to realise that political pluralism, meaning the existence of an opposition to the government, organised and ready to replace it by peaceful means, is the *sine quo non* of democracy today, under capitalism or socialism. As Clegg says:

Democracy is not only a matter of choosing who shall govern, it is a matter of making that choice more than formal by allowing opposition between parties, so that the electorate may choose between men and parties. . . . We now believe that the dangers of power are so great that even when a socialist government is in office every opportunity must be given to its opponents to bring about its defeat—so long as they use democratic methods.[4]

Standing at the root of his argument, then, is the assertion that opposition is a necessary condition of political democracy as we know it and that opposition is as vital in a socialist as in a capitalist framework to prevent abuses of political power which will otherwise inevitably arise.

Now, from this premise, Clegg goes on to make a direct analogy from politics to industry. He claims that just as political democracy is based on the

From *Industrial Democracy* by Paul Blumberg, Schocken Books, 1969. Reprinted by permission of Paul Blumberg.

existence of an opposition, so therefore industrial democracy is also contingent upon the existence of an opposition within the industry to the prevailing power of management or ownership. What constitutes an effective industrial opposition for Clegg is a strong trade union organisation. The trade union within the factory is to management what the opposition political party is to the government in power. According to Clegg, 'the most important function of a trade union is to represent and defend the interests of its members. Trade unions owe their existence to the need felt by the workers for an organisation to oppose managers and employers on their behalf.'[5]

As political or—in this case—industrial pluralism tends to be his prime criterion for democracy in any system, Clegg's definition of industrial democracy tends, therefore, to be quite modest and bland, especially when compared to the ambitious dreams of socialists of a previous generation who viewed industrial democracy as a system of complete workers' management, administered either by trade unions or by other forms of elected workers' representatives. Not so for Clegg, however. In fact, armed with his new theory of democracy, Clegg believes that the key elements in any system of industrial democracy are merely: *1*, the existence of a trade union strong enough to oppose management; and *2*, a management which accepts trade unionism as a 'loyal opposition' and is willing to compromise and come to terms with it in the interests of industrial harmony and unity. As Clegg says:

> . . . industrial democracy consists, in part, of the opposition of the trade unions to the employer, and, in part, of the attempt of the employer to build his employees into a team working together towards a common purpose. . . .[6]

Now, it is not clear in this early work, *Industrial Democracy and Nationalisation*, whether Clegg believes that industrial democracy is attainable in private as well as in publicly-owned industry. Indeed, logically it should be, for if industrial democracy consists of no more than trade union opposition and a management which accepts this opposition, then certainly this kind of 'industrial democracy' has been attained and is compatible with private ownership of industry. However, in this work, Clegg, a prominent Fabian, does not go

quite this far; he refers occasionally to 'capitalist authoritarianism' and it is clear that he still retains a sentimental, if not logical, attachment to socialism. Indeed, perhaps it was sentiment that caused Clegg to delay for nine years what seemed an obvious logical jump, i.e., to realise that if industrial democracy consists primarily of the existence of trade union opposition, then capitalism offers this as well as does socialism; and, if this is so, then nationalisation is actually unnecessary because the dream of industrial democracy—Clegg's version of it anyway—is already fulfilled under capitalism. Clegg, in fact, does ultimately reach this conclusion in a later work, *A New Approach to Industrial Democracy*, and we shall examine its major hypothesis later.

Having established to his own satisfaction the argument that the major purpose of trade unions is to act as an industrial opposition, he goes on to argue that for several reasons trade unions should never attempt to share the job of management with management itself. First of all, Clegg disputes the technical ability of trade unions to administer industry, and believes that they could not do so even if they chose. 'To take a serious part in the planning of large-scale industry', he argues, 'requires a high degree of technical knowledge, or briefing by technical experts. Hardly any of those who represent the workers have either of these advantages.'[7] Elsewhere he asserts that 'trade unions have not the technical, administrative, and commercial experience to run a large-scale industry'.[8]

A second argument against extending trade union power into the management of industry pertains to the question of democracy within the trade unions. Clegg argues that as a fighting organisation, a trade union must be granted a certain amount of indulgence for its frequent violations of democratic procedure, but one should be fully aware that penetration by unions into the realm of managerial responsibility means that these undemocratic practices are sure to accompany the unions as their power spreads. Clegg argues that an undemocratic voluntary organisation (such as a trade union) is far more tolerable in a free society than one which is not voluntary as trade unions would be if they assumed total responsibility for industrial management.[9]

Finally, we come to Clegg's primary reason for opposing trade union encroachment into management and it is a reason which stems from his initial discussion of the nature of industrial democracy. If, as Clegg asserts, industrial democracy is defined in terms of the existence of organised and autonomous trade unions, then any act or policy which would jeopardise the independence of trade unions from management or which would deflect union policy from its proper role as opposition, would to that degree undermine industrial democracy. As Clegg says:

The trade union cannot ... become the organ of industrial management; there would be no one to oppose the management, and no hope of democracy. Nor can the union enter into an unholy alliance for the joint management of industry, for its opposition functions would then become subordinate and finally stifled.[10]

If the trade unions were to participate in management, they would inevitably be drawn into an organisational role conflict, with the workers as the ultimate losers, for the workers' primary need is to have a force behind them which is in every respect free and independent of management, which bears no responsibility for management's decisions, and which is not in any way obliged to defend management policy. For this reason, according to Clegg, 'the conception of trade union leaders getting together with the board of a nationalised industry round a table which has no sides in order to solve together all the problems of industry, is both false and dangerous'.[11]

In addition, unions in a managerial role would inevitably begin to share the managerial *Weltanschauung* and would take on new concerns for productivity, profit margins, and the like. Clegg argues, for example, that the acceptance of wage restraint by British unions during Labour's first post-war government 'led them to use arguments about inflation, about prices and profits which they would have scorned even so recently as during the last war. . . .'[12]

Clegg also discusses and dismisses quickly the proposal that another group of workers' representatives, outside of the trade unions, should assume managerial authority. In such a case, Clegg asserts (in a vastly oversimplified way) that there would be a struggle to the death between the two organisations as both would claim to represent the workers. Confronted by this threat to its power as the sole voice of the workers within the plant, the trade union would undoubtedly attempt to capture control of the workers' management organs by getting its nominees placed. If this were successful there would be a reversion to trade union management and all the disadvantages mentioned above. If unions were unsuccessful in capturing workers' management bodies, then, according to Clegg, union power would be smashed and there would, again, be no effective workers' opposition to management.

Clegg argues, therefore, that any attempt by modern-day 'industrial democrats' or enthusiasts of workers' control to extend the influence of workers or their unions or other workers' representatives into the realm of management threatens to destroy the very basis of industrial democracy as it exists today, the autonomous trade unions. Advocates of workers' control would create an industrial despotism, not an industrial democracy because they would destroy independent trade unions which are the bulwark of industrial pluralism which in turn is the essential component of industrial democracy. Clegg believes that the kinds of complete workers' control envisaged by those firm believers in total industrial self-government is possible only 'if industry is operated by small independent groups of free associates'.[13] Unfortunately, however, such workers' control is incompatible with the irreversible large-scale organisation of industry today. But this should not be a cause of concern. Rather, Clegg advises that, like Molière's *bourgeois gentilhomme* who never realised he had been speaking prose all his life, those contemporary worshipers of workers' control should realise that industrial democracy need not be a remote aspiration, but rather is an accomplished fact, and lies in the existence of a free trade union movement whose activities are accepted by modern management.

If industrial democracy operates imperfectly in the public sector today in England, then Clegg's remedy is not to scrap the entire machinery of the public corporation in favour of thoroughgoing workers' participation, but rather a few very modest proposals to improve its operations such as methods to improve selection of industrial leaders, reform of promotion, hiring, and educational policies and improvement in the joint consultation machinery.

We place our hope . . . in the eagerness of boards to build up good relations, in the wide use of their powers of appointment and promotion, in the democratisation of promotion and training systems, and in the extension and improvement of schemes for educating managers in new methods for democratic leadership.[14]

I find Clegg's arguments both logically and empirically weak, and thus desperately in need of correction. First of all, his definition of democracy is simplistic and inadequate, for he tends to believe that the mere existence of an opposition has certain magical properties which guarantees democracy wherever it is found. The truth of the matter, however, is that opposition, though one means of achieving democracy, is neither a necessary nor a sufficient condition of democracy. For example, there are historically many circumstances where opposition has existed but where political democracy was completely absent. Medieval society saw conflicts between rival royal and aristocratic élites for power and was thus partially pluralistic, but certainly not democratic in any meaningful sense. In England before the second Reform Act which extended the suffrage widely, there was political opposition, political rivalry between Whigs and Tories, but little democracy as far as the vast majority of the population was concerned.[15]

On the other hand, there are numerous examples of democracy, mainly on a small scale, which have flourished without any organised opposition—the town meeting, the dissenting chapel, the trade union lodge, the consumers' co-operative.[16] And modern Mexico has achieved a measure of political democracy without the presence of a meaningful opposition political party.

I believe, therefore, that to define democracy exclusively in terms of opposition is a mistake; democracy is much more appropriately defined as the *accountability* of leadership to an electorate which has the power to remove that leadership. In this sense, the role of opposition is to make accountability effective by facilitating the selection of alternate sets of leaders. It should be made clear, however, that the mere existence of political opposition, without accountability, does not assure democracy.

Clegg himself realises the importance of accountability to democracy when he discusses nationalised industry, and he argues correctly that industries must, if they are to be democratically organised at all, be accountable in some fashion to the public. With respect to the socially owned sector, he argues that '. . . we must have some means of public accountability and control'.[17]

Now, if we are correct in arguing that democracy is best defined in terms of accountability, rather than in terms of opposition, then surely one must conclude that there is very little democracy—industrial or otherwise—in the ordinary trade union-organised factory as Clegg claims there is. For although the trade unions do constitute an opposition, nevertheless the employer is only minimally accountable to the union or the workers for decisions which lie outside the immediate job area. Thus, trade union opposition in itself does not constitute a sufficient condition for genuine industrial democracy.

But suppose we grant Clegg's definition of democracy as being synonymous with the existence of organised opposition. Even if we do so, his argument fails and the analogy he has made from politics to industry will not stand. Remember that Clegg has argued that in government the 'essence' of democracy is organised opposition and that in industry the same is true, so that the existence of trade union opposition is sufficient to guarantee industrial democracy. However, the crucial condition of any true multi-party system, or any system where political opposition exists, is that one or more parties is always ready and able to *replace* the party in power. An 'opposition' whose role is confined to protesting, making suggestions or criticising, but which can never itself *assume power*, is not an effective or a genuine opposition at all.

Now, it is obvious that British trade unions, in the public as well as the private sector, can never 'replace' their employer and become the ruling power in industry as, for example, the Labour party may replace the Conservative party in government. Clegg himself is quite aware of this, for as he admits parenthetically, 'The trade union is thus industry's opposition—*an opposition which can never become a government*.'[18] Further on, he states the idea again, but this time more explicitly.

The aim of a parliamentary opposition is to defeat and replace the government. A trade union can never hope to become the government of industry, unless the syndicalist dream is fulfilled [which Clegg believes is impossible].[19]

What Clegg does not seem to realise is that with this admission his analogy between political and industrial democracy completely breaks down and his entire argument lies in ruins. If trade unions have no power to replace the present government of industry but are merely able to challenge management in a carefully delineated sphere of its activity—the job area—then in terms of Clegg's own definition, there is no pluralism, no choice, no alternative, and no opposition—in short, no democracy. Nowhere does Clegg meet this issue.

In summary: *1*. Clegg's definition of democracy is faulty. He defines it in terms of the formal existence of an opposition rather than in terms of the accountability of leadership to the led. As employers are not accountable to their employees or to trade unions for the vast majority of their decisions, industrial democracy cannot be said to exist in the ordinary trade union-organised enterprise. *2*. Even if we accept Clegg's definition of democracy as synonymous with the existence of opposition, industrial democracy is still absent in public and private enterprise, for the trade union does not constitute a genuine opposition in the full sense of the word, i.e., one that is ready and able to assume power and replace the present leadership. If this is true, then industrial democracy is something still to be attained and not, as Clegg argues, something to be cherished as an accomplished fact. . . .

Clegg's approach, as we have said, is to state his principles boldly and then turn and run from them as the contradictory evidence pours in. His first principle, for example, is that trade unions must always remain independent of both the state and of management if they are not to compromise their essential freedom to oppose which would jeopardise industrial democracy. 'This principle', according to the author, 'seems to prevent unions from sending direct representatives to serve on the boards of nationalised industries. That would compromise their independence.'[20] But then Clegg examines at some length the West German experiment in codetermination in which labour representatives are accorded one half of the seats on the Supervisory Boards in the steel and coal industries and one third of the seats on the Supervisory Boards in most other German industries. (The German Supervisory Boards are roughly comparable to American corporate boards of directors.) In the steel and coal industries both the union federa-

tion (DGB) and the appropriate industrial union (Metal Workers or Mine Workers Union) directly select many of the labour members of the Supervisory Boards. In addition union officers are very frequently selected to sit on these boards. Data collected in the 1950s from thirty-five mining and twelve steel enterprises revealed that sixty-three of the 252 labour representatives on the supervisory boards were union functionaries, from locals, industrial unions, and the federation. An additional 105 were plant workers, of which 99 were representatives of the plants' works council, a workers' defence organisation with collective bargaining functions. Undoubtedly most of the 105 plant worker representatives were also trade unionists.[21]

In all probability, the proportion of trade unionists on supervisory boards has *increased* since this data were collected, for in the early days of codetermination there was a great shortage of qualified union personnel due to the Nazi decimation of trade union leadership and the initial lack of training and preparation of trade unionists for board positions.[22] The unions also play a large role in the selection of the Labour Director in each coal and steel company who is one of three members of top management. These labour directors are very frequently old trade unionists.[23]

Now, reasoning *a priori* from Clegg's first principle, one would conclude that such an arrangement would deal a death blow to German trade union independence and thus to 'industrial democracy' in that country. But is this the case? According to Clegg himself, this is emphatically *not* the case and he readily admits that '. . . it cannot be shown that the German unions have lost their independence under codetermination'.[24] He adds that:

Above all, no widespread unofficial movement has been called into being to protect the workers against representatives who can no longer represent them because they have 'gone over to the other side'.[25]

This is true 'despite the considerable salaries, fees, and other perquisites which go with membership on the boards [and to an even greater extent to the labour directors in top management, Clegg might have added] and the responsible way in which the workers' representatives have exercised their managerial authority'.[26]

If codetermination has not weakened trade union independence and industrial democracy among German unions as a whole, then perhaps it has done so in the Metal Workers and Mine Workers Unions which play a larger role in codetermination than unions in other industries. But Clegg concedes that this also is not the case.

There is certainly no evidence that codetermination has weakened the metal workers and mine workers in comparison to other unions in the *Deutsche Gewerkschaftsbund.* On the contrary, they are two of the strongest links in its armour.[27]

Forced to admit that worker and trade union representation on supervisory boards and in positions of top management 'appears to contravene the rule enjoining trade union independence',[28] and that in general 'it is difficult to reconcile codetermination with the three principles'[29] stated early in the book, he casts around for an explanation of why codetermination has 'done no obvious harm'. He asks rhetorically:

Why has it not undermined the independence of the German unions? If British unions with their greater strength, longer traditions and more continuous progress fear that the acceptance of joint responsibility with management for the running of industry would undermine their independence and destroy their value as unions, then surely the weaker and less stable unions of West Germany ought to have suffered badly from codetermination. But they have not.[30]

Trying to turn a rout into a strategic withdrawal, Clegg attempts to explain the anomaly. In brief, his explanation is that codetermination gives unions only a *partial* share in management; a larger share would certainly be dangerous. According to this explanation, however, we would expect the German Metal Workers and Mine Workers Unions which have a greater voice in management than other German unions to be less independent than other unions, but we have seen that this is not the case.

A more convincing rebuttal to Clegg's argument is apparent when we turn from the experience of West Germany to that of Israel where trade union participation in management is not partial at all but *total*. But even here, according to Clegg himself, the Histadrut 'appears to have maintained its independence',[31] even though it is inextricably tied into ownership and management. Histadrut, again in Clegg's words, 'has not realised the fears of those [i.e., Clegg himself!] who think trade unions cannot avoid corruption if they lose independence from management.[32]

In need of another patch to mend his badly tattered hypothesis, Clegg tries one that he hopes will do the job. He begins tentatively by allowing himself to hope that 'perhaps this state of affairs [successful Histadrut management combined with maintenance of its autonomous trade union functions] cannot continue'. He goes on:

Israel's experience as an industrial country is very brief. [But Histadrut has managed and owned enterprises for forty years or more.] It is very difficult to believe it [trade union independence] could continue if Histadrut's share in industrial ownership expanded to include the great majority of industrial undertakings. [But he does not explain why he believes this is so, and it is certainly not self-evident.] But for the moment it is so, and an explanation must be found.[33]

Clegg eventually 'finds' an explanation for Histadrut's success, but it is, to this writer at any rate, *ad hoc*, vague, and unsatisfactory.

Although Israel's own trade union movement is relatively young, many of the men and women who built it had long experience of the working and tradition of labour movements in other countries. Some of them had been amongst the most capable, the most trustworthy, and the most independent-minded in those labour movements. Consequently, far greater strength and self-reliance were implanted into the Israeli trade unions than could have developed if they had been a purely indigenous growth. It is this which has enabled them to bear the strain of a power and responsibility which otherwise would have broken them.[34]

So, although this principle of industrial democracy was initially based upon rigid and inflexible structural imperatives, now we see that it can be easily contravened by trade unionists who are 'experienced', 'capable', 'trustworthy', and 'independent-minded', and thus able to build up a strong trade union movement which can weather the storm of managerial responsibility. But if this can be done in Israel, then why not elsewhere, and if it is possible elsewhere, then why the need for strict trade union independence from management? And in that case, what has become of Clegg's cardinal principle of industrial democracy?

Not quite satisfied with this explanation of Histadrut's success in Israel, Clegg invokes an alternate hypothesis.

... in the past the Histadrut has left the boards of its own concerns to run their own firms, and has been able to do so because the Israeli movement threw up a number of dynamic entrepreneurs eager for industrial expansion and very ready to accept responsibility. Consequently left-wing circles attacked the Histadrut industry on the grounds that it was no better than private industry—not that the Histadrut management had the Histadrut unions and shop stewards in their pockets.[35]

It is indeed true that trade union enterprises in Israel traditionally have had considerable autonomy from the Histadrut. Clegg, in pointing to this independence, treats it as a curiosity or a quirk; he does not realise that in managerial autonomy lies the key to the successful trade union management of industry. Clegg has correctly pointed out that in trade union management there is a great danger of the development of conflicting loyalties and of a general undermining of the traditional role of the trade union as a workers' defense organisation. Any trade union, then, which seeks active participation in management, must carefully *isolate* its trade union functions from its managerial functions, and in this way the autonomy of each can be protected. The Histadrut did just this long ago by creating the *Hevrat Ovdim*, the separate holding company for Histadrut enterprises, and in giving considerable managerial autonomy to the boards of the enterprises and to their directors. With this done, the trade union as a defense organisation is not endangered and meaningful collective bargaining between the 'two halves' of the organisation remains possible.

Trade union management has been ridiculed and caricatured by those opposed to it by reference to the story of the trade union secretary who demands a wage increase and then goes round to the other side of the table and, as manager, denies it. However, it is inconceivable that any trade union which also possesses managerial responsibility would not recognise the necessity for a rigid organisational segregation of trade union functions from managerial functions. Arguing from the point of view of the feasibility and not necessarily the

desirability of trade union management, what is obviously needed to ensure trade union independence and to prevent the development of conflicting loyalties, are two hierarchies, independent from one another, but both responsive and accountable to the rank and file.

Actually, the Israeli experience totally refutes almost all of Clegg's arguments.[36] Although there is little space here for an elaborate discussion of the Histadrut as a test of Clegg's major arguments, the following points should be made.

I. Granted that the Histadrut has had a rather unique history, nevertheless, the assertion that trade unions are somehow by their very nature intrinsically incompetent and unable to organise and operate modern industry will not stand in the light of the record of this trade union organisation, as Clegg himself has had to admit. It is hardly a matter of dispute that the Histadrut, since its founding in 1920, has not only managed to organise 90 per cent of the working population, but has proved its technical and managerial ability in running modern industry. Histadrut's major industrial holdings (in the so-called *Koor* group) employed some 9,000 workers in the mid-1960s and comprised a vital share of Israeli basic industry (iron and steel, building materials of all kinds, glass, rubber, electrical equipment, and much more). The labour economy, in short, is in the vanguard of the industrialisation of the country, accounting for about 25 per cent of total GNP and employment.[37] In addition to its industrial holdings, the Histadrut is directly or indirectly involved in agriculture (via the collective settlements of various kinds), construction (through the large and venerable *Solel Boneh* construction firm, one of the first and most influential of all Histadrut enterprises), transportation (the wide network of transport co-operatives), plus diverse fields of commerce, finance and services.

The Histadrut has had no difficulty holding its own with the private sector of the economy and its strength has never been greater. It is well known that many important Histadrut enterprises today were originally purchased from private investors who were ready to close down operations or move them out of the country because of their inability to make them profitable. Such Histadrut hallmarks as *Phoenicia* (glass) and *Vulcan* (foundries) were purchased from private capitalists, not originally with the idea of making a profit, but of maintaining and expanding employment for settlers. And although Histadrut acquired these firms at the low ebb of their fortunes, the labour organisation eventually went on to make them thoroughly solvent and prospering organisations.

Finally, as for the productivity of its workers, the Histadrut has proved itself an able competitor of private industry. In mining and manufacturing, construction, and transportation and communication, the productivity of workers in the Histadrut sector exceeds that of workers in the private sector.[38]

II. Clegg fears that trade union management would lead to a new form of industrial despotism, not to industrial democracy, because, by taking responsibility for management, the unions would be unable to protect their workers' interests. This has also been contradicted by the Histadrut experience. First, workers in Histadrut firms are organised into an autonomous National Organisation of Workers in Histadrut Enterprises, and at the plant level, relations between management and the workers' committee are characterised by a genuine 'two sided bargaining approach'.[39] In brief, a healthy conflict of interest exists between the two groups. Second, there is regular grievance machinery in *Koor* firms to settle differences which arise between the union and management. It is significant that most of the levels through which grievances pass are weighted in favour of the trade union, and Derber found that *Koor* personnel managers thought that this grievance procedure was unfair to management. But workers had their complaints, too, and believed that management usually came out on top. Third, at least one study has shown that Histadrut managers tend to think like managers in the private sector, and, more important, trade union leaders representing workers in the Histadrut sector tend to think like trade union representatives in private enterprise, i.e., they have worker-oriented attitudes and have not been co-opted by management in any sense.[40] Fourth, the trade unions in Histadrut plants have *more* power and influence over management than they do in private establishments. Especially regarding discipline, transfers, promotions and the like, the Histadrut management regularly consults the workers' representatives, and to a degree un-

known in the private sector.[41] Fifth, wages and conditions in *Koor* plants are generally superior to those in private industry and are recognised as such by the workers who regard an appointment in a *Koor* factory as a privilege: job security is much greater, wages are as high or higher, and fringe benefits are 10–20 per cent better.[42]

Finally, management's authority in Histadrut enterprises does not take the form of despotic, arbitrary, and unchecked rule over groups of docile workers who have been abandoned by their trade union, as suggested by Clegg's thesis, but, on the contrary, management tends to be weak and timid, from the level of the foreman upwards. . . .[43]

NOTES

1. See, e.g., C. A. R. Crossland, 'What Does the Worker Want?' *Encounter* (February 1959), pp. 10–17. Clegg has also influenced foreign scholars. See, e.g., N. Das, *Experiments in Industrial Democracy* (Asia Publishing House, N.Y. 1964).

2. Blackwell, London 1951.

3. Blackwell, London 1960.

4. *Industrial Democracy*, p. 14.

5. Ibid., p. 131.

6. Ibid., p. 121.

7. Ibid., p. 73.

8. Ibid., p. 5.

9. Ibid., pp. 28 ff.

10. Ibid., p. 131.

11. Ibid., p. 133.

12. Ibid., p. 91. It is paradoxical that the Labour Government, which implicitly shares Clegg's views, is now attempting 'to integrate the trade unions in the machinery and ethos of planned capitalism', via wage restraints, increasing labour productivity, and so on, in order to lift the performance of the lagging British economy. See Tony Topham, 'The Campaign for Workers' Control in Britain', *International Socialist Journal*, 2 (August 1965), p. 473.

13. *Industrial Democracy*, p. 139.

14. Ibid., p. 126.

15. Royden Harrison, 'Retreat from Industrial Democracy,' *New Left Review*, 1 (July–August 1960), p. 34.

16. Ibid.

17. *Industrial Democracy*, p. 41.

18. Ibid., p. 22, emphasis added.

19. Ibid., p. 24.

20. Clegg, *A New Approach to Industrial Democracy*, p. 22.

21. Abraham Shuchman, *Codetermination: Labor's Middle Way in Germany* (Public Affairs Press, Washington, 1957), p. 148.

22. See W. M. Blumenthal, *Codetermination in the German Steel Industry* (Industrial Relations Sections, Dept. of Economics and Sociology, Princeton University, Princeton, N.J. 1956), Research Report Series No. 94, p. 29.

23. Shuchman, op. cit., p. 152.

24. *A New Approach*, p. 94.

25. Ibid., p. 55.

26. Ibid.

27. Ibid., p. 54.

28. Ibid., p. 56.

29. Ibid.

30. Ibid., p. 98.

31. Ibid., p. 67.

32. Ibid., p. 69.

33. Ibid., p. 102.

34. Ibid.

35. Ibid., p. 67.

36. For an extended discussion of the Histadrut in the light of Clegg's thesis, see my *Workers' Management in Comparative Analysis* (Ph.D. dissertation, University of California, Berkeley, 1966), ch. 5.

37. *Israel Economist*, 20 (August 1964), p. 143.

38. Haim Barkai, 'The Public, Private and Histadrut Sectors in the Isreaeli Economy', *Falk Project for Economic Research in Israel*. Sixth Report, 1961–3 (Jerusalem 1964), p. 39.

39. Milton Derber, 'Worker Participation in Industrial Management in Israel', (Institute of Labor and Industrial Relations, University of Ill. 1962), mimeographed, p. 21. Published in abridged form in *Industrial Relations*, 3 (October 1963). All page references are to the former.

40. Y. Rim and Bilha F. Mannheim, 'Factors Related to Attitudes of Management and Union Representatives', *Personnel Psychology*, 17 (Summer 1964), pp. 149–65.

41. Derber, op. cit., pp. 20–1.

42. Ferdynand Zweig, *The Israeli Worker: Achievements, Attitudes, and Aspirations* (Herzl Press, N.Y. 1959), pp. 161–3, 166, 217.

43. Ibid., p. 217.

CHAPTER SEVEN
Study Questions

1. How does Zwerdling explain the failures of the General Foods participation program?

2. Describe the varieties of worker participation programs evident in this chapter. Be careful to be clear about where and how they differ.

3. Describe some reasons why the makeup of future labor populations would provide self-interested reasons for companies to allow employees rights to participate in corporate decision making.

4. If employees are to participate in workplace policy setting, what sorts of information need they have access to?

5. How much interest do you believe employees in the general workplace have in participating in decisions at the shop-floor level of the firm? At the board level? What explanations are there for that level of interest?

6. Why does McCall claim that there are moral reasons for a universal employee right to participation in corporate decisions?

7. Northrup sees participation programs as providing unions with an inordinate amount of power, which leads to inefficiency. How does Blumberg suggest that can be avoided? Do you believe that workers who participate in corporate decisions will argue for decisions that would harm the economic viability of the company?

8. Do you believe that ordinary workers can be trained to participate as intelligently as current managers in the decisions that confront corporate management? Is there any evidence for or against your view in the preceding articles?

9. What is the difference between Blumberg's analysis of democracy and Friedman's analysis in Chapter 2? Which seems more appropriate to you?

CHAPTER EIGHT

WHISTLEBLOWING AND LOYALTY

■

CASE STUDY
Gellert v. Eastern Air Lines

Dan Gellert worked for Eastern Air Lines as a first officer (co-pilot) on L-1011 passenger planes. On two occasions the altitude hold on his airplane became disengaged upon slight contact with the control wheel. The altitude hold is an automatic control which keeps the plane flying at a predetermined altitude. When this control was on, an indicator light on the control panel was lit. When the control was disengaged, the light went off. Since no warning buzzer accompanied the light going off, it was possible for the pilots to be temporarily unaware of the change. Gellert's experiences with this problem occurred before a crash of an L-1011 in the Everglades west of Miami while approaching the Miami Airport.

After his first incident, Gellert reported it to a superior flight officer and wrote a letter to Eastern's vice president of operations. Then-Vice-President Frank Borman replied that the matter was being investigated. When the National Transportation Safety Board investigated the Everglades crash, Gellert sent letters to the chairman of the board and the president of Eastern expressing a desire to testify as Eastern's representative at the hearings. Eastern in-

stead sent its most experienced L-1011 pilot, but granted Gellert leave without pay or expenses to attend the hearings as a witness.

Gellert was not satisfied with the NTSB report. After it was released he filed a petition with NTSB asking that some of its findings be reconsidered. When the NTSB denied his petition, he wrote lengthy letters to the FBI and to Borman criticizing safety features of the L-1011. In the letter to Borman, Gellert included a copy of his letter to the FBI.

Eastern was troubled by the tone of the letters and asked their company psychiatrist and neurologist to evaluate them. The doctor concluded that the "construction, tone, intent and implications" of the letters indicated a psychiatric disorder. After examination by Eastern's medical department, Gellert was described as suffering from "monomania," so preoccupied with his cause, or "seeking justice for" himself, that it would not be "completely safe" for him to fly aircraft at that time. On the basis of this report, Gellert was removed from flight status and placed on sick leave with pay. Eastern also published the report of the company's doctor for its employees and the Airline

Pilots Association to read. Some time later Gellert was re-evaluated, found fit, and returned to flight status.

Gellert's troubles at Eastern continued. He was reprimanded for altering the destination of a pass standardly issued to pilots. He contended that the issue was not serious and that the reprimand constituted harrassment for his earlier activities. Later Gellert mailed in a request for change of duty. After a long delay Eastern responded by claiming that the request form was bare of any information. Gellert denied this and charged continued harassment. Finally, Gellert claimed that there was intentional tampering with the planes he was piloting as retaliation for his earlier actions. On one occasion he charged that someone had sabotaged his plane, causing one motor to lose most of its oil. On another occa-sion, an altimeter was improperly measuring the plane's altitude by hundreds of feet.

Gellert eventually sued Eastern Air Lines for breach of contract, intentional infliction of severe mental distress, and defamation. He also asked the courts to require Eastern to institute certain safety procedures.

Gellert saw himself as a crusader for airline safety. Eastern saw him as a troubled, and troublesome, employee. What moral issues are involved here? Can you offer a general evaluation of this case? Independent medical witnesses testified, after reading his letters, that Eastern was justified in originally grounding Gellert. How does this affect your analysis? Was Gellert fair to Eastern? Was Eastern loyal to Gellert? How would your views change if Gellert quit his job? If he were fired?

Introduction

EMPLOYEE WHISTLEBLOWING IS the act of complaining about an unethical, illegal, or dangerous corporate practice. As Gene James says, the whistleblower acts to disclose what he or she considers to be corporate wrongdoing.

Whistleblowing is an important moral and political issue in business ethics for two reasons. First, in deciding whether to blow the whistle, an employee usually confronts a dilemma posed by threats to him and his family if he discloses corporate misdeeds. Since corporate reprisals against whistleblowers are the rule rather than the exception, a prospective whistleblower must choose between the harms caused by the corporate wrongdoing and the potential damage to self and dependents. This choice between two undesirable circumstances is not simply a conflict between morality and self-interest, because persons can have moral obligations concerning their own and their families' welfare. Resolving this dilemma by determining the relative moral significance of obligations to prevent wrongdoing and obligations to protect one's family requires careful consideration of the issues involved. Business ethics discussions of whistleblowing attempt to provide moral guidance by clarifying under just what conditions the need to disclose wrongdoing supercedes a concern for one's own or one's family's welfare.

Whistleblowing is an important issue in business ethics for a second reason also. When an employee discloses corporate wrongdoing, the employee's behavior is in conflict with a traditional view of the employee as possessing duties of loyalty and confidentiality. There is a second conflict posed by employee whistleblowing, then, between moral obligations to prevent wrongdoing and obligations to one's employer. Business ethics discussions must attempt to determine the scope of these potentially opposing obligations by integrating the obligations of persons as employees with the moral and political rights and obligations persons possess as members of human societies. Thus, whistleblowing prompts discussions of the place of business institutions within a broader social context. The articles of this chapter address these two important moral and social aspects of whistleblowing. These two aspects will involve us in discussions of both the morality of disclosing corporate wrongdoing and the appropriateness of government responses to such disclosures.

Phillip Blumberg claims that new views of the duties of employees are slowly emerging from recent extensions of corporate social responsibility. Blumberg claims that these new views of the duties of employees conflict with the traditional legal approach to employment law. He describes in detail how employees traditionally have been held by the Law of Agency to have duties of loyalty, obedience, and confidentiality, which provided for few rights to engage in public disclosure of corporate wrongdoing and even fewer rights to protection from reprisal if they did blow the whistle. This lack of protection for whistleblowers is also discussed in the article by Gene James and in the short comment by John McCall, both of whom emphasize that the traditional employment-at-will doctrine in practice allowed employers to discharge employees for any reason or for no reason at all. The list of legal employee duties and the lack of legal employment security placed employees in a precarious position. Underscoring this is the fact that the legal periodical index until the late 1970s listed articles dealing with employer-employee relations under the general heading of "Master-Servant"! Blumberg, however, sees the need for change in this traditional view of employment, and he quotes Justice Felix Frankfurter's admonition that the employee's obligations under the Law of Agency must be limited by other important social and moral considerations.

As an example of a consideration that could limit the traditional duties of loyalty, obedience, and confidentiality, think about the constitutional right of freedom of speech. The framers of our Constitution, in giving free speech a special protection, recognized that freedom of speech provided for important social goods and that it expressed a belief in the fundamental worth of each person as an autonomous, self-determining being. Of course, freedom of speech is not an absolute right, since we could not be free to shout "fire" in a crowded theater or to slander maliciously the character of another. However, the reader should consider in just what circumstances freedom of speech is unjustly limited when employers retaliate for information disclosure by employees. Can a distinction be drawn between disclosing patented information to competitors and disclosing illegal or immoral practices to the public? Can such a distinction have any implications for when an employee duty of confidentiality ought to be limited by society's interest in promoting free speech?

Another consideration that might limit employee duties according to Frankfurter's admonition is proposed by Tom Donaldson in his book *Corporations and Morality*. Donaldson suggests that every person, as a moral agent, has the obligation to behave responsibly. However, an employer threat of retaliation places obstacles in the path of employees who have a responsibility to warn the public of potential harms. Thus, a moral consideration that people are obligated to behave responsibly might be seen as a legitimate basis for limiting legal duties of employee confidentiality and the legal right of employers to fire at will.

The selection by Ron Duska suggests that the traditional belief that employees owe loyalty to their employer is mistaken. Duska feels that the obligation of loyalty seems reasonable only because the employment relationship is conceived on the basis of an improper analogy. Thus, Duska argues that the belief that there is a serious moral conflict between obligations of loyalty and obligations to prevent harm is confused. Instead, he suggests that the burden of proof is on the employer to show why an employee should not disclose information about corporate wrongdoing.

Gene James, on the other hand, does not reject an employee obligation of loyalty altogether. He does, however, claim that whistleblowing is morally required or permissible in more cases than other commentators have allowed. He finds too restrictive such traditional limitations on whistleblowing as a requirement that internal channels be exhausted before the disclosure is made public. James notes that because circumstances vary, such limitations might discourage whistleblowing when it is obviously appropriate or even necessary for the protection of the public. Similarly, James rejects a moral injunction against anonymous whistleblowing by indicating that on some occasions anonymity could be the morally best policy. All in all, James's analysis is a thoughtful investigation of what ordinarily recognized moral responsibilities might imply about the propriety of whistleblowing. Students should consider carefully his arguments against those who take a more conservative approach to the morality of public disclosure of corporate wrongdoing.

At the conclusion of his article, James suggests that some whistleblowers deserve legal protection from employer reprisals. In a brief comment that follows James's article, John McCall outlines some of the mechanisms proposed for protecting whistleblowers. McCall, while agreeing the protection is needed, is skeptical about the chances any of these proposals have for providing real protection to employees who disclose wrongdoing. By implication, his comment suggests that the dilemma of choosing between disclosing wrongdoing and avoiding harms to self and family will continue so long as employers have the sole power to control the salary and position of employees.

PHILLIP I. BLUMBERG

Corporate Responsibility and the Employee's Duty of Loyalty and Obedience: A Preliminary Inquiry

I. INTRODUCTION

The nature of the American corporate world is changing, reflecting changing concepts of the objectives, role and responsibilities of business. The public corporation as a social and economic organization is undergoing a process of re-examination which has not yet run its course, and the ultimate outcome of which one may still not safely predict. There is general acceptance of the concept of corporate social responsibility with the major public corporation assuming a role of increasing significance in social problem solving. Although highly controversial and not generally accepted, there is also increasing expression of a new view of the large American corporation as a social institution to achieve social objectives, rather than as an economic institution to be operated for economic objectives for the benefit of share-

holders. It is inevitable, therefore, that as a corollary, new views will also emerge with respect to the changing relationship between the corporation and the groups vitally affected by it, particularly its employees, as well as such other groups as consumers, suppliers, and the public generally.

II. RECENT DEVELOPMENTS

This article constitutes a preliminary inquiry into aspects of a problem that the author believes will become an area of dynamic change in the corporate organization and in time will produce significant change in established legal concepts. It is concerned with the impact of the new view of the corporation upon traditional concepts of the duties of loyalty and obedience of the employee to his employer, firmly recognized in the law of agency.

This impact has been illustrated by a number of recent developments, which have a common core: the right of the employee of the large public corporation to take action adverse to the interests of his employer in response to the employee's view as to the proper social responsibility of his corporate employer. . . .

III. THE RESTATEMENT OF AGENCY

A review of the relevant provisions of the *Restatement of Agency* provides an obvious starting point for consideration of the new view of the role and duties of the employee.[1]

A. *The Duty of Obedience*

Section 383 and *Section 385* state the agent's duty to obey the principal. Section 385(1) imposes upon the agent "a duty to obey all reasonable directions" of the principal.[2] Comment *a* points out:

In determining whether or not the orders of the principal to the agent are reasonable . . . *business or professional ethics* . . . are considered.[3] (emphasis added)

Comment *a* continues:

In no event would it be implied that an agent has a duty to perform acts which . . . are *illegal or unethical.* . . .[4] (emphasis added)

Thus, Comment *a* expressly excludes matters contrary to "business or professional ethics" or "illegal or unethical" acts from those which an agent would be required to perform. This frees the agent from participation in such behavior and authorizes him to withdraw from the agency relation if the principal persists. It in no way authorizes him to disclose such directions of the principal, or not to comply with an instruction of the principal not to disclose any information about the principal's affairs, even in those cases where he is privileged not to perform in accordance with the principal's instructions. The duty exists not only so long as the agent remains an agent but continues after the agency has been terminated as well.[5]

Section 385(2) provides:

(2) Unless he is privileged to protect his own or another's interests, an agent is subject to a duty not to act in matters entrusted to him on account of the principal contrary to the directions of the principal. . . .[6]

The Comments make it clear that "an interest" which the agent is privileged to protect refers only to an economic interest, such as a lien[7] or his business reputation.[8] There is no suggestion that an interest which "he is privileged to protect" includes the public interest.

B. *The Duty of Loyalty*

Section 387 expresses the general principle that:

an agent is subject to a duty to his principal to act solely for the benefit of the principal in all matters connected with his agency.[9]

Comment *b* emphasizes the high degree of the duties of loyalty of the agent by stating that they "are the same as those of a trustee to his beneficiaries." It provides, however, that:

The agent is also under a duty not to act or speak disloyally . . . except in the protection of his own interests or those of others. He is not, however, necessarily prevented from acting in good faith outside his employment in a manner which injuriously affects his principal's business.[10]

and provides the following illustration:

3. A, employed by P, a life insurance company, in good faith advocates legislation which would require a change in the policies issued by the company. A has violated no duty to P.[11]

Thus, the agent is free to act "in good faith outside his employment," even in a manner which injures his principal's business, but is subject to a duty identical with that of a trustee with respect to "all matters connected with his agency." Under the comment and illustration, the General Motors employee may campaign in good faith for legislation imposing costly antipollution or product safety controls on automobile manufacturers, but he occupies a position equivalent to a trustee with respect to information about General Motors operations which he has acquired in the course, or on account, of his employment.

Section 394 prohibits the agent from acting:

for persons whose interests conflict with those of the principal in matters in which the agent is employed.[12]

The numerous examples in the comments relate to competitors or adverse parties in commercial transactions or parties with adverse claims and make it plain that the reference to conflicting "interests" means economic interests.

C. *The Duty of Confidentiality*

Section 395 imposes a duty upon the agent:

not to use or to communicate information confidentially given him by the principal or acquired by him during the course of or on account of his agency . . . to the injury of the principal, on his own account or on behalf of another . . . unless the information is a matter of general knowledge.[13]

Comment *a* emphasizes that the agency relation "permits and requires great freedom of communication between the principal and the agent." It expands the agent's duty by stating that the agent:

also has a duty not to use information acquired by him as agent . . . for any purpose likely to cause his principal harm or to interfere with his business, although it is information not connected with the subject matter of his agency.[14]

Comment *b* extends the duty beyond "confidential" communications to "information which the agent should know his principal would not care to have revealed to others."[15] Both Comments *a* and *b* refer to protection of the principal against competition, but it is clear that this is merely one of the interests of the principal protected by the section.

Comment *f* creates a privilege, significantly enough for a public, not an economic, interest:

An agent is privileged to reveal information confidentially acquired . . . in the protection of a superior interest of himself or of a third person. Thus, if the confidential information is to the effect that the principal is committing or is about to commit a crime, the agent is under no duty not to reveal it.[16]

This is the only illustration in the *Restatement* that the term "interest" may embrace something of a non-economic nature. The public interest in law enforcement is deemed a "superior interest" giving rise to a privilege to reveal otherwise confidential information.

If construed to include disclosure to any person, and not solely to law enforcement agencies, Comment *f* would support the "public interest disclosure" proposal to the extent it relates to "illegal" matters, without regard to the nature or seriousness of the offense. Section 395, Comment *f*, however, refers only to commission of a "crime." This contrasts with Section 385(1) relating to the duty of obedience which refers not only to "illegal" but also to "unethical" acts and to "business or professional ethics." The inclusion of these latter elements in Section 385(1) and their omission in Section 395 would indicate that the release of confidential information privileged under Section 395 does not extend beyond criminal acts.

Although Section 395 refers only to the agent's use or communication of information "on his own account or on behalf of another" and does not literally prohibit use or communication of such information for the benefit of the public, Comment *a* prohibits such use "for any purpose likely to cause his principal harm or to interfere with his business." Comment *a* thus would appear to expand the duty of the agent beyond acts "on his own account or on behalf of another" to include disclosures made to advance the "public interest," which were not related to commission of a "crime" privileged under Comment *f*.

D. *Privileged Conduct*

Section 411 makes "illegality" a defense for an agent's nonperformance. Comment *d* extends the defense to acts:

which are criminal . . . [or] although not criminal, are so contrary to public policy that an agreement to perform them will not be enforced.[17]

This follows the common-law rule that the principal cannot complain of the agent's failure to enter into agreements which would have been unenforceable, since even if the agent had performed, the principal would not have been able to enforce the agreement made by the agent.[18]

Section 411, referring to "illegality" or acts which are "criminal" or "contrary to public policy" closely, but not precisely, follows Section 385(1), Comment *a* which refers to "illegal or unethical" acts. Both Sections 411 and 385(2) dealing with the agent's privileged refusal to act contrast with Section 395 dealing with privileged disclosure which is restricted solely to "crime."[19]

Section 418 confirms the exception contained in Section 385 that:

An agent is privileged to protect interests of his own which are superior to those of the principal, even though he does so at the expense of the principal's interests or in disobedience to his orders.[20]

Again, the crucial question is the meaning to be ascribed to "interests." Comment *a* contains the usual emphasis on the agent's economic interests. As in the case of Section 385(2), Section 418, Comment *a* permits the agent to perform a contract unenforceable under the Statute of Frauds "to protect his financial interests or reputation" or to protect "a security interest in the principal's goods."

Comment *a* also provides that:

Similarly the agent has no duty to commit a tort or a minor crime at the command of the principal.[21]

This reference to "tort or a minor crime" may be compared with the references to "illegal or unethical" acts in Section 385(1), Comment *a*, and to acts which are "criminal" or "contrary to public policy" in Section 411 dealing with essentially the same problem.

In summary, except in the single area of "crime," the *Restatement* provides no support for the view that the employee may disclose nonpublic information about his employer acquired as a result of the employment relationship in order to promote the superior interest of society. While prohibiting affirmative acts of the employee such as disclosure, the *Restatement* relieves the employee of any duty to obey or act for the employer not only in the case of "crime" or "illegality" but also in case of "unethical acts" or acts "contrary to public policy" or constituting a tort.

The duties of obedience, loyalty, and confidentiality enunciated by the *Restatement* and the carefully circumscribed privileged exceptions clearly proscribe the "public interest disclosure" proposal suggested by Mr. Nader. We must recognize, however, that the *Restatement* drawn from the common-law cases is drafted in terms of economic activity, economic motivation, and economic advantage and formulates duties of loyalty and obedience for the agent to prevent the agent's own economic interests from impairing his judgment, zeal, or single-minded devotion to the furtherance of his principal's economic interests. The reference in Section 395, Comment *f* permitting the agent to disclose confidential information concerning a criminal act committed or planned by the principal is the sole exception to a system of analysis that is otherwise exclusively concerned with matters relating to the economic position of the parties. Thus, the question may fairly be asked to what extent the *Restatement* and the common-law decisions are useful in the analysis of a proposal that rests on the concept of an agent's primary obligation as a citizen to the society, transcending his economic duty to the principal.

Are doctrines resting on a policy of protecting the economic position of the principal against impairment by reason of an agent's effort to achieve economic gain properly applicable to the employee who releases non-public information about his employer without intent to obtain economic advantage for himself—and in fact at considerable economic risk to himself—and motivated by a desire to promote the public good rather than to injure the principal (although such injury may in fact result)?

The duties of loyalty and obedience on the part of the agent are unquestionably central to the agency relationship, irrespective of economic considerations. But these duties, as the *Restatement* itself recognizes, have limitations. To paraphrase Mr. Justice Frankfurter's well-known admonition: To say that an agent has duties of loyalty and obedience only begins analysis; it gives direction to further inquiry. It is thus not enough to say that the agent has duties of loyalty and obedience which will be impaired. One must inquire more deeply and ascertain the outer perimeters of the agent's obligations by balancing the conflicting considerations. On this critical question of how far the duties of loyalty and obedience extend, the *Restatement* enunciating the traditional rules in their economic setting provides limited guidance. . . .

NOTES

1. For the purposes of this paper, "agent" should be regarded as interchangeable with "employee."

2. *Restatement (Second) of Agency* § 385(1) (1958) (hereinafter cited as *Restatement*).

3. *Id.* § 385(1), Comment *a. See* W. Bowstead, *Agency* 111 (13th ed. 1968) ("In the case of a professional man, he will be bound to a considerable extent by the rules and ethical standards of his profession and he could not be required to perform an act which was contrary to those rules or standards.")

4. *Restatement* § 385(1), Comment *a.*

5. *Id.* § 396. *See* W. Bowstead, *Agency* 134 (13th ed. 1968); R. Powell, *Law of Agency* 314 (2d ed. 1961).

6. *Restatement* § 385(2).

7. *Id.* § 385(2), Comment *f* gives as an example an agent's security interest in the nature of a lien on goods sent to him to sell.

8. *Id.* § 385(2), Comment *f* (An agent is privileged to perform an authorized contract which is unenforceable under the Statute of Frauds, "although the principal directs him not to do so, in situations in which it is

customary for the defense of the Statute of Frauds to be waived and in which the agent's business reputation would suffer by his nonperformance.")

9. *Restatement* § 387.

10. *Id.* § 387, Comment *b.*

11. *Id.* § 387, Comment *b*, Illustration 3.

12. *Id.* § 394.

13. *Id.* § 395.

14. *Id.* § 395, Comment *a.*

15. *Id.* § 395, Comment *b.*

16. *Id.* § 395, Comment *f; see* Willig v. Gold, 171 P.2d 754, 757 (Cal. App. 1946) (Counsel "cites no case, and we are sure none can be found, that an agent is under a legal duty not to disclose his principal's dishonest acts to the party prejudicially affected.")

17. *Id.* § 411, Comment *d.*

18. Thomas Cheshire & Co. v. Vaughan Bros. & Co., (1920) 3 K.B. 240 (C.A. 1920); Cohen v. Kittell, 22 Q.B.D. 680 (1889); Webster v. DeTastet, 7 Term Rep. 157 (1797); *see* F. Tiffany, *Handbook of the Law of Principal and Agent* 376 (2d ed. 1924); W. Paley, *Law of Principal and Agency* 8 (1856).

19. It is possible to envision an act which is "illegal" but not a "crime." There is no indication that the draftsmen of the *Restatement* were attempting to make such a distinction.

20. *Restatement* § 418.

21. *Id.* § 418, Comment *a.*

RONALD DUSKA

Whistleblowing and Employee Loyalty

Three Mile Island. In early 1983, almost four years after the near meltdown at Unit 2, two officials in the Site Operations Office of General Public Utilities reported a reckless company effort to clean up the contaminated reactor. Under threat of physical retaliation from superiors, the GPU insiders released evidence alleging that the company had rushed the TMI cleanup without testing key maintenance systems. Since then, the Three Mile Island mop-up has been stalled pending a review of GPU's management.[1]

The releasing of evidence of the rushed cleanup at Three Mile Island is an example of whistleblowing. Norman Bowie defines whistleblowing as "the act by an employee of informing the public on the immoral or illegal behavior of an employer or supervisor."[2] Ever since Daniel Ellsberg's release of the Pentagon Papers, the question of whether an employee should blow the whistle on his company or organization has become a hotly contested issue. Was Ellsberg right? Is it right to report the shady or suspect practices of the organization one works for? Is one a stool pigeon or a dedicated citizen? Does a person have an obligation to the public which overrides his obligation to his employer or does he simply betray a loyalty and become a traitor if he reports his company?

There are proponents on both sides of the issue—those who praise whistleblowers as civic heroes and those who condemn them as "finks." Glen and Shearer who wrote about the whistleblowers at Three Mile Island say, "Without the *courageous* breed of assorted company insiders known as whistleblowers—workers who often risk their livelihoods to disclose information about construction and design flaws—the Nuclear Regulatory Commission itself would be nearly as idle as Three Mile Island . . . That whistleblowers deserve both gratitude and protection is beyond disagreement."[3]

Still, while Glen and Shearer praise whistleblowers, others vociferously condemn them. For example, in a now-infamous quote, James Roche, the former president of General Motors said:

Some critics are now busy eroding another support of free enterprise—the loyalty of a management team, with its unifying values and cooperative work. Some of the enemies of business now encourage an employee to be *disloyal* to the enterprise. They want to create suspicion and disharmony, and pry into the proprietary interests of the business. However this is labelled—industrial espionage, whistle blowing, or professional responsibility—it is another tactic for spreading disunity and creating conflict.[4]

From Roche's point of view, whistleblowing is not only not "courageous" and deserving of "gratitude and protection" as Glen and Shearer would have it, it is corrosive and not even permissible.

Discussions of whistleblowing generally revolve around four topics: (1) attempts to define whistleblowing more precisely; (2) debates about whether and when whistleblowing is permissible; (3) debates about whether and when one has an obligation to blow the whistle; and (4) appropriate mechanisms for institutionalizing whistleblowing.

In this paper I want to focus on the second problem, because I find it somewhat disconcerting that there is a problem at all. When I first looked into the ethics of whistleblowing it seemed to me that whistleblowing was a good thing, and yet I found in the literature claim after claim that it was in need of defense, that there was something wrong with it, namely that it was an act of disloyalty.

If whistleblowing was a disloyal act, it deserved disapproval, and ultimately any action of whistleblowing needed justification. This disturbed me. It was as if the act of a good Samaritan was being condemned as an act of interference, as if the prevention of a suicide needed to be justified. My moral position in favor of whistleblowing was being challenged. The tables were turned and the burden of proof had shifted. My position was the one in question. Suddenly instead of the company being the bad guy and the whistleblower the good guy, which is what I thought, the whistleblower was the bad guy. Why? Because he was disloyal. What I discovered was that in most of the literature it was taken as axiomatic that whistleblowing was an act of disloyalty. My moral intuitions told me that axiom was mistaken. Nevertheless, since it is accepted by a large segment of the ethical community it deserves investigation.

In his book *Business Ethics*, Norman Bowie, who presents what I think is one of the finest presentations of the ethics of whistleblowing, claims that "whistleblowing . . . violate[s] a *prima facie* duty of loyalty to one's employer." According to Bowie, there is a duty of loyalty which prohibits one from reporting his employer or company. Bowie, of course, recognizes that this is only a *prima facie* duty, i.e., one that can be overridden by a higher duty to the public good. Nevertheless, the axiom that whistleblowing is disloyal is Bowie's starting point.

Bowie is not alone. Sisela Bok, another fine ethicist, sees whistleblowing as an instance of disloyalty.

The whistleblower hopes to stop the game; but since he is neither referee nor coach, and since he blows the whistle on his own team, his act is seen as a *violation of loyalty* [italics mine]. In holding his position, he has assumed certain obligations to his colleagues and clients. He may even have subscribed to a loyalty oath or a promise of confidentiality. . . . Loyalty to colleagues and to clients comes to be pitted against loyalty to the public interest, to those who may be injured unless the revelation is made.[5]

Bowie and Bok end up defending whistleblowing in certain contexts, so I don't necessarily disagree with their conclusions. However, I fail to see how one has an obligation of loyalty to one's company, so I disagree with their perception of the problem, and their starting point. The difference in perception is important because those who think employees have an obligation of loyalty to a company fail to take into account a relevant moral difference between persons and corporations and between corporations and other kinds of groups where loyalty is appropriate. I want to argue that one does not have an obligation of loyalty to a company, even a *prima facie* one, because companies are not the kind of things which are proper objects of loyalty. I then want to show that to make them objects of loyalty gives them a moral status they do not deserve and in raising their status, one lowers the status of the individuals who work for the companies.

But why aren't corporations the kind of things which can be objects of loyalty? . . .

Loyalty is ordinarily construed as a state of being constant and faithful in a relation implying trust or confidence, as a wife to husband, friend to friend, parent to child, lord to vassal, etc. According to John Ladd "it is not founded on just *any* casual relationship, but on a specific kind of relationship or tie. The ties that bind the persons together provide the basis of loyalty."[6] But all sorts of ties bind people together to make groups. I am a member of a group of fans if I go to a ball game. I am a member of a group if I merely walk down the street. I am in a sense tied to them, but don't owe them loyalty. I don't owe loyalty to just anyone I encounter. Rather I owe loyalty to persons with whom I have special relationships. I owe it to my children, my spouse, my parents, my friends and certain groups, those groups which are formed for the mutual enrichment of the members. It is important to recognize that in any relationship which demands loyalty the relationship works both ways and involves mutual enrichment. Loyalty is incompatible with self-interest, because it is something that necessarily requires we go beyond self-interest. My loyalty to my friend, for example, requires I put aside my interests some of the time. It is because of this reciprocal requirement which demands surrendering self-interest that a corporation is not a proper object of loyalty.

A business or corporation does two things in the free enterprise system. It produces a good or service and makes a profit. The making of a profit, however, is the primary function of a business as a business. For if the production of the good or service was not profitable the business would be out of business. Since non-profitable goods or services are discontinued, the providing of a service or the making of a product is not done for its own sake, but from a business perspective is a means to an end, the making of profit. People bound together in a business are not bound together for mutual fulfillment and support, but to divide labor so the business makes a profit. Since profit is paramount if you do not produce in a company or if there are cheaper laborers around, a company feels justified in firing you for the sake of better production. Throughout history companies in a pinch feel no obligation of loyalty. Compare that to a family. While we can jokingly refer to a family as "somewhere they have to take you in no matter what," you cannot refer to a company in that way. "You can't buy loyalty" is true. Loyalty depends on ties that demand self-sacrifice with no expectation of reward, e.g., the ties of loyalty that bind a family together. Business functions on the basis of enlightened self-interest. I am devoted to a company not because it is like a parent to me. It is not, and attempts of some companies to create "one big happy family" ought to be looked on with suspicion. I am not "devoted" to it at all, or should not be. I *work* for it because it pays me. I am not in a family to get paid, but I am in a company to get paid.

Since loyalty is a kind of devotion, one can confuse devotion to one's job (or the ends of one's work) with devotion to a company.

I may have a job I find fulfilling, but that is accidental to my relation to the company. For example, I might go to work for a company as a carpenter and love the job and get satisfaction out of doing good work. But if the company can increase profit by cutting back to an adequate but inferior type of material or procedure, it can make it impossible for me to take pride in my work as a carpenter while making it possible for me to make more money. The company does not exist to subsidize my quality work as a carpenter. As a carpenter my goal may be good houses, but as an employee my goal is to contribute to making a profit. "That's just business"!

This fact that profit determines the quality of work allowed leads to a phenomenon called the commercialization of work. The primary end of an act of building is to make something, and to build well is to make it well. A carpenter is defined by the end of his work, but if the quality interferes with profit, the business side of the venture supercedes the artisan side. Thus profit forces a craftsman to suspend his devotion to his work and commercializes his venture. The more professions subject themselves to the forces of the marketplace, the more they get commercialized; e.g., research for the sake of a more profitable product rather than for the sake of knowledge jeopardizes the integrity of academic research facilities.

The cold hard truth is that the goal of profit is what gives birth to a company and forms that particular group. Money is what ties the group together. But in such a commercialized venture, with such a goal there is no loyalty, or at least none need be expected. An employer will release an employee and an employee will walk away from an employer when it is profitable to do so. That's business. It is perfectly permissible. Contrast that with the ties between a lord and his vassal. A lord could not in good conscience wash his hands of his vassal, nor could a vassal in good conscience abandon his lord. What bound them was mutual enrichment, not profit.

Loyalty to a corporation, then, is not required. But even more it is probably misguided. There is nothing as pathetic as the story of the loyal employee who, having given above and beyond the call of duty, is let go in the restructuring of the company. He feels betrayed because he mistakenly viewed the company as an object of his loyalty. To get rid of such foolish romanticism and to come to grips with this hard but accurate assessment should ultimately benefit everyone.

One need hardly be an enemy of business to be suspicious of a demand of loyalty to something whose primary reason for existence is the making of profit. It is simply the case that I have no duty of loyalty to the business or organization. Rather I have a duty to return responsible work for fair wages. The commercialization of work dissolves the type of relationship that requires loyalty. It sets up merely contractual relationships. One sells one's labor but not one's self to a company or an institution.

To think we owe a company or corporation loyalty requires us to think of that company as a person or as a group with a goal of human enrichment. If we think of it in this way we can be loyal. But this is just the wrong way to think. A company is not a person. A company is an instrument, and an instrument with a specific purpose, the making of profit. To treat an instrument as an end in itself, like a person, may not be as bad as treating an end as an instrument, but it does give the instrument a moral status it does not deserve, and by elevating the instrument we lower the end. All things, instruments and ends, become alike.

To treat a company as a person is analogous to treating a machine as a person or treating a system as a person. The system, company, or instrument get as much respect and care as the persons for whom they were invented. If we remember that the primary purpose of business is to make profit, it can be seen clearly as merely an instrument. If so, it needs to be used and regulated accordingly, and I owe it no more loyalty than I owe a word processor.

Of course if everyone would view business as a commercial instrument, things might become more difficult for the smooth functioning of the organization, since businesses could not count on the "loyalty" of their employees. Business itself is well served, at least in the short run, if it can keep the notion of a duty to loyalty alive. It does this by comparing itself to a paradigm case of an organization one shows loyalty to, the team.

Remember that Roche refers to the "management team" and Bok sees the name "whistleblowing" coming from the instance of a referee blowing a whistle in the presence of a foul. What is perceived as bad about whistleblowing in business from this perspective is that one blows the whistle on one's own team, thereby violating team loyalty. If the company can get its employees to view it as a team they belong to, it is easier to demand loyalty. The rules governing teamwork and team loyalty will apply. One reason the appeal to a team and team loyalty works so well in business is that businesses are in competition with one another. If an executive could get his employees to be loyal, a loyalty without thought to himself or his fellow man, but to the will of the company, the manager would have the ideal kind of corporation from an organizational standpoint. As Paul R. Lawrence, the organizational theorist says, "Ideally, we would want one sentiment to be dominant in all employees from top to bottom, namely a complete loyalty to the organizational purpose."[7] Effective motivation turns business practices into a game and instills teamwork.

But businesses differ from teams in very important respects, which makes the analogy between business and a team dangerous. Loyalty to a team is loyalty within the context of sport, a competition. Teamwork and team loyalty require that in the circumscribed activity of the game I cooperate with my fellow players, so that pulling all together, we can win. The object of (most) sports is victory. But the winning in sports is a social convention, divorced from the usual goings on of society. Such a winning is most times a harmless, morally neutral diversion.

But the fact that this victory in sports, within the rules enforced by a referee (whistleblower), is a socially developed convention taking place within a larger social context makes it quite different from competition in business, which, rather than being defined by a context, permeates the whole of society in its influence. Competition leads not only to winners but to losers. One can lose at sport with precious few serious consequences. The consequences of losing at business are much more serious. Further, the losers in sport are there voluntarily, while the losers in business can be those who are not in the game voluntarily (we are all forced to participate) but are still affected by business decisions. People cannot choose to participate in business, since it permeates everyone's life.

The team model fits very well with the model of the free-market system because there competition is said to be the name of the game. Rival companies compete and their object is to win. To call a foul on one's own teammate is to jeopardize one's chances of winning and is viewed as disloyalty.

But isn't it time to stop viewing the corporate machinations as games? These games are not controlled and are not over after a specific time. The activities of business affect the lives of everyone, not just the game players. The analogy of the corporation to a team and the consequent appeal to team loyalty, although understandable, is seriously misleading at least in the moral sphere, where competition is not the prevailing virtue.

If my analysis is correct, the issue of the permissibility of whistleblowing is not a real issue, since there is no obligation of loyalty to a company. Whistleblowing is not only permissible but expected when a company is harming society. The issue is not one of disloyalty to the company, but the question of whether the whistleblower has an obligation to society if blowing the whistle will bring him retaliation. I will not argue that issue, but merely suggest the lines I would pursue.

I tend to be a minimalist in ethics, and depend heavily on a distinction between obligations and acts of supererogation. We have, it seems to me, an obligation to avoid harming anyone, but not an obligation to do good. Doing good is above the call of duty. In-between we may under certain conditions have an obligation to prevent harm. If whistleblowing can prevent harm, then it is required under certain conditions.

Simon, Power and Gunneman set forth four conditions:[8] need, proximity, capability, and last resort. Applying these, we get the following.

1. There must be a clear harm to society that can be avoided by whistleblowing. We don't blow the whistle over everything.
2. It is the "proximity" to the whistleblower that puts him in the position to report his company in the first place.
3. "Capability" means that he needs to have some chance of success. No one has an obligation to jeopardize himself to perform futile gestures. The whistleblower needs to have access to the press, be believable, etc.
4. "Last resort" means just that. If there are others more capable of reporting and more proximate, and if they will report, then one does not have the responsibility.

Before concluding, there is one aspect of the loyalty issue that ought to be disposed of. My position could be challenged in the case of organizations who are employers in non-profit areas, such as the government, educational institutions, etc. In this case my commercialization argument is irrelevant. However, I would maintain that any activity which merits the blowing of the whistle in the case of non-profit and service organizations is probably counter to the purpose of the institution in the first place. Thus, if there were loyalty required, in that case, whoever justifiably blew the whistle would be blowing it on a colleague who perverted the end or purpose of the organization. The loyalty to the group would remain intact. Ellsberg's whistleblowing on the government is a way of keeping the government faithful to its obligations. But that is another issue.

NOTES

1. Maxwell Glen and Cody Shearer, "Going After the Whistle-blowers," *The Philadelphia Inquirer*, Tuesday, Aug. 2, 1983, Op-ed Page, p. 11a.

2. Norman Bowie, *Business Ethics* (Englewood Cliffs, N.J.: Prentice-Hall, 1982), p. 140. For Bowie, this is just a preliminary definition. His fuller definition reads, "A whistle blower is an employee or officer of any institution, profit or non-profit, private or public, who believes either that he/she has been ordered to perform some act or he/she has obtained knowledge that the institution is engaged in activities which a) are believed to cause unnecessary harm to third parties, b) are in violation of human rights or c) run counter to the defined purpose of the institution and who inform the public of this fact." Bowie then lists six conditions under which the act is justified. pp. 142–143.

3. Glen and Shearer, *ibid.*

4. James M. Roche, "The Competitive System, to Work, to Preserve, and to Protect," *Vital Speeches of the Day* (May 1971), 445. This is quoted in Bowie, p. 141 and also in Kenneth D. Walters, "Your Employee's Right to Blow the Whistle," *Harvard Business Review*, 53, no. 4.

5. Sisela Bok, "Whistleblowing and Professional Responsibilities," *New York University Education Quarterly*, Vol. II, 4 (1980), p. 3.

6. John Ladd, "Loyalty," *The Encyclopedia of Philosophy*, Vol. 5, p. 97.

7. Paul R. Lawrence, *The Changing of Organizational Behavior Patterns: A Case Study of Decentralization* (Boston: Division of Research, Harvard Business School, 1958), p. 208, as quoted in Kenneth D. Walters, op. cit.

8. John G. Simon, Charles W. Powers, and Jon P. Gunnemann, *The Ethical Investor: Universities and Corporate Responsibility* (New Haven: Yale University Press, 1972).

GENE G. JAMES
In Defense of Whistleblowing

INTRODUCTION

Whistleblowing may be defined as the attempt by an employee or former employee of an organization to disclose what he or she believes to be wrongdoing in or by the organization. The name comes from the fact that like blowing a whistle to call attention to a thief, whistleblowing is an effort to make others aware of practices one considers illegal, unjust, or harmful. Whenever someone goes over the head of immediate supervisors to inform higher management of wrongdoing, the whistleblowing is *internal* to the organization. Whenever someone discloses wrongdoing to outside individuals or groups such as reporters, public interest groups, or regulatory agencies, the whistleblowing is *external*.

Most whistleblowing is by people presently employed by the organization. However, people who have left the organization may also blow the whistle. The former may be referred to as *current* whistleblowing, the latter as *alumni* whistleblowing. If the whistleblower discloses his or her identity, the whistleblowing may be said to be *open*; if the whistleblower's identity is not disclosed, the whistleblowing is *anonymous*.

Whistleblowers differ from "muckrakers" because the latter do not have any ties to the organizations about which they seek to disclose wrongdoing. They differ from "informers" and "stool pigeons" because these words are most often used of people who disclose wrongdoing for self-interested reasons such as to obtain prosecutorial immunity. The term "whistleblower," on the other hand, is usually used to refer to people who disclose wrongdoing for moral reasons. However, unless whistleblowing is *defined* as disclosing wrongdoing for moral reasons, the distinction between whistleblowing and informers cannot be a sharp one. Thus, although most whistleblowers blow the whistle for moral reasons, one cannot take for granted that because a whistleblower attempts to disclose wrongdoing, his or her motive must be praiseworthy.

Whistleblowers almost always experience retaliation. If they work for private industry, they are likely to be fired. They also receive damaging letters of recommendation and may be blacklisted so they cannot find work in their profession. If they are not fired, or work for government agencies, they are still likely to be transferred, demoted, given less interesting work, and denied salary increases and promotions. Their professional competence is usually attacked. They are said to be unqualified to judge, misinformed, and so forth. Since their actions seem to threaten both the organization and their fellow employees, attacks on their personal lives are also frequent. They are said to be traitors, "rat finks," etc. They are also said to be disgruntled, known troublemakers, people who make an issue out of nothing, self-serving, and doing it for the publicity. Their life styles, sex life and mental stability may be questioned. Physical assaults, abuse of their families, and even murder are not unknown as retaliation to whistleblowing.

WHISTLEBLOWING AND THE LAW[1]

The law does not at present offer whistleblowers very much protection. Agency law, the area of common law which governs relations between employees and employers, imposes a duty on employees to keep confidential any information learned through their employment which might be detrimental to their employers. However, this duty does not hold if the employee has knowledge that the employer either has committed, or is about to commit, a felony. In this case the employee has a positive obligation to report the offense. Failure to

do so is known as misprision and makes one subject to criminal penalties.

The problem with agency law is that it is based on the assumption that unless there are statutes or agreements to the contrary, contracts between employees and employers can be terminated at will by either party. It therefore grants employers the right to discharge employees at any time for any reason or even for no reason at all. The result is that most employees who blow the whistle on their employers, even those who report felonies, are fired or suffer other retaliation. One employee of thirty years was even fired the day before his pension became effective for testifying under subpoena against his employer, without the courts doing anything to aid him.

This situation has begun to change somewhat in recent years. In *Pickering v. Board of Education* in 1968 the Supreme Court ruled that government employees have the right to speak out on policy issues affecting their agencies provided doing so does not seriously disrupt the agency. A number of similar decisions have followed and the right of government employees to speak out on policy issues now seems firmly established. But employees in private industry do not have the right to speak out on company policies without being fired. In one case involving both a union and a company doing a substantial portion of its business with the federal government, federal courts did award back pay to an employee fired for criticizing the union and the company, but did not reinstate or award him punitive damages.

A few state courts have begun to modify the right of employers to dismiss employees at will. Courts in Oregon and Pennsylvania have awarded damages to employees fired for serving on juries. A New Hampshire court granted damages to a woman fired for refusing to date her foreman. A West Virginia court reinstated a bank employee who reported illegal interest rates. The Illinois Supreme Court upheld the right of an employee to sue when fired for reporting and testifying about criminal activities of a fellow employee. However, a majority of states still uphold the right of employers to fire employees at will unless there are statutes or agreements to the contrary. Only one state, Michigan, has passed a law prohibiting employers from retaliating against employees who report violations of local, state or federal laws.

A number of federal statutes contain provisions intended to protect whistleblowers. The National Labor Relations Act, Fair Labor Standards Act, Title VII of the 1964 Civil Rights Act, Age Discrimination Act and Occupational Safety and Health Act, all have sections prohibiting employers from taking retaliatory actions against employees who report or testify about violations of the acts.

Although these laws seem to encourage and protect whistleblowers, to be effective they must be enforced. A 1976 study[2] of the Occupational Safety and Health Act showed that only about 20% of the 2300 complaints filed in fiscal years 1975 and 1976 were judged valid by OSHA investigators. About half of these were settled out of court. Of the 60 cases taken to court at the time of the study in November 1976, one had been won, eight lost and the others were still pending. A more recent study[3] showed that of the 3,100 violations reported in 1979, only 270 were settled out of court and only 16 litigated.

Since the National Labor Relations Act guarantees the right of workers to organize and bargain collectively, and most collective bargaining agreements contain a clause requiring employers to have just cause for discharging employees, they would seem to offer some protection for whistleblowers. In fact, however, arbitrators have tended to agree with employers that whistleblowing is an act of disloyalty which disrupts business and injures the employer's reputation. Their attitude seems to be summed up in a 1972 case in which the arbitrator stated that one should not "bite the hand that feeds you and insist on staying for future banquets."[4] One reason for this, pointed out by David Ewing, is that unions are frequently as corrupt as the organizations on which the whistle is being blown. Such unions, he says, "are not likely to feed a hawk that comes to prey in their own barnyard."[5] The record of professional societies is not any better. They have in general failed to come to the defense of members who have attempted to live up to their professional codes of ethics by blowing the whistle on corrupt practices.

THE MORAL JUSTIFICATION OF WHISTLEBLOWING

Under what conditions, if any, is whistleblowing morally justified? Some people have argued that it

is always justified because it is an exercise of free speech. But, the right to free speech like most other rights is not absolute. Thus, even if whistleblowing is a form of free speech, that does not mean it is justified in every case. Others have argued that whistleblowing is never justified because employees have obligations of absolute loyalty and confidentiality to the organization for which they work. However, because the actions of organizations often harm or violate the rights of others, and one has an obligation to prevent these if one can, a universal prohibition against whistleblowing is not justifiable.

Assuming that we reject such extreme views, what conditions must be satisfied for whistleblowing to be morally justified? Richard De George believes that whistleblowing is morally permissible if it meets the following three conditions:

1. The company must be engaged in a practice or about to release a product which does *serious* harm to individuals or to society in general. The more serious the harm, the more serious the obligation.
2. The employee should report his concern or complaint to his immediate superior. If no appropriate action is taken, then
3. The employee should take the matter up the managerial line. Before he is obliged to go public, he should exhaust the resources for remedy within the company.[6]

For whistleblowing to be morally obligatory De George thinks two other conditions must be satisfied:

4. The employee should have documentation of the practice or defect. . . . Without adequate evidence his chances of being successful . . . are slim.
5. The employee must have good reason to believe that by going public he will be able to bring about the necessary changes.[7]

De George believes that because of the almost certain retaliation whistleblowers experience, whistleblowing is frequently morally permissible but not morally obligatory. He holds that this is true even when the individual involved is a professional whose code of ethics requires him or her to put the public good ahead of personal good. He argues, for example:

The myth that ethics has no place in engineering has . . . at least in some corners of the engineering profession . . . been put to rest. Another myth, however, is emerging to take its place—the myth of the engineer as moral hero. . . . The zeal . . . however, has gone too far, piling moral responsibility upon moral responsibility on the shoulders of the engineer. This emphasis . . . is misplaced. Though engineers are members of a profession that holds public safety paramount, we cannot reasonably expect engineers to be willing to sacrifice their jobs each day for principle and to have a whistle ever at their sides. . . .[8]

He contends that engineers have an obligation only to do their jobs the best they can. This includes reporting observations about safety to management. But engineers do not have an "obligation to insist that their perceptions or their standards be accepted. They are not paid to do that, they are not expected to do that, and they have no moral or ethical obligation to do that."[9]

There are a number of problems with this analysis of whistleblowing.

The first condition is far too strong because it requires that there be *de facto* wrongdoing before whistleblowing is morally justified, instead of requiring that whistleblowers have evidence which makes it extremely probable that wrongdoing is occurring. All that should be required of whistleblowers in this regard is that they be diligent in gathering evidence and act on the basis of the best evidence available to them. They should not be held to a more rigid standard than is usually applied to moral actions.

What constitutes serious and considerable harm? Must the harm be physical? Since De George was writing on business ethics, it is understandable that he only discussed whistleblowing involving corporations. But businesses, like governments, can be guilty of wrongs other than physically harming people. Should one, e.g., never blow the whistle on such things as invasions of privacy?

If the harm is physical, how many people's health or safety must be endangered before the harm can be said to be considerable? And do professionals not have an obligation to inform the public of dangerous products and practices even if they will lose their jobs? Even though some Ford engineers had serious misgivings about the safety of Pinto gas tanks, and several people were killed when tanks exploded after rear end crashes, De George says that Ford engineers did not have an obligation to make their misgivings public. He maintains that although engineers are better qualified than other people to calculate cost versus safety, decisions about acceptable risk are not primarily engineering but managerial decisions. He believes that under ideal conditions the public itself would make this kind of decision. "A panel of informed people, not necessarily engineers, should decide . . . acceptable risk and minimum standards."[10] This information should then be relayed to car buyers who he believes are entitled to it.

One of the reasons it is difficult to decide when employees have an obligation to blow the whistle is that this is part of the larger problem of the extent to which people are responsible for actions by organizations of which they are members. The problem arises because it is extremely difficult to determine when a given individual in an organization is responsible for a particular decision or policy. Decisions are often the product of committees rather than single individuals. Since committee members usually serve temporary terms, none of the members who were involved in a particular decision may be on the committee when it is implemented. Implementation is also likely to be the responsibility of others. Since committee membership is temporary, decisions are often made that contradict previous decisions. Even when decisions are made by individuals, they seldom have control over the outcome of the decisions.

The result is that no one feels responsible for the consequences of organizational decisions. Top management does not because it only formulates policy; it does not implement it. Those in the middle and at the bottom of the chain of authority do not, because they simply carry out policy. If challenged to assume moral responsibility for their actions, they reply "I'm not responsible, I was simply carrying out orders" or "I was just doing my job." But, as De George points out, absence of a feeling of obligation does not mean absence of obligation.

Whenever one acts in such a way as to harm, or violate the rights of others, one is justly held accountable for one's actions. This is true regardless of one's occupation or role in society. Acting as a member of an institution or corporation does not relieve one of moral obligations. To the contrary, because most of the actions we undertake in such settings have more far-reaching consequences than those we undertake in our personal lives, this *increases* rather than decreases our moral obligation. The amount of responsibility one bears for organizational actions is dependent on the extent to which: (a) one could foresee the consequences of the organizational action, and (b) one's own acts or failures to act are a cause of those consequences. It is important to include failures to act here because frequently it is easier to determine what will happen if we don't act, than if we do, and because we are morally responsible for not preventing evil as well as for causing it.

Although the foregoing discussion is brief and the ideas not fully worked out, if the criteria which are presented are applied to the engineers in the Pinto case, I think one must conclude they had an obligation to blow the whistle. They knew the gas tanks were likely to explode, injuring or killing people if Pintos were struck from behind by cars traveling thirty miles per hour. They knew that if they did not blow the whistle, Ford would market the cars. They were also members of a profession who, because of their special knowledge and skills, have a particular obligation to be concerned about public safety.

De George thinks that the Ford engineers would have had an obligation to blow the whistle only if they had also known that doing so would have been likely to prevent the deaths. But we have an obligation to warn others of danger even if we believe they will ignore our warnings. This is especially true if the danger will come about partly because we did not speak out. De George admits that the public has a right to know about dangerous products. If that is true, it would seem that those who have knowledge about such products have an obligation to inform the public. This is not usurping the public's right to decide acceptable risk; it is supplying them with the information necessary to exercise the right.

De George also believes we are not justified in asking engineers to blow the whistle if it would threaten their jobs. It is true that we would not be justified in demanding that they blow the whistle if that would place their, or their families', lives in danger. But this is not true if only their jobs are at stake. Engineers are recognized as professionals and accorded respect and high salaries, not only because of their specialized knowledge and skills, but because of the special responsibilities we entrust to them. All people have a *prima facie* obligation to blow the whistle on practices that are illegal, unjust or harmful to others. But engineers who have special knowledge about, and are partially responsible for, dangerous practices or products have an especially strong obligation to blow the whistle if they are unsuccessful in getting the practices or products modified. Indeed, if they do not have an obligation to blow the whistle in such situations, then no one ever has such an obligation.

A number of people have argued that for external whistleblowing to be justified it is necessary for the whistleblower to first make his or her concern known within the organization. "Surely," says Arthur S. Miller, "an employee owes his employer enough loyalty to try to work, first of all, within the organization to attempt to effect change.[11] De George even states that for whistleblowing to be morally justified one must have first informed one's immediate supervisor and exhausted all possible avenues of change within the organization. The problems with this kind of advice are: (1) it may be one's immediate supervisor who is responsible for the wrongdoing, (2) organizations differ considerably in both their mechanisms for reporting, and in how they respond to wrongdoing, (3) not all wrongdoing is of the same type. If the wrongdoing is one which threatens people's health or safety, exhausting all channels of protest within the organization could result in unjustified delay in correcting the problem. Exhausting internal channels of protest can also give people time to destroy evidence needed to substantiate one's allegations. Finally, it may expose one to possible retaliation which one would have some protection against if one reported the wrongdoing to an external agency.

It has also been argued that anonymous whistleblowing is never justified. It is said, e.g., that anonymous whistleblowing violates the right of people to face their accusers. The fact that the whistleblower's identity is unknown also raises questions about his or her motives. But, as Frederick Elliston points out, anonymous whistleblowing can both protect whistleblowers from unjust retaliation and prevent those on whom the whistle is blown from engaging in an *ad hominem* attack to draw attention away from their wrong-doing. As he also points out, people should be protected from false accusations, but it is not necessary for the identity of whistleblowers to be known for this to be done. "It is only necessary that accusations be properly investigated, proven true or false, and the results widely disseminated."[12] Discovering the whistleblower's motives is also irrelevant as far as immediate public policy is concerned. All that matters is whether wrongdoing has taken place and, if so, what to do about it.

It has also been argued that anonymous whistleblowing should be avoided because it is ineffective. In fact, if anonymous whistleblowing is ineffective, it is more likely to be a function of lack of documentation and follow-up testimony than due to its anonymity. Moreover, anonymity is a matter of degree. For whistleblowing to be anonymous it is not necessary for the whistleblower's identity to be unknown to everyone, only to those on whom the whistle is blown and the general public. A few key investigators may know his or her identity. It should also not be forgotten that one of the most dramatic and important whistleblowing incidents in recent years, Deep Throat's disclosure of Richard Nixon's betrayal of the American people, was an instance of anonymous whistleblowing.

FACTORS TO CONSIDER IN WHISTLEBLOWING

I have argued that because we have a duty to prevent harm and injustice to others, which holds even though we are members of organizations, we have a *prima facie* obligation to disclose organizational wrongdoing we are unable to prevent. The degree of the obligation is dependent on the extent to which we are capable of foreseeing the consequences of organizational actions and our own acts or failures to act are causes of those consequences. It is also dependent on the kind and extent of the wrongdoing. Even a part-time or temporary employee has an obligation to report serious or extensive wrongdoing. But, in general, professionals who occupy positions of trust and special responsibilities, have a stronger obligation to blow the whistle than ordinary workers.

Although we have an obligation to document wrongdoing as thoroughly as possible, we can only

act on the basis of probability, so it is possible for the whistleblower to be in error about the wrongdoing and the whistleblowing still be justified. Whether we have an obligation to express our concern within the organization before going outside depends on the nature of the wrongdoing, the kind of organization involved and the likelihood of retaliation. Whether we have an obligation to blow the whistle openly rather than anonymously depends on the extent to which it helps one avoid unfair retaliation and is effective in exposing the wrongdoing. The same is true of alumni as opposed to current whistleblowing.

Since whistleblowing usually involves conflicting obligations, a wide range of variables and has far-reaching consequences for all people involved, decisions to blow the whistle are not easily made. Like all complicated moral actions, whistleblowing cannot be reduced to a how-to-do list. However, some of the factors whistleblowers should take into consideration, if they are to act prudently and morally, can be stated. The following is an attempt to do this.

Make sure the situation is one that warrants whistleblowing. Make sure the situation is one involving illegal actions, harm to others, or violation of people's rights, not one in which you would be disclosing personal matters, trade secrets, customer lists, etc. Or if disclosure of the wrongdoing would involve the latter, make sure that the harm to be avoided is sufficiently great to offset the harm from the latter.

Examine your motives. Although it is not necessary for the whistleblower's motive to be praiseworthy for the whistleblowing to be justified in terms of the public interest, examination of one's motives will help one in deciding whether there is a situation which warrants whistleblowing.

Verify and document your information. If at all possible, try to obtain evidence that would stand up in court or regulatory hearings. If the danger to others is so great that you believe you are justified in obtaining evidence by surreptitious methods such as eavesdropping or recording telephone calls, examine your motives thoroughly, weigh carefully the risks you are taking and try to find alternative and independent sources for any evidence you discover. In general, though it is advisable to avoid surreptitious methods.

Determine the type of wrongdoing you are reporting and to whom it should be reported. Determining the exact nature of the wrongdoing can help you decide both what kind of evidence to obtain and to whom it should be reported. For example, if the wrongdoing involves illegal actions such as the submission of false test reports to government agencies, bribery of public officials, racial or sexual discrimination, or violation of safety, health or pollution laws, then determining the nature of the laws being violated will also indicate which agencies have authority to enforce those laws. If, on the other hand, the wrongdoing consists of actions which are legal, but nevertheless contrary to the public interest, determining this will help one decide whether one has an obligation to publicize the actions and, if so, in what way. The best place to report this type of wrongdoing is usually a public interest group. Such an organization is more likely than the press to: (1) be concerned about and advise the whistleblower regarding retaliation, (2) maintain confidentiality, (3) investigate the whistleblower's allegations to try to substantiate them rather than sensationalize them by turning the issue into a "personality dispute." If releasing information to the press is the best way to remedy the situation, the public interest group can help with or do this.

State your allegations in an appropriate way. Be as specific as possible without being unintelligible. If you are reporting violation of a law to a government agency and it is possible for you to do so, include information and technical data necessary for experts to verify the wrongdoing. If you are disclosing wrongdoing which does not require technical information to substantiate it, nevertheless be as specific as possible in stating the type of illegal or immoral action involved, who is being injured and in what ways.

Stick to the facts. Avoid name calling, slander and being drawn into a mud-slinging contest. As Peter Raven-Hansen wisely points out: "One of the most important points . . . is to focus on the disclosure. . . . This rule applies even when the whistleblower believes that certain individuals are re-

sponsible. . . . The disclosure itself usually leaves a trail for others to follow to the miscreants."[13] Sticking to the facts also helps the whistleblower minimize retaliation.

Decide whether the whistleblowing should be internal or external. Familiarize yourself with all available internal channels for reporting wrongdoing and obtain as much data as you can on both how people who have used these channels were treated by the organization and what was done about the problems they reported. If you are considering blowing the whistle on an immediate supervisor, find out what has happened in the past in this kind of situation. If people who report wrongdoing have been treated fairly and problems corrected, then use internal channels to report the wrongdoing. If not, decide to what external agencies you should report the wrongdoing.

Decide whether the whistleblowing should be open or anonymous. If anonymous, decide whether partial or total anonymity is required. If anonymous, also make sure your documentation is as thorough as possible. Finally, since anonymity may be difficult to preserve, anticipate what you will do if your identity becomes known.

Decide whether current or alumni whistleblowing is required. Sometimes it is advisable to resign one's present position and to obtain another position before blowing the whistle. This protects one from being fired, receiving damaging letters of recommendation or even being blacklisted from one's profession. Alumni whistleblowing may also be advisable if one is anticipating writing a book about the wrongdoing. Since this can be profitable, anyone doing this has a particularly strong obligation to examine his or her motives to make sure they are morally praiseworthy.

Find out how much protection is available for whistleblowers in your industry, state, or federal agency. Follow any guidelines that have been established and make sure you meet all qualifications, deadlines, etc., for filing reports.

Anticipate and document retaliation. Although not as certain as Newton's law of motion that for every action there is an equal reaction, whistleblowers whose identities are known can expect retaliation. Thus whether you decide to work within the organization or go outside, document every step with letters, records, tape recordings of meetings and so forth. Unless you do this, you may find that regulatory agencies and the courts are of no help.

Consult a lawyer. Lawyers are advisable at almost every stage of whistleblowing. They can help you determine if the wrongdoing violates the law, aid you in documenting information about it, inform you of any laws you might yourself be breaking in documenting it, assist you in deciding to whom to report it, make sure reports are filed on time, and help you protect yourself against retaliation. However, since lawyers tend to view problems within a narrow legal framework, and decisions to blow the whistle are moral decisions, one must in the final analysis rely on one's conscience.

BEYOND WHISTLEBLOWING

What can be done to eliminate the wrongdoing which gives rise to whistleblowing? One solution would be to give whistleblowers greater legal protection. Another would be to try to change the nature of organizations so as to diminish the need for whistleblowing. These solutions are, of course, not mutually exclusive.

Many people are opposed to legislation protecting whistleblowers because they think it is unwarranted interference with the right to freedom of contract. However, if the right to freedom of contract is to be consistent with the public interest, it cannot serve as a shield for wrongdoing. It does this when threat of dismissal prevents people from blowing the whistle. The right of employers to dismiss at will has been previously restricted by labor laws which prevent employers from dismissing employees for union activities. It is ironic that we have restricted the right of employers to fire employees who are pursuing their economic self-interest, but allowed employers to fire employees acting in behalf of the public interest. The rights of employers to dismiss employees in the interest of efficiency should be balanced against the right of

the public to know about illegal, dangerous and unjust practices of organizations. The most effective way to achieve this would be a federal law protecting whistleblowers.

Laws protecting whistleblowers have also been opposed on the grounds that: (1) employees would use them as an excuse to mask poor performance, (2) they would create an "informer ethos" within organizations, and (3) they would take away the autonomy of business, strangling it in red tape.

The first objection is illegitimate because only those employees who could show that an act of whistleblowing preceded their being dismissed or penalized, and that their employment records were adequate up to the time of the whistleblowing, could seek relief under the law.

The second objection is more formidable. A society that encourages snooping, suspicion and mistrust is not most people's idea of the good society. Laws which encourage whistleblowing for self-interested reasons such as the federal tax law which pays informers part of any money that is collected, could help bring about such a society. However, laws protecting whistleblowers from being penalized or dismissed are quite different. They do not reward the whistleblower; they merely protect him or her from unjust retaliation. It is unlikely that federal or state laws of this sort would promote an informer society.

The third objection is also unfounded. Laws protecting whistleblowers would not require any positive duties on the part of organizations, only the negative duty of not retaliating against employees who speak out in the public interest. However, not every act of apparent whistleblowing should be protected. Only people who can show they had probable reasons for believing wrongdoing existed should be protected. Furthermore the burden of proof should be on the individual to show this. People who cannot may be justly penalized or dismissed. If the damage to the organization is serious, it should also be allowed to sue. Since these conditions would impose some risks on potential whistleblowers, they would reduce the possibility of frivolous action.

If, on the other hand, someone who has probable reasons for believing wrongdoing exists, blows the whistle and is fired, then the burden of proof should be on the organization to show that he or she was not fired for blowing the whistle. If it is found that the whistleblowing is the reason for the dismissal, the whistleblower should be reinstated and awarded damages. If there is further retaliation after reinstatement, additional damages should be awarded.

What changes could be made in organizations to prevent the need for whistleblowing? Some of the suggestions which have been made are that organizations develop effective internal channels for reporting wrongdoing, reward people with salary increases and promotions for using these channels, and appoint senior executives, board members, ombudspersons, etc., whose primary obligations would be to investigate and eliminate organizational wrongdoing. These changes could be undertaken by organizations on their own or mandated by law. Other changes which might be mandated are requiring that certain kinds of records be kept, assessing larger fines for illegal actions, and making executives and other professionals personally liable for filing false reports, knowingly marketing dangerous products, failing to monitor how policies are being implemented, etc. Although these reforms could do much to reduce the need for whistleblowing, given human nature it is highly unlikely that the need for whistleblowing can ever be totally eliminated. This is why it is important for there to be laws which protect whistleblowers and for us to state as clearly as we can both the practical problems and moral issues involved in whistleblowing.

NOTES

1. For discussion of the legal aspects of whistleblowing see Lawrence E. Blades "Employment at Will vs. Individual Freedom: On Limiting the Abusive Exercise of Employer Power," *Columbia Law Review* 67 (1967); Phillip Blumberg "Corporate Responsibility and the Employee's Duty of Loyalty and Obedience: A Preliminary Inquiry," *Oklahoma Law Review* 24 (1971); Clyde W. Summers, "Individual Protection Against Unjust Dismissal: Time for a Statute," *Virginia Law Review* 62 (1976) Arthur S. Miller, "Whistle Blowing and the Law" in Ralph Nader, Peter J. Petkas and Kate Blackwell, *Whistle Blowing*, New York, 1972, Grossman Publishers; Alan F. Westin, *Whistle Blowing!*, New York, 1981, McGraw-Hill; Martin H. Marlin, "Current Status of Legal Protection for Whistleblowers," forthcoming paper delivered at the Second Annual Conference on Ethics in Engineering, Illinois Institute of Technology, 1982. See also Gene G. James "Whistle Blowing: Its Nature and Justification," *Philosophy in Context*, 10, (1980).

2. For a discussion of this study which was by Morton Corn see Frank von Hipple, "Professional Freedom and Responsibility: The Role of the Professional Society," *Newsletter on Science, Technology and Human Values*, 22, January 1978.

3. See Westin, op. cit.

4. See Marlin, op. cit.

5. David W. Ewing, *Freedom Inside the Organization*, New York, 1977, E. P. Dutton, pp. 165–6.

6. Richard T. De George, *Business Ethics*, New York, 1982, Macmillan, p. 161. See also De George "Ethical Responsibilities of Engineers in Large Organizations," *Business and Professional Ethics Journal*, 1, No. 1, Fall 1981, pp. 1–14. He formulates the first criterion in a slightly different way in the last work, saying that the harm must be both serious and considerable before whistleblowing is justified.

7. Ibid.

8. De George "Ethical Responsibilities of Engineers in Large Organizations," op. cit., p. 1.

9. Ibid., p. 5.

10. Ibid., p. 7.

11. Miller, op. cit., p. 30.

12. Frederick A. Elliston, "Anonymous Whistleblowing," forthcoming in *Business and Professional Ethics Journal*.

13. Peter Raven-Hansen "Dos and Don'ts for Whistleblowers: Planning for Trouble," *Technology Review*, May 1980, p. 30. My discussion in the present section is heavily indebted to this article.

JOHN J. McCALL
Strategies for Protecting Whistleblowers

Our traditional approach to employment derives from English common law, and it has its contemporary American expression in the 1958 Restatement of Agency Law. This Law of Agency finds employment agreements to be terminable at will by either employee or employer. It also defines the obligations of employees who, in general, are considered to have broad obligations of loyalty to their employer.

These obligations of loyalty prohibit employees from engaging in activities that harm the economic interests of the employer. Standardly, exceptions to this duty of loyalty were allowed for few reasons. Employees, however, had the right to refuse orders or to speak against the interests of the employer if his actions were unethical, illegal, or a violation of some public policy that aimed at the general interest of the society. The employment-at-will doctrine, however, meant that employees who exercised their rights of speech or refusal in these areas were subject to dismissal. For example, no serious legal protection against retaliatory discharge was provided for an employee who warned the public about unsafe products.

Recently, however, state courts have begun a piecemeal attempt to extend protection to employees who exercise their legal rights under these three exceptions to the duty of loyalty. The basis of this broader protection is most often found in the courts' interpretations of the "public policy exception" to the employment-at-will doctrine. Courts are often now more liberal in their interpretation of what counts as public policy, and they occasionally will find a wrongful discharge of employees who refuse orders or who complain about practices that, though violations of public policy, had little chance of causing serious harms. Instances of this expanded protection are numerous and easy to find. An early and trend-setting case was the 1959 ruling of a California court in *Peter-men v. Teamster's Local 396*, which found a cause of action for an employee who was fired for refusal to give false testimony at legislative hearings. A more recent but similar case is the 1981 Michigan

court ruling in *Trombetta v. Detroit, Toledo and Ironton Railroad Co.*, where the issue was a refusal to give false testimony at state air pollution hearings. In these cases, the discharge of employees was found to undermine clearly established policies for the protection of the public.

Perhaps at the forefront of this move towards greater security for employees is the attempt to protect employees who "blow the whistle" about corporate products or practices that they consider dangerous or unethical. (While "whistleblowing" usually refers to employees going public with their information, courts have also extended some protection to employees who simply complain to their superiors about company practices.) For example, in 1978 a West Virginia court ruled in *Harless v. First National Bank* that an employee was wrongfully discharged for complaining about installment loan overcharges. And in *Sheets v. Teddy's Frosted Foods, Inc.*, an employee was found to have a cause of action over a discharge for internal complaints about substandard and underweight materials used in food products.

These cases set precedents for support of employees who attempt to shield the public from harms caused when their employers act against policies that the state could reasonably establish for the protection of its citizens. The court decisions in these cases provide evidence that there is some sentiment in our society for reciprocal protection of employees who act to protect our general welfare. Thus, the society has begun to consider institutional mechanisms for protecting whistleblowers by providing them some measure of economic security. This short comment will review some of the common proposals for protecting whistleblowers and will discuss the strengths and weaknesses of those respective proposals.

COURT PROTECTION

One proposal would have the courts protect the jobs of whistleblowers much as they have been doing in the above cases. However, we have to decide whether we wish to protect all or only some whistleblowers from retaliatory discharge. If the courts provided blanket protection to all discharged whistleblowers by allowing them a cause of action against their former employers, there is the danger that we would permit or encourage vindictive and retaliatory actions by disgruntled employees. Public "complaints" by such employees may pose a serious threat to the economic interests of the firm (and to the interests of those who depend upon the firm), since an allegation about an unsafe product or an illegal practice could hurt the company's sales significantly.

To avoid encouraging unjustified and damaging instances of whistleblowing, some have suggested that courts protect only those whistleblowers whose complaints about potential harms or violations of public policy are reasonably grounded or correct. While this proposal protects corporate interests from the unjustified harms described above, it fails to protect adequately the welfare of those who justifiably blow the whistle. For, with the current absence of uniform federal standards, state courts have been very uneven in interpreting the public policy exception to employment at will. In recent cases in New Jersey, Pennsylvania, and Missouri, courts, because they did not find clear and substantive violations of public policy, failed to grant a legal cause of action to employees who complained about what they reasonably believed to be dangerous or illegal practices. Whistleblowers, then, even when they have solid grounds for their complaints, have no guarantee that their complaints will be judged to have protection under the public policy exception.

Even with a more uniform interpretation of public policy, though, court protection for justifiable whistleblowers will be weak. For this court mechanism provides protection only when discharged employees bring suit. However, even employed workers usually have little chance of winning a suit before their financial resources are exhausted; corporations can extend court proceedings through legal maneuvers until the whistleblower can continue no longer. In addition, even if the whistleblower was successful in her suit, she likely would receive either reinstatement or a financial settlement. With reinstatement, the courts

realistically cannot prevent subtle forms of retaliation against the employee, which would either freeze her salary or force her to resign in frustration. Financial settlements, on the other hand, usually will not provide economic security and the discharged employee will surely have tremendous difficulty finding alternative employment. It would appear that the attempt to provide protection to whistleblowers through the courts will unjustifiably threaten the firm or will fail to provide significant protection for even justified whistleblowers.

A PUBLIC CLEARINGHOUSE

An alternative proposal suggests the creation of a public clearinghouse that could receive anonymous complaints. If the complaining parties are not identified when the clearinghouse releases the information, corporate reprisals against whistleblowers would be less likely. This proposal, however, presents what some see as an unjustifiable threat to the economic health of the firm by allowing vindictive complaints. The public clearinghouse proposal could avoid this difficulty only if it required substantial proof and/or investigated the authenticity of the whistleblower's charges. The length of time necessary to establish the authenticity of the charges, though, might mean that avoidable and severe public harms could occur while that investigation was underway. This is a particularly significant problem, since the charges made by whistleblowers are often hard to substantiate without protracted dispute. Again, there seems to be a conflict between protecting the interests of the firm from unjustifiable damages and protecting the welfare of others from improper actions of the firm.

OMBUDSMAN

Another common suggestion for an institution to deal with whistleblowing proposes the creation of an independent ombudsman within the corporation to whom employees could direct their complaints. This mechanism certainly protects the economic interests of the firm, since the information or complaint is not made public. However, whether this procedure provides adequate protection for the public or for the complaining employee is far from clear. There are numerous well-known cases where the use of internal channels has resulted in both the burying of the complaint and the retaliatory discharge of "insubordinate" employees. This approach to whistleblowing satisfies the society's desire to protect the welfare of some whistleblowers (as well as its own welfare) only if the internal mechanism is operated sincerely and only if the management of the corporation is committed to avoiding practices that cause harms or violate public policy. However, this is to say that the internal complaint procedure for dealing with society's whistleblowing concerns is effective only when the circumstances requiring whistleblowing are unlikely to arise. On the other hand, corporations that do not have that commit-ment are the very corporations in which instances of whistleblowing are probably needed.

SUMMARY

Thus, the current direction of legal rulings indicates that society wants to encourage instances of whistleblowing and wants to protect the interests of those who blow the whistle justifiably. This requires that there be some institutional procedure that protects those with serious complaints. However, we have seen that none of the three common proposals appears an adequate institutional response to society's concerns. Students are encouraged to see if additional proposals for dealing with whistleblowing can avoid the above problems.

CHAPTER EIGHT
Study Questions

1. Define whistleblowing. Why is it a serious moral issue?

2. What is employment at will? How does it relate to the traditional legal duties of employees? What are those duties as identified by Blumberg?

3. Should an employee feel a duty to be loyal to his or her employer?

4. Why would public disclosure of corporate wrongdoing be justifiable?

5. Do you find any relationship between a right to freedom of speech and an employee duty of confidentiality?

6. Should some whistleblowers be protected against corporate reprisals? When? What does James have to say about this question? How can whistleblowers be protected?

7. What advice would you offer to prospective whistleblowers? Does your advice differ from James's advice?

CHAPTER NINE

*H*EALTH
AND SAFETY

CASE STUDY

OSHA's Cotton Dust Standard

The Occupational Safety and Health Act directs the Secretary of Labor to establish standards for control of toxic materials in the workplace. It requires the secretary to set the standard "which most adequately assures, to the extent feasible, on the basis of the best available evidence" that no employee will suffer impairment of health. On December 28, 1976, OSHA proposed a new permanent standard to replace existing cotton dust standards. After holding public hearings around the country and soliciting comments from industry, workers, physicians, economists, scientists and others, OSHA issued its final standard on June 23, 1978. Including an accompanying statement of findings and reasons, the standard was 69 pages long.

Byssinosis, commonly known as "brown lung" disease in its more severe forms, is a respiratory disease primarily caused by inhaling cotton dust. Cotton dust is present in the air during the processing, weaving, knitting, or handling of cotton. Estimates have at least 35,000 present or former cotton mill workers, or 1 in 12 such workers, suffering from the most disabling form of byssinosis. Other esti-

mates have 100,000 active and retired workers suffering from some form of the disease. Byssinosis was not recognized as a distinct occupational hazard associated with cotton mills until the early 1960s.

Cotton industry groups, including the American Textile Manufacturers Institute and the National Cotton Council of America, filed suit to challenge the validity of the cotton dust standard. Their major challenge was that OSHA had not, but should have, used cost-benefit analysis in determining the appropriate standard.

In establishing the cotton dust standard, OSHA interpreted the law to require adoption of the most stringent standard possible to protect health, bounded only by technical and economic "feasibility." "Feasible" was taken to mean "capable of being done." Legislative history indicates that Congress itself mandated that worker health should override considerations of cost. The Congress had specifically chosen "feasible" rather than "cost-benefit" when enacting the OSHA law. The U. S. Court of Appeals upheld OSHA's interpretation of the law in all major respects and rejected the industry's contention that the benefits of the standard must outweigh its costs.

Much of the Supreme Court debate which followed centered upon the phrase "to the extent feasible." The majority, which ruled in favor of the OSHA standard, reasoned that cost-benefit analysis is not required of OSHA regulations. The majority ruled that "feasible" meant that the most stringent standard should be used wherever technologically and economically possible. The implication was that only economic viability, and not simply high costs, could count against the health and safety of employees.

In a dissenting opinion, Justice William

Rehnquist argued that "economic feasibility" was too vague to decide the issue either way. He argued that OSHA's legislative history showed that the phrase "to the extent feasible" was a compromise between those who favored and those who rejected cost-benefit analysis. As such, it masked a fundamental policy disagreement in Congress. Since Congress "abdicated its responsibility for making a fundamental and most difficult policy choice," interpretation of this phrase is nothing other than a bureaucratic decision of the Executive Branch. Since "economic feasibility" clearly implies that costs should be considered, OSHA should not ignore cost-benefit analyses.

Introduction

WHAT ARE THE responsibilities which a business has for the health and safety of its workers? What is the proper role of government in protecting worker health and safety? Should government regulators establish standards aiming at the prevention of injury, or should government action be limited to providing legal remedies for harms done in the workplace? Is it possible to assign costs to worker death or injury? If so, how much is a life worth? If not, should health and safety issues override all considerations of costs, including even the economic viability of a business or an entire industry? This chapter will examine these and other issues of worker health and safety.

Although no one is against health and safety, a great deal of controversy surrounds this issue. Few government regulatory agencies are as embattled as the Occupational Safety and Health Administration (OSHA), for example. Yet, despite the controversies, there is widespread agreement about the value and importance of workplace health and safety. For this reason, many of the debates in this chapter focus more upon procedures and techniques for ensuring safety and health than upon the goals at which those procedures aim. Government regulation as the means for achieving these goals, of course, will be a central topic of debate in these readings.

Before entering these debates it will prove helpful to consider the value and importance of health and safety. First, if anything can be said to have intrinsic value, it would be a healthy life. Except in the most extreme circumstances, life is better than death, health is better than illness, and bodily integrity is better than injury. Besides this intrinsic value, health and safety also have significant instrumental value. That is, they are very useful, if not necessary, for acquiring other things of value. However, unlike other instrumentally valuable things, like money, health and safety are necessary for almost any other good that we seek. Whatever one desires, chances are that being safe and healthy will greatly improve the possibility of satisfying that desire.

If we stress the intrinsic value of health and safety, then there is a presumption that concern with health and safety should outweigh more instrumental values like money or property. Thus, one interpretation of OSHA's cotton dust standard was that once cotton dust was established to be dangerous, possible steps should be taken to eliminate it. On the other hand, if we stress the instrumental value of health and safety, then there is a tendency merely to balance its worth against other instrumental values. Many people are uncomfortable, however, when forced to make a trade-off between health and safety and dollars and cents. Accordingly, despite universal assent to the value of health and safety, the precise role it should play in determining business's responsibility to workers is unclear.

Even when the value of health and safety is clearly established, there is a wide variety of means available for pursuing that goal. At one extreme would be voluntary agreement reached through a bargaining process between employer and employee. In this view, the value of health and safety is left open and is to be determined by individual employees. Those who place an extremely high value on workplace safety will be unwilling to work in a high-risk position for any price. Others who value health and safety, like money, for its more instrumental role, will be more willing to accept a high-risk job in return for higher wages. Either way, bargaining between employer and employee is thought to be the best reason for protecting worker health and safety.

There are problems with this individualistic approach, however. As Mark MacCarthy argues, risks confronting individuals vary significantly from the risks that confront groups. For example, an individual coal miner might find it attractive to risk his own safety for a higher wage. But, if this could not be done without jeopardizing the well-being of fellow miners who are less willing to take the risk, individual bargaining would prove to be an unsatisfactory means for protecting worker health and safety.

It seems that in many workplaces the health and safety of one worker cannot be separated from the health and safety of his or her co-workers. For this reason, a more collective approach seems preferable. Historically, worker compensation laws were the first major means that society used in pursuit of worker health and safety. As Barbara McLennan points out, worker compensation laws represented a "no-fault system under which employees suffering from work-related injuries or diseases receive benefits on the basis of compensation schedules established under state law." In the course of her analysis, McLennan raises some of the serious problems with this approach.

First, worker compensation laws essentially are a means for providing compensation for economic and not health loss. As such, they see health and safety as instrumentally valuable and seek to replace a loss of this value with another instrumental valuable, money. Compensation basically took the form of money paid for loss of earnings. Suffering or injury itself was not compensated. Also, different states had different payment schedules, which meant that the loss of an arm in Maine was compensated at a different rate than a similar loss in California. A growing inflation rate during the 1970s generally meant that increases in compensation rates lagged behind increases in overall cost of living. Developing as they did from laws during the early years of the Industrial Revolution, worker compensation laws tended to emphasize workplace safety and ignore work-related diseases. Finally, and perhaps most importantly, these laws did nothing to prevent injuries. As no-fault compensation laws, this approach to workplace safety and health provides virtually no incentive for preventing harms. The laws are reactive; they make up for harms done but do little to prevent harms from occurring in the first place.

An alternative means for securing worker health and safety is known as an "injury tax." Essentially, this would involve charging employers a fee, or "tax," for injuries suffered at their workplaces. The money would then be used to compensate injured workers and, since the tax is tied to number of injuries, this approach would also provide incentives for employers to prevent accidents.

However, there are problems with this approach. First, once again we have an equation of economic loss with health loss. Workers are compensated only for loss of economic earnings. Also, some critics charge that unless the taxes were sufficiently high, there would be little incentive for employers to prevent accidents. For some employers, it might make economic sense simply to pay the tax rather than pay for workplace improvements. In this way, the "tax" is more like a license to operate an unsafe or unhealthy workplace. Finally, as its name implies, an injury tax would also tend to emphasize injuries at the expense of work-related diseases. To provide a real incentive, it is essential that the tax be assessed soon after the harm, clearly connected to the incident and in clear reaction to it. Penalties ambiguously or lately assessed likely will be ineffective. However, this means that workplace diseases, many of which do not develop for many years later, will unlikely be compensated through the injury tax. A more effective means for preventing both injuries and diseases is needed.

One solution is to establish health and safety standards for the workplace. The Occupational Health and Safety Administration was established by Congress to pursue this alternative. Working in conjunction with all involved parties, OSHA is to set standards that would prevent accidents or diseases wherever "feasible." Standards, rather than taxes or compensation, were thought to be the most reasonable means for securing worker health and safety. First, as a cooperative process, standards would avoid the adversarial appearance of "taxes" or fines. Standards aim to prevent harm rather than compensate for it after it has occurred. Although initial compliance costs might be high, once established, standards would not be a continual drain on economic resources. Standards seek to avoid the problem of trying to place a price tag on health or safety. Finally, standards are equally concerned with preventing both injury and disease.

However, OSHA has been surrounded by controversy from its start. In his thorough analysis of the normative and conceptual issues involved in worker health and safety, Mark MacCarthy evaluates much of this controversy. MacCarthy describes and examines the problems involved with setting standards that are concerned with economic, moral, social, and political values. Unless these complexities are acknowledged, MacCarthy sees little chance of a successful health and safety policy.

One common objection to OSHA standards claims that they are too expensive. In 1978 the Business Roundtable commissioned the accounting firm of Arthur Andersen & Co. to study the incremental costs incurred by compliance to regulatory standards, including OSHA. Arthur Andersen's report, reprinted in part here, presents a mixed picture of regulatory costs. Incremental costs were considered to be those direct costs of actions taken to comply with regulations that would not have been taken in the absence of regulation. Among the conclusions of this report were the fact that the incremental costs represented only a "small portion" of the companies' total health and safety expenditures. There were significant differences in costs between different industries, with three—chemicals, rubber products, and primary metals—accounting for 52% of OSHA incremental costs. Toxic and hazardous substances were the major area of OSHA costs. Not surprisingly, many of these observations are critical of OSHA's procedures. One criticism is that despite increased costs, national standards have done little to improve worker health and safety.

However, some defenders of OSHA argue that while overall injury rates may not have changed significantly, rates for those accidents that OSHA is most likely to prevent—e.g., injuries from unprotected machinery—have decreased. Other injuries, ranging from strains and overexertions to some diseases, may actually have increased. Various explanations have been offered for this, including an increased tendency to report minor injuries in a more safety-conscious work environment and the cumulative effects of long-term exposure to harmful substances. The important point is that overall rates may not be a fair way to judge OSHA's effectiveness.

While agreeing with critics in business that OSHA has been ineffective, other critics offer altogether different explanations of this ineffectiveness. Focusing specifically on mine safety, Dan Curran presents significant empirical support for the claim that health and safety regulation has been a mostly symbolic gesture. In attempting to balance the interests of industry and workers, regulators often appear to be effective when in fact they have little real impact. Extending his research to the more general OSHA case, Curran concludes that while worker perception of health and safety has been changed by OSHA, this law has done little to improve the situation.

Of course, given a commitment to worker health and safety, critics of OSHA's approach should be challenged to provide an alternative for securing these goods. Any alternative would need to possess the strength of OSHA without, at least, some of its defects. At this point, the options are unclear.

BARBARA N. McLENNAN
Product Liability in the Workplace: Product Liability Legislation and Worker Compensation Laws

Worker compensation laws in the United States represent a theoretically no-fault system under which employees suffering work-related injuries or diseases receive benefits on the basis of compensation schedules established under state law; the costs related to employee compensation benefits are treated by employers as normal costs of doing business and are passed on directly to the consumer in the prices of products sold. At the same time, product liability litigation against manufacturers and sellers of industrial equipment involved in workplace accidents has grown substantially in recent years. Product liability tort law has traditionally been a reparations system based on the concept of fault.

Today, employers and employees often engage in protracted litigation due to attempts by injured workers to obtain recovery beyond amounts permitted in state worker compensation statutes. This litigation generally aims at shifting at least some of the economic costs of worker injuries to third parties outside the direct employer-employee relationship (primarily, manufacturers and insurers). Such product liability litigation is partially a reaction to reputedly inadequate benefit levels provided by the current worker compensation system

as well as an attempt to shift costs to parties (such as manufacturers and insurers) often better capable of bearing these costs than employers.

A number of legislative proposals currently being considered in Congress attempt to establish uniform national standards and procedures for product liability litigation. All of these bills contain sections that deal with the relationship between product liability litigation and worker compensation laws.

This article presents a brief history of the development of worker compensation statutes in the U.S. and an overview of the extent and nature of U.S. workplace injuries. A brief survey of current state laws is included as well as an analysis of the major problems facing the current system. The article then analyzes the provisions of several currently proposed statutes relating to the relationship between product liability and worker compensation laws and concludes with some general propositions that must be addressed by any logical federal approach to protecting workers in the workplace.

Contemporary United States worker compensation laws derive from statutes modelled on early nineteenth century Austrian and Prussian compensation systems which were designed to protect employees in the mining and railroad industries. In 1838 Prussia adopted the principle that employers would be held liable for industrial accidents and railroads would be held liable for injuries to passengers or employees; railroads were permitted the defenses of showing accidents were caused by the negligence of the person injured or by an Act of God. In 1854, Prussia required certain employers to contribute to local "sickness associations" and in 1876 adopted a voluntary insurance act; in 1884, Prussia adopted a complete state-run worker compensation system. Great Britain adopted a worker compensation act in 1897 that applied only to specified hazardous industries; in 1906 coverage was made general.

Under the German system, employers were required to post security for compensation and the system was enforced by an administrative agency. The British system did not require security for compensation and left enforcement to court action by the injured worker.

The passage of these statutes was a response to the development of heavy industry and manufacturing technology in the middle and late nineteenth century. Increased industrialization and the spread of factories had created a situation in Europe (and the United States) where injuries to workers in the workplace became frequent. Indeed, they came to be regarded as a normal, expected part of the process of manufacturing.

APPLICATION OF COMMON LAW

In Britain and the United States, in the preindustrial period when relatively fewer people worked in factories, common law principles were applied in lawsuits arising from accidents in the workplace. Workers could sue employers for negligence if their injuries were the result of defective or poorly maintained equipment.

However, to prove negligence an injured worker had to prove that his employer had breached a duty which caused the damage he had sustained. Under the common law, employers had specified duties: to provide safe equipment and a safe workplace; to provide sufficient numbers of competent co-workers so work could be safely performed; to warn workers of unusual hazards; and to enforce proper safety rules. If an employer had performed these duties, he could not be held liable for injuries to workers arising from employment.

These principles continued to be applied in the later industrial period when accidents became numerous and more dangerous. Under the common law "fellow-servant rule," an employer could use as a defense the negligence of a fellow worker in injury cases. In addition, employers could also claim the defense of contributory negligence on the part of the employee. This doctrine held that the slightest lack of ordinary care on the part of the injured worker barred him from recovering damages.

Another doctrine by which employers could avoid liability in court was that of "assumption of the risk"—employers could claim that employees had assumed the risks entailed in their labor by accepting their jobs in the first place. Under this doctrine, employees who take work enter into implied contracts in which they assume certain risks: the ordinary risks of employment; the extraordinary risks of employment, if they might reasonably be expected to know of them; and the risks of incompetence or carelessness of fellow workers.

The overall result of the application of the common law to cases of worker injury was to make it very difficult for injured workers to obtain full recovery for damages in court. Workers were generally unable to overcome the defenses available to employers; their fellow workers were reluctant to testify as witnesses against employers and workers often did not have sufficient resources to sue in court anyway.

There were some judicial attempts to modify the common law defense of employers in these circumstances. A number of jurisdictions modified the fellow-servant rule to exclude all employers' common law duties. Courts in some states also held that employees did not assume the risk of an employer's violation of a safety statute.

At the same time, a number of states passed employer's liability statutes designed to ensure that employees would be no worse off than strangers when injured due to the negligence of their employer or an employer's servants. A number of states abrogated the fellow-servant rule for railway companies, and some shifted the burden of proof in a claim of contributory negligence from the plaintiff to the defendant. Some abolished the defense of assumption of the risk when the employer was at fault.

Judicial and legislative attempts to modify the common law defenses made little impact by the early twentieth century when worker injuries were common and often very severe. Workers' injuries resulted in heavy court loads and numerous impoverished families at a time when few public benefits were available to the poor, disabled, and unemployed. Studies conducted by several state commissions on the plight of injured employees at the time proved to be shocking; for example, a 1908 New York study found that 43 percent of fatal industrial accidents resulted in no compensation for the employees' survivors. Studies in several states found that the system operated to leave injured workmen's families destitute.

In 1910, the first U.S. worker compensation law of general application was passed, on the British model, by the state of New York. This act provided compulsory worker compensation in certain hazardous jobs and optional coverage in others. The compulsory section of the law was held unconstitutional by the New York Court of Appeals on the grounds that it violated the state's due process clause, but the state constitution was quickly amended and a new law passed in 1913. Other states followed, and in 1917 the U.S. Supreme Court upheld the validity of several different types of state worker compensation statutes.

Today, workers in all of the fifty states, the District of Columbia, Guam, Puerto Rico, American Samoa, the U.S. Virgin Islands, employees of the U.S. federal government under the Federal Employees Compensation Act, and employees covered by the Longshore Act are covered by worker compensation statutes. Most early American laws followed the 1897 British model; however, Washington and Ohio followed the German model under which employers contributed to a state insurance trust fund set aside for providing compensation to injured workers. Early U.S. laws were simple social insurance schemes, very limited in scope and coverage; over the course of the twentieth century, state laws have been considerably broadened.

STATUTES IN THE UNITED STATES

Injury on the job, as broadly defined by current worker compensation statutes, is a major cause of death and disability in the United States. There have been over two million disabling injuries (including deaths) to workers on the job in every year between 1970 and 1980, although death rates have consistently declined since 1945. In 1980, there were thirteen thousand deaths on the job and 2.2 million disabling injuries.

In 1982, most worker compensation systems were compulsory, although New Jersey, Texas, and South Carolina have elective systems. Fourteen states permit exemptions for employers with fewer than five employees; agricultural workers are not covered in fourteen jurisdictions. Twenty-four states apply worker compensation laws to domestic service.

Benefits vary widely by jurisdiction. Today, worker compensation statutes provide medical benefits for injured workers, payments for temporary and permanent total disability, payments over varying periods for partial disabilities, benefits for surviving spouses and children in death cases, and burial allowances; some jurisdictions also provide for disfigurement. In most jurisdictions injury includes the result of occupational disease as well as injury due to accident; accidental injury is generally very broadly defined, usually including any injury that takes place on the employer's premises in connection with work (including transportation to and from work and injuries that take place before or after working hours).

Income benefits for total disability range from two-thirds of wages to 80 percent of spendable earnings with varying weekly payment maximums. The maximum weekly payment by jurisdiction varies between $112 in Mississippi to $942 in Alaska.

A number of states require an offset for social security disability payments; several jurisdictions offset unemployment compensation. Different states have different time limits and only seventeen jurisdictions make any provision for automatic cost of living increases to offset the cost of inflation.

Under current worker compensation statutes, employers and their insurers bear the cost of worker injury on a no-fault basis. Under current arrangements, both labor and employers, however, are dissatisfied. Labor complains that the benefit levels are inadequate, and employers complain that judicial interpretations too broadly define covered injuries, accidents, and causation.

The basic purpose of worker compensation laws has been to provide no-fault compensation for economic loss, not for physical injury; compensation therefore takes the form of cash benefits to workers for impairment of earning capacity and to dependents in case of death. Compensation for pain and suffering has never been allowed, though states do have varying schedules that compensate for lost limbs regardless of reduction in earning capacity. With the rapid increase in the rate of inflation over the 1970s, worker compensation benefit levels (which generally are not indexed for inflation) have, in real terms, been significantly reduced. During this period, workers have more and more turned to product liability lawsuits in an effort to receive greater compensation for their injuries.

RIGHTS UNDER COMPENSATION

Under current law, a worker injured on the job has two potential sources of possible recovery. He can receive workers' compensation payments from his employer, or he can sue a third party—for example, the manufacturer or seller of any product involved in his injury or their insurers—on grounds of either negligence or strict tort.

In general, an employee cannot sue a negligent employer; under most state worker compensation statutes employers who pay the statutorily required worker compensation are protected from further legal action, even if their own negligence contributed to their employees' injuries. Indeed, most jurisdictions have held that negligent employers may not be sued or joined by a third party as a joint tortfeasor either under contribution or indemnity principles.

State worker compensation laws therefore limit the liability of negligent employers to a statutory maximum payout, regardless of the number or severity of injuries for which they are directly or indirectly responsible. In recent years, a number of states have allowed a third party (usually, a manufacturer or seller), held liable for an employee's injuries, to recover contribution from a negligent employer; however, these jurisdictions limit contributions only to the extent of the employers' worker compensation liability. Employers' liabilities are therefore limited to the state worker compensation maximums. In large settlements, third-parties must bear the overwhelming proportion of the cost burden—even where the negligence is primarily the employer's.

The overall result has been a quid pro quo between employers and employees. Employers have given up the common law defenses in exchange for limitation in liability, and employees have given up the possibility of full recovery from employers for partial, but certain, recovery from the worker compensation system.

Under current law, benefits are provided to the individual disabled worker (or, in case of death, to his survivors). Payments are established to reflect lost earning capacity and not the severity of the disability or the needs of the worker's family. All persons, with the same specific disabilities, are treated identically.

In recent years, in addition, workers' compensation payments have not kept pace with rising rates of inflation, and real benefit levels have therefore declined. In 1981, only seventeen jurisdictions in the United States provided automatic cost of living increases in total disability cases. Of these seventeen, three (California, Idaho, and Virgin Islands) allow these adjustments only after a stated time period (one or two years); one jurisdiction (District of Columbia) limits cost of living adjustments to a five-percent maximum.

The vast majority of jurisdictions have seen the purchasing power of worker compensation benefits erode. In every jurisdiction benefits are based on a proportion of average weekly wages, and wage levels in the United States have not kept pace with increases in price levels over the last decade when measured in constant dollars.

Most jurisdictions in the U.S. provide worker compensation benefits equal to two-thirds of average weekly wages for total disability, although four jurisdictions provide a somewhat higher proportion (though less than full earnings); two states provide less than two-thirds for total disability. Thus, the value of worker compensation benefits, in every jurisdiction based on a proportion of average weekly wages, have declined proportionally and in real terms.

PRODUCT LIABILITY LITIGATION

A survey by the Insurance Services Office of 24,000 product liability claims closed between July 1, 1976, and March 15, 1977, found that, although workplace injuries accounted for only 11 percent of the product liability accidents which resulted in claims payments, they accounted for 42 percent of total bodily injury payments. The average claim payment for workplace injuries was $97,884—much higher than the overall average. This survey found that 58 percent of total dollars paid for workplace accidents were in cases involving possible employer negligence where the employer made no contribution to the payments.

A survey conducted by the National Machine Tool Builders Association found that only 13 percent of workplace product-related accidents were the result of the mechanical failures of the machines. In 18 percent of the cases, machines were poorly maintained by the employer, and in 63 percent of the cases, the employer failed to guard the machine properly. This survey found that, in 56 percent of the cases, injured workers had been on the job less than six months prior to the accident; 65 percent had not received proper training from their employers on how to safely operate the machines involved.

Product liability litigation over worker injuries has therefore inflicted substantial costs on manufacturers, sellers, and their insurers, even where employers have acted negligently. The costs to these manufacturers include not only the payments to injured workers but increases in the costs of product liability insurance. Beyond that, legal costs of defense in product liability cases are also very high in terms of executive and engineering time spent in responding to discovery requests. The system has been a windfall for lawyers. The American Insurance Association has estimated that, for every 66 cents an injured worker receives, 77 cents is collected in legal fees.

RECENT PROPOSAL: MUPLA

In 1979, the Secretary of Commerce published a Model Uniform Product Liability Act. Also, in the 97th Congress, product liability legislation relating to worker compensation has been proposed by Congressman Shumway, Congressman LaFalce, and Senator Kasten. Each takes a very similar approach to the issue, and all of them purport to be responding to the same difficulty: an underfunded worker compensation system which varies substantially from state-to-state, overlapping an increasingly costly system of worker reparations through product liability litigation.

The authors of MUPLA determined, after considerable study and effort, that the best solution to the problem of overlap between worker compensation and product liability litigation would be reform and development of the current worker compensation system as a sole source of recovery in product-related workplace accidents but only if the worker generally received increased benefits compared to present state standards. The authors concluded, however, that a model product liability law was "an appropriate vehicle for making alterations of that dimension in Worker Compensation law."

MUPLA attempts to retain the no-fault, limited employer liability basis of the worker compensation system but also attempts to increase employer incentives to keep workplace equipment and conditions safe. Subsections (A) and (B) forbid subrogation actions. Subsection (A) provides that a product seller's liability will be reduced by the amount awarded in a state worker compensation proceeding (including the present value of future benefits) regardless of whether the employer was at fault; subsection (B) abolishes an employer's right of subrogation, contribution, or indemnity when an employee's injury results in a products liability claim. Subsection (B) also holds that an employer's worker compensation insurance carrier shall have no right of subrogation against the product seller.

Under these provisions, an injured employee would receive the same benefits as under the current system, but worker compensation insurance carriers and self-insuring employers would be unable to shift liability to manufacturers. The MUPLA approach would also substantially reduce the amount of litigation transaction costs, because in cases of employer negligence there would be no three-party litigation as to the relative percentages of fault of employers and manufacturers.

Subsection (C) of MUPLA protects product sellers; a product seller may sue to reduce a judgment by the amount of worker compensation benefits or to recoup that amount from an employer, if the product seller has paid that amount in the judgment. Subsection (C) applies even where employers were not at fault.

Under MUPLA, multiple proceedings would continue. There would still be separate worker compensation and product liability claims arising from the same injury.

OTHER APPROACHES

The Shumway bill, H. R. 5214, takes an approach to worker compensation closely modelled on MUPLA. It adds a subsection (D) which specifically states that "no third party tortfeasor may maintain any action for indemnity or contribution against the employer of the person who was injured."

The LaFalce bill, H. R. 5261, attempts to establish federal product liability tort law standards. In so doing, it follows MUPLA and H. R. 5214 closely.

Under H. R. 5261, in product liability cases for bodily injuries, where the injured party is entitled to state worker compensation, third parties may not bring actions against the injured worker's employer. Also, employers and their worker compensation insurance carriers are barred from any lien on any judgment received in products liability actions, nor do they have any right of subrogation against third parties. Employers cannot be deemed responsible in product liability actions involving the assessment of comparative responsibility. H. R. 5261 follows MUPLA and H. R. 5214 in providing that products liability damages will be reduced by the amount of state worker compensation benefits received.

The Kasten bill is S. 2631; like MUPLA and H. R. 5214, it attempts to establish a uniform product liability law. It follows these other proposals in that it also provides that workers' compensation benefits due an employee would be deducted from any product liability awards to the employee and requires that worker compensation benefits be exhausted before a product liability action on the same injury can be pursued in the courts. Findings in any worker compensation action are barred from use as evidence in any other action or proceeding. S. 2631 also provides that an employer (or its insurer), unless a product seller has expressly

agreed to indemnify the employer, would have no right of subrogation against the manufacturer or other seller.

S. 2631 protects employers from actions by third party tortfeasors for implied indemnity or contribution in product liability actions for damages by injured workers entitled to worker compensation benefits. Employers and their insurers also are protected from product liability suits (and any other action other than a worker compensation claim) by present or former employees, where these employees are eligible for worker compensation.

The Kasten bill, which has the support of the Reagan Administration, would limit employer liability to the amount in current worker compensation statutes. It would also, much as the other proposals, allow the current system of separate claims under both worker compensation and product liability to continue.

The four product liability bills, though very similar, are not identical. Shumway adopts MUPLA language but adds several paragraphs spelling out the rights of product sellers to bring actions to reduce any product liability judgment by the amount of worker compensation benefits to which an employee is subsequently determined to be entitled. Shumway also specifically adds a section stating that no third-party tortfeasor may maintain an action for indemnity or contribution against an employer of an injured person entitled to workers' compensation in any products liability action on the same injury. LaFalce uses different language but adds no new concepts. Kasten adds several additional sections which require injured persons to exhaust worker compensation remedies before a court may entertain product liability claims and state that the determination of worker compensation benefits by the trier of fact in a product liability action may not have binding effect and be used as evidence in any other proceeding. Kasten's language with respect to third-party tortfeasors is identical to Shumway.

CURRENT SYSTEM

Workplace injuries constitute a major source for product liability litigation under current law. The system is chaotic, uneven across state jurisdictions, and unpredictable in outcome; it has been repeatedly criticized in congressional hearings by manufacturing and insurance groups. Nevertheless, it is also clear that the current system of worker compensation, based on fifty state statutes, several federal statutes, and court interpretations in all of those jurisdictions, is also inadequate. It also varies substantially across state boundaries; benefits do not reflect fault or loss of earning capacity; and benefit levels are generally inadequate in economic terms. The current system is costly but protects and limits the liability of employers; frequently, however, workplace accidents are caused by employer negligence and carelessness.

Currently proposed product liability legislation can only make a very small contribution to the rationalization of the problem. Provisions of the various product liability legislative proposals relating to worker compensation are all very similar: they limit subrogation actions and the number of legal transactions, but they retain the current state limits to employer liability; they also retain the current system by which worker compensation claims and product liability litigation can be brought on the same injury.

Serious proposals to reform the current worker reparations system have been proposed by a number of specialists in the area. These generally emphasize the need to reduce the overall cost of the compensation system while insuring that incentives be maximized for those who are best able to correct dangerous working conditions. The present system, which requires two proceedings to assess fault and damages (product liability actions and worker compensation claims) is perceived as duplicative and inefficient. Manufacturers and sellers are viewed as, in effect, subsidizing employers, regardless of fault, by paying tort costs which, in the absence of worker compensation statutes, would be borne by employers. To overcome this inefficiency, it has been suggested that manufacturers be integrated into the worker compensation system, sharing the costs and raising the level of benefits; this approach would close out the possibility for litigation, including product liability litigation, outside the worker compensation structure.

Other proposals advocate limiting the scope of outside product liability litigation through the collective bargaining process. Noting that the amounts paid for product liability insurance by manufacturers now overwhelmingly go to lawyers and insurance carriers, and not to injured employees, it has been argued that unions ought to agree to bar third-party tort claims by employees in exchange for greater worker compensation benefits.

Other countries have acted in this area; Britain, for example, abolished its worker compensation system in 1947. Currently, British workers must utilize the court system and sue for compensation in injury cases. It should be noted that British workers are more highly unionized than their American counterparts and can rely on the resources of their unions in these disputes. It appears unlikely that such an approach to the problem would be taken in the U. S.

All current proposals for serious reform would have the effect of raising costs to employers. For this reason, even the minimal proposals included in current product liability legislation are being opposed by some business and insurance groups. They fear that passage of any such provision would lead to basic reform of the current worker compensation laws, increase benefits, and raise employer contribution costs; they also fear the loss of the no-fault principle and eventual permission of lawsuits against negligent employers. Legal groups have also been critical of product liability legislation in general, the worker compensation provisions in particular, presumably fearing a loss of business if product liability legislation is limited in some way.

Product liability legislation may not be an appropriate vehicle for major reform of the worker compensation system, but consideration of the issue focuses attention on the inadequacies of the current worker compensation system. In addition, overall working and economic conditions have changed over the years.

CONCLUSION

The total number of disabling injuries (including deaths) since 1970, per year, has stayed virtually the same, and the rate of death has declined substantially over the last twenty-five years. Given these recent trends, and the prospect for more widespread automation and robotization of dangerous jobs in the future, it may now be an opportune time to open full debate on the logical approach to worker compensation. Worker injury is no longer considered a normal part of manufacturing as it was in the late nineteenth century. Machinery is not as inherently dangerous with proper maintenance and worker training. Employers have, under the common law, always been held responsible for proper maintenance and training of their workforce.

In these circumstances the unlimited no-fault structure of worker compensation can be questioned. Product liability legislation can provide a forum for debating whether it makes sense, in the late twentieth century, to limit employer liability for damages for injuries in the workplace on the basis of a theory developed in nineteenth century working conditions.

The worker compensation system today is not the only source of benefits to injured workers. Other programs which provide worker benefits are the Social Security disability system, unemployment insurance, and national and state welfare programs (where injured workers and their families are in need, e.g., Food Stamps, Aid to Families with Dependent Children, and Medicaid). Under these programs, loss of earning capacity is compensated on a no-fault basis; indeed, some states offset the amount of worker compensation benefits received by the benefits available in one or another of these other programs.

Worker compensation has never been considered a "welfare" system and it has never had any of the negative connotations associated with welfare. It is a system of providing workers with a means of support when they have been injured on the job. Worker compensation has never been means tested; the formulas for benefit levels are related, in every jurisdiction, to varying proportions of workers' lost earnings capacity due to injury.

For worker compensation to be retained, however, the benefit level must be increased so that injured workers and their families are not forced to avail themselves of various other welfare programs. This will be necessary if worker morale is to be raised and the volume of litigation reduced. If workers could live on worker compensation benefits, they would have less incentive to sue in court for increased compensation—especially when so high a proportion of the relief achieved through court settlements remains in the pockets of attorneys.

Providing increased worker compensation benefit levels will require higher costs to employers; also, an improved worker compensation system should reduce the costs to manufacturers and insurers of product liability litigation. Any final resolution must balance the costs and incentives to all the parties, and this will inevitably mean integrating the manufacturer into the system because manufacturers have greater resources for paying the requisite benefit levels than do many employers. After all, a solution that puts many employers out of business altogether is certainly not one that would be supported by labor or management. The issue facing policymakers is how to reform the current system to provide decent benefit levels to workers, while retaining a reasonable allocation of costs among employers, manufacturers, and insurers.

If the worker compensation system is not reformed and benefits remain inadequate, it is clear that product liability litigation over worker injury, in spite of all attendant difficulties and shortcomings, will grow. Worker injury in the workplace remains a widespread problem; many individuals and families are affected, as are employers, manufacturers of workplace equipment and their insurers. If a reasonably acceptable benefit level cannot be established under the current system, courts and legislatures are not likely to limit the possibility for the injured to achieve recovery in court on the basis of long accepted common law tort concepts and traditions. Under such circumstances, it would be unjust and inequitable to deny a fair hearing to injured workers who cannot achieve decent levels of recovery elsewhere under the established legal system.

MARK MacCARTHY

A Review of Some Normative and Conceptual Issues in Occupational Safety and Health

I. INTRODUCTION

Controversy has surrounded public policy toward occupational safety and health at least since the establishment of the Occupational Safety and Health Administration (OSHA) in 1971. Political, legal, and economic conflicts have surfaced in debates over the existence and nature of rights to safety and health on the job, the use of economic criteria in setting safety and health standards, and the principles that are to guide public policy in this area. Many of these issues were raised in recent court cases. In *Industrial Union Department, AFL-CIO v. American Petroleum Institute* (the benzene case), the Supreme Court decided that OSHA must make a threshold determination of significant risk before lowering the permissible exposure level of a toxic substance. In *American Textile Manufacturers Institute, Inc. v. Donovan, Secretary of Labor* (the cotton dust case), the Supreme Court upheld OSHA's policy of setting exposure levels for toxic substances at the lowest feasible level. In February 1981, the Reagan Administration issued an Executive Order addressing these problems. It sets the maximization of net benefits to society as the goal for all regulatory agencies and bars any major regulatory action unless its potential benefits to society outweigh its potential costs. Controversy continues over the appropriateness of this cost-benefit approach to occupational safety and health.

Although legal, political, and economic perspectives dominate these debates, the best means of improving the quality of public policy decisions concerning occupational safety and health is by clearly understanding the philosophical issues involved. This article identifies and describes the major issues of occupational safety and health that

are in need of and amenable to philosophical clarification. It begins with a discussion of the nature of occupational risk that emphasizes the crucial distinction between individual health risks and group outcomes, draws attention to some features of occupational health risks that separate them from other threats to health, and notes the unequal distribution of these risks. In the next section, the discussion turns to the ethical basis for public control of occupational risk. Collective action to reduce health threats in the workplace is required to protect workers' rights, to ensure a more equitable distribution of occupational risks, and to implement the shared public values that lie behind the concern for workplace safety. The following section discusses the appropriate criteria for setting public policy on occupational safety and health. The economic techniques of cost-benefit and cost-effectiveness analysis are examined, and the argument is made that these analytic techniques neglect normative considerations and can incorporate them only in inappropriate and misleading ways. Further, the use of cost-benefit and cost-effectiveness analysis as the sole or principal rules for policy in this area would tend to undermine the convictions that motivate public concern about the issue of occupational safety and health. The final section surveys alternative public policy principles, including cost containment approaches, risk-averse strategies, and the current official OSHA policy of feasibility analysis. The incompleteness of these approaches suggests the need for the development of a decision framework that would more adequately integrate health and economic information while allowing concerns over workers' rights, distributive justice, and public values to influence public policy materially.

II. THE NATURE OF OCCUPATIONAL RISK

Before addressing the major philosophical questions, several preliminary remarks may help to identify the special nature of the occupational safety and health problem. First, individual risks must be distinguished from group outcomes. Risk, in general, is the probability of an adverse outcome. Occupational risk is the probability of an injury or illness due to hazards in the workplace. These hazards, such as noise, toxic substances, or unguarded machinery, often produce a regular, predictable number of injuries and illnesses in the exposed worker population. At the individual level, the outcome is hypothetical; an individual worker may or may not be killed, injured, or made ill by workplace hazards. At this level, workers take their chances. In many situations, however, the outcome at the group level can be accurately predicted, and one may, then, expect a certain number of illnesses and injuries to appear in the exposed worker population as a whole. At this level, chance gives way to certainty.

A. The Individual and the Group

This distinction between the risk each individual takes and the overall outcome for the group is a conceptual distinction, related to the difference between statements about individuals and statements about the groups to which individuals belong. This distinction raises two questions regarding many kinds of risks. Consider, for example, coffee, which is allegedly involved in cancer of the pancreas. If coffee is involved in producing half of all pancreatic cancers, a noncoffee drinker aged fifty to fifty-four has seven chances in one hundred thousand of developing cancer of the pancreas in any single year. A coffee drinker's chances are doubled or tripled to approximately fourteen to twenty-one out of one hundred thousand. Should a person, then, avoid this extra risk by not drinking coffee? A different question arises with respect to the population as a whole. If coffee is implicated in producing half of all pancreatic cancers, then the consumption of coffee in the United States produces about twelve thousand of these cancers annually. Should steps be taken to reduce this number?

In the first example, we focus on the decision of the individual agent. His or her choice is essentially a private one. In the second case, we are concerned with the balance between two collective goals: the protection of public health and the provision of other social goods, including individual freedom of choice. This is a paradigm problem in public decision making.

This example illustrates the logical difference between the question, "Is this risk too great for me?" and the question, "Does the social value of this risky activity balance the certain harm that can be expected to result from it?" An answer to the first question is not necessarily an answer to the second. The distinction between questions concerning individual risk and questions concerning group outcomes (and group responsibility for these outcomes) parallels the difference between private and public choice.

In the area of occupational safety and health, the distinction between individual risk and group outcome is reflected in the difference between two approaches to public health. Economists typically take an individualistic approach. They are concerned with the rational choices individuals might make when confronted with a probability or an uncertainty about some harm. The other approach, more typical of doctors and other public health professionals, concerns predictable group outcomes and whether they are acceptable. The difference in focus is related to a difference in public policy goals: in the one instance, the problem is that the probability of an actual outcome is too large for the individual to accept; in the other, the aggregate outcome is too severe for society to tolerate.

It is fair to suggest that the label "risk" encourages, even if it does not strictly imply, an individualistic self-regarding (as distinct from group-regarding) approach to occupational safety. That may seem appropriate. Individuals face risks; it is they who bear them. The most familiar context in which people evaluate risks is personal—are the chances of being killed in an automobile or airplane accident too great for me? Will cigarettes give me cancer? Is this job too risky for me? Will coffee ruin my pancreas? These are familiar questions which we, as individuals, ask ourselves.

Yet there are other questions concerning risk which we may ask ourselves not as self-regarding individuals but as members of a society. We may wonder, for example, whether the yearly toll of automobile deaths is socially acceptable. Are risks imposed by various products—cigarettes and coffee among them—of the sort that should be left to individual discretion? The problem of workplace safety, at least as much as the problem of highway safety or product safety, has a public dimension.

The sheer amount of injury or death may be an appropriate cause of public as well as individual concern. From the individual point of view, a probability of death or injury, say one in a thousand, remains the same whether ten or ten million people take the same risk. From the social point of view, however, the difference is important: it could mean the loss of a thousand lives. How should we respond as a nation to these numbers? When occupational safety and health information is presented in terms of individual probabilities only, an evaluation typically follows in terms of the individual, not the group. By describing the problem this way—in terms of individual risks rather than community costs—we may commit ourselves to a subtle but powerful bias toward individualistic rather than community norms and values.

B. Hazards to Health

Occupational hazards are threats to health. These threats are special in that what may be lost—life or functional capacity—is irreplaceable. In the case of loss of life or limb, the irreplaceability is obvious. But the functional impairment of lungs or ears caused by exposure to hazards is also often irreversible, and the impairment becomes permanent. Techniques to reverse these effects are sometimes available, but in many instances, for example, chelation therapy for lead poisoning, the cure can be worse than the disease.

In addition, people cannot always be compensated for a loss of health. Damage to one's health is not altogether like damage to one's automobile. The insurance received for a damaged car, in principle at least, restores the owner to the earlier level of well-being. Compensation, in short, can be paid in full. In occupational fatalities, however, the precondition for any compensation is precisely what is lost. Any payment that could feasibly be made to workers with permanent disabilities, moreover, would not be compensatory in the technical sense

that the workers would just as soon have the compensation payment as their ability to walk or breathe. Normally, spending money, or what money can buy someone with diminished capacities, on disabling injuries and illnesses may be better than not doing so, but prevention may be better still.

Health is a precondition for a wide variety of other activities; it is an instrumental good. In fact, health is a precondition for such a wide variety of other activities that it is best viewed not simply as a value in itself, but as a condition of many or most other values. As such, it is not only an individual good, but also an element of social infrastructure, that is, an item that is needed to make possible the basic social and economic activities we engage in. From this point of view, maintaining an adequate public health system is in the same category as providing an adequate transportation system: widespread defects in either would have serious consequences for almost everything else we do. In contrast, other commodities have a much smaller range of activities that depend on them. If bicycles, three-piece suits, and garbage cans are not available, then certain desirable and socially worthwhile activities are foreclosed. But the range of such activities is small compared to the range of activities that depend upon public health or an adequate transportation system.

Health and physical integrity are also intrinsically valuable. They are social requirements not only in the sense that they are needed for other activities, but in the sense that they are desirable in and of themselves. They are primary goods in that they are things that all rational people want regardless of whatever else they want. This does not imply that risk minimization is a primary good, for this entails that people who risk their lives for good reason, for example, to conquer Mt. Everest or to free others from oppression, are irrational. Rather, the idea is that what is being risked—health—is a primary good that even risk takers would prefer not to lose.

C. Risk in the Workplace

The conditions under which risks occur in the workplace differ from those associated with other activities, for example, participation in recreational sports. People sometimes seek or actively court danger. The danger itself is sometimes satisfying because, among other things, it provides an opportunity for people to test themselves. Hence, dangerous sports like hang gliding are popular. In this sport—as in other risks people seek—the participants feel that their responses are crucial and they are engaged by and prove themselves against challenging conditions.

Risks encountered on the job are typically quite different. First, while it is possible that police officers, fire fighters, and other workers sometimes seek and take satisfaction in the dangers they face, this is not true of most workers. Those put at risk by toxic chemicals, for example, hardly feel challenged by the hazards they confront. These risks do not call upon workers to show special strength or dexterity. They may feel as if they were sitting ducks instead. In general, workers would like to avoid or minimize occupational hazards they face.

Secondly, risks on the job typically have no natural consequences that are desired. Coffee and cigarettes produce feelings of well being. Hence, despite the risks involved, people are willing to spend large amounts of money to consume these items. Occupational risks are quite different in that, by and large, they have only undesirable natural consequences. Natural consequences of occupational risk that are genuinely relished are hard to locate, and certainly are not sufficient in themselves to outweigh these risks in the minds of those who must bear them. For this reason, workers, perhaps like financial investors, would have to be compensated in some way to be persuaded to take risks.

A third distinction can be made between risks encountered on and off the job. Many risks, from children's games to casino gambling, have a social meaning. When risk taking has trappings of moral import, what is at stake is less important than the fact that undergoing the risk helps to structure social life. Esteem, honor, dignity, respect, and status all flow from withstanding symbolic gambles. In unusual occupations, such as airplane testing, occupational risks can become symbolically important in just this way. For most workplace risks, however, such "status gambling" may have less to do with heightening the meaningfulness of life and more to do with manipulation and self-deception. The transformation of occupational risks into symbolic risks can either be imposed deliberately on

workers as a way of avoiding hazard control or can be spontaneously generated by workers themselves as a defense mechanism to cope with their powerlessness. What seems clear, however, is that typical occupational hazards are not deliberately sought and that, if they were suddenly removed or greatly reduced, the "status gambling" attitudes fostered by the hazards would either wither away or find another focus.

Finally, exposure to occupational hazards is, by and large, involuntary. For most people in our society, work is unavoidable. If individual workers find themselves facing unacceptable occupational risks they cannot simply withdraw from the market. They must choose among available occupations—and so some must accept risky jobs. This does not mean that workers are coerced into taking risky jobs in the same way that draftees are. But external conditions frequently limit options so severely that coercion is not needed. The labor market sometimes structures risks so that those who bear them are not the informed, mobile risk-bearers of economic theory. Adequate information is often lacking; the power to insist on less risk does not exist; and there is no possibility of mobility. These limitations on choice characterize occupational as opposed to recreational or aesthetic risks.

D. The Distribution of Occupational Risk

Those who gain from risky work are not always those who do it. When hazardous working conditions lead to lower production costs, consumer prices go down and profits of business firms go up. But workers may suffer as a result. The distribution of risks among various industries, moreover, is plainly unequal. Some occupations and industries are extremely dangerous, while others are comparatively safe. This unequal distribution of risk is made all the more problematic because the burden of occupational risk apparently falls hardest on the comparatively disadvantaged.

Those who bear occupational risks, moreover, sometimes form small specific groups—vinyl chloride workers and native American uranium miners are examples. Others form large, but identifiable, social groups, as is the case with cotton textile workers, coal miners, and steelworkers. These workers tend to share common attitudes and interests that make them recognizable as a group. They are likely to regard occupational risk reduction as a matter of group interest. Risks associated with riding in automobiles or consuming saccharin-sweetened drinks or breathing polluted air, on the other hand, are likely to cut across recognizable social divisions. People face these latter risks either as isolated individuals or as members of rather more abstract and encompassing aggregates. This fact raises questions concerning the distribution of risk, not only among individuals, but also among groups.

Finally, the circumstances of occupational risk are unique because of the political dimension they introduce. Labor and management approach each other as adversaries on a wide variety of workplace issues. Very often an issue concerning occupational safety will also be an issue concerning the control of the workplace. The presence of job hazards is then used as an example of how things can go wrong if management is allowed unrestricted discretion in making decisions concerning the organization and pace of work. On the other hand, militant action in favor of reducing occupational risks can sometimes be resisted, not because management is opposed to risk reduction, but because of a feeling that labor is too forcefully infringing upon management prerogatives to organize production. The general issue concerning control over the workplace therefore colors the issue of occupational risk.

III. ETHICS AND GOVERNMENTAL INVOLVEMENT IN OCCUPATIONAL SAFETY AND HEALTH

The previous discussion suggests that occupational safety and health is at least partly a matter of moral and social concern. But the justification of government involvement in the area is more and more frequently being stated in terms of market failure, not moral principle. The labor market, it is argued, does not provide sufficient information for workers and management to make informed decisions about occupational risk. Furthermore, because of transaction costs, it would be more efficient to let government set national standards based upon a centralized body of knowledge concerning safety and health problems, especially in the areas where

risks are likely to be misperceived or the effects are chronic rather than acute. In addition, the government provides compensation programs that prevent workers and management from bearing the full social costs of workplace illnesses and injuries. The government may legitimately, then, enforce a limited amount of command and control regulation to deal with these information gaps and externalities.

This justification of government involvement is based upon considerations of efficiency in the satisfaction of personal preferences. According to this view, the labor market does not provide an amount of safety on the job that maximizes the satisfaction of these individual preferences. Behind the market failure justification for government involvement there lies a utilitarian principle. Several other ethical bases for government involvement exist, however, that are not derived from a utilitarian tradition. For analytical purposes, the following discussion divides these justifications into those based on workers' rights, those based on distributive justice, and those based on public values.

A. Workers' Rights

The framework of individual rights provides one ethical perspective on the problem of occupational safety and health. This framework emphasizes that people should be treated as ends and not as mere means. People have rights that protect them from others who would enslave them or otherwise use them for their own purposes. In bringing this idea to bear on the problem of occupational safety, many people have thought that workers have an inalienable right to earn their living free from the ravages of job-caused death, disease, and injury. Philosophers have offered strong defenses of the right to be free of the infliction of cancer on the job. Behind this contention lies the idea that people need rights to protect them from unreasonable health hazards where they earn their living. If the unrestricted market does not automatically satisfy this right to safety on the job, then the government must intervene in order to protect it.

What does it mean to say that someone has a right to safety and health on the job? According to one view, people have rights to something when they have a valid claim upon society to protect them in the possession of it. This general idea does not specify whether the entitlement in question is negative (noninterference) or positive (recipience), or partly both. The right to safety and health on the job has sometimes been seen as derivative from the right not to be killed or severely injured by others. From this perspective, workers would have a negative right to noninterference and protection against persons who threaten life or limb in a direct way. On the other hand, a right to safety and health on the job can be construed as a species of a positive right to life. From this perspective, workers are entitled to that share of society's resources needed to provide a minimum level of protection against hazards on the job. This minimal level of protection obviously varies with the available resources of the community. For a given amount of resources, the minimal standard may not be the optimal level at which to provide safety and health on the job, but it provides a floor below which protection should not be allowed to fall.

This right to minimum protection on the job is held by workers but it imposes duties on employers. These duties require employers to refrain from the use of hazardous materials or processes that would impose a significant risk of killing or seriously injuring workers—a negative duty corresponding to a negative right. Additionally, or alternatively, these duties could be construed to require adequate levels of protection against serious threats to worker safety and health—a positive duty corresponding to a positive right. These employer duties call for the expenditure of resources to provide safety on the job, either in the form of opportunity costs or actual expenditures. The allocation of resources to the fulfillment of this duty has a certain priority over their allocation to the production of other commodities. The existence of a right to safety on the job, then, implies that the pursuit of private interest must take the provision of safety and health on the job as something of a side-constraint, although not necessarily an absolute one.

A right to occupational safety and health would also have a certain priority over collective or social goals. According to one popular theory, rights are political trumps to the effect that the collective good is not a sufficient justification for imposing some loss or injury on the individuals holding these rights. A more moderate view would allow some compromises between the satisfaction of

rights and the satisfaction of common goals. Even if a more moderate view is adopted, however, a right to occupational safety and health could not be overridden by relatively minor increases in the satisfaction of some collective interest.

The assignment of a safety right to workers still allows the possibility of trading the right for additional wages. A right to safety, however, could also be viewed as inalienable. On this view, market transactions involving the exchange of *minimum* safety and health protections for wages would not be allowed. The reason for this is to ensure that everyone would enjoy the substance of the right. This restriction does not necessarily prohibit *all* wage/risk transactions. One possibility would be to permit employers to charge workers (via lower wages) for the provision of extra safety over and above the social minimum. A further possibility would be to allow employers to charge for the provision of the social minimum. One could argue that just as a right to safe consumer products allows manufacturers to charge extra to make their products free of unreasonable risks, so a right to occupational safety allows employers to charge extra to make their workplaces free of unreasonable risks. On the other hand, one could argue that the unavoidability of work makes the consumer product analogy inappropriate. On this view, the cost of providing worker safety is a cost of doing business, and must be passed on to the consumer or taken out of profits.

Some people propose that jobs with unreasonable risks should be made available to workers if the alternative is unemployment. On the average, let us say, workers will be better off taking these risky jobs than being unemployed. It would therefore be rational for them to accept these jobs. Why prohibit them from doing so? This way of stating the issue may be misleading. A better way may be to ask whether these risky jobs should be made available at all. In effect, the provision of unsafe jobs offers one way of providing employment for the unemployed. It has to be evaluated, therefore, against other strategies for reducing unemployment, including a deliberate national policy of full and safe employment. One argument for such a policy might be that, in its absence, workers would face a choice between jobs with unreasonable risks and no jobs at all.

The framework of individual rights, then, may

provide principles that justify government intervention in the area of occupational safety and health. Furthermore, the principle of ensuring minimal levels of safety and health protection provides some guidance in setting levels of effort in mandated programs. There are, however, some limitations on the framework of individual rights.

The first reason the individual rights framework is limited is that it does not determine any particular level at which safety should be provided to workers. The right to safety and health on the job is not a right to an absolutely risk-free workplace, but only to a minimum amount of safety and health on the job. But what is the level of safety to which workers are entitled? Some philosophers have argued that workers have the right to the maximum feasible level of safety. But is this true? Suppose a worker faces an extremely low level of risk, so low that the worker cannot distinguish it from zero. This risk can, however, be lowered or eliminated at a large, but affordable, cost. Is this worker entitled to demand the safety expenditure as a matter of right? Recall that this expenditure is purely for a trivial reduction in the already small probability of illness or injury. It is not a case of someone demanding a large expenditure in order to avoid his or her own death or serious injury. It seems that no worker has such a right, and so no worker, except, perhaps, in special cases, has the right to the maximum feasible level of safety. This is not to argue that a collective goal of maximum feasible safety is unjustified, but it does suggest that if it is to be justified, one must look elsewhere than to a theory of individual rights.

Once the idea of rights to maximal feasible safety is abandoned, no other choice for an appropriate level appears satisfactory. One way to see the difficulty is to note that the framework of rights focuses on the problem of occupational safety and health at the individual level. At this level, the problem is that workers are facing too high a probability of injury or illness on the job. But what probability of injury or illness on the job is a violation of an individual's rights? What probability of violating an individual's rights is itself a violation of his or her rights? The choice of one probability rather than another may appear arbitrary, and there seems to be no satisfactory mapping of other considerations onto these probabilities.

One attempt to deal with this problem introduces the idea of a standard threat. Rights provide guarantees not against all possible threats to their enjoyment, but only against standard threats. The notion of a standard threat is complex, but involves the ideas that the threats are (1) pervasive, common, ordinary; (2) serious; and (3) remediable, or feasibly resisted. What threats are standard is in part an empirical question, and may vary from context to context. This idea of standard threats probably captures the heart of the intuition that rights are involved in occupational safety and health. It does not, however, provide guidance as to what levels of risk are consistent with an individual's rights.

A second reason the individual rights framework may be inadequate lies in its attention to minimal levels of protection. It ties the right to safety and health to the notion of a minimally decent level of protection, assuming that those who lay claim to maximal levels, as a matter of right, are wrong. But the question for public policy is best approached as this: what is the optimum level of protection to provide? The Occupational Safety and Health Act, for example, goes beyond the requirement to provide minimal levels of protection and suggests an interpretation of the optimal level of protection as the highest feasible level. To the extent that it does this, the Act appears to go beyond the mere assignment of rights at a certain level of safety, and moves into the area of enforcing widely accepted public values concerning safety and health on the job.

Finally, the individual rights framework fails to do justice to some of our considered judgments concerning the public health impact of safety and health hazards on the job. It may be, for instance, that the probabilities of harm facing each worker are so low as to escape the charge of posing a *significant* risk. Nevertheless, the number of people exposed may be so large that a significant number of cases appears. At this point it may be reasonable to conclude that an insufficient level of protection is being provided, despite the fact that the risk facing each worker is perfectly consistent with the protection of his or her rights.

B. *Distributive Justice*

A second reason for the government to be involved in the area of occupational safety and health is to eliminate or reduce inequities in the distribution of occupational risks. The following example may clarify our intuitions about the idea of equal protection against occupational threats. Suppose firms were taxed at a fixed rate for each unit of worker exposure to a toxic substance. The result of this would be to encourage firms to control exposures up to the point where it becomes cheaper to pay the tax. Firms that could reduce toxic exposures cheaply would provide more protection for their workers than would firms that could reduce toxic exposures only at great expense. Workers would therefore receive unequal protection against toxic substances depending upon whether their employing firm faced high or low marginal abatement costs.

Why is this example unsettling? Certain intuitions about distributive justice are touched, but exactly what are they? Suppose that different plants provide unequal protection, but none is so lax that it violates the threshold level of protection guaranteed by right. Is any worker being treated unfairly? What if no rights were being violated, but there were extreme inequalities in protection? What if the extra risks were borne disproportionately by the powerless and the poor?

A review of several approaches to distributive justice may provide a way to address these questions. Utilitarian and procedural views regarding distributive justice provide some guidance. A utilitarian approach to the distribution of occupational risks would call for whatever distribution maximizes total or average utility. If we suppose, in the spirit of welfare economics, that ideal markets maximize utility, or at least achieve Pareto optimality, the most natural application of the utilitarian approach to occupational safety and health would result in support for market mechanisms, except in the case of demonstrated market failure. In the above example, this would therefore call for setting the tax so as to produce the efficient level of protection against health impairment. The utilitarian approach, then, supports the intuition that a distribution of risks based upon abatement costs may be just.

A utilitarian approach to justice may be contrasted with a procedural approach. It provides that whatever distribution results from fair principles of acquisition and transfer is just. Hence, no overriding aim in the distribution of safety and health

on the job needs to be specified, and no governmental action is needed to achieve a predetermined end state. Instead, occupational risks are allocated in an occupational risk market in which workers receive wage premiums for risky work. The model here is a gamble in which the conditions are fair, the bets are made voluntarily, no one cheats, etc. In a fair gamble involving money, whatever distribution of cash results is just. In this view, the occupational risk market, to the extent that it resembles a fair lottery, would be governed by pure procedural justice in which there is no independent criterion for the right result. Those who hold this view would reject the setting of a "toxic exposure" tax as an imposition of a social goal that illegitimately overrides just principles of transfer and acquisition.

Utilitarian and procedural approaches to distributive justice, then, tend to work against a policy goal of reducing inequalities in the distribution of occupational risk. The utilitarian would substitute overall efficiency for that goal; the procedural approach would deny that any goal should be set. A more hopeful basis for this policy may lie in egalitarian conceptions that tie justice to equality on a theoretical level. The following are several possible principles of justice in the distribution of occupational risk that could be examined in such an egalitarian framework.

The first principle declares that extreme inequality in the dangers associated with different jobs is in itself objectionable. It is not fair on this view that illnesses and injuries should be concentrated in particular jobs, occupations, and industries. The mere inequality in risk, and not just its distribution among nonoccupational groups, is objectionable. Some policy implications of this view are that high-risk industries should be targeted first, that exposure levels to toxic substances should be set at background levels, and that where risks cannot be eliminated they should be spread more equally among a larger population.

A second principle objects to extreme inequality in the prevalence of occupational illnesses and injuries among certain nonoccupational groups. It is not fair, on this view, that occupational illnesses and injuries should fall disproportionately on the poor, minorities, and the powerless. Nor should extra risks fall on people in morally irrelevant groups such as those who work in medium-size establishments or those for whom abatement costs are especially high. The difference between the two principles is that the first objects to any unequal distribution of occupational risks while the second objects only when the distribution has been determined in what seems an unjust way. A policy implication of the second principle is that special attention and effort should be given to those groups that experience extra occupational risk because they are poor, powerless, or victims of illegitimate discrimination.

These two principles each suggest that large increases in efficiency would be needed to balance the loss in equity resulting from the application of market principles such as a "toxic exposure" tax. A third principle might propose that, if occupational risk is concentrated in groups that are already disadvantaged, programs for the reduction of occupational risk should have priority over programs to reduce risks that are spread more evenly throughout the general population. Thus, if we have to choose between saving an equal number of asbestos workers and motorists, equity considerations should make us favor the asbestos workers.

All three distributive principles are in need of further theoretical support. They do not, moreover, specify the extent to which these egalitarian goals should be pursued in the face of conflicts with other goals. In addition, they are silent on the overall level of protection we should provide. They, therefore, do not determine the level of effort at which government programs in this area should operate. More complete guidance for occupational safety and health policy might be found by referring to widely shared public values that lie behind the concern over workplace safety.

C. Public Values

The concept of public values provides an important ethical justification for government involvement in occupational safety and health. This perspective is based on a distinction between individuals' preferences for their own personal welfare and their values and moral principles concerning the kind of society they think desirable or the collective policies they think worthwhile. These public values can concern the rules to be followed in the pursuit of private interests (such as property rights) or they can address some concrete common concern like national defense or environmental quality. When adopted by the community these public values become collective goals.

Not all public values are well defined. There is often no consensus supporting them; the criteria for community acceptance are not always clear. Yet in the case of occupational safety and health these concerns are not always problematical. One public value at stake in the question of government involvement in occupational safety and health, for example, is the uncontroversial belief that a society in which fewer people are killed or seriously disabled on the job is, other things being equal, better than a society in which more people are killed or seriously disabled on the job. This value may derive from a more basic judgment that people have a dignity and a worth that make it wrong to use them as mere means to any end including efficiency. This judgment leads to the idea that a special regard for the health and safety of workers is required to avoid treating them simply as components in the production process. This moral ideal underlies the passage of the Occupational Safety and Health Act, which established job safety and health as a national goal.

From the perspective of public values, the problem of occupational safety and health is not simply that occupational risks are inequitably distributed and that individuals are receiving less protection against threats to their safety and health on the job than they are entitled to by right. The problem is, in addition, that the level of injury and illness may be unacceptably high, even if rights are respected and the distribution of job risk is equitable. Both rights and justice are important public values. But if too many workers are killed or disabled on the job, the public may determine that the meager level of effort devoted to the reduction of this toll displays a disregard for the value we place on human life.

This evaluation of occupational safety is not necessarily accomplished by examining risks at the individual level. We may want to prohibit hazardous activities that are fully rational for each individual even when there are no violations of rights or justice involved. Recall the coffee example mentioned earlier. For a more extreme example, imagine a nonoccupational death lottery in which people could accept a risk of death in return for a cash payment. The death risks and the payments could probably be arranged so that many people would play. But deliberation regarding whether to allow such a death lottery would concern more than the size of the death risk, the monetary compensation involved, and the individuals or groups likely to play. It would also concern such matters as whether a sufficient respect for the value of life was displayed by this type of transaction, and whether the value of individual choice in the matter outweighed the damage done to the value of life. Also relevant would be the purposes behind the death lottery and the social outcomes to be expected, which would vary even if the individual-level death risks did not.

In the occupational risk market, where the group outcomes are often regular and predictable, the perspective of public values would similarly require a direct consideration of the importance of the activities producing these outcomes. The role of government would be to reflect this evaluation and to regulate or prohibit certain activities on the job when the outcomes that would result violate this public judgment.

To approach occupational safety on the basis of public values, however, is to encounter a familiar problem. The approach justifies some degree of government involvement, but does not specify the level. Moreover, it has a special difficulty in explaining why society has more of an interest in regulating the outcomes of occupational risks than in regulating other risk-taking behavior. The beginnings of an answer are to be found in the social nature of employment, the fact that it is not an avoidable activity, and the irreversible and non-compensable nature of injury and death. But more work would have to be done to distinguish the cases so as to avoid the use of principles that would also justify intrusiveness and intolerance.

IV. ECONOMIC CRITERIA

While moral principles involving rights, justice, and public values may help to justify centralized programs regulating occupational safety and health, they do not completely determine the level of government effort required. It has been suggested that various *economic* criteria may be used to supplement these moral principles in determining a desirable level of effort. This section examines the economic approach to occupational safety and health. It focuses on the difficulties in applying economic techniques in this area, notes some tensions between the use of these techniques and the normative considerations just discussed, and attempts to sketch an appropriate role for these techniques.

According to this economic approach, the goal of occupational safety and health policy should be to minimize the sum of workplace accident costs and workplace accident prevention costs, or equivalently, to maximize the difference between the benefits of workplace safety programs and the costs of these programs. A number of techniques have been proposed to achieve this goal. They divide into cost-effectiveness and cost-benefit rules. A program is cost-effective when it maximizes its objectives for a given cost, or minimizes its cost for a given objective. A program is cost-beneficial when its benefits exceed its costs. The cost-benefit criterion goes beyond the cost-effectiveness criterion in assigning a monetary value to the benefits involved, thereby allowing direct comparisons of the positive and negative consequences of a program in monetary terms. In examining the economic approach it is helpful to treat these criteria separately.

A. Cost-Effectiveness

Cost-effectiveness criteria were never intended to determine levels of safety. They presuppose that the desirable level of effort has already been set or that some cost constraint has already been imposed. The major use for cost-effectiveness approaches is not in setting levels, then, but in achieving in an efficient way goals determined on some other basis. Even this role, however, is limited by the need to balance efficiency against other values.

Despite this inherent limitation, cost-effectiveness can be a useful measure of the desirability of alternative workplace safety and health programs. Consider, for example, the problem of what to do about noise in the workplace. Suppose that one program calls for the use of engineering controls as a way of preventing cases of hearing impairment; another calls for the use of hearing protectors that prevent the same number of cases of hearing impairment, but at a much lower cost. In this hypothetical example, a cost-effectiveness approach would favor the use of the less expensive hearing protectors. Only rarely, however, is the choice quite that simple. The actual controversy in the case of noise in the workplace is whether hearing protectors do in fact provide the same level of protection as engineering controls. If the less expensive hearing protectors provide less protection, then the fact that they are less expensive does not make them more cost-effective. Alternative programs can be compared with respect to cost-effectiveness only when they achieve the same level of effect or impose the same costs.

Some misunderstandings of this point have resulted in the idea that a program that imposes the lowest average or marginal cost per accident avoided is cost-effective, while programs with higher unit costs are not cost-effective. This is not so. If the program that avoids more accidents or injuries has higher unit costs, this may reflect the familiar fact of diminishing returns, and indicates that if we want to avoid more incidents it will simply cost us more per incident to do it. Relative to our objectives, each program may be equally efficient.

Some analysts who use a cost-effectiveness framework propose to equalize the marginal cost per incident avoided. An example of this approach would be to set different levels of exposure to toxic substances for different industry segments depending upon the cost required to control exposures. If this is done, then the number of cases avoided will be maximized for any given level of expenditure. However, the distribution of cases avoided will differ from that determined by a policy that requires equal protection for all. To equalize the marginal cost of safety conflicts with considerations of distributive justice that could motivate government programs. More telling, perhaps, in the context of trying to determine levels, is that this cost-effectiveness rule does not specify at what level marginal costs should be set, or what should be the total social cost of the regulation.

Another cost-effectiveness rule would concentrate attention on the accidents or injuries that can be avoided most cheaply. The policy recommendation here is to set priorities and levels for safety programs on the basis of the lowest unit costs. The rationale is this: if we proceed up the supply curve

for lives saved in this way, then no matter where we stop spending, we will have maximized the number of lives saved for the amount spent. One difficulty with this recommendation is that it is likely to conflict both with the goal of targeting high risk industries and groups first and with the goal of providing equal protection across groups. Moreover, it does not take account of the total number of lives saved by a particular safety program. For example, when we choose which of two toxic substances to regulate first, it may be better to give priority to the substance that produces more illnesses and fatalities rather than the one that has the lowest per unit prevention costs. This would maximize the number of lives saved in a given period of time although it would be at an increased cost per life saved. Finally, the policy of saving the "cheapest" lives first does not solve the problem of levels since it does not specify at what point we should stop spending to save lives.

B. Cost-Benefit

From within a cost-benefit framework, the limitations on cost-effectiveness criteria appear to stem from the lack of a monetary value for the benefits of occupational safety and health programs. The cost-benefit approach attempts to move beyond the cost-effectiveness approach by placing a monetary value on these benefits. Cost-effectiveness analysis measures the benefits of safety and health programs in their natural units—lives saved, number of cases of hearing impairment avoided, and overall reductions in occupational illnesses and injuries. Cost-benefit analysis transforms these "naturally" measured benefits into monetary terms by specifying an appropriate monetary value. Since the economic costs of safety and health programs are already in dollar units, a direct comparison of benefits and costs is possible in terms of a single common measure. With this common metric, it is possible to examine clearly whether the benefits of a safety and health program exceed the costs.

A formal cost-benefit analysis, then, requires monetary values for the lives saved and illnesses avoided by safety and health programs. But these items are not typically bought and sold on markets, and so there is no prevailing price to use as a measuring rod. There has been much research, therefore, attempting to measure these benefits indirectly. However, a review of the two principal methods used to value the benefits of programs that save lives reveals severe technical and theoretical difficulties. The first method attempts to assess the social cost of lost lives. Essentially, this amounts to estimating the future earnings of those whose lives would be saved by the program and discounting this estimate to its present value. The benefits of life-saving programs are then measured as reductions in these social costs. Critics argue cogently that the social cost approach confuses the contribution people make to the gross national product with their social worth; the value of their livelihood with the value of their lives. It has the ethically unacceptable implications that poor people are worth less than the rich, women are worth less than men, blacks worth less than whites, and old people who have no income worth nothing at all. To remedy these difficulties, it has been suggested that a second approach be tried that uses the traditional economic criterion of willingness to pay.

This willingness-to-pay approach is the favored approach in the economics profession, largely because it has a solid basis in welfare economics. A straightforward application of this traditional criterion is blocked, however, by the fact that there appears to be little sense in asking what payment an individual would make to escape certain death. The accepted solution to this problem is to ask a different question: what would individuals be willing to pay to reduce the probability of death when these probabilities are very small? The monetary value of a person's life is not determined by this procedure, but a monetary value of personal safety is. Once this value is available, then a monetary value of the benefits of a life-saving program can be calculated as the number of people at risk times the probability of death times the value of safety.

The most widespread method of calculating the value of safety is based upon labor market studies. The labor market is assumed to function as an occupational risk market in which worker demand curves for safety and management safety supply curves intersect in a series of equilibrium points. Attempts are then made to measure the slope of the curve that these market equilibria trace out. This slope represents the wage differential for extra risk and is used as a measure of the value of safety.

There are some technical problems with this approach. First, the evidence is mixed on the existence of these compensating wage differentials. Some studies show the expected positive coefficient, indicating that hazardous work pays more; some show a negative one, indicating that hazardous work pays less; and some show a coefficient that cannot be statistically distinguished from zero at the usual levels of confidence, suggesting that level of risk has *no* influence on wage rates. It is not even clear that there is a risk market then. Second, even if a positive coefficient is found, it does not represent a worker demand curve for safety, but the intersection of worker demand curves and management supply curves. For small changes in the risk of death this does not matter, since, at market equilibrium, the amount workers are willing to pay for safety is theoretically the same as the amount management is willing to spend on it. But, conceptually, it is important to note that the estimated coefficient measures management willingness to supply safety as much as it measures worker demand for it. Third, the estimated coefficient may or may not represent an adequately functioning risk market. Lack of knowledge, power, or mobility may prevent workers from expressing their full desire for compensation. Fourth, since the loss of life cannot be measured objectively, there is no way to tell whether the observed compensation is adequate or not.

Further, a dilemma threatens the entire wage differential approach to estimating the value of safety. If risk markets are fully functioning, then workers receive full compensation for bearing risk, and there is no need for government intervention, because any mandated program above and beyond those already in place would cost management more than the fully compensated workers are willing to pay for it. On the other hand, if the markets are not fully functioning, then the estimated value of safety bears no systematic relation to the real value. It would then be illegitimate to value the benefits of a program designed to increase occupational safety in a malfunctioning occupational risk market on the basis of unreliable estimates of the value of safety drawn from these very same malfunctioning markets.

There is an even more fundamental objection to the wage differential measure. A formal cost-benefit analysis needs a measure of what people are willing to pay for a program that saves lives. What the wage differential coefficient represents, however, is willingness to pay for personal safety, not life-saving programs. The two are by no means the same. The value we want is what people are willing to spend for a social program that will fundamentally alter the options available on the occupational risk market; we, therefore, want to measure individual preferences for structural changes in the labor market. Wage differentials, however, represent people's preferences within a given structure of occupational risk, not what they would prefer in a labor market with an altered structure. It is possible that valuation under the present and the altered structure are systematically related, but individual preferences for structural change in the occupational risk market would have to be measured somehow before this could be established. But if they can be estimated directly, why bother with a surrogate measure?

These difficulties apply to estimates of the wage differentials for injury and non-fatal illness as well. It appears then that the attempt to value the benefits of occupational safety and health programs via wage differentials is not likely to produce useful estimates. If so, the option of using cost-benefit criteria to set levels of effort for government occupational safety and health programs is considerably less attractive.

Economic cost-benefit criteria in general suffer from a more basic limitation that makes them less desirable as public policy guides. They are designed to promote efficiency in the satisfaction of personal preferences. The notions of Pareto optimality and Kaldor-Hicks efficiency that underlie these criteria are admittedly one-sided in their neglect of individual rights, distributive justice, and public values. For this reason, economic criteria may underdetermine the level of governmental effort required in the area of occupational safety and health. Only if some further reason justifies giving pride of place to efficiency in the satisfaction of private preferences can economic criteria, as traditionally applied, be the principal basis for setting levels of effort in this area.

It may be possible to use ingenious techniques to incorporate distributional considerations and other public values into cost-benefit analyses. Even so, economic criteria may still have a limited role in occupational safety and health decisions. The political preferences and moral ideals of citizens are poorly represented in a market or surrogate market approach. People sometimes want certain social goals to be achieved, not because there is any personal gain in it for them, but simply because they think it is the right thing to do. The only way an economic analysis can capture these public ideals is by first pricing them. The defect in this procedure is not simply that people are not used to placing a monetary value on their ideals, but that it substitutes a measure of the strength of a preference for an evaluation of an ideal. The evaluation of an ideal, however, is a completely normative undertaking, and is properly done through public discussion, argument, and debate, rather than by assessing the intensity of people's preferences. It might be better, then, to see if the ideals that stand behind our public commitment to occupational safety and health can enter materially into public policy without first being priced by economic techniques.

If economic criteria are not to be the sole basis for occupational safety and health policy, what role should they play in this area? Some economists recommend that cost-benefit criteria be used as basic guidelines in standard-setting, qualified, if necessary, by equity and other considerations. Others recommend that cost-benefit analysis be done to measure the efficiency impact of policies only. The idea would be to balance economic efficiency as one of a number of perhaps equally important social values. This multidimensional approach may be attractive; it requires us, however, to specify techniques other than those available within cost-benefit analysis to balance efficiency against other normative considerations. The following section examines some possible ways in which this may be done.

V. ALTERNATIVE PUBLIC POLICY PRINCIPLES

Economic criteria cannot be the sole basis for public policy toward occupational safety and health because they do not adequately take into account the public concerns that motivated government involvement in this area. The Occupational Safety and Health Act was passed to make the workplace *safer*, not necessarily *more efficient*. The public remains concerned, moreover, with the nature of workplace hazards, their distribution, and the degree to which workers have a say in controlling the risks they face on the job. However, in attempting to carry out its mandate, OSHA has been criticized for failing to take into account important economic constraints. If we accept the conclusion of the previous section, that economic criteria cannot be the sole basis for occupational safety and health policy, the question arises whether principles can be devised or guidelines suggested that would both respect economic limits and satisfy public values. Three current proposals for doing this will be described here. One suggestion would be to put a total or unit cost constraint on workplace safety expenditures. Another approach draws upon decision-theory to formulate risk-averse strategies. A final approach is the OSHA strategy of feasibility analysis.

A. Cost Containment Strategies

The first cost containment strategy is to adopt a limit on the total amount that can be spent on worker safety and health in a given period. One proposal to do this is the regulatory budget. According to this idea, the level of resources to be mandated each year on occupational safety and health programs would be set by Congress. OSHA could not mandate expenditures above this level, although firms could spend more than the mandated amount if they wished. While the details of this proposal are not fully worked out, the general idea is widely discussed and has some congressional support. Its chief strength is that by fixing a budget outside the process of setting safety and health standards it allows the use of the cost-effectiveness rules discussed earlier to determine an appropriate level of worker protection. For example, the cost-effectiveness policy of saving the "cheapest" lives first could be followed and a stopping point would be reached when the budget was exhausted.

There are several objections to this idea. First, the proper size of the budget cannot be deter-mined on cost grounds alone. A large expenditure on safety and health may be worth every penny, while a small expenditure may be wasteful. A safety expenditure that would return net economic benefits, for example, could be ruled out by a regulatory budget. Second, by focusing attention on the cost of regulations, the regulatory budget encourages the development of inexpensive regulations, not effective ones. Third, there are a host of practical and administrative difficulties whose resolution appears unlikely.

A second cost containment strategy would be to cap the unit cost of occupational safety and health program. Suppose, for example, that it could be decided to spend no more than $3 million per life saved in an occupational safety program. Then OSHA could mandate safety programs up to the point where the marginal or average cost to save a life equals $3 million. Programs that would save lives at greater unit cost would not be pursued.

It is important to note that this proposal differs from the proposal to determine appropriate levels of safety by estimating what individuals are willing to pay for personal safety on the job. The individual willingness-to-pay measure relies on market or surrogate market analyses, and does not capture people's political preferences for structural change in the occupational risk market. The unit cost containment strategy, however, need not rely on market-like analyses; nor need it only reflect personal preferences for safety. Congress, for example, could reflect a collective decision to pay no more than a certain amount for avoiding a workplace fatality. Or surveys could be taken to discover not what people are willing to pay for their own safety, but how much people are willing to spend per life saved to increase safety for workers in general. One could, therefore, reject the estimates of the value of safety drawn from labor market studies, and still adopt a unit cost constraint strategy.

This suggestion maintains some of the advantages of the economic criteria discussed earlier, namely, a sense of overall efficiency and some consistency across programs. There are disadvantages as well. It is not clear that all the benefits of occupational safety and health programs can be treated in this way. Reaching some kind of political consensus on life-saving programs is not totally out of the question, but occupational safety and health programs prevent permanently disabling illnesses and injuries that often lead to premature death. Under a cost containment approach, how should the benefits of avoiding byssinosis, a chronically disabling lung disease affecting cotton textile workers, be evaluated against the benefits of avoiding silicosis, a different chronically disabling lung disease affecting sand blasters and miners? Do we have special surveys? Does Congress reflect a national consensus on each and every type of occupational disease and injury? Clearly, much would have to be delegated to OSHA for administrative judgment under such a strategy. But once removed from the political arena in this way the normative justification for these decisions, namely, that they reflect a national consensus, is much weaker.

There is a second difficulty. It may be unwise to apply the same cost constraint to all programs that save lives in the workplace. If the same cost constraint is applied universally to all occupational hazards, economic factors become the primary concern, while other considerations become less important. But other factors should remain equally important: the nature of the risk, how many people are at risk, how voluntarily it is assumed, who bears the cost, who gets the benefits, whether there is something especially dreadful about the hazard, how much individual freedom has to be sacrificed in order to eliminate it, exactly what economic goods might become more expensive, and so on. Once all these other considerations are given their full due, it is likely that the implied cost per life saved for different programs will differ considerably. Enforcing a consistency along the cost dimension, then, is a way of discounting the importance of equally important factors.

It may at first seem that, since the programs designed to save lives on the job accomplish their goal at a certain cost, any decision to proceed with such a program must be based upon cost considerations. There is, in other words, an implicit value of life-saving present in each decision to proceed. It may seem, then, that calling for the adoption of a unit cost containment figure simply makes explicit a previously hidden decision criterion and therefore opens it up to public debate. This position, however, confuses a consequence of a decision with a basis for it. A decision may imply the acceptance of a certain cost to save a life, but this figure may not have been a primary reason for making the decision. It may not even have formed any part of its justification. It may be that after an explicit

decision has been made to save certain lives that a cost per life saved figure can be inferred. When a decision is based on a balance of other factors, the unit cost results from this weighing but does not determine it. Hence, it is not always correct to describe a cost of life figure as a hidden decision criterion.

A more general problem faces these cost containment approaches: both seem to address the problem of setting levels of occupational hazard control from the wrong direction. They set a cost constraint on some basis or other and allow this decision to determine indirectly the level of protection to be offered. But the problem is in setting the right level of protection, as opposed to simply controlling regulatory costs. Why not determine this level directly? Why not set the level of protection desired in some reasonable way and then let this determine unit and total costs? Strategies other than cost containment may, therefore, be more promising.

B. Risk-Averse Strategies

Risk-averse strategies do not set levels of effort in occupational safety and health programs by employing a fixed cost constraint. Instead, they approach occupational illnesses and injuries as undesirable events whose probability of occurrence should be minimized. One risk-averse rule calls for zero risk, where this is technologically feasible. This rule, of course, gives economic costs no weight and is equivalent to treating risk reduction as lexically prior to all other endeavors. A more balanced rule is obviously needed. It does not follow, however, that zero risk is never a reasonable goal. A ban on the use of asbestos, for example, would reduce the occupational risk of asbestos-related diseases to zero and may in fact be the best policy to deal with this particular hazard, if there are competitive nontoxic substitutes available. It may not be possible to reduce all risks to zero, but this provides no argument against zero risk as a goal in particular cases.

Other risk-averse strategies do not aim at reducing the risks of occupational injury or illness to zero. The *maximin* and *minimax regret* rules are borrowed from the literature of decision theory and sometimes applied to problems in occupational safety and health. The maximin rule directs attention to the most disastrous possible outcome of each regulatory alternative under consideration and requires the decisionmaker to choose the alternative which has the most favorable worst possible consequence. The minimax regret rule is similar. It tells the decisionmaker to focus on the largest foregone benefit of each regulatory alternative and to choose the alternative having the smallest foregone benefit. The foregone benefit of a regulatory alternative would be determined by comparing the consequences of adopting it with the consequences of adopting some other regulatory option. These rules are risk averse with respect to occupational injuries and illness because they do not discount the magnitude of these adverse outcomes by the probabilities of their occurrence.

An example may clarify the use of these rules in the context of occupational safety and health. Suppose the problem is deciding how to regulate a substance that may be a mild, moderate, or strong carcinogen. The maximin rule would direct attention to the possibility of its being a mild carcinogen when considering an extremely stringent alternative, such as a ban, and would focus on the possibility of its being a strong carcinogen when considering the possibility of no regulatory action at all. The decision would then be made by comparing these worst cases. The minimax regret rule would ask the questions: (1) what have we lost by regulating stringently if this substance turns out to be only a mild carcinogen?; and (2) what have we lost by regulating loosely if this substance turns out to be a strong carcinogen? The decision would then be made by comparing these two estimates of loss.

These rules have a number of advantages. First, they do not ignore economic costs the way that a zero risk policy does, for, in comparing the worst cases of foregone benefits, some comparisons of economic costs to possible health gains must be made. Furthermore, these rules may be the best available when exact estimates of the probabilities involved cannot be obtained at reasonable cost. Finally, in situations involving small probabilities of enormous harm, these rules can be useful because the harm may be so catastrophic that even a small probability of its occurrence must be avoided. Thus, these rules are most helpful where the consequences of not regulating quickly and effectively could be genuinely catastrophic and the costs of regulating are relatively modest.

These rules, however, cannot be made the sole basis for decision making. They are not as attractive when the probabilities of harm are more exactly known because they focus attention on the worst cases even when the probabilities involved are vanishingly small. When catastrophic harm is not involved, this may be bad policy. The focus on the worst cases and the disregard for the size of the probabilities involved could, step by step, over a long period of time, impose deadweight economic losses that are themselves catastrophic. Furthermore, these rules presuppose some method of weighing economic costs against health benefits but do not provide help in choosing such a method. A different approach that would provide some guidance in weighing economic costs against health benefits is needed.

C. Feasibility Analysis

The policy of OSHA under Dr. Eula Bingham was to set standards regulating exposure to toxic substances based upon a criterion of feasibility. This feasibility approach avoids the fixed cost constraint of the cost containment approach, and provides a way of directly setting desirable levels of protection. Like the risk-averse strategies, it generally attempts to minimize threats to safety and health on the job, and yet it provides a bit more guidance in the area of weighing economic costs against health benefits.

The policy, in the most general terms, calls for the lowest *feasible* level of toxic exposure in the workplace, which is consistent with a literal reading of section 6(b)(5) of the Act. The approach of the agency to regulation may be pictured, roughly and generally, as follows. The agency asks first whether a substance is hazardous, that is, whether any material impairment to health would follow from exposure to it. If no, the agency does nothing. If yes, OSHA tries to determine the level of exposure at which no material impairment would take place. OSHA's generic policy for carcinogens sets this level at zero in the absence of proof to the contrary. If this zero-level is not technologically feasible, the agency then selects the lowest exposure level that can be met with reasonably available technology. If the affected industries cannot afford to achieve this level, the agency then requires the lowest economically feasible exposure standard. The criterion of economic feasibility might require some firms to close down, namely, those that could not remain profitable and at the same time meet the standard. The industry as a whole, however, could not be crippled or destroyed.

In principle, the constraint of feasibility is simply a matter of what can be done, and the goal of the regulation of toxic substances is to provide the maximum possible protection against material impairment of health. Notice that this approach does not countenance an explicit balancing of costs and benefits in *particular* cases. This is not because the advantages of safety and health on the job do not have to be compared to economic costs and other losses. The reason no trade-offs are permitted in determining particular permissible exposure levels is that the balance between occupational safety and health and other values has already been set by Congress when it in effect declared that lowest feasible level standards are worth whatever trade-offs are necessary in terms of economic costs and other values. Balancing worker health against other values, in short, must be done as part of overall national policy, but the agency cannot substitute its judgment of the proper balance in particular cases for the congressional directive to promulgate lowest feasible level standards.

Despite its consideration of costs, feasibility analysis clearly allows the promulgation of extremely protective standards. Affected industries contend that some of the standards passed under the feasibility criterion are overly stringent. Inevitably, this criterion for setting occupational safety and health standards has received attention in the federal courts. OSHA's use of feasibility analysis was challenged when it set a standard lowering the exposure level for benzene from ten parts per million (ppm) to one ppm. The American Petroleum Institute (API) challenged the standard before the United States Court of Appeals for the Fifth Circuit, and on preenforcement review won a judgment declaring the standard invalid on the grounds that it was based on conclusions that could not be supported by the administrative record. In particular, the lower court found that the agency had failed to show that the 1 ppm exposure limit was reasonably necessary to provide for safety in the workplace. OSHA appealed to the Supreme Court, the case was argued October 10, 1979, and on July 2, 1980 the Court affirmed the judgment of the lower court by a margin of five to four. Two questions were presented for decision in

this case. First, and most prominent, was whether a standard regulating occupational exposure to toxic substances must satisfy a cost-benefit test. The second question concerned the quantity and quality of health effect information needed to support such a standard.

The Supreme Court ruled that the agency had exceeded its authority in lowering the benzene standard from ten ppm to one ppm because it had not determined that benzene posed a significant risk of material health impairment below the ten ppm level of exposure. But the ruling did not affect the use of feasibility analysis by the agency. In effect, the ruling imposed an additional constraint of determining the existence of a significant health risk at particular levels of exposure before a toxic substance could be regulated. This ruling shifted the burden of proof onto the agency to show that a particular substance posed a health hazard at the regulated levels of exposure. OSHA could no longer justify setting a particular exposure level by noting that no safe level of exposure had yet been determined, and that, therefore, the lowest feasible level of exposure was required. The quantity and quality of health effect information OSHA was required to obtain before regulating was, therefore, greatly increased.

The benzene decision was silent on the question of setting exposure levels by balancing costs and benefits. Hence, one option in the post-benzene climate of opinion was to retain the lowest feasible level of exposure policy, but supplement it with a significant risk threshold test. It was open to the agency to operate under a policy that exposure limits should be set at the lowest feasible levels which are reasonably necessary or appropriate to eliminate significant health risks. While this would supplement the feasibility criterion with a significant risk criterion, it would not require the balancing of costs and benefits in setting particular levels of exposure. It would allow the possibility of determining the significance of the health risks at one decision level and the affordability of the costs at another level. The principle that if it is worth regulating at all, it is worth regulating to the lowest feasible level would remain intact.

OSHA took advantage of this option in its defense of the cotton dust standard. In 1978, the agency had promulgated a final rule limiting exposures to cotton dust in the cotton textile industry.

The American Textile Manufacturers Institute, Inc. (ATMI) sought to have the standard invalidated in preenforcement review before the United States Court of Appeals for the District of Columbia, but, in October 1979, the Court of Appeals upheld the standard. ATMI appealed to the Supreme Court, oral arguments were held in January 1981, and on June 17, 1981 the Supreme Court affirmed the judgment of the lower court.

The question presented for review in this case was the cost-benefit question that had been left unresolved in the benzene decision. In particular, the question was whether OSHA was required to show that the improvements in the health of workers that could be expected to follow enforcement of the cotton dust standard were significant in light of the economic costs the standard would impose on industry. OSHA took the position that such cost-benefit comparisons were not required, and furthermore, that the Act prohibited the agency from engaging in individualized cost-benefit comparisons in particular rule-making cases. The individual cost-benefit judgments were prohibited because they would interfere with the congressional mandate to promulgate standards imposing the lowest feasible level of significant health risk.

The Supreme Court upheld OSHA's position in this case, ruling that the agency was not required to employ cost-benefit analysis to set particular standards regulating exposure to toxic substances. Further, the Court declared that any such standard less protective than one based upon feasibility analysis was inconsistent with the Act. In effect, then, the Court barred the agency from using cost-benefit criteria to set toxic substances standards, enjoining it instead to use feasibility analysis.

Several issues remained unresolved by this decision. The use of cost-benefit analysis to determine which toxic substances could be regulated first was not addressed. In addition, the question of whether cost-benefit analysis could be applied to safety standards was not answered. Finally, the role of other economic approaches, such as cost-effectiveness analysis, was not made clear.

Despite these unresolved issues, the general model of decision making that emerges from the cotton dust case is virtually the same as the prebenzene model. As before, the agency can be pictured as asking a series of questions. First, is there a significant risk of material impairment of worker health at current levels of exposure? If no, then do

nothing. If yes, then determine the level at which this risk is not significant. OSHA no longer claims the authority to use a zero-risk policy at this point; instead it assesses each carcinogen or toxic substance separately, for even if there is no absolutely safe level above zero exposure, the remaining risk may or may not be significant. The determination of significant risk can be made on health grounds, without balancing costs and benefits. Consideration of economic and technological matters takes place later in the process and follows the same feasibility approach as before the benzene decision. As a result of the cotton dust decision, the present Assistant Secretary at OSHA, Thorne G. Auchter, has revised an initial plan to use cost-benefit analysis in a review of the cotton dust and lead standards.

Despite the victory in court, feasibility analysis has some limitations as a model for decisionmaking in occupational safety and health. The threshold test of significant risk which was imposed upon OSHA by the benzene decision is far from clear. Among the questions that must be confronted are these: (1) Does "significance" apply to the magnitude of the risk per individual or the magnitude of the expected outcome, that is, the number of deaths or injuries? (2) Must a chemical or other hazard pose a significant risk in itself, or should the unit for regulation consist of a group of chemicals that act synergistically? (3) May policy questions be cleanly separated from factual questions in assessing significance of risk? (4) What should be done, if anything, about hazards that do not pass the threshold test of significant risk but can be eliminated or greatly reduced at little or no cost?

The notion of feasibility, that provides the equivalent of a cost constraint in this approach, is also far from clear. How seriously must an industry be harmed before a standard is no longer economically feasible? Are there criteria for feasibility that impose an effective constraint on the agency? Beyond these questions of clarity, the idea that no trade-offs are allowed in particular cases raises questions of balance. For example, when several toxic substances are used in the same industry it may be economically feasible to control each substance individually, but not all at the same time. Surely some trade-offs would have to be made in instances like this. The lack of clarity in the concept of feasibility and the likely need to balance costs and benefits in particular rule-making cases may lead to a situation in which balancing judgments are in fact made, but are publicly justified in terms of feasibility.

There is still, therefore, a pressing need for principles that will help to make these balancing judgments. This does not mean, however, that formal cost-benefit analysis is the most desirable approach. The use of economic information is absolutely essential in the occupational safety and health area, and cost-benefit criteria can be useful in assessing the effect of standards on economic efficiency. But cost-benefit analysis does not provide a proper framework for balancing all the relevant values that have to be taken into consideration in setting health and safety standards. It is crucial to recognize, then, that not all balancing need be based exclusively on cost-benefit comparisons. A distinction must be drawn between justifying a level of effort in an occupational safety and health program on the basis of a comparison of the monetary value of the associated costs and benefits, and justifying such a program by weighing the reasons for and against it and deciding that, all things considered, the level of effort in the program is worthwhile. The first method is simply the cost-benefit approach and in effect treats efficiency as the only, or the most important, consideration. The second method considers efficiency, and might sometimes give it pride of place, but also considers individual rights, justice, and competing public values as reasons for or against a level of effort in a program. In the first case, the basis of decision is already given, and the crucial questions are technical. In the second case, most of the technical questions remain, although some are less urgent (for example, the monetary value of safety), but the bases for decision making are unclear. It is here that much further work needs to be done.

VI. CONCLUSION

By calling attention to the fact that occupational safety and health is one of many desirable goals of public policy, proponents of cost-benefit analysis

have opened the door for integrating job safety into the framework of a coherent, overall industrial policy. However, the cost-benefit approach and the cost-containment strategies discussed earlier are inherently unable to incorporate all the considerations relevant to occupational safety and health. Risk-averse strategies and feasibility analysis are also incomplete. In formulating a new approach to occupational safety and health policy within an industrial policy framework, the conceptual and normative issues raised earlier cannot be ignored. Hazards in the workplace do not merely increase the chances of injury for individuals—they also increase the overall toll of injury and illness for the nation. Moreover, workplace risks are fundamentally different from the voluntarily assumed risks of everyday life because they do not typically challenge the skills of those who must withstand them, they are rarely intrinsically enjoyable or symbolically important, and they normally involve a conflict of interest between labor and management characterized by imbalances of power, information, and mobility. Finally, the distribution of occupational risks among individuals and groups is arbitrarily unequal.

These points suggest that safety on the job is a matter of community interest, not individual discretion, and they lead to several normative guidelines for collective action. First, there is a need to preserve people's rights to protection against unreasonable health threats while they are earning their livelihood. Second, efforts should be made to achieve a more equitable distribution of the occupational risks that cannot be easily eliminated. Finally, social action is required to realize widely shared public values, such as the conviction that conditions of work should reflect a concern and respect for workers' dignity and autonomy, that lie behind the group interest in workplace safety. Although these normative considerations do not determine an overall level of effort, much less the details of particular regulatory actions, their neglect by decisionmakers will inevitably lead to an impoverished occupational safety and health policy.

ARTHUR ANDERSEN & CO.

Executive Summary Highlights

BACKGROUND

In early 1978, the Business Roundtable retained the accounting firm of Arthur Andersen & Co. to develop a study which measured certain "incremental" costs incurred in 48 Business Roundtable member companies in one year—1977—to comply with the regulatory requirements of six federal government agencies and programs—the Environmental Protection Agency (EPA), Equal Employment Opportunity (EEO), Occupational Safety and Health Administration (OSHA), Department of Energy (DOE), Employee Retirement Income Security Act (ERISA) and Federal Trade Commission (FTC).

The 48 participating companies operate in more than 20 industries. They comprise an important, though relatively small, segment of the U.S. economy. All the participants are large corporations, many of them international although only their domestic operations were included. No small businesses participated. Some industries were well represented, others not at all. For these reasons, Arthur Andersen & Co. did not attempt to extrapolate the results of the study to all businesses in the economy.

What the study shows, however, for the first time and in great detail, are certain incremental costs imposed by specific regulations on specific industries. No other study yet made provides the public-at-large, the business community, Congress and the regulatory agencies themselves with such specific detail of the disparate cost effects that individual regulations and agencies have among industries. The study identifies regulations that impose high incremental costs and those that impose low incremental costs. The study is also a pioneering effort in establishing a credible methodology for measuring the directly attributable incremental costs of individual regulations.

The Business Roundtable and Arthur Andersen & Co. believe that in conducting this study, business has made a valuable contribution to the regulatory reform process.

The business community has incurred substantial costs on behalf of the safety and health of its employees, the protection of the environment and other factors associated with good corporate practices. Additional costs have been incurred to respond to demands of the marketplace and to labor pressures. In addition, the federal government has established regulations formalizing many of the practices already in place and adding thousands of new regulatory requirements that impose yet another layer of costs.

The incremental costs in this study were defined as a portion of this last layer—the direct costs of those actions taken to comply with a regulation that would not have been taken in the absence of that regulation.

These incremental costs were based upon (1) information drawn from companies' accounting, engineering and other business records, and (2) informed judgment as to which actions would have been taken in the absence of regulation.

Incremental costs represent a portion of the costs of regulation to society. In addition to incremental costs, there are many less visible secondary effects that cause substantial incremental costs to the companies and to society generally. Examples of these effects of regulations include losses in productivity of labor, equipment and capital, delays in construction of new plant and equipment, misallocation of resources, and lost opportunities.

Many companies observed that the costs of secondary effects were substantially higher than incremental costs. However, those costs are very difficult to measure and it was decided to exclude them from incremental costs.

OVERALL RESULTS RELATED TO OSHA

Companies participating in the study reported incremental costs of $184 million incurred during 1977 for compliance with OSHA regulations.

Companies reporting incremental OSHA costs classified such costs principally as operating and administrative with lesser amounts classified as capital, research and development and direct product.

The companies participating in the study are all relatively large and for many years have had programs to provide safe working conditions and protect their employees from hazards in the work place. In computing the incremental costs of OSHA regulations, the companies excluded from incremental costs all of those expenditures that would have been a part of their safety and health programs in the absence of OSHA's regulations. Those expenditures, which far outweighed incremental costs reported in the study, included most costs of medical services, personal protective equipment, fire protection and protection against hazardous conditions, substances and operations. Based on the field visits made by Arthur Andersen & Co., it was evident that only a small portion of participating companies' worker safety and health expenditures were identified as incremental costs in this study.

The costs that were considered to be incremental were those associated with the added burden of coping with OSHA regulations, inspections and reporting and other actions caused by requirements imposed by OSHA which the companies considered to be beyond what was necessary to provide safe and healthful working conditions.

Three industries—chemicals and allied products, rubber and miscellaneous products and primary metals—accounted for 52% of OSHA incremental costs. However, they represent only 18% of the employees of the participating companies. This illustrates the significant differences in incremental cost impact of OSHA among industries, ranging from $6 per employee per annum in the banking industry and $11 per employee in the communications industry to $220 per employee per annum in the chemical industry.

DISCUSSION OF HIGH COST AREAS OF OSHA REGULATION

Toxic and Hazardous Substances

Toxic and hazardous substances regulation caused the highest 1977 incremental costs related to OSHA. Companies identified incremental costs as being in response to either existing, proposed or anticipated OSHA regulations dealing with toxic and hazardous substances.

Existing OSHA regulations for toxic and hazardous substances are included in the Code of Federal Regulations, Title 29, Chapter XVII, Part 1910, Subpart Z. These regulations address the following specific substances:

- Over 300 air contaminants (e.g., carbon monoxide, chlorine, hydrogen sulfide and coal dust)
- Asbestos
- Benzene
- Vinyl chloride
- Coke oven emissions
- 15 other substances suspected of causing cancer

For each of these substances, the regulations set allowable exposure levels and require the application of administrative or engineering controls to attain compliance. Also, for certain substances suspected of causing cancer, OSHA requires the establishment of a regulated area in the workplace where the substance is present and the provision of periodic physical examinations and training of employees potentially exposed to the substance.

Proposed OSHA regulations identified for the study in the area of toxic and hazardous substances relate to the following matters:

- Establishing standards covering approximately 70 additional substances suspected of causing cancer.
- Lowering the permissible limits for exposure to absestos fibers.
- Establishing exposure limits for cotton dust.
- Establishing standards covering work practices in hot environments.
- Establishing an identification system for hazardous substances as a means of alerting all concerned to inherent hazards.

Anticipated OSHA regulations that could be identified in the area of toxic and hazardous substances dealt with workplace monitoring for nitrosamines and chlorinated hydrocarbons and research, monitoring and record-keeping procedures undertaken in anticipation of future regulations for specific potentially toxic or hazardous substances.

Companies reporting incremental costs for toxic and hazardous substances regulations classified costs principally as operating and administrative or capital, with lesser amounts classified as research and development and direct product.

Although this area of OSHA regulation had significant impact upon many industries, the majority of incremental costs reported in this study for OSHA's toxic and hazardous substances regulations was reported by companies in two industries—the chemicals and allied products industry and the primary metals industry.

Chemicals and Allied Products Industry. Fully half of the incremental costs reported as attributable to OSHA regulations for toxic and hazardous substances were incurred by participating companies in the chemicals and allied products industry. To comply with the regulations, companies installed new or improved dust collection systems and vapor control equipment to limit worker exposure to various substances—principally asbestos, benzene and certain of the 300 air contaminants identified in the regulations. Companies also modified workplace practices or their raw materials and established procedures for testing and detailed monitoring of personnel and the workplace.

Some of the chemical companies reported that they undertook extensive efforts to compile an inventory of all chemicals present at their locations to aid in control of potentially toxic substances.

Of the $12 million of incremental costs for compliance with *proposed* OSHA regulations dealing with toxic and hazardous substances, over $8 million was reported by companies in the chemicals and allied products industry. These costs were incurred primarily as a result of OSHA's proposed generic carcinogenic standards. In 1977, OSHA proposed certain standards for 70 substances that were determined to be potentially carcinogenic. The standards would apply as well to substances generically related to the 70 named. The proposed standards would require that exposure to each substance be reduced to and maintained at the

lowest level feasible, regardless of the substance's potency. Further, the required exposure levels would have to be achieved solely by engineering methods, irrespective of other practical alternatives. The chemical companies participating in the study reported that during 1977, they undertook various studies to determine the potential impact of the proposed regulations on their operations and to determine the feasibility of implementing sufficient engineering controls.

Most of the $4 million for *anticipated* OSHA regulations for toxic and hazardous substances was also reported by companies in the chemicals industry. The costs were incurred primarily as a result of the Standards Completion Project, a joint effort by OSHA and the National Institute of Occupational Safety and Health (NIOSH). The incremental costs incurred by participating companies in 1977 were related to the establishment by companies of a data base for the various substances covered by the project, including worker exposure and health factors in cases where the substances are present.

Primary Metals Industry. Of the total $60 million of incremental costs reported by all companies, $11 million was reported by companies in the primary metals industry.

Most of the $11 million reported by companies in the primary metals industry was reported by steel companies, and about 80% of steel companies' costs was incurred in controlling coke oven emissions. The costs resulted from engineering controls such as stage charging, a method that slows the introduction of coal into the oven, and work practices including the planning of implementation programs, monitoring of personnel and the workplace, provision of medical examinations and use of protective clothing.

Occupational Health and Environmental Control

Companies reported $30 million of incremental costs for occupational health and environmental control regulations. This area of OSHA regulation deals with standards for ventilation systems, radiation exposure and noise exposure. The incremental costs of $30 million reported were attributable primarily to noise regulations. There are two main reasons why control of noise resulted in higher incremental costs than ventilation systems and control of radiation exposure. First, because OSHA standards for ventilation systems come into play principally when the workplace has a substance covered by the toxic and hazardous substances area of OSHA regulation, companies classified most of their incremental costs of ventilation as attributable to the OSHA regulations for toxic and hazardous substances. Second, in the case of radiation exposure, most companies indicated that before the establishment of OSHA regulations they had been meeting the exposure and monitoring standards of the Nuclear Regulatory Commission. Therefore, the incremental radiation costs reported in the study were due primarily to the posting of warning signs and other minor actions, which resulted in nominal costs.

The OSHA regulation on noise exposure quantifies the tolerable noise level. When that level is exceeded, the employer must use feasible administrative or engineering controls to meet the tolerable level. If such controls are not adequate, personal protective equipment may then be used to reduce worker noise exposure to the prescribed level.

Incremental research and development and capital costs were incurred in meeting the feasible engineering control requirement by installing silencing apparatus or sound-deadening material to facilities, machinery and equipment or by acquiring new, more silent machinery and equipment. Operating and administrative costs resulted principally from maintaining new capital items acquired to meet the noise regulations and from audiometric testing and record-keeping for compliance with the regulations.

General Administration and Knowledge of Regulations

Companies Incurred Significant Costs in Keeping Abreast of Changing OSHA Regulations. Companies reported incremental costs of $22 million for general administration and knowledge of regulations.

Most of the cost was classified as operating and administrative, resulting from the following types of actions taken by the companies:

- ☐ Keeping abreast of existing, proposed and anticipated OSHA regulations.
- ☐ Preparing written responses to proposed OSHA regulations.
- ☐ Conducting education and staff training programs.
- ☐ Conducting workplace inspections by company management.
- ☐ Other overall administration of OSHA compliance not identified with a specific area of OSHA regulation.

Machinery and Machine Guarding

Companies Incurred $12 Million of Incremental Costs in Complying with OSHA Regulations on Machinery and Machine Guarding. OSHA's regulations for machinery and machine guarding generally require that one or more methods of machine guarding be provided to protect the operator and other employees from hazards such as those created at the point of operation by moving parts, flying chips, sparks and similar hazards. The regulations establish specifications for the guarding of equipment and general requirements for inspection and maintenance of the equipment.

Companies participating in the study reported $12 million of incremental costs incurred during 1977 in order to bring their operations into compliance with this area of OSHA regulation.

As most of the OSHA regulations for machinery and machine guarding had been in existence for several years before 1977, a great part of the incremental capital expenditures in 1977 were a result of companies having to comply after their applications to OSHA for variances were denied. Incremental costs resulted from a variety of actions ranging from the installation of relatively simple guarding devices to the acquisition and installation of sophisticated robot systems for the mechanical handling of material. Companies resorted to the latter when they decided that the regulations made manual handling of material uneconomical or impractical.

The reported operating and administrative costs were due primarily to the incremental expense of operating and maintaining new capital items acquired to comply with this area of OSHA regulation.

Walking-Working Surfaces

Participating companies reported $9 million of incremental costs incurred in 1977 for compliance with OSHA regulations related to walking-working surfaces. These regulations establish standards for railings and covers to guard floor and wall openings, and they set specifications for the design and construction of stairs, ladders and scaffolding.

Materials Handling and Storage

OSHA regulations for materials handling and storage apply mainly to powered industrial trucks and cranes used in the handling of industrial materials. The regulations establish equipment performance standards, testing requirements, maintenance and inspection routines and operating procedures. The regulations also establish rated capacities for various types of slings, chains, ropes and cables used in conjunction with materials handling equipment, and provide for the periodic testing and inspection of such devices. In some cases, the regulations require that the periodic inspections be supported by fully documented, dated and signed reports indicating the condition of the equipment.

Participating companies reported $8 million of incremental cost for complying with OSHA regulations in the area of materials handling and storage. Of that amount, 75% was classified as operating and administrative expense.

COMPANY OBSERVATIONS

During the course of the study, many of the companies reported their observations about the impact of OSHA regulations on their operations. Following are the most significant of these observations.

Toxic and hazardous substances regulations caused the highest 1977 incremental costs related to OSHA. Companies in the two industries most heavily impacted—chemicals and allied products and primary metals—made several critical observations.

Chemical Companies Questioned the Reasonableness of Required Exposure Limits. Most of the chemical companies in the study agreed with the need to monitor and control worker exposure to toxic substances. However, they expressed concern over the reasonableness of the specific limits set for the exposure levels and the specific procedures required by OSHA as the means of control.

Present exposure levels established by OSHA for toxic substances are based, for the most part, on toxicology studies performed on small laboratory animals from mammalian species. The tests do, in fact, show an element of risk implicit in the substances. The companies in the study contended, however, that it is often not at all clear that the exposure levels prescribed by OSHA have been correctly extrapolated from the toxicology tests to human beings. The companies said they believe that OSHA's regulations go further than present scientific knowledge would dictate.

Chemical Companies Also Expressed Concern over OSHA-Mandated Methods of Compliance. The second principal concern expressed by participating companies was the methods of compliance prescribed by OSHA. In the past, companies have used a combination of engineering controls, such as equipment modification and ventilation systems, and personal protective equipment, such as masks and respirators, to achieve control. OSHA regulations require that all possible engineering controls be implemented first and subsequently, if excess exposure persists, personal protective equipment be used. Companies noted that it is easier for OSHA to determine whether or not the engineering controls exist than it is for OSHA to monitor whether or not employees consistently use protective gear. The companies believe, however, that the actions required to achieve a given level of protection with engineering controls are often far more costly than achieving the same level of protection with personal protective equipment.

Certain companies in the study reported that the major element of their incremental cost of complying with this area of OSHA regulation was the burden of record-keeping. They indicated that even when they meet prescribed exposure levels using "the best engineering technology available," they still must expend effort in maintaining required documentation regarding workplace monitoring and employee medical surveillance activities.

Chemical Companies Are Concerned that Threshold Limit Values for Toxic and Hazardous Substances Will Be Unnecessarily Low.

Companies expressed concerns regarding the Standards Completion Project, an anticipated regulation for toxic and hazardous substances. Under the Standards Completion Project, a joint effort of OSHA and NIOSH, permissible exposure limits have been set for some 400 substances. These are limits derived from the threshold limit values (TLVs) originally established by the American Conference of Governmental Industrial Hygienists, an independent organization. While most participating companies view the original TLVs as reasonable, they indicated significant concern that the Standards Completion Project would establish uniform, inflexible, burdensome and costly measuring, monitoring, reporting, record-keeping and medical requirements without consideration of the various levels of hazards presented, which in many cases the companies believe to be inconsequential. Companies noted that the standards propose initiation of costly atmospheric measurements and medical surveillance for all substances, without regard to relative risk, at a level of one-half the TLV. Companies believe that, if adopted in their present form, the standards would greatly limit the use of respiratory equipment as a means of worker protection.

Companies in the Primary Metals Industry Stated Concerns about OSHA's Standards on Coke Oven Emissions.

Companies expressed concerns about the maximum allowable exposure level established by OSHA for coke oven emissions and concern about the requirement that engineering controls be exhausted before resorting to the less costly alternative of personal protective equipment. Companies believe the OSHA-prescribed exposure level is much more stringent than that supported by toxicological studies. Companies also believe that respirator equipment alone would provide adequate protection for workers.

Many Companies Questioned the Value of First Exhausting All Feasible Engineering Controls in Meeting Required Noise Levels.

While participating companies generally indicated no strong adverse reaction to the objective of the existing OSHA-prescribed noise levels, many believe that the requirement to exhaust all feasible engineering controls before resorting to personal protective equipment is not cost justified. They would have relied on personal protective equipment for the ears to meet the performance standard, a far less costly solution. Companies observed that ear protection equipment is now available that will provide protection without interfering with normal communication, warning horns on forklift trucks or other warning sounds.

Companies believe that OSHA's insistence on engineering controls rather than personal protective equipment is motivated by two factors.

☐ Engineering controls are passive. They do not require any compliance actions on the part of the workers.

☐ Engineering controls are easier for OSHA to administer. The OSHA inspector can simply tour the workplace with a meter and check the decibel reading.

Whatever the reasons, companies believe that the insistence on engineering controls by OSHA allows companies little flexibility and causes higher costs of attaining a given level of protection for workers.

Companies believe the problem may become even more significant in the future in view of OSHA's proposed regulation to reduce tolerable noise levels even further. In anticipation of such a regulation, one of the participating companies analyzed the potential cost impact on its operations. That company's analysis showed that meeting the lower proposed noise level would require further expenditures over the next five years of between $500 million and $1 billion for the installation of engineering controls. For the past twenty years, the same company has followed a hearing conservation program that focuses on the prevention of hearing impairment for each of its workers. The program relies heavily upon periodic hearing tests for workers, followed by administrative controls and/or ear protection specifically prescribed to meet the needs of the individual worker based upon his or her susceptibility to hearing loss in his or her particular job circumstances.

The results of the program have been good and the company believes that its workers face a lower risk of hearing impairment than they would if the company confined itself to meeting either the existing or proposed tolerable noise level standards prescribed by OSHA.

The company's current cost for the hearing conservation program is less than $2 million per year, compared to the estimated $500 million to $1 billion it would have to spend over the next five years to meet the OSHA-proposed noise level standard using engineering controls.

Companies Suggest that OSHA Issue Regulations on a Scheduled, Periodic Basis. Several companies indicated that they required significant manpower to keep current with changes in OSHA regulations. The impact of OSHA regulations is pervasive throughout each company, and the regulations cut across many of the companies' functions—manufacturing, warehousing, transportation, engineering, sales, medical, personnel administration and legal. Companies suggested that their efforts to keep current could be reduced if, rather than issuing changes throughout the year, OSHA would establish a timetable whereby changes would be made on a quarterly basis on a specific date, except for emergency measures, which would be initiated at unscheduled times. In that way, companies would not have to scrutinize each day's Federal Register for new regulations or changes proposed by OSHA.

Participating Companies Observed that Adoption of National Consensus Standards into Law Has Done Little to Improve the Safety or Health of Their Employees but Has Substantially Increased Costs. The national consensus standards, which emanated in large part from voluntary guidelines, were adopted by OSHA beginning in 1971 as authorized by the Occupational Safety and Health Act. The standards in many cases are very specific in directing quantities, configurations, levels and dimensions. When used as absolute requirements by OSHA inspectors, which

has generally been the case in the opinion of the participating companies, the standards become easier to enforce because of the elimination of the judgment factor. However, the companies maintain that this rigid approach leads to unnecessary expenditures because of the inability to exercise judgment regarding alternate means of compliance. The companies believe that the costs they considered incremental did little to improve worker safety or health.

The major impact of OSHA's adoption of national consensus standards was felt in the six years prior to 1977, so that 1977 was not a year of high incremental costs related to OSHA. The issue of conformity with the standards had generally been thrashed out with OSHA in the years between 1971 and 1977, during which time most of the resultant costs were incurred.

Companies Observed that OSHA's Prescribed Inspections of Certain Materials Handling Equipment at the Beginning of Each Shift Is Ineffective. An OSHA standard requires powered industrial trucks and cranes to be inspected at the beginning of each work shift (three times per day for most participating companies). Most companies stated that prior to OSHA's requirement for formal inspection and documentation, they emphasized equipment safety by establishing procedures whereby trained operators of equipment continually evaluated the safety attributes of the equipment during its operation. Companies believe that the formal inspections imposed by OSHA not only cause unproductive use of time each day but, because of constant repetition, become superficial. In the companies' view, the daily formal inspections are unproductive and do not substitute for proper safety training of operators.

In response to the OSHA requirement for documented reports of inspections of certain equipment, some companies have contracted with outside testing organizations to inspect and certify the equipment in accordance with the OSHA standards. Whether such reports were prepared by outside organizations or by the companies themselves, the related costs were considered to be incremental.

With respect to the operation of overhead cranes, one company reported that even though

OSHA regulations require cranes to be equipped with a brake, and their cranes are so equipped, the operators do not use the brakes since their abrupt stops result in dangerous swings of the load being carried. Instead, when the crane is rolling in a particular direction, the operator moves the control lever through the neutral position to the power setting for the opposite direction to achieve a controlled stop.

The Effectiveness and Efficiency of OSHA Regulations Dealing with Worker Safety May Be Improved by Emphasizing Performance Standards.

In its regulations dealing with worker safety, as distinct from worker health, OSHA has relied upon specification standards as the primary means of achieving the stated goal of improved worker safety. Volumes of OSHA regulations cover the design and construction of equipment and facilities as well as specific procedures to be followed on the job. Companies said that, while such specifics make compliance relatively easy to determine, there is little evidence that OSHA's specifications are the only ones resulting in safe conditions. For example, it is quite simple to verify the height of a railing and, thus, compliance with one of OSHA's walking-working surface regulations. However, it has not been demonstrated that a railing height of 42 inches, as regulated, is any safer than a railing that is 44 inches or 40 inches high. Companies, therefore, believe that the cost of changing the railing height by a small amount is unnecessary and burdensome. Companies made similar observations with respect to the requirements of OSHA's regulations on machinery and machine guarding.

Participating companies have suggested that a better foundation for regulation would be the establishment of performance standards directed to a quantifiable measure of employee safety. Such standards would not alter the objective of worker safety, but they would provide companies greater flexibility in applying appropriate alternate methods to meet the objective.

Accident rates are generally suggested as the best yardstick of safety performance. Some standardization would, of course, be necessary in order to set goals and monitor performance with respect to them. Companies noted that perhaps the best measure would be the number of reportable incidents during a certain number of worker-hours. Such standards could be developed for specific industries as defined by the Standard Industry Classification (SIC) system.

Companies said that if OSHA's safety regulations were expressed in terms of such performance standards, the enforcement role of OSHA could be reduced, or at least OSHA could concentrate such efforts on workplaces with accident rates in excess of the standard. Also, performance standards would be easier for companies to relate to and accept in economic terms as being compatible with such corporate objectives as reducing the costs of lost time and insurance resulting from employee accidents. With regulations stated in terms of performance standards, companies would be able to pursue the most cost effective means of attaining the standard. In different situations the methods used might be through a combination of equipment and facilities specifications, organizational changes or training of workers in safe practices.

Revocation of 900 "Nuisance Standards" in 1978 Will Result in Few Cost Savings for Studied Companies.

Recognizing some of the problems and limitations inherent in the national consensus standards that OSHA adopted, Congress, in the DOL-HEW appropriations bill for fiscal 1977, directed OSHA to eliminate so-called "nuisance standards." OSHA formed a task force to identify standards that were:

☐ Obsolete or inconsequential,

☐ Concerned with comfort or convenience as distinct from safety,

☐ Directed toward public safety or property protection as distinct from worker safety,

☐ Encumbered by unnecessary detail, or

☐ Adequately covered by other general standards.

After the findings of the task force were exposed for public comment, OSHA revoked approximately 900 of its general industry standards in November 1978.

In revoking the approximately 900 general industry standards, OSHA assessed the potential economic impact of the proposed revocation and concluded "that the subject matter of the proposal was not a major action which would necessitate further economic impact evaluation or the preparation of an Economic Impact Statement."

Arthur Andersen & Co.'s analysis of the revoked standards indicates that participating companies incurred only small amounts of incremental costs in 1977 in complying with these standards. However, the action by OSHA is perceived by the companies as a progressive step in the simplification of regulations and the elimination of unnecessary requirements whenever possible.

DANIEL J. CURRAN

Regulating Safety: A Case of Symbolic Action

I. INTRODUCTION

Since the late 1800's, the presence of the U.S. Federal Government in the industrial sphere has been expanded progressively by a series of laws establishing so-called "regulatory" bureaucracies. While the earliest legislation focused directly on economic and competitive practices, contemporary regulatory laws have tended to address the issue of public welfare. Regardless of the legislative orientation, the actual impact of these legal efforts often comes into question.

For many scholars, regulatory legislation generally has had minimal impact and frequently appears to have been little more than "symbolic" gestures intended to placate a disgruntled populace while maintaining the status quo in industry. As illustrated by Arnold's discussion of the Sherman Anti-Trust Act of 1890, much early regulatory legislation clearly exhibited this quality:

The effect of this statement of the ideal [Sherman Act] and its lack of enforcement was to convince reformers either that combinations did not exist, or else that ... they were about to be done away with. ... The crusade was not a "practical" one ... [it was] purely ceremonial (1937: 208, 211).

Most recently, this concept of symbolic legal action has been applied to critique the performance of various federal health and safety agencies (Berman, 1978; Calavita, 1983; Deutsch, 1981). The present analysis of the U.S. Coal Mine Health and Safety Act of 1969 pursues this theme, arguing that while the government through the 1969 Act moved to create a large, visible agency in the Mining Enforcement and Safety Administration (MESA) the organization did little to effect change in the coal-fields.[1] The law was in ways a "symbolic" solution. Symbolic, not in the sense that it represented a conscious attempt by legislators to deceive those concerned, but rather symbolic in that the law, with its "dualistic" nature, could not effectively alter working conditions. In other words, the law serves a dual function in that it attempts to project a positive image of the state as protector of mine workers, while simultaneously assisting coal operators. O'Connor refers to this phenomena as the "mutually contradictory functions" of the state, i.e., the need to "legitimate" itself to the people and the need to aid industry in capital accumulation (O'Connor, 1973:6).

The 1969 Act is typical of most federal legislation in the rhetoric used to illustrate the lawmakers' concern for the people and their well-being, as evidenced in the initial congressional declaration recorded in the Act:

The first priority and concern of all in the coal mining industry must be the health and safety of its most precious resource—the miner (U.S. Congress; 1969:4).

Indeed, the congressional commitment to improve the working environment in the mines is overwhelming when one considers the extended scope of the law with its implementation of mandatory health and safety standards.[2] Moreover, the establishment of MESA under Title V of the Act reinforces the pro-worker aspect of the law. Again, one must keep in mind the argument forwarded regarding the role of federal regulatory agencies in this legitimating process. As Edelman posits, the main function of many regulatory statutes and agencies is "the resolution of tension," by functioning to "induce a feeling of well being" among the general population (Edelman, 1964: 38–39). This "symbolic satisfaction of the disorganized" is initially achieved by presentation of these government organizations as saviors of the taxpayers, consumers, or other disadvantaged groups in society and by the declaration that these organizations will operate in an impartial, equalitarian manner to protect all. Once these agencies have been established and the public discontent quelled, Edelman argues that the regulatory agencies fulfill only a "symbolic" function for the "disorganized" segments of the population who had been instrumental in the passage of the original legislation. Edelman explains that often after the initial battle to secure the passage of such bills, the disorganized have depleted their power resources, both financial and political, while the "regulated" or "organized" element maintain their extensive power base and are thereby able to further influence the law creation process beyond this initial phase. It is this substantial force which insures that the sections of the legislation favorable to their interests will be implemented by the regulatory agencies. Consequently, legislation of apparent import to the disadvantaged segment of the society is transformed or sabotaged through the influence of powerful interest groups.

To illustrate this process the present analysis focuses on three major issues. First, it will examine the implementation and enforcement of the law by surveying the activities of the bureaucratic agency responsible for its administration. Second, it will reflect on the legislation's impact on the industry and its workers. And finally, parallels between this analysis of coal legislation and other regulatory laws, like the Occupational Safety and Health Administration (OSHA) Act, will be discussed.[3]

II. THE 1969 ACT: IMPLEMENTATION AND ENFORCEMENT

A. The Growth of the MESA Bureaucracy

Under the provisions of the 1969 Act, the federal government committed itself to an extensive program for improving mine health and safety. As part of this commitment, the government expanded the existing bureaucratic structure to meet the needs of the mining industry. From the passage of the Act to 1977, the monetary expenditures allocated for enforcement steadily increased, both at the administrative and inspection levels of the organization. In fact, as Table 1 shows, the MESA coal mine budget increased fourfold over an eight-year time span. This is especially noteworthy considering the economic recession experienced by the U.S. during the latter part of this period which resulted in substantial budget cuts in many areas of governmental activities. But while the agency was granted these enormous increases, often the funds were used in areas extraneous to the actual inspection process. For example, in 1978, MESA's coal mine division requested additional funding totaling $3,522,000: $1,100,000 was allocated to develop and implement a computerized management information system; $900,000 to develop a revised coal dust control program; and the remainder was used to maintain the current level of operations, i.e., promotions and within-step increases for inspection and support personnel. Therefore, only a limited amount of this increase was directly involved in the actual development of new field-related programs.

At the same time, the size of the bureaucracy in relation to the number of mine inspectors also increased linearly from 406 to 1313 as reflected in Table 1. The increase in the inspection force is even more dramatic when one considers that the ratio of mines per inspector declined from 11.0 to 1 in 1970 to a rate of 3.5 to 1 in 1977.

Considering the rapid expansion of the MESA bureaucracy over this limited eight-year span, one would naturally conclude that the presence of the agency in the mines would increase proportionately. But such is not the case, as Table 1 indicates. The number of inspections did rise substantially in the initial four years to a high in 1973 of 90,004.

TABLE ONE

Mining Enforcement and Safety Administration Facts and Figures 1970–1977

	MESA Budget	Inspection Personal	Active Mines	Mine/Inspec- tor Ratio	Number of Inspections	Inspections/ Inspector Ratio
1970[1]	$13,093,000	408	4495	11.0	8,709	25.1
1971[1]	29,384,000	989	4347	4.0	26,863	26.4
1972	29,793,000	1075	3578	3.3	59,481	55.3
1973	32,035,000	1171	3117	2.7	90,004	76.9
1974	35,663,000	1098	4157	3.7	78,996	71.9
1975	39,843,000	1266	4470	3.5	74,176	55.7
1976	45,528,000	1312	4492	3.4	64,850	48.7
1977	53,648,000	1375	4929	3.5	55,950	39.9

[1]Activities were financed as part of the Bureau of Mines, but are shown comparatively as a separate appropriation.

Source: Annual Report of the Secretary of the Interior under the Federal Coal Mine Health and Safety Act of 1969, 1970–77, U.S. Department of the Interior, Budget Justification 1970–77.

After this point, however, the number of inspections declined precipitously. Thus, while the average number of mines per inspector varied little after 1972, the number of inspections performed varied greatly.

This situation indicates that while the physical responsibility did not change over time, for some reason from 1973 to 1977 the volume of inspections declined. During the process of interviewing MESA personnel, two explanations were offered for this transition. The first, given by an assistant administrator in MESA Technical Support Division when confronted by statistics contained in Table 1, was that the agency had altered its policy on types of inspections from an emphasis on spot inspections to one on regular health and safety. But this assertion is not supported by MESA statistics over the years. In contrast to this administrative rationale, an interview with a MESA field inspector stressed the massive bureaucratic red tape as the factor preventing the inspector from performing his "proper role in the coal mine." The inspector argued that this extended paperwork significantly reduced the amount of time he had daily to spend in the mines.

Theoretically, two similar arguments can be forwarded to explain this phenomena. First, this tendency is similar to the one described by Edelman (1964), where he posits that after initial fanfare to open the regulatory agencies providing the "symbolic" visibility needed to placate concerned citizens, there will be little done to actually address the problems. Second, the pattern of enforcement displayed here is remarkably similar to the pattern found in Stearns' (1979) Swedish occupational study, where preliminary increases in inspections were followed by a gradual decrease. Her analysis speaks to the dialectical relationship between contradictions, conflicts, and resolutions to explain how a bureaucracy grows but simultaneously reduces its actual presence or effectiveness. In her discussion of the Swedish mining industry, Stearns states that the government's promise to enhance health and safety conditions in the mines was basically a response to the 1969 wildcat strike by miners, as was the case in the present analysis. Furthermore, she posits, "that the creation of a bureaucracy which would ostensibly protect worker safety and health without in fact interfering with profits, was a solution to a basic dilemma of Sweden's political economy" (Stearns, 1979: 9). Sweden's commitment is given substance first by personnel and budget increases, and by the enforcement of regulations through inspection. Once the problem or issue causing the conflict has been defused, the state will gradually reduce surveillance while maintaining the "symbolic" structure through further increases. In Stearns' words, "increase the bureaucracy but decrease its surveying power" (1979: 10).

The facts point to such a situation existing in the present study. Law addresses conflict in the coalfields, conflict which might cause national economic crises. The response takes the form of a large, visible bureaucracy to enforce this law. An eventual decline in agency inspection efforts is experienced while the same bureaucracy continues to expand. All of the data then hint of "symbolic" legitimation by the state. An assessment of fines for violations of the 1969 Act provides further evidence of this reality.

B. The Assessment Problem

Under the 1969 Act, the government for the first time granted federal mine authorities the power to assess monetary penalties. Under section 109 (a) (1), the Secretary could assess a civil penalty not to exceed $10,000 for each such violation. In computing such a penalty, the inspector was to consider the six criteria: (1) the history of previous violations; (2) the size of the operator's business; (3) whether the operator was negligent; (4) the effect upon the operator's ability to continue in business; (5) the gravity of the violation; and (6) the demonstrated good faith of the operator in attempting to achieve rapid compliance after notification of a violation. Between January 1970 and August 1976, approximately $66 million in civil penalties were assessed against coal operators in accordance with these criteria. The average assessment per violation was around $90. Of this total $66 million, $60 million was settled for only $25.5 million, a recovery rate of only 41 percent. Why? Basically because the Act also provides broad legal remedies for use by coal operators in appealing an assessed penalty. An operator can appeal a fine before an Administrative Law Judge of the Office of Hearings and Appeals. In addition, an operator has further recourse under the Act through a trial by jury in Federal Court to contest a penalty sought by the Secretary. Litigation of contested penalties in Federal Courts is handled by the Justice Department.

It was argued by critics of the Act that such a review process would hamper the assessment of fines and thereby reduce the effectiveness of the enforcement process. For example, from 1970 to 1977 over 704,000 violation notices were issued to coal mine operators, each being assessed a civil penalty. At the close of 1976, MESA had collected only $29 million in penalties. This means that the average assessment collected per violation was $48.23. In addition, there were $5 million in proposed penalties awaiting administrative appeal by coal mine operators, either at an informal MESA review or a formal hearing before an Administrative Law Judge. Another $5 million in assessed penalties were awaiting collection in Federal Courts.

The civil penalty program under the 1969 Mine Safety Act was a failure primarily because of two major shortcomings—low penalties and delay in collection. If the purpose of the civil penalty under the Act was to insure that individuals responsible for the operation of a mine would comply with the standards established, fines of a sufficiently high level must be assessed to deter individuals. A 1976 Senate Subcommittee drew a similar conclusion in its report:

To be successful in this objective, a penalty should be of an amount which is sufficient to make it more economical for an operator to comply with the Act's requirements than it is to pay the penalty assessed and continue to operate while not in compliance (U.S. Congress Committee on Labor and Public Welfare, 1976).

This senate committee does not stand alone in its appraisals of the situation, as the Congress, the Executive, and other branches of the government have also directed criticism at the inadequacies of the civil penalty program. For example, the General Accounting Office, in December 1974, concluded:

Civil penalties are assessed by the Federal Government to help insure that coal mine operators comply with health and safety standards. As we have found several times in the past, Interior's procedures in assessing and collecting penalties needed to be improved because ... penalties paid were much lower than the amounts originally assessed and were a questionable deterrent to noncompliance (U.S. Congress Committee on Labor and Public Welfare, 1976).

The civil penalties assessed against the Scotia No. 1 Mine, which exploded twice in March 1976, killing 26 men, provides a vivid example of the low level of civil penalties, even for a chronic violator. From January 3, 1974 until the date of the explosion, inspectors discovered 62 violations of the ventilation standards alone at the mine. As incredible as it may seem, the amounts assessed and collected for these recurring violations actually *decreased* as the number of violations increased. According to MESA reports, the violations which Scotia settled with the agency had an average cost of $121.35 each. Considering the size of Scotia's parent company, Blue Diamond Coal Company, and the fact that it marketed more than $30 million worth of coal a year, the penalty assessments represented a cost of less than two cents per ton. This amount is easily absorbed during production and is viewed as a "cost of doing business." Obviously, such penalties do not deter.

Low assessments and even lower collections are the norm for repeated violators. The Scotia situation is the rule, not the exception. The extremely low level of the current penalties serves to assure the coal operators that they may freely violate the Act's standards as long as they are willing to pay a negligible sanction upon their unsafe method of operation. The Senate Subcommittee concluded:

Mine operators still find it cheaper to pay minimal civil penalties than to make the capital investments necessary to adequately abate unsafe or unhealthy conditions; and there is still no means by which the government can bring habitual and chronic violators of the law into compliance (U.S. Congress, Senate, 1976).

An examination of the 22-mine subsample from which the preceding data on the Scotia Mine were derived provides additional insight into the gross inadequacies of the assessment system. These data display the extent to which the appeal process affects the enforcement power of the Act. From April 1976 to December 1977, violation and assessment data were compiled on each of the 22 mines. Table 2 shows the average number of violations, initial and current or final assessments for all mines surveyed, and the average for the Peabody and Consolidation Coal Companies, the first and second largest producers of coal respectively. On the basis of this limited study, it is apparent from examining the total statistics that first, the initial assessment is low—an average of $162.94 per

violation; and second, that the review process results in an overall loss of 22 percent in the recovery rate. By contrasting these total figures with the statistics of the major corporations, the loopholes provided by this review process are even more evident. The Peabody mines averaged 45 percent more violations, with each fine being 8 percent higher than the sample mean of $162.94. Peabody managed to reduce the average fine to $109.86 (16 percent lower than the final or current assessment of total mines), which means MESA was realizing a recovery rate of only 62 percent. The statistics for Consolidation Coal Company reflect the same tendency. Indeed, the review process provides a valuable escape for the major coal operators.

More conclusive evidence for this assertion is provided when one analyzes only the major fines, those over $1,000, as done in Table 3. Here, after a minimum two years had elapsed since assessment, approximately half of the 78 major fines continued to be appealed. Of those settled, the recovery rate was a mere 29.5 percent of the initial assessment. Only two of the nineteen $10,000 penalties were fully paid, while the average recovery rate was 20 percent. Individual mines provide further support: Drake Mine No. 3, controlled by Gulf Oil Corporation, four $10,000 penalties with no final assessment—recovery rate of 0 percent; Harmac Mine of Consolidation Coal Company, three $10,000 fines with a recovery rate of 15 percent; and Deer Creek Mine, Peabody Coal Company, six $10,000 assessments, 27 percent recovery, one paid in full, and one still under review.

These mines, all owned or controlled by large corporations, are typical of the pattern manifested in the assessment process. The majority of civil penalties are assessed at a level insufficient to deter the operator. Economically, it is more sensible to continue operation in non-compliance and pay fines rather than correct the hazardous conditions. If the penalty is assessed at a sufficiently ample level, the operator can fight it indefinitely to have the fine reduced as illustrated above.

In sum, the source of this inadequacy is the Act itself since, (1) it does not set a minimum level on assessment, and (2) it allows for the lengthy review process. The overall assessment program must be considered a failure on the basis of these data and a boon to the powerful corporations in the industry. The procedure established to settle assessment

TABLE TWO

Average Violations, Assessments, and Recovery Rate, 22-Mine Subsample, 1976–1977

	Number of Violations	Initial Assessment	Current Assessment	Recovery Rate
Total mines	650	$105,911 ($162.94)[1]	$ 82,734 ($127.28)	78%
Peabody Coal Co. Mines (2)	941	165,252 ($175.61)	103,374 ($109.86)	62%
Consolidation Coal Co. Mine (1)	784	124,401 ($158.67)	86,108 ($109.83)	69%

[1]Parentheses indicate average assessment per violation.

Source: MESA Accident Prevention Study, 1975–1977.

disputes provides for a series of judicial appeals where the operator could attempt to overturn an inspector's decision or try to reduce the amount of the fine assessed. Under this system, the large operators are at a definite advantage since their corporate legal staff could usually succeed in a substantial reduction in fines while the smaller operators without this legal assistance must pay full assessments. The significance of the bias of the 1969 Act in favor of the powerful is apparent too in the evaluation of the impact of the legislation on marginal operators.

III. THE 1969 ACT: ITS ULTIMATE IMPACT

A. Closing Marginal Operators

Having discussed the enforcement biases of the 1969 Act, the analysis turns now to a discussion of two other critical outcomes of this legislation. The first is the elimination of the distinction between gassy and non-gassy mines. Prior to the 1969 Act, federal authorities had classified certain mines as non-gassy—that is, having low methane levels—and did not require these operations to meet certain safety standards. Characteristically, these mines were controlled by small independent operators which, according to the Bureau of Mines' own studies, had displayed an excellent safety record in past years. Because of this past performance, these small companies asserted that there was virtually no basis to justify the reclassification of non-gassy mines as gassy on safety grounds as provided in the 1969 Act. Their sentiments on the passage of this

measure are summarized in the following statement of Robert Halcomb, a representative for the small operators, before the Congressional Committee on Coal Mine Health and Safety:

Unfortunately, coal mine safety is inextricably wound up in the politics of the coal industry. Many of the proposals made in the name of safety have little to do with the safety of the individual miner, but a great deal to do with the vested interests of the most powerful forces in the coal industry, the large operators and the union.

The principal effect of the elimination of the distinction between gassy and non-gassy mines, however, would be that it will effectively put out of business the vast majority of the small mines in the country. The effect will be to increase substantially the unemployment of miners in the Appalachian areas of the country where the government is now spending billions of dollars to increase employment.

These small mines will be put out of business principally because they cannot afford the expenditures required to purchase the equipment that is now required in gassy mines (U.S. Congress, 1969: 556–557).

If Holcomb and other critics were correct in their assessment, the impact of this provision would be the closure of marginal independent operations and a subsequent increased dominance of the coal industry by larger firms. In addition, the measure would precipitate greater unemployment in an already economically depressed industry which, in turn, would result in the government incurring additional social expenses to help the affected population. Unfortunately, they were accurate in their predictions.

The year immediately following the enactment of the 1969 Act marked the final year in which underground mines outnumbered surface mines

TABLE THREE

Assessment Totals for Major Violations 22-MESA Mine Subsample, 1975–1977

Initial Assessment Civil Penalty	Number of Violations	Number of Penalties Appealed	Number of Penalties Disposed	Final Total Assessment	Final Recovery Rate
10,000	44	25	19	38,460	20.2%
9,500	1	0	1	5,500	57.9
9,000	3	3	0	0	0.0
7,500	3	0	3	1 1,078	49.2
5,000	6	5	1	2,500	50.0
7,000	1	0	1	2,000	28.5
4,000	2	1	1	3,500	87.5
3,500	1	0	1	1,000	28.5
3,000	1	0	1	3,000	100.0
2,500	1	0	1	1,500	60.0
2,000	2	2	0	0	0.0
1,500	5	2	3	3,900	86.6
1,300	2	0	2	700	26.9
1,200	1	0	1	375	31.2
1,100	2	0	2	1,060	48.1
1,000	3	0	3	2,300	76.7
Total	78	38	40	$76,873	29.5%

Source: MESA Accident Prevention Study, 1975–1977

in the U.S. After the initial year of enforcement, there was a 22 percent drop in the number of underground mines and an 18 percent increase in surface mines. There was no significant change in total national production. Of 588 underground mines which shut down, 70.7 percent were located in Kentucky and West Virginia, states characterized by a predominance of small privately owned, non-gassy mines. In early 1974, MESA administrator Jack Day indicated that of the remaining 1000 mines which were formerly considered to be non-gassy, only 50 percent had come into compliance with 1969 standards. On March 30 of that year, the Department of the Interior was required by law to order these mines to close, while acknowledging in its own reports that the closure would result in a drop in national coal production of more than 5 percent and the unemployment of some 6,000 miners. The following statement, taken from the Washington Star-News of March 24, 1974, clearly depicts the sentiments of the small mine operators confronted with this dilemma:

Harman, (coal operator) 45, will lose his $125,000 investment in mining equipment, which will become worthless because it does not meet the new safety standards. Harman estimates it would cost at least $200,000 to buy new equipment, so he has decided to go out of business. "I thought somebody would come to their senses before it came to this," Harman said. "I've put my life into coal and now I've lost everything because of the federal requirements" (Washington Star News, 1974: A2).

Harman's estimate of the costs was conservative since, in most operations, the cost of the spark-contained equipment ranged as high as $500,000 per mine, often greater than the total value of the coal in the mine itself.

From these data, it can be argued with justification that, as in the case of Kolko's (1963, 1965) analyses of the railroad and meat packing industries, it was the small marginal operators who were the first to succumb to the power and demands of the new government agency. In their stay, surface mines typically owned and operated by the large coal corporations would make up for lost production, increasing their control over the coal market.

B. Safety in the Mines: The Final Judgment

In the final analysis, the ultimate criterion upon which this law must be judged is its performance in the reduction of death and injury in the mines. Defenders of the agency are quick to point out that over the eight-year period, the fatality rate (deaths per million man hours) dropped from .55 in 1970 to .34 in 1977 as reflected in Table 4. However, it should be noted that utilization of this statistic as an evaluative measure is somewhat problematic because the small number of deaths per year cause the rate to fluctuate severely. The significance of this decline in the mortality rate is further reduced when one considers that this low rate in 1977 is about three times greater than the casualty rate experienced in European mines more than twenty years ago. On the other hand, the disabling injury rate which is generally considered a highly reliable indicator reflects an annual increase in injuries since 1974. Therefore, after eight years of operation the agency has had little effect on safety conditions in the mines in spite of extensive bureaucratic growth. In fact, it can be argued that the incidence of injuries would have risen substantially if it had not been for a massive shift in the mode of production from traditional underground to surface mining. In 1977, the disability injury rate in underground mines was 52.68 in contrast to 18.56 in surface operations (Caudill, 1977: 492). In sum, the 1969 Act and MESA bureaucracy did not effectively alter working conditions.

DISCUSSION

On the basis of this analysis one would tend to argue that, in effect, the Federal Coal Mine Health and Safety Act of 1969 was basically a symbolic action with the regulatory bureaucracy, MESA,

generally functioning as a legitimating agent for the state and capital. Both the law and the agency served to placate and reassure the miners through "symbolic activities" without altering existing economic arrangements in the coalfields. The law, while being the most comprehensive coal mine legislation in U.S. history, contained numerous legal loopholes through which the state and industry could easily manipulate the Act to fulfill their interests. Through its pro-worker rhetoric, the law calmed the conflicts and crises in the coalfields during the late sixties, and the establishment of MESA perpetuated the positive image of the government as protector of the miners. This is most apparent when one considers MESA's continued bureaucratic growth as the volume of inspections gradually tapered off after an initial push in the coalfields. Again, this bureaucratic growth projected an image of continuous governmental interest without interfering with profit accumulation.

Unfortunately, this scenario is not unique to coal legislation, for as noted at the outset, much recent regulatory activity follows a similar pattern. By far the closest parallel which can be drawn here is the performance of OSHA. Declared by President Nixon in 1970 as "Perhaps one of the most important pieces of legislation to pass in this Congress," the OSHA Act was quickly recognized as an ineffective agent in the workplace (Public Paper of the Presidents, 1970: 1160). Labor's disenchantment with OSHA, both the Act and the bureaucracy, soon surfaced as witnessed by the comments of Kenneth Peterson, the legislative representative of the AFL-CIO, and John Sheehan of the United Steelworkers of America at a 1973 Senate Committee on Appropriations. Peterson stated that "after two years of operations under the Occupational Safety and Health Act, the entire program has never gotten off the ground" (U.S. Congress Senate 1973: 6427). Sheehan continued, "It is our contention that . . . the Administration is *deliberately underfunding and misguiding OSHA*" (1973: 6433, emphasis in the original). But perhaps the most relevant statement for the present analysis is that of Anthony Mazzocchi, legislative director of the Oil, Chemical and Atomic Workers Union to the *New York Times*: "The [OSHA] Act has done a great deal to improve workers' perception about the situation, but it hasn't yet done much to improve the situation" (quoted in Brody, 1974:20). Here again, a

TABLE FOUR
Disabling Injury and Fatal Rates, 1970–1977

Year	Underground Disabling Rate	Surface Disabling Rate	Total Disabling Rate	Fatal Rate
1970	——	——	37.41	.55
1971	——	——	35.44	.41
1972	58.33	25.22	46.66	.58
1973	51.91	27.22	40.89	.48
1974	36.90	17.16	29.24	.45
1975	39.29	18.07	30.59	.42
1976	47.71	19.33	39.92	.37
1977	52.83	18.56	37.77	.36

Source: Annual Report of the Secretary of the Interior under the Federal Coal Mine Health and Safety Act of 1969, 1970–1977.

law touted as progressive by its makers fails to achieve its declared objectives.

In conclusion, while the government has enacted numerous regulatory laws, they have been typically ineffective in attaining their goals. Several characteristics have been identified which serve to explain this failure:

1. Regulatory laws frequently are phrased in an ambiguous manner exhibiting a "dualistic" nature, i.e., placating labor while assisting industry. This "symbolic" action makes prosecution difficult.

2. The laws typically mandate weak penalties while providing sufficient legal loopholes to reduce assessed fines.

3. Often the law results in reduced competition as marginal companies succumb to federal statutes while major corporations continue operation virtually unaffected.

4. The failure of regulatory legislation and their enforcement illustrates the influence of the powerful on the legislative process at the expense of the rest of the citizenry.

NOTES

1. Coal mining has a rate of work-related injuries and illnesses which exceeds the national industry rate by approximately 15 percent. One out of every 1500 mine workers is killed on the job or dies from work-related injuries or illnesses, compared to 1 out of every 12,400 in other professions (U.S. Congress, Senate, 1977: 80). In 1981, the hazards of coal mining resulted in the death of 133 miners and left another 18,720 disabled (U.S. Dept. of Labor, 1981: 4).

2. While government officials have acknowledged the dangerous nature of this industry, the passage of all significant coal legislation can partially be attributed to a succession of catastrophic mine disasters which heightened awareness of the working conditions in the mines. For example, in the five years preceding the enactment of the Organic Act of 1910 which established the U.S. Bureau of Mines, there were a total of 85 major mine disasters resulting in the deaths of 2,640 workers. The overall number of fatal accidents during the 1905–09 period was 12,664 with a high in 1907 of 3,197 when eight separate mine explosions killed a total of 1,148 miners. As a response to this situation, Congress intended that the Bureau of Mines function primarily as an agency to promote health and safety by conducting research to assist and advise the mining industry. The obvious shortcoming in this arrangement was the lack of inspection authority under the law which specifically denied "any right or authority in connection with the inspection or supervision of mines ... in any state" on the part of Bureau employees (U.S. Congress, House 1969: 4). In other words, the Congress had created a relatively powerless bureaucracy, and the Bureau of Mines remained in this advisory status until 1952 when federal inspectors were given limited authority to issue Notices of Violation and Orders of Withdrawal under Public Law 82-522, the Federal Mine Safety Act (U.S. Congress, House, 1969: 6).

In sum, these laws were characteristically weak, severely limiting the power of federal agencies in the coal mines. It can be argued that these acts have traditionally functioned as legitimating agents in the capitalistic state; that is, they have been utilized to placate disgruntled groups in society without altering the existing economic structure (Habermas, 1973; O'Connor, 1973).

3. The study taps four major data sources. First, national statistics published in the *Annual Report of the Secretary of the Interior on the Administration of the Federal Coal Mine Health and Safety Act* and other agency publications were utilized to evaluate the major national issues in the implementation and enforcement of the Act. Second, data from a MESA sample of 85 randomly selected underground mines were used to evaluate the impact of accident and educational programs, technical counseling, and various modes of inspection on the reduction of injuries at the individual mine level. This research, conducted as part of an Accident Prevention Program, contains data collected monthly for the period January to September 1976. Third, from the 85-mine sample, a 22-mine secondary sample was drawn for use in a series of detailed case studies intended to supplement the two prior data sources. Included in this subsample are the Scotia Mine, the site of a 1976 disaster resulting in the deaths of 23 men, and the Stearns Justin Mine, where UMWA miners conducted a two-year strike over safety conditions. And fourth, interviews were conducted with MESA Inspectors and Administrators to assess their options on the Federal Health and Safety Program.

4. For discussion of OSHA assessments, see Brody (1974: 20).

BIBLIOGRAPHY

Arnold, Thurman W. (1937) *The Folklore of Capitalism.* New Haven, Conn.: Yale University Press

Berman, Daniel M. (1978) *Death on the Job.* New York: Monthly Review Press

Brody, Jane (1974) "Many Workers Still Face Health Perils Despite Law." *New York Times*, March 4: 20

Calavita, Kitty (1983) "The Demise of the Occupational Safety and Health Administration." *Social Problems* 30(4):437–447

Caudill, Harry (1977) "Dead Laws and Dead Men: Manslaughter in a Coal Mine." April 23 *The Nation* 492

Deutsch, Steven (1981) "Introduction: Theme Issue on Occupational Safety and Health." *Labor Studies Journal* 6(1):3–6

Edelman, Murray (1964) *The Symbolic Use of Politics.* Urbana, Ill. University of Illinois Press

——— (1971) *Politics as Symbolic Action.* Chicago: Markham Publishing Company

Habermas, Jurgen (1973) *Legitimation Crisis.* Boston: Beacon Press

Kolko, Gabriel (1963) *The Triumph of Conservatism.* New York: The Free Press

——— (1965) *Railroads and Regulations.* Princeton, N.J.: Princeton University Press

O'Connor, James (1973) *The Fiscal Crisis of the State.* New York: St. Martin's

Stearns, Lisa (1979) "Fact and Fiction of a Model Enforcement Bureaucracy: The Labor Inspectorate of Sweden." *British Journal of Law and Society* 6:1–23

CHAPTER NINE

Study Questions

1. Much of the Supreme Court disagreement in the cotton dust case concerned the meaning of "feasible." Do you believe that the interpretation of feasible as "wherever possible" is too strong?

2. What, exactly, is the difference between the *intrinsic* and *instrumental* value of health and safety?

3. How does group risk differ from individual risk? Should individuals be allowed to take greater risks for higher pay in all cases? When not?

4. How would you compare "strict products liability" as discussed in Chapter 3 with workers compensation as discussed by Barbara McLennan?

5. Since many of the firms examined in the Business Roundtable–Arthur Andersen study already had taken voluntary measures to secure worker health and safety, the "incremental cost" involved, in effect, is the cost of legally requiring compliance to health and safety standards. Are these costs worth legally requiring what was voluntarily being done anyway?

6. What criteria have been discussed for determining levels of protection for safety and health? What problems are there in the use of these various criteria?

DUE PROCESS

CASE STUDY

Sheets v. Teddy's Frosted Foods

From November 1973 to November 1977, Emard Sheets was employed by Teddy's Frosted Foods, Inc., as a quality control director and operations manager. Teddy's Frosted Foods is a Connecticut-based company which produces frozen food products. During these years, Sheets received periodic raises and bonuses which indicated that his job performance was satisfactory.

In his capacity as quality control director, Sheets began to notice deviations from specifications contained in Teddy's standards and labels. Some vegetables were found to be substandard and some meat was underweight. Besides the moral wrong involved here, these deviations violated Connecticut law. Besides prohibiting misleading and mislabeled packaging, the law provided for fines and jail sentences for anyone involved in the violation, regardless of whether or not they had actually intended to defraud or mislead. As quality control manager, Sheets conceivably could have been prosecuted for these deviations.

In May 1977, Sheets complained in writing to his superiors about the use of substandard and underweight products. He did not report his discovery to anyone outside of the company. His recommendations for more selective purchasing were ignored. On November 3, 1977 Sheets was fired. In the words of a later judicial decision, "he was actually dismissed in retaliation for his efforts to ensure that the defendant's products would comply with the applicable law."

Sheets sued in Connecticut court, claiming that he was unjustly fired. He claimed that there was a violation of an implicit employment contract and that his firing violated public policy by undermining the Connecticut labeling law. He argued that the facts of his case exempted him from the employment-at-will rule.

Teddy's argued, and a lower court agreed, that Sheets was an employee hired for an indefinite term and was dischargeable at will. If Sheets were free to quit at any time and for any reason, the employer should be free to fire at any time and for any reason. Besides, there was little real chance that Sheets would ever be prosecuted for such minor violations. Finally, it was pointed out that the Connecticut legislature had recently considered and rejected a bill requiring a "just cause" before dismissal.

The Connecticut Supreme Court decided in favor of Emard Sheets. The court reasoned that public policy, as represented in the Connecticut labeling law, overruled the employer's right to discharge at will. The court also ruled that Sheets' claim was importantly different from the "just cause" bill which was rejected by the legislature. "Just cause," according to the court, would require an employer to proffer a proper reason for dismissal and forbid arbitrary or capricious dismissals. The Sheets case sought damages for an instance when an

"employee can prove a demonstrably improper reason for dismissal." The court concluded that Sheets had proven this and decided in his favor.

What are some examples of a "proper reason" to dismiss someone? Improper reasons? Would no reason at all, or an arbitrary reason, be improper? How would this case differ if Sheets had been a whistleblower and complained to public officials? Should an employer be able to collect damages from an employee who quits for no reason? For an improper reason? What would be an improper reason to quit a job?

Introduction

ALONG WITH ISSUES of health and safety, job security is among the most pressing employee concerns. This chapter considers the restrictions, if any, that should be placed upon an employer's ability to fire or discipline an employee.

In cases of legal punishment and sanctions, citizens are protected from illegitimate use of authority by the right of due process. Before a government authority can exercise control over a citizen, certain conditions upon the use of that authority must be met. Trials by jury, consistency with legal precedents, right to legal counsel, and public hearings are only some of the ways in which citizens are protected from the unjustified use of government authority. Should employees have similar protections to ensure that an employer's authority to fire or discipline not be abused? Should employers be required to follow certain procedures, for example granting a hearing before an impartial arbitrator, before dismissing or disciplining an employee? Or should employers have the right, in the words of one court, to discharge "for good cause, for no cause, or even for cause morally wrong"?

Due Process in Law. The legal concept of due process is often traced to the Magna Carta. In that document, *per legem terrae* ("by the law of the land") guaranteed citizens, or at least the barons, protection from the arbitrary will of the king. From that point on, the king's authority over the barons was restricted; it was required to be in accord with the common law, the "law of the land."

The American Declaration of Independence can be seen as a similar reaction against the arbitrary use of government authority. To ensure that such abuses would not continue, the U.S. Constitution's Fifth Amendment states that "No person shall . . . be deprived of life, liberty, or property, without the due process of law. . . ." The Fourteenth Amendment later explicitly prohibited states from depriving "any person of life, liberty, or property, without due process of law." All government actions that could control the lives of citizens were thus brought under the protection of due process.

This is not to say that the nature and extent of due process in law is clearly established. Due process is among the most vague of all the constitutional rights. Legal debates over the proper interpretation of due process have continued to this day. We do not need to examine these debates here, but one issue deserves note.

In discussions of due process, there is a long-established distinction between *substantive* and *procedural* due process. In general, due process rights protect a person from arbitrary and illegitimate uses of authority. This protection can be guaranteed in two ways. First, we could exempt specific goods from government control. By granting citizens a right to free speech and thereby generating a government obligation to respect this right, the U. S. Constitution identifies one illegitimate action. Substantive due process would be all those rights that citizens can claim against their government. A government conforms to the requirements of substantive due process whenever it respects all of the specific rights its citizens have.

A government conforms to the requirements of procedural due process, on the other hand, whenever it follows certain procedures in exercising its authority over citizens. In this sense, procedural due process is a right added to the list of specific rights of substantive due process. For example, the "exclusionary rule," which prevents the prosecution from using evidence obtained illegally, is a procedural due process rule. The Constitution does not grant citizens the right not to have such evidence used against them in court, but the Supreme Court has ruled that this is an illegitimate means for prosecuting criminals. Although the government has the authority to prosecute criminals, it cannot do so in just any way; certain procedures must be followed.

In the employment context, we can say that an employer respects employees' substantive due process rights whenever she respects the specific rights that employees have. Thus an employer who obeys all the labor laws, doesn't frustrate union activities, pays above the minimum wage, respects the employees' privacy, allows participation in decision making, operates a safe and healthy workplace, etc., would be conforming to the requirements of substantive due process. (This list, of course, is subject to determining the specific rights that employees do have. Previous chapters have pursued that question in greater detail.) However, if that employer decided that she no longer wanted a particular person working for her and dismissed him for no reason at all, she would not be violating the substantive due process rights. Accordingly, this chapter is concerned primarily with procedural due process. We shall consider the nature and rationale of fair dismissal procedures in employment. Previous chapters in Part Three can be understood as having analyzed the specific rights that guarantee substantive due process.

Employment at Will and Due Process. Let us say that procedural due process involves a set of procedures that guarantees to an individual protection from arbitrary and unjustified uses of authority. As Thomas Scanlon claims in our first reading, in any society or institution some people will have the power to control or intervene in the lives of others. In employment, managers have the power to fire workers, vice presidents have the power to control managers, foremen have the power to tell workers what to do, etc. Although most people agree that such power is legitimate, not everyone agrees upon the justification that makes it legitimate.

One justification holds that the legitimacy of this power rests upon the consent of the controlled. In this contractual view of employment, employees voluntarily enter into a relationship in which their lives (at least at work) will be controlled by others. They do this, of course, in return for certain benefits (pay, health and retirement insurance, job security, etc.). By consenting to this situation, employees themselves justify this control.

Another justification might be argued from grounds of economic efficiency. Basically a utilitarian argument, this view holds that society will be better off when its economic institutions are organized in this way. It would be inefficient or impossible to operate a business that did not grant some people the right to control others.

In our second reading, Lansing and Pegnetter suggest that a justification of this second type was behind the early legal framework for cases of employee discharge. The traditional legal rule was known as "employment at will," and it held that employers could fire an employee for no reason at all.

Employees' jobs were at the discretion, or "will," of the employer. Lansing and Pegnetter argue that in an era when economic development required businesspersons to take risks and expand, courts developed the employment-at-will rule to protect industry from risks and to encourage economic growth. Basing the legal decision in the principle of mutuality of obligation in contract law, courts reasoned that if employees were free to quit "at will," employers must be able to fire at will.

The employment-at-will rule has survived, if not altogether unchallenged, to the present. It is central to this chapter in that employment at will denies the validity of any procedural due process right. To say that an employer can fire "for good cause, for no cause, or even for cause morally wrong," is to say that employees have no protection from the arbitrary uses of authority. To defend due process in this context will require abandonment of the employment-at-will rule.

There were some initial limitations on the employment-at-will rule. Government employees, for example, were not subject to it. This was because of the peculiar nature of their employer. Their employer is the only institution explicitly obligated by the Constitution not to deny due process rights. Citizens who work for their government retain all of their civil rights in the workplace. Union workers who are covered by collective bargaining agreements also typically are exempt from the employment-at-will rule. Due process rules are among the most common elements of a union contract. (It should be pointed out that at present less than 25% of all American workers are covered by such agreements and virtually no "white collar" workers are unionized.) Finally, some specific grounds for dismissal or discipline are prohibited by law. Thus, employment at will does not cover cases in which an individual is fired or disciplined for reasons of race, sex, religious beliefs, age, etc. Although this prevents some "morally wrong" causes from being used, it is still allowable to fire for "good cause" or "no cause."

We will consider two arguments in favor of due process and, implicitly at least, against employment at will. One argument holds that due process is a requirement of morality and as such it overrides the economic efficiency claim. Thomas Scanlon claims that due process is "grounded in a conception of the moral requirement for [all] social institutions." Due process is "a condition upon the moral acceptability" of any institution that has the power to control the lives of others. In this view, morality requires that individuals be protected from arbitrary and preventable harm.

A second defense of due process denies the economic efficiency claim that supported the employment-at-will rule. Lansing and Pegnetter claim that the era when this protection of the employer was necessary for economic development has passed. They suggest why "mutuality of obligations" should no longer govern the employment relationship.

In response to these claims, Donald Martin argues that the civil right of due process should not extend to the private sector. Rejecting the analogy between government and industry (and presumably, therefore, Scanlon's claim that due process is a condition upon the moral acceptability of any institution), Martin argues that "market processes, more than political processes" can better protect individuals. Finally, Martin claims that such procedures will be too inefficient and too costly for both employers and employees.

T. M. SCANLON[1]
Due Process

In this paper I will offer a general account of how the absence of "due process" can give rise to legitimate claims against institutional actions. I will be concerned particularly to show in what ways claims to due process are grounded in moral principles of political right and how far they depend rather on strategic judgments about the prudent design of social institutions. My account will provide a demarcation of the area within which due process claims are appropriate—an area much broader than "state action"—and provide at least a rough framework for determining when given procedures are adequate responses to these claims. I will also offer an account of substantive due process and undertake to explain why it is that when a legal right to due process is recognized courts, in enforcing this right, will find themselves making substantive as well as merely procedural decisions.

The account I will offer sticks close to the truism that due process is concerned with protection against arbitrary decisions, and one can find a place in my account for many of the phrases that have been used in interpreting the Fifth and Fourteenth Amendments to the United States Constitution. But while I will have a certain amount to say in the abstract about the role of courts in providing and enforcing due process, my account is a philosophical and not a legal one. It is grounded in a conception of the moral requirements of legitimacy for social institutions and not on what the law of the United States or any other country actually is. I hope that what I have to say may be of some use in legal arguments about constitutional rights to due process of law, but I have not undertaken to defend my theory as an interpretation of the constitution.

I

The requirement of due process is one of the conditions of the moral acceptability of those institutions that give some people power to control or intervene in the lives of others. Institutions create such power in several ways. They do so directly by giving some the authority to command others and providing the force to compel obedience to these commands. Less directly, but no less effectively, institutions give some people a measure of control over others by securing their control over resources or opportunities that are important ingredients in the kind of life that people in the society want to live. I have referred to these forms of control in terms that emphasize their negative and threatening aspects, but they are an aspect of social life one could not reasonably seek to avoid altogether. To begin with, some dependence of this kind is in a trivial sense unavoidable. To the extent that any one person has the right and ability to determine how some choice is to be made, others are to that degree "subject to his will." In addition, nontrivial forms of authority are important and valuable means to many social goals.

But even if rights and powers giving some people a measure of control over others must be a feature of any plausible system of social institutions, the way in which these rights and powers are distributed is one of the features of social institutions that is most subject to moral criticism and most in need of justification. Questions of due process become interesting only on the supposition that such justifications can be given. The importance of due process arises from the fact that these justifications are in general limited and conditional. Even a person's rights to move his body and to dispose of his possessions as he sees fit are limited by requirements that he not bring specified kinds of harm to others. More interestingly, the authority of public officials is, typically, not only limited (e.g., by their jurisdiction) but also conditional. Thus they are empowered not simply to disburse a certain benefit or impose a certain burden but rather to do so *provided* certain specified conditions are met. For example, the authority of a judge to order penalties or fines, and the authority to issue or revoke licenses are both of this form. Authority not tied to special justifying conditions is in fact quite rare. (Perhaps the presidential power to pardon is an example.)

This conditional character is typical not only of the authority of public officials but also of that of persons occupying positions of special power in nongovernmental institutions such as schools, colleges, and businesses. School administrators have the authority to suspend or expel students on academic or disciplinary grounds and to impose other disciplinary penalties. Employers have the right (absent specific contractual bars) to fire workers when this is required by considerations of economic efficiency, and perhaps also when it is necessary as a means of discipline within the firm. In each case, these limits and conditions on a given form of authority flow from the nature of the justification for that authority. The authority of school administrators and employers is presumably to be defended on the ground that it is crucial to the effective functioning of these enterprises.[2] But there would be no prospect of constructing on this basis a defense for unconditional authority to fire or suspend someone for any reason whatever; e.g., because you didn't like his looks, his politics, or his religion, or because he was unwilling to bribe you.

But once de facto power to suspend or fire is conferred, one may ask what reason there is to believe that it will not be exercised in these unjustifiable ways. Thus, beyond the requirement on institutions that the power they confer be morally justifiable, there is the further moral requirement that there be some effective guarantee that these powers will be exercised only within the limits and subject to the conditions implied by their justification. In some cases, nothing need be done to provide such a guarantee. It may happen that, given the motives and the scruples which those in a particular position of power can be expected to have, and given the structural features of their position (e.g., the competitive pressures active on them), there is little reason to expect that they will act outside their authority. Where this is not the case—when obvious temptations or even just clear opportunities for laxness or capriciousness exist— an effective counter may be provided by a system of retrospective justice, levying penalties for the improper use of power and requiring compensation for those injured.

Beyond (or in addition to) this, further guarantees may be provided by introducing special requirements on the way in which those who exercise power make their decisions. Due process is one version of this latter strategy. It aims to provide some assurance of nonarbitrariness by requiring those who exercise authority to justify their intended actions in a public proceeding by adducing reasons of the appropriate sort and defending these against critical attack. The idea of such proceedings presupposes, of course, publicly known and reasonably specific rules with respect to which official actions are to be justified.

The authority to decide whether the reasons advanced are adequate may be assigned to different persons or bodies by different procedures. If the grounds and limits of a given decision maker's authority are well known and taken seriously in a community, then even a hearing procedure that allows him to preside and pronounce the verdict may be a nonnegligible check on the arbitrary use of his power since he will presumably place some value on not being publicly seen to flout the accepted standards for the performance of his job. But in general the assurances provided by a system of due process will be credible only if there is the possibility of appeal to some independent authority which can invoke the coercive power of the state to support its decisions.

Appeal to the courts offers greater assurance against arbitrariness, in part, because of the expectation that the judge will be less a party to the original dispute than the decision maker himself, but also because a judge is presumed to have a greater commitment to an ideal of procedural justice and a greater long-term stake in his reputation as a maker of decisions that are well founded in the relevant rules and principles. At each stage in the appeals process other than the last, these factors of personal motivation will be supplemented by the more explicit threat of being overruled. When we reach the ultimate legal authority, of course, we will in practice be relying on personal commitment, pride, and aspiration alone and on the existence of a public conception of the ground and limits of this authority, which serves as a basis for public approbation or disapprobation of the way it is exercised.

II

Due process is only one of the strategies through which one may seek to avoid arbitrary power by altering the conditions under which decisions are made. It may be contrasted with strategies that seek to make power less arbitrary by making the motives with which it is exercised more benign; for example, by allowing decisions to be made by elected representatives of those principally affected. Rule by such elected representatives is an acceptably nonarbitrary form of authority in a given situation to the extent that it is reasonable to believe that the complex of motives under which representatives act—the desire to be reelected, the need for financial support, loyalty to and shared feelings with one's region or group, the desire to be a "good representative" in the generally accepted sense of this phrase, the desire to be esteemed in the society of representatives and politicians, etc.—will add up to produce decisions reasonably in accord with the rights and wishes of those governed.

As I have mentioned, the mechanisms of a system of due process also depends upon motives—e.g., on the professionalism of judges—but such a system need not in general attempt to influence the authority whose decisions it is supposed to control in favor of the interests of the affected parties. Indeed, the notion of due process is most often invoked in cases (such as the employment case discussed above, or cases of school or prison discipline) where it is assumed that the decision-making authority whose actions are to be checked will be moved (quite properly) by considerations largely separate from the interests of the persons most directly affected. The idea of a right to due process is thus much broader in application than that of a right to participation or representation; it involves the recognition of those subject to authority as entitled to demand justification for its uses and entitled to protection against its unjustified use but not necessarily as entitled to share in the making of decisions affecting them.[3]

The fact that imposition of due process requirements thus involves minimal alteration in the established relations of power makes it a particularly easy remedy for courts to invoke. Its acceptability is also increased in a society like our own by the extraordinary high public regard for legal institutions and the procedures that are typical of them. Given these facts one might expect that insofar as it falls to the judiciary to deal with important social conflicts the remedy of due process is likely to be over utilized.

I have not attempted to say what the *right* to due process is. The moral basis of my account of due process lies in something like a right, namely the idea that citizens have a legitimate claim against institutions which make them subject in important ways to the arbitrary power of others. But it is not easy to say in general when those who have such a claim are entitled specifically to what I have called a mechanism of due process. I described above a range of controls on the exercise of power extending from cases in which authority can be regarded as self-policing to systems of retrospective justice to systems of due process with increasing levels of judicial review.

Moral principles of political philosophy do not determine which of these mechanisms is required in any given case. This is a question of strategy that can be answered only on the basis of an analysis of the factors active in a particular setting. The situation is analogous to the case of representation. One might set forth as a principle of political philosophy that just institutions should provide means for people to participate effectively in decisions affecting them provided that power is distributed equally and that its exercise will not enable some to override the rights of others. But political philosophy can tell us little about what kinds of participatory and/or representative institutions will satisfy the requirement of effective and equal participation in a given case. The choice of suitable forms may depend on local tradition, the distribution of economic and social power in the society, the nature of other primary divisive conflicts, and other variables.

In deciding whether mechanisms of due process are required and in assessing the adequacy of particular mechanisms the main questions seem to be these:

1. How likely is it that a given form of power—if unchecked—will be used outside the limits of its justification?

2. How serious are the harms inflicted by its misuse?

3. Would due process be an effective check on the exercise of this power?

4. Would the costs of a requirement of due process in cases of this kind be excessive? Is the additional effectiveness of due process over other forms of control worth the additional cost?

The costs at issue here will include, in addition to the delay of decisions and the costs of mounting the procedures themselves, the personal and social costs of depersonalizing decisions and reducing them to rules and procedures.

Due process, as I have characterized it, will be most effective where there exist reasonably clear, generally understood standards for exercise of the authority in question, standards which can serve as the background for public justification and defense of decisions. As the relevant standards—and even the starting points for arguments for and against the propriety of a given decision—become less and less clear, the constraints on the decision maker in a due process proceeding become progressively weaker, and the power of these decision makers itself comes to seem more and more arbitrary. The same thing may be true when the relevant standards—while quite precise—become less and less generally understood until finally they are the preserve of a small group including only the hearing examiners, their staff, and the main combatants.

The variation in the forms of due process mechanism that seem appropriate to different situations is not due solely to the different ways in which effective protection against arbitrary decisions can best be given. The procedures with which we are familiar in civil and criminal trials, disciplinary proceedings, and administrative hearings serve a variety of different functions in addition to the general one of providing protection against arbitrary power; and some of the features of these proceedings may be explained by these additional purposes. Thus, for example, many hearings are not merely fact-finding or rule-applying mechanisms; they also serve an important symbolic function as public expressions of the affected parties' right to demand that official acts be explained and justified. If the hearing is to serve this function, the procedures followed should be ones that take the complainants' objections seriously and place them on a par with the claims of authority. This provides an argument for adversary proceedings, for the right to counsel, and for the rights to call witnesses and cross-examine opposing witnesses which go beyond whatever advantages these procedures may have as mechanisms for ensuring a "correct outcome."[4] An argument of this kind is at its strongest in the case of a criminal trial or other proceedings in which a person is accused of wrongdoing. An accused person has an interest in having the opportunity to respond to the charges against him and to present what he takes to be the best defense of his action. This interest would not be met merely by ensuring that all the facts and the relevant legal arguments in the defendant's favor will somehow be brought before the court. There is a crucial difference between having these facts presented and having them presented as a defense by the accused or by someone speaking for him with his consent and participation. To the extent that this interest is a component in the rationale for the procedures of a criminal trial, it would be a mistake automatically to take these procedures as a model for what due process requires generally.

A different mix of purposes is represented in disciplinary proceedings in a school or university. Officials of an educational institution have, in addition to general duties to treat students coming before them fairly and not to use their power in an arbitrary manner, special fiduciary obligations to be concerned with its students' intellectual and personal needs.[5] It is therefore not sufficient merely that disciplinary proceedings follow clear and fair rules and that accused students be informed of their rights and given the opportunity to rebut charges against them. The institution may also be itself obligated (in a way that the state in a criminal trial is not) to investigate cases with the aim of uncovering evidence favorable to the defendant. It should also undertake to inform an accused student of the various alternatives open to him and counsel him in deciding what course to follow.[6] One would expect to see these special obligations reflected in differences between the procedures followed in cases of student discipline and in cases where faculty members or other employees face dismissal. But the requirements of *due process* in these cases are the same.[7]

III

I have described due process as one of the conditions for the moral legitimacy of power-conferring institutions. Suppose that a right to due process as I have described it were to be recognized as a legal right within a given legal system. What might a court be deciding in determining in a certain case that this right had been violated? There seem to be three possibilities:

1. The court may decide that, given the nature of the authority in question, the nature of the harms likely to result from its improper use, and the likelihood of its being used improperly, procedural safeguards are required that were not followed in the given case. Here the court is appraising the decision-making process from the outside in its capacity as the guarantor of the legal right to (procedural) due process.

2. On the other hand, the court may decide that while the procedures followed in the given case were formally adequate the reasoning accepted in these tribunals was faulty or in any case insufficient to justify the decision in question on the required grounds. Here the court is playing a role as one of the appeals stages in an established system of due process. Whether judicial authority to make decisions of this kind is required as a deterrent against tendentious verdicts at earlier stages is itself a question of procedural due process of type (1).

3. Finally, the court may decide that, while the procedures followed in the given case were formally adequate and the reasoning offered in support of decisions unexceptionable, the rules that were applied in these proceedings must themselves be rejected because they exceed the assigned authority of the decision maker in question. Such rules (e.g., the disciplinary code of a school, prison, or labor union) might be struck down on the ground that their enforcement would infringe some specific constitutional guarantee (e.g., some First Amendment right), but this is just one way in which it might be shown that a given rule exceeded the authority of the agency in question. This same conclusion could also be reached by arguing that, given the nature of the institution in question, the given rule could not possibly be taken as part of its writ.

This third case is substantive due process as I understand it. Substantive due process decisions in their most characteristic and controversial form are those based not on any explicit constitutional limitation but rather on appeal to the nature of the authority whose power is in question. The notion of the nature of an institution is one likely to raise legal and philosophical eyebrows. It appears to be an attempt to resolve legal or moral issues by appeal to definitions, and it is apt to provoke questions as to where such definitions are supposed to come from. Surely, it will be urged, social institutions do not have "essences" which can be discovered and used as the basis for authoritative resolution of philosophical or legal controversies. But an important social institution enabling some to wield significant power over others is unlikely to exist without some public rationale—at the very least an account put forth for public consumption of why this institution is legitimate and rational. This will include some conception of the social goals the institution is taken to serve and of the way in which the authority exercised by participants in the institution is rationally related to those goals. If the institution is not merely rationalized by those wishing to maintain its power, but in fact generally accepted as legitimate then some conception of this sort will be fairly generally accepted in the society and rendered coherent with other aspects of the prevailing views. Such a conception may be more or less clearly articulated. It is almost certain to be vague and incomplete in some areas and may be gradually shifting and changing. But something of this kind will almost surely exist and can serve as a basis for argument.

In an argument of the kind I have in mind, an appeal to the current conception of an institution—even in its clearest and most explicit features—need not be final. One must also be prepared to defend the social goals appealed to as in fact valuable and to defend the forms of authority defined by the institution as rational means to those goals and as acceptable given the costs they involve. When a defense of this kind is given within the context of a due process proceeding, the social goals and judgments of relative value to which it appeals must themselves be defended by appeal to contemporary standards (or by an argument about what standards in the relevant area ought to be given other beliefs and values people in the society hold.) But while the limits of debate are in this sense set by prevailing views, the fact that the dominant conception of an institution is not taken at face value but must be shown to be coherent and consistent with other social values provides a measure of independence and allows for criticism through which the prevailing conception of an institution can be extended, clarified and altered.

Appeals of this sort to the nature of social institutions lie behind many quite convincing commonsense political arguments, and even though our conception of an institution is often partly in doubt and in places controversial such appeals can yield quite definite conclusions. It seems to me clear, for example, that a labor union could not use its power of expulsion to collect dues to be used to support a particular religious group but that it could, at least in some cases, compel dues members to pay to support a political candidate or party. And this conclusion follows, I think, from our conception of the nature and purposes of a union rather than from any specific constitutional or statutory limitation.

Such arguments by appeal to the nature of an institution occupy a kind of gray area between considerations of rights and considerations of good policy. Take, for example, the question of academic freedom. It seems to me that the doctrine of academic freedom has its basis in the idea that the purposes of academic institutions are the pursuit and teaching of the truth about certain recognized academic subjects as defined by the prevailing canons of those subjects.[9] Relative to this conception of the purposes of academic institutions, it is rational that they be organized in such a way that the primary motivation of scholars and teachers will be to report and to teach whatever appears to them to be the truth about their subjects. In particular, if teachers and scholars are subject to power which is likely to be used to influence them to teach and report doctrines favored by certain people whether or not these doctrines appear to them to be the truth about their subjects, then it is rational (provided the costs are not too high) to shield them from this power.

The doctrine of academic freedom is generally defended as one such shield. The restraints it imposes on the authority of administrators and trustees over teachers are directly tied to a particular conception of the purposes of an academic institution. They would make no sense (or only a different and more limited kind of sense) as applied to a religious school whose main purpose was the dissemination of a particular faith or to a school founded for the purpose of offering an education which included a nonstandard version of some recognized subject, e.g., biology without evolution or some unorthodox version of history.

As I have described it, academic freedom appears more as a counsel for the rational design and wise administration of certain kinds of academic institutions than as a matter of right. But such a counsel of rationality may be transformed into a right through the application of a general moral or legal principle of due process, limiting the authority of academic officials to those powers and prerogatives that are consistent with and rationally related to the rationale for and purposes of their institutions. To defend the right of academic freedom so conceived, one must be prepared to defend the relevant kind of academic institutions as worth having and their activities as worth the costs of safeguarding them through this means. . . .

IV

I have argued that the basis of due process requirements lies in a condition on the legitimacy of power-conferring institutions. Since the state is only one such institution among many, it follows that the range of possible application of due process requirements is much broader than the extent of "state action." This conclusion seems to me to be in accord with our intuitions about particular cases. In considering rights to due process in cases of suspension or expulsion of students, for example, it seems arbitrary to distinguish between institutions on the basis of whether or not they receive state or federal funds. This seems arbitrary, first, because the very serious dislocation of a student's career which in our society can result from expulsion from college is not significantly different in the two cases. Nor is the likelihood of arbitrary action by administrators acting in the absence of procedural safeguards less in one case than the other. Given the importance attached to gaining admission to college, and the lack of real bargaining power on the part of applicants, student's freedom of choice in deciding what college to attend can scarcely be expected to serve as an effective check on administrator's authority, and the decision to attend a particular school can scarcely be taken as authorization of whatever powers the administrators of that school may wish to claim. At any rate, there seems to be little difference with respect to these matters between private and public institutions.

But while judicial enforcement of due process requirements does not seem to me to be limited to cases of state action, there does seem to me to be an area of activity, which might be called the sphere of purely voluntary organizations, within which due process requirements apply only with reduced force. In this section I will attempt to characterize this area more clearly and examine the ways in which the claims of due process seem to be reduced.[8] I will also indicate how the notion of state action retains some content and force even though it does not mark the outer limits of due process enforcement.

Even given the similarities noted above, the difference between state-supported institutions and private institutions might still be crucial for due process if the costs of imposing due process requirements on the two kinds of institutions were significantly different. But, at least as long as we confine our attention to procedural due process, and as long as we are concerned with colleges and universities in the traditional sense, this is not the case. One can imagine a religious school in which the tenets of the faith required relations of authority which would be entirely inconsistent with due process requirements of the usual kind. In such a case, the cost of imposing due process rights would be quite high, amounting to the serious alteration, if not the destruction, of valued aspects of institutional life. A school of this kind would be extremely special in offering not merely education of the kind required for the careers at which most members of the society aim but rather a special form of life chosen for its own sake by those few who happen to value it. Those who attend such an institution thus accept its requirements voluntarily in a stronger sense than those who accept the

requirements of, say, Princeton or the University of Michigan or Harvard Law School, institutions which are principal means of access to some of the most highly desired positions in the society.

But as far as the weakening of procedural due process requirements is concerned, it is the former feature—the direct clash between the forms of due process and the goals of the institution— rather than its high degree of voluntariness that is crucial. For even where institutions are thoroughly voluntary, if the costs to individuals of the misuse of official authority are high and the chance of such misuse significant then there will be a prima facie case for procedural due process safeguards. In the present example, this prima facie case is overridden by the unusually disruptive consequences of due process forms.

In voluntary institutions of this kind, it is at least partly accurate to see the authority of institutional officers to order, discipline, and expel members as arising from a contract, and to see the limits and conditions of this authority as fixed by the terms on which members (voluntarily) enter. Since even full voluntariness at time of entry into membership does not preclude great inequality in the power unilaterally to interpret and act on the terms of the membership "agreement," the need to impose procedural due process is not eliminated by the voluntary nature of the institution.

But substantive due process is very different. It amounts to the power of a court to arrive at an independent judgment of the limits and conditions of the authority of the group and its officers, a judgment based on a conception of the nature of the institution that need not be determined by the understanding of its members. Where an institution is truly voluntary, this represents a serious inroad into the freedom of individuals to enter into such arrangements as they wish and to define the terms of their own association.

But few of the most significant institutions of society are voluntary in this strong sense. When institutions are not fully voluntary, there are limits on the degree to which it is permissible to allow present members or present officers freely to determine the conditions under which others may have access to the benefits their institution provides. These limits are in part determined by the nature of the institution in the sense described above.

Let me return to the case of traditional colleges and universities. Some limits on changes in university requirements and policies may arise from the requirement of fair warning and the obligation to comply with the legitimate exceptions of students already enrolled. In determining what expectations are (or were) legitimate, we may appeal to the "idea of a university" as it was understood at the time these students enrolled. Here appeal to the nature of an institution helps us to fill in a vague or incompletely articulated agreement. But the idea of a university may be invoked in a stronger sense in setting the limits on requirements for admission or requirements that are to apply only to students who enroll in the future.

It seems at the outset that almost any requirements of this kind would be immune from substantive due process review provided they were plausibly related to normal educational purposes or could be brought under the heading of educational experimentation. For requirements that are evidently idle or perverse, the matter is not so clear. I am thinking here of such things as a policy of restricting admission to persons over six feet tall or a university policy requiring freshmen to speak only when spoken to and to serve as lackeys to older students and faculty.

If we think that courts should not intervene to review and possibly strike down such policies, this is presumably because we feel that freedom to try out new and different educational forms is a good thing, that competitive pressures between institutions will curb excesses, and that the existence of many comparable alternative institutions prevents idiosyncratic policies adopted by one school from imposing a very high cost on would-be applicants. Such considerations are crucial to the case for nonintervention given the place universities occupy as means of access to the most desired positions in our society. If these conditions should fail to hold—if certain restrictions on admission unrelated to plausible academic purposes should cease to be merely the idiosyncrasy of a few particular institutions among many and should come to be quite general, thereby effectively excluding a group of people from university education and all those careers to which it is the main avenue of approach—then the case for judicial intervention on substantive due process grounds would be strong.

This is what has happened in cases of discrimination. What once was or might have been an idle

preference which some institutions could be allowed to cater to—like a preference for people over six feet tall—comes to have unacceptable consequences once it becomes a general pattern. This preference then ceases to be an acceptable ground for admissions decisions. Antidiscrimination judgments of this kind can be seen as substantive due process decisions based on arguments about the nature of an institution in the sense discussed above. The judgment that university admissions officers cannot follow a white-only policy is based on the judgment that a university cannot take being an all-white institution as one of its defining purposes. It cannot do so because the cost of allowing educational (and other) institutions so to define themselves is, in the circumstances, unacceptable. What is the cost? It is, first, that a whole group of people will be effectively blocked from important areas of social life. Of course, any set of criteria—if uniformly employed by all the institutions in a given category (e.g., all universities)—will act as a bar to some "group," namely those who fail to meet these particular criteria. Perhaps any such exclusion, when it is sufficiently uniform, always represents a cost which must be considered. But it is crucial to the costs typical of cases striking us as discrimination that the criteria of exclusion express attitudes that are demeaning to those towards whom they are directed. Once circumstances arise in which such attitudes are widespread and have been generally acted upon—once, that is, discrimination of a certain kind has become a problem—the cost of allowing institutions to define themelves as excluding the group discriminated against become very high. This may provide grounds for refusing to allow institutions so to define themselves even in areas of national life in which such a definition would pose no threat of systematic exclusion. For example, it would not be acceptable to form a lily-white professional sports team in 1975 even though this would pose no threat to black athletes.

The conclusion of a substantive due process argument of this kind barring institutional discrimination against blacks is not that institutional policies must be "color blind." A university admitting blacks only would not be objectionable on the grounds I have mentioned: there is at present no risk of whites being excluded from higher education generally or from any important range of institutions within it. A policy of excluding whites need not be based on antiwhite attitudes, and, even if it were, the threat posed to their self-respect and standing in the society would be insignificant. Finally, an institution with such a policy could conceivably be thought to serve significant cultural value. (A similar asymmetry exists in the United States of 1975 between institutions excluding women and institutions for women only.)

I have suggested that the conclusion of a substantive due process argument against discrimination is to be stated negatively as the judgment that there are certain purposes which institutions may not be allowed to adopt as part of their defining rationale or to appeal to in justifying their policies.[9] It might be suggested that such judgments could as well be stated positively as, for example, the judgment that universities must employ only admission criteria rationally related to their central academic purpose. I want to make two comments about this alternative formulation.

First, if this requirement is understood narrowly, as the claim that since the central purpose of universities is education, they must employ academic excellence, demonstrated or projected, as their sole criterion for admission, then the proposal is one that has never been imposed and should not be. Obviously, colleges and universities should be able to choose their own special character and be free in choosing students to supplement strictly academic criteria with other desiderata related to the kind of institution they wish to be. Substantive due process decisions which ruled out this kind of variation, even to the extent of requiring that nonacademic criteria be restricted to a tie-breaking role in admissions, would be mistaken. This shows, I think, that the correct arguments must be understood negatively—as ruling out certain purposes and standards rather than demanding others.

Second, it is a mistake to think that criteria of academic excellence are themselves sacrosanct. I have stressed the fact that universities are gateways to the most generally desired positions in our society. Criteria of academic success bear some relation to plausible efficiency-based criteria for selection to these positions. But this connection certainly can be, and for many positions no doubt commonly is, overrated. In any event, the general use of standard academic criteria for admission to

colleges, universities and professional schools has costs, both in tending to preserve some forms of discrimination and in creating its own form of stratification, and these have to be weighed against its value as a means to increased efficiency. I am not here arguing that this balancing comes out against academic criteria. I am only pointing out that the standard of merit which they represent, while it may have great appeal both for its own sake and as a hard-won refuge from arbitrary and discriminating practices, still has to be defended as worth the costs it involves.[10]

Let me summarize the discussion of this section. There is an important distinction between those institutions of a society that are truly voluntary and those that, because they are the means of access to benefits desired by most in that society, are so important to life in the society that their power cannot plausibly be justified merely by saying that anyone who does not wish to deal with them on their own terms may simply refrain from dealing with them. Obviously, an institution that is truly voluntary at one time can cease to be so at another as conditions and mores change. Perhaps colleges and universities were once truly voluntary in our society; now they are not. Procedural due process requirements apply to voluntary as well as to nonvoluntary institutions, but for substantive due process the distinction is crucial. The authority that truly voluntary institutions have over their members can plausibly be seen as derived from consent, and their more general justification lies simply in the value of allowing individuals to associate for whatever purposes they may choose.[11]

But as an institution ceases to be truly voluntary and comes to be the mechanism for providing some important good, some further justification for its power is required. This justification typically rests on the institution's role in providing the good in question, and the authority of individuals within the institution must then be defended as part of a rational and acceptable mechanism for providing that good. Thus, in the case of nonvoluntary institutions, there arises both a case for and a basis for criticism on substantive due process grounds. But this does not mean that a court would be justified in imposing on any such institution its conception of what is required by the central function of that institution. Institutional autonomy and variety among institutions providing the same good remain important values. Even where institutions of a certain kind are not fully voluntary, the ability of individuals to choose among various institutions of this kind may constitute an adequate safeguard against capricious restrictions or unwarranted requirements. But when the exercise of institutional autonomy leads to systematic exclusion or to the imposition of other unacceptable social costs then judicial intervention may be called for to delimit the purposes with respect to which institutional policies are to be justified.

A remark on "state action." The state is a nonvoluntary institution of the strongest kind. Everyone in the society is subject to its requirements, and most are required to support its activities whether they wish to or not. The activities of the state, however, are varied. Some of these, when considered with respect to their particular purposes, are in themselves what I have called nonvoluntary institutions (state-supported universities are an example); others are more akin to voluntary institutions (national parks and the support of scholarly research seem to me to fall into this category).[12]

But all of these activities, since they are supported by tax money, are the undertakings of a particular nonvoluntary institution. Accordingly, they are subject to conditions and limitations flowing from the nature of this institution, conditions and limitations that may not apply to other (voluntary or nonvoluntary) organizations pursuing the same purposes (e.g., nonpublic universities, private recreational areas, or foundations for the support of scholarly research). Thus, for example, tax-supported institutions may be barred from adopting religious or political activities as part of their function even though comparable private institutions may do so, and tax-supported institutions may be subject to especially stringent requirements of fairness in the distribution of their benefits. These conditions and limitations could be enforced under the heading of substantive due process as applied to the particular nonvoluntary institution of the state. But, since the state is only one nonvoluntary institution among many, this is a special case of substantive due process. To show that substantive due process applies to a given institution one need not show that it is an activity of the state but only that it, like the state, should be recognized as not truly voluntary.

NOTES

1. In revising this paper I have benefited from the responses of the commentators and discussants at the meeting at which the first version of the paper was delivered and from comments by members of the Society for Ethical and Legal Philosophy and members of Ronald Dworkin's seminar on the philosophy of law, all of whom heard later versions. I am grateful to the members of these audiences for their patience and help, and especially to Bruce Ackerman and Ronald Dworkin for many helpful discussions on the subject of this article.

2. Of course one also has to justify *having* such institutions given their costs.

3. Contrast Selznick, *Law, Society and Industrial Justice* p. 275: "... there is latent in the law of governance [as exemplified by due process] a norm of participation. ... a legal order should be seen as transitional to a polity."

4. The inadequacies of a purely instrumental justification for trial procedures is pointed out by Laurence Tribe in "Trial by Mathematics," 84 Harv. L. Rev. 1329–93.

5. See W. A. Seavey, "Dismissal of Students: 'Due Process,'" 70 Harv. L. Rev. (1957) 1406–10; also, the unsigned note "Judicial Control of Actions of Private Associations" 76 Harv. L. Rev. (1963) 983–1100, esp. pp. 1002 ff.; and Z. Chafee, "The Internal Affairs of Associations Not for Profit," 43 Harv. L. Rev. (1930) 993–1029. I am grateful to Owen Fiss, who called my attention to the last two articles after the original version of this paper had been written.

6. This implies that what would normally be regarded as fair adversary proceedings may not be enough. It is sometimes suggested that, for reasons like those considered here, adversary procedures are not appropriate at all for university discipline and that something more like traditional avuncular "dean's justice" better allows for the appropriate combination of concerned investigation, personal counseling, and rendering of justice. But the potential for arbitrariness here is apparent and familiar. One obvious alternative is a division of labor between (probably adversary) tribunals to apply the rules and separate officials to counsel and assist in uncovering the facts.

7. An alternative explanation of these differences would be that due process itself requires something different where the accused persons are young. But the special obligations of school officials seem to go beyond what general paternalistic arguments are usually taken to require.

8. For a discussion of the law relating to voluntary associations, in which many of the intuitive distinctions used here are clearly and perceptively drawn, see the sources referred to in note 5 above.

By distinguishing, in the following discussion, between "purely voluntary" institutions and institutions that are "not fully voluntary" I do not mean to suggest that those who participate in institutions of the latter sort, e.g. as students in universities, do so *involuntarily*. All I am saying about such institutions is that, given the costs of refusal to participate in them, the authority they exercise over their members cannot be defended simply by appeal to the members' consent as expressed in their willingness to "join".

9. My analysis of discrimination is in this way similar to that offered by Ronald Dworkin in his "The Right to Go to Law School—The DeFunis Case," *New York Review of Books* 23 (Feb. 5, 1976) pp. 29–33. But I do not proceed, as he does, from a general theoretical distinction according to which all preferences to associate with or not to associate with others are suspect.

10. See Thomas Nagel, "Equal Treatment and Compensatory Discrimination," *Philosophy and Public Affairs* 2 (1973) 348–63.

11. In deciding how large a price nonmembers may be asked to bear in order that we can associate for our own private purposes one may, of course, have to take into account what those purposes are. The point is only that with respect to the substance of its power over *members*, the particular purposes of a voluntary association do not have the same justificatory role as they do in the case of nonvoluntary institutions.

12. Some clarification of the nation of a voluntary institution is needed. Our concern is with forms of power some people are able to wield over others, and within a single institution several different forms of power may be involved. Thus, for example, a social club exercises one form of power over members, another over those who seek membership, and another over its employees. With respect to the first two, it is a purely voluntary institution; with respect to the last not so. Thus, the governmental agencies referred to are like voluntary organizations in the power they have over beneficiaries but like businesses or other employers in their authority over those they hire.

What about research-supporting agencies like NSF and NEH? Are the recipients of their grants like beneficiaries or like employees? The answer to this question depends on the role such support has in the economy of the relevant branch of academia. If grants provide temporary support for breaks within other long-term employment, they seem to belong to the voluntary sphere; but not so if they constitute continuing support without which a career of research in the field would be economically impossible.

PAUL LANSING AND RICHARD PEGNETTER

Fair Dismissal Procedures for Non-union Employees

When most prospective employees discuss their future employment situation with their prospective employers, the usual topics of discussion are wages, hours, vacation time, health benefits, etc. It is rare that the topic of grounds for termination will ever arise in this discussion, but it is an area that is becoming increasingly relevant to both parties. Both parties may be unaware that in the majority of employment situations in this country, the employer can legally fire the employee for no reason at all under what is known as the "employment-at-will rule." The status of at-will employees has been and is now the subject of legal examination, and various limitations have been placed on the legal right of the employer to fire his employee. This article will trace the development of the termina-

tion-at-will rule, discuss recent inroads made into that rule, and culminate in a proposal for the disposition of employment termination complaints.

HISTORY OF THE TERMINATION-AT-WILL RULE

The American law of term-of-employment contracts emanated from the common law of England. In 1562, the Statute of Laborers fixed the term of hiring for certain occupations at one year but would allow evidence of custom or trade usage to rebut this presumption. This rule was based upon the presumption that injustice would result in the absence of such a rule. For example, it would be unfair for the owner of a large farm to hire workers during the planting and harvesting seasons but to discharge them during the unproductive winter season in order to avoid feeding them.

This rule of termination of employment remained in effect in this country until the middle of the nineteenth century when the emergence of the general theory of contract law became the dominant concept. In effect, the law of contract said that the parties to a contract assumed certain legal obligations that the legal system would enforce, but the parties to the contract freely entered into that contract and therefore their intentions were to be the source of their relationship. Notions of freedom of contract served to effectuate several important goals at this time in American history. First, it was thought that parties who were free to contract would allocate their property and skill for the benefit of the entire society. Second, freedom of contract would permit the individual to strive for self-determination and control over his own affairs. Lastly, courts would only have to interpret the agreement the parties had made.

In adopting the new theories of contract, the common law recognition of the implied-in-law obligations prohibiting an unjust termination by either party came under scrutiny. The protective restraints which had been developed were repudiated by a rule formulated by a treatise writer in 1877:

With us the rule is inflexible, that a general or indefinite hiring is *prima facie* a hiring at will, and if the servant seeks to make it out a yearly hiring, the burden is upon him to establish it by proof. . . . [I]t is an indefinite hiring and is determinable at the will of either party. . . .[1]

The principal consequence of this rule was a drastic limitation in the employer's duties to the employee. Relying on the new rule, courts rejected the customary presumption that indefinite hirings were for one year and concluded that hirings for an indefinite period should be presumed terminable at will. Under this approach, if the intention of the parties had been to have a one-year employment contract, that would have been so stated in their contract.

By the beginning of the twentieth century, this doctrine had become the prevailing rule governing the right to discharge. However, it should be noted that the rule was adopted in an era of an emerging industrial society, a period of tremendous economic development when entrepreneurs ran heavy risks. So that these risks might be minimized and industry encouraged to expand, the courts created a legal framework to protect the employer. This protection of industry was accomplished, in part, by generally incorporating the law of employment into a developing body of contract law. Using the contractual principle of mutuality of obligation, it was reasoned that if the employee can quit his job at will, then the employer must also have the right to terminate the relationship at will.

At the time of the adoption of the termination-at-will rule in the middle of the nineteenth century, less than half of all employed people were wage and salary workers. By 1950 it was 80% and by 1970, 90%. It is clear that laissez-faire individualism in employment situations is gone and that declining opportunities for self-employment have made America a nation of employees. However, the courts have strictly adhered to the traditional rule that in the absence of a statute or agreement specifically limiting the right of discharge, the employer may discharge his employee at any time for any reason.

The termination-at-will employment contract received its greatest support in two early twentieth century Supreme Court cases, *Adair v. United States* and *Coppage v. Kansas*. In both cases, the employee involved lost his job because of his membership in a labor union and not because of his work performance. In both cases, the Supreme Court struck down the anti-yellow-dog contract legislation which made it a crime for an employer to discharge an employee for union activity. The Court found that an employer's right to hire and fire at will was a constitutionally protected property right. Implicit in these opinions is the idea that the right of the employer and the employee to determine the terms of employment must remain undisturbed by the courts or legislatures. The Court's belief was that the doctrine of freedom of contract ought to prevail even if the bargaining power of the parties is grossly unequal.

LEGISLATIVE ENACTMENTS

The assumption that an employee is on an equal footing in the modern employment relationship to bargain with his employer regarding a wrongful discharge is absurd. Only the most unusual employee possesses sufficient bargaining power to insist upon a restriction of the dismissal power. Although the employer has traditionally been granted an enormous amount of discretion by the employment-at-will rule, recent developments have restricted the employer's right to discharge and have given the employee some protection from arbitrary action by the employer.

The National Labor Relations Act of 1935 was one of the first statutes to curtail the employer's absolute right to discharge his employees. The NLRA makes unlawful the discharge of the employee as a result of his exercising the rights to organize and join a labor organization and to bargain collectively with the employer. Additionally, the NLRA has fostered the growth of collective bargaining, which in turn has led to a new body of labor law limiting arbitrary discharges in two ways. The first is statutory regulation. In upholding the constitutionality of the NLRA, the Supreme Court in *NLRB v. Jones & Laughlin Steel Corp.* noted that the NLRA did not interfere with the normal exercise of the right of discharge, but was aimed only at prohibiting employers from using the right of discharge as a means of intimidation and coercion. In essence, however, *NLRB v. Jones & Laughlin Steel Corp.* was a partial rejection of the philosophy espoused in *Adair* and *Coppage* since the NLRA does place a limitation on the employer's absolute power to discharge.

There has been extensive additional statutory regulation of the power to disclose since the enactment of the NLRA. This legislative activity has resulted in a patchwork scheme which safeguards only certain categories of employees from wrongful discharge. These categories include public employees, veterans, debtors, and the aged, who receive legislative protection from the employer's power to discharge. In addition, other statutes restrict the power to discharge as a means to effectuate other social policies but not because of a direct concern with the dismissal power. For example, statutes have been enacted prohibiting any discharge on the basis of race, color, religion, national origin or sex.

The second limitation on arbitrary discharge has come from the collective bargaining contracts themselves. These contracts contain legally enforceable grievance arbitration provisions, as discussed below.

COLLECTIVE BARGAINING

A major result of the enactment of labor legislation in this country has been the growth of the union movement and the mechanism of collective bargaining. One of the primary reasons for this development has been the desire of individual employees, who possess little if any bargaining power when dealing with employers, to band together and obtain greater leverage for their goals. Counteracting the undervaluation of job security by unorganized, individual employees has been one of the main objectives in the collective bargaining process. Over 90 percent of collective bargaining agreements in the United States limit the employer's power to discharge an employee.

Of course, the critical limitation upon the collective bargaining process is that a great majority of the American work force does not belong to a labor union. Less than a quarter of the American working population is now covered by collective bargaining agreements. In addition, there are indications that union membership is shrinking, due to increased automation and the growing number of professional and white collar workers who choose not to join organized labor.

Another limitation on the collective bargaining process is that the union maintains almost exclusive control over the right to utilize the grievance procedure. It is therefore possible that an individual employee who feels he has been wrongfully dismissed may have no legal outlet for his protest should the union decide not to go along with the individual employee.

For labor, the most advantageous aspect of the development of the collective bargaining process has been the establishment of binding arbitration procedures for grievance disputes. The governing principles used by arbitrators have not been based on the common law but on the social reality of the relationship between employee and employer.[2] The existence of this new framework of principles is reflected by the variance between the common law and arbitral approaches when an employee is discharged for what the union contends is insufficient cause during the term of the agreement.

Rejecting the principle of an unrestricted power to discharge by the employer, arbitrators have implied just cause or other requirements into the bargaining contract.

The Supreme Court began to lend its support to the development of this private system of jurisprudence in *Textile Workers Union v. Lincoln Mills*. In that case, the Court interpreted section 301 of the Labor Management Relations Act as a mandate to federal courts to specifically enforce grievance-arbitration provisions of collective bargaining agreements. Just as the traditional attitude of the courts was not to interfere in the private contracts made between employers and their employees, so the courts have taken the position that they will, for the most part, not interfere in the contracts made between employers and unions and the collective bargaining arrangements made therein.

JUDICIAL ACTION

Although the legal system has abandoned the nineteenth century belief that there should be no restriction on the right to discharge by an employer, the majority of employees remain unprotected in this country. For the most part, unless a case falls within one of the exceptions noted above, courts have generally invoked the rule that an employee has no recourse against the employer who has terminated his at-will employment. In recent years, however, some courts have taken closer scrutiny of the employment-at-will cases that have come before them. The result has been a few decisions granting relief to the employee who has been wrongfully discharged.

One basis for qualifying the employer's right to terminate employment at will has been the public policy argument. Under this rationale, the employee at will has an action for wrongful discharge based on the injury society suffers as a result of the employer's conduct. In *Peterman v. Teamsters Local 396*, an employee was discharged after disobeying his employer's order to testify falsely before a state legislative committee. The court held that a discharge based upon retaliation for refusal to commit perjury was wrongful, emphasizing the fact that perjury was a criminal offense and was clear evidence of a strong public policy against it.

In so concluding, the court granted the employee a cause of action against his employer.

Some other courts faced with similar fact situations have also granted employees a right of action. For example, recoveries have been allowed where an employee was dismissed because he had refused to alter pollution control reports required by the state, or because he accepted jury duty. However, the cases emphasize that an infringement of the employee's private interests alone is not enough and that a community or societal interest must be violated in order to seek relief under this exception. A further restriction on the use of this public policy argument is that it is available only if no alternative remedies are available. Therefore, although a public policy exception to the termination-at-will rule does exist, it is applicable only in limited circumstances.

The second judicial basis for qualifying the employer's right to terminate employment at will has been the good-faith modification argument. In *Monge v. Beebe Rubber Co.*, plaintiff alleged that she was discharged because she refused to go out with defendant's foreman. In suing for breach of her employment contract, the court stated that "the employer's interest in running his business as he sees fit must be balanced against the interest of the employee in maintaining his employment, and the public's interest in maintaining a proper balance between the two." Applying this rationale, the court held that a termination which is motivated by bad faith, malice or retaliation constitutes a breach of the employment contract.

The *Monge* decision is a limited exception to the employer's general right of termination because the court relied upon contract principles as the basis for its decision. Under this approach, where an employee can prove a bad-faith motivation for the termination of his services, the employer will be liable for lost wages due to the bad-faith discharge. However, because the action is of a contract nature, the plaintiff will be precluded from damages for emotional distress and from punitive damages.

OTHER RECENT DEVELOPMENTS

It should be noted that neither the public policy nor the good-faith argument limits the employer to a right to dismiss only for just cause. The United States is one of the few industrial countries in the world that does not provide general legal protection against unjust dismissals.[3] Recognizing the need to maintain management's right to manage, most other countries nevertheless have developed a statutory scheme within the last ten years by which alleged unjust dismissals may be effectively handled. All Common Market nations, Sweden, and Norway have some statutory protection against unjust dismissals. These statutes usually require that a probationary period of employment be completed (usually six months) before statutory protection exists, and that advance notice of the termination be given for a dismissal to take effect. Compensation, rather than reinstatement, is the most common remedy available under these statutes, and most impose a limit on the amount of compensation. Most disputes arising under these statutes are heard in either special labor courts or industrial tribunals.

In light of our federal government's failure to respond to the termination-at-will situation, some states are considering or have recently enacted legislation of their own. For example, the Connecticut legislature had bills introduced in 1973 and 1975 that would provide just-cause protection to unorganized employees. In South Carolina, the Department of Labor by statute mediates disputes between employers and unorganized employees where involuntary terminations are involved. In Michigan, there is presently a bill (the Bullard bill) before the legislature which provides that an employer cannot suspend or discharge an employee except for just cause and sets up a procedure to hear complaints under that standard.

It is clear that the nineteenth century philosophical view of America as a laissez-faire, free enterprise, and individualistic society is no longer necessary to accomplish the economic development which was required at that time. The doctrine of complete freedom of contract which was a useful legal tool for accomplishing that goal is also no longer required or in use. The legal notion of unconscionability of contracts is clearly an inroad into the freedom of contract doctrine by the recognition that all parties to a contract do not have equal bargaining power. While some inroads have been made into the termination-at-will doctrine, it is time that the United States join the other industrialized nations of the world who have provided a complete statutory scheme to deal with the problem. Following are our suggestions.

SUGGESTIONS FOR REGULATING EMPLOYMENT CONTRACTS

Federal/State Regulation

A threshold question in providing employees with an appeal mechanism for unjust dismissal is whether such a system should be established through federal or state legislation. Some familiar and serious issues arise immediately. If federal legislation is the exclusive vehicle for unjust-dismissal regulation, the issue of federal intrusion into states' rights becomes, if nothing else, a political problem. On the other hand, if state legislation is the exclusive basis for an appeal system, the very real possibility exists that many states will fail to provide such legislation. This is clearly evident in the establishment of bargaining rights for state and local government employees, where only about 30 states have passed comprehensive bargaining legislation for such public employees.

A solution which would best meet both of these concerns is a mixture of federal legislation with state options similar to the Occupational Safety and Health Act. Under this approach, there would be a comprehensive federal law which would apply in any state which had failed to enact a substantially equivalent statute protecting against unjust dismissal. Such a mixture would ensure that all employees would be afforded protection, irrespective of state residence. At the same time each state could retain control of the operation of the dismissal appeal system by adopting its own legislation. A maximum limit of two years from the date of the federal legislation would be provided for the states to act to avoid the operation of the federal system in that state.

Coverage

The protection afforded by fair dismissal legislation would extend to all employees, but with several major qualifications or exceptions. One qualification would limit coverage to employers with ten or more employees. Unique intra-organizational pressures may result from the operation of a formal grievance system within a small work organization. Employee-employer problems and their solutions can become too personalized to permit effective remedies. Further, the notion of a size restriction is reflective of public policy in other legislation. Federal and state fair employment laws directed at discrimination impose such limits on coverage.

An exception would also apply to employees currently covered by negotiated contracts or civil service systems. The intention of fair dismissal legislation is to establish protection for employees who are now without any protection, not create a maze of dual procedures. Virtually all negotiated contracts and civil service systems contain grievance and appeal mechanisms which include dismissal within their scope. Supervisors and managers would be excluded from coverage in a manner consistent with the NLRA. The industrial relations literature and judicial decisions emphasizing a conflict-of-interest potential and the need to maintain a cohesive management team will not be repeated here. And, while it is acknowledged that several state public employee bargaining laws extend coverage to supervisors, the wisdom of such an approach has not been conclusively demonstrated. Consequently, a fair dismissal law should exclude supervisors and managers in the same way and for the same reasons embodied in most collective bargaining legislation for private and public sector employees. Finally, new, probationary employees would also be excluded to provide employers with an opportunity to evaluate employees before awarding status as "permanent" employees. An employee would be considered in permanent status after successfully completing six months of employment.

Scope of Procedure

The central core of a fair dismissal system must be that employees will be disciplined or discharged only for "just cause." The apparent simplicity of such a statement of the scope of the procedure conceals a plethora of more detailed considerations. The concept of discipline (which is not to be imposed without just cause) must be broad enough to include both dismissal and other major actions such as demotion and suspension. The major reason for encompassing nondischarge disciplinary actions such as suspension or demotion is to ensure the integrity of the system's protection. If nondischarge penalties were not included, abuses like one year "suspensions" or "transfers" to unattractive, lower paying work would escape the protection of the system. Also, if the positive, corrective nature of progressive discipline is to be encouraged, proper lesser penalties which may eventually be used as part of a discharge action must be subjected to review under the appeal mechanism.

In addition, the meaning of "just cause" must be established. The experience and decisions of over 30 years of grievance arbitration in the United States has generated a clear set of standards to measure just cause. They include the following principles:

1. Work rules and production standards are to be transmitted to all employees so that the employees have *foreknowledge* of expected work behavior. The essence of this standard is that employees have a right to be made aware of work rules in advance, not to learn of rules only as a result of unknowingly violating a regulation.

2. The system of penalties for violations of the work standards are to be given to employees so they are *forewarned* of the consequences for violating work rules. Again, the standard assumes that employees have a right to know in advance that improper action will result in a generally specified penalty.

3. The use of work standards and penalties are to be applied to all employees in a *fair and consistent* manner. The standard here is that two employees who commit essentially the same offense should be subjected to the same discipline.

4. Penalties will be imposed as part of a system of *progressive discipline* wherever possible in a fashion to ensure correct work behavior. This means that discipline is primarily used in the work place as a remedial tool and the ultimate penalty of discharge is presumed appropriate only for serious first offenses, such as stealing, or repeated lesser offenses like absenteeism.

While the above four principles are sometimes further subdivided by arbitrators, the important point is that a well-founded body of the "law of the shop" on disciplinary matters has been developed to a sophisticated and effective level which is available to delineate "just cause" in the proposed statutory system.

Procedural Structure

The procedure proposed to insure fair dismissal practices is composed of two main elements. One is a system to provide for an initial effort to conciliate dismissal appeals and develop a resolution satisfactory to both parties. The second element is an arbitration mechanism with the authority to impose a binding decision on the parties.

Conciliation. The value of a nonadjudicative system to resolve employee-employer disputes has been well tested in American industrial relations. In the broadest sense, it is highly successful in resolving collective bargaining disputes over new contract terms. Agencies such as the Federal Mediation and Conciliation Service have demonstrated an ability to assist the parties in achieving mutually acceptable agreements and avoiding strikes or the use of public employment adjudicative procedures in the form of fact-finding or interest arbitration.[4]

More specifically for the dismissal appeal structure proposed here, the opportunity for mutual settlement of employee grievances prior to arbitration has been a cornerstone of union-management relations under collective bargaining. The evidence clearly shows that few grievances ever need resolution through a decision imposed by an outside arbitrator. Instead, most grievances are settled by the parties at internal levels or steps of the grievance procedure. The steps of the procedure preceding arbitration force the parties to test the evidence and the correctness of their positions thoroughly prior to risking their case before the binding authority of an arbitrator. The result of such an internal effort by the parties is usually a mutually agreed resolution and the avoidance of an externally imposed outcome, a basic goal of the collective bargaining system.

However, several essential ingredients in the collective bargaining system for dismissal appeals are absent for at-will employees. There is no multi-stage, internal grievance system and no union representative to facilitate a mutual resolution. The substitute proposed here is the use of a conciliation stage preceding the submission of a dismissal appeal to arbitration. The conciliation would be provided by full-time conciliators in the service of a public agency. This stage of the dismissal appeal system would have several features and advantages. The conciliation service would be provided free to the parties at public expense and could be invoked by either party in a dismissal dispute. The most significant impact of this feature would be its availability as a mechanism to help avoid adjudication of the dispute. As will be discussed below, the parties must share the cost of the arbitration system proposed. For many employees, the costs of both a conciliation stage and an arbitration stage would often be prohibitive.[5] Consequently, many employees would be financially excluded from any appeal for their dismissal claim. In addition, the conciliation stage would be a mandatory prerequisite to taking a dismissal appeal to arbitration. This requirement would insure at least an opportunity for the noted advantages of a settlement between the parties. By facilitating more objective communication between the parties and forcing the parties to critically examine the validity of their positions, conciliation could frequently assist the parties to avoid arbitration.

The system would also require that the dismissal dispute be taken to the conciliation agency within seven calendar days of the employer's action against the employee. This requirement would ensure that the action could be reviewed by the parties and the conciliator while supporting evidence is fresh and available. For its part, the conciliation agency would be required to schedule a conciliation meeting within two weeks of the notice of appeal. This requirement would further aid in quick attention to the dispute and would minimize the impact of any back-pay provisions if a remedy became appropriate. A further requirement would be to limit the conciliation effort to a single conciliation session. This requirement would aid in controlling costs for the agency responsible for conciliation and, perhaps more important, help protect the employer's time commitment to the process from abuse by nonmeritorious or frivolous appeals.

A final note should be made regarding the conciliation agency and costs. If the fair dismissal law and its appeal system are adopted as a state function, numerous existing state agencies could be assigned the conciliation function as an expansion of their current activities. About 20 states have public and/or private sector labor relations boards which currently provide mediation services among their other duties. Several of these agencies are already providing grievance mediation—the Michigan Employment Relations Commission, for example. These state employment relations boards or commissions would be likely vehicles for dismissal appeal conciliation services at minimal additional public expense.

Arbitration. If the parties were unable to resolve the dispute through conciliation, either party could make a timely request for arbitration. The arbitration mechanism would be statutorily available to provide fairness and finality in settling the dispute. Again, many of the tested and proven elements of union-management contract grievance arbitration could be incorporated into the statutory system. The statute would provide that either party could invoke arbitration. This would assure that any attempt to use dilatory tactics could be thwarted. In particular, since arbitration would be compulsory, an employer could not avoid arbitration by withholding mutual consent to place the issue before an arbitrator. In addition, a party's appeal to arbitration would be required to have been made within one week of the date of the conciliation hearing to be timely. This would guarantee a speedy decision regarding an appeal to final adjudication. The same value of immediacy and the avoidance of extended deliberation cited earlier as the reasons for a time limit on invoking conciliation apply here.

A cornerstone to the appeal system would derive from the cost of arbitration. A request for arbitration would be accepted only if accompanied by an escrow of $500 or an amount equal to one week's wages, whichever was less; the employer would be required to post an equal amount in escrow. Both payments would be held by the state conciliation agency for payment of the arbitrator's

fee.[6] Any charges for expenses and professional services by the arbitrator would be paid from the escrow fund. Money remaining after payment would be divided equally for return to the parties. Charges in excess of the escrow fund would be absorbed by the state. A prepayment requirement is essential in avoiding abuse of the arbitration appeal mechanism. By attaching a cost to the appeal of a nonmeritorious or frivolous case, employees will be forced to weigh and evaluate the decision to seek arbitration, rather than only concerning themselves with cost *after* an award has been rendered. Additionally, the parties will defray all or a major part of the cost of arbitration for the public. The value of a shared cost to the parties in screening legitimate claims has been well documented under collective bargaining grievance arbitration.

Upon receipt of a proper request for arbitration, the conciliation agency would provide the parties with a list of three certified, neutral arbitrators from a panel of ad hoc arbitrators maintained by the agency. Each party would have the right to strike the name of one arbitrator. The remaining arbitrator would hear the case. This procedure would permit a measure of mutual determination or selection of the adjudicator by the parties. The preference for a mutual selection of the arbitrator, with its resulting greater acceptance of the award by the parties, has been noted by various industrial relations research studies and the Supreme Court's application of federal labor law.

To further insure time efficiency and aid in the control of costs—both arbitration costs and potential back pay award penalties—the arbitration process will normally allow for only one day of hearing with the award to be rendered within two weeks of the hearing. Exceptions to the single day of hearing could be permitted in special circumstances at the discretion of the arbitrator. The allowance of one day should adequately comport with experience in contract grievance arbitration and civil service appeal procedures where evidence shows that most disciplinary grievances involve a single day of hearing.

Procedural requirements for the arbitration hearing would be kept informal, again similar to contract grievance arbitration. Employees and employers could be represented by anyone of their choosing, including themselves.[7] No formal rules of evidence would be imposed and the arbitrator's expertise would serve as a sufficient protection for the weight accorded to various forms of evidence. Informality would insure that employees without the ability to retain counsel would not be prevented from proceeding to arbitration once the filing escrow had been provided. The arbitration process would require that the employer proceed first. This requirement would reflect the fact that action against the employee was taken by the employer. However, no strict burden of proof would attach to the requirement to proceed first. In keeping with the experience of contract grievance arbitration, the arbitrator of statutory dismissal appeals would decide cases on the basis of the preponderance of evidence. The normal measure to be met would be that the employer had "just cause" for the disciplinary action taken against the employee.

Another important facet of the system is the remedy power of the arbitrator. The remedy provided in cases where discipline was not found to be for just cause would be either to make the employee whole for any lost wages and benefits or to adjust the penalty to conform to the offense. As in contract grievance arbitration, there normally would be no costs or damages awarded as a part of any remedy. One exception to the limit of a make-whole remedy should be established to reflect the absence of a collective bargaining relationship and union representation, with its concomitant financial assistance for the appellant. The exception would be that in cases where the employer acts without just cause *and* without good faith toward the affected employee, the employee could be awarded costs and damages by the arbitrator. This option would aid in deterring employers from abusing their economic superiority and taking arbitrary and capricious disciplinary action against employees.

Finally, the arbitration award would be insulated against judicial review on the merits of the decision. As under the law of the *Steelworkers* trilogy developed for contract grievance arbitration, only procedural irregularities would serve as the basis for judicial examination of an arbitrated dismissal dispute. The value of speed and finality cited in the trilogy by the courts is even more

applicable to the statutory appeal mechanism proposed here, where considerable financial burden is placed on the employee as part of the screening premise for nonmeritorious claims.

SUMMARY

The vast majority of the American labor force is employed by business or service enterprises. Only about one-fourth of these employees are covered by collective bargaining contracts which provide protection against dismissal without just cause. The remainder of the private sector labor force continue their employment "at will." With few limitations, such as those associated with race or sex discrimination, these "at will" employees may be subjected to unjust dismissal at any time. The courts have moved to fill the void in protective legislation in only a highly limited fashion. The American approach to protection against unjust dismissal is in stark contrast to systems in Western Europe where most employees enjoy statutory guarantees that discharge will be for proper cause.

The problem of unjust dismissal protection for American workers could be similarly resolved by federal legislation. The legislation proposed in this paper would provide a system of conciliation, followed by arbitration, for most employees not currently covered by either a collective bargaining agreement or a civil service system. The procedure would permit employees to challenge disciplinary actions which were imposed by an employer without just cause. Employees and employers would share part of the cost of the arbitration step of the procedure, while conciliation would be provided at no cost to the parties by a government agency. The system would continue many of the features proven to be successful in contract grievance procedures which end in arbitration.

The proposal for statutory protection against unjust dismissal for non-unionized employees could be incorporated into the American system and its institutions with minimal adjustment. The discipline appeal procedure outlined would extend the protection already in place for unionized and civil service employees to most of the remaining American workforce. The use of existing state labor boards and agencies would substantially reduce the cost of such a system. In addition, the sharing of some arbitration costs by employers and the employee who filed an appeal under the procedure would further reduce cost and help protect against nonmeritorious grievances. The adoption of the proposed system for unjust dismissals would ensure that this vital aspect of American human resource management would match the protection already provided for employees in Western Europe.

NOTES

1. "Both parties to a contract must be bound or neither is bound." *Corbin, Contracts* § 152 at 2 (1963).
2. An arbitrator is a neutral third party who settles the dispute and whose decision is binding on both parties.
3. The United States is the only major industrial nation in the free world without such a scheme. *See* Note, *A Remedy for Malicious Discharge of the At Will Employee: Monge v. Beebe Rubber Co., 114 N.H. 130, 316 A.2d 549 (1974), 7 Conn. L. Rev.* 758 (1975).
4. Federal Mediation and Conciliation Service figures show that during 1977, 1978, and 1979, the number of closed disputed mediation cases in which the Service participated totaled 23,450, 20,257 and 20,414, respectively. Of these, strikes were involved in 13.3%, 13.4%, and 14.2%, respectively. *FMCS Rpt.* (1979) at 19.
5. This cost, including representation and the fee charged by the arbitrator, has been estimated by unions at over $2,000. *See* Zalrisky, *Arbitration: Updating a Vital Process,* 83 *The American Federationist* 1 (1976).
6. The actual cost per case by arbitrators in 1979 was $911.83. FMCS Thirty-Second Annual Report 35 (1979).
7. BNA, *supra* note 68, at 132. In addition, the NLRB states that "any individual employee or a group of employees shall have the right at any time to present grievances to their employer . . . without the intervention of the bargaining representative. . . ."

DONALD L. MARTIN

Is an Employee Bill of Rights Needed?

The perception of the corporation as an industrial form of government in which management plays the role of the governor and labor the role of the governed has been particularly popular since the end of World War II. "Industrial democracy" has been the slogan of the labor movement in the industrial relations community. This analogy has recently given rise to demands for an "Employee Bill of Rights." Such a bill would guarantee the worker the same *due process* that the Constitution guarantees the citizen. It would protect the worker from the arbitrary and inequitable exercise of managerial discretion.

WHERE THE INDUSTRIAL DEMOCRACY ANALOGY FALTERS

But the industrial democracy analogy surely must be false. Two important considerations obviate it. First, a crucial distinction between government at any level and private economic organization, corporate or otherwise, is the right entrusted to

government to exercise legitimate and reasonable force in its relations with its citizens. Second, the cost to a citizen of switching affiliation between governments is far greater than the cost to an employee of switching affiliations between firms. Since governments will surely violate public trust through their police powers, and since the costs to citizens of changing leaders or residences are relatively high, citizens will seek institutions to insulate themselves from the arbitrary and exploitative use of such powers by their elected and appointed representatives. These institutions include the first ten amendments to the United States Constitution (the Bill of Rights) and the Fourteenth Amendment (guaranteeing due process).

THE PROBLEM OF THE MONOPSONISTIC LABOR MARKET

Something close to an analogous use of exploitative power in the private sector occurs in the world of monopsonistic labor markets. In those labor markets, would-be employees have few, if any, alternative job opportunities, either because of an absence of immediate competitive employers or because of the presence of relatively high costs of moving to available job alternatives in other markets. With few or no job alternatives, workers are more likely to be the unwilling subjects of employer prejudice, oppression, and personal discretion than if labor market competition prevails.

No one would claim that the American economy is completely free of monopsony power. There is not a shred of evidence, on the other hand, that such power exists in the large American corporation of today. Indeed, there is impressive evidence to suggest that monopsony is not likely to be found in large, private corporations. Robert Bunting's examination of labor market concentration throughout the United States among large firms, for example, finds that employment concentration (measured by the fraction of total employees in a geographic area who are employed by the largest reporting firm in that area) is related inversely to labor market size, while firm size is correlated positively with labor market size.

It is well known that monopsonistic powers reside in the collusive owners of professional sports teams, precisely because these powers are exempt from antitrust laws in the United States. Professional sports firms, however, do not number among the large corporations at which "Employee Bill of Rights" proposals are directed.

Interestingly, monopsonistic power in the labor market may be a significant factor at the local government level. Evidence of monopsony exists in such fields as public education, fire and police protection, and nursing.

THE NATURE OF EMPLOYER-EMPLOYEE AGREEMENTS

The Constitution of the United States does not extend the Bill of Rights and the due process clause of the Fourteenth Amendment to the private sector unless agents of the latter are performing public functions (*Marsh v. State of Alabama*, 66 S. Ct. 276 [1946]). Instead of interpreting this limitation as an oversight of the founding fathers, the preceding discussion suggests that the distinctive treatment accorded governments reflects the conscious belief that market processes, more than

political processes, yield a degree of protection to their participants that is closer to levels that those participants actually desire. It also suggests that this inherent difference justifies the institutionalization of civil liberties in one form of activity (political) and not in the other form (market).

This interpretation is consistent with the repeated refusal of the United States Supreme Court to interfere with the rights of employers and employees (corporate or otherwise) to make mutually agreeable arrangements concerning the exercise of civil liberties (otherwise protected under the Constitution) on the job or in connection with job-related activities. (The obvious legislative exceptions to this generalization are the Wagner Act of 1935 and the Taft-Hartley Act of 1947. These acts proscribe the free speech rights of employers with regard to their possible influence over union elections on their own property, while allowing labor to use that same property for similar purposes.)

In the absence of monopsonistic power, the substantive content of an employer-employee relationship is the result of explicit and implicit bargaining that leaves both parties better off than they would be if they had not entered into the relationship. That both are better off follows because each is free to end the employment relationship at will—unless, of course, contractual relationships specify otherwise. Americans have demonstrated at an impressive rate a willingness to leave current employment for better pecuniary and nonpecuniary alternatives. During nonrecessionary periods, employee resignations contribute significantly to turnover statistics. In an uncertain world, the workers who resign generate valuable information about all terms and conditions under which firms and would-be employees can reach agreement.

THE COSTS OF WORKPLACE CIVIL LIBERTIES

If information about each party to employment and information about potential and actual performance are costly, both firms *and* employees seek ways to economize. Indeed, the functions of a firm, from the viewpoint of employees, are to screen job applicants and to monitor on-the-job activities. A firm's final output is often a result of the joint efforts of workers rather than a result of the sum of the workers' separate efforts. This jointness of production makes individual effort difficult to measure, and on-the-job shirking becomes relatively inexpensive for any given employee. The reason is precisely that all employees must share the cost of one employee's "goldbricking." As a consequence, shirking, if done excessively, threatens the earning opportunities of other workers. Other white-collar crimes, such as pilfering finished products or raw materials, have similar consequences.

To protect themselves from these threats, workers use the firm as a monitoring agent, implicitly authorizing it to direct work, manage tools, observe work practices and other on-the-job employee activities, and discipline transgressors. If employers function efficiently, the earnings of workers will be higher than if the monitoring function were not provided.

Efficient *employer* activities, however, may appear to others, including some employees, to be flagrant violations of personal privacy from the perspective of the First, Fourth, Fifth, and Ninth Amendments to the Constitution. These employer activities, on the contrary, are the result of implied agreements between employers and employees, consummated by demand and supply forces in the labor market. The reduction in personal liberty that workers sustain in a firm has a smaller value for them, at the margin, than the increase in earning power that results. Thus, limitations on personal liberty in a firm, unlike such limitations in governments, are not manifestations of tyranny; they are, instead, the product of a mutually preferred arrangement.

It should not be surprising that higher-paying firms and firms entrusting more valuable decision-making responsibility to some employees would invest relatively more resources than would other firms in gathering potentially revealing information about the qualifications of prospective employees and about the actions of existing employees. Since the larger a firm is, by asset size or by employee number, the more likely it is to be a corporation, it should also not be surprising that corporations are among the firms that devote relatively large amounts of resources to gathering information of a personal nature about employees.

Prohibiting the gathering of such information by superimposing an "Employee Bill of Rights" on the employment relationship has the effect of penalizing a specific group of employees. This group is composed of those persons who cannot otherwise compete successfully for positions of responsibility, trust, or loyalty because the high cost of information makes it unprofitable for them to distinguish themselves from other workers without desirable job characteristics. Thus, federal protection of the civil liberties of employees in the marketplace may actually harm those who wish to waive such rights as a less expensive way of competing.

Under an "Employee Bill of Rights" the process of searching for new employees and the process of managing existing employees are relatively more costly for an employer. This greater cost will be reflected not only in personnel policy but also in the cost of producing final outputs and in the prices consumers pay for them. An effect of an "Employee Bill of Rights" would be limited dimensions on which employees may compete with each other. Although there are precedents for such limitations (for example, federal minimum wage laws), it is important to recognize that this kind of protection may have unintended effects on the welfare of large numbers of employees. The anticompetitive effects of institutionalizing due process and civil liberties have long been recognized by trade unions. These effects constitute an important reason for the interest unions have in formalizing the procedures employers use in hiring, firing, promoting, demoting, rewarding, and penalizing union employees. It is false to argue, nevertheless, that an absence of formal procedures and rules in nonunionized firms is evidence that workers are at the mercy of unfettered employers, or that workers are more likely to be exploited if they are located in corporations rather than in noncorporate forms of organization.

Even the most powerful corporations must go to an effectively competitive labor market for their personnel. Prospective employees see arbitrary and oppressive personnel policies as relatively unattractive working conditions requiring compensation of pecuniary and nonpecuniary differentials over and above what they would receive from alternative employments. Those workers who want more certainty in the exercise of civil liberties pay for that certainty by forgoing these compensating differentials. This reasoning suggests that the degree of desired democracy in the labor market is amenable to the same forces that determine wages and working conditions. There is neither evidence nor persuasive arguments that suggest that workers in large corporations somehow have been excluded from the process that determines the degree of democracy they want.

CHAPTER TEN
Study Questions

1. What would be an improper reason for dismissing an employee? Is no reason at all an improper reason? Would randomly firing one employee as warning to others be an improper reason?

2. What are the similarities between a large corporation and a political state? What are the dissimilarities?

3. What exactly is the difference between procedural and substantive due process?

4. Do you believe that independent arbitrators could successfully ensure due process, or would a more active government policy be required?

5. Should employees be required to offer a "just cause" before they quit? What is a "just cause" anyway?

PART FOUR

BUSINESS
AND SOCIETY

*A*FFIRMATIVE ACTION

CASE STUDY

United Steelworkers of America v. Weber

For generations, blacks in America were denied jobs, were denied equal pay and promotions when they did get jobs, and were generally relegated to unskilled and semi-skilled positions. Even many of these jobs were lost to increasing automation. Black unemployment was much higher than white and steadily worsening.

Congress passed the Civil Rights Act of 1964 to change all this. Title VII of that act reads, in part, that "It shall be an unlawful employment practice for any employer, labor organization, or joint labor-management committee controlling apprenticeship or other training or re-training, including on-the-job training programs to discriminate against any individual because of his race. . . ." The legislative history of the act indicates that Congress believed that this would "open employment opportunities for Negroes in occupations which have been traditionally closed to them." But did the act prohibit any and all discrimination "because of . . . race," or only the insidious discrimination that historically had plagued blacks?

In 1974, United Steelworkers of America

and Kaiser Aluminum entered into a collective-bargaining agreement that contained a plan "to eliminate conspicuous racial imbalances" in Kaiser's skilled craftwork positions. Future selection of trainees for these positions would be on the basis of seniority, except that 50% of the positions would be reserved for blacks until the percentages of blacks in these jobs approximated the percentage of blacks in the local labor force. At one Kaiser plant in Gramercy, Louisiana, for example, only 5 out of 273 (1.83%) skilled craftsworkers were black, despite the fact that 39% of the workforce in the Gramercy area was black.

During the first year of the Kaiser-USWA plan, seven black and six white trainees were selected at the Gramercy plant. Several white workers who were denied admission to the training program had more seniority than the most senior black trainee. One of those rejected workers, Brian Weber, filed suit claiming that the Kaiser-USWA plan violated the section of Title VII quoted above. A district court and, later, a court of appeals decided in favor of Weber, concluding that the plan did violate Title VII's prohibition against discrimination "because of race." Upon appeal, the Supreme Court overruled these decisions and found in favor of the Kaiser-USWA plan.

The majority opinion reasoned that a literal interpretation of the law without examination of the legislative history was misplaced. They reasoned that Congress sought to overcome the inequalities that resulted from past discrimination against blacks and that, therefore, a voluntary plan between employers and unions that had the same goals was consistent with the act. The minority opinion argued that the law explicitly prohibited any discrimination on the basis of race. In the words of Justice William Rehnquist, "Were Congress to act today specifically to prohibit the type of racial discrim-ination suffered by Weber, it would be hard pressed to draft language better tailored to the task than that found" in the section from Title VII quoted above.

What, if anything, is the difference between the type of discrimination suffered by blacks for generations and that suffered by Weber? How might plans like Kaiser-USWA harm young white males? Is seniority a fair standard to use in determining qualifications? How would your views change if the Kaiser-USWA plan had been required by Congress, rather than voluntarily established? To avoid such plans ultimately resulting in insidious discrimination against young white males, must they be ended somewhere? Where?

Introduction

ALMOST EVERYONE RECOGNIZES the existence of affirmative action or preferential treatment programs. And almost everyone admits that these programs at least intend to improve the economic and social condition of specific minority or disadvantaged groups. However, not everyone recognizes that the terms "affirmative action" and "preferential treatment" refer to programs of widely varying strength. And certainly, not everyone agrees about the propriety of these programs. (The article by James Jones in this chapter shows that even the Supreme Court is deeply divided about the constitutionality of these programs.) It will be helpful if we sketch the range of such programs and if we outline the types of argument offered for and against specific programs.

Unfortunately, when people discuss affirmative action and preferential treatment programs, they often fail to note that these programs can range from relatively weak attempts to ensure open advertising of employment opportunities to numerical requirements for hiring individuals from target groups. They also often fail to note that affirmative action can operate in employment decisions, housing programs, and higher education admissions policies. In addition, there is some confusion over the reference of the terms "affirmative action" and "preferential treatment."

Usually, "affirmative action" is a term reserved for programs that go beyond a passive acceptance of equal opportunity for all who *happen* to apply. Thus, affirmative action programs typically attempt to secure applicants from minority or disadvantaged groups. Preferential treatment policies, on the other hand, extend to members of select minority or disadvantaged groups a different sort of consideration than that extended to members of other groups. Thus, either "affirmative action" or "preferential treatment" can be applied to all of the following policies:

1. The attempt to guarantee that job openings, housing notices, etc. are advertised openly so that disadvantaged persons *could* become aware of them.

2. The requirement that advertisements be targeted for minorities.

3. The creation of remedial training or special educational programs for disadvantaged minorities.

4. Encouraging or requiring that minority applicants be chosen over others if qualifications are roughly equal.

5. Choosing a minority applicant who meets specific standards of competence even when candidates with stronger credentials are available.

6. Making minority status itself count in one's favor without making it an absolute requirement for a position (as veterans preference programs in civil service hiring count military service in one's favor).

7. Setting numerical goals or quotas for minority representation in employment or professional school admissions.

Obviously, this list is not exhaustive; there are any number of other possible policies. This list only means to emphasize the variety of programs that function under the names "affirmative action" and "preferential treatment." Of course, the reader is advised to question just what sorts of programs are at issue in each of our readings. If one is not cautious about this, one might be misled into accepting or rejecting a particular program on the basis of arguments that properly apply only to some other policy.

The arguments supporting or objecting to these policies fall into broadly identifiable types. Critical arguments usually focus either on the supposed harmful consequences of the proposed programs or upon their purported injustice. Arguments concerning potential harmful consequences often claim either that the programs lead to inefficiency because they foster the hiring of less competent workers or that policies of preference for target minorities will encourage the attitude that members of these groups are inferior and "unable to make it on their own." Note that the former consequentialist argument is not an objection to policies 1 through 4 above. A traditional response to the second consequentialist argument suggests that if, for example, blacks succeed after being given places in medical schools under preferential admissions policies, others in the society will be less able to support a belief that blacks are not appropriate candidates for the medical profession. A similar point is made in the selection by Ronald Dworkin in this chapter.

Objections to affirmative action or preferential treatment programs as unjust usually claim that they violate the rights of nonminorities. For example, many claim that in hiring decisions the most qualified candidate has a right to be given the job. Preferential treatment policies are held to violate this right of the most qualified when those with lower qualifications are chosen because of their minority status. This position argues that a just society is a meritocracy where benefits are distributed on the basis of individual qualifications. (Note again that this objection cannot serve as a criticism of the fourth policy above.)

A number of responses to this merit objection to affirmative action can be found in the articles of this chapter. Ronald Dworkin notes that the concept of "qualification" is vague. Do a person's qualifications for medical school increase if he has quick hands for surgery, or are Medical College Admissions Test scores the only relevant qualification? Could a person's black skin mean that he could be more qualified to offer medical care to a particular segment of the society? Dworkin argues that no specific set of abilities or characteristics can be identified as qualifications in the abstract; it is perfectly possible for society's changing needs to mean that an aspect of a person is a qualification for a position at one time while it may not be at another time.

Richard Wasserstrom also argues against this merit objection to preferential treatment. Wasserstrom claims that our society is currently far from a meritocracy; he can be seen as implicitly criticizing the merit argument for demanding that the merit criterion be applied only to those who are already disadvantaged. More importantly, Wasserstrom claims that many of the standard qualifications used for distributing benefits or positions are in fact things over which individuals have little control or responsibility; natural intelligence and the quality of one's secondary education are classic examples.

Wasserstrom argues that it is improper to use aspects beyond a person's control to determine who deserves the benefits of the society. If one person does not morally deserve to have greater natural intelligence than another (and surely no one *deserves* that), how can one then have a right to be given a position of greater status or wealth solely because of that intelligence?

Alan Goldman seems to disagree with Wasserstrom on this matter. Although Goldman believes that jobs are not simply property that employers can disperse as they please (he claims that society has a legitimate right to demand some constraints on hiring, i.e., by requiring equality of opportunity), he also believes that the interests of society are best served when the most qualified applicants are chosen over the lesser qualified. Goldman also contends that once society establishes a standard rule for hiring, individuals will plan their lives on the basis of that rule. If society alters its standard hiring policy and, hence, frustrates the expectations created by its traditional policy, it treats its members unfairly and unjustly. Thus, Goldman appears to believe that there are grounds for a claim that the most qualified candidate has a right to be given the job, since our society has traditionally hired on a merit basis.

In assessing the debate between Goldman and Wasserstrom over merit hiring, it will be helpful to recognize that Goldman considers questions about hiring criteria and salary scales to be separate issues. On the salary issue Goldman admits the apparent injustice of advantaging or disadvantaging people on the basis of personal characteristics over which they have little control. Thus, he implicitly allows that the distribution to the most qualified of greater benefits in the form of salary and status may not be justified. And he allows this for the very reasons that led Wasserstrom to defend preference. The reader should ask whether it is practically possible for society to restructure its salary scales while still awarding jobs on the basis of standard qualifications. If this is not possible, the reader should consider Wasserstrom's suggestion and weigh the seriousness of frustrating the expectations of the most qualified against the strength of appeals for preferential treatment based on the needs of the disadvantaged.

A second justice objection to preferential treatment programs derives from a common belief that persons have a right to be treated equally. The article by Lisa Newton provides a philosophical expression for this common objection by noting that if standard discrimination against blacks was wrong because it failed to treat them equally, then the "reverse discrimination" preference policies are also wrong. Both Wasserstrom and Dworkin respond to this objection by noting that any criterion of hiring or admission will discriminate between people on the basis of some personal characteristic (e.g., skill or intelligence). Thus, they claim that discrimination cannot be wrong in and of itself. Rather, they believe that systematic discrimination against blacks and women was wrong because of the disrespect it exhibited for members of these groups. They believe that preferential treatment, on the other hand, does not necessarily exhibit disrespect for white males. Moreover, they also claim that such programs have social advantages (eliminating serious inequalities or providing better medical care for some members of the society) which were not present in systematic discrimination against blacks and women. These articles should lead the reader to consider just what it is about traditional systematic discrimination that makes it so wrong. Does the discrimination present in preferential treatment have any of these characteristics?

Just as the arguments critical of affirmative action or preferential treatment fall into broadly identifiable categories, so too do the arguments attempting to justify those policies. Traditionally, arguments supporting some sort of preferential treatment for disadvantaged groups are either forward or backward looking in their justifications. Backward-looking arguments claim that some policy is needed to compensate victims of injustice for *past* wrongs they have suffered. Forward-looking justifications are not so concerned with providing restitution to wronged individuals. Instead they argue that affirmative action or preferential treatment programs will make for a morally better society in the long run. The article by

Ronald Dworkin provides an example of the forward-looking approach. Dworkin sees affirmative action programs as moving us toward a more ideal society where power and status are not as unevenly distributed along racial or sexual lines.

Our selections do not include an overt example of the compensatory approach. The following description, however, will allow the reader to understand the compensatory argument and the issues it raises. The classic compensatory argument holds that blacks and women deserve compensation for the unjust discrimination they have suffered in the past. Failing to compensate these groups will simply perpetuate the injustice. Hence, a policy of preferential hiring or admissions can be justified because of the demand that injustices be compensated for.

An obvious objection to this argument is that the serious injustices that deserve compensation were inflicted on blacks and women who are no longer alive. Thus, the objection would claim that preferential treatment of current blacks and women is unnecessary. In response to this objection, some would claim that current blacks and women have suffered competitive disadvantages because of the effects of the socialization process. They claim that even blacks and women who have not been actual victims of overt discrimination "get the message" from discrimination against other members of their groups that society considers them less important because of their race or sex. Since a person's self-perception is formed by his or her interactions with others, some would argue that blacks and women have lower levels of self-confidence and self-esteem than they would if society had treated their groups differently. Members of these groups, then, must work all that much harder against self-doubt if they are to overcome the competitive disadvantages they supposedly suffer through the socialization process. The compensatory argument claims that the best way to compensate these victims of an unjust socialization is to provide them with the conditions necessary for increased confidence and self-esteem. In our society, that means that blacks and women ought to be given some preference in employment decisions.

The success of this compensatory justification appears to turn on the ability to make a case for the factual claim that all blacks and women are victims of injustice. If this claim cannot be argued, then it would appear that affirmative action will often "compensate" persons who have not been victims. The reader is challenged to offer specific suggestions about how blacks and/or women could be subtly but importantly damaged because of the way society socializes its members. Perhaps some material for such suggestions can be found in the article by Claire Renzetti, who describes the relative economic circumstances of these groups. The reader is also challenged to see if similar arguments can be constructed for other groups.

A further objection to the compensatory argument for preferential treatment claims that even if certain members of the society deserve compensation for past injustices, it is unfair to impose the entire costs of that compensation on the young white males who would have received the positions had preference policies not been in effect. A possible response to this objection might be that someone will lose the position under any policy. Thus, the fact that a young white male would otherwise have received the position is no objection unless it can also be argued that he deserved the position. That would seem to suggest that the objection presupposes that standard merit criteria are the only just criteria for awarding positions. The difficulties with that position have already been outlined. Moreover, many would suggest that failure to use preferential treatment allows young white males to benefit from the unjust competitive disadvantages inflicted on blacks and women. So, some would argue that preferential treatment programs do not deny young white males anything to which they have a right; rather, these programs only remove an undeserved advantage.

This introduction shows that the acceptability of affirmative action is a complex topic. The reader needs to consider carefully the numerous issues raised here and by the articles that follow. Does affirmative action violate anyone's rights? Is it necessary for providing restitution to victims of injustice?

Does it have negative effects on society as a whole or on those it aims to benefit? Are there other means that would just as effectively move society in the direction of greater equity? Will equality of opportunity alone allow minority and disadvantaged groups to improve their relative social position? What explains the fact that women characteristically find employment in occupations of lower salary and status?

To arrive at a reasonable assessment of affirmative action policies, the reader must attempt to provide cogent answers to these questions. It might help if students would trace the themes of this introduction through the articles that follow, and if they would outline the point/counterpoint of the arguments between critics and defenders of affirmative action.

CLAIRE M. RENZETTI

One Step Forward, Two Steps Back: Women, Work and Employment Legislation

INTRODUCTION

Since the early 1960's an unprecedented volume of employment litigation on behalf of women workers has been heard by American courts. Undoubtedly, the vast majority of these suits has been brought under Title VII of the 1964 Civil Rights Act which forbids employment discrimination on the basis of sex as well as race, color, religion, or national origin.[1] In addition, the Equal Pay Act and Executive Order 11246 established further prohibitions against sex discriminatory employment practices.[2]

Given these various avenues of legal redress now open to women workers, we might expect their position in the labor force to have improved significantly relative to men. Indeed, if we accept the dire predictions of critics of this legislation, we are inevitably led to conclude that substantial numbers of essentially unqualified women are actually replacing men in all job categories, as employers scramble to avoid lawsuits and to fill minority "quotas."[3] Putting conservative hysteria aside, however, we are left with the empirical question of whether or not such statutes have proven to be effective tools in remedying the employment in-

equity historically suffered by women. The purpose of the present paper is to address this question through an analysis of recent occupational and earnings data for males and females. In so doing, the extent of sex segregation in the labor force will be discussed along with some of the weaknesses of relevant employment legislation and the prevalent stereotypes about women which continue to operate against them in the labor market.

TRENDS IN OCCUPATIONAL OPPORTUNITIES FOR WOMEN

Since 1960, the percentage of the female population sixteen years and older participating in the labor force has risen steadily from 39 percent to 51 percent in June 1980.[4] As economist Francine Blair observes:

[T]he profile of the female labor force now corresponds more closely to the total female population. . . . Thus, it is rapidly becoming more difficult to consider working women as an unrepresentative or atypical group.[5]

Nevertheless, while the percentage of female labor force participation has uniformly increased, women are still employed primarily in traditional female occupations. The data in Table 1 bear this out. We find, for example, that in 1981 men holding professional, technical, managerial, and administrative positions accounted for approximately 36 percent of all male job-holders and 73.5 percent of male white-collar workers.[6] At the same time, only 41 percent of female white-collar workers held professional, technical, managerial, and administrative occupations. While nearly 73 percent of the female work force was employed in white-collar jobs, the majority held clerical positions. In fact, clerical work remains the single largest employment category for women and accounts for 52 percent of the female white-collar labor force.[7]

Even in blue-collar work, women are still virtually excluded from the relatively high-status, high-income positions. Referring again to Table 1 we find that 21 percent of employed men in 1981 were craftsmen and kindred workers (which includes foremen and supervisors). They represented over half of all male blue-collar workers. On the other hand, little more than 2 percent of the working women in 1981 were craftsmen and kindred workers—only about 15 percent of all women holding blue-collar jobs.

Finally, we see in Table 1 that service work remains a stronghold for women workers. In 1981, nearly 13 percent of the female labor force was employed in service work and over 94 percent held service jobs in fields other than private household labor. Importantly, analyses of employment trends since 1960 show a dramatic decline in the percentage of women employed in private household or domestic labor, while female employment in other service occupations has slightly increased.[8] But before we conclude that this transition indicates significant upward mobility for women, we must bear in mind that service work encompasses such traditional female occupations as hairdresser, waitress, dental assistant, practical nurse, and nurses' aid. Moreover, as the percentage of women in private household labor has decreased, the percentage of women in clerical work has steadily increased. Thus, occupational mobility for women workers has been largely horizontal in nature—i.e., from one "pink-collar" job to another.

These data demonstrate quite convincingly that occupational segregation by sex remains a reality in today's labor market. This is not to deny, of course, that women have made progress in penetrating the male-dominated work world. But as Elizabeth Almquist observes, "The absolute occupational position of men and women has improved steadily since 1870, but men's position has improved much faster than women's since 1950."[9] Further research substantiates this argument. For instance, of the 250 occupations listed by the U.S. Bureau of the Census, half of all female job-holders are employed in only 17 whereas half of all male workers are employed in 65. One quarter of working women are employed in just five jobs—secretary-stenographer, household worker, elementary school teacher, bookkeeper, and waitress.[10] In short, claims that a large segment of the female labor force is successfully entering non-traditional jobs appear to be markedly exaggerated.

Despite the prevalence of occupational sex segregation a commonly-held sociological truism has evolved which maintains that in those jobs that men and women do share, they now receive equal pay for their equal work. However, a close examination of available data calls this assertion into question. The findings in Table 2, for example, clearly indicate that, holding age and education constant, women's mean earnings are consistently lower than those of men. Strikingly, while education correlates directly with income by determining both the type of job and the entry level of the job for which one qualifies, we find that women workers earn substantially less than their male counterparts with the same number of years of education. In fact, a woman with 5 years or more of college can expect an annual salary less than that of a man who has only graduated from high school. A woman college graduate working full-time will earn on the average less than a man with fewer than 12 years of education.

The data in Table 2 also reveal the stagnant earnings pattern of working women. Not surprisingly, older men take home considerably higher wages than young men with the same number of years of education. The differential is especially pronounced among men who have attended college. For instance, a 64-year-old man with 1–3 years of college earns about 58 percent more than a 25-year-old man in the same educational category. Men 64 years of age with 4 years of college earn almost 112 percent more than their 25-year-old counterparts and those with 5 or more years of

TABLE ONE

Occupation of Longest Job in 1981 for Year-Round Full-Time Civilian Workers, 18 Years Old and Over by Sex

Occupation of Longest Job	Male	Female
Total	100.0% (N = 41,715)*	100.0% (N = 23,312)
White-collar workers	49.1	72.9
Professional, technical, and kindred workers	18.5	20.2
Managers and administrators (exc. farm)	17.9	10.0
Sales workers	6.4	4.7
Clerical and kindred workers	6.2	38.0
Blue-collar workers	40.5	13.8
Craft and kindred workers	21.0	2.1
Operatives (exc. transport)	9.6	10.1
Transport equipment operatives	5.2	0.4
Laborers (exc. farm)	4.6	1.0
Service workers	6.8	12.7
Private household workers	**	0.7
Service workers (exc. private household)	6.8	12.0
Farm workers	3.4	0.4
Farmers and farm managers	2.4	0.2
Farm laborers and supervisors	0.8	0.2

*Percentages may not total 100 due to rounding.
**Less than 0.05%.

Source: U.S. Bureau of the Census. Current Population Reports. *Money Income of Households, Families, and Persons in the United States: 1981.* Table 52, p. 184.

college earn 71 percent more. Turning our attention to women, however, we find that 64-year-olds with 1–3 years of college have a mean annual earnings only about 14 percent higher than 25-year-olds in that educational group. Similarly, 64-year-old female college graduates and those with 5 or more years of college earn 35 percent and 34 percent more respectively than their 25-year-old educational peers. These findings lend support to an earlier Department of Labor study which concluded that:

Women aged 30 to 34 had the highest average income among women—$9,629. This amount is only slightly higher than the median figure for each age group between 25 and 69 years. However, the $17,347 peak income for men which occurred among those 45 to 49 years, was significantly greater than the income of younger men aged 25 to 29—at the beginning of their careers.[11]

Men, therefore, appear to enjoy a progressively rising lifetime earnings curve while that of women is virtually flat, "indicating that most women's jobs are dead-end, with little promotional opportunity and with few instances in which wages increase as a function of time or seniority."[12]

The data in Tables 3 and 4 further illustrate the male/female earnings gap. First, using Table 3 we can compare the average annual earnings of 25–34-year-old men and women workers in select occupations while holding educational attainment constant. Across the board, women earn less than men with the same job title and, although the

TABLE TWO

Mean Earnings in 1979 for Year-Round, Full-Time Workers 21 to 64 Years Old,
by Years of School Completed and Sex

Present Age	MALE					FEMALE				
	Less than 12 years	High School	College			Less than 12 years	High School	College		
			1 to 3 years		5 years or more			1 to 3 years		5 years or more
		4 years		4 years			4 years		4 years	
21 years	11,212	15,260	13,200	11,375		9,063	10,362	10,501	12,370	16,289
22 years	12,373	17,385	16,780	13,846	18,123	9,329	10,833	11,392	11,695	15,066
23 years	13,055	16,947	17,147	15,348	20,211	9,904	11,098	11,725	13,956	13,220
24 years	13,876	17,755	18,727	18,539	19,306	9,600	11,595	12,648	14,626	14,285
25 years	16,512	19,723	19,638	20,683	22,497	9,421	12,431	13,535	14,759	16,879
26 years	16,107	19,723	20,744	22,046	21,718	9,790	13,104	13,836	15,873	17,180
27 years	16,204	20,610	21,261	21,680	22,158	10,633	12,837	14,671	16,105	18,021
28 years	19,705	21,494	21,699	23,505	23,418	9,603	12,763	14,981	16,759	18,537
29 years	16,627	21,782	22,276	24,824	28,264	11,288	13,366	17,756	16,873	18,791
30 years	18,261	21,508	23,631	25,684	27,046	10,674	14,531	15,489	17,840	20,600
31 years	16,717	22,306	23,644	27,942	28,607	10,956	14,466	15,546	17,967	21,056
32 years	18,891	24,106	24,156	28,553	32,009	10,733	12,719	15,501	17,433	21,550
33 years	18,692	23,749	25,240	30,096	33,353	9,727	14,221	15,397	19,844	21,817
34 years	17,181	24,695	26,719	30,013	34,352	12,441	14,748	15,944	18,212	21,390
35 years	20,876	27,108	27,779	32,272	37,167	11,954	14,906	16,819	18,221	25,797
36 years	22,511	26,858	30,091	34,618	37,421	9,902	13,785	15,583	18,529	30,981
37 years	20,499	26,705	31,013	36,451	40,113	10,845	15,175	17,553	17,917	23,154
38 years	19,941	27,875	29,721	38,165	42,803	11,147	14,788	18,428	20,924	23,762
39 years	18,038	27,497	33,746	38,988	41,052	13,460	13,768	16,839	17,272	23,286
40 years	23,160	26,729	30,796	34,500	39,586	13,044	13,289	14,958	17,204	22,326
41 years	20,882	25,819	27,532	34,809	42,805	10,117	13,951	15,290	17,385	22,878
42 years	22,312	24,614	27,126	34,895	41,147	10,144	14,815	15,959	16,122	31,589
43 years	29,416	27,226	33,030	35,882	43,197	15,037	13,734	23,856	17,606	22,842

differential narrows slightly among professionals, it is nevertheless acute for both white-collar and blue-collar workers. Female computer specialists, for instance, earn on the average less than $78 for every $100 a male computer specialist earns. But the gap is widest in retail sales where women earn only $43 for every $100 earned by men.

Significantly, the data in Table 4 indicate that women's economic position in the labor market has actually worsened in recent years. Comparing male and female workers of all ages, Table 4 shows that, in general, in 1950 women earned about $65 for every $100 earned by men while in 1970—seven years after the passage of the Equal Pay Act—their median earnings dropped to 57 percent of those of men. In examining specific occupational categories, a similar picture emerges; the male/female wage gap increased in virtually every

Present Age	MALE		College			FEMALE		College		
	Less than 12 years	High School 4 years	1 to 3 years	4 years	5 years or more	Less than 12 years	High School 4 years	1 to 3 years	4 years	5 years or more
44 years	21,531	26,763	28,524	41,940	40,826	11,714	13,626	16,878	18,840	22,677
45 years	23,153	27,415	37,558	37,641	45,380	10,977	15,330	16,709	24,348	32,018
46 years	22,554	27,304	28,527	37,833	42,714	10,139	17,794	15,035	29,569	22,450
47 years	22,917	27,705	28,861	38,181	45,188	12,026	15,308	20,658	21,781	23,390
48 years	22,325	28,373	31,969	43,132	44,867	12,450	14,384	14,813	17,021	20,980
49 years	22,749	29,307	36,615	41,984	46,171	10,516	17,304	17,058	20,763	27,734
50 years	21,060	26,880	29,267	42,448	43,890	10,207	17,797	15,875	17,749	22,931
51 years	22,491	30,166	33,337	43,999	43,812	12,174	16,493	14,807	20,476	24,019
52 years	23,750	28,003	33,732	43,009	43,382	10,065	14,929	17,640	18,915	26,319
53 years	20,998	26,179	28,937	43,107	44,603	10,678	14,404	14,498	19,335	22,174
54 years	26,728	27,061	31,641	43,358	41,441	10,967	14,216	15,938	30,431	23,415
55 years	21,779	25,790	32,123	41,389	48,007	12,775	14,106	17,859	25,906	22,956
56 years	21,818	27,358	30,060	40,747	42,143	11,512	16,116	16,164	17,556	25,581
57 years	22,387	26,597	33,698	40,509	42,786	10,999	15,174	17,032	29,791	34,174
58 years	21,417	26,160	38,882	42,836	45,789	13,535	16,504	15,880	23,432	23,770
59 years	22,403	27,755	29,653	37,537	41,335	10,724	15,478	19,103	25,094	21,465
60 years	20,095	26,819	26,855	41,258	48,284	10,706	14,407	16,826	19,508	19,583
61 years	21,467	25,257	29,551	42,519	49,024	10,554	16,164	17,943	33,216	20,736
62 years	17,979	26,452	32,531	41,877	50,206	15,312	13,398	12,948	18,155	32,166
63 years	23,411	26,261	31,550	41,409	43,251	13,552	19,697	18,079	20,924	23,276
64 years	23,968	26,779	31,000	43,813	38,575	12,447	14,382	15,400	20,172	22,632

Source: U.S. Bureau of the Census. Current Population Reports, Series P-60, No. 139, *Lifetime Earnings Estimates for Men and Women in the United States: 1979*. Table B-1, p. 28.

area, except in professional work where it remained relatively stable and in farm work where it showed some improvement. It is tempting, of course, to argue that these statistics may be too dated to yield an accurate comparison of the contemporary wages of men and women, but other studies using data as recent as 1977 reach identical conclusions.[13]

The obvious question at this point is why—

why, after nearly twenty years of litigation under federal laws which bar employment discrimination, is job segregation by sex still the norm in the workplace? And why is the magnitude of the male/female wage differential larger today than it was before such legislation was passed?

The answers to these questions are many and varied. To some extent our data may be explained in terms of the steady rise in female labor force

TABLE THREE

Earnings and Occupation of Males and Females, Age 25–34 by Years of School Completed. Working 50–52 Weeks: 1970.

Occupation—Total	Male	Female	Educational Attainment	Ratio Female/Male
Professional	11,158	7,548	4 yrs. college	67.6
Computer specialists	12,918	10,045	5 yrs. college +	77.8
Teachers, college and university	10,887	8,363	5 yrs. college +	76.8
Engineering and science technicians	9,926	7,229	5 yrs. college +	72.8
Managers	12,103	8,110	4 yrs. college	67.0
Sales managers and dept. heads	10,854	8,166	4 yrs. college	75.2
School admin. (college)	11,866	8,517	5 yrs. college +	71.8
Sales workers	11,468	6,363	4 yrs. college	55.5
Salesmen and sales clerks (retail)	8,095	3,482	4 yrs. h.s.	43.0
Clerical workers	9,291	5,974	4 yrs. college	64.3
Bank tellers	6,549	4,456	4 yrs. h.s.	68.0
Bookkeepers	7,784	4,856	4 yrs. h.s.	62.4
Payroll and timekeeping clerks	8,090	5,485	4 yrs. h.s.	67.8
Craftsmen	8,927	5,589	4 yrs. h.s.	62.6
Operatives	8,122	4,521	4 yrs. h.s.	55.7
Transport operatives	8,265	5,256	4 yrs. h.s.	63.6
Laborers	7,340	4,511	4 yrs. h.s.	61.5
Farmers and managers	5,920	3,622	4 yrs. h.s.	61.2
Farm laborers	5,099	2,767	4 yrs. h.s.	54.3
Service workers	7,881	3,928	4 yrs. h.s.	49.8
Private household workers	2,739	1,795	1–3 yrs. h.s.	65.5

Source: Population Profiles, Unit #15: "Women in American Society: A Historical and Demographic Profile," Mary Ellen Reilly and Leon F. Bouvier (1976).

participation which has brought about a corresponding increase in the number of women in entry level (and hence, low-paying) positions. But this theory fails to account for the fact that unlike men, women's status and earnings do not significantly increase as a function of experience and seniority. Secondly, the inherent weaknesses in the employment laws themselves cannot be overlooked as causal factors. For example, the Equal Pay Act defines wage discrimination in limited but nonetheless complex terms, leading judges to arrive at varying interpretations of the "equal skill, effort, and responsibility" clause. As a result, the courts often hand down contradictory decisions in closely related cases.[14] At the same time, Equal Pay Act suits frequently reveal an employer's flagrant violation of Title VII, but this is generally ignored by the courts since the Act itself forbids only wage discrimination, not sex segregation.[15] Exacerbating the problem is the lack of unity among the agencies charged with enforcing the laws.[16] Thus, while it's true that both the Department of Labor and the EEOC can bring suit against the same employer and move for consolidation of the cases, this rarely occurs because of "the lack of in-depth communication between the two agencies."[17]

TABLE FOUR

Median Earnings of the Experienced Labor Force by Occupation for 50–52 Weeks Worked by Sex

	1970			1960			1950		
Occupation	*Male*	*Female*	*Female as % of Male*	*Male*	*Female*	*Female as % of Male*	*Male*	*Female*	*Female as % of Male*
Total	8,633	4,925	57.0	5,307	3,118	58.8	3,090	2,003	64.8
Professional	11,535	7,117	61.7	7,124	4,186	58.8	4,311	2,615	60.7
Managers	11,409	6,207	54.4	6,926	3,800	54.9	4,158	2,382	57.3
Sales workers	9,634	3,819	39.6	5,639	2,370	42.0	3,364	1,658	49.3
Clerical workers	8,087	5,260	65.0	5,206	3,546	68.1	3,213	2,255	70.2
Craftsmen	8,762	5,370	61.3	5,699	3,555	62.4	3,395	2,280	67.2
Operatives	7,489	4,386	58.6	4,897	2,911	59.4	2,969	1,926	64.9
Laborers	6,323	4,110	65.0	4,018	2,863	71.3	2,392	1,912	79.9
Farmers and managers	5,328	2,759	51.8	2,458	916	37.3	1,655	854	51.6
Farm laborers	3,833	2,651	69.2	1,919	821	42.8	1,129	474	42.0
Service workers	6,582	3,695	56.1	4,012	2,102	52.4	2,502	1,445	57.8
Private household workers	3,534	1,635	46.3	2,075	922	44.4	1,505	799	53.1

Source: Population Profiles, Unit #15: "Women in American Society: A Historical and Demographic Profile," Mary Ellen Reilly and Leon F. Bouvier (1976).

Prevalent stereotypes about women in general, and working women in particular, also help to preserve sex-based employment discrimination. Common among them are the assumptions that a woman's primary commitment is to her family rather than to her career, and that a woman is naturally suited for certain kinds of jobs but not others because of her unique physical constitution, temperament, or some other sex-linked trait. These attitudes, in turn, generate other prejudices: (1) that women workers have higher rates of turnover and absenteeism because of their family responsibilities; (2) that women work for extra spending money or out of boredom and, therefore, have low career aspirations and low productivity; and (3) that repetitive, tedious tasks which require manual dexterity but little physical strength are especially appropriate for women.

That there is no empirical evidence to support these beliefs does not make them any less powerful, for what is important here is that they are widely held and that people use them to guide their actions.[18] In the workplace this translates into hiring practices which channel women away from positions requiring continuity, geographical mobility, participation in extensive job-training programs, long overtime hours, or complex technical skills. The job evaluation systems typically used by employers to set wage rates for specific occupations also have built-in biases which consistently result in positions identified as "women's work" being undervalued.[19] And once large numbers of women are employed in a previously male-dominated position, the job itself is considered "feminized" and tends to become characteristically low-paying, low-status, and dead-end.[20]

But women confront these prejudices even before they look for employment. As a recent study by the American Association of Colleges (AAC) concluded, sexism in our educational institutions often leads women to lower both their academic and their career aspirations. According to the AAC:

In college classes . . . men are called on more frequently and get more credit for the ideas they express. . . . Professors interrupt women more frequently, are less likely to encourage them to participate in discussions and rarely make eye contact with women students. Women also tend to miss out on informal contact with faculty members, which dims their chances for personal recommendations and teaching assistantships. . . .[21]

In light of these findings it should come as no surprise that the Department of Labor reports that, although there has been a tremendous increase in the number of female degree-earners, women college grads are still "more likely to be found in clerical positions and less likely to hold managerial posts than are their men counterparts."[22] Perhaps what is more startling is that women have made modest gains for themselves despite the many barriers.

CONCLUSION

Our discussion thus far has not presented recent employment legislation in a very favorable light, but the changes it has effected should not be minimalized. Under the Equal Pay Act, for instance, the courts have ruled that men and women performing substantially equal work deserve equal pay regardless of their job titles, thereby undermining the common practice of assigning different titles to virtually identical jobs carried out by men and women in order to justify their differential pay.[23] In addition, Title VII has been instrumental in striking down discriminatory pre-employment selection tests, restrictive state employment laws such as those prohibiting women from working at night, double standards of employment such as policies requiring only female employees to remain single, and the "old boy networks" fostered by word-of-mouth recruiting.[24]

Clearly these laws have made visible dents in many of the discriminatory traditions of the patriarchal work world, but the system itself is far from collapse. To the contrary, it is currently being buoyed by the deregulatory zeal and anti-feminism of the White House.[25] While President Reagan promises to slash federal spending and cut bureaucratic red tape, many of his policies will likely weaken the legislation most important to women workers. The Department of Labor has already taken the initiative in this regard by announcing its plans for a wholesale revision of

Affirmative Action regulations. The Department's proposal eliminates certain penalties and reporting requirements, and relies chiefly on voluntary rather than legal action to encourage the hiring of women and minorities.[26] This program essentially leaves federal contractors free to police themselves, but given their long history of sex discrimination it is rather doubtful that they will now make a concerted effort toward equality on their own. What is more significant, however, is that Labor's actions represent just one aspect of the government's general retreat from women's rights, signaling that the hard-won victories of the 1960's and 70's could soon be replaced by the setbacks of the 1980's.

NOTES

1. Title VII does allow employment decisions based on sex, religion, or national origin (but not race) in situations where it can be demonstrated that any of these factors is a bona fide occupational qualification (BFOQ). Consequently the BFOQ remains the chief defense of employers charged with discrimination under Title VII. See Barbara Allen Babcock, Ann E. Freedman, Eleanor Holmes Norton, and Susan C. Ross, *Sex Discrimination and the Law: Causes and Remedies*, (Boston: Little, Brown and Co., 1975), pp. 229–246.

2. The Equal Pay Act of 1963 makes it illegal for an employer to pay employees of one sex lower wages than employees of the opposite sex when both men and women perform jobs which require equal skill, effort, and responsibility, and are carried out under similar working conditions. However, if the differential payment is based on a seniority system, a merit system, a system which measures earnings by quantity or quality of production, or any additional factors other than sex, it is permissible under the Equal Pay Act. In contrast, Executive Order 11246 applies only to employers who hold contracts with the federal government. But in addition to prohibiting employment discrimination, it also requires such employers to take affirmative action to ensure the recruitment and hiring of minority job applicants. The significance of Executive Order 11246 lies in the fact that it covers about one third of the work force including most individuals employed by schools and universities. See Babcock, et al., op. cit., pp. 440–559.

3. For an excellent discussion of the affirmative action controversy, see J. Stanley Pottinger, "Race, Sex, and Jobs: The Drive Toward Equality," *Change Magazine* 4 (October, 1972), pp. 24, 26–29.

4. United States Department of Labor, Bureau of Labor Statistics, *Perspectives on Working Women: A Databook*,

(Washington, D.C.: U.S. Government Printing Office, 1980), p. 3.

5. Francine D. Blau, "The Data on Women Workers: Past, Present, and Future," in *Women Working*, ed. A. H. Stromberg and K. Harkness, (Palo Alto, CA: Mayfield Publishing Co., 1978), pp. 37–38.

6. The percentage of major occupational category is calculated by the percentage of the total labor force in the specific sub-category divided by the percentage of the total labor force in the major occupational category. For instance, the percentage of male white-collar workers who hold professional, technical, managerial, and administrative positions is calculated by dividing the percentage of the total male labor force in these occupational sub-categories (36 percent) by the percentage of the total male labor force in the major occupational category of white-collar workers (49 percent). In 1981, therefore, the percentage of male white-collar workers holding professional, technical, managerial, and administrative jobs was about 73.5 percent.

7. Only 2 percent of all secretaries are male and, while there have emerged a number of "super-secretaries" employed by the presidents of major corporations and earning a salary upward of $25,000 a year, they constitute a minority of America's 2.5 million secretaries as well. The current average annual secretarial wage is $12,000; some secretaries earn as little as $8,000 and, regardless of salary, the job carries with it little prestige even for the "super-secretaries." Nevertheless, U.S. labor forecasters predict that 250,000 new secretarial positions will be available each year through 1985 and that they will be filled almost exclusively by women. See Lee May, "Cream of the Secretarial Crop and Some Still Bring the Coffee," *Philadelphia Inquirer*, (December 6, 1981), p. 3-H.

8. See, for example, Claire M. Renzetti and Daniel J. Curran, "Women, Crime, and Gender Roles: A Critical Reappraisal," paper presented at the Annual Meetings of the American Society of Criminology, Washington, D.C., 1981.

9. Elizabeth M. Almquist, "Women in the Labor Force," *Signs* 3 (Summer 1977), p. 847.

10. Ruth G. Blumrosen, "Wage Discrimination, Job Segregation and Women Workers," *Women's Rights Law Reporter* 6 (Fall/Winter 1979–80), p. 23; Blau, op. cit., 43–44.

11. United States Department of Labor, Office of the Secretary, Women's Bureau, *The Earnings Gap Between Women and Men*, (Washington, D.C.: U.S. Government Printing Office, 1979), p. 5.

12. Blumrosen, op. cit., p. 25.

13. See, for example, United States Department of Labor, Office of the Secretary, Women's Bureau, op. cit., p. 1. Here it is argued that women must work "nearly 9 days to gross the same earnings men grossed in 5 days." See, too, "Women Paid Less for Comparable Work, Says Federal Study," *Equal Opportunity in Higher Education* 7

(September 7, 1981), p. 6; "Women Doctorate Holders Lag Behind Male Peers," *Equal Opportunity in Higher Education* 7 (October 5, 1981), p. 9; and Blumrosen, op. cit.

14. Compare, for instance, *Hodgson v. Brookhaven General Hospital,* 426F.2d 719(5thCir.1970), *on remand,* 65L.C. 32,520(N.D.Tex.1971) with *Hodgson v. Good Shepherd Hospital,* 327F.Supp.143(E.D.Tex.1971); and *Brennan v. Goose Creek School District,* 519F.2d53 (5thCir.1975) with *Walker v. Columbia University,* 407F.Supp.1370(S.D.N.Y.1976).

15. According to Babcock, et al., op. cit., p. 507, "unthinking equal pay courts . . . have even established legal standards which might encourage companies to violate Title VII by sex segregating workers."

16. Equal Pay Act suits are brought by the Department of Labor and Title VII suits are brought by the Equal Employment Opportunity Commission (EEOC). The Office of Federal Contract Compliance has the responsibility of enforcing Executive Order 11246.

17. Babcock, et al., op. cit., p. 448.

18. For a discussion of research debunking the myths about women workers, see Babcock, et al., op. cit., pp. 192–202, and pp. 205–213.

19. For a thorough analysis of the relationship between sex discrimination and job evaluation systems, see Blumrosen, op. cit., pp. 30–39. See also Norma Briggs, "Guess Who Has the Most Complex Job?" in Babcock, et al., op. cit., pp. 203–205.

20. Blumrosen, op. cit., pp. 22–25.

21. "College Classroom 'Chilly' for Women, Study Says," *Equal Opportunity in Higher Education* (January 25, 1982), pp. 5–6. A number of early psychological studies reached the similar conclusion that both men and women devalue the same work when it is attributed to a woman rather than a man. See especially the now-classic studies by Sandra Bem and Daryl Bem, "Case Study of a Nonconscious Ideology: Training the Woman to Know Her Place" in *Female Psychology: The Emerging Self*, ed. Sue Cox, (Chicago: Science Research Associates, 1976), pp. 180–190; and Philip Goldberg, "Are Women Prejudiced Against Women?" in *Toward a Sociology of Women*, ed. C. Safilios-Rothschild, (Lexington, MA: Xerox College Publishing, 1972), pp. 10–13.

22. "Men, Women Graduates Go Separate Ways, Labor Study Shows," *Equal Opportunity in Higher Education* 7 (February 9, 1981), p. 7; and "Women Earning More Degrees Than Ever," *Equal Opportunity in Higher Education* 7 (June 1, 1981), p. 10.

23. *Schultz v. Wheaton Glass Co.*, 412F.2d259 (3dCir.1970), *cert. denied*, 398 U.S. 905.

24. For an extensive examination of relevant cases, see Babcock, et al., op. cit., pp. 229–559; and Wendy Williams, *Babcock, Freedman, Norton, Ross' Sex Discrimination and the Law 1978 Supplement*, (Boston: Little, Brown and Co., 1978), pp. 77–172.

25. Many observers maintain that the present federal administration is blatantly anti-woman. As an example, they point not only to Reagan's budget-cutting, but also to his unquestioning acceptance of George Gilder's economic philosophy. Gilder's recent book, *Wealth and Poverty*, which Reagan has recommended to his cabinet, blames working women for most of the country's present economic problems, denounces equal pay for equal work, and states that there is no such thing as an intelli-

gent feminist. See Aaron Epstein, "Civil Rights Advocates Fear Reagan is Retreating," *Philadelphia Inquirer* (September 27, 1981), pp. 1–H and 5–H; and Vera Glaser, "Feminists Fear a White-House Anti-Woman Bias," *Philadelphia Inquirer* (May 24, 1981), p. 3-E.

26. "Administration Dispute Over Affirmative Action Rules Nears Resolution," *Equal Opportunity In Higher Education* 9 (June 13, 1983), p. 5.

LISA H. NEWTON

Reverse Discrimination as Unjustified

I have heard it argued that "simple justice" requires that we favor women and blacks in employment and educational opportunities, since women and blacks were "unjustly" excluded from such opportunities for so many years in the not so distant past. It is a strange argument, an example of a possible implication of a true proposition advanced to dispute the proposition itself, like an octopus absent-mindedly slicing off his head with a stray tentacle. A fatal confusion underlies this argument, a confusion fundamentally relevant to our understanding of the notion of the rule of law.

Two senses of justice and equality are involved in this confusion. The root notion of justice, progenitor of the other, is the one that Aristotle (*Nichomachean Ethics* 5.6; *Politics* 1.2; 3.1) assumes to be the foundation and proper virtue of the political association. It is the condition which free men establish among themselves when they "share a common life in order that their association bring them self-sufficiency"—the regulation of their relationship by law, and the establishment, by law, of equality before the law. Rule of law is the name and pattern of this justice; its equality stands against the inequalities—of wealth, talent, etc.— otherwise obtaining among its participants, who by virtue of that equality are called "citizens." It is an achievement—complete, or, more frequently, partial—of certain people in certain concrete situations. It is fragile and easily disrupted by

powerful individuals who discover that the blind equality of rule of law is inconvenient for their interests. Despite its obvious instability, Aristotle assumed that the establishment of justice in this sense, the creation of citizenship, was a permanent possibility for men and that the resultant association of citizens was the natural home of the species. At levels below the political association, this rule-governed equality is easily found; it is exemplified by any group of children agreeing together to play a game. At the level of the political association, the attainment of this justice is more difficult, simply because the stakes are so much higher for each participant. The equality of citizenship is not something that happens of its own accord, and without the expenditure of a fair amount of effort it will collapse into the rule of a powerful few over an apathetic many. But at least it has been achieved, at some times in some places; it is always worth trying to achieve, and eminently worth trying to maintain, wherever and to whatever degree it has been brought into being.

Aristotle's parochialism is notorious; he really did not imagine that persons other than Greeks could associate freely in justice, and the only form of association he had in mind was the Greek *polis*. With the decline of the *polis* and the shift in the center of political thought, his notion of justice underwent a sea change. To be exact, it ceased to represent a political type and became a moral

From *Ethics*, 83:4, (July 1973), pp. 308–312. Reprinted by permission of The University of Chicago Press. A version of this paper was read at a meeting of the Society for Women in Philosophy in Amherst, Massachusetts, November 5, 1972.

ideal: the ideal of equality as we know it. This ideal demands that all men be included in citizenship— that one Law govern all equally, that all men regard all other men as fellow citizens, with the same guarantees, rights, and protections. Briefly, it demands that the circle of citizenship achieved by any group be extended to include the entire human race. Properly understood, its effect on our associations can be excellent: it congratulates us on our achievement of rule of law as a process of government but refuses to let us remain complacent until we have expanded the associations to include others within the ambit of the rules, as often and as far as possible. While one man is a slave, none of us may feel truly free. We are constantly prodded by this ideal to look for possible unjustifiable discrimination, for inequalities not absolutely required for the functioning of the society and advantageous to all. And after twenty centuries of pressure, not at all constant, from this ideal, it might be said that some progress has been made. To take the cases in point for this problem, we are now prepared to assert, as Aristotle would never have been, the equality of sexes and of persons of different colors. The ambit of American citizenship, once restricted to white males of property, has been extended to include all adult free men, then all adult males including ex-slaves, then all women. The process of acquisition of full citizenship was for these groups a sporadic trail of half-measures, even now not complete; the steps on the road to full equality are marked by legislation and judicial decisions which are only recently concluded and still often not enforced. But the fact that we can now discuss the possibility of favoring such groups in hiring shows that over the area that concerns us, at least, full equality is presupposed as a basis for discussion. To that extent, they are full citizens, fully protected by the law of the land.

It is important for my argument that the moral ideal of equality be recognized as logically distinct from the condition (or virtue) of justice in the political sense. Justice in this sense exists *among* a citizenry, irrespective of the number of the populace included in that citizenry. Further, the moral ideal is parasitic upon the political virtue, for "equality" is unspecified—it means nothing until we are told in what respect that equality is to be realized. In a political context, "equality" is specified as "equal rights"—equal access to the public

realm, public goods and offices, equal treatment under the law—in brief, the equality of citizenship. If citizenship is not a possibility, political equality is unintelligible. The ideal emerges as a generalization of the real condition and refers back to that condition for its content.

Now, if justice (Aristotle's justice in the political sense) is equal treatment under law for all citizens, what is injustice? Clearly, injustice is the violation of that equality, discriminating for or against a group of citizens, favoring them with special immunities and privileges or depriving them of those guaranteed to the others. When the southern employer refuses to hire blacks in white-collar jobs, when Wall Street will only hire women as secretaries with new titles, when Mississippi high schools routinely flunk all black boys above ninth grade, we have examples of injustice, and we work to restore the equality of the public realm by ensuring that equal opportunity will be provided in such cases in the future. But of course, when the employers and the schools *favor* women and blacks, the same injustice is done. Just as the previous discrimination did, this reverse discrimination violates the public equality which defines citizenship and destroys the rule of law for the areas in which these favors are granted. To the extent that we adopt a program of discrimination, reverse or otherwise, justice in the political sense is destroyed, and none of us, specifically affected or not, is a citizen, a bearer of rights—we are all petitioners for favors. And to the same extent, the ideal of equality is undermined, for it has content only where justice obtains, and by destroying justice we render the ideal meaningless. It is, then, an ironic paradox, if not a contradiction in terms, to assert that the ideal of equality justifies the violation of justice; it is as if one should argue, with William Buckley, that an ideal of humanity can justify the destruction of the human race.

Logically, the conclusion is simple enough: all discrimination is wrong prima facie because it violates justice, and that goes for reverse discrimination too. No violation of justice among the citizens may be justified (may overcome the prima facie objection) by appeal to the ideal of equality, for that ideal is logically dependent upon the notion of justice. Reverse discrimination, then, which attempts no other justification than an appeal to equality, is wrong. But let us try to make the conclusion more plausible by suggesting some of the implications of the suggested practice of reverse discrimination in employment and education. My argument will be that the problems raised there are insoluble, not only in practice but in principle.

We may argue, if we like, about what "discrimination" consists of. Do I discriminate against blacks if I admit none to my school when none of the black applicants are qualified by the tests I always give? How far must I go to root out cultural bias from my application forms and tests before I can say that I have not discriminated against those of different cultures? Can I assume that women are not strong enough to be roughnecks on my oil rigs, or must I test them individually? But this controversy, the most popular and well-argued aspect of the issue, is not as fatal as two others which cannot be avoided: if we are regarding the blacks as a "minority" victimized by discrimination, what is a "minority"? And for any group—blacks, women, whatever—that has been discriminated against, what amount of reverse discrimination wipes out the initial discrimination? Let us grant as true that women and blacks were discriminated against, even where laws forbade such discrimination, and grant for the sake or argument that a history of discrimination must be wiped out by reverse discrimination. What follows?

First, are there other groups which have been discriminated against? For they should have the same right of restitution. What about American Indians, Chicanos, Appalachian Mountain whites, Puerto Ricans, Jews, Cajuns, and Orientals? And if these are to be included, the principle according to which we specify a "minority" is simply the criterion of "ethnic (sub) group," and we're stuck with every hyphenated American in the lower-middle class clamoring for special privileges for *his* group—and with equal justification. For be it noted, when we run down the Harvard roster, we find not only a scarcity of blacks (in comparison with the proportion in the population) but an even more striking scarcity of those second-, third-, and fourth-generation ethnics who make up the loudest voice of Middle America. Shouldn't they demand *their* share? And eventually, the WASPs will have to form their own lobby, for they too are a minority. The point is simply this: there is no "majority" in America who will not mind giving up just a bit of their rights to make room for a favored

minority. There are only other minorities, each of which is discriminated against by the favoring. The initial injustice is then repeated dozens of times, and if each minority is granted the same right of restitution as the others, an entire area of rule governance is dissolved into a pushing and shoving match between self-interested groups. Each works to catch the public eye and political popularity by whatever means of advertising and power politics lend themselves to the effort, to capitalize as much as possible on temporary popularity until the restless mob picks another group to feel sorry for. Hardly an edifying spectacle, and in the long run no one can benefit: the pie is no larger—it's just that instead of setting up and enforcing rules for getting a piece, we've turned the contest into a free-for-all, requiring much more effort for no larger a reward. It would be in the interests of all the participants to reestablish an objective rule to govern the process, carefully enforced and the same for all.

Second, supposing that we do manage to agree in general that women and blacks (and all the others) have some right of restitution, some right to a privileged place in the structure of opportunities for a while, how will we know when that while is up? How much privilege is enough? When will the guilt be gone, the price paid, the balance restored? What recompense is right for centuries of exclusion? What criterion tells us when we are done? Our experience with the Civil Rights movement shows us that agreement on these terms cannot be presupposed: a process that appears to some to be going at a mad gallop into a black takeover appears to the rest of us to be at a standstill. Should a practice of reverse discrimination be adopted, we may safely predict that just as some of us begin to see "a satisfactory start toward righting the balance," others of us will see that we "have already gone too far in the other direction" and will suggest that the discrimination ought to be reversed again. And such disagreement is inevitable, for the point is that we could not *possibly* have any criteria for evaluating the kind of recompense we have in mind. The context presumed by any discussion of restitution is the context of rule of law: law sets the rights of men and simultaneously sets the method for remedying the violation of those rights. You may exact suffering from others and/or damage payments for yourself if and only if the others have violated your rights; the suffering you have endured is not sufficient reason for them to suffer. And remedial rights exist only where there is law: primary human rights are useful guides to legislation but cannot stand as reasons for awarding remedies for injuries sustained. But then, the context presupposed by any discussion of restitution is the context of preexistent full citizenship. No remedial rights could exist for the excluded; neither in law nor in logic does there exist a right to *sue* for a standing to sue.

From these two considerations, then, the difficulties with reverse discrimination become evident. Restitution for a disadvantaged group whose rights under the law have been violated is possible by legal means, but restitution for a disadvantaged group whose grievance is that there was no law to protect them simply is not. First, outside of the area of justice defined by the law, no sense can be made of "the group's rights," for no law recognizes that group or the individuals in it, qua members, as bearers of rights (hence *any* group can constitute itself as a disadvantaged minority in some sense and demand similar restitution). Second, outside of the area of protection of law, no sense can be made of the violation of rights (hence the amount of the recompense cannot be decided by any objective criterion). For both reasons, the practice of reverse discrimination undermines the foundation of the very ideal in whose name it is advocated; it destroys justice, law, equality, and citizenship itself, and replaces them with power struggles and popularity contests.

RONALD DWORKIN

The Rights of Allan Bakke

On October 12, 1977 the Supreme Court heard oral argument in the case of *The Regents of the University of California v. Allan Bakke*. No lawsuit has ever been more widely watched or more thoroughly debated in the national and international press before the Court's decision. Still, some of the most pertinent facts set before the Court have not been clearly summarized.

The medical school of the University of California at Davis has an affirmative action program (called the "task force program") designed to admit more black and other minority students. It sets sixteen places aside for which only members of "educationally and economically disadvantaged minorities" compete. Allan Bakke, white, applied for one of the remaining eighty-four places; he was rejected but, since his test scores were relatively high, the medical school has conceded that it could not prove that he would have been rejected if the sixteen places reserved had been open to him. Bakke sued, arguing that the task force program deprived him of his constitutional rights. The California Supreme Court agreed, and ordered the medical school to admit him. The university appealed to the Supreme Court.

The Davis program for minorities is in certain respects more forthright (some would say cruder) than similar plans now in force in many other American universities and professional schools. Such programs aim to increase the enrollment of black and other minority students by allowing the fact of their race to count affirmatively as part of the case for admitting them. Some schools set a "target" of a particular number of minority places instead of setting aside a flat number of places. But Davis would not fill the number of places set aside unless there were sixteen minority candidates it considered clearly qualified for medical education. The difference is therefore one of administrative strategy and not of principle.

So the constitutional question raised by *Bakke* is of capital importance for higher education in America, and a large number of universities and schools have entered briefs *amicus curiae* urging the Court to reverse the California decision. They believe that if the decision is affirmed then they will no longer be free to use explicit racial criteria in any part of their admissions programs, and that they will therefore be unable to fulfill what they take to be their responsibilities to the nation.

It is often said that affirmative action programs aim to achieve a racially conscious society divided into racial and ethnic groups, each entitled, as a group, to some proportionable share of resources, careers, or opportunities. That is a perverse description. American society is currently a racially conscious society; this is the inevitable and evident consequence of a history of slavery, repression, and prejudice. Black men and women, boys and girls, are not free to choose for themselves in what roles—or as members of which social groups—others will characterize them. They are black, and no other feature of personality or allegiance or ambition will so thoroughly influence how they will be perceived and treated by others, and the range and character of the lives that will be open to them.

The tiny number of black doctors and professionals is both a consequence and a continuing cause of American racial consciousness, one link in a long and self-fueling chain reaction. Affirmative action programs use racially explicit criteria because their immediate goal is to increase the number of members of certain races in these professions. But their long-term goal is to *reduce* the degree to which American society is overall a racially conscious society.

The programs rest on two judgments. The first is a judgment of social theory: that America will continue to be pervaded by racial divisions as long as the most lucrative, satisfying, and important careers remain mainly the prerogative of members of the white race, while others feel themselves systematically excluded from a professional and social elite. The second is a calculation of strategy: that increasing the number of blacks who are at work in the professions will, in the long run, reduce the sense of frustration and injustice and racial self-consciousness in the black community to the point at which blacks may begin to think of themselves as individuals who can succeed like others through talent and initiative. At that future point the consequences of nonracial admissions programs, whatever these consequences might be,

could be accepted with no sense of racial barriers or injustice.

It is therefore the worst possible misunderstanding to suppose that affirmative action programs are designed to produce a balkanized America, divided into racial and ethnic subnations. They use strong measures because weaker ones will fail; but their ultimate goal is to lessen not to increase the importance of race in American social and professional life.

According to the 1970 census, only 2.1 percent of US doctors were black. Affirmative action programs aim to provide more black doctors to serve black patients. This is not because it is desirable that blacks treat blacks and whites treat whites, but because blacks, for no fault of their own, are now unlikely to be well served by whites, and because a failure to provide the doctors they trust will exacerbate rather than reduce the resentment that now leads them to trust only their own. Affirmative action tries to provide more blacks as classmates for white doctors, not because it is desirable that a medical school class reflect the racial makeup of the community as a whole, but because professional association between blacks and whites will decrease the degree to which whites think of blacks as a race rather than as people, and thus the degree to which blacks think of themselves that way. It tries to provide "role models" for future black doctors, not because it is desirable for a black boy or girl to find adult models only among blacks, but because our history has made them so conscious of their race that the success of whites, for now, is likely to mean little or nothing for them.

The history of the campaign against racial injustice since 1954, when the Supreme Court decided *Brown v. Board of Education,* is a history in large part of failure. We have not succeeded in reforming the racial consciousness of our society by racially neutral means. We are therefore obliged to look upon the arguments for affirmative action with sympathy and an open mind. Of course, if Bakke is right that such programs, no matter how effective they may be, violate his constitutional rights then they cannot be permitted to continue. But we must not forbid them in the name of some mindless maxim, like the maxim that it cannot be right to fight fire with fire, or that the end cannot justify the means. If the strategic claims for affirmative action are cogent, they cannot be dismissed simply on the ground that racially explicit tests are distasteful. If such tests are distasteful it can only be for reasons that make the underlying social realities the programs attack more distasteful still.

The New Republic, in a recent editorial opposing affirmative action, missed that point. "It is critical to the success of a liberal pluralism," it said, "that group membership itself is not among the permissible criteria of inclusion and exclusion." But group membership is in fact, as a matter of social reality rather than formal admission standards, part of what determines inclusion or exclusion for us now. If we must choose between a society that is in fact liberal and an illiberal society that scrupulously avoids formal racial criteria, we can hardly appeal to the ideals of liberal pluralism to prefer the latter.

Professor Archibald Cox of Harvard Law School, speaking for the University of California in oral argument, told the Supreme Court that this is the choice the United States must make. As things stand, he said, affirmative action programs are the only effective means of increasing the absurdly small number of black doctors. The California Supreme Court, in approving Bakke's claim, had urged the university to pursue that goal by methods that do not explicitly take race into account. But that is unrealistic. We must distinguish, as Cox said, between two interpretations of what the California court's recommendation means. It might mean that the university should aim at the same immediate goal, of increasing the proportion of black and other minority students in the medical school, by an admissions procedure that on the surface is not racially conscious.

That is a recommendation of hypocrisy. If those who administer the admissions standards, however these are phrased, understand that their immediate goal is to increase the number of blacks in the school, then they will use race as a criterion in making the various subjective judgments the explicit criteria will require, because that will be, given the goal, the only right way to make those judgments. The recommendation might mean, on the other hand, that the school should adopt some nonracially conscious goal, like increasing the number of disadvantaged students of all races, and then hope that that goal will produce an increase in the number of blacks as a by-product. But even if that strategy is less hypocritical (which is far from

plain), it will almost certainly fail because no different goal, scrupulously administered in a nonracially conscious way, will in fact significantly increase the number of black medical students.

Cox offered powerful evidence for that conclusion, and it is supported by the recent and comprehensive report of the Carnegie Council on Policy Studies in Higher Education. Suppose, for example, that the medical school sets aside separate places for applicants "disadvantaged" on some racially neutral test, like poverty, allowing only those disadvantaged in that way to compete for these places. If the school selects these from that group who scored best on standard medical school aptitude tests, then it will take almost no blacks, because blacks score relatively low even among the economically disadvantaged. But if the school chooses among the disadvantaged on some basis other than test scores, just so that more blacks will succeed, then it will not be administering the special procedure in a nonracially conscious way.

So Cox was able to put his case in the form of two simple propositions. A racially conscious test for admission, even one that sets aside certain places for qualified minority applicants exclusively, serves goals that are in themselves unobjectionable and even urgent. Such programs are, moreover, the only means that offer any significant promise of achieving these goals. If these programs are halted, then no more than a trickle of black students will enter medical or other professional schools for another generation at least.

If these propositions are sound, then on what ground can it be thought that such programs are either wrong or unconstitutional? We must notice an important distinction between two different sorts of objections that might be made. These programs are intended, as I said, to decrease the importance of race in the United States in the long run. It may be objected, first, that the programs will in fact harm that goal more than they will advance it. There is no way now to prove that that is so. Cox conceded, in his argument, that there are costs and risks in these programs.

Affirmative action programs seem to encourage, for example, a popular misunderstanding, which is that they assume that racial or ethnic groups are entitled to proportionate shares of opportunities, so that Italian or Polish ethnic minorities are, in theory, as entitled to their proportionate shares as blacks or Chicanos or American Indians are entitled to the shares the present programs give them. That is a plain mistake: the programs are not based on the idea that those who are aided are entitled to aid, but only on the strategic hypothesis that helping them is now an effective way of attacking a national problem. Some medical schools may well make that judgment, under certain circumstances, about a white ethnic minority. Indeed it seems likely that some medical schools are even now attempting to help white Appalachian applicants, for example, under programs of regional distribution.

So the popular understanding is wrong, but so long as it persists it is a cost of the program because the attitudes it encourages tend to a degree to make people more rather than less conscious of race. There are other possible costs. It is said, for example, that some blacks find affirmative action degrading; they find that it makes them more rather than less conscious of prejudice against their race as such. This attitude is also based on a misperception, I think, but for a small minority of blacks at least it is a genuine cost.

In the view of the many important universities who have such programs, however, the gains will very probably exceed the losses in reducing racial consciousness over-all. This view is hardly so implausible that it is wrong for these universities to seek to acquire the experience that will allow us to judge whether they are right. It would be particularly silly to forbid these experiments if we know that the failure to try will mean, as the evidence shows, that the status quo will almost certainly continue. In any case, this first objection could provide no argument that would justify a decision by the Supreme Court holding the programs unconstitutional. The Court has no business substituting its speculative judgment about the probable consequences of educational policies for the judgment of professional educators.

So the acknowledged uncertainties about the long-term results of such programs could not justify a Supreme Court decision making them illegal. But there is a second and very different form of objection. It may be argued that even if the programs *are* effective in making our society less a society dominated by race, they are nevertheless unconstitutional because they violate the individual constitutional rights of those, like Allan

Bakke, who lose places in consequence. In the oral argument Reynold H. Colvin of San Francisco, who is Bakke's lawyer, made plain that his objection takes this second form. Mr. Justice White asked him whether he accepted that the goals affirmative action programs seek are important goals. Mr. Colvin acknowledged that they were. Suppose, Justice White continued, that affirmative action programs are, as Cox had argued, the only effective means of seeking such goals. Would Mr. Colvin nevertheless maintain that the programs are unconstitutional? Yes, he insisted, they would be, because his client has a constitutional right that the programs be abandoned, no matter what the consequences.

Mr. Colvin was wise to put his objections on this second ground; he was wise to claim that his client has rights that do not depend on any judgment about the likely consequences of affirmative action for society as a whole, because if he makes out that claim then the Court must give him the relief he seeks.

But can he be right? If Allan Bakke has a constitutional right so important that the urgent goals of affirmative action must yield, then this must be because affirmative action violates some fundamental principle of political morality. This is not a case in which what might be called formal or technical law requires a decision one way or the other. There is no language in the Constitution whose plain meaning forbids affirmative action. Only the most naïve theories of statutory construction could argue that such a result is required by the language of any earlier Supreme Court decision or of the Civil Rights Act of 1964 or of any other congressional enactment. If Mr. Colvin is right it must be because Allan Bakke has not simply some technical legal right but an important moral right as well.

What could that right be? The popular argument frequently made on editorial pages is that Bakke has a right to be judged on his merit. Or that he has a right to be judged as an individual rather than as a member of a social group. Or that he has a right, as much as any black man, not to be sacrificed or excluded from any opportunity because of his race alone. But these catch phrases are deceptive here, because, as reflection demonstrates, the only genuine principle they describe is the principle that no one should suffer from the prejudice or contempt of others. And that principle is not at stake in this case at all. In spite of popular opinion, the idea that the *Bakke* case presents a conflict between a desirable social goal and important individual rights is a piece of intellectual confusion.

Consider, for example, the claim that individuals applying for places in medical school should be judged on merit, and merit alone. If that slogan means that admissions committees should take nothing into account but scores on some particular intelligence test, then it is arbitrary and, in any case, contradicted by the long-standing practice of every medical school. If it means, on the other hand, that a medical school should choose candidates that it supposes will make the most useful doctors, then everything turns on the judgment of what factors make different doctors useful. The Davis medical school assigned to each regular applicant, as well as to each minority applicant, what it called a "benchmark score." This reflected not only the results of aptitude tests and college grade averages, but a subjective evaluation of the applicant's chances of functioning as an effective doctor, in view of society's present needs for medical service. Presumably the qualities deemed important were different from the qualities that a law school or engineering school or business school would seek, just as the intelligence tests a medical school might use would be different from the tests these other schools would find appropriate.

There is no combination of abilities and skills and traits that constitutes "merit" in the abstract; if quick hands count as "merit" in the case of a prospective surgeon, this is because quick hands will enable him to serve the public better and for no other reason. If a black skin will, as a matter of regrettable fact, enable another doctor to do a different medical job better, then that black skin is by the same token "merit" as well. That argument may strike some as dangerous; but only because they confuse its conclusion—that black skin may be a socially useful trait in particular circumstances—with the very different and despicable idea that one race may be inherently more worthy than another.

Consider the second of the catch phrases I have mentioned. It is said that Bakke has a right to be judged as an "individual," in deciding whether he is to be admitted to medical school and thus to the medical profession, and not as a member of some group that is being judged as a whole. What can that mean? Any admissions procedure must rely on generalizations about groups that are justified only statistically. The regular admissions process at Davis, for example, set a cutoff figure for college grade-point averages. Applicants whose averages fell below that figure were not invited to any interview, and therefore rejected out of hand.

An applicant whose average fell one point below the cutoff might well have had personal qualities of dedication or sympathy that would have been revealed at an interview, and that would have made him or her a better doctor than some applicant whose average rose one point above the line. But the former is excluded from the process on the basis of a decision taken for administrative convenience and grounded in the generalization, unlikely to hold true for every individual, that those with grade averages below the cutoff will not have other qualities sufficiently persuasive. Indeed, even the use of standard Medical College Aptitude Tests (MCAT) as part of the admissions procedure requires judging people as part of groups because it assumes that test scores are a guide to medical intelligence which is in turn a guide to medical ability. Though this judgment is no doubt true statistically, it hardly holds true for every individual.

Allan Bakke was himself refused admission to two other medical schools, not because of his race but because of his age: these schools thought that a student entering medical school at the age of thirty-three was likely to make less of a contribution to medical care over his career than someone entering at the standard age of twenty-one. Suppose these schools relied, not on any detailed investigation of whether Bakke himself had abilities that would contradict the generalization in his specific case, but on a rule of thumb that allowed only the most cursory look at applicants over (say) the age of thirty. Did these two medical schools violate his right to be judged as an individual rather than as a member of a group?

The Davis Medical School permitted whites to apply for the sixteen places reserved for members of "educationally or economically disadvantaged minorities," a phrase whose meaning might well include white ethnic minorities. In fact several whites have applied, though none has been accepted, and the California Court found that the special committee charged with administering the program had decided, in advance, against admitting any. Suppose that decision had been based on the following administrative theory: it is so unlikely that any white doctor can do as much to counteract racial imbalance in the medical professions as a well-qualified and trained black doctor can do that the committee should for reasons of convenience proceed on the presumption no white doctor could. That presumption is, as a matter of fact, more plausible than the corresponding presumption about medical students over the age of thirty, or even the presumption about applicants whose grade-point averages fall below the cutoff line. If the latter presumptions do not deny the alleged right of individuals to be judged as individuals in an admissions procedure, then neither can the former.

Mr. Colvin, in oral argument, argued the third of the catch phrases I mentioned. He said that his client had a right not to be excluded from medical school because of his race alone, and this as a statement of constitutional right sounds more plausible than claims about the right to be judged on merit or as an individual. It sounds plausible, however, because it suggests the following more complex principle. Every citizen has a constitutional right that he not suffer disadvantage, at least in the competition for any public benefit, because the race or religion or sect or region or other natural or artificial group to which he belongs is the object of prejudice or contempt.

That is a fundamentally important constitutional right, and it is that right that was systematically violated for many years by racist exclusions and anti-Semitic quotas. Color bars and Jewish quotas were not unfair just because they made race or religion relevant or because they fixed on qualities beyond individual control. It is true that blacks or Jews do not choose to be blacks or Jews. But it is also true that those who score low in aptitude or admissions tests do not choose their levels of intelligence. Nor do those denied admission because they are too old, or because they do not come from a part of the country underrepresented in the school, or because they cannot play basketball well, choose not to have the qualities that made the difference.

Race seems different because exclusions based on race have historically been motivated not by some instrumental calculation, as in the case of intelligence or age or regional distribution or athletic ability, but because of contempt for the excluded race or religion as such. Exclusion by race was in itself an insult, because it was generated by and signaled contempt.

Bakke's claim, therefore, must be made more specific than it is. He says he was kept out of medical school because of his race. Does he mean that he was kept out because his race is the object of prejudice or contempt? That suggestion is absurd. A very high proportion of those who were accepted (and, presumably, of those who run the admissions program) were members of the same race. He therefore means simply that if he had been black he would have been accepted, with no suggestion that this would have been so because blacks are thought more worthy or honorable than whites.

That is true: no doubt he would have been accepted if he were black. But it is also true, and in exactly the same sense, that he would have been accepted if he had been more intelligent, or made a better impression in his interview, or, in the case of other schools, if he had been younger when he decided to become a doctor. Race is not, in *his* case, a different matter from these other factors equally beyond his control. It is not a different matter because in his case race is not distinguished by the special character of public insult. On the contrary the program presupposes that his race is still widely if wrongly thought to be superior to others.

In the past, it made sense to say that an excluded black or Jewish student was being sacrificed because of his race or religion; that meant that his or her exclusion was treated as desirable in itself, not because it contributed to any goal in which he as well as the rest of society might take pride. Allan Bakke is being "sacrificed" because of his race only in a very artificial sense of the word. He is being "sacrificed" in the same artificial sense because of his level of intelligence, since he would have been accepted if he were more clever than he is. In both cases he is being excluded not by prejudice but because of a rational calculation about the socially most beneficial use of limited resources for medical education.

It may now be said that this distinction is too subtle, and that if racial classifications have been and may still be used for malign purposes, then everyone has a flat right that racial classifications not be used at all. This is the familiar appeal to the lazy virtue of simplicity. It supposes that if a line is difficult to draw, or might be difficult to administer if drawn, then there is wisdom in not making the attempt to draw it. There may be cases in which that is wise, but those would be cases in which nothing of great value would as a consequence be lost. If racially conscious admissions policies now offer the only substantial hope for bringing more qualified black and other minority doctors into the profession, then a great loss is suffered if medical schools are not allowed voluntarily to pursue such programs. We should then be trading away a chance to attack certain and present injustice in order to gain protection we may not need against speculative abuses we have other means to prevent. And such abuses cannot, in any case, be worse than the injustice to which we would then surrender.

We have now considered three familiar slogans, each widely thought to name a constitutional right that enables Allan Bakke to stop programs of affirmative action no matter how effective or necessary these might be. When we inspect these slogans, we find that they can stand for no genuine principle except one. This is the important principle that no one in our society should suffer because he is a member of a group thought less worthy of respect, as a group, than other groups. We have different aspects of that principle in mind when we say that individuals should be judged on merit, that they should be judged as individuals,

and that they should not suffer disadvantages because of their race. The spirit of that fundamental principle is the spirit of the goal that affirmative action is intended to serve. The principle furnishes no support for those who find, as Bakke does, that their own interests conflict with that goal.

It is of course regrettable when any citizen's expectations are defeated by new programs serving some more general concern. It is regrettable, for example, when established small businesses fail because new and superior roads are built; in that case people have invested more than Bakke has. And they have more reason to believe their businesses will continue than Bakke had to suppose he could have entered the Davis medical school at thirty-three even without a task force program.

There is, of course, no suggestion in that program that Bakke shares in any collective or individual guilt for racial injustice in America; or that he is any less entitled to concern or respect than any black student accepted in the program. He has been disappointed, and he must have the sympathy due that disappointment, just as any other disappointed applicant—even one with much worse test scores who would not have been accepted in any event—must have sympathy. Each is disappointed because places in medical school are scarce resources and must be used to provide what the more general society most needs. It is hardly Bakke's fault that racial justice is now a special need—but he has no right to prevent the most effective measures of securing that justice from being used.

RICHARD WASSERSTROM
A Defense of Programs of Preferential Treatment

Many justifications of programs of preferential treatment depend upon the claim that in one respect or another such programs have good consequences or that they are effective means by

which to bring about some desirable end, e.g., an integrated, equalitarian society. I mean by "programs of preferential treatment" to refer to programs such as those at issue in the *Bakke* case—

From *National Forum (The Phi Kappa Phi Journal),* vol. LVIII, no. 1 (Winter 1978), pp. 15–18. Reprinted with permission of the author.

programs which set aside a certain number of places (for example, in a law school) as to which members of minority groups (for example, persons who are nonwhite or female) who possess certain minimum qualifications (in terms of grades and test scores) may be preferred for admission to those places over some members of the majority group who possess higher qualifications (in terms of grades and test scores).

Many criticisms of programs of preferential treatment claim that such programs, even if effective, are unjustifiable because they are in some important sense unfair or unjust. In this paper I present a limited defense of such programs by showing that two of the chief arguments offered for the unfairness or injustice of these programs do not work in the way or to the degree supposed by critics of these programs.

The first argument is this. Opponents of preferential treatment programs sometimes assert that proponents of these programs are guilty of intellectual inconsistency, if not racism or sexism. For, as is now readily acknowledged, at times past employers, universities, and many other social institutions did have racial or sexual quotas (when they did not practice overt racial or sexual exclusion), and many of those who were most concerned to bring about the eradication of those racial quotas are now untroubled by the new programs which reinstitute them. And this, it is claimed, is inconsistent. If it was wrong to take race or sex into account when blacks and women were the objects of racial and sexual policies and practices of exclusion, then it is wrong to take race or sex into account when the objects of the policies have their race or sex reversed. Simple considerations of intellectual consistency—of what it means to give racism or sexism as a reason for condemning these social policies and practices—require that what was a good reason then is still a good reason now.

The problem with this argument is that despite appearances, there is no inconsistency involved in holding both views. Even if contemporary preferential treatment programs which contain quotas are wrong, they are not wrong for the reasons that made quotas against blacks and women pernicious. The reason why is that the social realities do make an enormous difference. The fundamental evil of programs that discriminated against blacks or women was that these programs were a part of a larger social universe which systematically maintained a network of institutions which unjustifiably concentrated power, authority, and goods in the hands of white male individuals, and which systematically consigned blacks and women to subordinate positions in the society.

Whatever may be wrong with today's affirmative action programs and quota systems, it should be clear that the evil, if any, is just not the same. Racial and sexual minorities do not constitute the dominant social group. Nor is the conception of who is a fully developed member of the moral and social community one of an individual who is either female or black. Quotas which prefer women or blacks do not add to an already relatively overabundant supply of resources and opportunities at the disposal of members of these groups in the way in which the quotas of the past did maintain and augment the overabundant supply of resources and opportunities already available to white males.

The same point can be made in a somewhat different way. Sometimes people say that what was wrong, for example, with the system of racial discrimination in the South was that it took an irrelevant characteristic, namely race, and used it systematically to allocate social benefits and burdens of various sorts. The defect was the irrelevance of the characteristic used—race—for that meant that individuals ended up being treated in a manner that was arbitrary and capricious.

I do not think that was the central flaw at all. Take, for instance, the most hideous of the practices, human slavery. The primary thing that was wrong with the institution was not that the particular individuals who were assigned the place of slaves were assigned there arbitrarily because the assignment was made in virtue of an irrelevant characteristic, their race. Rather, it seems to me that the primary thing that was and is wrong with slavery is the practice itself—the fact of some individuals being able to own other individuals and all that goes with that practice. It would not matter by what criterion individuals were assigned; human slavery would still be wrong. And the same can be said for most if not all of the other discrete practices and institutions which comprised the system of racial discrimination even after human slavery was abolished. The practices were unjustifiable—they were oppressive—and they would have been so no matter how the assignment of victims had been made. What made it worse, still, was that the institutions and the supporting ideology all interlocked to create a system of human oppression whose effects on those living under it were as devastating as they were unjustifiable.

Again, if there is anything wrong with the programs of preferential treatment that have begun to flourish within the past ten years, it should be evident that the social realities in respect to the distribution of resources and opportunities make the difference. Apart from everything else, there is simply no way in which all of these programs taken together could plausibly be viewed as capable of relegating white males to the kind of genuinely oppressive status characteristically bestowed upon women and blacks by the dominant social institutions and ideology.

The second objection is that preferential treatment programs are wrong because they take race or sex into account rather than the only thing that does matter—that is, an individual's qualifications. What all such programs have in common and what makes them all objectionable, so this argument goes, is that they ignore the persons who are more qualified by bestowing a preference on those who are less qualified in virtue of their being either black or female.

There are, I think, a number of things wrong with this objection based on qualifications, and not the least of them is that we do not live in a society in which there is even the serious pretense of a qualification requirement for many jobs of substantial power and authority. Would anyone claim, for example, that the persons who comprise the judiciary are there because they are the most qualified lawyers or the most qualified persons to be judges? Would anyone claim that Henry Ford II is the head of the Ford Motor Company because he is the most qualified person for the job? Part of what is wrong with even talking about qualifications and merit is that the argument derives some of its force from the erroneous notion that we would have a meritocracy were it not for programs of preferential treatment. In fact, the higher one goes in terms of prestige, power and the like, the less qualifications seem ever to be decisive. It is only for certain jobs and certain places that qualifications are used to do more than establish the possession of certain minimum competencies.

But difficulties such as these to one side, there are theoretical difficulties as well which cut much more deeply into the argument about qualifications. To begin with, it is important to see that there is a serious inconsistency present if the person who favors "pure qualifications" does so on the ground that the most qualified ought to be selected because this promotes maximum efficiency. Let us suppose that the argument is that if we have the most qualified performing the relevant tasks we will get those tasks done in the most economical and efficient manner. There is nothing wrong in principle with arguments based upon the good consequences that will flow from maintaining a social practice in a certain way. But it is inconsistent for the opponent of preferential treatment to attach much weight to qualifications on this ground, because it was an analogous appeal to the good consequences that the opponent of preferential treatment thought was wrong in the first place.* That is to say, if the chief thing to be said in favor of strict qualifications and preferring the most qualified is that it is the most efficient way of getting things done, then we are right back to an assessment of the different consequences that will flow from different programs, and we are far removed from the considerations of justice or fairness that were thought to weigh so heavily against these programs.

It is important to note, too, that qualifications—at least in the educational context—are often not connected at all closely with any plausible conception of social effectiveness. To admit the most qualified students to law school, for example—given the way qualifications are now determined—is primarily to admit those who have the greatest chance of scoring the highest grades at law school. This says little about efficiency except perhaps that these students are the easiest for the faculty to teach. However, since we know so little about what constitutes being a good, or even successful lawyer, and even less about the correlation between being a very good law student and being a very good lawyer, we can hardly claim very confidently that the legal system will operate most effectively if we admit only the most qualified students to law school.

To be at all decisive, the argument for qualifications must be that those who are the most qualified deserve to receive the benefits (the job, the place in law school, etc.) because they are the most qualified. The introduction of the concept of desert now makes it an objection as to justice or fairness of the sort promised by the original criticism of the programs. But now the problem is that there is no reason to think that there is any strong sense of "desert" in which it is correct that the most qualified deserve anything.

Let us consider more closely one case, that of preferential treatment in respect to admission to college or graduate school. There is a logical gap in the inference from the claim that a person is most qualified to perform a task, e.g., to be a good student, to the conclusion that he or she deserves to be admitted as a student. Of course, those who deserve to be admitted should be admitted. But why do the most qualified deserve anything? There is simply no necessary connection between academic merit (in the sense of being the most qualified) and deserving to be a member of a student body. Suppose, for instance, that there is only one tennis court in the community. Is it clear that the two best tennis players ought to be the ones permitted to use it? Why not those who were there first? Or those who will enjoy playing the most? Or those who are the worst and, therefore, need the greatest opportunity to practice? Or those who have the chance to play least frequently?

We might, of course, have a rule that says that the best tennis players get to use the court before the others. Under such a rule the best players would deserve the court more than the poorer ones. But that is just to push the inquiry back one stage. Is there any reason to think that we ought to have a rule giving good tennis players such a preference? Indeed, the arguments that might be given for or against such a rule are many and varied. And few if any of the arguments that might support the rule would depend upon a connection between ability and desert.

Someone might reply, however, that the most able students deserve to be admitted to the university because all of their earlier schooling was a kind of competition, with university admission being the prize awarded to the winners. They deserve to be admitted because that is what the rule of the competition provides. In addition, it might be argued, it would be unfair now to exclude them in favor of others, given the reasonable expectations they developed about the way in which their

industry and performance would be rewarded. Minority-admission programs, which inevitably prefer some who are less qualified over some who are more qualified, all possess this flaw.

There are several problems with this argument. The most substantial of them is that it is an empirically implausible picture of our social world. Most of what are regarded as the decisive characteristics for higher education have a great deal to do with things over which the individual has neither control nor responsibility: such things as home environment, socioeconomic class of parents, and, of course, the quality of the primary and secondary schools attended. Since individuals do not deserve having had any of these things vis-à-vis other individuals, they do not, for the most part, deserve their qualifications. And since they do not deserve their abilities they do not in any strong sense deserve to be admitted because of their abilities.

To be sure, if there has been a rule which connects, say, performance at high school with admission to college, then there is a weak sense in which those who do well at high school deserve, for that reason alone, to be admitted to college. In addition, if persons have built up or relied upon their reasonable expectations concerning performance and admission, they have a claim to be admitted on this ground as well. But it is certainly not obvious that these claims of desert are any stronger or more compelling than the competing claims based upon the needs or advantages to women or blacks from programs of preferential treatment. And as I have indicated, all rule-based claims of desert are very weak unless and until the rule which creates the claim is itself shown to be a justified one. Unless one has a strong preference for the status quo, and unless one can defend that preference, the practice within a system of allocating places in a certain way does not go very far at all in showing that that is the right or the just way to allocate those places in the future.

A proponent of programs of preferential treatment is not at all committed to the view that qualifications ought to be wholly irrelevant. He or she can agree that, given the existing structure of any institution, there is probably some minimal set of qualifications without which one cannot participate meaningfully within the institution. In addition, it can be granted that the qualifications of those involved will affect the way the institution works and the way it affects others in the society. And the consequences will vary depending upon the particular institution. But all of this only establishes that qualifications, in this sense, are relevant, not that they are decisive. This is wholly consistent with the claim that race or sex should today also be relevant when it comes to matters such as admission to college or law school. And that is all that any preferential treatment program—even one with the kind of quota used in the *Bakke* case—has ever tried to do.

I have not attempted to establish that programs of preferential treatment are right and desirable. There are empirical issues concerning the consequences of these programs that I have not discussed, and certainly not settled. Nor, for that matter, have I considered the argument that justice may permit, if not require, these programs as a way to provide compensation or reparation for injuries suffered in the recent as well as distant past, or as a way to remove benefits that are undeservedly enjoyed by those of the dominant group. What I have tried to do is show that it is wrong to think that

programs of preferential treatment are objectionable in the centrally important sense in which many past and present discriminatory features of our society have been and are racist and sexist. The social realities as to power and opportunity do make a fundamental difference. It is also wrong to think that programs of preferential treatment are in any strong sense either unjust or unprincipled. The case for programs of preferential treatment could, therefore, plausibly rest both on the view that such programs are not unfair to white males (except in the weak, rule-dependent sense described above) and on the view that it is unfair to continue the present set of unjust—often racist and sexist—institutions that comprise the social reality. And the case for these programs could rest as well on the proposition that, given the distribution of power and influence in the United States today, such programs may reasonably be viewed as potentially valuable, effective means by which to achieve admirable and significant social ideals of equality and integration.

ALAN H. GOLDMAN
Justice and Hiring by Competence

The issue to be settled in this paper regards a general rule for hiring or awarding scarce desirable positions in society. In recent political debates on the subject of reverse discrimination or preferential hiring, the principle of hiring by competence has seemed to remain sacrosanct, at least if one can judge by the lipservice paid to it by all sides of the discussion. Proponents of affirmative action go to great lengths to distinguish minority "goals" from quotas. While strict quotas for raising percentages of blacks and women employed by a fixed date, which would result in strong reverse discrimination, are acknowledged to be incompatible with the maintenance of strict competence standards, percentage goals for minorities toward which good faith efforts are made are held to

encourage minority hiring while maintaining existing standards. Opponents of the policy on the other hand seem to feel that by demonstrating how academic standards of excellence suffer and most qualified individuals fail to get positions through pressure for reverse discrimination, they thereby show affirmative action programs in universities to be unjust.

But despite apparent unanimity regarding the principle in the context of this public debate, it has recently come under attack in more sophisticated philosophical circles from both the left and the right. Libertarians argue or imply that corporations or organizations with positions to fill can give them to whomever they choose, that society has no right to interfere in this free process. Corporations like individuals have the right to control their legitimately acquired assets and to disburse them to whom they choose, and the right to freely hire is part of this more general right. Egalitarians on the other hand hold the principle of hiring by competence unjust in rewarding initial undeserved advantages and purely native talents. Individuals do not deserve those initial advantages for which they can claim no responsibility, and hiring by competence alone often rewards just such chance talents and advantageous initial social positions. I will argue here against these attacks.[1] I will be concerned with two central questions: (1) Does society have the right to impose and enforce any rule of hiring against corporations with positions to fill? (2) If the answer to (1) is affirmative, which principle of hiring ought to be adopted from the point of view of justice? I will argue against libertarians in this area that society does have the right and duty to enforce a principle, and against egalitarians that hiring by competence is just, that with several qualifications it is as just as human nature allows, and that even without them it is more just than seemingly egalitarian alternatives.

I. THE LIBERTARIAN POSITION

The first question to be faced here is why one system of hiring can be judged more just than another at all, i.e. why the award of jobs by private corporations as opposed to the award of other benefits by private individuals involves considerations of justice rather than simply questions of right and wrong. There are situations in which individuals or corporations can make wrong, even overall morally wrong decisions, without treating anyone unjustly or unfairly. To say that principles of hiring are a matter of distributive social justice is to imply that certain individuals acquire distributive *rights* to certain positions, and that to refuse them these positions is to refuse to grant them what is legitimately due them. The libertarian denies that any such rights exist. He argues that just as Mary has the right to marry whom she pleases, so a private corporation with benefits in the form of jobs to award has the right to hire whom it pleases without interference.[2]

No one acquires a right to marry Mary, and similarly, argues the libertarian, no one acquires a

right to a benefit from a private corporation which it has not contracted away. It will be useful in criticizing this position to see how far this analogy can be pressed. The difference between the case of Mary and that of the corporation cannot lie in the fact that a person's vital interests are affected by the job he works at, since his vital interests appear equally affected by his spouse, and yet as we said no one acquires a right to marry Mary—she can choose as capriciously as she wants. Thus we cannot argue simply from the fact that it makes a great deal of difference to people what jobs they get to the conclusion that society has a right to enforce a certain rule of hiring against private corporations. Nor does the converse seem to create a distinction, for if Mary's right to choose derives from the fact that her vital interests are involved as well, the same holds true of the corporation's vital interests in its personnel. Since a corporation's welfare and even continued existence depends upon who occupies its various positions, it can be argued that these choices should be left to it. It seems then that just as Mary has the right to choose a husband who will make her unhappy in the long run, i.e. she treats no one unjustly in doing so even if some other suitor would make a perfect spouse, so a corporation has the right to hire total incompetents if it chooses to act so unwisely. Nor can we argue simply that a corporation has no right to hire whom it pleases since the consequences of such freedom are bad (given present biases against minorities). For we perhaps can think of more scientific (or traditional?) ways to match spouses in comparison to which free choice has bad long range consequences for happiness, yet we would not want to deny Mary that right, nor contract it away ourselves. Even gains to her own interest or happiness do not justify interference with Mary's free choice, so that her right to choose derives from more than calculation of interests in particular cases. So in the case of a corporation, while it is difficult to see how hiring the most competent could damage its long range interests, perhaps it has a right to ignore those interests if it so chooses.

Are the cases then really totally analogous in relevant ways? First, although interests seem parallel as seen above, are the basic rights involved indeed similar? In Mary's case the general rights underlying her particular freedom in this case include a right over her own body and the freedom to control her life as she sees fit. That these rights, especially the first, have wide scope and absolute priority within their domains is in the interest of all to recognize. In the case of the corporation, the rights presumably involved are at most weaker versions or narrower cases of these: namely the right to property and that of free association. A corporation may be said to have a property right in the positions it chooses to fill in virtue of having legitimately acquired the assets with which to fund the positions. A corporation like an individual has a right to control those goods or assets which it has legitimately acquired. And the right to control its own assets is empty unless it is free to disburse them as or to whom it chooses. Since present members of the corporation must associate with new appointees, the freedom to associate with whom one pleases may also be cited in support of the libertarian position here. An enforced rule for hiring may force present members to work closely with others against their will, making their work unpleasant for them. And the friction created by this forced close association may be detrimental to the continued smooth operation of the company organization.

Clearly the right over one's body, which applies in the case of Mary's marriage, is more basic than the right to external property, which applies in the hiring case (whether or not Locke is right in claiming that the latter can be derived from the former), and the freedom to control one's life broader and more precious in total than that of free association. It can nevertheless be argued that just as the former rights constitute the paramount considerations in Mary's case, so do the latter in the case of the corporation. The corporation's property rights to control the disbursement of its assets and the right of free association of its members can be held to imply a specific right to hire whom it pleases without interference from society. In relation to the analogy with Mary's specific right to choose a spouse following from her rights over her own body and to control her life plan, the central questions here are first, whether Mary's rights always entail that she cannot treat others unjustly in choosing a spouse (i.e. whether these rights are absolute in this sphere), and second, whether there might be other rights involved in the case of the corporation, but not in Mary's case, which limit or override those to which it can appeal in support of free choice. To the extent that Mary's specific right to marry whom she pleases is not absolute, and to the extent that the two cases are disanalogous regarding the rights and interests involved, we cannot argue from Mary's case to an absolute right to hire freely of the corporation.

It should first be noticed regarding the question of the scope of Mary's right that she can treat Dick unfairly or unjustly despite her right to choose, if she has led him on and then rejected him in favor of another at the altar. There are situations in which someone might acquire a legitimate expectation to marry Mary and be treated unjustly or unfairly by her subsequently. This might lead us to suspect that injustice in hiring as well has to do with thwarting legitimate expectations arising from previous efforts. But what could render expectations of individuals to jobs legitimate, given the corporation members' rights of property and free association? It might be held that the only parallel would be a corporation's refusing a job to an individual promised that position, but there are contract laws to prevent that from occurring, and the libertarian acknowledges the state's duty to enforce contracts freely made. (At least the rights in question, as in Mary's case, are already shown to be somewhat limited in scope.)

But there is a difference from the average case of whom one chooses to marry in that whether corporations have competent people or not affects the goods they produce for the rest of society, while whom one marries affects basically only oneself. If Mary happened to be a seventeenth century queen of England and her marriage affected how the country was ruled, she would lose her right to choose whom she pleased, and her subjects could complain of a choice being unfair to them. Similarly it seems society can complain if it fails to get necessary goods and services because of incompetents in positions of responsibility. If one corporation hires incompetents or relative incompetents because of discriminatory practices, it will soon be driven out of business in a competitive situation, but if there is such a practice generally in a whole sector of the economy, the public can complain for the price it pays for such lack of efficiency. To assume that competition will root out all such practices is to oversimplify motives and knowledge of both producers and consumers, and this assumption has proved empirically false.

It may be asked, however, how a social interest in more material goods and services can override recognized rights of individuals or private corporations within the society, like the rights of property and free association here. To determine a social interest is not necessarily to demonstrate the right of society or the state to further that interest, especially when individual or private corporation rights are apparently ignored in the process. For one principal purpose of recognizing individual rights within a system of social justice is to protect individuals from losses whenever utilitarian calculations run against them in particular cases. The recognition of the right to property, for example, means that a person will not be dispossessed whenever another is in greater need, although such forced transfer would raise total or average utility in particular cases. Therefore the rights to property and free association, it could be argued by analogy, should not be overridden here by the social interest in maximizing goods and services. A private corporation with assets to disburse for jobs should be free to hire whom it pleases, even when this results in lower efficiency in its production of goods and services. Efficiency cannot be permitted to override recognized rights, or our rights and freedoms would be fragile indeed. Thus while it may be in the interest of all, even of those in power in corporations, to have the most competent hired, there may exist rights to ignore the maximization of interest satisfaction, as in the case of marriage choices.

While I accept the above account of rights as far as it goes, it presents an oversimplified picture when used only in conjunction with appeal to property and free association rights in the context of this libertarian argument for freedom in hiring. What is ignored is the fact that recognition of particular rights, like that of property, is established in the first place in relation to a set of varied social values including welfare, and that such rights are therefore rarely (never?) unlimited in scope, but include exceptive clauses recognizing rights established in relation to other values. My right to dispose of my property as I please does not include a right to dispose of my knife in an editor's chest; my right to use my property according to my own wishes does not include a right to play my stereo at deafening volumes; and my right to spend my assets as I like does not allow me to buy nerve gas,

even if I keep it sealed in my basement vault. The above examples represent restrictions of freedom to prevent harm, annoyance or potential harm, but these are not the only possible cases. In the initial formulation of rules and rights the value of freedom may be weighed against those of equality or equity, and welfare, for example. This is compatible with the fact that welfare or utility considerations are no longer applied once the rights have been established and their scopes defined. Thus while it may be in the interest of all to recognize a right to personal property, this right may include an exceptive clause regarding filling jobs by corporations, again in the interest of all. This does not mean that property rights are to be overridden in specific cases for net gains in social welfare—property would be too precarious in that case—but general exceptive clauses of narrower scope (than any net gain in welfare) are compatible with the existence and protection of specific rights like that of property.

We have not yet won the argument with the libertarian, however. For his position is precisely that freedoms, including those of disbursing property and associating with those of one's choice, may only be limited to prevent harm. And a defender of this position would undoubtedly want to press the distinction here between the interests of individuals in maximizing available goods and services and any potential harm to them from the exercise of these freedoms on the part of corporations in hiring. I am not sure, however, that the distinction between harm and utility can be drawn at all in relation to many positions of responsibility in society, such as pilots, surgeons, police and even automobile, home or toy manufacturers. Relative incompetents in these positions represent not only losses in efficiency, but serious potential harm. Thus the harm principle itself, if it allows prevention of unnecessary risk or potential harm, which it must to be at all plausible, may require enforcement of a rule for hiring the most competent in many positions. On a deeper level it may be questioned whether considerations of freedom can be so sharply differentiated from considerations of equality and welfare when designing basic institutions or establishing rules and recognizing rights. To approach this question in this present context, we must first examine how considerations of equality or equity figure in the issue of hiring by competence, for this is somewhat less obvious than the relevance of social welfare or utility.

There is in fact another right involved in this issue which libertarians ignore—what is generally recognized as the right to equality of opportunity. To allow jobs to be awarded capriciously, especially given deep-seated prejudices known to exist in our society, is to deny equal opportunity for goods in a most blatant fashion. An equal opportunity for jobs is the necessary condition for an equal chance to all other basic goods. Thus the right of equal opportunity, if recognized at all, must also be acknowledged to figure more prominently in the issue of a social rule for hiring than the right to property or free association. The reason for this unequal weight is that the right to property as well as that of free association continue to exist although limited by exceptive clauses regarding corporations' doling out jobs, as they continue to exist with clauses involving limited redistributive taxation or open housing in the name of equality. But equal opportunity for social goods does not exist at all without equal opportunity for jobs. While redistributive taxation, open housing, and integrated schools are advocated in the name of this right, they amount to little when jobs can be denied to those who have managed to acquire superior qualifications with their help. The enforcement of some rule for hiring stipulating criteria not based purely upon inborn or initial chance factors is the first prerequisite for equality of opportunity, since decent jobs are not only of highest value in themselves, but means to most other valuable things.

This admittedly may not bother the thoroughgoing libertarian. For he will most likely recognize no such right as that to equal opportunity, nor give it any weight at all against the maximization of individual freedoms in regard to property and association. He holds that people have a right (short of harm) to what they have freely and legitimately acquired, and that no general right like that of equal opportunity should be recognized which involves repeated violations of individuals' rights to their acquired property. Have we then finally reached in regard to this issue an impasse in moral argument, uncovered an ultimate clash in moral attitude? Rather than admit this we can plausibly continue the argument by accusing the libertarian first of failing to assume a moral attitude on this

issue at all, and second of inconsistency in his appeal to the absolute value of freedom over equality.

We can first point out then that part of what it means to assume a moral attitude is to recognize the moral equality of others (implied in a recognition of their subjectivity, i.e. feelings, points of view. etc.)—to accept rules which could be willed from their positions in the social context, or at least by neutral agents. If this recognition of moral equality or moral community within a system of social rules is to be given content as well as form, it means that the rules must not only apply to all, but as far as possible operate to the good of all. It also means that there is a presumption of equality not only in worth but in material conditions, which must be weighed against other values such as that of freedom in the formulation of more specific moral rules. A minimal moral outcome of this balancing (too minimal for egalitarians) is to formulate rules which result not in equality of goods, but in something approaching an equal chance to acquire goods through effort. Hence the recognition and protection of this right in social rules, such as a rule for hiring, seem a minimal condition for a moral social system. To bring this argument down to the specific issue at hand, its upshot is that rules protecting equality of opportunity, and specifically the recognition that society has the right to enforce some fair rule for hiring against private corporations, are necessary if distributions of property and other goods are to be just.

I have been speaking thus far as if freedom here is to be balanced against equality and welfare, but also indicated above that absolute liberty with respect to property and association may not result in the overall maximization of freedom desired by the libertarian. For poverty and the lack of satisfaction of basic needs which poverty entails constitute an impediment to freedom as well, to the basic freedom to formulate and pursue a meaningful life plan and control one's life as one desires. This is perhaps the most essential liberty of all, and if it is denied through the operation of a social or economic system which leaves some in need so that others may totally control their property, we can view this as an unwarranted conventional constraint upon liberty (property is only protected in the first place by the social system). It follows that any rule of hiring which results in more goods and services, as long as some of these trickle down to those whose freedom is compromised by want, can be adopted not only in the name of welfare or utility, but to increase freedom as well. This does not mean in general that every increase in welfare is to be counted as an increase in freedom as well, or that despotic states with higher GNP's are to be preferred, but only that no social system can be justified in the name of freedom which leaves those at the bottom constrained within the circle of dire poverty. A society with severe racial biases and no rule for hiring results in that situation. Thus we again arrive at the conclusion that society has the right to impose some rule for hiring against private corporations, this time in the name of freedom. Restrictions upon the freedom of corporations to choose capriciously or invidiously in hiring are necessary to protect or create freedom for those for whom equality of opportunity is its necessary condition.

If rules for hiring are then justified through considerations of utility or welfare and equality of opportunity, why not equal opportunity to marry Mary, or the adoption of mating rules which can be shown to maximize happiness or compatibility in the long run? Do the above arguments apply equally to this case, and if so mustn't they be dismissed in light of our intuitions against social rules for marriage choices? In answer to the first part of the first question, equal opportunity to marry Mary would amount only to an equal opportunity to win her favor, for that is the only relevant qualification we can presently think of for marrying her (we have no independent reliable criteria for what will make her happy in the long run). We might say that equality of opportunity for passing this purely subjective test exists already (Mary's favor might be won by one who could not have been predicted in terms of knowledge of her prior preferences), or given that Mary has certain relatively fixed prejudices, we might deny the possibility of enforcing any rule (except education against such biases) to create equal opportunity for passing this purely subjective test. In answer to the second part of the question, even if we had independent criteria for happiness in marriage as we do for successful job performance, since whom Mary marries affects herself far more than others, others having at most a peripheral interest, we can

leave the choice and its consequences to her. Regarding the consideration of social welfare, the welfare of others is not involved in the average marriage cases as it is in who occupies various productive positions. Regarding the consideration of equal opportunity for those applying for jobs versus marriage consents, equality of opportunity in the latter case is not a necessary condition for equal chances at other goods, hence not a necessary condition for basic freedoms or a just social system overall, as it is in the case of jobs. For all these reasons none of my above arguments imply by analogy that society has the right to enforce a rule for mating against Mary.

These last points of difference apply as well to the more important and difficult cases of an individual hiring someone for temporary help, or the small businessman who gives a job to his son. Must we to be consistent apply our rule to all such cases and deny these freedoms as well? The first distinction between the case of the small business or private individual and the large corporation is the interest of the public in their products and services. If a small business is the only source of a vital service or product in a given area, it may be reasonable to demand competents in positions of responsibility. Otherwise it may be unreasonable to demand the proprietor to take the time and bear the cost to advertise the position, etc. (this is especially clear in the case of my hiring someone to unload my rented truck, or similar cases). The right of free association is also more central in the case of a small business, and this was part of the reasoning of Congress in applying nondiscriminatory regulations only to businesses with more than twenty-five employees. Since these differences are real, and since equality of opportunity and social welfare do not require that literally every position in society be open to all, but only a certain proportion of them, we may in applying these rationales establish a rule for hiring only for corporations over a certain size, recognizing that the drawing of a precise line will be somewhat arbitrary.

Thus my argument to the effect that certain individuals acquire rights to certain jobs and that corporations treat them unjustly if they are denied those positions involves two steps; first, society has the right in the name of social utility and equality of opportunity to establish a rule for hiring and enforce it against private as well as public corporations and organizations; second, by satisfying this social rule through effort an individual comes to deserve the position in question. The second step is dependent upon the first, which has been established in this section (the second step will be more prominent in the next). I have now provided criteria for the acceptability of a rule for hiring, i.e. social utility and protection of equal opportunity, without having completely shown how a single rule could meet both. In demonstrating that hiring by competence is the correct rule, we must consider the counterarguments of the egalitarian.

II. THE EGALITARIAN POSITION

If the argument of the last section is correct, that is if a rule for hiring is to be justified in terms of social utility and equality of opportunity, it seems easy to show that hiring by competence qualifies as a just distributive principle. Many major theories of distributive justice, especially liberal theories, agree that practices are to be preferred which result in Pareto improvements, i.e. in benefits to some without loss to others. In regard to social utility, it can be argued that hiring by competence results not only in improvements over alternatives of this sort, but in the production of more goods for everyone in society (strong Pareto improvements). Hiring the most competent analytically entails increased goods and services, for competence is defined in terms of the ability to perform in a job by satisfying social demand. (I assume here the ability to judge competence according to qualifications, a difficulty which does not in any case affect the argument that we should *aim at* competence.)

The egalitarian attempts to refute the above justification by arguing that those abilities relevant to awarding jobs on the basis of efficiency, which is the basis for hiring in a pure market economy with only profit motives operating, are irrelevant from the point of view of justice; that in rewarding native talent, intelligence and social position (which even if acquired required an ability for acquisition for which the agent can claim no responsibility), the practice of hiring by competence involves rewards which are arbitrary from a moral point of view. Individuals deserve only those benefits which they have earned. They do not deserve their native advantages and so do not deserve those benefits,

including good jobs, which flow from them throughout their lives. A child born rich and intelligent stands a far better chance than do other children of acquiring competence qualifications for desirable positions later in life, yet he cannot be said to deserve that better chance from the point of view of justice, nor thus the job which he eventually gets. Thus increments to social welfare from hiring by competence are a matter of social utility from which questions of justice must be separated. The egalitarian appears to have uncovered a conflict between the two criteria for a just rule advanced in the first section, i.e. maximization of utility through hiring by competence seems inconsistent with equality of opportunity in the present social context, and he claims the moral predominance of considerations of equality over those of social utility.

I do not think that any such radical separation of analyses of justice and efficiency could accord with our intuitions regarding the former, as these are aroused by specific examples. Although we may not all be Utilitarians, it seems we must grant that welfare does at least count as a positive consideration, and certainly at the extreme involved in this issue. Following Nicholas Rescher,[3] I would argue that a practice or rule which generates a sum total of goods of 15 units to be distributed in a hypothetical society of 4 individuals in shares of 4, 4, 4, 3 is preferable from the point of view of justice to one which generates 8 units to be distributed in shares of 2, 2, 2, 2, despite its greater inequality. In other words, those who could have received 4 units under the first plan could legitimately claim injustice at being reduced so as to equal the lowest share under the second, other things being equal. If a claim of injustice or unfairness at being so reduced in moving from the first socio-economic plan to the second is justified, then aggregate utility in itself must be a consideration of distributive justice, and plans must be prima facie preferable which result in larger aggregates. To deny this is perhaps to grant too large a moral force to the feelings of envy and pride. For even the person with the lowest share in our hypothetical case is better off under the first plan than the second, except for the fact that he sees others around him with more. There may seem to be a complication here in that those with less relative income (even though more absolute) may be in a worse position to bid for scarce goods. But these alternatives in relation to choices between hiring by competence or other rules for hiring may be taken to refer to goods available, and not simply income. The argument is that more goods will be available to all if competents occupy productive positions, and this is what the egalitarian wrongly claims to be irrelevant to the choice of a just rule for hiring.

Even if we continue to insist upon a radical separation of justice (in a narrow sense) from efficiency, it seems we must admit that the latter can override the former from a moral point of view when it comes to hiring or filling positions of responsibility. It may be, for example, that those best qualified to be brain surgeons do not most deserve the benefits of those positions from a radically egalitarian view of justice, but surely egalitarians would want them to have the jobs anyway (even if they are not the ones on the operating tables). We pointed out in the last section other jobs as well in which incompetents represent not only losses in goods and services, but potential harm of a serious sort. When we think of all the cases of severe harm such as bodily injury or death which occur from defective products or incompetents conducting vital services, it is clear that lowering ranges of competence further would be something to avoid even if at the expense of equality or fairness in the narrowest of senses to job applicants. Since jobs carry responsibilities as well as benefits, society can legitimately complain if its welfare is sacrificed by a policy which leaves those responsibilities unfulfilled. And victims of avoidable irresponsibility (avoidable through a different system of distributive justice or alternative rule for hiring) can complain not only of incompetence or inconvenience, but of injustice. Another way of expressing this is to say, as we said in the last section, that the public has a right to be spared such avoidable harm.

There might nevertheless be held to be several assumptions involved in the last paragraphs which can be questioned. An opponent could argue that in holding that hiring by competence alone creates more goods for all I am restricting the scope of the concept of goods to that of material productivity reflected in material wealth, and furthermore assuming that such greater wealth (from following this rule as opposed to alternatives) will filter down to those who end up in less lucrative posi-

tions (but might have done relatively better under some alternative rule). Regarding the first assumption, this appears to ignore the dignity or lack of dignity attached to certain positions and presuppose that those denied more prestigious positions because of lack of talent or training would be willing to sacrifice a sense of importance, etc. for material benefits. It may be that those with relatively less competence for desirable positions will nevertheless have more and better material goods available to them overall if there is a general rule for hiring the competent as opposed to alternatives, but they may be willing to sacrifice some of this quantity and quality for more equal chances at prestigious positions and the self-respect they carry. Regarding the assumption that the results of greater productivity will filter down (accepted for the sake of argument in the last sentence), this is sound only for an equalitarian distribution of products throughout society, but the complaint against hiring by competence alone in market economies is not simply that it denies dignity to those less qualified for higher positions, but that it lowers their material income as well. Less desirable positions almost invariably have lower pay scales as well, and hence it is questionable whether those occupying them will have maximum benefits under the rule for hiring the most competent, despite the higher total aggregate of goods produced under that system.

In reply to the first charge, it is not necessary to debate or maintain a restriction of primary or basic goods to material wealth in order to defend my position. That part of the justification of hiring by competence having to do with utility depends not upon considerations regarding those applying for particular jobs, but regarding the rest of society or the public as a whole, who could justly complain not only of loss of material goods and vital services, but of increased potential harm, if those with less than maximal competence were granted positions with social responsibility. It still might be that relative incompetents would be willing to accept these sacrifices and risks under a different rule, but another essential point is that given the inequality of benefits attached to various positions in the economic structure, raising those with less competence simply lowers those with more, and does not result in any more equalitarian distribution of final products. Those who end up with the lower positions under any alternative rule would certainly be worse off than those incompetent for desirable positions at present, given the same inequality in distribution and a lower aggregate of goods and services. And even with the unequal distribution, there is likely to be enough difference in productivity between systems which award jobs to competents versus those which award incompetence equally, that any gain achieved by other individuals in moving from the former system to the latter would be short lived.

Still, an equalitarian could argue that although moving away from hiring by competence would not in itself result in a more equal distribution of goods, a more random process would at least tend to equalize the chances of all individuals for acquiring the benefits of an unequal distribution. The emphasis can again be placed upon achieving true equality of opportunity. There remains the moral dissatisfaction with a system which rewards native advantages, for we feel at least in the abstract that only those characteristics should be rewarded for which an agent can legitimately claim responsibility. This dissatisfaction is warranted, and it is partly for this reason that ideal theories of justice which legitimize hiring by competence add the qualification that there must be equality of opportunity for acquiring competence. To this qualification regarding education or training can be added another regarding rewards for jobs, for the reward scale for different jobs is at least theoretically independent from the criterion on the basis of which the jobs are awarded. While it is not even the case now that those jobs requiring the longest training or highest intelligence are those with the highest rates of compensation (alas!), the pay scale rather being determined for the most part by social demand and political muscle, there are other factors such as intrinsic agreeableness or disagreeableness of the job which ought to be taken into account. Unlike moving away from the practice of hiring by competence, the readjustment contemplated here toward equalization of pay scales would perhaps not result in great losses of efficiency, since executives would not in any case resign to become sanitation workers. I have my doubts, however, about many doctors, and in any case social demand would still have to play a significant role for reasons of utility (given present attitudes). But the conclusion of relevance to our immediate topic following from these considerations is that inequalities in benefits and unjust rewards for native differences would be better corrected by adjustments to the pay schedule and within the educational system than by a randomization of the process of hiring for jobs. What is most unjust about the present practice of hiring by competence (aside from the fact that those in power often fail to follow the rule to which they pay lipservice) is the final unequal distribution of benefits which results, and the fact that some have initial headstarts toward those benefits which are insurmountable. But these injustices could be corrected without alterations in the rule for hiring itself or the drastic sacrifices in social welfare that would entail.

Although the above lays the groundwork for later points in this section, I have not yet done justice to the egalitarian argument, for it is exactly at this point that it can be resurrected. Its claims are perhaps not meant to be applied to ideal situations in the educational system and regarding different pay scales, and in such situations my more radical opponent might even agree that hiring by competence is legitimate. Rather they are intended to apply to a society whose educational system fails to make adequate efforts to correct for initial inequalities and whose system of economic rewards is far from just. Given that those jobs often pay most which also carry the greatest social esteem and are the most agreeable or interesting, given that some, no matter how hard they try, simply do not have the native intelligence, talent or initial economic and social advantage to achieve those positions, and given that the educational system does not even encourage those who might succeed but currently lack motivation, the argument is that any system of hiring attached to this situation which freezes these inequalities is unjust in its distributive results. And if the results of a distributive system are unjust, so is the system. Thus, it can be argued, given the intractability of the unequal and unfair results of the system, it would again be more just to equalize chances for the unequal shares by randomization, for example, rather than hiring by competence. The point can again be pressed that equal chances to unequal shares are fairer than unequal chances to unequal shares. (A realistic egalitarian would require randomization only for those above a minimal level of competence—he would have to recognize some lower limits of efficiency.)

But the egalitarian still seems to ignore the separability of the pay scales and educational system from the rule for hiring. These are conceptually detachable not simply because the former could be made more just independently from alterations to the rule, but more importantly because the justification of the rule appealed to totally other factors. The questionable steps in his above argument consist in the claims that a system of hiring attached to an unjust schedule of rewards is therefore itself unjust in its results, and therefore also unjust in itself. These premises would be legitimate in this case only if the justification of hiring by competence relied upon appeal to its final distributive results in terms of relative shares to those hired versus those turned down. But the justification offered above was independent of the justice or injustice of the schedule of rewards attached to different positions, appealing rather to the welfare of the general public in terms of goods and services, to protection against discrimination, and to honoring legitimate expectations derived from previous efforts (to attain competence). Even if the efforts of some are unjustly doomed to failure, or if some are not encouraged to make the effort through neglect, it still seems preferable to reward those who have made efforts and succeeded than to ignore effort entirely. It is true that the final distribution of benefits (jobs plus their rewards) will be unjust if *either* the basis for assigning positions *or* the relative schedule of rewards is unjust, but this does not mean it will not be more unjust if fair principles are violated regarding the former as well as the latter.

That the egalitarian argument fails becomes more clear if we seriously consider its alternative to hiring by competence, for the central question in this section is whether randomization is more just as claimed, given the present educational system and pay scales. Is a job lottery, which equalizes chances for desirable positions, the ideal of distributive justice in this area, given present inequalities as frozen into education and pay scales? The general principle, as we have seen, which does seem sound in genèral, is that when shares are unalterably unequal, it is fair, other things being equal, to equalize chances for unequal shares; but

of course the crucial issue here, which is generally the case in debates on equality, is whether other things are equal, here regarding job applicants. The central problem for establishing any rule of hiring is the stipulation of criteria regarding which characteristics of individuals are to be considered relevant in awarding the positions. Is winning a lottery to be the only relevant characteristic? It seems at first glance (but I believe at first glance only) the most truly egalitarian.

The central complaint against hiring by competence without sufficient compensatory mechanisms in the educational system was that it tended to reward initial differences for which the agents could claim no responsibility. But certainly a process of random selection in the job market, aside from losses in efficiency, comes out worse on this score. It can be admitted that differences in competence for various positions constitute reasonable barometers of prior efforts to acquire competence only where the educational system has attempted to correct for initial inequalities. But even when such remedial efforts are lacking, the acquisition of competence still represents the expenditure of some effort in a socially desirable way, although the effort is not strictly proportional to the degree of competence acquired. The question is whether it is more just to ignore socially productive effort altogether and make all reward a matter of pure chance, which seems implausible or inconsistent if the only complaint against hiring by competence was that it rewarded chance factors to some degree. The effect of a lottery at any level is to negate differences in previous efforts, and if the cost of negating initial social differences (which can be equalized otherwise) is to render all effort meaningless as a measure of desert as well, it hardly seems worth it from the point of view of distributive justice.

The argument in favor of randomization now becomes that although it awards jobs on the basis of pure chance, at least it equalizes the chances—if benefits are to be doled out according to rolls of the dice, at least the dice should not be loaded. While the dice are loaded at present in favor of the rich, the talented and the intelligent, randomizing the process of hiring restores the balance which should have been restored by the neglectful educational and economic systems. In reply it could be argued first that in the original Book of Life all had equal chances at intelligence, etc., which is just a colourful way of saying that how intelligent you are or who your parents happen to be *is* a matter of chance from your point of view: it is simply a matter of chance operating further in the past. It makes a difference whether the chance factor operated in the past or in the present in the form of a job lottery, however, since in the interim have occurred the efforts of those who have attained requisite skills. Second, there is an important difference ignored in the above argument between correcting for inequalities in the educational or tax systems and annihilating them at the final bell in the hiring process. For there is a limit to the justifiable neglect of those with superior talents, motivation and monetary assets, and their efforts should be ignored no more than those less fortunate once reasonable attempts have been made to motivate the latter and make their success possible.

The real contrast still reduces to that between rewarding chance versus rewarding effort and past and potential social contribution, and it still seems that a random lottery for hiring is the worst of all possible worlds by these criteria. Where there is no ulterior social purpose in the reward of some benefit than the distribution of some windfall good, and where furthermore no previous actions of the individuals in question can be seen to create differential rights or deserts to the goods, a random process of choosing is fairest. This follows from the presumption of equality of persons deduced in the first section. But when positions are assigned for socially productive purposes, and when individuals are therefore encouraged to direct their efforts towards fulfilling these purposes, past and potential productivity achieved through these efforts cannot be justly ignored. The same points apply to a lesser extent to randomization for those above a certain minimal level of competence, and in any case the egalitarian's reasoning must lead him to suggest this only for reasons of efficiency and not justice, which he takes to be distinct. Total randomization functions as the ideal of egalitarian justice in this area (given that jobs and their rewards must be unequal), and it is therefore relevant to argue as I have that it is a misconceived ideal.

The argument regarding socially productive

effort can lead us to question further whether the supposed egalitarian ideal really represents a net increase in equality. It can first be maintained that randomization in any case detracts from liberty—the liberty to pursue the career of one's choice. It is assumed by proponents that a lottery would increase this liberty for many, since it would allow all who wish to pursue a given position to do so merely by entering the lottery. But the meaningful pursuit of what one considers valuable and worth achieving involves effort and even struggle, and part of the enjoyment of reward is the feeling of success after effort. Such real pursuit is rendered meaningless by being ignored in awarding positions by chance. The same argument can be put in terms of equality and the denial of equal right—here equal right to pursue value and acquire through effort what one considers worthwhile, as well as or perhaps equivalent to equal right to dignity. Dignity, or a sense of personal worth, beyond the mere dignity of being human often mentioned in equalitarian arguments, derives from a sense of having accomplished, not won by chance. But an equal right to jobs at all levels is bought at the expense of an equal chance to meaningful achievement through effort (certainly in the early and formative years).

It might be held that a randomization of rewards and recognitions does give an equal right to this type of pursuit—namely no right at all. This might seem a pyrrhic victory for the egalitarian, but might at least show that my argument here cannot be stated in terms of equality, but only in terms of balancing other values against that of equality. But when some have directed the efforts of their early years to attaining skills needed for some type of position they hope to occupy, and then see these positions filled through a chance process by others, who acquire at least a small chance of hanging on to them without having achieved the same level of competence through the same degree of effort, there is an inequality and unfairness involved. If to avoid this unfair waste lotteries are pushed further back into the early years, so that individuals know the positions they are to occupy from the beginning and so do not make efforts in the wrong direction, the only relevant differences between this determination and the operation of original chance differences against which the egalitarian complains would be that this assignment of positions would be more rigid and would involve losses in social utility, as compared with more open and widespread competition for productive positions.

The egalitarian could further argue that in his system a sense of dignity or achievement can be developed through performing well on the job rather than in the process of acquiring it, and that his system equalizes chances for the former type of achievement. Aside from the fact, as mentioned above, that this downgrades accomplishments culminating the first twenty-five years or so of a person's life, the dignity of even those who acquire positions through a random process would most likely not be appreciably enhanced (could they be expected to perform well, having never found the need to do so before while awaiting the lottery?), and the prestige of the positions themselves and the self-respect that goes with them would soon diminish with the knowledge that they were gotten by chance. If anyone could enter any lottery for any position, then no one could pursue positions or feel any satisfaction in having achieved them. If competence were nevertheless later demanded on the job, and a sense of satisfaction were supposed to derive from having performed well at that level in demanding positions, there would result a series of firings and hirings until competent people filled the positions anyway, with a net increase in resentment for those who proved and could have been predicted to be incompetent. If not everyone can enter all lotteries, but only those who have achieved a certain level of competence through effort, and a sense of achievement is to be derived from having acquired that level, why ignore all achievements beyond that level? (If a number of individuals applying are at the same level, there will have to be some other means of choosing anyway, possibly preferably random.) While we do not want to reward purely native characteristics, and to do so is generally unfair, it is an empirical fact which makes my argument somewhat easier that there are few desirable positions for which successful performance demands only native characteristics.

These last arguments really rely upon the abstractness of the notions of liberty and equality, to which other writers have pointed as well, upon the fact that "Liberty" and "Equality" are generally

emotive laden shorthand for "liberty to do x" and "equality with respect to y." With regard to the latter, the above points illustrate that the crucial question is always what factors should be given equal weight in any decision or distribution, that giving certain factors equal weight often militates against considering others. What I have been suggesting is that equality of opportunity should be defined not in terms of equal or random chances at goods including jobs, but in terms of real and equal chances to achieve success through effort. Proponents of randomization would presumably base their stand regarding the ambiguity of "equality" upon the claim that the most equalitarian and least meritocratic criterion is to consider people equal just in virtue of being human wherever possible, rather than more narrowly specifying the criteria for the distribution of goods, and that this is the purpose of the job lottery. I argued in the first section that this broad criterion of humanity is relevant in generating a right to have basic needs satisfied and a presumption of equality of conditions from which deviations must be justified. This much is implied in the recognition of the common humanity or distinct subjectivity of others who share a moral community. But unequal efforts and social productivity do seem to justify differences in benefits, and it is doubtful that the egalitarian criterion can be applied at all in the case of job hiring. It has to be admitted right off that a job lottery attempts to consider people equal not simply in virtue of being human, but in virtue of want (desire for a particular position), or in virtue of having entered the lottery, since those who do not want the position enough to enter the lottery will not be considered. But then it becomes questionable whether equal weight is being given to want or degrees of want, since all degrees over the minimal necessary to enter the lottery is discounted. It seems that a better or fairer way to measure want would be in terms of wanting enough to have made the effort to acquire competence, and we are brought back to the argument on rewarding socially productive effort rather than luck.

The final point to be raised regarding effort and its just rewards is that even if hiring by competence is not most just in relation to abstract moral principles, the fact that society regards it as just or has adopted it as a working rule legitimizes certain expectations arising from successful efforts to satisfy that rule. Although I maintained in the first section that an individual's acquiring a right to a position is dependent upon a society's right to establish a rule for filling that position, it is somewhat independent of which rule society adopts. Individuals living in a community must for the most part direct their efforts toward socially acceptable goals, and if these efforts are constantly thwarted after the fact by changes in social criteria for success, the psychological effect is devastating, and society is to be held responsible. While this conservative line of reasoning is abused or overstated if used to apologize gross injustice in the status quo, it does create a presumption in favor of honoring prior commitments of the community in relation to its accepted rules, just as there is a presumption which can nevertheless be overridden in favor of keeping promises, even when what is promised is not independently morally best. Thus we can speak of rights in practice or rights created through satisfaction of socially accepted rules for social rewards (even when these rules are not written into law).

Such rights in practice function only as insurance in this context, however, if my previous arguments establish the overall justice of hiring the most competent as opposed to alternative general distributive rules. While I believe the practice is overall just, what remains nevertheless ultimately to bother us about hiring by competence is that some people will not be able to acquire maximal qualifications for some positions no matter how hard they try. Some people simply do not have the native intelligence, and any system of distributing jobs in which efficiency is an important consideration will forever bar these individuals from positions in the upper echelon. I maintain that if this is sad or seems unfair, it is nevertheless a fact of life

which cannot be justifiably improved by alternative rules of hiring. The point was made above that no matter how narrowly we construe the concept of justice and just reward, no one would advocate randomizing hiring of surgeons by hospitals. The corresponding more general point is again of relevance here. For it is generally just those positions which stress or require excellence or intelligence, thus barring individuals lacking these qualities, which we would least want to open to a random process because of their high social utility. Social welfare and often safety demands maximum competence in just such positions. The egalitarian must seem like the sceptic regarding knowledge of the external world in the philosophy classroom when he attacks hiring competents in such positions, i.e. as not to be taken with real seriousness in practice. Thus we are left with the proposal that if we tend to be egalitarians in the economic sphere, the only intelligent program is to press for compensatory programs creating equality of opportunity as far as possible, and for readjustment of pay scales, no matter how difficult or utopian the latter sounds in itself.

NOTES

1. For libertarian arguments, see Robert Nozick, *Anarchy, State, and Utopia* (New York, 1974), ch. 7, 8; also Judith Thomson, "Preferential Hiring," *Philosophy & Public Affairs*, vol. 2 (1973), pp. 364–384. For the egalitarian position see Thomas Nagel, "Equal Treatment and Compensatory Discrimination," *Philosophy & Public Affairs*, vol. 2 (1973), pp. 348–363; also John Rawls, *A Theory of Justice* (Cambridge, 1971), pp. 75–90.

2. The analogy is from Thomson, *op. cit.*

3. Nicholas Rescher, *Distributive Justice* (Indianapolis, 1966), ch. 1, 2, 5.

JAMES E. JONES

"Reverse Discrimination" in Employment

Judicial Treatment of Affirmative Action Programmes in the United States

THE CORRUPTION OF A CONCEPT

The controversy over reverse discrimination did not become acrimonious until rather late in the modern civil rights revolution. One reason, in my opinion, lies in the fact that at first the civil rights revolution had little practical impact upon Whites. It was not until theoretical rights began to be exercised in practice that opposition developed on a large scale. As long as the Executive Order[1] programmes of presidents and governors were confined to the "jaw-bone phase"[2] and Title VII[3] litigation was concerned largely with procedural and conceptual issues, only limited attention was given to so-called reverse discrimination. However, once affirmative action began to take off[4] and the focus of Title VII litigation shifted to the adoption of affirmative action plans to remedy discrimination, entrenched interests were threatened. Employers, unions and innocent White employees were put at risk and attacks on the bona fides of affirmative action began in earnest. Allegations of reverse discrimination became a key element in such attacks.

The term "reverse discrimination" is of rather recent vintage in American law, particularly in the law on equal employment opportunity (EEO). With the aid of a computer we searched the recorded cases[5] and the earliest derivation of the term we discovered was in a dissent to a 1964 New York State court case, *Balaban v. Rubin*.[6] In this case the majority sustained the action of a school board in drawing boundaries with a view, among other things, to improving racial balance in the new school. The dissent asserted:

This . . . is the reverse of anti-discrimination. The principle of anti-discrimination is that each person shall be treated without regard to race, religion or national origin. It is discrimination to admit a person because he is a Negro, Pole, Catholic, Anglo-Saxon, Jew, and so on. If persons can legally be admitted because they belong to any of these groups, then they can be excluded for the same reasons. Such a result would be contrary to the equal protection clause of the federal and state Constitution. . . .[7]

The Rise and Fall of "Reverse Discrimination" in EEO Law

The earliest federal cases we discovered both concerned employment. In *Howard v. St. Louis-San Francisco Railroad Co.*,[8] a 1965 case brought under the Railway Labour Act and crowning a 40-year struggle by Black "train porters" to be classified, paid and promoted with full seniority as "brakemen", the Court said that to allow the Blacks to use their seniority as trainmen could result in White brakemen, junior to them in years of service, being ousted from their jobs. This the Court characterised as "a kind of discrimination in reverse."[9]

In *Quarles v. Philip Morris, Inc.*,[10] the first case under Title VII of the 1964 Civil Rights Act in which the term occurs, a number of principles emerged. First, the Court determined that Congress did not intend to freeze an entire generation of Negro employees into discriminatory patterns that existed before the Act was passed. Therefore it required that Negro employees who had seniority in race-segregated departments of the company be allowed to use all of it in competition with Whites for job vacancies and promotions anywhere in the plant. The Court held, however, that Congress did not require that Negroes discriminatorily denied employment be preferred over White employees with employment seniority: that would constitute "reverse discrimination".

One aspect of the *Quarles* case, the "effects or consequences" concept subsequently endorsed by the Supreme Court in *Griggs v. Duke Power Co.*[11] and relating to the present effects of past discrimination, had a substantial impact upon the development of Title VII law. Ironically, the reverse discrimination line in *Quarles* was a "throw-away", having nothing to do with the case. It was repeated by the Court of Appeals of the Fifth Circuit in *Local 189, United Papermakers and Paperworkers v. United States*,[12] again as an example of what the law did not require. It was not a meaningful part of either decision, but it obviously provided a usable concept for future litigation. If complainants could show that a proposed action constituted reverse discrimination, arguably the action violated Title VII. It should be noted that *Local 189* and *Quarles* were decided very early in the development of Title VII law (in 1968 and 1969) when a statement by any authority was quickly seized on in the controversy over the direction the law should take.

"Reverse discrimination" was an analytical element in the *Quarles* case but not essential to the outcome. In *Franks v. Bowman*,[13] however, the relief requested for individuals discriminatorily refused employment was denied by the lower court as "fictional seniority", which under the *Quarles* and *Local 189* analysis was "reverse discrimination". The Supreme Court rejected this analysis as having no foundation in the law or its legislative history.

The next year, the Supreme Court rejected, or at least seriously restricted, the remaining contribution of those cases.[14] It concluded that seniority systems did not violate the law merely because they telescoped into the present past discriminatory hiring or placement practices. The contrary view had been expressed by eight courts of appeals in more than 30 decisions.[15] The Court also ruled that actions taken before the EEO Act was passed, though they would be in violation of the law if taken now, were beyond relief under this law.[16] So by 1977, when the reverse discrimination debate was in full swing, the legal basis of the concept had ironically been rejected by the highest court of the land.

Affirmative Action Makes Its Mark

Had it not been for the Executive Order programme in the field of equal employment opportunity, the debate over reverse discrimination would have died down after the Supreme Court decisions on seniority. The modern thrust into affirmative action begins with efforts to give meaning to that term as it was used in Executive Order 10925 of 1961[17] and continues today with the implementation of other Executive Orders.[18] A development that strengthened the Executive Order programme—and inevitably led to charges of reverse discrimination—was the introduction of the Philadelphia Plan by the Federal Government in the late 1960s.[19] Executive Orders already required government contracting agencies to write into their contracts specific clauses respecting fair employment practices, including a provision that the contractor would take affirmative action to ensure that job applicants are employed and are treated during employment without regard to race, colour, religion, sex or national origin.[20] In mid-1969 the Secretary of Labour issued an order setting out the conditions that construction contractors in the Philadelphia area would have to meet if they were to bid successfully for federally assisted contracts. These included specific goals and timetables for the employment of minority group members in six skilled crafts. The Government's action was challenged and, after losing in the federal district court, the plaintiffs took the case to the Court of Appeals of the Third Circuit.[21]

The complainants contended that the Philadelphia Plan was illegal and void for the following reasons:

1. It is action by the Executive Branch not authorised by the Constitution or any statute and beyond executive power.
2. It is inconsistent with Title VII of the Civil Rights Act of 1964.
3. It is inconsistent with Title VI of the Civil Rights Act of 1964.
4. It is inconsistent with the National Labour Relations Act.

5. It is substantively inconsistent with and was not adopted in procedural accordance with Executive Order No. 11246.

6. It violates due process because *(a)* it requires contradictory conduct impossible of consistent attainment; *(b)* it unreasonably requires contractors to undertake to remedy an evil for which the craft unions, not they, are responsible; *(c)* it arbitrarily ... singles out the five-county Philadelphia area for discriminatory treatment without adequate basis in fact or law; and *(d)* it requires quota hiring in violation of the Fifth Amendment.

This was a very significant case for a number of reasons, the most notable being that it was one of the first challenges to the Executive Order and, if the Government had lost it, the entire affirmative action effort might have been aborted.

In addition to claiming a violation of the anti-preference provision of Title VII, the plaintiffs contended that the Philadelphia Plan violated the basic prohibition against discrimination by imposing racial quotas and violated the "due process" clause of the Fifth Amendment ("No person shall be ... deprived of life, liberty or property without due process of law ...") because a decision to hire Black employees necessarily involved a decision not to hire qualified White employees—in other words, reverse discrimination.

The Court rejected all of these contentions and sustained the Government's plan. Two years later in *Associated General Contractors of Massachusetts, Inc. v. Altshuler*, [22] the First Circuit Court of Appeals reviewing a similar affirmative action plan in construction but one with even more stringent requirement than the Philadelphia Plan, sustained the goals and timetables against allegations of illegal quotas and reverse discrimination.

These cases show that there are two contexts in which the colour-conscious quota issues have been constitutionally treated and upheld. The first is where courts, pursuant to a federal statute (including Title VII), have ordered remedial action for past discrimination. These cases are instances of remedy imposed after adjudication. Clearly this type of remedy is not novel. [23] The second context in which race has been recognised as a permissible criterion for employment is in affirmative action programmes, not as a result of adjudication of

discrimination charges against specific defendants but as a matter of general policy and practice either by the executive, some other administrative agency, or the legislature. The Court of Appeals in the Philadelphia Plan case discussed above clearly recognised that the affirmative action covenant in the plans at issue was no different in kind from covenants specified in invitations to bid for contracts. It opined that the plan did not impose a punishment for past misconduct but rather exacted a covenant for present performance. The distinction between affirmative action programmes as undertakings required as a matter of general policy and affirmative action programmes as a remedy for adjudicated discrimination is significant. It is the difference between the tort, malicious injury concept and a public policy requirement directed towards changing a social condition.

Despite the failure of the Philadelphia Plan challenge, several attacks were launched against the Government's use of goals and timetables. In the overwhelming majority of cases the programmes were sustained, but the enemies of affirmative action did not desist, regardless of the growing list of defeats in the federal courts. Efforts in Congress to prohibit affirmative action requirements by attaching riders to the Labour Department's appropriations met with decisive defeat after extended discussions of the alleged horrors of employment quotas imposed by the Government. [24]

In addition to appropriation riders, when revisions of Title VII of the Civil Rights Act were being considered in 1972 attempts were made to enact specific legislation which would prohibit the use of quotas. [25] Not only did Congress reject these but it enacted section 718 of Title VII of the Civil Rights Act of 1972, which gives increased legislative validity to the affirmative action plans required under the Executive Orders.

These victories were followed by further developments of great significance to the reverse discrimination controversy. First, the Federal Government generalised the affirmative action requirement that had been validated in construction and applied goals and timetables to most other contractors. [26] Second, the US Congress incorporated the affirmative action idea with varying degrees of specificity into a large number of federal programmes. These included 10 programmes relating to educational benefits, a minority business enterprise programme, programmes to help elderly members of minority groups and provide domestic assistance to persons who do not speak English fluently, the State and Local Fiscal Assistance Act of 1972, as amended (the Revenue Sharing Act), and many others. Additionally, many state and local bodies have adopted comparable programmes so that it is doubtful whether anyone now knows the full extent of affirmative action obligations throughout the country.

DeFUNIS TO BAKKE: FIVE MORE YEARS OF ACRIMONIOUS DEBATE (1974-79)

By 1974, then, there was an abundance of affirmative action programmes, and although they had won approval by a substantial number of federal courts the critical issue of the constitutionality of affirmative action had still not been addressed by the US Supreme Court.

The first major case to reach the highest court of any state was *DeFunis v. Odegaard*.[27]

Marco DeFunis, a White male, was denied admission to the University of Washington School of Law although more than 30 applicants with lower academic credentials, all members of minority groups, were admitted. DeFunis sued in the state court alleging he had been denied admission solely on the basis of race, contrary to equal protection of the laws. The trial court agreed and a divided Supreme Court of the State of Washington reversed. The United States Supreme Court granted *certiorari*.[28] Thirty briefs were filed in the Supreme Court addressing the multitude of complex constitutional issues, but the Court, sharply divided, ruled that the case was moot.

Heated debates over the underlying issues continued for the next five years. *Bakke v. Regents of the University of California*[29] not only provided fuel for the continuing debates, but offered the US Supreme Court another opportunity to enter the fray. Unfortunately, the Supreme Court's disposition of the *Bakke* case did less to resolve the conflict than the deep division in the intellectual community deserved.

The *Bakke* case concerned a special programme for admitting minorities to the Medical School of the University of California at Davis.

Sixteen of 100 slots in the entering class were specifically reserved for minority candidates who were, however, also eligible for the other 84. This was the process that Bakke, who had been turned down for admission several times, challenged as unconstitutional, as a violation of Title VI ("Nondiscrimination in federally assisted programmes") of the Civil Rights Act of 1964, and as a violation of the Constitution of the State of California. The trial court in California found that the special programme operated as a racial quota because minority applicants were rated only against one another and the 16 places in the class of 100 were reserved for them. This, the court said, violated the federal Constitution, the state Constitution, and Title VI. However, the Court refused to order Bakke's admission because he failed to prove that without the special programme he would have been admitted to the Medical School.

On appeal, the Supreme Court of California held that the programme violated the equal protection clause of the Fourteenth Amendment of the federal Constitution because Bakke had been rejected on the basis of his race in favour of another who was less qualified as measured by the standards applied without regard to race. The Court ordered Bakke to be admitted to the Medical School and enjoined the University of California-Davis from considering the race of any applicant in its admission process.

The Supreme Court of the United States granted *certiorari* to consider the important constitutional questions raised. A record number of *amicus curiae* briefs were filed, and when the Court finally issued its decision, all sides claimed victory. One description of the outcome was that it was a 4-1-4 decision (the Supreme Court consists of nine justices). Four justices, Brennan, White, Marshall and Blackmun, fully accepted the Davis programme. They held that the Government may take race into account when it acts not to demean or insult any racial group, but to remedy disadvantages minorities have suffered by past racial injustice, at least when appropriate findings have been made by judicial, legislative or administrative bodies with competence to act in the areas concerned. Mr. Justice Powell joined the four by indicating that he was prepared to accept a system that takes race into account as *one factor* in selection, and he would approve even numerical goals where there had been a finding of prior illegal discrimination by a competent administrative or legislative agency. Four justices, Stevens, Stewart, Rehnquist and Burger, ruled that the university's programme was prohibited by Title VI of the Civil Rights Act of 1964 because the intent of Congress in that Act was that any such programme be colour-blind. Therefore it was unnecessary to take a position in this case on the constitutional issue of the use of race quotas to achieve a specific remedial effect.

The sum of the Supreme Court's treatment left much to be desired. Although there seemed to be five clear votes, a majority, for the proposition that under certain circumstances racial classification and actions based thereon would pass constitutional muster, with the shift of Justice Powell on one critical issue, there were five votes that said the Davis programme was illegal. At the very least five justices concluded that the racial classifications and the use of specific remedies were not *per se* unconstitutional. That four justices took refuge behind the will of Congress as manifested in Title VI left unresolved the question of their views on the constitutionality of the Congress's deciding to require or *permit* affirmative action. With such a cloud over the meaning of the *Bakke* case, the debate over the desirability and legality of affirmative action continued. One effect of the decision, at least as it affected education, was that the faint-hearted or the doubtful were moved to restrict affirmative action efforts. On the other side of the ledger, encouraged by a five-vote majority that race could be relevant, the more resolute proponents of affirmative action were moved to devote their attention to the specifics of their various programmes to ensure that they met Justice Powell's concerns. The Federal Government, which had supported the California-Davis programme before the Supreme Court, continued its posture that such programmes were constitutional.

While the world was waiting for the Supreme Court's disposition of the *Bakke* case, the Fifth Circuit Court of Appeals issued an opinion in *Weber v. Kaiser Aluminum and Chemical Corp.*[31] The *Weber* case was a Title VII challenge to a voluntary affirmative action programme providing for a one-to-one ratio in selection for an on-the-job training programme for skilled craft jobs in Kaiser's Gramercy (Louisiana) plant. This plan, which

formed part of the collective bargaining agreement between the company and its union, was adopted partly in order to comply with Executive Order 11246. The company previously had no training programmes and had hired its skilled craftsmen directly from the streets. The Court of Appeals ruled that the plan violated Title VII by discriminating against Whites since it had not been determined or shown that Kaiser was guilty of any past discrimination.

Observers viewed *Weber* as an opportunity for the Supreme Court to pronounce comprehensively on the issue of reverse discrimination. The Court of Appeals went out of its way to determine that even if the plan were in response to the Executive Order, the Order was invalid as it was in conflict with Title VII provisions that all preferences based on race violated the Act.

The Supreme Court in a 5-2 decision ruled that the plan was not prohibited by Title VII.[32] Mr. Justice Brennan for the majority of the Court reasoned that to interpret Title VII as prohibiting voluntary preferences of the kind agreed to by the parties in this case would be inconsistent with the clear concerns that Congress expressed in enacting the statute.[33] The majority opinion in the case is a rather curious one as it addresses only the validity of *voluntary* affirmative action plans in the context of Title VII. It is all the more curious because, although the incidents giving rise to the case occurred in 1974, no discussion appears in any of the opinions of the legislative history of Congress's 1972 amendments to the 1964 Act. The Court behaved as if Congress had shut up shop and never discussed the relationship between affirmative action and Title VII after its debates of 1964. It could be argued that, as thus discussed, the ruling offers stronger support of affirmative action than might otherwise have been the case. What it plainly establishes is that a private employer and a union, or an employer alone, can voluntarily act to eliminate manifest racial imbalance in traditionally segregated jobs where no official body—judicial, legislative or administrative—has established that there was discrimination by that employer. Such conduct does not violate Title VII.

Unfortunately, the Court missed the opportunity to address directly many of the critical issues which were raised in the lower court. While recognising the value of judicial restraint, one still wonders at the Court's reluctance to gasp the nettle. The affirmative action/reverse discrimination issue had plagued the country for a decade, particularly in employment. If ever a more wide-ranging opinion was justified, it was in the *Weber* case. And yet the Court once again spoke with uncertain voice and the debates continue.[34]

The scholarly law journals tend to lag a season behind the Supreme Court. There has been a modest amount of post-*Weber* comment and, no doubt, there is work in progress which will make its appearance next season. Meanwhile, before we have digested *Weber*, the Supreme Court decided *Fullilove v. Klutznick* on 2 July 1980.[35] This case may be the Supreme Court's fundamental contribution to disposing of the reverse discrimination issue but it would be too optimistic a reading of *Fullilove* to conclude that it will end the controversy. There were three opinions among the justices voting to sustain the programme under attack and two opinions among the three dissenting justices.

At issue was a constitutional challenge to the requirement in a congressional spending programme that, unless an administrative waiver is granted, 10 per cent of the federal funds granted for local public works projects must be used by state or local grantees to procure services or supplies from businesses owned and controlled by members of the statutorily defined minority group (this was the minority business enterprise programme mentioned earlier). There is no question that this is classification by racial or other minority criteria and that it provides a "preference" for members of the groups so defined. In the district court the validity of the programme was upheld in *Fullilove v. Kreps*.[36] The Court of Appeals of the Second Circuit affirmed, holding that even by the most exacting standards of review the programme passed constitutional muster;[37] considering the programme in the context of many years of governmental efforts to remedy past racial and ethnic discrimination, it was difficult to imagine any purpose for the programme other than to remedy such discrimination.

In the Supreme Court a plurality opinion written by Chief Justice Burger and joined by Justices White and Powell, after reviewing the legislative history and the administrative procedures relevant to the minority business enterprise programme,

declared that: "A programme that employs racial or ethnic criteria, even in a remedial context, calls for close examination."[38] The Court noted that even Acts of Congress are not immune from scrutiny and that it must look closely to determine whether Congress had overstepped its constitutional power. The Court concluded that the objectives of the legislation were within the power of Congress, that the limited use of racial and ethnic criteria in the context presented was a constitutionally permissible means for achieving those objectives, and that the Act did not violate the equal protection component of the due process clause of the Fifth Amendment.

It rejected the contention that, even in a remedial context, Congress must be wholly colourblind. With regard to the objection that the programme impermissibly deprived non-minority businesses of access to at least a portion of the government contracting opportunities generated by the Act (the reverse discrimination charge), the Court recognised that the objective of remedying historical impairment of access could have the effect of awarding elsewhere some contracts which would otherwise have been awarded to non-minority businesses that may themselves be innocent of any prior discriminatory acts. It noted that the failure of non-minority firms to receive certain contracts was an incidental consequence of the programme, not part of its objective. Similarly, it conceded that past impairment of access by minority firms to public contracting opportunities may have been an incidental consequence of "business as usual" by public contracting agencies and among prime contractors, but the Court concluded that it was not a constitutional defect in the programme that it might disappoint the expectations of non-minority firms. It declared: "When effectuating a limited and properly tailored remedy to cure the effects of prior discrimination, such a 'sharing of the burden' by innocent parties is not impermissible."[39]

On the charge that the programme excluded certain groups, the Court noted that it was legitimate for the legislature to take one step at a time to remedy part of a broader problem. Congress had not sought to give select minority groups a preferred standing in the construction industry but to place them on a more equitable footing with respect to contracting opportunities.[40] Perhaps the most telling statement from the Burger plurality opinion was the following:

Congress, after due consideration, perceived a pressing need to move forward with new approaches in the continuing effort to achieve the goal of equality of economic opportunity. In this effort, Congress has necessary latitude to try new techniques such as the limited use of racial and ethnic criteria to accomplish remedial objectives; this especially is so in programmes where voluntary co-operation with remedial measures is induced by placing conditions on federal expenditure. That the programme may press the outer limits of congressional authority affords no basis for striking it down. . . . Petitioners have mounted a facial challenge to a programme developed by the politically responsive branches of government. . . . Congress must proceed only with programmes narrowly tailored to achieve its objectives, subject to continuing evaluation and reassessment; administration of programmes must be vigilant and flexible; and, when such a programme comes under judicial review, courts must be satisfied that the legislative objectives and projected administration give reasonable assurance that the programme will function within constitutional limitations.[41]

Mr. Justice Powell, although joining the opinion of the Chief Justice, also set forth his view separately for the purpose of applying the analysis of his opinion in the *Bakke* case. He stated with greater specificity what must be done if competent legislative or administrative bodies are to be successful in imposing race-conscious remedies.

Mr. Justice Marshall, joined by Justices Brennan and Blackmun, concurred in the judgment of the Court but wrote separate opinions for a particular purpose. Agreeing with their fellow justices that programmes which contain suspect classification are subject to strict scrutiny and can be justified only if furthering a compelling governmental purpose, and even then only if no less restrictive alternative is available, the Marshall group wrote to reinforce the position they took in *Bakke*, namely that principles outlawing the irrelevant or pernicious use of race are inapposite to racial classifications that provide benefits to minorities for the purpose of remedying the present effects of past discrimination.

Such classifications [they wrote] may disadvantage some Whites but Whites as a class lack the "traditional indicia of suspectness": the class is not saddled with such disabili-

ties, or subjected to such a history of purposeful unequal treatment, or relegated to such a position of political powerlessness as to command extraordinary protection from the majoration process. Because the consideration of race is relevant to remedy the continuing effects of past racial discrimination, and because governmental programmes employing racial classifications for remedial purposes can be crafted to avoid stigmatisation, we conclude that such programmes should not be subjected to conventional "strict scrutiny"—scrutiny that is strict in theory but fatal in fact.[42]

Justices Rehnquist and Stewart joined in a dissent, the burden of which was that the Constitution is colour-blind and neither knows nor tolerates classes among citizens, and that on its face the provision at issue in this case denied equal protection of the law. Their sentiments were summarised as follows:

The Fourteenth Amendment was adopted to ensure that every person must be treated equally by each state regardless of the colour of his skin. The Amendment promised to carry to its necessary conclusion a fundamental principle upon which this nation had been founded— that the law would honour no preference based on lineage. Tragically, the promise of 1868 was not immediately fulfilled, and decades passed before the states and the Federal Government were finally directed to eliminate detrimental classifications based on race. Today, the Court derails this achievement and places its imprimatur on the creation once again by government of privileges based on birth.[43]

In their view, under the Constitution, we may not practise racism even temporarily as an experiment.

Mr. Justice Stevens, who also dissented, seems to come down somewhere between the position of the Chief Justice and that of the Rehnquist/Stewart dissent. He was not convinced that the Constitution contains an absolute prohibition on classification by race, but he believed it is up to Congress to demonstrate that any unique statutory preference is justified by a relevant characteristic that is shared by members of the preferred class. In his opinion Congress failed to make that demonstration in the programmes under scrutiny and consequently failed to discharge its duty to govern impartially as required by the Constitution.[44]

Two things may be said about the impact of this decision on the continuing debate regarding reverse discrimination/affirmative action. The view that racial classifications *per se* violate the Constitution managed to garner only two votes (Stewart and Rehnquist). Marshall, Brennan, and Blackmun would have sustained even the *Bakke* programme and took a more flexible view of what governments may do. They found no constitutional impediment to this programme and will no doubt continue to approve efforts to remedy discrimination in this fashion. Burger, joined by White and Powell, gave clear indication that all future programmes using racial classifications are going to be scrutinised on a case-by-case basis. Add to Powell's recitation of the safeguards required by such programmes Stevens's unhappiness with the extent to which Congress complied with those requirements this time, we can anticipate continued assaults upon the principle of affirmative action under the guise of seeking review of specific programmes. The Supreme Court, it seems, rather than resolving the issue, has ensured that debate over it will be prolonged. The Burger plurality opinion is a very narrow approach which suggests trouble for other programmes which might not be able to fit into the structure established by the Public Works Employment Act of 1977 and the history of administration of the minority business enterprise programme.

On the plus side, it seems clear that all six of the majority believe deference is due to the legislature, as a coequal branch of government, and that resolution of the conflict more appropriately belongs in the political arena. Even the dissent of Stewart and Rehnquist points in that direction.

That the debate will be continued is guaranteed by the Supreme Court's docket for 1981.[45] If the position outlined in the Burger plurality opinion (and seemingly endorsed by Mr. Justice Stevens) prevails, we can anticipate a steady flow of cases seeking Supreme Court review until all of the issues have been addressed.

CONCLUSION

The term "reverse discrimination" is a corruption no matter in which sense it is used. If it is used to describe denial of a right or a benefit or an expectation to a White because Blacks or other minorities are being given preference, it is a corruption of the law. The Supreme Court has ruled (Mr. Justice Marshall for a unanimous Court) that Title VII of the Civil Rights Act of 1964 and the Reconstruction Era Civil Rights Act prohibit discrimination on grounds of race—White, Brown or Black.[46]

Whenever race or ethnic background is used as a distinguishing factor in programmes benefiting the members of groups so identified, such programmes are attacked as "reverse discrimination". Up to a point, the term is apt—that is, these programmes do identify the group, not for the purpose of stigmatising, excluding or abusing its members, but to ensure that they are included and helped. Thus it is true that this is the reverse of the purposes for which these groups were classified for so many years in the United States, and that the attention given them under modern affirmative action programmes is the reverse of the treatment they received in the past. But this is not what those who use the term "reverse discrimination" mean. What they mean is that their group risks losing some right, benefit or expectation while other groups receive or will receive special attention and that this is, or should be, illegal.

Acceptance by the courts or other governmental entities of the notion of "reverse discrimination" would put the country in an impossible position. The only feasible way to remedy the underparticipation of some groups (e.g. in employment) is to devise programmes specifically aimed at the members of these groups. For example, if underutilisation of women and Blacks is the problem, it would be patently idiotic to craft a remedial programme that ignored sex or race.

The social purpose of affirmative action programmes is to achieve a distribution throughout occupational and professional categories, or other life chances, that is appropriately representative of the diversity of our population generally. To achieve this objective, some individuals in an underutilised group will necessarily be "windfall" beneficiaries of altered, and hopefully improved, economic circumstances. Unfortunately, some individuals in other groups whose participation is average or above will—if opportunities are not unlimited—be unintentionally restricted or forced to lower their expectations. To label such programmes "reverse discrimination" is to determine legality and constitutionality through the use of undefined terminology.

Analysis of the use made in law of the term "reverse discrimination" easily reveals what is at issue. Discrimination is not defined in equal employment opportunity law; rather its meaning has emerged through judicial decisions. There is discrimination—invidious discrimination—which is not in violation of Title VII or of other civil rights legislation.[47] What the law has endeavoured to do is to determine which kinds of discrimination are *actionable*. The reverse discrimination lobby would have the law prohibit any *benign* conduct based on race, by government or by private parties compelled by government, because any such programme would exclude some group.

Is there no justification for governmental attention to the plight of minorities in modern America? Is there no evidence of racial underparticipation in the benefits of America? Mr. Justice Marshall in his separate opinion in the *Bakke* case summarised the modern condition:

The position of the Negro today in America is the tragic but inevitable consequence of centuries of unequal treatment. Measured by any benchmark of comfort or achievement, meaningful equality remains a distant dream for the Negro. . . . [There follow statistics demonstrating that Blacks are on average at a clear disadvantage in respect of life expectancy, infant mortality, income and employment.]

The relationship between these figures and the history of unequal treatment afforded to the Negro cannot be denied. At every point from birth to death the impact of the past is reflected in the still disfavoured position of the Negro.

In light of the sorry history of discrimination and its devastating impact on the lives of Negroes, bringing the Negro into the mainstream of American life should be a state interest of the highest order. To fail to do so is to ensure that America will forever remain a divided society.[48]

Americans are great believers in statistics and there is no way that the figures cited by Mr. Justice Marshall can be explained as accidental. One can, of course, take refuge in the belief that Black Americans are genetically inferior and, coupling this view with a notion of social Darwinism, conclude that the minority population's participation rate is what that population deserves. Another approach, of course—and one seemingly acceptable to Mr. Justice Rehnquist and Mr. Justice Stewart—is that regardless of the country's history and any current conditions of imbalance, the Constitution requires colour-blindness, and any effort to deal with this

problem that involves classification by race and specific attention to the group so classified violates constitutional principles.

There is substantial evidence that the representatives of the majority of Americans reject the Rehnquist-Stewart approach and, whether or not they reject the genetic inferiority view, they accept the obligation of society to do something about the severe imbalance. One of the difficulties with the political response over the past decade, as was also the case in the 1860s, has been that legislative bodies have felt it necessary to include other groups as well as Blacks in the special programmes to make them politically palatable. Thus we see attention also given to women, the Spanish-speaking, the Indians and the Aleuts. History documents that the impact of invidious discrimination in this country has been felt most cruelly and perniciously by Blacks, but neither political power nor moral persuasiveness has ever been great enough for programmes to be crafted solely for their benefit.

Despite the continuing attacks on affirmative action programmes in periodic court cases and in the legal and intellectual journals, these programmes have gained wide acceptance over the past ten to 12 years. There are so many federal programmes on the subject that no one seems to have an exact count; the estimate is that Congress has enacted some 60 to 80 such laws.[49] Nor is there any estimate of how many programmes have been enacted by states, cities and counties, through legislation or executive action, though evidence again indicates that the number is substantial. . . .[50]

The continued viability of affirmative action programmes in the field of job opportunities will also, of necessity, be heavily dependent upon the economic health of the country, as sharing the burdens of past discrimination is more acceptable when job opportunities are abundant. For this reason the future of affirmative action/reverse discrimination will now depend less on legal theories or philosophical ideals than on economic and political realities.

NOTES

1. Executive Orders are administrative decrees used by the President to implement certain policies without the

need for full Congressional approval. However, should an Executive Order have financial implications, the Congress must give its acquiescence if the Order is to be fully implemented. The same applies, *mutatis mutandis*, to orders issued by state governors.

2. J. Jones: "Federal contract compliance in Phase II: the dawning of the age of enforcement of equal employment obligations," in *Georgia Law Review* (Athens (Georgia)), Summer 1970, pp. 756 ff.

3. Title VII ("Equal employment opportunity") of the Civil Rights Act of 1964 is reproduced in full in *Legislative Series* (Geneva, ILO), 1964–USA 1. For an analysis of this Title see J. E. Means: "Fair employment practices legislation and enforcement in the United States," in *International Labour Review*, Mar. 1966, pp. 237–242.

4. See J. Jones: "The bugaboo of employment quotas," in *Wisconsin Law Review* (Madison (Wisconsin)), 1970, pp. 341 ff.

5. Using Lexis, a computerised system for retrieving legal documents, we first requested all opinions containing the term "reverse discrimination" and then all those containing both "reverse" and "discrimination" or "discriminatory" within five words of each other. The second search recovered terms such as "discrimination in reverse" and "reverse racial discrimination".

At the federal level we found 221 opinions using "reverse discrimination" or a similar term. Fifty cases which did not concern employment discrimination were immediately discarded, and 60 more were found to be not relevant to the analysis. In another 19 cases the term "reverse discrimination" was merely a party's allegation that was not accepted by the court. In 25 cases the term was not relevant to the decision.

We studied most closely the remaining 67 in which "reverse discrimination" was a synonym for "unlawful". In 30 cases the court labelled the contested consent decree, or affirmative action or the desired relief "reverse discrimination" and struck it down. In 37 cases the court upheld the decree or programme or granted relief by announcing that it was not "reverse discrimination". (Note that these statistics concern the use of the term "reverse discrimination", but not the state of the law on affirmative action. In some instances, both trial and appellate court decisions in the same case are included. Also, some opinions on affirmative action do not discuss "reverse discrimination". Those cases do not appear in the statistics.)

After announcing the conclusion "reverse discrimination", the courts rarely reasoned further. If the target group received a preference, it was "reverse discrimination" and unlawful. One partial exception in the US Court of Appeals, Second Circuit, in *Kirkland v. New York State Dept. of Correctional Services*, 520 F.2d 420 (1975). The Kirkland test has two prongs: first, there must be a "clear-cut pattern of long continued and egregious racial discrimination" and second, the effects of the affirmative action must not fall on a small, identifiable group.

6. *Balaban v. Rubin*, 14 N.Y. 2d 193, 199 N.E. 2d 375 (1964).

7. 14 N.Y. 2d, p. 199, 199 N.E. 2d, p. 378.

8. *Howard v. St. Louis-San Francisco Railroad Co.*, 244 F.Supp. 1008 (E.D. Mo. 1965).

9. Ibid., p. 1012. The job of train porter was indistinguishable from brakeman except that Blacks who performed all of the duties that brakemen did had extra tasks including sweeping, general cleaning and helping passengers. For doing more work they received less pay. For the entire sordid story see *Howard v. Thompson*, 72 F.Supp. 695, reversed 191 F.2d 442, affirmed sub nom. *Trainmen v. Howard*, 343 U.S. 768 (1952).

10. *Quarles v. Philip Morris, Inc.*, 279 F.Supp. 505 (E.D. Va. 1968).

11. *Griggs v. Duke Power Co.*, 401 U.S. 424 (1971). See also A. W. Blumrosen: "Strangers in paradise: *Griggs v. Duke Power Co.,* and the concept of employment discrimination", in *Michigan Law Review* (Ann Arbor (Michigan)), 1972–73, pp. 59 ff.

12. *Local 189, United Papermakers and Paperworkers v. United States*, 416 F.2d 980 (5th Cir. 1969), *cert. denied*, 397 U.S. 919 (1970).

13. *Franks v. Bowman Transportation Co., Inc.*, 424 U.S. 747 (1976).

14. *International Brotherhood of Teamsters v. United States*, 431 U.S. 324 (1977).

15. There are 11 United States courts of appeals in 10 circuits composed of three or more states and one circuit for the District of Columbia.

16. *United Airlines, Inc. v. Evans*, 431 U.S. 553 (1977).

17. Executive Order 10925, *Title 3 Code of Federal Regulations: 1959–1963 compilation* (Washington, 1964); pp. 448–454. See also Means, op. cit., pp. 220–221.

18. Sex-based discrimination was prohibited by Executive Order 11375, *Title 3 Code of Federal Regulations: 1966–1970 compilation* (Washington, 1971), pp. 684–686. Enforcement was transferred from 11 separate compliance agencies to the Secretary of Labour by Executive Order 12086, *Title 3 Code of Federal Regulations: 1978 compilation* (Washington, 1979), pp. 230-234.

19. See "The Philadelphia Plan: equal employment opportunity in the construction trades", in *Columbia Journal of Law and Social Problems* (New York), May 1970, pp. 187 ff.; Leithen: "Preferential treatment in the skilled building trades: an analysis of the Philadelphia Plan", in *Cornell Law Review* (Ithaca (New York)), 1970, Vol. 56, pp. 84 ff.; and Jones: "The bugaboo of employment quotas", op. cit.

20. The prohibition of sex-based discrimination was added in 1967 by Executive Order 11375. See note 30.

21. *Contractors' Association of Eastern Pennsylvania v. Secretary of Labor*, 442 F.2d 159 (3d Cir. 1971), *cert. denied*, 404 U.S. 854 (1971).

22. *Associated General Contractors of Massachusetts, Inc. v. Altshuler*, 490 F.2d 9 (1st Cir. 1973), *cert. denied*, 416 U.S. 957 (1974).

23. See *Rios v. Enterprise Association Steamfitters Local 638 of U.A.*, 501 F.2d 622 (2d Cir. 1974), p. 629, for a list of the eight circuit Courts of Appeals that approved the imposition of a quota remedy once discrimination was found.

24. "The Philadelphia Plan: a study in the dynamics of executive power", in *University of Chicago Law Review* (Chicago), Summer 1972, pp. 723 ff.

25. Ibid., pp. 747–757.

26. Order No. 4, *Code of Federal Regulations* (Washington, 1979), Vol. 41, part 60-2, pp. 310 ff.

27. *DeFunis v. Odegaard*, 82 Wash. 2d 11, 507 P.2d 1169 (1973).

28. *Cert. granted*, 414 U.S. 1038 (1973).

29. *Bakke v. Regents of the University of California*, 18 Cal.3d 34, 553 P.2d 1152 (1976).

30. *Cert. granted*, 429 U.S. 1090 (1977).

31. *Weber v. Kaiser Aluminum and Chemical Corp.*, 563 F.2d 216 (5th Cir. 1977).

32. *United Steelworkers of America v. Weber*, 443 U.S. 193 (1979).

33. Justices Stewart, White, Marshall and Blackmun joined Brennan's opinion, with Justice Blackmun also filing a separate concurrence. Justices Burger and Rehnquist dissented. Justices Stevens and Powell did not take part in the case.

34. See H. Edwards: "Affirmative action or reverse discrimination: the head and tail of Weber", in *Creighton Law Review* (Omaha (Nebraska)), 1980, Vol. 13, pp. 713 ff.; idem: "Preferential remedies and affirmative action in employment in the wake of Bakke", in *Washington University Law Quarterly* (St. Louis (Missouri)), 1979, No. 1, pp. 113 ff.; and "Some post-Bakke-and-Weber reflections on reverse discrimination", in *University of Richmond Law Review* (Richmond (Virginia)), 1980, Vol. 14, pp. 373 ff.

35. *Fullilove v. Klutznick*, 100 S. Ct. 2758 (1980).

36. *Fullilove v. Kreps*, 443 F.Supp. 253 (S.D.N.Y. 1977).

37. *Fullilove v. Kreps*, 584 F.2d 600 (2d Cir. 1978).

38. *Fullilove v. Klutznick*, op. cit., p. 2771.

39. Ibid., pp. 2777-2778.

40. Ibid., p. 2778.

41. Ibid., pp. 2780-2781.

42. Ibid., pp. 2795-2796.

43. Ibid., p. 2802. The Fourteenth Amendment applies to the states. The Due Process Clause of the Fifth Amendment performs the office of both the Due Process and Equal Protection Clauses of the Fourteenth Amendment in requiring the Federal Sovereign to act impartially.

44. Ibid., pp. 2813–2814.

45. The Court will hear one challenge to a state affirmative action programme, and two other challenges of city affirmative action programmes seek review.

46. *MacDonald v. Santa Fe Trail Transportation Co.*, 427 U.S. 273 (1976).

47. See, for example, *International Brotherhood of Teamsters*, op. cit.; *United Airlines*, op. cit.; and *General Electric Co. v. Gilbert*, 429 U.S. 125 (1976).

48. *Regents of the University of California*, op. cit.; separate opinion of Justice Marshall, pp. 387 and 395–396.

49. Telephone conversation with James D. Henry, Associate Solicitor of Labour for Civil Rights, US Department of Labour, 7 July 1980.

50. The *Fair Employment Practice Manual* (Washington, Bureau of National Affairs). Vol. 8-8a (1981), reports 20 states and the District of Columbia as having taken some type of affirmative action initiative. Seven states have enacted statutes. Nineteen, including five that also have statutes, have acted by Executive Order or administrative rules.

CHAPTER ELEVEN
Study Questions

1. What explanations are there for the wage differentials between blacks or women and white males in the same occupations and with the same educational backgrounds?

2. The Constitution requires that all citizens be provided equal protection under the laws. Lisa Newton interprets the right of equal citizenship to prohibit preferential treatment for minorities in affirmative action programs. Do you believe that this constitutional right to equality should be seen as prohibiting those programs? Are there any distinctions between citizens that can be made by the law in a manner consistent with this right to equality? Can a right to equality, whether moral or constitutional, require that all persons be treated in the same fashion?

3. A merit approach to hiring or admissions emphasizes the qualifications of applicants. What sorts of qualifications would indicate that one merited admission into college? On what grounds do you distinguish between aspects of persons that are qualifications and aspects that are not? Are discriminations that college admissions officers make between people on the basis of these qualifications fair?

4. Affirmative action programs are meant to improve the lot of minority or disadvantaged groups. Left-handed golfers are a minority group. Do they deserve to benefit from affirmative action? How do you determine when a minority group should benefit from affirmative action? On the basis of that determination, which groups do you feel ought to benefit from affirmative action?

5. If affirmative action programs aim at improving the social and economic conditions of minorities, when would those conditions improve enough to eliminate the programs?

6. What problems are there for affirmative action programs when they would result in the hiring of incompetent workers?

7. Are all forms of discrimination based on race equally objectionable?

8. Many object to affirmative action because it places the burden of correcting society's wrongs on only one segment of the society—young white males. Certainly under these policies young white males often fail to get jobs they otherwise would have gotten. Is this unjust? When does the imposition of a cost create an injustice?

CHAPTER TWELVE

*E*NVIRONMENT

CASE STUDY

Dumping Dioxins

No environmental issue has attracted as much public concern during recent years as the dumping of toxic wastes. No toxic waste has generated more of this concern than dioxin. Both the Agent Orange and Times Beach controversies involved dioxin contamination. Yet, while the controversy continues, some businesses must make daily decisions about disposal of dioxins.

Dioxin itself has no practical use or benefits. It is a contaminant of other useful products, created in the process of manufacturing herbicides, wood preservatives, and bacteria cleansers. It has been called the most toxic substance known to man, but the evidence for this is ambiguous. Dioxin is over 2,000 times more deadly than strychnine in guinea pigs, yet its toxicity varies tremendously across species. It is 5,000 times less lethal in hamsters than in guinea pigs, 300 times less lethal in dogs, 70 times less lethal in monkeys. Other than skin rashes, its effect on humans is unclear. While scientific studies have been inconclusive, it has been claimed as the major cause of deaths and sicknesses in Vietnam veterans

who were exposed to dioxin-contaminated Agent Orange.

Although some industry studies suggest that dioxin is formed in many different combustion situations, including fireplaces and car exhaust pipes, the most serious cases of contamination can be traced to waste disposal methods of chemical companies or private waste haulers. Disposal of dioxin raises the following issues for chemical manufacturers.

First, there is no established evidence that dioxin in trace amounts, one part per billion or so, causes serious harm to humans. As long as consumers demand certain herbicides, dioxin-contaminated wastes will require disposal. Further, present law only requires a 60-day notice before disposing dioxin. Although there are various detoxification technologies available, including burning and exposure to ultraviolet light, it is not illegal to bury the waste. In fact, it costs significantly less to dump these wastes than to detoxify them. The EPA also allows smaller companies to dispose of toxicants at solid waste landfills and municipal dumps. Often called the "small-generator exemption," this rule allows individual firms to dispose of up to one ton of toxic wastes a month without EPA monitoring or official record-keeping. Finally, firms can hire independent private haulers to dispose of these wastes and thereby pass along responsibility. Accordingly, dumping dioxin wastes in small amounts can be a legally and economically sound business decision. Is it a morally sound decision?

Introduction

OF ALL THE issues examined in this book, concern with the environment is, in a sense, the least controversial. No one wants to breath polluted air. No one desires to drink tainted water. No one wants to live atop a toxic waste dump. No one desires that a plant or animal species should become extinct. Few are unconcerned with the quality of the environment that will be inherited by our children and grandchildren. All other things being equal, we would all desire to live in a clean, safe, and ecologically stable environment.

Of course, "all other things" are not equal. None of these desirable states of affairs can be secured without paying a price. Industrial closings, lower productivity, loss of jobs, and lower living standards are some of the results that critics of the environmental movement foresee if we quickly and vigorously pursue policies aimed at cleaning up the environment. Undesirable economic consequences are generally the most common and most serious objections raised against environmental policies by the business community. The selections in this chapter, therefore, pay special attention to the relation between environmental goals and economic consequences.

Before we begin this analysis it will be helpful to make a distinction between issues of *pollution* and issues of *conservation*. Those issues that involve contaminating the natural environment with harmful products are pollution issues. Concern with preserving the natural environment we shall call conservation issues. Many philosophers (and others) believe that this distinction involves importantly different moral issues.

From the moral point of view, pollution is important because it represents a potential harm to human beings. Moral rights are generally understood as providing people with protection from harm. In this way, moral discussions about pollution often involve consideration of human moral rights. Do we have a right to a clean and livable environment? If so, how is this right justified? How does it arise? How do environmental rights compare with other rights? How should we adjudicate conflicts between environmental rights and other rights? Much of the philosophical analysis of pollution focuses on these questions, with special emphasis upon conflicts between environmental and property rights.

Conservation issues do not so obviously involve the rights of currently living people. It would be difficult to show how strip-mining or clear-cutting timber harvesting or snail-darter extinction actually harms anyone. Rather, moral discussions of conservation issues usually focus upon the moral status of things other than living humans. Do natural objects, e.g., trees, mountains, lakes, animals, species, have moral rights? How would such rights relate to the rights of humans? If natural objects do not have rights, do they possess some intrinsic goodness or value that deserves protection? Do future generations of people have rights that would entail duties on our part to conserve resources? How would we best discharge an obligation to conserve? These and other questions dominate the philosophical analysis of conservation.

Whether or not a clear distinction between pollution and conservation can be maintained, the reader should be sensitive to diverse philosophical issues that underlie much of the environmental discussion. Merely to say that a clean and healthy environment or a preserved natural resource is a *desirable* thing often conceals complex and important moral issues.

Turning to pollution issues, this chapter begins with a short description of acid rain. The selection is from a League of Women Voters publication that outlines the nature, causes, and costs of acid rain. Although as yet the diagnosis is not accepted by all, especially by industry sources, prevailing scientific opinion locates the source of much acid rain in the sulfur dioxide emissions of industry smokestacks in the Ohio Valley and Far West. This description of acid rain will provide a useful example while evaluating the debates in the selections that follow.

Our next few readings turn specifically to the question of the economic costs of environmental policies. The U. S. Council on Environmental Quality, in its 11th Annual Report, claims that in general the data shows that there is little impact upon productivity by environmental regulations. The council defends environmental regulations on a number of grounds. First, the contributions that regulation makes to productivity are often ignored or unmeasured. Safe and healthy workplaces, clean air and water, and fertile reclaimed land certainly can add to economic productivity, although this fact is often ignored by critics. Further, the council points out that economic incentives are being used to control pollution. Such incentives aim at making it more economically efficient to comply with rather than ignore or fight environmental regulation. Finally, the council claims that studies have shown that the EPA is better at estimating compliance costs than the private sector. Since these private estimates are often the basis of criticisms of EPA policies, this is a crucial fact indeed.

In the following selection, Freeman, Haveman, and Kneese present a more detailed analysis of the costs of environmental regulation. A number of arguments support their conclusion that "while achieving major environmental improvements is likely to be very costly, the amounts are not so great as to require a significant reduction in our material well-being." The authors also consider some implications of pollution and offer an important analysis: It is often the poor who get most hurt by pollution; who, in other words, pay the costs of not enforcing the environmental regulations. Finally, the authors consider some policies, including cost subsidies and adjustment assistance, aimed at reducing the economic hardships of compliance.

Various objections are raised to this economic approach to pollution regulation. Perhaps the most serious challenge is raised against the entire economic approach itself. David Pearce develops an extensive critique of the economic approach to pollution problems. Pearce evaluates and rejects many of the economic recommendations made by economists. Neither cost-benefit analysis, the free market, standards, nor charges (taxes) can resolve the current environmental crisis. To believe that the economic approach can solve our problems is "dangerously naive." On the other hand, to reject economics and its methods is also to make a mistake. A more integrated approach combining both economics and ecology is needed.

Turning more directly to conservation issues, John Baden and Richard Stroup consider various methods for managing our national forests. Their analysis easily can be extended to the management of all natural resources, including not only forests but lakes, rivers, mountain ranges, and even animal life.

In their analysis, Baden and Stroup suggest that the aim of our environmental policies should be to achieve "efficiency and equity." Efficiency, in the economic sense we have considered in earlier chapters, would guarantee optimal use of resources. More people have more of their preferences satisfied in an efficient distribution than otherwise. This aim seems consistent with democratic values like pluralism and majority rule. Equity, on the other hand, should ensure that efficiency not be achieved unfairly or unjustly.

Baden and Stroup argue that property rights, properly understood, hold the key to a solution of our problems. By selling national forests to private parties we can achieve a net improvement in both efficiency and equity. They suggest that people will be less likely to exploit, waste, or destroy their own property than they are when that property is held in common. An example can help explain their point.

Certain whale species are on the verge of extinction. In the open ocean no one "owns" the whales, they are there for the taking, and Russian, Japanese, Canadian, and American whalers have been taking them for generations. The entire whale population has been exploited for generations and it is now close to extinction.

On the other hand, there is virtually no chance that chickens, cows, or dogs will become extinct. All of these animals can be privately owned and it is the owners who make certain that they will not become extinct. Some of these owners do this in order to make money, but others, for example dog owners, do this because of their concern for the dogs themselves.

So, the argument goes, private ownership of natural resources provides the best means for guaranteeing the preservation of those resources. Owners, whether their motivation is profit or something more ecologically benign, have the incentive to preserve resources. This incentive does not exist when the resources are unowned or owned publicly.

Mark Sagoff criticizes this approach to conservation along many of the same lines that David Pearce criticized the economic approach to pollution. Sagoff argues that the approach that aims at efficiency and equity "will result in commercial sprawl," and will "appall ethical judgment and aesthetic taste." Sagoff believes that non-economic principles must be used in making environmental decisions.

One criticism of Sagoff would characterize these other principles as "elitist" and anti-democratic. People have many different desires and, in a democracy at least, no individual desires should dominate. Who is to say that your desire for a wilderness and backpacking national park is better than my desire for one that has motels, fast-food stands, and amusement parks? Only a market solution can guarantee an optimal satisfaction of these various desires.

Against this criticism, Sagoff believes that the time has come to find arguments to support those desires, be they ethical or aesthetic, that are characterized as "elitist." In yet another version of a debate we've seen before, Sagoff claims that not all consumer preferences are equal, that some are better than others, and that, therefore, some deserve to be satisfied before others. Sagoff believes that reasoned arguments can be given in support of this view.

In our final selection, Annette Baier examines the question of the rights of future generations. Baier believes that there is nothing incoherent about seeing future persons as having rights. Further, she believes that there are good reasons for us to recognize obligations to these future persons. Among these are obligations to renew what we use, to pass on what we ourselves have received from previous generations, and to try to leave things, at least, no worse off than we found them.

THE LEAGUE OF WOMEN VOTERS

Acid Rain: The Invisible Enemy

Picture a soft spring rain dancing on a clear blue lake, with a backdrop of tall pines and rugged hills—hardly a typical scene for an antipollution campaign. It's hard to recognize an enemy you can't see. It's hard to look at that pastoral vista and realize that the lake may be lifeless and the rain may be the reason why. Most Americans have heard of acid rain, but few know what it is or where it comes from. Strictly speaking, the term is as deceptive as that peaceful lakeside scene. Scientists prefer the more accurate "acid deposition." But in many ways, the image of rain—the primeval sustainer of life now become the transmitter of lethal, invisible pollution—makes the more popular term a good description of the complex acid rain problem.

WHAT IS ACID RAIN?

The measurement used to determine whether a substance is acid or alkaline (basic) is known as the pH scale. On the scale of 0 to 14, a value of 7 is neutral, with lower numbers indicating progressively greater acidity; values above 7 denote progressively greater alkalinity. Since the pH scale is logarithmic, apparently small increments in pH measurements may in fact tell of serious changes. The 10-fold increase between numbers means that a pH of 6.0 is ten times more acidic than 7.0; 5.0 is one hundred times more acid than 7.0; 4.0 is one thousand times more acidic, and so on. Normal rain is slightly acidic—about pH 5.6—due to naturally occurring chemicals in the atmosphere. However, the average pH of rainfall over the northeastern United States and eastern Canada, where acid rain has taken its greatest toll, is now 3.9–4.3 (about the acidity of lemon juice), with many individual storms registering much lower. It is a growing problem in other areas of the country as well, most notably in the Southeast. In the Northeast, the cumulative effects of acid rain are particularly critical, partly because of the lack of natural buffering agents in the soil and bedrock. One result is that more than 280 once-pristine lakes in the Adirondack Mountains of New York have gradually become too acidic to support fish and other organisms. Hundreds more are in trouble, although to a nonexpert, the trouble may be hard to see. Large fish kills and other dramatic signs of pollution are rare. Instead, as the pH level decreases, fish and other species simply disappear, succumbing slowly to the effects of acid or the increased concentration of heavy metals that the acid leaches from surrounding soils. Reproductive failures and the breakdown of the food chain also take their progressive toll until, by the time the pH level of the lake drops to about 4.5, all life is gone. Of course, this simplified description masks myriad biological and chemical complexities. But scientists have no shortage of real-world laboratories as they work to unravel those complexities on the shores of dead and dying lakes. Other researchers have documented the adverse effects of acid rain on buildings and monuments, and the evidence linking acid rain to crop and forest damage is becoming more and more evident. Scientists are increasingly concerned about human health effects, as well, particularly through the contamination of drinking water.

The process that spawns this invisible kind of pollution—a process that typically begins scores or hundreds of miles from the scene of precipitation—is as complex as its effects. To simplify again, acid rain is formed when sulfur dioxide (SO_2) and nitrogen oxides (NO_x) react with moisture in the atmosphere to form sulfates and nitrates, which are eventually washed out by rain—or perhaps by snow or fog. Dry acid deposition occurs when the SO_2 and NO_x fall to the ground and then are converted to acids when they are mixed with moisture. The "raw materials" for the creation of acid

From *The National Voter,* Vol. 32, No. 4, (Winter 1983), pp. 23–26. Reprinted by permission of The League of Women Voters, Wash., D.C. 20036.

rain—sulfur dioxide and nitrogen oxides—are the by-products of fossil fuel combustion. Coal-burning utilities generate two-thirds or more of the SO_2 and about 30 percent of the NO_x in the atmosphere; cars, trucks, and other mobile sources account for much of the rest of the NO_x.

BLOWING IN THE WIND

Utilities in the Ohio Valley are responsible for the highest output of sulfur dioxide in the United States, and it is there that prevailing scientific opinion traces the source of much of the acid rain problem in the eastern part of the country. Under the gun to meet tough air-quality standards in their own backyards, many utilities over the last decade raised their emissions stacks to facilitate the dispersal of pollutants—contrary to the intent of the Clean Air Act, which aimed at *controls* rather than dispersal. This "solution" only transferred the problem—via strong west-to-east wind currents that pick up pollutants from these towering stacks and transport them over great distances. The political problem with this phenomenon of "long-range transport" is that once SO_2 molecules pour out of an Ohio smokestack, for instance, it is impossible to identify them positively with the acid raindrops falling on a lake in New York or a trout stream in West Virginia. That makes it difficult for some decision makers to accept that reducing SO_2 emissions in the Midwest, or elsewhere, will help to reduce the acidity of rain falling far "downwind." Nevertheless, a growing body of scientists around the world, led in this country by the prestigious National Academy of Sciences (NAS), warns that as long as millions of tons of SO_2 and NO_x—proven to be destructive to health and environment—are poured into the atmosphere every year, the law of gravity will surely bring the consequences down somewhere. According to a 1981 NAS report, "continued emissions of sulfur and nitrogen oxides at current or accelerated rates, in the face of clear evidence of serious hazard to human health and to the biosphere, will be extremely risky from a long-term economic standpoint as well as from the standpoint of biosphere protection."

Some experts argue that more research is needed into all aspects of the acid rain issue before control strategies are initiated. However, the League of Women Voters of the United States and other members of the National Clean Air Coalition strongly endorse the NAS position that, while continuing research is vital, the nation simply cannot afford to further delay curbs on the most obvious culprits in the unfolding—and spreading—acid rain story. The League is vigorously supporting efforts to incorporate acid rain control provisions into the reauthorization of the Clean Air Act, which has been the focus of major battles on Capitol Hill for over a year. ... A League-backed provision introduced in Congress ... calls for reducing SO_2 emissions by 10 million tons by 1990. The reduction quotas for each of 31 states in an acid rain control region east of the Mississippi River would be apportioned through a formula based on relative contribution to the SO_2 emission problem. The LWVUS is also fighting hard to counter automakers' pressure for a relaxation of the Clean Air Act's auto-emission standards for NO_x.

COSTS AND BENEFITS

How to count the dollars associated with the causes and cures of acid rain? Estimates prepared by ICF, Inc. for the National Clean Air Coalition showed that a 10-million-ton SO_2 clean-up over 10 years would cost about $2.5 billion a year. By contrast, the NAS has estimated that damage from acid rain amounts to about $5 billion a year. The Administration comes down on the side of those calling for a closer look at the remaining "unknowns" in the acid rain equation before Congress acts. Part of Administration officials' concern is that, since many of the most poorly controlled power plants are in the Ohio Valley, new emissions standards could fall most heavily on the economically hard-hit Midwest. Some midwestern utilities have claimed that the proposed emission reduction targets could mean electricity rate increases of more than 50 percent for residential consumers and almost 80 percent for industrial customers. However, the ICF study commissioned by the National Clean Air Coalition projected that a 10-million-ton reduction would translate into an average increase of only 2 percent in utility rates in affected states. Moreover, consumers in states bearing the steepest percentage increases would still be paying less for electricity in 1990 than those in the states hardest hit by acid rain. Thus, according to the coalition, acid rain control strategies amount to a "shift to more equitable distribution of costs among the states that contribute to the acid rain problem and the states that suffer the most damage." Indeed, recent evidence has shown that acid rain damage is more and more a nationwide problem. Alarmingly, low pH readings have been recorded from Minnesota's Boundary Waters Canoe Area to the Teseque watersheds of New Mexico's Santa Fe National Forest to the Great Smokey Mountains of North Carolina and Tennessee. The record low pH level reported so far was 1.5—equivalent to battery acid—in a rainstorm over Wheeling, West Virginia. Surveys have consistently shown that Americans are willing to pay and to share the costs of a clean environment. There is no question that the longer the delay in tackling the acid rain problem, the higher those costs—in dollars, as well as in serious damage to health and environment—are sure to be. It is time for citizens and officials alike to begin to fight the "invisible enemy," before it wreaks a great deal more quiet but long-lasting destruction.

COUNCIL ON ENVIRONMENTAL QUALITY
11th Annual Report (1980)

The Council estimates that the nation spent approximately $37 billion in 1979 to comply with federal environmental protection requirements—approximately 1.5 percent of the gross national product. It has been suggested that these expenditures may be slowing the growth of productivity. Although studies on the subject are not conclusive, available data suggest that environmental controls have had little impact on productivity.

Regulators have begun to consider economic incentives, including various offset policies which permit one industrial facility to increase air pollution emissions if another facility is willing to reduce them. The purpose of such policies would be to maintain desired levels of environmental quality at a lower overall cost to the nation. The Supreme Court has also begun to consider the issue of costs and benefits in reviewing cases involving environmental regulation.

REGULATION AND PRODUCTIVITY

Between 1948 and 1965, productivity in the United States—measured in terms of dollar value of output in the private sector (corrected for inflation) per hour of paid employment—grew at an average annual rate of approximately 2.5 percent. But in recent years, the rate of productivity growth has slowed substantially. Between 1965 and 1973, the average annual rate of growth was 1.6 percent per year. Between 1973 and 1978, it slowed to 0.8 percent per year. In 1979, for only the second time since World War II, productivity actually fell by 0.9 percent (1974 was the other year). In the first half of 1980, productivity was declining at an annual rate of 1.7 percent. This continuing decline is of concern because increased productivity might make it possible for wages to rise without accompanying price increases. Productivity gains are thus a key element in the effort to control inflation.

Environmental and other forms of regulation are among the many factors that may have slowed productivity growth, but there are others as well. The post-World War II rural-to-urban migration into new jobs in high-productivity manufacturing has ended. Large numbers of unskilled workers have entered the labor force, especially in the cities. Recent increases in energy prices may have encouraged the substitution of labor for energy-intensive capital equipment, and cyclical fluctuations in economic activity may have inhibited investment in new plants and equipment. Finally, there has been a shift in the economy from manufactured goods, which lend themselves to automation and thus increased productivity, to personal and other services, which generally do not.

It is important to determine what effect each of

these factors has on productivity. Regulation may reduce productivity—as traditionally measured—if, for example, it diverts labor or capital from the production of goods to the production of safe workplaces or clean air or water. Regulation might also slow productivity growth by delaying the construction of new industrial facilities or requiring their location in areas not convenient to suppliers or transportation lines, thus increasing costs. Similarly, uncertainty about future regulation could adversely affect the development of new and potentially productive technologies.

In any consideration of the relationship between regulation and productivity, however, it is essential to recognize that safe workplaces, clean air and water, unspoiled vistas, reclaimed land, and other benefits of environmental regulation are seldom included in estimates of national productivity. Thus imposition of air or water pollution abatement measures or other regulation will almost always produce a reduction in *measured* output but an increase in unmeasured benefits. Although reductions in productivity because of stagnation or decline in measured output are always of concern, they are acceptable if the unmeasured benefits of regulation are of greater value to society than those that are lost. To the extent that this shift from measured to unmeasured output is responsible for declining productivity growth, the "problem" is only an artifact of our current measurement system.

In the past several years, economists have tried to determine statistically the individual contributions of the many factors that affect the rate of productivity growth, as traditionally measured. The first attempt to quantify the impact of environmental regulation on productivity growth appeared in 1978. Using estimates of annual nonresidential business expenditures on pollution abatement (much like those presented later in this chapter), the study tried to determine the probable increase in productivity had the labor and capital used for pollution control been used for normal production instead. In its calculations, the study assumed that all resources devoted to pollution control would have been used for production and that those resources were of average productivity.

The study found that between 1967 and 1969, pollution abatement expenditures reduced the annual rate of growth of productivity 0.05 percent. Between 1969 and 1973, the effect was estimated at 0.10 percent, and between 1973 and 1975, 0.22 percent, i.e., the annual rate for 1975 would have been 0.822 rather than 0.080. The difference may seem small, but the size of the national income makes the absolute dollar amounts of output foregone substantial.

Both of the study's underlying assumptions are open to question, however. First, it is unlikely that all the money used for pollution control from 1967 to 1975 would have been spent on conventional production. Two of those years were recession years during which additional output would have been difficult to sell. Assuming a dollar-for-dollar displacement, then, probably leads to overestimation of the impact of regulation on productivity. Second, in general, the most productive resources are utilized first, the least productive, last. Thus if environmental regulation requires the diversion of existing labor and capital or the addition of new resources, the resources diverted are likely to be less productive than those devoted to the continued production of conventional output. In this respect also, it is likely that the study overestimated the adverse effects of regulation. These tendencies toward overestimation are offset to some extent by the fact that the study ignored the indirect, and perhaps significant, effects of regulation on productivity growth resulting from delay and siting effects, for example. It is thus difficult to draw definitive conclusions about the overall effects of regulation on productivity growth from this study.

The author of this study recently applied this same approach to more recent data on pollution abatement expenditures and data then available on GNP. He calculated that between 1975 and 1978, expenditures on air and water pollution control and solid waste disposal reduced the rate of productivity growth 0.08 percent—about one-third the effect that these controls were thought to have had between 1973 and 1975. The later calculations suggest that, although environmental regulation was still adversely affecting the rate of productivity growth in the late 1970s, as conventionally measured, its impact appears to be diminishing.

Numerous studies have attempted to quantify the effects of various factors on the slowdown in productivity growth. These reviews suggest that some of the factors mentioned above may play larger roles in the decline in productivity growth than does environmental regulation. One review of the studies concluded that "in no case are pollution abatement regulations assigned more than 20 percent [or about 0.2–0.4 percent] of the responsibility for the decrease in productivity growth. The typical estimate of the role of environmental regulations is in the range of 5–15 percent [about 0.05–0.3 percent]."

ECONOMIC INCENTIVES

Economic incentives may be effective in controlling pollution. Possible incentives might be effluent charges (fees that must be paid for each unit of pollution discharged) or marketable permits (legally enforceable entitlements to discharge that are fixed in number and exchangeable among polluters). Under certain conditions, both effluent charges and marketable permits are considered capable of vastly reducing the cost of improving environmental quality by taking advantage of variations in the costs of pollution control among dischargers—variations determined for the most part by the kind of raw material and process involved.

The Environmental Protection Agency's bubble and offset policies (the former allows a polluter to increase air emissions in one portion of a facility if it will reduce emissions elsewhere in the same facility, where costs may be lower; the latter permits an increase in emissions in one part of a geographic area if the polluter either reduces pollution elsewhere in that area or persuades another polluter to do so) are attempts to make use of economic incentives within the current regulatory framework.

EPA is also considering several other incentive-based approaches. Transferable Emissions Reduction Assessments (TERAs) might be used if the emission controls required under State Implementation Plans (SIPs) were insufficient to meet the ambient air quality standards established under the Clean Air Act. Normally, the long process of a SIP revision would be necessary in such circumstances. Under the TERA approach, if a 10 percent reduction in overall emissions were required to meet the standards in a particular area, every pollu-

tion source in that region would be directed to cut its emissions 10 percent. But if one source could find another comparable source in the area able to reduce its emissions at a reasonable cost and then persuade that source to cut back 20 percent (in exchange, say, for financial considerations), the first source could avoid a cutback. In other words, firms could either make the reductions themselves or find offsetting reductions elsewhere. Such a procedure could have a cost-saving advantage and speed up the process of environmental improvement.

EPA is considering other incentive-based approaches to prevent significant deterioration (PSD) in areas where air quality is better than national standards. The Clean Air Act limits the extent to which air quality can be diminished in such areas. EPA must determine which sources may "consume" the incremental degradation that is permitted. This increment could be allocated on a first-come, first-served basis as sources apply for new permits. But other systems of allocation could also be used:

□ Variable offsets—a potential new source could purchase some emissions entitlements from existing sources but less than it expects to emit (because some degradation is permitted)

□ Emission density zoning—emissions entitlements would first be limited and then tied to particular parcels of land in PSD areas

□ Emissions fees—potential sources would pay for the additional degradation that they cause, and the price would rise as air quality approached the minimum permitted quality.

All three methods of allocating allowable increases in degradation are based on differences in the costs of pollution control among sources.

The Clean Air Act distinguishes between new and existing sources of pollution. In general, new sources are held to much stricter performance standards (new source performance standards, NSPS) than existing ones on the premise that environmental quality will gradually improve as existing sources are retired; in time, all sources will be subject to strict controls. Critics of this approach argue that it may unintentionally result in old plants being operated long past the point at which they would otherwise have been retired in order to avoid the strict controls on new sources. There is little evidence available on the extent to which new plant construction is being delayed, but it may be worth thinking about ways to secure the same reductions in emissions that would result from strict NSPS without discouraging new plant construction.

One way to achieve this goal would be to allow new sources of pollution to operate under less stringent controls than those now required if they can secure equal or perhaps even greater than offsetting reductions from other new or existing sources in the same geographical area. Pollution would then be reduced by the same amount as under the NSPS approach, but some of the disincentive to introduce new sources would be removed. In some cases, securing emission reductions from existing sources (which are often largely uncontrolled) would be less costly than the higher removal efficiencies called for under existing new source performance standards.

An additional benefit of using the offset approach in the NSPS might be improved productivity secured by use of more sophisticated technology in new plants and equipment that allow each worker to produce more than before. Thus environmental quality might be maintained without loss of productivity.

Another and different kind of economic incentive might increase the accuracy of the information that polluters provide to regulatory agencies in advance of standard setting. When EPA is considering imposition of a standard, it needs to know the cost to a company of meeting that standard. Under current practice, the company has an incentive to exaggerate the cost to make the regulation appear unjustifiable (some evidence of the accuracy of both private and government estimates of compliance costs is discussed later in this chapter). If in fact companies are exaggerating compliance costs, they are depriving regulatory agencies of potentially the most reliable cost data, that from the affected firms.

What can be done to prevent exaggeration of expected compliance costs? One possibility is to link penalties for violations to compliance cost estimates—that is, to make the penalty for noncompliance with an established regulation dependent upon the previous estimate of the costs of compliance. Then a company would be free to claim that compliance with a proposed regulation would be unjustifiably costly, but future penalties for noncompliance would be greater than if the firm had provided a more realistic estimate of costs.

Linking noncompliance penalties to compliance cost estimates might make it possible to improve *ex ante* analysis (analysis prior to issuance of regulations) of the impacts of regulation by providing more accurate information than is now available. For such a system to have legal sanction, the affected firms would have to make their cost estimates official, increasing the resources needed to estimate costs, resources otherwise available for production. The usefulness of such an approach, then, depends upon the value of improved estimates of compliance costs compared to the additional effort entailed by such estimates.

Still another means of obtaining more accurate information on the costs of complying with environmental regulation is suggested by recent action taken by the Securities and Exchange Commission. The SEC ordered two very large firms—U.S. Steel and Occidental Petroleum—to disclose to their stockholders potential liabilities arising from pollution control costs or other environmental activities. The SEC found that between 1973 and 1977, U.S. Steel had not adequately disclosed to its stockholders the costs associated with coming expenditures on air and water pollution control, thus making its financial condition appear better than was actually the case. Occidental, the SEC found, had failed to inform stockholders of possible liabilities arising from waste disposal practices of its subsidiary, Hooker Chemical, at Love Canal.

If firms were required to incorporate in reports to the SEC and to report to stockholders the same estimates of pollution control compliance costs that they provide to regulatory agencies, exaggerated estimates to agencies might become less common. Presumably, firms would not want to alarm stockholders with the prospect of large liabilities for pollution control. Neither would they want regulatory agencies to think that potential new regulations were costless.

COST-BENEFIT ANALYSIS AND THE COURTS

Unsettled issues in the setting of regulations include the extent to which regulatory agencies must demonstrate the benefits of their proposed actions and the relationship that these benefits must bear to the costs of regulation. The Supreme Court considered in part the first of these issues in 1980.

In July 1980, the Supreme Court handed down a decision in *Industrial Union Department, AFL–CIO v. American Petroleum Institute et al.* The Court upheld in part a 1978 ruling by the U.S. Court of Appeals for the Fifth Circuit. The Fifth Circuit had ruled in favor of the American Petroleum Institute (API) that the Occupational Safety and Health Administration (OSHA) could not tighten the standard limiting worker exposure to benzene from 10 parts per million to 1 ppm without first conducting a cost-benefit analysis of the proposed change. OSHA had argued that some of the costs and benefits of the proposed change were unquantifiable and that it was prohibited by law from considering the costs of regulation except to determine that industry was capable of bearing them.

By a 5–4 majority, the Supreme Court upheld the circuit court's invalidation of the benzene standard on grounds that OSHA had failed to produce evidence that a "significant risk of harm exists" at the old standard that would justify the proposed revision. Rather, OSHA had merely asserted that the change would afford workers more protection.

The Court chose not to rule on whether benefits had to be completely and precisely quantified or had to bear some reasonable relationship to costs.

EXPENDITURES ON ENVIRONMENTAL QUALITY

Each year the Council has estimated current and future expenditures for pollution abatement and other measures to protect or enhance environmental quality. These estimates serve several purposes. They can be used to help determine the macroeconomic effects of federal environmental regulation, and they can be compared with broad-scale estimates of the benefits associated with environmental regulations. Because of their high level of aggregation, however, the CEQ estimates cannot be used to evaluate the benefits and costs of specific standards or provisions of the Clean Air Act, the Clean Water Act, or similar legislation. Such evaluations are clearly of great importance when changes are considered in specific provisions of environmental statutes.

As Table 1 indicates, CEQ estimates that the nation spent $36.9 billion in 1979 to comply with federal environmental protection regulations. (Spending necessitated by federal regulation is termed "incremental" by CEQ). The $36.9 billion amounted to approximately 1.5 percent of GNP in 1979, 0.2 percent higher than in past years. The increase was caused by spending on new regulations, the effects of which are only now beginning to be felt. The Toxic Substances Control Act and the Surface Mining Control and Reclamation Act are the most prominent examples.

Air and water pollution controls (mandated by the Clean Air Act and Clean Water Act) accounted for 95 percent of incremental expenditures, $35.0 billion. Of this amount, air pollution control accounted for $22.3 billion—$1.5 billion of which was spent by federal, state, and local governments for the control of air pollution at hospitals, military installations, incinerators, and other municipal disposal sites. The control of air pollution from automobiles, trucks, buses, and motorcycles cost $8.1 billion. Electric utilities spent $8.4 billion for air pollution control; all other industrial sources spent $4.3 billion. The $22.3 billion for air pollution control was divided rather evenly between operation and maintenance expenses and annual capital costs (which include interest and depreciation).

Of the $12.7 billion in incremental water pollution control expenditures in 1979, municipalities spent $6.0 billion for waste water treatment. Industrial sources other than electric utilities spent another $6.0 billion for water pollution control; utilities accounted for the remaining $0.7 billion.

Approximately $1.9 billion spent in 1979 was expended on the reclamation of land following strip mining (under the Surface Mining Control and Reclamation Act), the control of toxic substances (under the Toxic Substances Control Act),

TABLE ONE
Estimated Incremental Pollution Abatement Expenditures[a], 1979–88 (billions of 1979 dollars)

PROGRAM	1979 Opera-tion and Mainte-nance	Annual Capital Costs[b]	Total Annual Costs	1988 Opera-tion and Mainte-nance	Annual Capital Costs[b]	Total Annual Costs	CUMULATIVE (1979–88) Opera-tion and Mainte-nance	Capital Costs[b]	Total Costs
Air pollution
Public	1.2	.3	1.5	2.0	.5	2.5	15.8	3.7	19.5
Private
Mobile	3.2	4.9	8.1	3.7	11.0	14.7	32.1	83.7	115.8
Industrial	2.0	2.3	4.3	3.0	4.1	7.1	25.8	33.0	58.8
Electric utilities	5.5	2.9	8.4	7.6	5.7	13.3	62.3	42.7	105.0
Subtotal	11.9	10.4	22.3	16.3	21.3	37.6	136.0	163.1	299.1
Water pollution
Public	1.7	4.3	6.0	3.3	10.0	13.3	25.1	59.2	84.3
Private
Industrial	3.4	2.6	6.0	5.4	4.5	9.9	42.0	34.0	76.0
Electric utilities	.3	.4	.7	.3	.9	1.2	2.9	6.5	9.4
Subtotal	5.4	7.3	12.7	9.0	15.4	24.4	70.0	99.7	169.7
Solid waste
Public	<.05	<.05	<.05	.4	.3	.7	2.6	2.0	4.6
Private	<.05	<.05	<.05	.9	.7	1.6	6.4	4.4	10.8
Subtotal	<.05	<.05	<.05	1.3	1.0	2.3	9.0	6.4	15.4
Toxic substances	.1	.2	.3	.5	.6	1.1	3.6	4.6	8.2
Drinking water	<.05	<.05	<.05	.1	.3	.4	1.3	1.4	2.7
Noise	<.05	.1	.1	.6	1.0	1.6	2.6	4.3	6.9
Pesticides	.1	<.05	.1	.1	<.05	.1	1.2	<.05	1.2
Land reclamation	.3	1.1	1.4	.3	1.2	1.5	3.8	11.5	15.3
Total	17.8	19.1	36.9	28.2	40.8	69.0	227.5	291.0	518.5

a. Incremental costs are those made in response to federal legislation beyond those that would have been made in the absence of that legislation.
b. Interest and depreciation.

the protection of drinking water (under the Safe Drinking Water Act), the elimination or attenuation of noise (under the Noise Control Act), and the control of pesticides (under the Federal Insecticide, Fungicide, and Rodenticide Act). Land reclamation accounted for $1.4 billion of the $1.9 billion devoted to expenditures on other than air and water pollution control.

CEQ estimates that by 1988, expenditures necessitated by federal environmental measures will grow to $69.0 billion (in 1979 dollars), a real rate of growth of about 7.2 percent per year. Air and water pollution control will still account for the greatest share of incremental spending in 1988—$62.0 billion—but spending for other programs will grow to 10 percent of the total. By then, $2.3 billion will be required annually to control the disposal of hazardous and other wastes in compliance with the Resource Conservation and Recovery Act.

During the 10 years 1979–88, spending in response to the federal environmental quality regulations considered here is expected to amount to $518.5 billion. Of this cumulative incremental spending, air pollution control will total nearly $300 billion (58 percent), water quality programs will require about $170 billion (33 percent), and all other programs together will account for the remaining $50 billion. Of this $50 billion, $15.3 billion will be devoted to land reclamation and another $15.4 billion to control of the disposal of hazardous wastes. The control of hazardous substances will require $8.2 billion, and noise control measures will cost $6.9 billion.

In addition to estimating spending in response to federal environmental legislation, CEO has estimated total spending on pollution abatement and other environmental measures, including expenditures made in response to state or local environmental controls (which are sometimes quite stringent) or voluntary expenditures made for reasons of principle or private profitability. These estimates obviously require some assumptions about what industry, households, and government units would have spent on pollution control in the absence of federal regulations. These baseline expenditures, as they are called, are determined by examining environmental expenditures in the mid- to late 1960s prior to establishment of present federal environmental regulations and then extrapolating trends to the present. Because extrapolation of this kind is a particularly difficult task, estimates of total expenditures should be viewed as only broadly suggestive.

As shown in Table 2, spending on all environmental programs, either voluntary or in response to federal, state, or local statutes, is estimated at $735.0 billion between 1979 and 1988. Air pollution will account for $338.8 billion, water pollution for $250.0 billion, and solid waste disposal for $100.9 billion. The share of solid wastes in total

expenditures is much greater than its share in incremental spending because much of the spending on solid wastes is either voluntary or in response to state or local regulations. All other programs are expected to account for $45.3 billion of total expenditures between 1979 and 1988.

There is a great deal of uncertainty in these estimates. Although they are presented as point estimates (that is, as single numbers), they might better be presented as ranges because of the uncertainties involved in determining them. It should also be noted that these estimates reflect anticipated costs of compliance for environmental regulations in effect as of mid-1980. This year's totals reflect new methods for estimating compliance costs for several programs. Differences in methods explain some differences between this year's estimates and those in previous Annual Reports.

ACCURACY OF POLLUTION CONTROL COST ESTIMATES

A study conducted for EPA in 1980 attempted to assess the accuracy of some of the estimated costs of complying with federal environmental law. Because the study did not consider all industries and regulations or the cost of regulation to the public, its findings cannot easily be generalized to the aggregate estimates of federal environmental regulation compliance costs that CEQ makes. Nevertheless, the report gives some indication of the precision of compliance cost estimates.

The study compared *ex ante* estimates of pollution control costs for several industries made when a regulation was issued with actual expenditures that were eventually made. It examined estimates prepared by EPA and its contractors and estimates prepared by industry. Estimates were then adjusted for the fact that not all firms actually complied with the regulations; "compliance-adjusted" estimates were compared with actual expenditures.

The study examined estimates of compliance costs of best practicable technology (BPT) effluent guidelines for the iron and steel, pulp and paper, petroleum refining, and steam electric utility industries issued under the Clean Water Act, Clean Air Act requirements for scrubbers in the electric utility industry, and vehicle emissions standards for

TABLE TWO

Estimated Total Pollution Abatement Expenditures, 1979–88 (billions of 1979 dollars)

PROGRAM	1979			1988			CUMULATIVE (1979–88)		
	Operation and Maintenance	*Annual Capital Costs*	*Total Annual Costs*	*Operation and Maintenance*	*Annual Capital Costs[a]*	*Total Annual Costs*	*Operation and Maintenance*	*Capital Costs*	*Total Costs*
Air pollution									
Public	1.7	.4	2.1	2.8	.7	3.5	22.5	5.3	27.8
Private									
Mobile	3.2	4.9	8.1	3.7	11.0	14.7	32.1	83.7	115.8
Industrial	2.5	2.9	5.4	3.9	5.1	9.0	32.5	41.5	74.0
Electric utilities	6.3	3.5	9.8	8.5	6.5	15.0	71.1	50.1	121.2
Subtotal	13.7	11.7	25.4	18.9	23.3	42.2	158.2	180.6	338.8
Water pollution									
Public	3.7	8.2	11.9	5.4	14.2	19.6	45.4	99.7	145.1
Private									
Industrial	4.4	3.2	7.6	6.4	5.1	11.5	52.4	41.1	93.5
Electric utilities	.4	.5	.9	.4	1.1	1.5	3.6	7.8	11.4
Subtotal	8.5	11.9	20.4	12.2	20.4	32.6	101.4	148.6	250.0
Solid waste									
Public	1.7	.3	2.0	2.5	.6	3.1	21.8	5.3	27.1
Private	4.5	.7	5.2	7.5	1.6	9.1	61.3	12.5	73.8
Subtotal	6.2	1.0	7.2	10.0	2.2	12.2	83.1	17.8	100.9
Toxic substances	.1	.2	.3	.5	.6	1.1	3.6	4.6	8.2
Drinking water	.3	.4	.7	.5	.8	1.3	5.3	5.2	10.5
Noise	<.05	.1	.1	.6	1.0	1.6	2.6	4.3	6.9
Pesticides	.1	<.05	.1	.1	<.05	.1	1.6	.1	1.7
Land reclamation	.4	1.3	1.7	.4	1.4	1.8	4.5	13.5	18.0
Total	29.3	26.6	55.9	43.2	49.7	92.9	360.3	374.7	735.0

a. Interest and depreciation.

new light-duty automobiles required by the Clean Air Act.

The study report reveals that compliance cost estimates prepared by EPA or its contractors were lower than industry estimates for five of the six regulations examined; only the pulp and paper industry's estimate of the costs of meeting BPT effluent guidelines was below that of EPA. However, EPA estimates were not consistently high or low compared to actual costs. In two cases EPA appeared to underestimate costs, in three cases it appeared to overestimate costs, and for vehicle emissions standards, the estimates appeared to be too high in two model years and too low in a third.

Industry also overestimated compliance costs in some cases and underestimated in others. For the BPT guidelines in the iron and steel industry, the apparent overestimate was substantial, ranging from 2.5 to 3.5 times the actual cost. On the other hand, industry estimates of the cost of scrubbers to electric utilities and the cost of the BPT effluent guidelines in the pulp and paper industry were less than actual expenditures. Industry compliance cost estimates for vehicle emissions standards were both higher and lower than actual increases in sale prices resulting from the regulations.

Overall, the report shows that EPA appears to be slightly better at estimating compliance costs than are the affected industries. As Table 3 indicates, EPA's ratio of estimated-to-actual expenditures is more often nearer 1.0 than the ratio for corresponding industry estimates (a ratio of 1.0 means that actual expenditures were forecast exactly). In BPT guidelines for electric utilities and model year 1976 vehicle emissions costs, the EPA estimate was within 10 percent of eventual actual expenditures. The electric utility industry's estimate of scrubber costs was also within 10 percent of actual expenditures.

A first attempt to compare predicted and actual compliance costs, this study is a useful one. But it must be interpreted carefully. First, it is difficult to determine actual (*ex post*) expenditures incurred to comply with a regulation. The study used data reported by the Bureau of Economic Analysis, McGraw-Hill, the Bureau of Labor Statistics, and industry trade associations. Although these data are the best available on actual spending for pollution control, they do not differentiate between spending undertaken to comply with specific federal regulations and that undertaken because of state or local regulations or private profitability. Further, it is difficult to isolate pollution control spending from that for modern equipment and streamlined production processes, for example.

In addition, compliance data vary in quality. Thus it is not clear how accurate estimates of pollution control compliance costs are once they have been adjusted for industry compliance ratios. Such an adjustment will not affect the accuracy of EPA

estimates compared with those of industry (because both are adjusted in the same way). But the tendency of either party to over- or under-estimate actual costs is less apparent.

TABLE THREE
Ratio of Estimated to Actual Pollution Control Expenditures in Selected Industries

INDUSTRY AND REGULATION	RATIO
Electric utility scrubber	
EPA	0.74
Industry	0.91
Utilities (BPT guidelines)	
EPA	0.89–0.91
Industry	1.36–1.40
Pulp and paper (BPT guidelines)[a]	
EPA	1.27–1.49
Industry	0.75
Iron and steel (BPT guidelines)	
EPA	1.32–1.79
Industry	2.56–3.47
Petroleum refining (BPT guidelines)	
EPA	1.87–2.50
Industry	1.91–2.62
Automobile emissions standards[b]	
1974 model year	
EPA	1.32–1.45
Industry	0.72–1.74
1976 model year	
EPA	0.93–1.02
Industry	0.51–2.31

BPT = Best practicable technology.
a. EPA estimate, 1974–77; industry estimate, 1972–77.
b. Ratio of estimated to actual sale price increase as calculated by the Bureau of Labor Statistics.
Source: Putnam, Hayes & Bartlett, Inc., "Comparisons of Estimated and Actual Pollution Control Cost for Selected Industries," prepared for the U.S. Environmental Protection Agency, February 1980.

A. MYRICH FREEMAN, ROBERT HAVEMAN, AND ALLEN KNEESE

Environmental Management: Some Issues

THE COSTS OF POLLUTION CONTROL

Pollution control and environmental protection cannot be obtained without incurring significant costs. No one can state with certainty what the final bill for the whole economy will be. This is true partly because of the difficulties inherent in estimating and predicting on this scale and partly because we are still in the process of making some of the choices and decisions that will influence the size of the bill. The total costs will ultimately depend on three factors: how much environmental improvement we want; the state of the technology of pollution control and the rate of improvement in this technology over time; and the nature of the pollution control policies chosen to implement our environmental goals. As we have shown, some pollution control policies are better than others in terms of their ability to achieve pollution control objectives at least possible total cost.

The President's Council on Environmental quality has presented its estimates of the total costs for the six-year period 1970 to 1975. We have already referred to some of the individual components of them in earlier chapters. The totals are:[1]

For water pollution control	$38 billion
For air pollution control	23.7 billion
For solid waste control	43.5 billion
Total	$105.2 billion

Most of the solid waste figure represents continued expenditures for existing collection and disposal services. If we omit these, we obtain an estimate of the *incremental* expenditure for air and water—a total of $61.7 billion. A recently published survey by McGraw-Hill, Inc. reveals what industry esti-

mates it will have to invest in new pollution control equipment by 1976. Industry estimates that it will have to spend $22.8 billion through 1975. Planned expenditures for 1972 are $4.9 billion. An average annual spending of $5.7 billion per year over this period will be needed to meet their estimated total requirement.[2] In contrast, the Council on Environmental Quality estimates industry's capital requirements to be $18.7 billion; but in addition they foresee spending of $16.9 billion for annual operation.[3]

Both the Council on Environmental Quality's and McGraw-Hill's estimates of spending needs are rough approximations at best. We do not yet know enough about the costs of carrying out the pollution control policies we are in the process of developing. Yet, we can see enough of the picture to make several important observations. The first concerns the magnitude of these costs and our ability to pay the bill. Although the figures look large in themselves, they are relatively small in comparison with other relevant economic magnitudes. For example, the $61.7 billion total for six years or air and water, which is the highest official estimate yet published, is only about 6 percent of this year's gross national product and represents less than 25 percent of the *increase* in GNP that we can reasonably expect to occur because of economic growth over this period. Even the $105 billion figure which includes solid wastes comes to only about 40 percent of the expected economic growth "dividend." The question is not one of ability to pay, but rather one of priorities and *willingness* to redirect our economic resources from other things to pollution control.

Turning to industry's own estimate of required expenditures, pollution control spending is expected to be only 5.3 percent of total planned capital expenditures between now and 1975. This means that a doubling in the level of spending for pollution control by industry could be accommodated with only a 5.6 percent reduction in other capital spending. It is not that industry lacks the financial resources. Rather they lack an incentive to use more of these resources for pollution control.

While trying to put these large sounding totals in some kind of perspective, we do not want to minimize the political and economic difficulties in achieving a reallocation of resources of this magnitude. As resources are moved out of one sector of the economy, for example defense and aerospace, and into the pollution control equipment industry, there are likely to be bottlenecks, shortages, and so on. While a market economy with its resource mobility, price signals, and decentralized decision making is remarkably well-suited for bringing about the necessary economic adjustments, adjustment can never be instantaneous. One consequence may be temporary unemployment.[4] There are likely to be price increases as well. But there is no reason to expect either persistent depression and unemployment or a continuously rising general price level. These are problems of macroeconomic stabilization. And without trying to minimize the difficulties in achieving and maintaining full employment without inflation, we can say that an effective pollution control program creates no more serious obstacles to these twin objectives than a host of other regularly operating economic forces.

Our second observation concerns the benefits of good planning. Although the total (cost) figure may be small relative to the size of the economy, it is large enough in magnitude to provide high payoffs for efforts to economize in pollution control. A change in policy that would reduce the total costs of pollution control by 10 percent would result in a substantial savings of money over time running to many billions of dollars. Every effort should be made to develop policies that will achieve pollution control goals at least possible cost and that will induce the kind of technological change that would make pollution control less expensive.

Third, there are good reasons for believing that pollution control goals can be met at less than the estimated costs if improved management approaches, including effective economic incentives, are adopted. We have developed the details of this assertion in earlier chapters but it deserves

reemphasis. The available estimates focus on treatment of residuals streams already generated at the expense of other technologies that would enter into an optimum program for achieving environmental objectives. In the case of air pollution, for example, the emphasis is on treating gaseous residuals after generation—for example, removing substances from stack gases and providing "add-on" devices for internal combustion engines. Alternatives, such as fuel preparation, short-term fuel substitution during severe pollution episodes, switching to fuels having inherently low emissions, and substituting alternatives like steam or turbine engines for internal combustion auto engines are given less emphasis.

In the case of water, the neglect of alternatives to conventional approaches seems even more serious—perhaps because we know more about the range of potential choices. For example, the Delaware Estuary study showed that the use of even a relatively simple system of economic incentives, in the form of effluent charges, could cut in half the social cost of achieving water quality standards in that river in comparison with a conventional approach like uniform treatment. The saving in cost over a 25-year period was about $150 million. Furthermore, careful studies of a number of basins, including the Delaware, Miami, Potomac, Wisconsin, Raritan Bay, and others, reveal that a regional management approach, including such technologies as mechanical reaeration of watercourses and reservoir storage to regulate low flows operated in a manner closely articulated with waste water treatment operations, can greatly increase the effectiveness and efficiency of water quality improvement programs.[5]

Fourth, studies of a number of industries—including beet sugar, petroleum refining, canning, pulp and paper, and wool reprocessing—show that process changes and changes in the mix of inputs and outputs can often be less costly ways of reducing industrial wastes than treatment after the wastes have been generated. Any program aimed at achieving efficiency in the pursuit of environmental quality must take account of these facts.

Finally, these estimates represent a lot of capital investment for catching up and correcting past abuses. Probably more than three quarters of the expenditures would be investment. Accordingly, expenditures discussed above are likely to "hump" and then drop off considerably. One should not make too much of this point, however, because some further steps could turn out to be extremely costly. For example, it has been estimated that it might cost $90 billion to remove or recycle nutrients from all treated sewage effluents to protect streams and lakes from excessive enrichment and eutrophication. Separation of storm and sanitary sewers in the major cities to prevent the overloading of treatment plants after rainstorms could cost as much as $50 billion. And last there are no well-founded estimates of the costs of controlling non-point-source water pollution.

In summary, the estimates discussed here suggest that while achieving major environmental improvements is likely to be very costly, the amounts are not so great as to require a significant reduction in our material well-being. Nor is unemployment or inflation inevitable. However, this is a short-run conclusion, valid for perhaps a few decades. The implications of very long continued growth in population and material and energy conversion could be quite different. We offer some observations on this in a later section.[6] [Not included in this anthology.]

EQUITY AND POLLUTION CONTROL

Crudely put, the equity questions are: Who gets hurt by pollution, the rich, the poor, or everybody? And who will wind up paying the costs of controlling pollution? Given our failure to come to grips effectively with the general national problem of equity in income distribution, there is good reason to be concerned with the distributional impact of particular pollution problems and policies.

Benefits

With respect to who gets hurt by pollution and who would benefit from effective pollution control programs, the situation seems to be roughly as follows. The poor, and blacks in particular, are exposed to polluted air more than affluent whites.[7] One of the advantages of wealth is that it enables its possessors to buy protection from environmental insults such as air pollution. The wealthy can live in the best suburbs, drive in air conditioned cars, etc. Accordingly, improved air quality in center cities

would directly affect the poor and blacks more than the rich.

However, the ultimate impact of improved air quality on the distribution of income and welfare is more complicated. Economic reasoning suggests that improved air quality in part of an urban area will make the land under that air more valuable and raise land prices. In fact, as we pointed out in the previous chapter, investigators have found that air quality and land prices tend to be related in urban areas, with higher land values in areas of higher air quality, other things being equal. If the urban poor and blacks tend to rent their dwellings rather than buy them (which is true), it may turn out that in the long run some part of the benefits of air quality improvement will be passed on to the landlord-property owners in the form of higher rents. In other words, while urban dwellers will be better off because of better health and reduced damages and amenity losses, this gain will tend to be partially offset by higher costs of housing. Nevertheless, it appears, on balance, that the improvement would be pro poor.

Turning to water pollution control, the principal readily identifiable benefits are in the form of improved recreational opportunities and amenities. People with higher incomes tend to participate in the various forms of water-based recreation more often than those from lower income groups; and they tend to place a higher dollar value on amenities, largely because they have more dollars. Thus, it appears that water quality improvements would tend to accrue disproportionately to the more affluent. This tendency is modified somewhat, however, by the fact that major improvements in water quality would often be centered in or near large cities, thus providing more opportunities for water-based recreation close to where poorer people are concentrated.

Costs

First we must distinguish between two broad types of pollution control costs—real *resource costs* and *factor income costs*. The resource costs represent the land, labor, and capital, that must be devoted to altering production processes, to recycling and recovering materials so as to reduce the amounts of pollutants generated, and to collecting and treating wastes that would otherwise be discharged to the environment. The factor income costs represent those changes in labor and capital incomes due to pollution control measures.

Consider first the real resource costs. Where public agencies undertake the pollution control activity (for instance, municipal sewerage treatment), the resource costs are passed on to the taxpayer, or perhaps are covered by user charges levied on those who transmit their wastes to the plant. Where user charges are imposed on firms, and where firms undertake pollution control efforts of their own, the resource costs will be passed on to consumers, for the most part, in the form of higher prices for goods and services.

The resource costs are all real costs or opportunity costs because they represent opportunities foregone. All the resources used in pollution control could have been put to some other use. The cost to society is what their value would have been in their next best use. On the other hand, factor income costs are not necessarily real costs. Pollution control programs may result in changes in factor prices as some resources become less valuable, and their owners may thus experience a reduction in income. For example, an air pollution control program may result in a lower price for high sulfur content coal. The coal may still be mined and used, thus there is no real or opportunity cost; but coal mine owners will receive lower incomes on their holdings of land containing coal.

Factor income costs can, however, be real costs—especially in the short run. For example, as a result of a pollution control policy that raises the real costs to firms, output will have to be contracted as the price is increased to cover the higher costs. This follows from the law of demand. With lower total output some plants, and perhaps some firms, will have to reduce output and perhaps go out of business. If the released resources that have alternative uses, especially labor, are quickly employed in other activities at comparable wages, there are no factor income costs. But if the resources remain unemployed for some time, because of geographic immobility, or imperfect information on job alternatives, there is a significant factor income cost. Moreover, this cost is a real cost, since the unemployed resources could be producing something of value for society.

What is the likely incidence of these costs, that

is, who pays? Those resource costs that are passed on as higher prices are likely to have a regressive incidence on balance—like a sales or excise tax. By regressive we mean that lower income individuals will pay a higher *proportion* of their income in the form of these costs than will upper income individuals. This is because lower income people tend to spend a higher proportion of their income on goods and services in general. The incidence of the tax costs depends on what form of tax is used to raise the revenues. Local governments generally raise revenues by regressive sales and property taxes,[8] or equally regressive sewer charges based on water consumption or the size of the lot. The incidence of the real factor income costs, that is, those due to unemployment, is highly regressive in that the people who bear them have no income.

It is possible to design public policies to redistribute or shift some of these pollution control costs in the interest of greater equity in income distribution. There are two broad categories of cost shifting policies. The first deals with resource costs. It consists of various kinds of direct and indirect grants and subsidies designed to shift the costs from consumers as a group to taxpayers as a group, and within the group of taxpayers from lower income to higher income taxpayers. We call this a policy of *cost subsidy*. The second type of policy deals with real factor income costs, that is, those costs that arise from the slow or imperfect adjustment of resources, principally labor, to the changed economic conditions brought about by pollution control. Recognizing the parallel with similar provisions in our foreign trade laws, let us call this *adjustment assistance*. Both of these are discussed below.

Cost Subsidies

Cost subsidies can be either direct or indirect. Indirect cost subsidies can be accomplished by linking favorable tax treatment to certain kinds of pollution control activities. For example, the real cost of installing pollution control equipment can be reduced by permitting an accelerated depreciation of that equipment for corporate income tax purposes. Also, pollution control equipment can be exempted from sales taxes or real property taxes. Both types of indirect subsidy are now used by the federal and state governments. Direct subsidies consist of cash payments to municipalities and firms to reimburse them for some part of their pollution control costs. In Chapter 6 [not included in this anthology] we described the federal law that authorizes grants to municipalities to cover up to 55 percent of the construction costs for water pollution treatment plants. States are encouraged by this law to put up another 25 percent—reducing the locally borne costs to 20 percent of the total.

Who does this subsidy benefit? If the state and federal tax systems are more progressive than the local taxes used to finance the town's share (which they normally are), this shifting of costs benefits lower income taxpayers at the expense of higher income groups. If the municipality receiving the subsidy is also treating industrial wastes in its plant, it is required by federal law to recover only 20 percent of the cost of treating the industrial wastes from the companies. In this way, federal funds can be used to subsidize the control of industrial pollution. The benefit of this subsidy flows to the company and perhaps to consumers in the form of a lower price. To the extent that the latter is true, the subsidy tends to favor the lower income end of the scale.

However, before one advocates more widespread use of cost subsidization policies, even on distributional grounds, there are two important qualifications to be discussed. First, although cost subsidies can change the distribution of the burden between rich and poor, they also increase the total burden because they distort the economic incentives faced by dischargers. If dischargers are relieved of the responsibility of paying the full costs of treating their wastes, they have no economic incentive to reduce or control the volume of wastes being generated. The total of wastes to be treated will be too high and the total cost of a given level of pollution control will be higher than necessary. This is true whether the cost subsidy is going to municipalities or industry. Whatever equity benefits are gained by cost subsidies come at the expense of higher than necessary treatment costs. One must always ask the question: Are the equity gains worth the cost?

As for the second qualification, where cost subsidies go to firms, there is some likelihood that their benefits will not be passed on to consumers in the form of lower prices. For example, if a multiplant firm selling in a national market receives a subsidy for pollution equipment installed in one plant, this is not likely to affect the price at which the product is sold. Hence, the benefits would accrue to stockholders. Cost subsidies can also produce interregional transfers. For example, a state subsidy to a municipal treatment plant which is also treating industrial wastes could flow largely to out-of-state consumers or stockholders if the industrial discharger was producing for a national market or if stock ownership was spread across the nation.

In short, the matter of who benefits from existing cost subsidy programs presents a decidedly mixed picture; and it is very difficult to frame subsidy policies that do not result in gross inefficiencies. The latter may easily outweigh any intended redistributive effects. Moreover, as we have noted, cost subsidies may partly go to increase profits. Accordingly, although we believe that who bears the costs of pollution control is an important policy question, we take a dim view of present efforts at cost subsidy since it is not clear that any major distributional or equity benefits are being realized. However, we would not oppose cost subsidies that were clearly targeted on needy groups—an example might be the costs of automotive air pollution control systems for low income families.

Adjustment Assistance

Adjustment assistance consists of direct payments or other contributions to specific owners of factor inputs adversely affected by environmental control policy for the purpose of shifting the burden of adjustment to newly imposed environmental standards. This type of assistance is sometimes called "targeted" assistance. Although such payments are not presently part of any state or federal environmental policy, they appear to be both efficient and equitable.

If cost subsidies are ruled out, as we argue they should be, high pollution industries will be faced with rising costs, rising relative prices for their products, and shrinking markets. Some firms would be forced out of the industry, plants would be shut down, and labor and capital would be at least temporarily unemployed. The consequences could be particularly severe in those areas where factor inputs are relatively immobile, for example, in small towns and one-industry mill towns.

An appropriately designed *adjustment assistance* policy could go far toward ameliorating the adverse effects of the pollution control policy on labor and capital that would otherwise be unemployed for extended periods. There is a useful model for this in certain provisions of the Trade Expansion Act of 1962 and the Canadian-American Automotive Trade Agreement. Both of these agreements contain provisions for adjustment assistance where the lowering of tariffs has brought about economic hardship. According to the Trade Expansion Act, it must be shown that the tariff reductions were a "major" cause of idle facilities, lack of profits, or unemployment. If this can be established, then adjustment assistance is available both for labor and for business. Firms can obtain technical assistance in developing new products or lowering costs; they can obtain low-interest loans or loan guarantees for new equipment or conversion to a new activity where market conditions are better. Workers can obtain unemployment compensation and relocation allowances for moving to areas where the prospects of employment are better. Also workers are eligible for retraining programs and grants to support them while they learn new skills.

In addition to adjustment assistance for labor and capital, a well-conceived pollution-control adjustment-assistance program should make provision for financial aid to those towns that lose tax revenues because of the loss of industry. There is a very delicate problem in defining the conditions of eligibility and in providing for an appropriate body to judge that eligibility. Yet, experience with adjustment assistance for tariff cuts should make it possi-

ble to write regulations that are neither so strict as to defeat the intent of the program nor so liberal as to turn the program into a general subsidy for business and labor.

In contrast to our conclusions on cost subsidies, adjustment assistance policies are more likely to be consistent with achieving pollution control at least cost. Furthermore, adjustment assistance deals directly with the problem of easing the plight of those who are by circumstance forced to bear a disproportionate share of the total cost of pollution control. Adjustment-assistance serves to redistribute the costs of environmental improvement where these costs are borne by a few for the benefit of many.

NOTES

1. The President's Council on Environmental Quality, *Environmental Quality*—1971, Washington, D.C., 1971, p. 111.

2. *Business Week,* May 13, 1972, p. 77.

3. *Environmental Quality*—1971, op. cit.

4. This possibility is discussed in more detail in the next section.

5. See Allen V. Kneese and Blair T. Bower, *Managing Water Quality: Economics, Technology, Institutions,* Baltimore: The Johns Hopkins Press, 1968.

6. See pp. 156–161. [Not included in this anthology.]

7. This finding and other points in this section are based primarily on A. Myrick Freeman III, "The Distribution of Environmental Quality," in Allen V. Kneese and Blair T. Bower, eds., *Environmental Quality Analysis: Theory and Method in the Social Sciences,* Baltimore: The Johns Hopkins Press, 1972.

8. The extent of the regressivity of the property tax is not a settled issue. See Mason Gaffney, "The Property Tax Is Progressive," *National Tax Association Papers and Proceedings,* 1971.

DAVID PEARCE

*T*he *Economics of Pollution*

Homo economicus could scarcely be described as an attractive animal. His view of the world is conditioned by individual self-interest, and in so far as he recognizes obligations and duties, obeys his conscience, cares for others, or even acts out of malice, he tends to exist outside the realms of conventional economic theory. Since no one would suggest that human behaviour is motivated only by self-interest, it is all the more odd to see economics described as 'the science of human behaviour'. As a theory of how people behave when faced with situations in which they have to choose between alternatives, economics is therefore necessarily incomplete. But this incompleteness is not the main deficiency, for, once having defined economic man in a particular way, conventional economic doctrine then goes on to *prescribe* policies on the basis of criteria designed to realize the aims of economic man. In this way, *what is* becomes *what is good*. If it can be demonstrated that market forces cause doctors to have higher wages than miners, it becomes 'right' that doctors should earn more than miners. As a result, one economist has remarked, one purpose of economic theory becomes that of making those who *are* comfortable *feel* comfortable.[1] Positivists would strenuously deny any such subtle slip from the positive to the normative. But the dividing line is thin, and nowhere has the issue been highlighted more than in the current debate over the economic aspects of environmental deterioration.

On the one hand there are the advocates of the conventional wisdom, by far the majority, who argue that environmental problems are economic problems, that economics already possesses the tools of analysis and the policy weapons to solve those problems, and that policy should be prescribed on the basis of conventional economic criteria. On the other hand there are those who recognize in the life sciences a fundamental challenge to the application of economic theory. They tend to argue for largely unfamiliar ideas of 'stable states', with ecologic criteria being substituted, in the main, for economic criteria. And, as always in any debate over fundamentals, there are those who adopt a middle position, accepting some limitations on the ability of economics to prescribe policies for environmental problems, but believing, for the most part, that the criteria should remain those of the economist.

THE NATURE OF THE ECONOMIC DEBATE

Conventional economic theory is rigidly anthropocentric. More than this, its apparent concern with human welfare tends to be confined to current generations, with future generations being 'cared for' only in so far as capital goods are built up to provide an inheritance of material wealth.[2] This view is differentiated from the 'ecological' approach in several ways. Firstly, some members of the latter school of thought ascribe 'rights' to future generations, the most basic being a 'right' to existence. Secondly, these rights are frequently extended to other living species so that the presence of what we might call 'biotic altruism' is acknowledged. These considerations make it look as though what divides the schools of thought is a morality, a dispute over the area of concern that a current generation should exhibit when making its choices. In some cases there is indeed such a difference. Fallaciously, the conventional theorist sees this as adding an extra set of value judgements to a value-free 'science', and rejects the ecological approach on these grounds. The error lies in his failure to recognize that artificially defining the area of concern to cover only current generations is itself a value judgement, *par excellence*. Indeed,

From *Environment and the Industrial Society* by Nicholas Holmes, Westview Press, 1976. Reprinted by permission of Hodder & Stoughton, England. *Author's Note*—I am indebted to my colleagues Michael Common and Christopher Nash for valuable comments on an earlier draft of this chapter.

the whole idea of 'economic efficiency' centres around the basic normative proposition that resources *should* be allocated in such a way as to maximize the welfare of an existing generation. But even the definition of welfare is value-loaded. All policies involve gains for some people and losses for others. The economist compares the two by attempting to find what the losers are prepared to accept, to put up with their loss. If the money value of what the gainers are willing to pay exceeds the money value of compensation required, there is a 'net gain' to society and the policy is justified. We shall illustrate this idea shortly, but for the moment it is only necessary to note two things: first, consumer preferences determine what is economically desirable; second, those preferences are not expressed as political votes, but as votes weighted by market power. In general, the higher the voter's income the more his vote will count. Willingness to pay is dependent upon ability to pay. Unless the nation's material output is distributed between voters in the best possible way, unless it is 'optimal', economic votes will not meet the criterion for economic efficiency. To assume that it is optimal is itself a value judgement. On several scores then, conventional theory and doctrine is value-loaded. Since no rules can be derived for saying how many value judgements a social science should contain, the dispute between the conventional theorist and the 'ecological approach' cannot be resolved by reference to value-judgements. They may indeed differ, but they cannot be used to decide which approach is 'correct'.

As it happens, the two approaches also differ in positive content, in the facts of the matter. It is to the belated credit of conventional theory that it recognizes part of the interdependence between people. The behaviour of each person invariably affects the welfare of someone else. If that behaviour is offensive, like an act of pollution and if no mechanism exists whereby the polluter's selfish behaviour is automatically modified, there exists an 'external cost'; cost here meaning a loss in welfare. Since economic theory recognizes that all gains and losses must be included before deciding whether a policy is sound, the uncompensated losses of the sufferer must be allowed for. The idea that external costs should be 'internalized', that the polluter in our case should be induced to take account of the nuisance he causes, is the pivot of the conventional approach to environmental de-

terioration. In the next section we shall demonstrate how the correction is meant to take place.

The ecological approach, on the other hand, extends the idea of interdependence. First, it points out that external effects are not isolated instances to be corrected by piecemeal policies. They are endemic to the economic system, and this characteristic of external effects is not contingent upon the type of economic system in question, capitalist, socialist or otherwise. The 'pervasiveness' of external effects arises because of the simple operation of physical laws. Essentially, whatever is withdrawn from the environment in the form of a resource, whether material or energy, must return to the environment in a roughly equal mass according to the law of conservation of energy. The fact that the resources are transformed, so that coal returns as smoke and gases, for example, is essentially what makes a resource into a pollutant. But the critical point remains that the creation of external effects is endogenous to the system. As we shall see, this has implications for the type of policy that might be adopted for dealing with environmental problems.

Second, interdependence is extended to the relationships between man and his environment. Once the existence of ecological chain reactions is recognised, external effects become more difficult still to pin down and identify. DDT residues may affect other humans geographically distant from the source, or after a time-lag of several years. In the cases of nuclear waste, the time-lags may extend to hundreds or even thousands of years, imposing the external effect on a generation not yet in existence. More than this, the idea that something is a loss only if some individual places an economic value on it is rejected. If the quality of human existence, and even existence itself, is dependent upon a life-support system that contains animals, plants, insects, and so on, then intefering with that support system in any substantial fashion will generate 'costs' that are not at all likely to show in the conventional economist's balance sheet of gains and losses. What this really means is that the whole idea of an external effect is redundant since it can only be defined by assuming away the very picture of the world that the ecologist is providing. As two recent writers have suggested, the idea of an external effect presupposes 'that social and natural systems are enclosed in bounded sets with the contained systems functioning in isolation, linked only via physical material flows', whereas, 'an holistic view ... regards these systems as enclosed in unbounded subsets of a universal biospheric set.'[3] In this respect the physical distinction between systems is non-existent, since all elements are inextricably related.

Even this very broad division of the parties to the current debate indicates the size of the rift between them. The argument here is that while value judgements do indeed differ between the camps, the real source of disagreement emanates from different views of how economic systems operate. The conventional view sees the economic system in isolation from the environment. The ecological view does not. Which one is correct depends critically upon whether ecological relationships are in some sense sacrosanct. We shall return to this issue later, but will turn now to a closer look at the conventional theory and the policies it advocates.

CONVENTIONAL ANALYSIS

The conventional approach hinges, as we have seen, on the idea of an external effect. Acting out of self-interest, economic man tends to ignore the effects of his activities on others. The degree of disinterest is likely to be greater the further away in time or distance the effect occurs. It is an essential aspect of conventional analysis that external effects are almost entirely what Dr Holmes has called 'local effects', the well-defined and observable nuisances with which most of us are familiar. As we saw, the ecological approach criticizes this unjustified narrowness of scope.

The significance of external costs is substantial.[4] First, since the individual ignores them in making his decision, he operates at a level of activity which is not socially optimal. To put it another way, society would be better off if he accounted for the losses he imposes on others and reduced his activity accordingly. This can be demonstrated fairly easily. Suppose we can measure the gains and losses involved. Since we need a measure common to both gains and losses we choose money values. This is not deferring to materialism, however. All it is saying is that those who gain receive benefits for which they are willing to pay. Those who lose suffer a cost which they are able to express as a sum of money they would wish to receive as compensation. The table shows a hypothetical situation. The activity in question is producing a product for sale, say a paper product. The loss arises from water pollution due to effluent from the paper mill: the loss may be to commercial or recreational fishermen, to people living nearby, to occasional visitors, or even to downstream producers who have to install equipment to clean the water they extract from the river. The last column of the table shows the result of subtracting external costs from private benefits: it is a column of net *social* benefits.[5]

(1)	(2) Private Benefits (£)	(3) External Costs (£)	(4) Social Benefits = (2) − (3)
Output (units)			
1	100	50	50
2	600	150	450
3	1000	300	700
4	1300	500	800
5	1500	1000	500
6	1600	1700	− 100
7	1400	3000	− 1600

Now we can contrast what happens between a system where the polluter is allowed to ignore the external cost and a system where he is made to account for those costs. If our polluter is not obliged to take account of the nuisance he causes (and, by assumption, self-interest will prevent him from doing so) he will operate where the benefit *to him* is greatest. In our example he will produce 6 units, with a private benefit of £1600. But clearly this is not the best scale of activity for 'society' as a whole. If allowance is made for external costs, the polluter should produce at 4 units where *net social benefits* are highest. The effect of inducing the polluter to account for external costs is that he reduces his activity.

Why do external effects occur? The physical reasons are frequently obvious: no-one suggests that polluters *wish* to impose costs on others. Pollution tends to be a by-product of economic activity. On the other hand, the polluter does frequently have the choice of *how* much pollution to produce. He can, as we have seen, simply reduce the scale of his activity, or he can look for alternative technological processes by which to produce his output with less pollution. Self-interest explains why he does neither voluntarily: to reduce output is to reduce profits, while to change technologies is to adopt a costlier process (it couldn't be less costly or he would already have adopted it in the interests of self gain) and also reduce profits. But his self-interest would be modified if those who lose by his actions had enforceable and well-defined property rights in the river or air or land that is affected. The sufferer could then exact damages from the polluter, and, knowing this, the polluter would change his behaviour accordingly, just as we are careful to avoid damaging other people's houses or motor cars. But if the polluter knows the property rights of those he offends are loosely defined, or difficult to enforce, he may well accept the risk of polluting. This is exactly the situation with riparian law in the western world: the rights of those who suffer are fairly well defined but rarely enforced. When actions are taken, the polluter usually complains that the action will force him to close down and move his activity elsewhere, with a consequent loss of output and employment to the local community. The situation will be worse still where property rights are not defined at all: no resident has a right to sue for damages against aircraft noise, for example. And the oceans have no property rights attached to them, with the consequence that no one can sue anybody else for the dumping of radioactive waste, or for fish kills caused by pollutants. Hence the proper definition and enforcement of property rights in all resources is an oft-mooted long term proposal for 'solving' externalities and hence environmental problems.

There is an added feature of this inadequacy of current economic systems to define property rights. Suppose a property right were established in clean air, something that does not exist at the moment, then, technically, it would be possible for the owner of that right to sell clean air as a commodity on the market. But clean air is, in the economist's language, a 'public good'. Such goods have particular characteristics that make it difficult to establish a market in them. If they are supplied to one person, they are supplied to all. Thus, if our

clean air property owner provides clean air to you, he provides it for me. If I cannot be excluded from this provision it will pay me to pretend that I don't want clean air, wait for it to be provided to you, and then I can benefit without paying. (With 'private' goods you can exclude me if you are willing to pay the price and I am not: if you are willing to pay £1500 for a car and I am not, I have effectively been excluded from having the car.) To use the jargon, I become a 'free rider' and the existence of free riders means that no owner of the property right in clean air has any incentive to provide that good since he will not capture the true price the beneficiaries are willing to pay. He is more likely to use the air resource for some other purpose, e.g., as a 'sink' for airborne pollutants.

Our example contains many assumptions, explicit and hidden and we can see shortly what difficulties are involved in this kind of analysis. But some immediate conclusions of importance are already possible. First, once the polluter takes account of the external costs he imposes on others, he will reduce the scale of the offending activity. This shouldn't surprise anyone: we are all familiar with the simple idea that people shouldn't engage in offensive activities. But the significant thing in this case is that the offending activity is not *eliminated*. This may be surprising at first sight. Instead of calling a halt to the offending activity, we require the producer to operate at a lower level of activity where he still imposes some nuisance: in our example he still imposes an external cost of £500. Economists of the conventional school refer to this as the 'optimal amount of external cost'. In a nutshell, economic analysis of this kind tells us to reduce an offending activity but not to stop it altogether. If no other considerations were relevant, for example, it would tend to imply that legislation like the Clean Air Acts, forbidding pollution of certain types in certain areas, is not 'optimal'. It also means that we should *not* aim to clean up all rivers—perhaps some *should* stay as industrial sewers—or clean up all beaches. If correct, this would be a significant recommendation and, of course, a comforting one since a total clean-up policy would be politically difficult to operate and very costly. The general rule would be to weigh up the benefits and costs of any offending activity, and then ensure that the activity takes place at a level which maximizes net benefits. Not surprisingly then, those who advocate this approach tend to be firm believers in cost-benefit analysis, a method of appraisal which attempts to put money values on external costs in the way we have assumed possible in our examples.[6]

If we can suppose that the analysis is correct, the crucial question arises of how to achieve the 'optimum': i.e. how do we ensure that the producer of paper products in our example sells only 4 units and not the more profitable (to him) 6 units? It should be evident that if he operates as 'economic man' he will exhibit no conscience about his polluting activities. He won't therefore voluntarily operate at the optimum. However, the idea of inducing awareness and conscience into polluters is one we are familiar with. Campaigns to secure recycling of bottles or to ensure that open-cast mining operations take note of nuisance effects have something of this missionary flavour. But, in keeping with his analysis, the economist argues that we have to operate in a fashion which acknowledges the self-interest of the polluter. The first idea is therefore very simple, in theory anyway: tax the polluter in such a way that he produces at the 'optimum'.

Actually finding the right level of tax is not easy. In our example we require the polluter to pay a tax equal to the external cost he imposes on others. So, at 4 units of output he will pay £500. His private benefits will therefore be reduced from £1300 to £800. At 5 units he pays a tax of £1000 (the external costs he imposes at that level), making his net private benefit £1500 − £1000 = £500. Obviously then it will not pay to increase output beyond 4 units. Just to make sure that we have the right output level, consider the output of 3 units. He pays a tax of £300 and secures private benefits of £1000 − £300 = £700, i.e., less than he would achieve if he produced at 4 units. So, we have what appears to be a simple rule: tax the polluter according to the level of external cost he imposes and the tax will automatically induce the producer to operate at the 'right' level of activity. Notice that, although government has to interfere directly as far as this solution is concerned, once it has set the tax we can rely on the normal behaviour of the polluter, his self-interested behaviour, to achieve the right level. All that has happened is that we have added a further element to the producer's cost, consisting of the pollution tax.

FREE MARKETS AS A SOLUTION

Before looking in a little more detail at the 'tax solution', it is useful to look at some of the other corrective measures suggested by economists. Perhaps the most controversial argument has been advanced by Professor Coase of Chicago University.[7] Like many Chicago economists, Professor Coase found the idea of a tax a further example of unwarranted interference with the working of a free economic system. He pointed out that it is in the interests of both parties in the previous example to 'bargain' over the appropriate level of pollution. Suppose the polluter operates at the level of 6 units, which maximizes his personal benefits. If he were to reduce output to 5 units he would lose £100. But that reduction in output would reduce the external costs suffered by the recipient of the pollution by £700. Now of course the £700 may not accrue as hard cash. But it should represent the recipient's valuation of the gain in 'welfare' experienced by seeing the nuisance reduced. So, the argument runs, the polluter should be willing to accept any sum of money *greater* than £100 to reduce his output to 5 units, and the sufferer should be prepared to pay any sum of money less than £700 to secure the reduction. Obviously, we have a bargaining situation, with property rights vested in the polluter but not the loser. The loser can 'bribe' the polluter to reduce output: exactly what bribe will be necessary will be determined by their relative strengths and skills as bargainers. But we can repeat the exercise. For a reduction from 5 to 4 units, the polluter will accept any sum greater than £200 (the loss he would make if output fell to 4 units from 5), and the loser should be willing to pay £500 since his costs will fall by £500 from £1000 to £500. So a move to 4 units can be achieved by bargaining. Try the exercise again for a reduction from 4 to 3 units. A bargain is no longer mutually beneficial: the polluter would lose £300, the sufferer would gain only £200. So we have a 'bargaining optimum' at 4 units. It is no accident that this optimum coincides with the level that maximizes net social benefits.

Could it be then, that the system will take care of itself? That *Homo economicus* will operate in his own interests to achieve the optimal level of pollution by bargaining? There are technical criticisms of the 'Coasian solution', but the real problem lies in the unreality of the analysis.[8] Certainly bargains do take place: but in general they are conspicuous by their absence. The absence of bargains is perhaps explained by the costs of administering them: collecting protesters together, establishing contact, demonstrating that losses have occurred and bargaining. But if these costs are so high that no bargains take place then it could mean that bargains *should not* take place. This odd result arises because economists call anything involving the use of a real resource a 'cost', including time. Hence an administrative cost is a real resource cost. If those costs prevent a bargain taking place it can only mean that it is not worth incurring costs to secure a bargain. As one writer has remarked, there is something decidedly Panglossian about such a view: the absence of a bargain must be for the best, because if it wasn't for the best a bargain would take place.[9]

But under the umbrella of this potentially never-ending argument lie other important reasons for rejecting the 'bargaining' system. First, the important externality situations simply do not fit the context where people can come together and bargain. Air pollution is often widely dispersed and tracing the source of a nuisance can be very difficult. Nor are sufferers conveniently grouped into natural bargaining units. How would we bargain over ocean pollution, and with whom? What happens if the external costs occur years after the activity that generated them? How do future generations bargain with us to reduce the external costs we impose on them? What happens when the activity is a non-continuing one: i.e. a once-for-all event like secretly dumping cyanide in a river. In addition, if environmental quality is a 'public good', as suggested earlier, how would the polluter collect payments from the sufferers if there are free riders?

There are other problems too. Our hypothetical example assumes a particular pattern for benefits and costs as the polluter's activity increases. But in many respects, these patterns are themselves arbitrary. If, for example, the column of private benefits read 10, 100, 400, 900 etc. we would have a situation in which, if property rights are vested in the sufferer, the polluter would not *begin* production, even though net benefits might soon become increasingly positive. Only if he can

somehow 'jump' to an output of three units would he be able to start paying compensation.[10]

Nor, as we have seen, is bargaining a relevant solution in situations where competition between firms is limited; i.e. 'imperfect'. Essentially, if the firm produces so as to maximize profits he is already producing less than the socially desirable output. To reduce his output even further by bribes, is to perpetuate the inefficiency. If we add to all of this the strong possibility that external costs exist on a widespread scale, are difficult to evaluate, occur over wide distances and over time, the unreality of the 'bargaining' solution is only underlined.

Even if there were something attractive about letting the market look after itself, the idea that the 'sufferer should pay' is the result of armchair theorizing about a world that exists, at best, only in the textbooks.

Second, there is an important hidden value judgement in the analysis. Essentially, offender and offended are being treated on an equal footing and this runs counter to what we might call 'usual morality' when dealing with activities of this kind. The person who loses is frequently an innocent party and yet the Coasian solution is consistent with making the innocent party pay. This in turn suggests that there is profit in making threats, and, it is worth noting, that the rewards of blackmail could be higher than the profit obtained by carrying out the normal business of producing goods. For example, in our hypothetical case, the polluter reduces output from 6 to 4 units and 'loses' £300 of private benefits. But he gains whatever bribe the sufferers are prepared to pay, which could be as much as £1200. Logically, it pays the polluter to set up business where he can do as much damage as possible and bargain as hard as possible. This would be an undesirable result of a free market world even in terms of the 'economic efficiency' concept so far introduced. To all this must be added the fact that the loser is frequently the person who is least able to adjust his behaviour to accommodate an externality situation: those who live in noisy and polluted atmospheres, in high density and low amenity areas are also those with low relative incomes, least articulation and least capability of geographical movement to avoid the nuisance. On 'equity' grounds alone there can be little argument that it is the privileged who offend environmentally and the underprivileged who suffer.[11] To argue in this context that the losers must pay for their lack of privilege scarcely accords with any concept of justice that appeals.[12]

MAKING THE POLLUTER PAY

If, as seems correct, the idea of bargaining over external costs is rejected, then some form of tax or direct control to achieve the optimum level of pollution is required. The polluter must pay, and one method of making him pay is to tax him, as previously suggested.

The simple example used so far assumes that the choice facing society is to reduce the polluter's production of goods in order to reduce the level of external cost. But it is also possible that the firm could adopt some alternative *method* of production, a 'clean' technology, or that it could engage in the treatment of waste. The principle of maximizing net social benefit is equally applicable in this case. The cost of treating waste is a real cost: it means that resources must be used for that purpose and that therefore they cannot be used for some alternative purpose. Against these costs must be measured the benefits from waste treatment. If we know how external costs are related to waste treatment, we know immediately how benefits relate to costs.[13] The aim would then be to spend money on waste treatment up to the point where the difference between the resulting benefits (reducing damages) and the costs of treatment is greatest.

The tax approach to the problem may well achieve this result. That is, if a tax is imposed in the manner described, the polluter may well continue producing at his previous level of output, but with a different method of production brought about by the fact that he now bears the tax. In this case the tax is making it relatively costly to use 'dirty' technologies. Equally, if the sufferer holds the property rights and the polluter does not, it pays the polluter to invest in waste treatment up to the point where the cost of doing so is just equal to the compensation he would have to pay out for damages otherwise caused. All roads lead, in theory, to the optimum solution.

The tax solution need not involve the authorities in knowing the polluter's cost of waste treatment. But it does require some knowledge of damages. If, in our example, raising output from 5 to 6 units involves an extra amount of damage of £700, the 6th unit should be taxed at £700. It can then be left to the polluter to adjust his behaviour accordingly. If waste treatment is possible, the polluter will increase treatment as long as the cost of doing so is less than the tax imposed. One of the most popular criticisms of pollution taxes is that the consumer will eventually pay in the form of higher prices. This is true but it is in fact a *desirable* outcome of the tax policy. Essentially what happens is that prices rise because of the tax and hence demand for the product in question falls. Now that the price of the offending commodity has risen relative to other goods which are not similarly taxed, the latter will tend to be substituted for the former. In this way the *composition* of spending patterns is changed in favour of commodities with a lower pollution content.[14]

Anyone familiar with actual pollution problems will recognize the extreme degree of simplicity involved in this analysis. However, the exponents of the conventional approach would argue that actual problems differ only in complexity and that this complexity is usually manageable with computerized models. To take just one example, waste treatment in one direction will often create a waste disposal problem in another direction. It would be misleading, for example, to compare the costs of filtering dust from power station flue gases with the benefits of reduced air pollution, if, as often happens, there is then a problem of disposing of the toxic dust on nearby land. The principle of conservation of mass tells us that any treatment process will always entail some disposal problem. Good treatment involves transforming the pollutant into useful by-products (extracting vanadium from fly-ash for example, or fertilizer from sewage sludge—providing the fertilizer is not then a pollutant!) or reducing the pollutant to a form which can be assimilated by the environment. Even where this does not happen, however, the arguments suggest that it may pay to treat waste as long as the reduction in damages, allowing for the damages caused by any processed waste, outweighs the cost of treatment.

Another approach, and the one most widely adopted in anti-pollution policies, is the setting of 'environmental quality' standards. It should be evident by now that what the conventional theory would demand is that the standards should coincide with the point where net social benefits are maximized. Also, by the previous arguments, it should not make any difference in theory if the standard is expressed in terms of the amount of waste treatment that should take place, or in terms of the quality of the environment that should result. In practice, it will make some difference. Establishing a quality level for the receiving environment may make administration more difficult: if the quality level is not reached and there are dozens of polluters, it may be difficult to decide who is at fault. If the standards relate to the amount of treatment it should be possible to inspect treatment facilities and see if they meet the standards laid down. However, in the latter case the main problem lies in allocating an agreed limit of discharged waste to all the polluters. Unless the limits for each individual polluter are specified carefully, there is likely to be inefficiency in using resources for waste treatment.

However, the basic reason that society opts for quality standards is that the information necessary for calculating taxes is not available. We simply do not know what the 'damage function' looks like for reasons that will become clear later. (This does not rule out the use of taxes: they still provide a weapon for ensuring that *some* adjustment is made in the polluter's activities.) Hence the use of standards which appear ostensibly to be unrelated to any idea of maximizing net benefits. It is sometimes argued, however, that these standards may not be too far divorced from the 'optimal' standard. First, whatever standard is set implies something about benefits and costs. If a standard is set for the polluter in our hypothetical example and he can only meet that standard by reducing output to, say, 5 units, it has cost him £100 in lost private benefits. Equally, it has resulted in reduced external costs equal to the reduced damage resulting from the improved quality level: in this case £700. So net benefits are £600. The fact that they cannot be measured should not obscure the fact that the quality standard implies some level of net benefits. It makes sense therefore to talk about the *idea* of 'optimal' quality standards. And, if it were just a

matter of doing more research to find out how to value damages in money terms, we should engage in that research in order to set the appropriate quality level. Second, how are standards set? Usually the procedure is to establish 'tolerable' levels of pollution where the tolerance thresholds are set by human health standards (the presence of the sewage bacterium *Escherichia coli* in water, for example) or by standards necessary to maintain fish life (e.g. levels of dissolved oxygen), recreational facilities (swimming, boating) and so on. Now, since the damage function, if we knew it, would be heavily influenced by these tolerance levels—we would expect benefits to 'jump' when quality levels rose above these levels—there is some likelihood that setting standards will coincide with maximum net benefits.

In practice, one doubts if standards coincide in the manner suggested. Standards are more likely to be set by political bargaining. Thus if a polluting industry exerts political pressure it may have a major influence on setting standards at levels which suit the industry, but not society as a whole. There is good reason to suppose that many of the *de facto* environment standards in the western world are set in this way. Also, quality standards are set with reference to one threshold only, so that the likelihood of this particular threshold coinciding with maximum net benefits is small.

Taxes have at least one advantage over standards. Once a standard is set, the polluter will disregard the damage costs associated with effluent which does not exceed the standard. He will only incur costs once he exceeds the standard. Taxes, on the other hand, will be payable with respect to *all* damage incurred whether it is below or above the standard set. Hence the tax has the advantage of encouraging the firm to switch to 'cleaner' technologies, an incentive which still exists, but less forcefully, with the standard.

The serious problem with standards or charges for the amount of pollutant a firm may discharge is one of policing. If the polluter is faced with a difficult waste disposal problem he may secretly discharge waste at night and hope he will not be detected via any resulting fish kills or damage. This is a familiar problem and arises clearly with the cleaning of oil tankers at sea; some cleaning is permitted but there is little possibility of detection if waste is disposed of at the same time. Recent cases in Britain of the dumping of cyanide waste fit the same pattern.

But the overriding practical argument in favour of standards is that they avoid the problem of valuing the external cost, a problem which, as we suggest below, is more difficult than is usually imagined.

SOME CRITICISMS OF TAX SOLUTIONS

Taxing the polluter is increasingly likely to become an integral part of pollution abatement policies. But tax solutions have drawbacks and cannot therefore be relied upon to ensure an approach even to the kind of economic optimum we have so far been discussing. Any tax mechanism requires that we know what the benefits of abatement are, unless of course the tax is being used as one instrument to secure a given environment-quality standard set independently of economic criteria. But the benefits are usually not known and it is not difficult to see why. Frequently they are intangible and include things like the preservation of a view, or recreational fishing benefits, reduced risks of health hazards, preservation of wildlife, and so on. In general, the conventional economist argues that these benefits, however difficult to define, have a price. If pollution impairs a natural beauty spot we can ask what people would accept in compensation for the loss of the benefit, or what they would be willing to pay to restore it. The question at least is meaningful. And if it is meaningful there is no *conceptual* problem about placing a money value on the benefit. Most, but not all, economists accept this view. Those who do not, point to the distinct possibility that people do not always translate losses and gains into money values. It is important to understand what this means. Pollution abatement is not a free good: it uses up resources directly and indirectly, resources which could have been used for some other purpose, perhaps for things most of us would find attractive—hospitals, schools, playgrounds. There is always, in the economist's language, a 'trade-off'. If we have one thing, we go without something else. To say that people *cannot* place a money value on something is either to say there is no trade-off, or

that people place infinite values on some things. It means that there exists a 'dual' value system, that the values computed by the economist are not the only values, that some values override others. We suggested at the outset that this will be the case anyway: few people would be able to translate the loss of their own child into a money value or put a money value on a substantially increased risk of losing their own life. The conventional economist would argue to the effect that the most that people would be willing to pay to prevent a loss of this kind is their entire lifetime income and so there is at least a finite upper limit. But this kind of argument only proves what the conventional economist wants to prove using his own framework of analysis, in which 'willingness to pay' is always constrained by income. What the critics are saying is that the *framework* is irrelevant for some benefits and costs and that a proof in terms of that framework is not an answer to a criticism of the values economists generally accept. The reluctance of economists to accept this line of thought is understandable: if attaching money values to things produces a simple decision rule, it makes for a widespread relevance that, like most social scientists, economists want to possess. Hence the attraction of cost-benefit analysis. Equally, it is often argued that since there are always advantages and disadvantages to a scheme, cost-benefit analysis must be relevant. But if cost-benefit is saying no more than that we should compare the pros and cons of any move, it is saying nothing distinctive or unexceptional. The fact is that it does say more than this. It purports to find a single measure of costs and benefits—money values—*and* to attach weights to those costs and benefits, weights which reflect in one way or another some kind of relative social valuation of the outcomes.

The conclusion that our many value-systems cannot be squeezed into the framework of cost-benefit seems inescapable. If so, the idea of looking at pollution within that framework must be questioned. It does not make it irrelevant. Perhaps there are projects where benefits and costs are clearly defined conceptually and where the problems of valuation are not overwhelming. But it is as well to consider some further practical problems of applying taxes to see how far this is likely to happen.

A number of pollutants are synergistic: when

combined, they have effects out of proportion to the effects each one has individually. This means that the damage done by one pollutant cannot be calculated unless we know the likelihood that it will be accompanied by the other pollutant, and by the conditions necessary to create synergistic effects. The tax solution does not become irrelevant in these circumstances: it does become much more difficult to decide who should be taxed, and by how much.

The example of external costs we have been working with is obviously unrealistic. One polluter affects one sufferer. In practice, many polluters combine to affect many sufferers. This would again have only the effect of making life more difficult in terms of devising taxes if it were not for the further fact that external costs are not localized events unrelated to the rest of economic activity. The seminal work of Ayres and Kneese demonstrated this with the aid of *materials balance* analysis.[15] The essential theory is simple. We know that matter cannot be created or destroyed. We know too that economic activity draws on natural resources— coal, oil, timber, water, etc.—for the purpose of transforming those resources into 'goods' that are useful, i.e. satisfy wants. Whatever is taken from the environment in the form of resources must travel *through* the economic system, usually receiving continual physical information—crude oil to refined oil, plastics, synthetic fibres and so on—*and must reappear as material (and energy) to be disposed of when the transformation has produced the goods we want.* By the law of conservation of mass, what reappears as unwanted 'residuals' must be roughly equivalent in weight to the resources extracted to produce those goods. Not all residuals are pollutants, of course. Some are assimilated by the natural capacity of the environment to break down waste products. Some, like carbon dioxide, appear as a potential pollutant but mostly concentrated in the upper atmosphere and, as discussed in Chapter Two [not included in this anthology], arguments exist as to whether this is, or will ever be, a problem or not. But two crucial facts remain. First, the pollution problem is a necessary consequence of using up resources in the way we do. The more resources we use, in general, the more pollution there will be. Second, the process of transforming those resources will affect pollution—if we prefer our furniture to be made of

plastic and not of wood, we shall face a disposal problem in that plastic has no natural decomposers in the environment: neither have mercury or cadmium. So the *composition* of our desires for goods will determine the composition of the final outputs we produce and hence the composition of the residuals.

However, the point of looking at the problem in a materials balance framework is to demonstrate that external costs are not isolated, clearly defined occurrences. They are 'pervasive'. Since every good has a pollution content of one kind or another, all production causes externalities since all goods must return to the environment, usually in a form quite different to the resource they come from. If now we are to 'tax the polluter' what is entailed? Nothing less than a wholesale reshaping of the price structure of the economy: goods with high pollution content would have high prices, those with low content would have low prices. Public transport, for example, would be encouraged, private transport discouraged, since, pollution per head of transport user would be lower in the former case. The 'tax solution' is not affected in principle: but it does mean that it would have to be applied on a scale that one doubts very much is ever envisaged by those who advocate it. On the practical side, could we ever estimate the social damage caused by each and every good in the economy? If not, the tax solution as we have described it would not be relevant: it would be impossible to estimate the right 'social price' for each good. If the tax solution is seen as one element of a wider strategy, perhaps aimed rather more in hope than certitude at the securing of an economic optimum, then a tax proportional to the pollution content of each good should have the desired effect. But this is a long cry from cost-benefit analysis.

There are still other problems. If we consider an environmental benefit, like a clean river, how would we estimate benefits? We might value its commercial use for water or fishing, and its use as a recreational facility. Standard procedures exist, albeit dubious in many respects, for placing a money value on the recreational benefits. What is missing, however, is the value placed on the river by those who do not visit it. This may sound odd, but is clearly important. Some people like to hold open the 'option' of visiting the area if they want to.

Their loss of option if the river is polluted is nowhere accounted for in conventional cost-benefit analysis, nor is it easy to see how it could be. But still others may be upset by unclean rivers even though they never intend to exercise their option. They value the facility as part of their heritage, or because they ascribe some sort of 'right' to exist to the river's wildlife.

The standard reaction to this fact is to designate those who possess these values as 'sentimentalists', as if this in some way depreciates the relevance of these preferences. This objection is self-defeating even within the confines of economic analysis, however. For all that matters is that people *do* care. If the conventional economist insists that only preferences count and that it is not the economist's role to investigate their source, preferences arising from 'sentiment' must be accorded exactly the same weight as any other preference. There may be any number of reasons why people have a valuation. All that matters in terms of conventional economics is that they do have it. If these kinds of losses are excluded, we are effectively undervaluing the benefits of amenity and hence the external costs of pollution. Even on conventional criteria then, we are in danger of investing too few resources in pollution abatement.

If the pervasiveness of external costs and the existence of unaccounted 'demands' for environmental products are not sufficient reasons for doubting the relevance of tax policies alone, the ecologist is quick to point out that many of the costs of pollution are not known in sufficient detail for us to accommodate them in an economic framework. Suppose, for example, we were to carry out a cost-benefit analysis of crop spraying policies. Two kinds of effect are likely to be left out.

First, there will be the costs associated with effects of pesticide residues distributed geographically at great distance. The conventional economist replies that this is a matter of the 'state of the art': if we research into these effects we will learn to identify them and value them. Certainly, the research into long-range ecological effects is crucial. But this is not the real problem in the meantime. The fact is that the effects are not well defined. What matters then is how to behave, how to make decisions, in the context of uncertainty. Economics offers a number of rules, and we turn to some of

them in the final section. To date, however, cost-benefit analysts have shown no signs that they recognize that uncertainty defines the context of analysis for environment problems. Added to this, the ecologic effect may well be irreversible. What does the economist say about losses that can never be restored? It is extremely doubtful if he can say anything useful: to ask people what they would accept to go without something for ever is rather like asking the parent what compensation he will accept for losing his child. And the irreversible effect will not just be suffered by the current generation: future generations must go without it too. One of the arrogances of economics is the assumption that all future generations will have preferences similar to our own. Although economists aim to plan only for the current generation, since they do not know what future generations want, effectively what happens is that we leave a capital stock for future generations with the qualities *we* would expect to find in a desirable capital stock. This permits us to engage in activities with irreversible external effects: if we are not diminished by them, neither will our heirs. We shall return to this point shortly.

The second aspect of ecologic effects is their possible distribution in time. The effects of DDT were not recognized at the time of its introduction, save by the farsighted few and have begun to accrue now, many years after, due to the fact that the effects build up through time in the food chain. Again, the conventional economist calls for research into these effects and argues that they fit his pattern of thinking. But, in fact, if the effects accrue to future generations they are ignored. The declared intent of cost-benefit analysis is not realized. Time is in fact incorporated into the analysis in such a way that costs *now* appear more important than costs *later*. This is done by the procedure of 'discounting', a system of weighting gains and losses depending on *when* they occur. Discounting is justified because people, we are told, prefer their benefits in the present compared to the future, and, conversely, worry more about costs now than later. But this is entirely at odds with planning for future generations.

For all these reasons, we must be severely sceptical of anyone who tells us that economists already have the tools of analysis to deal with the environmental problem, already know what the solutions would look like and that the only problems are those of finding the right money values by which to determine the right taxes. The argument so far has been that, even on their own terms, the conventional economists see no problems for analysis because they do not question the theoretical and practical limitations of their own subject. This is perhaps not surprising: if someone invests a great deal of 'intellectual capital' in taking up a stance, they are unlikely to indulge in the kind of self-criticism that is called for. If we press the self-criticism a bit further, however, it may well be that the difficulties are even more serious and that 'conventional' economics has a severely limited scope. The concluding section suggests why this might be so.

ECOLOGY AND ECONOMICS

The misfortune of much of the silliness that has surrounded the current debate on the 'environmental crisis' is that it has obscured the relevance of ecology to the planning of resource use, and hence the relevance to economics. On the one hand we have the pessimists declaring that economics is irrelevant, as if there were no cost to solving a pollution problem, and at the other extreme we have conventional economists declaring that the 'science' of economics as they understand it already contains all that we need to analyse pollution problems and prescribe the appropriate remedy. The real issue is therefore whether, if there is 'crisis', economics can handle it in terms of prescribing how we should behave in order to deal with potential problems. The oddity of the conventional approach is that it is not clear how it can deal with this situation. If a 'crisis' is defined as a situation in which social costs are very substantial, even infinite in the worst event, cost-benefit must somehow incorporate the prediction of crisis in its balance sheet of losses and gains. Since many of the losses are not known until they have occurred, there is a danger that the only results from economic analysis will be to determine that a policy already undertaken should not have been. But this is not the object of policy-making and would be a remarkably hopeless outcome of economics if

the results of the policy turned out to be irreversible, locally or globally. What matters is that policy should somehow be determined beforehand: it should prescribe how we should behave, not how we should have behaved.[16] But if we then argue that cost-benefit studies can take account of *predicted* crises, we are doing no more than saying that activities which lead to crises should not be undertaken—simply because of the costs that will exceed the benefits. In this respect the analysis could not improve on a physical analysis of the situation, save in one respect: how do we 'value' crisis situations?

In other words, there is a role for some sort of cost-benefit analysis if the issue of valuation is a real one. But this raises the entire issue of what values the economist uses, what ethical premises he works with. The fact remains that those values are orientated to current generations, as we have seen. They contain no guarantee that they are 'survival orientated' and if this is true, we have to question what an 'economic optimum' means. Once this is recognized we can see why ecologist and economist find so little common ground. The conventional economist is saying that what we ought to do is get as near as humanly possible to a situation in which we maximize net social benefit. The ecologist, on the other hand, lays down what he believes to be the conditions for the existence of a society at some quality level. If we achieve economic optima we have no guarantee that we simultaneously achieve the ecologist's 'stable state'. And, if the ecologist is right, a stable state becomes a precondition for the existence of any society, whatever we maximize. In this way, economic activity may have to be constrained to meet ecologic conditions. There is nothing in the working of the economic system that guarantees the automatic fulfilment of the ecologic conditions. Since the latter are logically prior to the former, it is to the latter that we should first direct attention.

We can illustrate the idea by looking again at how the economist defined the 'optimal' amount of external cost. It occurred where the net social benefits from the polluting activity were maximized, and this was seen to coincide with some remaining amount of pollution. Compare this to a simple ecologic analysis. The ecologist would point out that what we call an 'externality cost' can only occur when the disposal of waste exceeds the assimilative capacity of the environment, or when the *form* of residual is not matched by a corresponding decomposer population in the environment. But the ecologist's stable state exists when disposed residuals are just assimilated by the environment. By definition then, any externality situation must correspond to an unstable state. If then we define an economic optimum to exist where some amount of externality exists, it follows that economic optima are also unstable in the ecologist's sense.

Does this matter? It depends on the validity, claimed by ecologists, for the relationship between stability and survival. And this is a scientific issue, very much dependent in turn on the validity of comparing ecosystems which exhibit stability without human interference with ecosystems that do contain man as an integral part. Certainly the evidence is clear that once man is introduced to a previously 'natural' ecosystem, that system exhibits signs of breakdown in terms of species other than man. Whether that breakdown applies equally to man, or will apply, is a critical issue. For the economist, however, the problem is how to behave until the answer is clear. Suppose the stability-survival connection is established. Then we must behave in such a way that ecologic preconditions are met (unless of course someone divines an external value judgement which declares that current generations have the 'right' to eliminate future generations, or at least reduce their chances of survival). If the ecologist is wrong, it may not matter what we do as long as we pay attention to the relevant costs and benefits.[17]

What is remarkable is that anyone should prescribe a policy of *ignoring* ecologic constraints without first establishing the truth of the ecologist's case. To adopt this attitude to policy-making is to engage in a peculiar form of Russian roulette, equivalent to what the game theorists call 'maximax'—hoping for the best situation to develop and choosing the best outcome of that situation. It seems self-evident that a safety-first policy is better and one could suggest 'minimax regret', another of the game theorist's rules. In this case we look at the worst outcomes and aim to minimize the amount of regret we could possibly suffer. If the worst fears of ecologists were realized, of course, 'regret'

might well be something that only our souls could experience. Nonetheless, it provides a framework within which to operate and suggests that no one should 'take risks' with the environment.[18]

However, even if the ecologist is wrong and man can and will somehow continue surviving at some acceptable quality level, it is right to question whether economic criteria based on current generation values provide the correct approach. If we relax the arrogant assumption that future generations will like what we like, it seems more sensible to plan so as to leave each successive generation with the right to choose among options, subject to the constraint that no option should be eliminated. The oddity of current economic criteria is that they advance the idea that we should aim to do the best with what we have by way of resources and the natural environment. If the natural environment diminishes in some way—perhaps by species elimination—conventional criteria simply demand that we do the best we can with the new, smaller set of resources. No loss is attached to the fact that the ability to choose is now constrained more than it was. But being free to choose is as much a benefit as having what we choose. 'Keeping the options open' by way of what Dennis Gabor has called, in a different context, 'open-ended planning' makes for more sensible planning for resource use.[19]

CONCLUSION

No science advances without self-criticism. To declare, as some economists have done, that economics already possesses the weapons of analysis and hence the potential answers to environmental problems is both to engage in a dangerously naïve approach to environmental issues, and to diminish the status of science. As Buckminster Fuller has pointed out, diversity in knowledge, the avoidance of 'brain slavery', is as much a condition for the survival of man,[20] as is the ecologist's requirement for species diversity. Economics *alone* offers no answers to environmental problems since the problems themselves raise questions about the relevance of the values on which economic prescription is based. It does offer weapons, and it does offer a framework for some problems. But to suggest more than this is to assert, without any indication of self-doubt, that the values underlying economics are ubiquitous, timeless, and unchallengeable.

NOTES AND FURTHER READING

1. Balogh, T., quoted in Daly, H. 'The Stationary-State Economy'. *The Ecologist*. July 1972.

2. Mercifully, this domination of economics by a bias towards the present generation is being eroded and 'intergenerational equity' is becoming an issue for serious attention.

3. Norton, G. A., and Parlour, J. W. 'The Economic Philosophy of Pollution: A Critique'. *Environment and Planning*. 1972. 4.

4. External costs are sometimes called 'social costs'. This is misleading to the extent that it implies that the use of resources for the production of benefit does not constitute a social cost and tends to imply that economic activity can be evaluated by looking at the external costs alone. See Pearce, D. W., and Sturmey, S. G. 'Private and Social Costs and Benefits'. *Economic Journal*. March 1966.

5. There is a major complication even with this simple example. We have assumed what economists call 'perfect competition', a somewhat mythical state of affairs in which there are infinitely many buyers and sellers so that each individual has no influence over the market price of the product. The more realistic situation is one of 'imperfect competition' in which individuals can dominate the market. Under 'imperfect' conditions, *even without external costs*, social welfare is not maximized by letting firms maximize profits. It cannot then be assumed that if external costs exist they have only to be subtracted from private benefits to measure social welfare. Basically, if competition is imperfect, column (4) above will not measure social welfare simply because column (2) is not a measure of social welfare without external effects.

This is an important, if technical, qualification. Most of the literature on external costs implicitly or explicitly assumes, unrealistically, perfectly competitive conditions. In terms of the ensuing analysis, 'bargaining' solutions are not relevant to imperfect competition although it is suggested that a tax solution could be devised to secure the overall optimum. For one of the few treatments of this point see S. Wellisz, 'On External Economics and the Government-Assisted Invisible Hand', *Economica*, November 1964.

6. For an over-view of the nature of cost-benefit, see Pearce, D. W. (1971) *Cost-Benefit Analysis*, Macmillan.

7. Coase, R. 'The Problem of Social Cost'. *Journal of Law and Economics*. October 1960.

8. A major aspect of this unreality—the assumption of perfectly competitive conditions—has already been noted. See 5, above.

9. Mishan, E. J. 'Pangloss on Pollution'. *Swedish Journal of Economics*. March 1971.

10. This corresponds to the very realistic situation in which the polluter operates under conditions of what the economist calls 'increasing returns'. It is also possible that an outcome similar to that which results from increasing returns can arise because of the very existence of external costs. Several economists have noted that the way in which benefits change with output is critically important for the neatness of the tax and bargaining solutions. But it is not widely recognized that the very fact that external costs exist may *cause* the benefit curve to behave in an odd way. See W. Baumol and D. Bradford, 'Detrimental Externalities and Non-Convexity of the Production Set', *Economica*, May 1972.

11. Of course, Coasians also tend to be those who argue that 'equity' considerations are not relevant to economic analysis. Space forbids a critique of this widespread but arbitrary view of how the subject matter of economics should be confined. It would be argued that the sufferers tend to place more value on the £1 they lose than the producer does on the £1 he gains. If so, a simple comparison of money values as in our example, would be illicit. To use the technical language, we would be saying that marginal utilities of income differ.

12. For a brilliant exposition of the relevance of concepts of justice to any social science, see Rawls, J. (1971) *A Theory of Justice*. Oxford University Press. Of course, the unfairness could operate the other way; if a housing estate is built near an already established factory that pollutes the local area, should the factory pay for the added suffering it now 'causes'? Considerations of this kind have led some writers to argue that the liability for payment should devolve on the party arriving later in calendar time. See Ng, Y. 'Recent Developments in the Theory of Externality and the Pigovian Solution'. *Economic Record*. March 1971.

13. This requires three steps. First we must know how treatment will affect the amount of waste discharged. Second, we must know how waste discharged relates to the quality of the river or air that acts as 'receiver' of the wastes. Third, we must know how the water or air quality relates to damage suffered, expressed in money terms. The first step is straightforward, but steps two and three involve considerable difficulty in practice. As far as step two is concerned, it involves many variable and often random factors—weather, seasons, stream flow, temperature, and so on. A great deal of current research is devoted to 'simulating' local environments to predict this behaviour and allow for it in environmental policy.

14. This also helps to explain why some economists see no real conflict between economic growth and the en-

vironment: part of their argument is that the total national output need not be altered but its *composition* may be changed so as to reduce pollution.

15. Ayres, R. U. and Kneese, A. (1969) 'Production, Consumption and Externalities'. *American Economic Review*. See also Kneese, A., Ayres, R. U., and d'Arge, R. (1970) *Economics and Environment*. Resources for the Future Series. I.B.E.G. Ltd.

16. Thus, to overcome the difficult problem of valuing the actual damages generated by pollution, one economist has popularized the idea of an 'iterative solution'. An arbitrary tax is selected and imposed. Since producers will know how their costs are affected, even if governments do not, they will adjust their behaviour. Once they have altered their activities, the authorities calculate the social costs *ex post*. If they have gone down by an amount *less* than the tax, the tax is lowered, and so on, until the tax rate is equal to the extra damage imposed. The idea is to avoid estimating the way in which damages respond to changes in activity. As it happens, however, the procedure is likely to involve as many problems of calculating *ex post* damages as would be involved in estimating the entire range. The difficulty is not one of finding the range, but of calculating what the damages are for *any* level of pollution. Secondly, the method involves waiting for the costs to occur before they are calculated. If the

damages are to health, or are irreversible, the method must result in very undesirable outcomes.

The method was suggested in W. Beckerman, 'Environmental Policy Issues: Real and Fictitious', in *Problems of Environmental Economics*, OECD, Paris, 1972.

17. For an outline of the contrast between the economist's and ecologist's approach see Pearce, D. W. 'An Incompatibility in Planning for a Steady State and Planning for Maximum Economic Welfare'. *Environment and Planning*, 1973. 5, 2.

18. This is roughly equivalent to Ciriacy-Wantrup's rule that the aim of the policy should be that of insuring against those losses that cannot be quantitatively evaluated. See S. V. Ciriacy-Wantrup, 'The Economics of Environmental Policy', *Land Economics*, 1971. However, if the ecologist is correct, the range of situations in which quantitative evaluation is impossible is larger than suggested.

19. Gabor, D. (1968) *Open-ended Planning*. Paper presented to OECD Seminar on Long-Range Planning and Forecasting.

20. Buckminster Fuller, R. (1970) 'Education for Comprehensivity'. In *Approaching the Benign Environment*. Macmillan. New York.

JOHN BADEN AND RICHARD STROUP

*P*roperty Rights, Environmental Quality, and the Management of National Forests

THE CONVENTIONAL VIEW ON PROPERTY RIGHTS

It is commonly asserted that American society places too much value on property rights, too many of these property rights are in private hands, and much too little value is placed on human rights. Variants of this view are associated with liberal and radical politics. They were extremely common in the flood of environmental crisis literature after Earth Day, 1970. This position is overly

simplistic and betrays a gross and perhaps dangerous ignorance of the social functions of property rights and the forces that determine their evolution.

We hope to explain here that a fundamental cause of inefficient resources use is an institutional structure that underweights, assigns to wrong parties, neglects, or otherwise fails to include, certain existing or potential property rights. We suggest efforts to modify rights in the national forests. In brief, we suggest that net improvements in both

This article has been revised from an earlier version by the same authors entitled "Private Rights, Public Choices, and the Management of National Forests," which appeared in *Western Wildlands*, 2, no. 4 (Autumn 1975), 5–13. Reprinted by permission.

efficiency and equity are likely to result if certain of the property rights in the national forests are sold to private parties.

THE EVOLUTION OF PROPERTY RIGHTS

In an extremely simple social environment property rights are of little importance. For a pure hermit like Robinson Crusoe before Friday, property rights were simply irrelevant. Property rights are tools used to organize society. They encourage constructive behavior, reduce uncertainty, and have a capacity for prediction that can result in long-range productive activities with a promise of potential rewards.

In effect, property rights specify how persons may be benefited or harmed. There is a clear relationship between the structure of property rights and the lawful ability of an individual to impose costs or external effects on others. An obvious example would be that of the paper company which, under one system of rights, may have society's implicit permission to use the atmosphere or watershed as an environmental sink for its wastes.

It is our basic argument that cultural shifts (or changing beliefs and values), changes in the relative values of resources, new technology, and increased social interdependence all may require the development of new property rights. With such changes, property rights can account for externally imposed costs to which the old system was insensitive. The movement in this direction is a primary thrust of the environmental movement. Further, it has historic precedents. New property rights will develop when relative values shift to make defining and enforcing these rights worthwhile.

For example, anthropological evidence establishes a close link between the development of private rights to land and the commercial fur trade involving the Indians of Northeastern North America. Property rights were modified by the Indians to reduce externalities, in this case the overhunting of game.

In the absence of property rights to animals or their habitat there is no sanctioned ability to control hunting and trapping. Under conditions of high demand, overkill or hunting beyond sustained yield would take place. Thus, success by one party on the trapline imposed external costs on following trappers.

Prior to the establishment of the fur trade, hunting and trapping were for domestic consumption only. Hence, demand for the game resource was low and externalities or imposed costs were negligible. Thus, there was no reason to have recognized property rights in land and associated resources.

With the development of the fur trade, the value of furs increased dramatically and as a result the scale of hunting increased. The negative externalities associated with free hunting became more than trivial and as a consequence, the property rights system was modified.

By the early 1700s territorial hunting and trapping arrangements based on kin ties developed in Quebec and Newfoundland. The Iroquois, for example, appropriated land two leagues square for each group. Similar developments were found among the coastal tribes of the Northwest. Rights among some of the latter tribes included inheritance.

In sum, property rights changed with changing conditions, especially the changing value of a resource. When it became economically beneficial, property rights developed that encouraged the conservation of fur-bearing animals, with the concomitant ability and incentive to prevent poaching.[1]

IMPLICATIONS OF PROPERTY RIGHTS FOR FOREST USE

Economic growth and development fundamentally involve the manner in which resources are used, producing utilities and disutilities. The response of decision makers to the opportunities for development are determined by the "rules of the game," or public laws and contracts. An important concern when considering the proposed development of Western lands is that certain important property rights will be unassigned, that the costs of negotiating these rights will be so high as to preclude efficient use of the resources, or that the structure of rights preclude optimum use of the resource. It can be demonstrated that without the cost of negotiation and transaction, production outcome would be identical regardless of who has rights to air and watersheds.[2] On the other hand, high costs of negotiating and enforcing rights can yield inefficient allocations. Other inefficiencies can be expected if the structure of property rights insulates resource managers from market or other public forces.

In the United States the rules of the game have traditionally fostered economic development, often at the expense of amenity resources. When resources were abundant and population low, this was socially optimal. There comes a time, however, when it is preferable to modify this bias and grant people rights to amenities.

Generally, then we face two related problems. First, some rights such as amenities, may be either unassigned or difficult to enforce. Second, management responsibilities may be assigned to those insulated from the preference of potential consumers. There is then less of a cushion to absorb the opportunity costs of providing amenities.

The pressure for changing the rules of the game will arise when the costs of these changes are outweighed by the projected benefits from the new rules. Thus, attempts to change the rules are productive activities to which resources can be devoted. As culture and technology change, increasing the value of a bundle of rights, the return on defining and enforcing these rights becomes greater. As high quality air, water, scenery, and back country have become scarce, and thus more valuable, individuals have attempted to better define their rights to these resources. This process will be a critical feature of the struggle for control of Western lands and resources. A failure to understand the importance of this contest over property rights will seriously disadvantage those of us interested in fostering quality management of our national forests. In terms of commodity production, a change in rules may lead to more nearly optimal regulation of the forests. Both of these advantages are likely to be lost through an inappropriate institutional structure.

INSTITUTIONAL PATHOLOGY AND THE BUREAUCRATIC MANAGEMENT OF NATIONAL FOREST LANDS

A bureaucracy is defined as an organization that (1) receives at least part of its budget from grants rather than exclusively from the sale of packageable goods; and (2) has managers who neither receive a portion of its profits as personal income nor personally absorb any of its losses. From the standpoint of public welfare, these features create the possibility of a pathological institution, that is, one that does not serve its supposed purpose. In the area of forest management, the danger is especially great.

It is reasonable to assume that bureaucrats, like other people, are primarily self-interested. As a rule, both bureaucrats and businessmen generate public benefits primarily as byproducts of efforts to enhance their own well-being. The private businessman offering services and products for sale is far more likely to pay attention to the preferences of the consuming public than is his public servant counterpart.

We are not prepared to argue that the bureaucrat is either less moral or less intelligent than his counterpart in the private sector. Given that non-priced products dominate the output of public agencies, it is exceedingly difficult to estimate the relative values of these products. No matter how intelligent or well-intended the public administrator, it is probably impossible for him to produce at the socially optimum level other than by luck. Without the benefit of the high-quality information generated by the market, he has no easy way to determine what the optimum level is. In the auto industry, decisions on how many autos of each style, size, color, etc. are difficult, but executives get daily reality checks, in the form of relative sales information to tell them when and where corrections should be made. Each customer makes his own choice, pays the price for added costs, and must live with his own decision. By contrast, the public sector consumer who has the same very small influence but will pay only a tiny share of added cost for added output, will typically be either apathetic or enthusiastically in favor of more of the goods *he* enjoys. Apathy, and indeed, ignorance on his part, is rational because in the public sector informed action will seldom influence what he is able to consume. He has to live with what the *public* chooses, regardless of his own actions.

In general, although there are massive amounts of waste in the public sector, and even some fraud and graft, the greatest inefficiency flows from very strong pressures on the bureaucrat to exceed the optimal size and scope, and hence the budget, of a public agency.[3]

For social efficiency, agencies should produce only to the point where the extra product is just worth the extra cost. Government agencies are fundamentally social tools to be employed when the opportunity costs of private action are excessive. Clearly then, the relative social value of any agency's production is a function of the state of the larger system. Budgets of the various bureaus should shift in response to changes in the relative social value of their products. It follows that the public spirited bureaucrat would occasionally argue that a portion of his budget should be allocated toward his competition in the public sector. As far as we know, this never happens. Pressures for growth apparently counter and swamp considerations of general welfare.

From the perspective of the self-interested administrator, there are very good reasons to argue for continuous expansion. The bureaucrat, because he lacks market information on the relative value of his product and those of other public agencies, suffers from the absence of an obvious and immediate reality check on what he wants to believe. Thus, it is easy for him to harbor the illusion that his agency has above average merit and therefore deserves above average budget increases.

If public welfare is to be optimized, public funds should be allocated in accord with the equimarginal principle. In the best of worlds funds would be shifted among agencies and their bureaus and offices in such a manner that the marginal benefits of those funds would be equal for each unit.

Unfortunately, however, in nonmarket activities we have only rough approximations of value produced. Hence, if there are systematic biases in the budgetary process, society would gain if certain functions were transferred from the political to the market allocation sector. This logic holds whether the agency's budget is either too large or too small. Many have argued, for example, that silvicultural segments of the Forest Service budget have been too small. Implicit in this position is the claim that the marginal benefits from additional investments are greater than those in alternative programs. This would imply that the private timber owner could increase his wealth by investing in more silvicultural practices.

In many cases waste is generated from the bureau being above optimum size, although substantial forces lead in this direction. For the bureau head, civil service rank, prestige, pay, and office amenities all are strongly related to the size of his bureau. (For example, in one university, for years only deans and above could have IBM typewriters.) In addition, expansion generates more possibilities for promotion. This enhances the ability to control those under his charge, since under Civil Service rules firings are nearly impossible to execute successfully. To gain control over inferiors the promise of promotions may be offered as inducements.

Of perhaps equal importance for the ambitious bureaucrat is the fact that a large proportion of his budget is "locked in" from previous years. This, of course, reduces the range of discretionary expenditures. New funds offer far more opportunities for flexibility and innovation.

Therefore, society may be better off if some public sector allocating functions were transferred to the private sector. Market forces could then determine the level of investment appropriate for the diverse preferences found in society. The problems of both over and under investment discussed above would be vitiated or, at the minimum, the costs of inappropriate investments would be borne by the private parties responsible for the errors. In the following section we consider some of the implications of selling property rights in the national forests.

EXPECTED IMPACTS OF SELLING NATIONAL FORESTS[4]

Proposed solutions to problems of managing the national forests range from small changes in criteria or practices to rather drastic changes in the form and function of management itself. Milton Friedman and others have suggested that government agencies should not manage these forests at all. Instead there would be private managers, and the present value of the forests would be captured for public use by auctioning off rights (title) to the lands in question.

The effectiveness of management, however measured, depends on the combination of information and incentives facing the decision maker, within his given context. In a market system with private ownership of rights, incentives and most information flow are handled through prices. We need not rely on good will, morality, or principle: greed will suffice. Within a market context people are of course free to ignore the wishes of others—expressed through bid and asked prices—but when prices are not distorted, resource users and owners sacrifice wealth exactly to the extent that they ignore those wishes. It is largely the efficiency of prices in transmitting information, and their effectiveness in providing incentive without coercion, which make the market system attractive.

The advantages claimed for this sort of resource management system include diversity, individual freedom, adaptiveness, the production of information, and a certain equity. Diversity is fostered because there is no single centralized decision maker, but many asset owners and entrepreneurs, each of whom can exercise his own vision. Those who correctly anticipate people's desires are most rewarded. Individual freedom is preserved as those who wish to participate in and support each activity may do so on the basis of willing consent. Adaptiveness is encouraged in both management and consumption, since prices provide immediate information and incentive. If only a few see scarcities or opportunities ahead, they can buy, sell, or provide expertise as a small group of consultants, and thus direct resource use without having to convince a majority. In this case profits will reward foresight and quick action, while losses discipline those who divert resources foolishly.

Production of information in a market situation is slowly being recognized for its own importance. Activities not marketed prove very difficult to manage rationally for there is little or no concrete evidence of how people really value them. We know, for example, how much people are willing to sacrifice for a thousand board feet of lumber, but how much would they pay for a day's access to a wilderness area? In the latter case we have only rough estimates. Even the most conscientious and competent manager cannot make good management decisions without knowledge of the absolute and relative values of his various outputs.

Finally, there is a measure of equity in having those people who use a resource pay for it by sacrificing some of their wealth. The proceeds from the sale of public assets could be distributed, or invested and perpetually distributed to the poor,

for example. Those using the forests would be required to pay, whether it be for recreation, timber harvest, or even research in a unique area.

Unfortunately, the orderly picture above does not fully describe all real world market situations. The prime villain in disturbing the beauty of the picture is what economists and political scientists call "externalities." Broadly, this means that asset owners or managers may not be in a position to capture all the benefits of their various actions. It is clear that in a market situation there is normally little incentive to provide goods or services that offer no return. If, for example, a forest owner could not (at low cost) exclude those recreationists who did not pay for access, receipts would understate recreational valuation, and he would have a diminished incentive to preserve or provide recreational opportunity. Among potential externalities are flood control, watershed provision, weather modification, animal habitat, biotic diversity, and environmental buffering. These effects might be partially internalized by placing restrictions on the title transfer, constraining the buyers to avoid certain socially costly decisions. But to the extent that this happens, the benefits of market organization and individually expressed preferences are eschewed. In practice management is generally left to those who have relatively little incentive to be guided by preferences expressed in relative prices. In sum, externality is recognized by many economists and political scientists as a necessary, but not sufficient, condition for government interference with markets. However, an important form of externality is pervasive also in all governmental forms of organization. At best, decision makers are held accountable by the threat of replacement. They do not directly receive the gains from better management (or costs from poor management) as private resource owners generally do.

Given the problems of market failures, people exercising "bad taste" or wanting "the wrong things," and the elimination of subsidy from those of us who now use the national forests at a reduced price, perhaps we should consider separating property rights from the land and selling only a portion of those rights now associated with the land. The rights sold would be those that can be effectively handled via market transaction.

Another fundamental law of political economy is that public goods, if privately supplied, tend to be under-supplied. The benefits of public goods cannot be captured via the market and people have a strong resistance to giving up valuable resources when the projected return is less than the cost. Thus, we should identify the public goods of the national forests and segregate them from the sale. Because the projected costs of enforcing property rights are so high, the provision of wilderness experiences is as much a public good as the examples given above. Thus if we want to prevent undervaluing these goods, we should keep them in the public sector and assign production responsibilities to a variety of competing agencies. The best argument for granting one agency a monopoly is one of economies of scale, and only occasionally would we anticipate such economies. Competition among the agencies, however, will benefit diverse public interests.

There are two obvious sets of rights that could be sold to private parties, rights to timber production and rights to grazing. However, there are interdependencies between these property rights and the public goods supplied by the forest. If general welfare is to be maximized, negative externalities must be controlled. Hence, the timber and grazing rights must be sold subject to constraints determined by potential impacts of harvesting and silvicultural practices upon the public goods.

Timber

Let us first consider selling timber rights. Note that it is not the land that would be sold, but rather the standing timber and the right to produce timber on some portion of the land. If the value of timber is expected to increase, then relatively intensive silviculture would be expected of the private operator, who had estimated both the costs and the benefits from various rates of harvest and levels of investment. The same incentives do not bear upon public managers insulated from market forces. The public manager is likely to find the prospect of increasing production more attractive than a rational consideration of the marginal benefits from this increase would indicate. Growing trees is fun. Growing more units per hectare is even more fun, and the implications of diminishing marginal returns are not very important to the bureaucratic silviculturalist.

Conversely, there are situations in which additional investments in silviculture are socially bene-

ficial. Yet the bureaucrat must rely upon political allocations for budget increases. He is competing in the public sector with alternatives such as a space program, a foreign military adventure, or expanded welfare programs. The primary issues are not efficiency and equity, but rather skills of political mobilization and leverage. Because elections come every two, four or six years, the discount rate in the public sector may be very high. Thus there is under-investment in programs whose payoff is more than an election or two away. Until we achieve two-year rotations of Douglas fir we might expect this bias to be controlling.

It is also possible for environmental groups to dominate decisions to such a degree that timber harvest is scheduled at suboptimal phasings. This constitutes a transgenerational transfer. All we could expect from economic analysis is an explication of these shifts of benefit flow and an estimation of their consequences. Under the existing system, socially optimum use is largely a matter of luck.

It is, however, exceedingly important that the rights to produce timber not preclude production of public goods. For example, hunting, camping, and hiking rights would still be held by the public and the timber operator would be accountable for the costs of increased erosion. If property rights for fishing the drainage were sold to political districts or private groups such as Trout Unlimited or American Sportsman, then there would be a party with vested interest in protecting the quality of the watershed. More importantly, these sporting groups would have established legally recognized property rights that could be protected by the legal process.

Selling timber rights to the national forests should not result in a shift to strictly short-sighted goals, such as immediate exploitation of logging to the detriment of long-run productivity. The owner of a forest may be 50 years old and expect to live only to 70; but, even if he wants to leave his heirs nothing, he will maximize his own returns by managing the forest in such a way as to maximize long-run expected value. He would thus sell out when he wants cash and would receive expected market value. Of course, if timber prices are expected to rise less rapidly than other prices, then immediate harvest may make sense both privately and socially, depending on timber growth rates and the effects of timber harvest on alternative forest land uses. Only in those cases when private owners cannot capture increased values of better management will they not be penalized for being short-sighted.

Grazing Rights

Substantial improvements could also be made in the allocation of rights to grazing and forage production. If demand for meat increases dramatically over the medium run, the value of forage will increase. Hence, the advantages from more effective management would be correspondingly greater. If the amenity values associated with wildlife populations, especially predators, increase, again greater advantages will come from improved property rights to these resources. In general, if either scarcity or culture increases the value of resources, then the payoffs from improved management also increase. In this section we argue that substantial improvements are likely to result from changes in the distribution of property rights for grazing on the national forests.

First, although existing practice suggests the contrary, subsidized rights for grazing privileges were not cast on gold tablets and distributed by God. (Such grazing privileges are measured in terms of "animal unit months" or AUMs. One AUM = pasture for one cow with calf for one month.) They represent an evolution, guided by the selective pressures of the political process, which transferred wealth from the general public to the holders of permits. The permittees then have been able to capitalize the value of these rights in the private lands which serve as a home base for their stock. Thus, the market value of a ranch with assigned AUMs is greater than an equally productive ranch that lacks AUMs on public lands. The maintenance of these rights is primarily, if not exclusively, a matter of administrative tradition rather than law. This tradition, however, is so well established that many western bankers will accept AUMs as partial collateral on a ranch mortgage. Normally, the government AUMs sell for much less than private AUMs, with the amount ranging from 10 percent to occasionally 100 percent of a market clearing price.

In the case we know best, one author of this essay receives about 700 percent more for the AUMs he sells from his land in Montana than does the Forest Service on land two to six miles away. Part of this difference may be due to the convenience afforded by corrals, loading chutes, etc., but most is accounted for by a windfall gain to the original holders of Forest Service AUMs. If the holder of Forest Service AUMs did not acquire them by buying a ranch with the value of the AUMs capitalized in its purchase price, he is being subsidized. If these values were capitalized in the sale of the ranch, the value of the AUMs constitutes a windfall gain to the original permittee.

Given that the holder of government AUMs has only imperfect property rights in his AUMs, he has a diminished incentive to make improvements on his land. Clearly these rights are politically determined and, hence, are inherently arbitrary. In the absence of clear and enforceable property rights in AUMs, we fully expect a suboptimal investment in long-run improvements. Further, the threat that these rights are temporary encourages overgrazing the land and treating it as a modified commons. Although the USFS regulates the number of animals permitted, many stockmen trespass additional animals on "their" unit. The costs of excessive use are distributed among the entire population in the form of diminished productivity of the land base. The costs of diminished wildlife habitat and increased erosion are entirely transferred to the general public.

Again, it seems reasonable to suggest that property rights to some of the forage produced by national forest lands be sold on the open market. Then the primary costs of overgrazing would be felt by those responsible for the errors. Furthermore, trespass animals would constitute theft from the federal government identical to other types of public theft and subject to the same range of criminal liabilities. When the property rights to government AUMs are sold, the public goods generated by these lands should be protected. If the domestic stock is sympatric with wildlife, some measures should be taken to protect the wildlife from competition. If an error is made in overestimating the number of AUMs sold for an area or if the value of wildlife increases relative to that of stock, then some of the AUMs could be bought back from the stockman at market value by exercising eminent domain. In contrast, if stock is symbiotic with valuable wildlife, as sometimes happens with deer and cattle, it may be efficient to subsidize stock. In the latter case, the stock produces positive externalities in terms of improved wildlife habitats.

Second, the stockman with grazing rights would have strong incentives to make production improvements. Improvements, however, would have to be restrained in order not to diminish other values without just compensation. For example, the holder of grazing rights would not be free to spray, chain, or otherwise decrease environmental quality.

The third advantage concerns a highly emotional topic, the predation of stock by wildlife. An increasing number of Americans place a growing value on such predators as lions and other cats, coyotes, wolves, and bears. Under current arrangements, individuals with subsidized grazing rights are free to kill these animals, and, moreover, this high social deprivation cost is subsidized by government hunters and trappers. Here economic inefficiencies are compounded by inequities.

Currently both interest and information are biased and concentrated in favor of the stockman. While a stockman is quite likely to attribute losses to predation, relatively few people will know that a government trapper took twenty lions from the Lincoln backcountry in one season. The public will be uninformed that twelve verified grizzly bears were killed for sheep predation on the Targhee since 1970 in a state that does not even have an open season on these bears and where the sheep holding pens were, for convenience, built near the center of the grizzly range.

If property rights in grazing were sold on the open market these conditions could improve substantially. Permits would be for forage and would not include any more rights to kill predators than those held by sport hunters. Violations of this provision of the sale would constitute poaching and

could result in the forfeiture of grazing rights without compensation. While the remote stockman would still kill some predators and, hence, deprive the public of a valuable resource, the potential costs of his doing so would increase from near zero to something substantial. Some shooting in "self-defense" would doubtlessly occur, but it might be difficult to convince a jury. More importantly, the use of poison baits would be in clear violation of the sale. Predation history or folklore is well known in most local areas. Hence, when grazing rights were auctioned, traditionally high-predator areas would receive lower bids than low-predator lands.

As usual, when the full range of costs and benefits are included, the market would be an efficient allocating device. If this proposal were adopted, by changing the structure of property rights we could anticipate substantial improvements, in equity and efficiency, over the current system, which maximizes the negative features of both bureaucratic and market means of resource allocation.

NOTES

1. To see how this process continued after the arrival of the white man, see "The Evolution of Property Rights: A Study of the American West," by T. Anderson and P. J. Hill, in *The Journal of Law and Economics, 18* (April 1975).

2. See "The Problem of Social Cost," by R. Coase, in *The Journal of Law and Economics, 3* (October 1960).

3. For a thorough treatment of this topic, see William Niskanén, *Bureaucracy and Representative Government* (Chicago: Aldine, 1971).

4. This section enlarges upon parts of Stroup and Baden, "Externality, Property Rights, and the Management of Our National Forests," *The Journal of Law and Economics, 16* (1973), 303–312.

MARK SAGOFF

Do We Need a Land Use Ethic?

I

Economists often argue that environmental problems are economic problems and require economic solutions.[1] They say that when externalities are internalized, the commons divided, and "fragile" values priced, the environment will be adequately protected.[2] Most environmentalists believe that this is only half true. Many of our environmental problems do have economic causes. Environmentalists tend to believe, however, that the solutions had better be ethical ones. An economic cure may be worse than the disease.

A policy is economically "efficient" insofar as it satisfies preferences which consumers reveal or would reveal in markets. These preferences call for environments that can be supplied and maintained at a profit. These include trailer parks, fast-food restaurants, golf courses, condominiums, and pinball arcades. Demand for these environments is assured because it is created along with the environments themselves.[3] Brian Harry, chief naturalist at Yosemite National Park when the MCA Corporation took over its management, put the matter succinctly. "People used to come here for the beauty and the serenity," he said. "Those who come now don't mind the crowds; in fact, they like them. They come for the action."[4]

In this essay, I argue that economic approaches to environmental policy succeed, in principle, to the extent that they satisfy aggregate consumer demand. Consumers are likely to demand what Harry calls "action." By *action* may be meant anything that an attractive man and woman can be photographed enjoying together in a state of undress or semi-undress. It may include virtually any activity of consumption, especially conspicuous consumption, that is shown on TV or written up in glossy magazines. Economic solutions to environmental problems could, then, provide the "action" that consumers demand. This might be done on the grand scale, for example, by converting wilderness areas into resort complexes and amusement parks. It happens on a smaller scale each time a woods or a marsh is replaced by a health spa, a gas station, or a fast-food stand.

This conversion of the natural into the efficient conflicts with many principles and convictions that ought to influence environmental policy, whether consumers act on them or not. These principles, which have nothing conceptually to do with what consumers are willing to pay for, may require us to protect even "useless" endangered species and their habitats. These principles and ethical convictions suggest that we owe more to a million year old wilderness than to regard it as a future site for strip mines and singles bars. A market or an economic approach to environmental policy, if it remains consistent and true to itself, is likely to convert nature into a place "where the action is." A policy based on moral conviction and aesthetic principle, however, would tend to preserve some environments for their own sake.

II

The land use ethic we have is primarily economic. It assumes that the *chooser* is always the *consumer*. It stands on the premise that consumers reveal their preferences in what they buy or would buy if the price were right. The goal is to satisfy the greatest number of the most intense consumer preferences at the least cost. Another goal may be to redistribute wealth or opportunities so that even the least wealthy people can buy what they most want. In a world in which resources are plentiful and demand is scarce—in Eden, for example—everyone can have a mansion by the sea. But in our world, it has to be a motel room. In our world you

© 1981. Reprinted by permission of *Environmental Ethics* and the author. *Author's Note*—Support is gratefully acknowledged from the National Endowment for the Humanities and the National Science Foundation, Grant No. 0SS-801809. Views expressed are those of the author, and not necessarily those of the NEH or the NSF.

have to franchise enough Pizza Huts and build gas stations to keep up with demand. You subdivide the old estates and unload the duplexes and the split foyers.

This land ethic takes it as a premise that consumer preferences reveal the values of our society. People want what they want—not what some public official thinks they ought to want. And they should have what they are willing to pay for: Winnebagos, powerboats, bowling alleys, movies. What argument can be given for failing to satisfy the wants of the vulgar mass . . . and pleasing the tastes of an affluent elite instead?

Once the question has been asked in this way, I believe, there is no way to answer it, but answers are attempted. Economists remind us that exploitation of the natural environment is often inefficient. They describe externalities, spillover effects, and pollution costs. They talk about the "shadow" price of "intangible" or "fragile" values. They speak in terms of the "problem of the commons"—as if that shows, somehow, the folly of translating natural beauty into urban blight.

I believe that this sort of thinking supports an economic approach to land use and land management. To worry about fragile values or the problem of the commons is not necessarily to criticize the economic ethic; it may be to defuse criticism. It is to make environmental law in the image of economic efficiency. It is to rest public policy on a platform of analytical sophistication in the service of consumer demand.

In this essay, I argue that an economic approach to land use leads to, or at least may justify, the destruction of our remaining waterfront and wilderness areas, even if fragile values and the problem of the commons are taken into account. Consumers do not share merely a natural commons: they also share roads, trailer parks, and fast-food stands. And they may find a lot of amenity in a cheap motel if it has its own swimming pool. The satisfaction of consumer preferences may involve the protection of highways as much as the protection of habitats—for we travel in off-road vehicles, snowmobiles, trailers, pickups, caravans, cabin cruisers, motorcycles, trail bikes, busses, houseboats, campers, broncos, vans, and Hobicats. The effect is obvious. The sprawl of the city will spread to the sea. If you do not believe me, look around.

III

Let me begin with the view that land has value primarily not *as land* but *as property*. We owe this thought directly to John Locke, particularly, to chapter 5 of the *Second Treatise of Government*. There, Locke writes:

God, who hath given the World to Men in Common, hath also given them reason to make use of it to the best advantage of Life, and convenience. The Earth, and all that is therein, is given to Men for the Support and Comfort of their being. And though all the Fruits it naturally produces . . . belong to Mankind in common, . . . yet being given to the use of Men, there must of necessity be a means *to appropriate* them some way or other before they can be of any use, or at all beneficial to any particular Man.[5]

Locke rests his argument on the observation that land has little or no value except when labor changes its character and thus, as it were, forces its favors. Locke says:

Land which is wholly left to Nature, that hath no improvement of Pasturage, Tillage, or Planting, is called, as indeed it is, *wast;* and we shall find the benefit of it amount to little more than nothing.[6]

And, again:

. . . *labour makes the far greatest part of the value* of things, we enjoy in this World: And the ground which produces the materials, is scarce to be reckoned in, as any, or at most, but a very small part of it. . . .[7]

And, again:

Tis *labour. . . which puts the greatest part of Value upon Land.*[8]

Although Locke adheres to a labor theory of value, he does not, therefore, deny that there are moral limitations on land ownership. To be sure, Locke contends that land, water, air, and minerals are virtually worthless in their natural state. Yet he did not infer from this that a person may rightfully possess *any* unowned resource into which he "mixes" his labor. Locke restricts ownership, at least at first, to that which an individual can use without waste or spoilage.[9] Second, Locke allows a rightful original claim to land only when there exists "enough and as good" for others.[10] If all, or almost all, of a resource is already owned, then an individual has arrived late: he must buy from others. And this he can do if he has *money*.

If the labor theory causes Locke to place these two moral limitations on the acquisition of property, the theory of money allows him to overcome these restrictions. As soon as people can trade for money, scarcity and spoilage no longer limit the amount of property one person may accumulate. As for the spoilage limitations, Locke says:

... a man may fairly possess more land than he himself can use the product of, by receiving in exchange for the overplus, Gold and Silver, which may be hoarded up without injury to any one, these materials not spoiling or decaying in the hands of the possessor.[11]

The use of money, so Locke argues, also permits a person to acquire resources rightfully even after they have become scarce. A person has only to buy them from someone who has a rightful title. And that a person will do, at least in theory, only if he can make a more profitable, more efficient, and therefore more beneficial use of the resource. Accordingly, Locke reasons that a person can "heap up" as much land and wealth as he can use or cause to be used economically—"the *exceeding of the bounds of his* just *property* not lying in the largeness of his possession, but the perishing of anything uselessly in it."[12]

A labor theory of value and a money theory of value—these Locke uses to transcend the moral limits he himself has placed on property ownership. Land, like any other resource, is worth only what you can get for it. It is worth what you can do with it or perhaps to it; its value is what you can sell it or its products for. Many texts in resource economics repeat this message. "In principle, the ultimate measure of environmental quality," says one standard introduction today, "is the value people place on these ... services or their *willingness to pay*."[13] The concept of economic efficiency—the idea that resources should be allocated to those who derive the greatest benefit from them—is not mentioned by Locke explicitly. Locke seems to believe, however, that something like this concept allows him to transform a natural right to the property one needs into an unlimited right of acquisition.

IV

I wish Locke could see Ocean City today. I wonder what he would say about the commercial holocaust that sweeps from Baltimore, Maryland to Norfolk, Virginia. I would tell him that it is all private property—all owned and properly franchised. I would show him that we have mixed our labor with the land—and our exhaust, sludge, cans, bottles, shopping carts, newspapers, tires, boxes, cigarettes, fenders, furniture, toxic chemical wastes, and everything else we can bury or throw away. Locke plainly had farms in mind as his paradigm of private property. What would he say about tract developments, chemical dumps, and commercial strips?

Locke, perhaps, might deplore what seem to be the consequences of his theory of property. Many of us would agree with him. Many have said that Locke's theory of natural property rights—and his view that government exists to protect those rights—rests on a mistake. But what mistake? Where did he, or we, go wrong?

Many writers have proposed answers to this question. They have suggested that Locke's theory is inadequate because it:

- □ leads to inequity and injustice;
- □ assumes that man has domination over nature or that nature exists simply for his sake;
- □ works only when resources are plentiful;
- □ ignores the ecological or biological function of the land;
- □ fails to consider the problem of the commons;
- □ neglects "fragile," "intangible," or "aesthetic" values.[14]

I believe that something is to be said for each of these criticisms. I argue, however, that none of them gets to the essential shortcoming of the Lockean ethic for the use of land.

That *property* is the origin of *inequality* is a thesis commonly argued—and brilliantly argued, for example, by Rousseau. His *Discourse on the Origin and Foundations of Inequality* makes the following observation against Locke:

... from the moment one man needed the help of another, as soon as they observed that it was useful for a simple person to have the provisions of two, equality disappeared, property was introduced, labor became necessary; and vast forests were changed into smiling fields which have to be watered with the sweat of men, and in which slavery and misery were soon seen to germinate and grow with the crops.[15]

If the only criticism to be made of Locke's theory of property is that it leads to inequality and injustice, then, it seems, we would know how to correct it, to make it perfect. We would outlaw slavery. We would redistribute wealth. We could restructure taxation, inheritance, education, health insurance, and other institutions to mitigate the effects of the concentration of wealth, or alleviate them entirely. The fact that we fail to do this is not a consequence of a Lockean approach to land as property. It is to be blamed, rather, on our unwillingness to distribute justly the wealth which a Lockean approach to land use creates.

If we took Locke to Ocean City, moreover, what would he see? Would he see a lot of people starving while a privileged few eat salmon and drink Chateaux Margaux? No. Locke would see just about everyone lined up for steamed crabs, ice cream, and beer. Not bad—for $3.95. To show Locke Ocean City is not to present to him the horrors of social inequality. It is to show him the horrors of social equality. Schlock on every block. K-Mart lowers the price. Who can complain when $250 on the used-car market buys an eight-cylinder, four-on-the-floor '73 Impala with mags and stripes? It goes from 0 to 80 in ten seconds flat. Not even the rich in the Honda CVCCs can do that. So what if it needs a muffler? Locke might point out that it is no accident that the last bastions of beauty on the Eastern Shore are the estates of the rich. There are a lot of compelling reasons to redistribute wealth in the United States—but environmental quality is not one of them. We already have plenty of people this side of the poverty line to crowd every Ho Jo, Go Go, Disco, and peep show that can be built between Rehoboth and Virginia Beach.

V

If social injustice is not the problem, what is? Lynn White, a historian of science and technology, in a well-known essay, has said that our environmental woes derive, in large part, from "Judeo-Christian attitudes toward man's relation to nature," attitudes which permit us to regard ourselves as "superior to nature, contemptuous of it, willing to use it for our slightest whim."[16] I am not sure to what extent the Judeo-Christian tradition represents nature as a subject for man's domination, and to what extent it presents nature as an object for respect and veneration, "for nature," as Sir Thomas Browne has written, "is the art of God."[17] Locke, as we have seen, does introduce his theory of property with the remark that God gave the Earth to men "for the Support and Comfort of their being."[18] May we infer from this that Locke's theory fails because it assumes that man dominates and is the steward of nature?

I do not think that this is the problem. Locke refers to Genesis in a rhetorical way; this does not show, however, that his theory depends upon a traditional or religious conception of man's relation to nature. Indeed, I do not believe that any conception of man's "place" in the universe is required by Locke's theory or entailed by it. Locke seems to start from the unavoidable needs and the natural rights which belong, or so he argues, to every individual.

Locke's theory depends, as I think, on the unobjectionable view that individuals have a right to secure their freedom and to pursue their happiness however they will as long as they respect the same right in others. They are to be constrained by government only to the extent necessary to protect the rights of others. This, anyway, seems to be part of Locke's conception of freedom: freedom, in general, is the ability of a person to do as he wishes and to get what he wants, except insofar as he is constrained by rules of competition and cooperation common to all.[19] And what is happiness? Happiness, we may think, is bound up with the satisfaction of desire. This is the reason that an economically efficient land use policy—one that maximizes the satisfaction of consumer wants over the long run—appears to many of us to be an ethical policy as well: It gives people what they desire. Locke's theory of property has this ethical appeal. It does not rest on a conception of man's place in nature. It asks us only to make such use of nature—for example, offshore drilling and highway construction—which, over the long run, gives more consumers more of whatever they demand.

Writers sometimes argue that Locke's theory of

property may work in a world in which resources are plentiful and await development, but it breaks down when resources become scarce. William Ophuls, for example, has written:

His [Locke's] argument on property by appropriation is shot through with references to the wilderness of the new World, which only needed to be occupied and cultivated to be turned into property for any man who desired it. Locke's justification of original property and the natural right of men to appropriate it from nature thus rests on cornucopian assumptions: there is always more left; society can therefore be libertarian.[20]

Much as I admire Ophuls' book, *Ecology and the Politics of Scarcity*, I believe that his criticism of Locke misses the point. Locke understands that it is not the availability but the scarcity of resources that creates property. Government protection of property is needed when people want things that are *not* free for the taking. "The great and *chief end* therefore, of Mens uniting into Commonwealths, and putting themselves under government, *is the preservation of their property*."[21] The power of government to protect property rights hardly rests on "cornucopian assumptions"; it rests on the fact that scarcity requires the division between mine and thine.

Some people have argued that Lockean notions of property, if enforced, are the best response we have to the problem of scarcity. William Baxter, for example, writes that "good conservation practices are implicit in carefully defined and enforced situations of ownership."[22] The reason is this. Those who own a resource in an enforceable sense, and can exclude others from its use, will exploit it gradually and carefully, in order to maximize future return. Thus, if you own an oil well, you would probably hold on to it, assuming that the price of oil will continue to rise, so that conservation is more profitable than exploitation. If you need quick cash you may mortgage the resource or you may sell it to someone who will hold it for long-term capital gain.

Any conceptual connection that may exist between conservation and well-defined and enforced situations of ownership, however, tends to break down in practice. Two problems seem formidable. The first is the problem of *agency*. Those who make decisions at the relevant levels in large corporations have their own personal success or careers in mind, rather than the long-term profitability of the organization. Thus, a short-term "good showing" is more important to them than is the eventual capital growth of the firm. Accordingly, executives may squander resources to make themselves look good on the balance-sheet, no matter what happens to the corporation or to the environment in the long run.

Second, while holding a resource may be more profitable than present consumption, an alternative investment may be even better. If the government offers risk-free securities at a twenty percent return annually, one is likely to sell everything one can to today's consumers in order to buy bonds; one might also liquidate resources to invest in fast-food retailing or some other business. To think that property rights can be a basis for conservation is to assume that conservation of resources is more profitable than *any* other investment that might be made with gains from immediate consumption. As long as "quick buck" investments exist, however, a lot of opportunities will be more attractive.

So far, I have discussed criticisms of Locke's theory from four points of view: first, that it leads to inequality and injustice; second, that it assumes man's "domination" of nature; third, that it works only when resources are plentiful; and fourth, that it fails to conserve for future generations. All of these criticisms are plausible but none is entirely convincing. We have yet to put our finger on a sure reason to believe that Locke's theory of property is inconsistent with a principled and dignified policy for the natural environment.

VI

Every well-socialized individual understands that one does not have a right to use one's property in a way that causes harm or injury to someone else. My property right to my hammer does not permit me to hit your head with it. Can we make Locke's theory of property consistent with environmental goals by hedging it with a doctrine of harm? Is the police power a sufficient ground on which government can limit the use of private property to favor public ends?

At first we may think that the answer to this question is yes. A doctrine of harm—especially ecological harm—is called for as a supplement to

Locke's labor theory of value. Locke, after all, believed that land, in the state nature leaves it in, is practically worthless. Readers almost three hundred years ago could believe Locke when he wrote:

We see in *Commons*, which remain so by compact, that 'tis the taking any part of what is common and removing it out of the state Nature leaves it in, which *begins the Property*; without which the Commons is no use.[23]

Now we know that land, air, and water, in the "state nature leaves them in" are enormously valuable—and that the labor which changes the state of these resources may destroy this value. Does this knowledge provide a way to apply Locke's theory to land use today?

I do not believe so. The reason is that our knowledge, while helpful in a general way, is often inadequate to make out specific causal connections. If I fill in my wetland or build a shopping mall over a salt marsh, what harm, exactly, have I done? Suppose your house floods ten years later and a hundred miles away. Am I at fault? Who is? Any paved area, any farm, any housing project may have also contributed. How much harm did each property owner cause? To ask this question is to see that no one can possibly answer it.

The Chesapeake Bay is the largest and richest estuary in the United States. It undergoes enormous changes even in a year. The crabs become scarce and public hearings are held. Who is at fault? The crabs become plentiful and the hearings end. The oysters are few and we are sure that pollution or overharvesting or *something* is the cause. But they may, as inscrutably, come back again. Islands disappear; shoreline washes away; the bay itself fills in. Is this our fault or is it "natural"? How much does the builder of a new bowling alley contribute to this?

Within the past few years, most farms in the Chesapeake region have followed an instruction to practice "no-till" agriculture in order to combat the erosion of the soil.[24] To do this they depend upon the use of herbicides, notably atrazine. Recently, several species of underwater vegetation in the bay have begun to disappear. Traces of atrazine have been found in some of these plants. Is atrazine in runoff destroying underwater vegetation? Is Hurricane Agnes the culprit? Could a predator be

doing the job? Is some combination of these—and any number of other conditions—responsible? All of these are possibilities.[25] How important is the vegetation to the ecology of the bay? Is it better to have the atrazine than the erosion? What is the amount of harm done by a farmer in Chestertown who tills half his land and applies simazine to the other half? (The question is grossly oversimplified, since, for example, different levels of nitrogen fertilizers, also pollutants, are used in no-till and traditional agriculture.) The research on these questions is likely to continue for a long time. Meanwhile, the underwater vegetation, for reasons perhaps known only to it, may return to the bay.

I submit that the problem of "pricing" or "internalizing" externalities in an ecological context, in many or most instances, simply defies solution. It can't be done. Linear chains of causality are not often found; events are the results of any number of interacting causes. Allied Chemical Corporation paid a $13 million fine for dumping Kepone in the James River in 1976. News reports at the time quoted statements to the effect that the organochloride pesticide could severely damage life in the Chesapeake Bay.[26] What damage has occurred or is likely, in fact, to occur? We simply do not know. It depends on too many conditions—e.g., on the market for oysters (now depressed); the occurrence of hurricanes; and the rate at which the chemical sinks under the sediment. Item: preliminary studies indicate that there is a potential for microbial degradation of Kepone.[27]

The doctrine of harm will not make Locke's conception of property rights workable in an ecological context. Harms exist: the use we make of our property may cause or contribute to these harms. But *which* use of *whose* property accounts for *how much* of what *specific harm*? You will sooner discover the philosopher's stone than find a way to answer that question.

VII

Earlier, I suggested that Locke's theory of property might be criticized for presupposing an "anthropocentric" view of the natural world. A better and more common criticism directs itself to the moral psychology which underlies the Lockean tradition. This represents us as possessive individuals each intent on maximizing his or her self-interest. Once this criticism has been made, it is easily developed in terms of the problem or "tragedy" of the commons. The words ring in our ears:

Ruin is the destination toward which all men rush, each pursuing his own best interest in a society that believes in the freedom of the commons. Freedom in a commons brings ruin to all.[28]

Readers of this essay are likely to be familiar with the way Garrett Hardin relates the "logic" of the commons to the problem of pollution. Hardin writes:

The rational man finds that his share of the costs of the wastes he discharges into the commons is less than the cost of purifying his wastes before releasing them. Since this is true for everyone, we are locked into a system of "fouling our own nest," so long as we behave only as independent rational, free-enterprisers.[29]

The solution which Hardin suggests—mutual coercion mutually agreed upon—intends to prevent the would-be "maximizer" from realizing the gains of pollution while distributing the costs. Is this what we need? Is a solution to the problem of the commons the key by which we can overcome the shortcomings of a Lockean land use ethic? Does it bring us closer to an alternative ethic?

I do not believe that Hardin goes much beyond Locke in providing a land use ethic or a guide for environmental policy. This may be seen when we ask what Hardin would have us to do, say, about the fellow who is tearing around in that '73 Impala without the muffler. What does Joe Macho have to gain by agreeing to a law which makes us all drive quiet CVCCs? The bomber is what he can afford. He may *like* the noise and not mind the pollution. *You* do. How can you stop him? You could *pay* him to stop driving—or to drive something else. But what gives you the right to fine him or to force him to do what suits *your* tastes, *your* interests?

You might argue that his noise and pollution cause harm—but that is what is sometimes called "subjective." To be annoyed at the noise may mean no more than you do not like it. The epidemiological evidence, moreover, will convince no one that there is more cancer, say, in Ocean City than on Nantucket, where there is less pollution. Hardin, incidentally, suggests we sell the nation's parks or charge for their use, to keep crowds away.[30] But the crowds enjoy what they find—otherwise they would not come. They can smell the lavatories—but this may be *efficient*, not inefficient, park use. An inefficient policy would charge a high admittance price so that only a few could enjoy the luxury of "unspoiled" nature. (One can do that, incidentally, on a much vaster scale, simply by contemplating the stars.) Hardin favors and would protect his own interests. One person's trailer home is another's fouled nest.

Hardin's conclusion is this: we should organize competition so as not to get in each other's way. This advice lies well within the tradition of Hobbes, Locke, and Adam Smith. Hobbes called for coercion, in the form of the Leviathan, to provide one public good, security; Hardin adds environmental quality to this list. Locke did not believe that people would voluntarily respect property rights; he thought governments had to exist to enforce them. And Adam Smith did not argue that the Invisible Hand operates *in nature* but *in markets*. And markets are created and maintained by the enforcement of property and contract. This *is* mutual coercion mutually agreed upon. It is hard to find anything in Hardin—which is not also in Hobbes and Locke.

What is crucial in the tradition of Hobbes and Hardin is the appeal to rational self-interest. Rational self-interest is supposed to make us agree to rules which govern competition and enhance cooperation in ways that benefit all. Sounds good. But rational self-interest may be satisfied when a magnificent wilderness is converted into a tacky amusement park. Rational self-interest is served by technologies that make us independent of natural processes and therefore more able to destroy them. I know that without fusion power or something like that we must rely on photosynthesis and the nitrogen cycle. If we accept an economic land use ethic, however, the only limits that stand between us and the worst excesses of exploitation are technological. When a safe, clean, abundant, and inexpensive source of energy is found, then, apparently, these limits will vanish. Nothing then prevents the self-interest or preference of consumers from creating an environment completely dominated by highways, shopping centers, housing projects, motels, and endless commercial strips.

Rational self-interest, at any rate, is an untenable basis for public policy because it is unenforceable. Suppose we agree to laws regulating pollution. Who would enforce them? The policeman. The inspector. But if they were self-interested, they would take bribes. We could bring them before a judge. But she would take gifts, stock, free passes, sexual favors, or something, if she acted with a single eye to her self-interest. We might appeal to the President—but the regress is obvious. At some point, someone has to do something not because it is in his or her self-interest but because it is right. Why not start this at the beginning? Why not introduce principles, not merely preferences, into a public policy? Why not protect the environment not because that will satisfy insatiable and often contemptible consumer demand, but because it is what we can believe in and take pride in for reasons of an utterly different kind?

VIII

We come now to the last refuge of the liberal mind. It involves the shadow pricing of "intangible" or "soft" variables.[31] This is the attempt to price not only our *interests* but our *principles* and *beliefs* as market externalities. It may be understood, in the context of the Lockean tradition, as a last effort to interpret political issues in economic terms. It is a way of representing *contradiction* as *competition*. It attempts to represent differences of *opinion*, which should be settled through debate, ending, if necessary, in a vote, as if they were conflicts of *interest*, requiring a cost-benefit analysis, ending in a bottom line. Economists rescue the principle of efficiency from its likely ugly consequences for the environment not by introducing other principles or views, but by the incredible ruse of giving approaches to environmental policy that oppose theirs a surrogate market or shadow price. They may do this, for example, by asking environmentalists how much they are willing to pay for the mere knowledge that a species is protected or that a wilderness is not despoiled. Economists who know how to frame and whom to ask these questions can "show" that any policy that is morally, aesthetically, or culturally important is "efficient" as well.

This approach by the economist to environmental policy has a fascinating relation with classical utilitarian theory. The utilitarians were concerned about the fact that many intense pleasures come from tawdry or tasteless sources. (Prostitution is an example.) Few were as hardy as Bentham: few would agree that poetry is less valuable than pushpin if it produces less pleasure. More might agree with Mill that Socrates dissatisfied is better than a pig satisfied. But if this is true, why do we make "satisfaction"—e.g., consumer satisfaction—the basis of public policy? Why should markets—even if we assume that they maximize "satisfaction"—determine what we do to the environment?

The answer economists sometimes give is this. Even if people enjoy pinball and do not read Pushkin they may still have a certain respect for Pushkin. This deserves a market price. The mere availability of poetry, in other words, is a benefit even for those who never read it. People enjoy knowing that some members of their society are artists, or whatever; therefore, there is an interest, although not one expressed in markets, in the arts. Transaction costs, free rider problems, or something of that sort, prevent people from "buying" these "aesthetic" or "moral" benefits. Economists have a way to "correct" this market failure. It is perfectly bizzare. Since they recognize that Socrates dissatisfied is better than a pig satisfied, they give Socrates' dissatisfaction a shadow price.

I do not have to criticize this tactic here.[32] Suffice it to say that it is the emotive theory of value run wild. Suffice it to say that it confuses what people believe in and care about with what they desire and will spend money on. Suffice it to say that economists who price the opinions of others need to listen, therefore, only to their own. Suffice it to say that market analysis, when carried on in these terms, is a subversion of public debate. Economic analysis, carried on in these terms, can do nothing to reveal or clarify values other than those of economists themselves. Cost-benefit analysis does not open up the "back room" of policy making to the light of day. It only explains away the loud knocking at the door.

IX

I have now exhausted the remedies and stratagems by which economists and others have tried to defend market-based and property-based solutions to environmental problems. I have argued that in spite of these remedies the cure remains at least as bad as the disease. It *is* the disease. A worn out and no longer useful form of thought approaches societal problems as if efficiency and equality were the only values involved. These values are important to our society, but they are not our only ones, and in the environmental area, they often function as red herrings drawn across the path we should follow. This is the path of public discussion and debate in which we assess the ethical principles and aesthetic ideals that make us, in a sense, "Nature's Nation."[33]

Those who are developing the field of environmental ethics contribute to this discussion and debate. The best contribution they may make, I believe, is to define and argue for principles other than those of efficiency and equality, which, as I have proposed, may have as much to do with causing as with resolving environmental problems. Those who argue that other ethical and aesthetic convictions should guide environmental policy, however, invite the charge that they are elitists, trying to protect the privileges of the affluent few by criticizing the demands of the less affluent many.[34] The only way to answer this attack, I believe, is to find arguments to show that the tastes of "elitists" (if that is what they are) can be argued for and are not merely the sort of preferences that markets create and satisfy. They must be shown to have a basis all of us can recognize and respect.

The way to do this may be to emphasize the distinction between objects that are valuable *as individual things* and objects that have value because of some *purpose* that they serve. The distinction between intrinsic and instrumental value is one of the oldest in philosophy. Those who love and admire the environment value it for what it is and "for its own sake"; they do not value it simply because of the "satisfaction" or utility it provides. This is also the way we appreciate friendship, freedom, truth, indeed, anything we believe has an intrinsic worth. This is the essence of appreciation. To appreciate is not to value the objects one enjoys; it is to enjoy the objects one values.

What is the value of a magnificent environment such as wilderness? What is a species worth, e.g., the Colorado squawfish or the snail darter? As well ask what is the value of a work of art, a friendship, or a significant moment in the past. These things may have no use; indeed, one who uses friends

soon no longer has them. The value of art, the value of history, the value of friendship, depend not on the uses they have (though these may be important), but on the meanings they have. They express what we are, what we believe in, and what we care about. We respect these things, and their value consists, perhaps, in what this respect tells us about ourselves. It assures us that we are not mere bundles of preferences, but human beings capable of more than desire; we are not merely self-interested consumers bent on achieving the lowest common denominator of satisfaction. To develop a land use ethic is to elaborate categories for public policy beyond those of efficiency and even equality. It is to bring into environmental law a concept of dignity to balance the concept of price.

NOTES

1. For an excellent annotated bibliography of literature arguing this point, see A. Fisher and F. Peterson, "The Environment in Economics: A Survey," *Journal of Economic Literature* 14 (1976): 1–31.

2. For a popular book representing many others, see William Baxter, *People or Penguins? The Case for Optimal Pollution* (New York: Columbia University Press, 1974).

3. For discussion, see Martin Kreiger, "What's Wrong With Plastic Trees?," *Science* 179 (1973): 446–55.

4. Steven V. Roberts, "Visitors are Swamping the National Parks," *New York Times*, 1 September 1969, p. 15. Quoted in Joseph Sax, *Mountains Without Handrails* (Ann Arbor: University of Michigan Press, 1980), p. 74.

5. *Second Treatise of Government*, chap. 5, sec. 26. (In *Locke's Two Treatises of Government*, Peter Laslett, ed. [Cambridge: Cambridge University Press, 1963]).

6. Ibid., sec. 42.

7. Ibid.

8. Ibid., sec. 32.

9. Ibid, sec 31.

10. Ibid., sec. 33.

11. Ibid., sec. 51.

12. Ibid., sec. 46.

13. A. M. Freeman, Robert Haveman, and Allen Kneese, *The Economics of Environmental Policy* (New York: Wiley & Sons, 1973), p. 23.

14. A large literature relating property and inequality includes the Rousseau essay mentioned below and Thorstein Veblens' *The Theory of the Leisure Class* (Boston: Houghton Mifflin, 1973). For Locke and man's dominion

over nature, see, for example, Kathleen Squadrito, "Locke's View of Dominion," *Environmental Ethics* 1 (1979): 255–62. Robert Nozick discusses Locke and the problem of scarcity in *Anarchy, State, and Utopia* (New York: Basic Books, 1974), pp. 175–82. R. Bryant discusses the problem of relating property regimes to ecology in *Land: Private Property, Public Control* (Montreal: Harvest House, 1972). The problem of property and the commons is widely discussed, e.g., in Garrett Hardin and John Baden, eds., *Managing the Commons* (San Francisco: W. H. Freeman, 1977). For a discussion and survey of attempts to relate fragile values or benefits to property data, see A. Myrick Freeman III, "Property Values and Benefit Estimation," in A. M. Freeman, *The Benefits of Environmental Improvement: Theory and Practice* (Baltimore: Resources for the Future, 1979), pp. 108–64.

15. J. J. Rousseau, *The First and Second Discourses*, Roger D. Masters, ed. (New York: St. Martin's Press, 1964), pp. 151–52.

16. Lynn White, "The Historical Roots of the Ecological Crisis," *Science* 155 (1967): 1204.

17. *Religio Medici* I. 16.

18. Locke, *Second Treatise*, sec. 26. Locke suggests that "natural *Reason*, which tells us that Men, being once born, have a right to their Preservation," is as good a basis as revelation to show that the Earth is "given" to man for his use (sec. 25).

19. I paraphrase Locke, *Second Treatise*, sec. 22.

20. William Ophuls, *Ecology and the Politics of Scarcity* (San Francisco: W. H. Freeman, 1977), p. 155.

21. Locke, *Second Treatise*, sec. 124.

22. Baxter, *People or Penguins*, p. 34.

23. Locke, *Second Treatise*, sec. 28.

24. See R. E. Phillips et al., "No-Till Agriculture," *Science* 208 (1980): 1108–14.

25. See *Proceedings of the Bi-State Conference on the Chesapeake Bay*, 27–29 April 1977, Commonwealth of Virginia Publication CRC #61, pp. 46–47, 121f.

26. Marvin Zim, "Allied Chemical's $20 Million Ordeal with Kepone," *Fortune*, 11 September 1978, p. 91.

27. *Proceedings*, p. 136.

28. Garrett Hardin, "The Tragedy of the Commons," *Science* 162 (1978): 1244.

29. Ibid., p. 1245.

30. Ibid., p. 1245.

31. I comment extensively on the relevant literature in "Economic Theory and Environmental Law," *Michigan Law Review*, forthcoming.

32. For criticism, see the article listed in previous note.

33. Perry Miller, *Nature's Nation* (Cambridge: Harvard University Press, 1967).

34. For discussion and bibliography, see Richard Andrews, "Class Politics or Democratic Reform: Environmentalism and American Political Institutions," *Natural Resources Journal* 20 (1980): 221–41, esp. 222.

ANNETTE BAIER

The Rights of Past and Future Persons

No one doubts that future generations, once they are present and actual, will have rights, if any of us have rights.[1] What difference is made if we say, not that they *will* have, but that they *do* have rights—now? I see two main points of difference—first, that those rights will then give rise to obligations on our part, as well as on their contemporaries' part; and, second, that what they have a right *to* will be different. In addition to whatever political and civil rights they have or will have, they will also each have a right to a fair share of what is then left of the earth's scarce resources. If they *now* have rights, they have rights to a share of what is *now* left of those scarce resources. To believe that they have rights is to believe that *we* must safeguard those rights and that, where the right is to a share, that we must share with them, and that the size of our share is affected by their right to share.

Should we believe that future persons not merely *will* have rights, but that they presently *do* have rights? To decide this I shall first consider whether any conceptual incoherence would result. Having eliminated that threat, I shall turn to the question of what rational or moral grounds there might be for the belief. I shall argue that some of the reasons for recognizing obligations to future persons are closely connected with reasons for recognizing the rights of past persons and that these reasons are good ones. In addition there are the obligations that arise from our responsibility for the very existence of those future persons, through our support of social policies that affect the size and nature of the human population in the future. I shall argue that we have good reason to recognize these obligations to future persons, whether or not we see them as arising out of their rights.

I turn first to the question of what we are committed to in asserting that a person has a certain right. I take it that this is to assert:

a. That at least one other person has an obligation to the right-holder. This obligation may be to refrain from interfering with some activity of the right-holder or to take some positive steps to secure for the right-holder what he or she has a right to. These steps may be ones that benefit the right-holder or some third party, as would be the case if I have promised a friend to feed his cat. He thereby has a right to my services that are intended to benefit the cat. Following Feinberg's[2] terminology, I shall say that the obligation is *to* the right-holder and *toward* whomever is the intended beneficiary.

b. There is, or there should and could in practice be, socially recognized means for the right-holder, or his or her proxy, to take appropriate action should the obligations referred to in (a) be neglected. This action will range from securing belated discharge of the obligation, to securing compensation for its neglect, to the initiation of punitive measures against the delinquent obligated person.

I think that this account covers both legally recognized rights and also moral rights that are more than mere "manifesto" rights,[3] since clause (b) requires that effective recognition could be given to such rights. Such effective recognition can of course be given only to a set of nonconflicting

rights, and so I assume that to claim anything as a right is to claim that its effective recognition is compatible with the effective recognition of the other rights one claims to exist.[4] To claim a moral right to something not effectively recognized as a right is to claim that it could without contradiction to other justifiably recognized rights *be* given recognition, that only inertia, ignorance, greed or ill-will prevents its recognition.

This account of what it is to have a right differs in another sense from the account that is more commonly given. The point of difference lies in the extension of power to claim the right from the right-holder to his spokesman, vicar, or proxy. This extension is required to make sense of the concept of rights of past or future generations. I think we already accept such an extension in empowering executors to claim the rights of the deceased whose wills they execute. The role of executor is distinct from that of trustee for the heirs. We recognize obligations both *to* and *toward* the legal heirs, and *to* the person who made the will. Where the legal heirs are specified only as the "issue" of certain persons known to the will-maker, we already accept the concept of an obligation, owed by the trustees, to look after the interests of such not-yet-determinate persons.

Can those who protect the rights of future persons be properly regarded as their spokesmen, claimants of their rights in the present, when they, unlike executors of wills, cannot be appointed by the original right-holder? The rights of past persons, claimed by their recognized spokesmen, are person-specific rights to have their legally valid powers exercised, while the rights in the present claimed for future persons will be general human rights. No one needs to be privy to the individual wills of future persons to claim their right to clean air. Already recognized spokesmen for known past persons, claiming their particular rights, need knowledge of them, their deeds, and their wishes, and so are sensibly required to have a special tie to the original right-holder, initiated by him. Spokesmen for future persons, claiming general rights, need no such tie.

If future generations have rights, then we, or some of us in some capacity, have obligations to and presumably also toward them, and their spokesman should be empowered to take action to see to it that we discharge those obligations. I see no conceptual incorrectness in attributing such rights. Admittedly we do not now recognize any person as the proper spokesman, guardian, and rights-claimant for future generations. But we could, and perhaps we should.

The fact that future generations are not *now* living persons is irrelevant to the issue, if, as I have argued, we are willing to speak of the rights of those who are no longer living persons. The fact that we do not and cannot have knowledge of the special characteristics and wishes of future generations is, I have claimed, also irrelevant to the recognition of their rights to basic nonspecial human requirements, such as uncontaminated air. Our dependence on fossil fuels may be, compared with the needs of past generations, quite special, and there may be good reason not to extrapolate that need into the distant future. But there is no reason to think that the need for air will be lessened by technological progress or regress in the future. Our ignorance of precisely *who* future generations will be, and uncertainty of how numerous they will be, may be relevant to the priority of our obligations to them, compared with obligations to the living, should conflicts arise; but it is not relevant to the reality of obligations to future persons, nor to the moral priority of such obligations over our tastes for conspicuous consumption or our demands for luxury and for the freedom to waste or destroy resources.

As lawful heirs of specific past persons, some of us may have a right to what those persons intended us to possess, should there be sufficient moral reason to recognize the disputed right to pass on private property and to inherit it. By contrast, we all inherit a social order, a cultural tradition, air and water, not as private heirs of private will-makers but as members of a continuous community. We benefit from the wise planning, or perhaps the thoughtless but fortunate conservation, of past generations. In so far as such inherited public goods as constitutions, civil liberties, universities, parks, and uncontaminated water come to us by the deliberate intention of past generations, we inherit them not as sole beneficiaries but as persons able to share and pass on such goods to an indefinite run of future generations. It was, presumably, not for this generation in particular that public spirited persons in past generations saved or sacrificed.

Rights and obligations are possessed by persons not in virtue of their unique individuality but in virtue of roles they fill, roles that relate to others. For example, children, *qua* children, have obligations to and rights against parents *qua* parents. My obligations as a teacher are owed to my students, whoever they may be. When I discharge obligations to them, such as ordering textbooks, I do not and need not know who those students will be. As long as I believe that determinate actual persons will fill the role of students, will occupy a position involving a moral tie to me, my obligations are real and not lessened by my ignorance of irrelevant details concerning those role-fillers. As long as we believe there will be persons related to us as we are related to past generations, then any obligations and rights this relation engenders will be real. Whether there will be such persons is something about which we can have well-based beliefs, especially as it is to some degree up to us whether to allow such roles to be filled.

The ontological precariousness of future generations that some see as a reason for not recognizing any rights of theirs is not significantly greater than that of the future states of present persons. In neither case does ignorance of details about the future, or the possible nonexistence in that future of those who would benefit from discharge of obligations in the present, affect the reality of our obligations. To make sacrifices *now* so that others may benefit in the future is always to risk wasting that sacrifice. The moral enterprise is intrinsically a matter of risky investment,[5] if we measure the return solely in terms of benefits reaped by those toward whom obligations are owed. Only if virtue is its own reward is morality ever a safe investment. The only special feature in a moral tie between us and future generations lies in the inferiority of our knowledge about them, not in the inferiority of their ontological status. They are not merely possible persons, they are whichever possible persons will in the future be actual.

So far I have found no conceptual reason for disallowing talk of the rights of future persons. Neither their nonpresence, nor our ignorance of *who* exactly they are, nor our uncertainty concerning how many of them are, rules out the appropriateness of recognizing rights on their part. The fact that they cannot now claim their rights from us puts them in a position no different from that of past persons with rights in the present—namely, a position of dependency on some representative in this generation, someone empowered to speak for them. Rights typically are *claimed* by their possessors, so if we are to recognize rights of future persons we must empower some persons to make claims for them.

Another thing that can be done with a right is to waive it. Past persons who leave no will waive the right that they had to determine the heirs of their private property. Since nothing could count as a sign that future generations waive their rights against us, then this dimension of the concept of a right will get no purchase with future generations, unless we empower present persons not merely to claim but also to waive rights of future persons. Waiving rights and alienating them by gift or exchange are both voluntary renunciations of what a right puts in the right-holder's secure possession. However, waiving rights, unlike alienating them, does not involve a transfer of the right. Since the rights that are transferred are always special rights, and the rights of future persons that we are considering are general ones, there can be no question of transferring such rights. But might a proxy waive them? Guardians of present persons (children, incompetents) do have the power to waive some rights on behalf of their wards, but the justification for this practice, and any exercise of it, depends upon the availability of special knowledge of what will and will not benefit the right-holder. It is barely conceivable that we or any official we appointed could have such knowledge of the special needs of some future generations. If we were facing the prospect of a nuclear war and foresaw that any immediate successor generations would live in the ruins of civilization as we have known it, we might judge that there was no point in trying to preserve, say, the Bill of Rights for one's successors, although they had a *prima facie* right to inherit it. One might on their behalf waive that right, in extreme conditions, and bury the Constitution, rather than prolong our agony to fight for it. But such scenarios are bizarre, since it is barely conceivable that those who would bequeath to future generations the effects of a nuclear war would care about the rest of their bequest, about the fragments that might be shored against our ruin. The benefits that might be gained for future generations by empowering any of their ancestors to waive some

of their rights seem minimal. Still, this is a question not of the conceptual absurdity of waiving a recognized right of future generations but of the practical wisdom of giving another this power.

I conclude that no conceptual error is involved in speaking of the rights of future generations. The concept of a right includes that of the justified power of the right-holder or his spokesman to press for discharge of obligations affecting his particular interests, or to renounce this power. The concept has already shown itself capable of extension to cover the rights of past persons and could as easily accommodate the rights of future generations if we saw good reason thus to extend it.

What might give us such a reason? I have already spoken of our position in relation to past generations whose actions have benefited us, either by planning or by good luck. The conservative way to decide the *moral* question is to ask whether we ourselves claim anything as a matter of right against past generations. Do we feel we had a *right* to be left the relatively uncontaminated water we found available to us, as a generation? Do we feel that the Romans, whose cutting down of forests left barren, eroded hillsides, violated a right of later generations? I think that we do not usually attribute to past generations the obligation to save for us, we do not accept their savings as only our just due, we do not usually condemn past generations where their actions have had bad effects in the present. But the reason for this may be that we are reluctant to attribute obligations where we are uncertain of the ability to meet them. Past generations, unlike ours, were rarely in a position to foresee the long-term effects of their actions, so are rightly not blamed by us for any harm they caused. Where what they did had good consequences for us, we accept these not as our due but as our good fortune. Where past generations deliberately saved or conserved for us, we accept their savings not as something they owed us, even when they may have believed they did owe it, but as something they chose to give us, where the "us" in question includes future generations.

It is possible that we stand to future generations in a relation in which no previous generation has stood to us; so that, although we have no rights against past generations, future generations do have rights against us. This is a possible position one might defend. Our knowledge and our power are significantly different even from that of our grandparents' generation, and might be thought to give rise to new moral relationships and new obligations. Before turning to consider how we might determine what those new obligations are, and how to find for them a common ground with old obligations, I want to look more closely at our relations to past generations and to ask if there is anything they might have done that would have given us a reason to blame them for failing in their obligations to us.

I take as an example of a benefit made possible by the actions of earlier generations my own education at the University of Otago in New Zealand. This university was founded extraordinarily early in the establishment of the colony because of the high priority the Scottish colonists gave to education and to its free availability. The existence of a distinguished university, and of the institutions supporting and financing it, was due to the efforts of people in my great grandparents' generation. Had they not made that effort, or had they or later generations established a university that only the wealthy could attend, I would have had no ground for complaint against them. They did not owe me a university education. But had an intervening generation allowed the university and its supporting institutions to founder, and done so from unwillingness to spend on its upkeep the resources that could be used for personal profit, I and my generation *would* blame those who failed to pass on the public benefits they themselves inherited. One obligation that every generation has toward subsequent generations is to leave "as much and as good" of the public goods previous generations have bequeathed them. This obligation arises as much from a right of past persons to have their good intentions respected as it does from any right of future persons, but I think there *is* a right to have passed on to one those public goods that, but for ill will or irresponsibility, would have been passed on. If I had been deprived of an education because a previous generation had destroyed an already founded university for the sake of its own greater luxury, I would feel that *my* rights, as well as those of the university's founders, had been overridden. It is interesting to note that the rights of past benefactors and their future beneficiaries give rise to one and the same obligation. Indeed, if we consider the motivation of the university's

founders, who were heirs to a Scottish tradition of investment in public education, we find that they saw themselves as much as *preservers* as creators, as passing on, in new and difficult conditions, a heritage they had themselves received. As one of their hymns put it:

They reap not where they laboured,
We reap where they have sown.
Our harvest will be garnered
By ages yet unknown.

The metaphor of seed and harvest is the appropriate one where what is passed on, sown, is the same good as was received or harvested from the earlier sowing by others. The obligation that each generation has, which is owed equally to past and future generations, is the obligation to preserve the seed crop, the obligation to regenerate what they did not themselves generate.

That this obligation can be seen as due, indifferently, to past or future persons shows something of considerable importance about obligations in general and about the moral community. Earlier I said that rights are possessed not in virtue of any unique individuality but in virtue of roles we fill. The crucial role we fill, as moral beings, is as members of a cross-generational community, a community of beings who look before and after, who interpret the past in the light of the present, who see the future as growing out of the past, who see themselves as members of enduring families, nations, cultures, traditions. Perhaps we could even use Kant's language and say that it is because persons are *noumenal* beings that obligations to past persons and to future persons reinforce one another, that every obligation is owed by, to, and toward persons as participants in a continuing process of the generation and regeneration of shared values.

To stress the temporal continuity of the moral community is not to deny that accumulating knowledge and increasing power make a difference to the obligations one has. Earlier I said that the reason we do not morally condemn earlier generations for those actions of theirs whose consequences are bad for us is the reasonable doubt we feel about the extent to which they knew what they were doing. If the overgrazing that turned grasslands into deserts were thought by us to have been a *calculated* policy to increase a past generation's nonrenewed wealth, at our expense, we would condemn them for it. Any obligations we have to generations future to us that find no exact analogue in obligations past persons owed us arise, I believe, both from special features of our known control over the existence and the conditions of life of future generations and from our awareness of what we owe to past generations. We are especially self-conscious members of the cross-generational community, aware both of how much, and how much more than previous generations, we benefit from the investment of earlier generations and of the extent to which we may determine the fate of future generations. Such self-consciousness has its costs in obligations.

Another sort of obligation we may have to future generations arises out of our failure to discharge other obligations to them. We, unlike earlier generations, are in a position to control population growth and to attempt to gear it to the expected supply of essential resources. Where we are failing to use this ability responsibly, we incur obligations to compensate our victims in a future overcrowded world for the harm we have thereby done them. Special efforts to increase, not merely to conserve, needed food and water resources are the appropriate accompaniment to our neglect of the obligation not to overbreed.

Our special position, relative to previous generations, in the procession of human possessors of knowledge and power, gives us the ability to end the sequence of human generations as well as to be self-conscious and deliberate in our procreative or regenerative activities. It is a consequence of my version of the cross-generational moral community that this power to end the human community's existence could justifiably be exercised only in conditions so extreme that one could sincerely believe that past generations would concur in the judgment that it all should end. I do not think that anyone, past, present, or future, has a right to exist, and certainly no merely possible person has such a right. But we do not need the rights of possible persons to restrain us from bringing about the end of human life, the rights of past persons and the very nature of membership in a moral community rule that out in all except the very direst circumstances. Just as we have no *right* to use up all scarce resources in our generation for our own luxury or whim but, rather, an obligation to renew what we

use, to pass on what we received, so we have no right to decree the ending of an enterprise in which we are latecomers. To end it all would not be the communal equivalent of suicide, since it would end not only our endeavors but those invested endeavors of all our predecessors. Only if they could be seen as concurring in the decision not to renew human life, or not to allow it to be renewed, could such a decision be likened to suicide.

I have said almost nothing about the theoretical basis for the obligations and rights I have claimed exist. Indeed, I am not sure that theories are the right sort of thing on which to ground assertions about obligations. In any case I shall not here go into the question of which moral theory would best systematize the sorts of reasons there are for recognizing the rights and obligations I have invoked. Kant's moral theory, if it could be stripped of its overintellectualism, Burke's account of a cross-generational community, if it could be stripped of its contractarian overtones, Hume's account of the virtues recognized by us humans who see ourselves as "plac'd in a kind of middle station betwixt the past and the future" who "imagine our ancestors to be, in a manner, mounted above us, and our posterity to lie below us,"[6] Rawls's idea of social union, of a continuing community in which "the powers of human individuals living at any one time takes the cooperation of many generations (or even societies) over a long period of time,"[7] if this could be used, as he does not use it, to give an account of the right as well as the good, all these give us assistance in articulating the reasons that we should recognize obligations of piety to past persons and responsibility to future ones. I do not think that either utilitarian theories or contractarian theories, or any version of any moral theory I am familiar with, captures the right reasons for the right attitudes to past and future persons. Perhaps we need a new theory, but the "intuitions" it will ground are, I believe, very old ones. I have relied, rather dogmatically, on those intuitions that I think are fairly widely shared, but before attempting to summarize in broad outline the factors relevant to our obligations to future generations I need to make clear a few points about the community in which such obligations arise.

First, it is not a community to which one

chooses to belong, but one in which one finds oneself. By the time any moral reflections arise, one is already heir to a language and a way of life, and one has already received benefits from those particular older persons who cared for one in one's initial extreme dependency and who initiated one into a way of life. This way of life typically includes conventions to enable one voluntarily to take on obligations as well as to renounce and transfer some rights; but not all obligations are self-imposed, and those that are arise from institutions, like that of promising, which depend for their preservation on other obligations that are not self-imposed. As Hume said: "We are surely not bound to keep our word because we have given our word to keep it."[8] We may, and usually do, "agree," as Hume put it, or go along with the customs we find in force, including the custom of promising and demanding that promises be kept, since we see the benefits of having such a practice; but any obligations there may be to support existent practices depend not on the prior consent of the obligated but on the value of the practice to all concerned and on their reliance on it.

Reliance creates dependency, and the second point I wish to make is that the relations that form a moral community, and which, once recognized, give rise to obligations, all concern dependency and interdependency. Some of these dependency relations are self-initiated, but the most fundamental ones are not. The dependency of child on parent, for example, is a natural and inevitable one, and the particular form it takes is socially determined but certainly not chosen by the child. Socially contrived dependencies shape, supplement, and balance natural and unavoidable dependencies. Rights and duties attach to roles in a network of interdependent roles, which if it is wisely designed will conserve and increase the common store of goods, and if it is fairly designed will distribute them equitably. Some morally significant and interrelated roles are ones we all occupy in sequence—the dependent child becomes the adult with children in his care, those who care for the dependent elderly themselves become old and in need of care. Similar to these roles in their reference to earlier and later persons, but unlike them in that we do not occupy them in temporal succession, are the roles of inheritor from past generations, executor and determiner of the in-

heritance of future generations. In filling these roles one both receives and transfers goods, but the transfer involved is of necessity nonreciprocal, only a *virtual* exchange, and the taking begins to occur too early to be by choice.

The third point is that the cross-temporal moral community in which one finds oneself is not restricted to those who share one's own way of life, but extends to all those with whom one stands, directly or indirectly, in dependency or interdependency relations. Although a seventeenth-century Scotsman may have had no ties, social or economic, with Maoris in New Zealand, or even any knowledge of them, he has indirect ties if his descendants have economic and social and political relations with them. Interdependency is transitive, and so relates me to all those with whom either earlier or later participants in my particular way of life have stood in interdependent relationships.[9] Thus the tie linking "those who are living, those who are dead, and those who are yet to be born"[10] is a cross-cultural one and brings it about that (at least) no one human is alien to me.

What facts about our own dependency relations to past and future generations are relevant to deciding what rights and duties those relations should entail? As far as our own duties to past and future generations go, the relevant facts are these: first our relatively privileged material position, compared with that of most members of most previous generations; second, our dependency for this on past generations as well as our own generation's efforts; third, our power to affect the lot of future generations; fourth, our comparatively extensive knowledge of the long-term effects of our policies; and fifth, the fact that when past generations conserved or saved deliberately for the sake of future generations (in creating parks, writing and fighting for constitutions) there is no reason to think that it was for us in particular, but rather that it was done on the assumption that we would pass on the inheritance. To sum up, the chief facts are our indebtedness to the past and our dangerously great ability to affect the future. We, like most of our forebears, are the unconsulted beneficiaries of the sacrifice of past generations, sometimes seen by them as obligatory, often in fact nonobligatory. If we owe something in return, what is it, and what can we do for those who benefited us? The most obvious response is to continue the cooperative scheme they thought worth contributing to, adapting our contributions to our distinctive circumstances. What is distinctive is our increased ability to plan and foresee the future (and to recognize the dangers of overplanning). If we say that all generations have owed it to the moral community as a whole, and to past generations in particular, to try to leave things no worse than they found them, then we too have that obligation. In addition, in as far as past generations, by supererogatory effort, left things *better* than they found them, we owe it to them to pass on such inherited benefits. We must not poison the wells, even such wells as we have deepened.

We, unlike our ancestors, are better able to judge and control what will benefit and harm our descendants, so our obligations are correspondingly more determinate. Does our special position warrant speaking of the rights of future generations and not just of our obligations toward them? I have argued that past generations have rights against us, that we not wantonly waste or destroy what they made possible for us to have, not intending it for us only. It would therefore be appropriate to recognize spokesmen for their rights. Should spokesmen for future generations, as well as for past generations, be empowered to ensure that we discharge our obligations, take our "trusteeship" seriously, and should we see our obligations as arising out of the rights of future generations?

When we speak of obligations as arising out of rights, we do several morally pertinent things. First, we put a certain emphasis on determinate interests that these rights protect and individuate our obligations by reference to these individual interests of persons. Second, we give a certain guarantee of moral priority to the protection of these definite central interests over negotiable goods. Third, we give the person whose interest a right protects a certain power of individual initiative to claim or demand or waive the right.[11] In all three aspects the concept of a right goes along with that of a certain individualist version of respect for persons and involves seeing obligations as arising out of this respect.

I have argued for a convergence of important interests of past and future persons, so that obligations to future persons do not stem from consideration of their interests alone. But their interests are of undeniable importance and merit a high priority, so that the first two dimensions of rights apply here. The third ingredient, respect for the rightholder's initiative in claiming a right, could only be fictionally present in the case of future generations, if we recognized a spokesman for them. I see no reason in principle why we should not speak of rights of future generations as well as of our obligations to them, but on the other hand I see nothing very important to be gained by doing so. As long as we recognize our obligations to consider the good of the continuing human community, it matters little whether we speak of the rights of future persons. Whether an official agency to execute our collective obligations were seen as a guardian of the interests of future persons or as a spokesman for their rights would make little difference to the responsibility of such an agency. To speak of their rights would be to commit ourselves to the priority of whatever rights we recognized over our own lesser interests. Until we are clear exactly what priority we are willing to give to the interests of future persons, and to which of their interests we will give this priority, it would be less misleading not to use the language of rights. We should first recognize that we have obligations, then devote ourselves to clarifying the precise content of these. If when that is done we find that we do believe we should give priority to certain definite individuated rights of future persons, we can then recognize and itemize such rights.

I have not detailed the content of our obligations to future persons, but have addressed myself only to the general question of whether there are any. I shall end by repeating the features of our own relationship with future persons that I have claimed to be relevant to these obligations. Future persons stand to us in several morally pertinent roles that give rise to obligations on our part:

1. As those who, like us, depend upon naturally self-renewing resources like air, soil, and water, which none of us produced, they are owed the use of these resources in an unpoisoned state.

2. As intended heirs, with us, of the public goods past generations created, often at great cost and sacrifice, they are owed their share in these goods.

3. As those whose existence we could have prevented, but which we owe it to past generations

not to prevent wantonly or for our own increased luxury, they have a right to a tolerable and so to a not-too-crowded existence. Our duty to the past is to ensure that, short of catastrophe, there be future persons. Our duty to those persons is to ensure that there not be too many of them.

4. As victims of our probable failure to meet the last mentioned obligation, they are owed some compensation from us. This means, for example, that we as a society should be working on methods to increase food supplies beyond those that would be needed should our justifiable population policies succeed.

I have claimed that there is no conceptual counter-reason, and that there is good moral reason, to recognize obligations to future generations, to recognize that either they, or past generations, or both, have a moral right to our discharge of such obligations. I agree with Golding that "if obligation to the past is a superstition, so is obligation to the future,"[12] and I have tried to suggest that, if both these are superstitions, then all obligation is superstition.

NOTES

1. I do not take it for granted that any of us do in any morally significant sense have rights. We do of course have legal rights, but to see them as backed by moral rights is to commit oneself to a particular version of the moral enterprise that may not be the best version. As Hegel and Marx pointed out, the language of rights commits us to questionable assumptions concerning the relation of the individual to the community, and, as Utilitarians have also pointed out, it also commits us more than may be realistic or wise to fixing the details of our moral priorities in advance of relevant knowledge that only history can provide.

2. J. Feinberg, "Duties, Rights and Claims," *American Philosophical Quarterly*, vol. 5, no. 2 (April 1966).

3. J. Feinberg, *Social Philosophy* (Englewood Cliffs, N.J.: Prentice-Hall, 1973), p. 67. The term 'manifesto rights' is from Joel Feinberg, who writes, "[I am] willing to speak of a special 'manifesto sense' of 'right,' in which a right

need not be correlated with another's duty. Natural needs are real claims, if only upon hypothetical future beings not yet in existence. I accept the moral principle that to have an unfulfilled need is to have a kind of claim against the world, even if against no one in particular.... Such claims, based on need alone, are 'permanent possibilities of rights,' the natural seed from which rights grow." (p. 67)

4. I assume that while it makes sense to speak of *prima facie* and possibly conflicting obligations, statements about rights gave final moral decisions, so there are no *prima facie* or conflicting rights.

5. I have discussed this in "Secular Faith," *Canadian Journal of Philosophy* (March 1979).

6. David Hume, *Treatise of Human Nature*, ed., Selby Bigge (Oxford University Press, 1968) p. 437.

7. John Rawls, *A Theory of Justice*, p. 525. Rawls uses this idea of a cross-temporal social union to explicate the concept of the good, but in his account of justice he restricts the relevant moral community, those who make an agreement with one another, to contemporaries who do not know their common temporal position.

8. David Hume, *Enquiry Concerning the Principles of Morals*, ed., Selby Bigge (Oxford: Clarendon Press, 1935), p. 306.

9. This transitivity of dependency and interdependency does not imply any strong cultural continuity; but I do assume that, where the dependency is recognized and so is obligation-engendering, there is sufficient common culture for some sort of understanding of intentions to be possible. Even if, as those like Michael Foucault believe, there is radical discontinuity in human culture, so that we are deluded if we think we can understand what Plato or Hume meant, it is nevertheless a significant fact that we try to understand them and that we get insight from those attempts. Indeed, part of the intention of any writer, artist, or producer of other meaningful human works, may be to provide something that can be reinterpreted. We do not need to see the heritage of the past to be fixed in form in order to value it, nor see future persons as strict constructionists, finding only our intentions in our works, in order to work for them.

10. Edmund Burke, *Reflections on the Revolution in France* (London: Macmillan, 1910), pp. 93–94.

11. H. L. A. Hart stresses this element in the concept of a right in "Are There Any Natural Rights?", *Philosophical Review*, vol. 64 (1955), and in "Bentham on Legal Powers" in *Oxford Essays in Jurisprudence*. Second Series, ed., A. W. B. Simpson (Oxford: Clarendon Press, 1973).

12. M. P. Golding, "Obligations to Future Generations," *Monist* (January 1972), p. 91.

CHAPTER TWELVE
Study Questions

1. In Chapter 9, we considered a "feasibility" standard for regulating worker health and safety. Would you recommend a similar standard for environmental regulation? Why or why not?

2. Do you think that it is fair to raise the price that midwesterners pay for electricity, which presently is at a rate below that paid in the East, in order to reduce the acid rain traceable to midwestern electric generating plants?

3. We apparently give some animals, e.g., dogs, legal rights such as protection against cruelty. Does it make sense to say that animals have *rights*? Why or why not? How about plants?

4. Do you think that it is legitimate that current generations' desire for luxury goods should jeopardize future generations' desire for necessary goods?

5. Are the obligations that U. S. citizens owe to Canadians concerning acid rain pollution the same obligation that they have to other U.S. citizens? Does America have obligations to undeveloped countries to conserve natural resources as strong (or as weak, or the same) as it has to future generations of Americans?

INDEX TO COURT CASES

INDEX